UNIVERSITY OF STRATHCLYDE
30125 00843966 2

ANDERSONIAN LIBRARY
WITHDRAWN
FROM
LIBRARY
STOCK
UNIVERSITY OF STRATHCLYDE

D1477915

Construction Manual for Polymers + Membranes

MATERIALS
SEMI-FINISHED PRODUCTS
FORM-FINDING
DESIGN

KNIPPERS
CREMERS
GABLER
LIENHARD

Birkhäuser
Basel

Edition Detail
Munich

Authors

Jan Knippers, Prof. Dr.-Ing.
Institute of Building Structures & Structural Design (itke)
Faculty of Architecture & Urban Planning, University of Stuttgart

Jan Cremers, Prof. Dr.-Ing. Architect
Faculty of Architecture & Design
Hochschule für Technik Stuttgart

Markus Gabler, Dipl.-Ing.
Institute of Building Structures & Structural Design (itke)
Faculty of Architecture & Urban Planning, University of Stuttgart

Julian Lienhard, Dipl.-Ing.
Institute of Building Structures & Structural Design (itke)
Faculty of Architecture & Urban Planning, University of Stuttgart

Assistants:
Sabrina Brenner, Cristiana Cerqueira, Charlotte Eller, Manfred Hammer, Dipl.-Ing.; Petra Heim, Dipl.-Ing.; Carina Kleinecke, Peter Meschendörfer, Elena Vlasceanu

Specialist articles:
Joost Hartwig, Dipl.-Ing.; Martin Zeumer, Dipl.-Ing. (Environmental impact of polymers)
Field of Study Design & Energy-Efficient Construction, Department of Architecture, Technische Universität Darmstadt

Carmen Köhler, Dipl.-Ing. (Natural fibre-reinforced polymers and biopolymers)
Institute of Building Structures & Structural Design (itke),
Faculty of Architecture & Urban Planning, University of Stuttgart

Consultants:
Christina Härter, Dipl.-Ing. (Polymers)
Institute of Polymer Technology (IKT), University of Stuttgart

Andreas Kaufmann, MEng (Complex building envelopes);
Philip Leistner, Dr.-Ing. (Building physics and energy aspects)
Fraunhofer Institute for Building Physics (IBP), Stuttgart/Holzkirchen

Alexander Michalski, Dr.-Ing. (Loadbearing structure and form)
Chair of Structural Analysis, Technische Universität Munich

Mauricio Soto, MA Arch. (Building with textile membranes)
studio LD

Jürgen Troitzsch, Dr. rer. nat. (Building physics and energy aspects)
Fire & Environment Protection Service, Wiesbaden

Editorial services

Editors:
Judith Faltermeier, Dipl.-Ing. Architect; Cornelia Hellstern, Dipl.-Ing.; Jana Rackwitz, Dipl.-Ing.; Eva Schönbrunner, Dipl.-Ing.

Editorial assistants:
Carola Jacob-Ritz, MA; Cosima Strobl, Dipl.-Ing. Architect;
Peter Popp, Dipl.-Ing.

Drawings:
Dejanira Ornelas Bitterer, Dipl.-Ing.; Ralph Donhauser, Dipl.-Ing.;
Michael Folkmer, Dipl.-Ing.; Marion Griese, Dipl.-Ing.;
Daniel Hajduk, Dipl.-Ing.; Martin Hämmel, Dipl.-Ing.;
Emese Köszegi, Dipl.-Ing.; Nicola Kollmann, Dipl.-Ing. Architect;
Simon Kramer, Dipl.-Ing.; Elisabeth Krammer, Dipl.-Ing.

Translation into English:
Gerd H. Söffker, Philip Thrift, Hannover

Proofreading:
James Roderick O'Donovan, B. Arch., Vienna (A)

Production & layout:
Simone Soesters

Reproduction:
Repro Härtl OHG, Munich

Printing & binding:
Aumüller Druck, Regensburg

Bibliographic information published by the German National Library. The German National Library lists this publication in the Deutsche Nationalbibliografie; detailed bibliographic data are available on the Internet at http://dnb.d-nb.de.

This book is also available in a German language edition
(ISBN 978-3-920034-41-6)

Publisher:
Institut für internationale Architektur-Dokumentation
GmbH & Co. KG, Munich
www.detail.de

Birkhäuser GmbH
PO Box 133, 4010 Basel, Switzerland
Printed on acid-free paper produced from chlorine-free pulp. TCF∞

ISBN: 978-3-0346-0733-9 (hardcover)
ISBN: 978-3-0346-0726-1 (softcover)

9 8 7 6 5 4 3 2 1

www.birkhauser.com

Contents

Preface

Whereas building with textiles can look back on thousands of years of tradition, plastics, or rather polymers, represent a comparatively new class of materials. So in that respect at first glance it might surprise the reader to discover both topics combined in one book. But this approach is less surprising when we consider the fact that it was not until the middle of the 20th century that membranes first found their way into architecture – as synthetic fibres and polymer coatings enabled the production of more durable, stronger textiles, which replaced the cotton cloth that had been used for tents up until that time. It was the development of modern synthetic materials that helped Frei Otto, Walter Bird and others to build their pioneering tensile surface structures, which quickly attracted attention and became widespread over the following decades.

At first, plastics were developed to provide substitutes for valuable and scarce natural resources such as ivory, shellac or animal horn, or to replace less durable materials such as cotton. Since the early 1950s, synthetic materials have been taking over our daily lives, symbolising the dream of a happy future brought about by technical progress. But the public's opinion of polymers started to change quite drastically towards the end of the 20th century. The reasons for this were the defects frequently encountered with polymers used for buildings and the rising costs, but particularly a growing environmental awareness in which synthetic materials no longer seemed to play a part. Consequently, as the historical review in Part A "Polymers and membranes in architecture" shows, the true polymer house has not enjoyed any success so far.
By contrast, the spread of the materials themselves throughout the world of everyday artefacts, likewise the building industry, has proceeded almost unnoticed. This is why polymers are now to be found everywhere in buildings, albeit less in visible applications and more in the technical and constructional make-up of a building; seals, insulation, pipes, cables, paints, adhesives, coatings and floor coverings would all be inconceivable these days without polymers.

In keeping with the tradition of the *Construction Manuals* series, this volume is devoted to the applications of polymers that shape architecture, and that includes loadbearing structure, building envelope and interior fitting-out. Descriptions of the common material principles – from the twin-wall sheet to the coated glass-fibre membrane – run through this book like a common thread. The parallels within the group of synthetic materials are pointed out in every chapter, emphasized irrespective of the differences in the constructional realisation and architectural application. It is this approach that distinguishes this publication because it is more customary to deal with building with textiles and building with polymers separately.

What all synthetic materials have in common is that they exhibit an extremely wide range of properties. By choosing a suitable raw material and modifying it during production and the subsequent processing stages, it is possible to match a material or product to the respective requirements very precisely. Such options are very often available to the designer, but not always. Part B "Materials" therefore first describes the basic materials, i.e. primarily polymers and fibres, and their production and processing technologies in detail. In doing so, the authors have attempted to bridge the gap between the polymers familiar from everyday use and the highly efficient polymers employed in the construction industry. These processes are intrinsic to an understanding of semi-finished products and forms of construction involving synthetic materials. The information goes well beyond the current state of the building art in order to do justice to the dynamic developments in this field. For example, materials researchers are currently intensively involved in the search for a substitute for oil-based polymers in order to reduce the consumption of finite resources and allow better recycling of end-of-life materials. Natural fibre-reinforced polymers and biopolymers therefore have a chapter all to themselves, even though these materials are of only secondary importance in the building industry at present and really only play a role in the automotive and packagings sectors.

The plastics and textile industries make use of specific technologies for the step from primary to semi-finished product, technologies that are otherwise unknown in the world of construction. Those technologies include very diverse aspects such as the processing of fibres to form textiles, the foaming of polymers and also processes like extrusion and injection-moulding. Following a general review of primary products, Part C "Semi-finished products" takes separate looks at reinforced and unreinforced polymers as well as films (often called foils) plus coated and uncoated textiles. One special characteristic of all polymers is that not only their mechanical, but also their building physics properties, e.g. permeability to light and heat, can be adjusted very specifically. The ensuing options are explored in detail.
The chapter covering the environmental impact of polymers is a response to the very emotional debate about the ecological characteristics of synthetic materials. In the form of insulating and sealing materials, polymers in many cases make an indispensable contribution to ecologically efficient building design, and their low weight means they have the potential for creating lightweight structures that use their building materials efficiently. The disadvantages, however, are the high energy input required during production, the extensive use of fossil fuels and the unsatisfactory recycling of these materials once their useful lives have expired. This chapter makes it clear that ecological assessments of constructions made from polymers can have very different outcomes depending on the raw materials, the constructional realisation and the architectural function, and that global statements on this subject are impossible.

Part D "Planning and form-finding" illustrates the similarities, but also the differences, between the various uses of polymer materials. The structural analysis of tensile surface structures and rigid polymer designs is normally handled in totally separate codes of practice and regulations. However, this comparative presentation shows that the principles shared by the materials and the resulting similarity between the creep and fatigue strength behaviour lead to related analysis concepts, even when the constructional realisation is totally different. Form-finding for membrane structures, however, calls for totally different procedures to those we are used to with other building materials. A profound understanding of the relationship between force and form is crucial here, and this aspect is dealt with fully in a separate chapter.

Practical and descriptive presentations of building with semi-finished and free-form polymer products, also foils and textile membranes can all be found in Part E "Building with polymers and membranes", which for the first time contains a detailed overview of design solutions. It is not just the building technology aspects that are investigated here, but also the significance of the materials in the building envelope in terms of building physics, which explains the attention given to the options of multi-layer and multi-leaf forms of construction.

The projects selected for Part F "Case studies" primarily comply with the criterion of an exemplary integration of polymers or membranes in a way that influences the architecture. The aim was to present a wide selection of building types and locations.
The case studies show that many possibilities – the integration of functions for redirecting daylight, generating energy or storing heat, to name but a few – are currently not exploited at all in buildings or at best are in their early days. Technologies already familiar in the automotive or aircraft industries, e.g. "smart" structures made from fibre composites with integral sensors and actuators, have not yet found their way into the construction sector. There is great potential here which will open up many possibilities in architecture. The development of synthetic materials is progressing apace. In order to do justice to this fact, the latest results from research, some of them not yet published, have been incorporated in the writing of this book.

In the past the publications available on polymers have been limited to very specific works of reference, e.g. for aviation or mechanical engineering. A compilation of the principles of the materials with respect to applications in architecture has not been undertaken so far, which is why a great deal of preparatory work was required for this book. We would therefore like to thank all those who have supported us: the consultants from various sectors, the students who prepared the drawings and the photographers of the University of Stuttgart's Werkstatt für Photographie.

The idea of bringing together polymers and membranes in one book is not only reflected in the title. The joint work on the chapters by all the authors led to a tight interweaving of the diverse fields of knowledge. This *Construction Manual* closes a gap in the specialist literature. We very much hope that it will contribute to an increased interest in these materials and, above all, to new applications in architecture.

The authors and publishers
August 2010

Part A Polymers and membranes in architecture

Fig. A Mobile membrane pavilion, Stuttgart (D), 2006, Julian Leinhard

Polymers and membranes in architecture

A 1

A 1 Hermann Staudinger explaining his molecular chain theory on which modern polymer chemistry is based.
A 2 The cover of the first issue of *Kunststoffe* (plastics), Munich, 1911
A 3 Radio with Bakelite case, Philips, 1931
A 4 "Jumo Brevete" desk lamp, France, c. 1945
A 5 "Rocking Armchair Rod" (RAR) from the Plastic Shell Group, 1948, Charles and Ray Eames
A 6 Stacking chair, 1960, Werner Panton

The discovery and development of polymers

Wood rots, metals are expensive, leather becomes brittle and horn warps! Humankind has for a long time been dreaming of replacing natural materials by synthetic ones that are easy to produce and work, long-lasting and readily available to everyone.
It was this dream that tempted the alchemists of past centuries to engage in the weirdest of experiments. With some success: in the Arabic world they distilled blossoms to make perfumes, in China they invented gunpowder and paper. A synthetic resin – obtained by repeated boiling of low-fat cheese and used for medallions and cutlery – was produced in Augsburg in southern Germany as long ago as the 16th century. One of the last great successes of the European alchemists was the discovery of porcelain. After much experimentation, they finally managed to produce that "white gold" in Meissen in former East Germany in the 18th century – more than 1000 years after China had done it!

From alchemy to chemistry

The change from practical alchemy to theoretical chemistry took place gradually with the rise of the natural sciences in the 17th and 18th centuries. And chemistry became a key science of the Industrial Revolution in the 19th century: the mass production of textiles called for new dyes as well as detergents and bleaching agents, foundries were looking to improve the production of metals, mines needed effective and safe lamps. Replacements for scarce and expensive natural materials such as ivory, horn, shellac, coral and silk were urgently required, and so the first steps on the road to modern synthetic materials were taken. The offer of a prize of US$ 10000 to the first person who could produce billiard balls from a synthetic replacement for ivory apparently provided the impetus for the development of celluloid.
The basic ingredient of celluloid is cellulose, the natural polymer that gives plants their stability. Adding a mixture of nitric and sulphuric acid alters the consistency of the cellulose and produces nitrocellulose, the raw material required for the production of celluloid. However, it took a long time and many experiments to find a suitable solvent and binder that would turn the nitrocellulose fibres into a workable polymer compound. Alexander Parkes presented a precursor, so-called Parkesine, at the 1862 World Exposition in London. However, owing to the rapid formation of cracks it was not successful. It was the American book printer John Wesley Hyatt who finally developed the technical method for producing celluloid by using camphor as a solvent. He applied for a patent for his method in 1870. This form of celluloid quickly became popular and was used not only for billiard balls, but also as an imitation for mother-of-pearl, tortoiseshell and horn for combs and hair accessories, and for toys, spectacles, toothbrushes, false teeth and, ultimately, for films. George Eastman, the founder of the Kodak company, started producing roll film made from celluloid in 1889 and thus made photography accessible to the masses.
By the end of the 19th century, manufacturers urgently needed a substitute for another expensive natural product associated with a very costly production method: silk. It was the French scientist Hilaire de Chardonnet who managed to produce an artificial silk based on cellulose. But, although this marked the beginning of the production of synthetic fibres, this form of artificial silk brought no long-term success because, like all products made from cellulose, it suffered from the serious disadvantage of being highly flammable.

Soon after this the Swiss chemist Jacques Brandenberger managed to produce an ultra-thin transparent foil: cellophane, which is still used today for packaging.
In order to replace shellac, a resin-like substance that is obtained in a laborious process from the secretions of the lac bug (*kerria lacca*) and therefore very expensive, the Belgian chemist Leo Baekeland developed the first completely man-made substance made exclusively from synthetic raw materials around 1905: Bakelite. The main constituent of Bakelite is phenol, a waste product of coke production which is consequently very cheap. Bakelite is an electrical insulator and only ignites above a temperature of 300 °C. It therefore proved to be suitable as a shellac substitute and was used primarily as

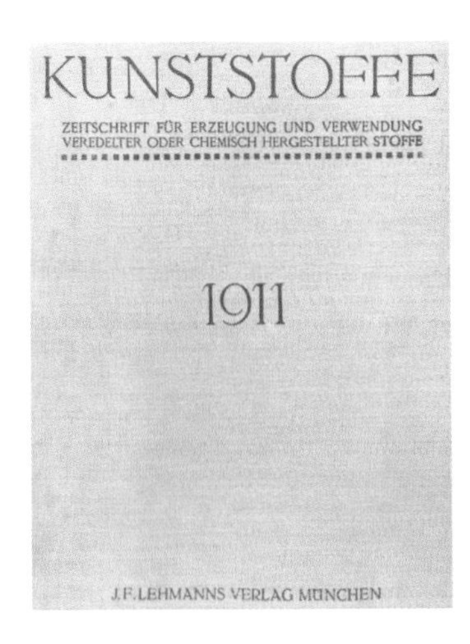
KUNSTSTOFFE

ZEITSCHRIFT FÜR ERZEUGUNG UND VERWENDUNG
VEREDELTER ODER CHEMISCH HERGESTELLTER STOFFE

1911

J.F. LEHMANNS VERLAG MÜNCHEN

A 2

A 3

a thin layer of insulation in the first electrical devices. At last the electrical engineering industry had the insulating material it had been searching for. Bakelite thus rendered possible the mass production of switches, ignition coils and radio and telephone equipment (Fig. A 3, see also "Phenol formaldehyde, phenolic resins", p. 46).

Polymer chemistry and industrial production

The German term for polymers or synthetic materials, *Kunststoffe*, was used for the first time in 1911, as the title of a trade journal, and established itself in the following years (Fig. A 2). However, the scientific basis for the production of polymers – polymer chemistry – was first developed in the early decades of the 20th century by Hermann Staudinger, professor of chemistry in Freiburg and Zurich (Fig. A 1). It was for this work that he was awarded the Nobel Prize in 1953.
In the early years the manufacture of celluloid, Bakelite and related materials was based on experience, speculation and chance. But a scientific basis rendered possible a fully focused development of synthetic materials: research into chemistry was transformed from experiments by creative individuals into strategically planned projects in large research departments. One example of the latter is nylon, the first completely synthetically produced and commercially exploited synthetic fibre. It is made from cold-drawn polyamide and was the result of 11 years of research by the American chemicals group DuPont. Led by Wallace Hume Carothers, who had succeeded in producing neoprene, a synthetic rubber, while working at DuPont in 1930, a 230-strong team was involved in the development of this synthetic fibre. When nylon was launched onto the market in 1938, it was initially in the form of bristles for toothbrushes and later for ladies' stockings. The first four million pairs of stockings were sold within a few hours of their appearance in New York stores in 1940! Working independently, a team at the I.G.-Farben industrie AG plant in Berlin succeeded in producing a polyamide fibre with a very similar structure in 1939; they called their product "Perlon". During the Second World War, these synthetic fibres, originally created for fashionable clothing, were used for parachutes. The polyester fibres so important for membrane structures these days were developed in England by J. R. Whinfield and J. T. Dickinson in 1940 and given the trade name "Trevira", also originally intended for clothing.

The oldest of the mass-produced polymers used these days is polyvinyl chloride, or PVC for short. Fritz Klatte, a researcher at the Griesheim-Elektron chemicals factory near Frankfurt am Main, patented a method for producing PVC as early as 1912. PVC was intended to replace the highly flammable celluloid. However, the outbreak of the First World War delayed the introduction of large-scale industrial production of PVC and it was not until the 1930s that this polymer could be mass produced for cable sheathing, pipes and numerous other commodities.
The majority of polymers appeared in quick succession in the middle of the 20th century:

- Polymethyl methacrylate (PMMA, acrylic sheet), 1933
- Polyethylene (PE), 1933
- Polyurethane (PUR), 1937
- Polyamide (PA), 1938
- Unsaturated polyester (UP), 1941
- Polytetrafluoroethylene (PTFE, Teflon), 1941
- Silicone, 1943
- Epoxy resin (EP), 1946
- Polystyrene (PS), 1949
- High-density polyethylene (PE-HD/HDPE), 1955
- Polycarbonate (PC), 1956
- Polypropylene (PP), 1957
- Ethylene tetrafluoroethylene (ETFE), 1970

Polymers in furniture and industrial design

Polymers are not even 100 years old – a great contrast to many of the other materials commonly used in the building industry. But the d esign options of these new materials were very quickly discovered and so it was not long before they became part of everyday building practice. Shapes that had been impossible in the past were now added to the vocabulary of industrial and furniture designers. Examples of this include the French desk lamp "Jumo Brevete" of 1945 made from Bakelite (Fig. A 4), or the range of foodstuffs containers made from

A 4

A 5

A 6

A 7

A 8

A 9

moulded thermoplastic polyethylene launched in 1946 by the Tupper Plastics Company, founded by former DuPont chemist Earl S. Tupper. In furniture the first really significant use of polymers for mass-produced articles began in 1948 with the seat shells of moulded, glass fibre-reinforced polyester designed by Charles and Ray Eames and marketed by the Plastic Shell Group (Fig. A 5, p. 11). Irwine and Estelle Laverne designed their "Champagne Chair" in 1957, with a seat shell of transparent, moulded acrylic sheet. They were inspired by the architect and designer Eero Saarinen, who two years previously had designed his "Tulip Chair". Perhaps the most important piece of polymer furniture ever, the stacking chair, first appeared in a design by Werner Panton in 1959 (Fig. A 6, p. 11). It was the first chair made from just a single material – rigid polyurethane foam (from 1970 onwards made from the styrene thermoplastic ASA/PC, later polypropylene; see also "Thermoplastic moulded items", p. 91) – using injection moulding and just one mould. It was in 1962 that Robin Day devised the "Polyprop", an extremely low-cost chair with the first polypropylene injection-moulded seat shell and legs made from bent steel tubes; some 14 million of these chairs have been sold since 1963!
Polymers were increasingly opening up new options thanks to the great flexibility of their material properties and the emergence of new production methods (e.g. polymer injection moulding), which also permitted new, more economic jointing principles to be used – a not insignificant factor. This process of expanding design and construction options, which would later become so important for the building industry, too, can be seen in the development of the LEGO building bricks system, which began life in the mid-20th century. Ole Kirk Christiansen, a Danish joiner who actually made wooden toys, was inspired by the children's building kit "Kiddicraft Self-Locking Building Bricks" (for which the Englishman Harry Fisher Page had been granted a patent) and began producing very similar building bricks in 1949, selling them under the name of "Automatic Binding Bricks", and from 1953 onwards under the LEGO brand. The first bricks were made from cellulose acetate, with the well-known studs on the top but completely hollow inside. With their firm but detachable connections and production by means of injection moulding, these bricks were a far cry from wooden building blocks. By 1958 hollow tubes had been incorporated inside to stabilise the connection between the bricks. That distinguished them even more so from the familiar options for fitting wooden blocks together.
The properties of the material itself were also optimised: since 1963 LEGO bricks have been made from the copolymer acrylonitrile butadiene styrene (ABS).
The example of the LEGO brick shows quite clearly that being able to adjust the material properties when designing the material plus moulding options can open up totally new configuration and jointing possibilities that go way beyond those of conventional materials. The huge popularity of building kits made from polymers (many others as well as LEGO) led to scores of people being subconsciously confronted with construction options from a very early age with constructions options other than those of classical building forms and materials.

The spread of polymers

Polymers are these days ubiquitous and produced in huge quantities. For example, bottles made from polyethylene terephthalate (PET) have been in widespread use since the mid-1990s. Returnable, reusable PET bottles, which are only about one-twelfth the weight of comparable glass bottles, can be returned and refilled about 10 times before they have to be reprocessed (approx. 40 reuses for glass bottles). Worldwide annual PET production amounts to approx. 40 million tonnes (2007), which accounts for about one-fifth of all polymers produced, and more than 125 million PET bottles were produced in 2003. The reuse rate, i.e. the proportion of recycled PET bottles as a percentage of the total quantity in circulation, was, for instance, 78 % in Switzerland in 2008 (more than 35 000 t, or more than one billion bottles).
The price of the main resource required for the production of polymers, i.e. petroleum, has so far remained comparatively low, a fact that has contributed to the enormous spread of polymer products throughout the world. But for the future we must ask ourselves how we wish to handle polymers when the price of their raw material starts to rise steeply. It is therefore likely that the development of biopolymers from renewable raw materials will become more and more important (see "Biopolymers", pp. 62–65). For example, polylactic acid (PLA) polymers made from lactic acid are already in wide use in the packaging industry. Although the market share is currently under 1 %, it is growing rapidly.
So, whereas the first polymers were made from natural cellulose and the transition to synthetic materials based on oil took place only gradually, 100 years later our newly acquired awareness of the finite nature of the earth's resources is triggering a reversal of this process.

The dream of the polymer house

During the Second World War, industry was producing goods almost exclusively for the armed forces. This situation had an effect on the emerging polymers industry – polymer production was mainly confined to parachutes, polyethylene cable sheathing for radar systems and lightweight, scratch-resistant polycarbonate turrets and cockpits for bombers. To achieve this, production capacities had to be stepped up very quickly: in the USA 5000 sheets of polycarbonate were being produced every month in 1937, but by 1940 the number had risen to 70 000!
After the war, these capacities were available for non-military uses once again. The search for new markets helped polymers to gain a foothold in all aspects of everyday life. For example, huge numbers of ladies' stockings could be produced for the market; the onslaught on American department stores when "nylons" finally became available again in the autumn of 1945 is legendary. Stockings, clothes and underwear made from nylon, Perlon or Trevira became incredibly popular in the post-war years. And household goods and packagings made from polyethylene or polypropylene were now suddenly appearing in every kitchen. As polymers proved successful for everyday items and were already being used for furniture, too, it seemed obvious to use them for buildings as well.

A 7 "Fly's Eye Dome" made from GFRP elements, USA, 1970, Richard Buckminster Fuller
A 8 Radome, USA, 1955, Richard Buckminster Fuller
A 9 Monsanto "House of the Future", demonstration building forming part of "Tomorrowland", Disneyland, California (USA), 1957, Richard Hamilton and Marvin Goody
A 10 "fg 2000", Altenstadt (D), 1968, Wolfgang Feierbach

A 10

First buildings of glass fibre-reinforced polymer (GFRP)
Lincoln Laboratories, a research institute belonging to the American Ministry of Defence founded in 1951 at the Massachusetts Institute of Technology (MIT), worked on the development of protective enclosures for radar stations, so-called radomes. As radar antennas sweep a circle and the sphere represents the smallest ratio of surface area to volume, Richard Buckminster Fuller's geodesic dome idea (1954) was taken up as a design principle. However, enclosures for radar stations needed to be free from metals as far as possible in order to avoid disrupting the electromagnetic signals. It was these requirements that led to the first assemblies made entirely of synthetic material. They consisted of manually laminated moulded parts with flanged edges for strength and for the connecting bolts. Glass fibre-reinforced epoxy or polyester resins were the materials used. The first dome employing this form of construction was erected on Mount Washington in 1955; many more followed for the radar stations of the Distant Early Warning Line in the Arctic (Fig. A 8). Today, they can be chosen more or less from a catalogue showing different versions and over 200 000 have been built to date.
Buckminster Fuller continued to work on the design principle of the polymer geodesic dome independently of these developments and in 1961 applied for a patent for his "Monohex" structure, which later also became known as the "Fly's Eye Dome" because of its circular openings fitted with acrylic sheet cupolas. In the patent he describes the production of these structures in timber, metal and GFRP. The first "Fly's Eye Domes" made from GFRP appeared in 1975 in three different sizes: 3.66 m (12 ft), 7.92 m (26 ft) and 15.24 m (50 ft). The smallest dome required just one moulded part and even the larger versions needed only two.

The polymer module for the house of tomorrow
It was not just a number of architects and research bodies who were expecting to see growth in the market for industrialised building. The chemicals industry was also hoping for a huge market in the building sector.

Monsanto "House of the Future" (USA)
In 1954 the Monsanto Chemical Company approached the MIT with the idea of developing a house made completely of polymers. Just one year later the MIT published a study entitled "Plastics in Housing", which described how the house of tomorrow might be. Flexible usage for changing families, easy relocation for increasing mobility and cost-effective housing for the growing middle classes were the main reasons behind building with polymers. All these aspects were to be demonstrated in a project that could be adapted to various plan layouts and local conditions through simple assembly and modifications. After two years of development and production, the first show house was built at "Disney World" in California in 1957 (Fig. A 9). Four cantilevering wings, containing living and sleeping quarters, were grouped around a square core mounted on a concrete base. The central core contained the rooms with high services requirements, i.e. kitchen, bathroom and WC. The outer envelope was a laminated sandwich construction in thicknesses between 7 and 11 cm, which were joined together to form hollow boxes capable of supporting the cantilevering wings. The core of the sandwich was a paper honeycomb filled with polyurethane (PUR) foam, the two facing layers 10 plies of glass fibre-reinforced polyester resin. Internal timber members stiffened the polymer construction at certain points. The many specialist publications [1] that accompanied the appearance of this building describe the windows as "washable plastic", which means they were probably made of acrylic sheet. Various plan layouts were also presented, but in reality modifying the arrangement was not so simple because of the many adhesive joints and seals. The weight of approx. 50 kg/m^2 each for the roof and the floor of the cantilevering wings was much lower than that of conventional forms of construction.
Inside the house, too, almost everything was made of polymers: shelves, kitchen cupboards and – naturally – the cutlery. All the technical devices that were expected to fill the homes of the future were also on display: video telephone, microwave, electric toothbrush and shelves extending/retracting at the touch of a button! [2]
Numerous polymer house prototypes appeared in rapid succession in the late 1960s. For instance, the catalogue to the "2nd International Plastic House Exhibition", held in Lüdenscheid, Germany, in 1972, contains illustrations of almost 90 houses and single-storey sheds built from polymers, with GFRP being used as the loadbearing or enclosing material.
The construction of the majority of these buildings was similar to that of the Monsanto design. What is remarkable is the contrast between the futuristic aspirations and the actual methods of production. Both the form of construction and the design language suggested industrial production. But in fact all these polymer buildings were built in small workshops using the simplest manual techniques.

fg 2000 (Germany)
It was in 1968 that the master model-maker Wolfgang Feierbach developed his "fg 2000" polymer house in Germany. His was the only polymer house system that was granted an approval for its sale and construction, and hence fulfilled the requirements for series production (Fig. A 10).
This building system consisted of slightly concave 1.25 × 3.40 m wall elements with rounded edges plus 1.25 × 10.50 m roof and floor elements, which were erected side by side to form the length of building required. The inner and outer "leaves" of the "fg 2000" were formed by 4 and 6 mm thick GFRP panels respectively. Between these there was an 8 cm core of rigid PUR foam as thermal insulation and stiffening material. The roof, floor and wall elements included preformed flanges connected by bolts; all joints were sealed with preformed strips of sponge rubber and polysulphide.
However, in this first prototype the diversity of the plan layout was severely restricted by the fact that all the panels were simply lined up side by side. A second prototype was therefore

A 11

A 11 "Zip-Up House", photograph of model, UK, 1969, Richard Rogers
A 12 "Futuro", Matti Suuronen
a Exterior view
b Interior view
A 13 The polyhedral housing modules of the Hübner family home, Neckartenzlingen (D), 1975, Peter Hübner and Frank Huster
A 14 In situ polyurethane foam building at the "International Plastic House Exhibition", Lüdenscheid (D), 1971, Peter Hübner

built in 1972, which included corner elements and self-supporting floor units that enabled the plan layout to be varied.

Zip-Up House (UK)
The "Zip-Up House" (1969) designed by the architect Richard Rogers is representative of a certain phase in English architecture in which the construction and the technology were the principal design features. The use of polymers for the loadbearing components is not obvious at first sight (Fig. A 11). The name "Zip-Up" stands for the assembly of individual sealed and highly insulated room modules made from 20 cm thick loadbearing sandwich panels, with the aluminium facing plies and the foamed polymer core acting together to create a stiff member. Like in vehicles, the joints and windows were sealed with synthetic rubber gaskets.
These self-supporting room modules spanning 9 m enabled a completely flexible interior layout and could be easily extended at a later date. The thermal insulation to these buildings was so good that in England a heating system was unnecessary.

Futuro (Finland)
The icon of all polymer houses is, however, probably the "Futuro", designed by the Finnish architect Matti Suuronen in 1968 (Fig. A 12). The concept of the house as a mobile unit, as an everyday article for everybody, is demonstrated by the "Futuro" like no other design. Its form makes abundantly clear that manned space flights were exerting a certain effect on the architecture of that period. It became the symbol of the space age and the unbroken belief in the boon of tomorrow's technology even though Suuronen stressed again and again that he only wanted to design a ski lodge!
The "Futuro" was an oblate spheroid measuring 8 m in diameter and 4 m high. It was made from eight identical, curved sandwich panels for the bottom half, another eight for the top half, and was mounted on a steel ring which made it possible to set up the building on rough terrain. The interior fitting-out was arranged concentrically, and with its fixed reclining seats and sanitary block was just as consistent in its design as the external form. By 1978 some 60 had been set up, meaning that "Futuro" could claim a modest economic success, in contrast to other polymer houses. [3]

Polymer houses as an expression of visionary ideas
The experiments with polymer houses took place at a time in which various utopias for the future of humankind were being formulated. Visions of future "mega cities" were triggered by the 1960 exhibition "Metabolism" in Tokyo and by the manifesto "Metabolism 1960 – The proposal for urbanism". The British architectural group Archigram published pictures of a "Walking City" or a "Plug-In City" influenced by pop culture. Flexibility and mobility were the key terms here and led to ideas of giant three-dimensional frameworks into which room modules were fitted.
The first polymer houses made in small batches attracted great interest from the public because they responded to such futuristic visions and made use of state-of-the-art polymer technology to do so. Polymers became an expression of an alternative culture, a subculture that began to emerge during this period. All over the world, avant-garde groups – oscillating between architecture and art – started to appear; besides Archigram in the UK, there were Ant Farm and Eat in the USA, Archizoom, Superstudio and UFO in Italy, and Coop Himmelb(l)au in Austria. They rebelled against the retrogressive tendencies of the architecture of that time, wanted to break away from conventional theory and practice. Experimentation with new forms and materials, like polymers, created the starting point for the development of new types of housing.

Building with polymers and the first oil crisis
However, the experiments with polymer houses ended in the mid-1970s just as swiftly as they had begun. The first oil crisis of 1973–74 brought about a rise in the price of the raw material, petroleum, and so polymer houses, which were expensive anyway, finally lost the chance to establish themselves on the market. In addition, humankind was gradually waking up to the fact that the earth's resources are finite, which meant that concepts such as Monsanto's "House of the Future" became ecologically questionable virtually overnight. In the years that followed, it also became clear that for a society where individuality was becoming more and more important, the idea of the industrially manufactured room module, which had once seemed to be the vision of the future, was now out of date. Polymers were so closely associated with such architectural notions that they had absolutely no chance of any further architectural development. The lack of experience with the design of such buildings plus poor workmanship led to building physics or constructional problems and so synthetic materials gained a reputation for being low-quality alternatives, a view that to some extent still persists today.

Room modules made from polymers – industrial prefabrication and batch production
An article by Peter Hübner published in the catalogue to the "1st International Plastic House Exhibition", held in Lüdenscheid, Germany, in 1971, captures the mood of this period: "It is not just cheap futuristic gossip to claim that in the coming decades people will live in houses, estates, yes, even towns and cities that are either wholly or partly based on synthetic materials ... Nothing more stands in the way of building and living in a world of plastics. Only ourselves at best because we find it difficult to accept something new. The hasty among us may be comforted by the fact that the evolution from the eternal flame to the perfectly functioning cigarette lighter also took more than just a few days." [4]
Hübner exhibited his tree house made from "in situ foam" at the exhibition, which represented a complete contrast to the precision of the industrial prefabrication that dominated the architectural ideas of that period (Fig. A 14).
The contract to provide 110 temporary room modules for kiosks, toilets and information pavilions on the site of the 1972 Olympic Games in Munich was the chance for the small-scale industrial production of these units. The room modules that Hübner devised for this were polyhedral, octagonal in plan with a side length of approx. 3.60 m. The walls consisted of three plies of corrugated cardboard that were subsequently coated with glass fibre-reinforced polyester resin. The built-in bathroom and kitchen items were made from deep-drawn polystyrene.

Hübner and his partner Frank Huster went on to develop this system of temporary room modules for permanent accommodation. He tested and demonstrated this by using the modules for his own house, which was built in just one day! This fact was expressed very neatly in the invitation he set out to guests: "The modules arrive in the morning, the guests in the evening" – an expression of his expectations for the buildings of the future. The vehicles loaded with 23 prefabricated "Casanova" modules left the Staudenmayer factory at 7 a.m. The foundations and building services had been prepared in advance in such a way that a mobile crane only had to lift the modules, already fitted with their services, into the appropriate positions. By the time the guests arrived for the opening ceremony in the evening, all the polymer elements had been assembled to form a complete house (Fig. A 13). Hübner tried to overcome the repetitive nature of the modules by employing diverse combinations. The main living quarters are linked by oversize openings, resulting in an almost open-plan layout; the modular arrangement of the system is not perceived as limiting space in any way. The house has been occupied since 1975 and as yet there have been no serious problems with the building fabric. Indeed, in 1985 and 1996 timber structures with green roofs were added.
Contrary to the supposition that systems such as these meant that humankind was standing on the brink of mass-produced housing, prefabricated room modules disappeared almost completely from architecture at the end of the 1970s. All that remained were polymer bathroom and sanitary units, which began to be produced in large numbers for hospitals and hotels in the mid-1970s.
Like many of his contemporaries, Hübner, too, turned away from topics such as series production and prefabrication and became involved in other, totally different, issues, especially ecological building.
The end of this period of experimentation with housing and building that had begun with so much enthusiasm is depicted by the inglorious end to the Monsanto house. Although it had been visited by 20 million people, it seems that there were no negotiations about further sales or considerations concerning small-scale production, and in 1967 the building was demolished. Easier said than done, however, because the demolition ball simply rebounded off the elastic building envelope! Instead, the house was surrounded by a wire rope and squashed – an operation that took two weeks. That showed that Monsanto had very little interest in demonstrating the idea of flexible, easily set up, easily relocated housing modules through a corresponding deconstruction plan. At this time obviously nobody believed any more in the future of this concept.

Polymers today

Defining architectural elements made from synthetic materials disappeared almost completely from architecture in the mid-1970s. However, since then, seals, insulation, coatings and many other items found virtually everywhere in buildings would be inconceivable without polymers. But their use as loadbearing and enclosing materials has remained mainly confined to niche markets where their durability and stability are especially important, e.g. covers to sewage treatment plants, walkways on offshore platforms, or installations in the chemicals industry.
The further development of polymers has since then taken place primarily in other technology sectors. Aircraft design played a pioneering role here as a result of the constant efforts to reduce weight and optimise aerodynamics. The first glider made from GFRP, christened "Phoenix", was produced at the University of Stuttgart as early as 1958. Airbus employed fibre composites for commercial aircraft for the first time in 1972; such materials account for 50 % of the latest aircraft, in the meantime even being used for parts of the fuselage that are crucial to safety. In order to save weight, a number of helicopters have a body made almost totally from fibre composites because every gram that can be saved reduces the power necessary for a vertical take-off. Similar materials are also being used in the construction of vehicles, boats and sports equipment. For example, there are racing cycles that apart from chain and bearings are made entirely of carbon fibre-reinforced polymers – they weigh less 3 kg! However, as such bicycles are very expensive to produce, a minimum weight for racing cycles has been laid down in order to avoid giving wealthy teams an unfair competitive advantage. By the time the first public footbridges made from glass fibre-reinforced polymers appeared in the late 1990s, viewed with great interest in construction circles, the semi-finished products and jointing techniques in use seemed to be almost hopelessly out of date compared with developments in other sectors of industry.
In architecture the new ideas regarding flowing forms and resolved spaces is reawakening interest in synthetic materials because sometimes polymers are the only way of achieving such random geometries. However, polymers are used today almost exclusively for cladding or facade elements only; their use for loadbearing or enclosing components, as in the polymer structures of the 1960s, remains confined to a few individual instances, e.g. the Itzhak Rabin Centre in Tel Aviv by Moshe Safdie (Fig. E 2.36, p. 184), or "The Walbrook" office building in London by Foster & Partners (see pp. 232–233). The continuous development of forms of construction suited to the materials and the demands of building is still in its infancy and the subject of current R&D work (see also "Potential, trends and challenges", pp. 24–27).

a

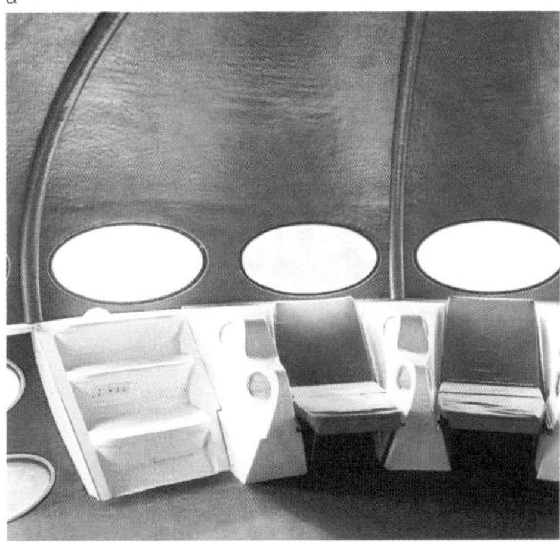

b

A 12

A 13

A 14

a

b A 15

Development of tensile surface structures

At first sight it seems strange to place building with membranes and building with polymers in the same context. Fabric constructions appeared many thousands of years before the first polymers and therefore are as old as humankind's attempts to protect itself against adverse weather. Only after we take a closer look do the similarities reveal themselves. Following the traumatic years of the Second World War, visionaries and utopians shook off the shackles of traditions and started searching for new forms of human co-existence, housing and building. One example of this is the work of Frei Otto, whose first lightweight tensile surface structures expressed a new understanding of building reflecting the works of nature. He can take credit for introducing the old idea of the tent into contemporary architecture around 1960; tent-like constructions had been used since ancient times solely as temporary, functional structures and were seen as unimportant in terms of architecture.
The roofs to Roman stadiums and theatres are good examples. Huge roofs made from lightweight cotton to provide shade were already in use during the reign of Julius Caesar. They were made from numerous individual pieces that could be moved and gathered together with ropes. The Romans made use of their experience with sailing ships for the design, construction and operation of these roofs, a fact that is reflected their name: *vela* (sail). The roof over the Colosseum in Rome, for example, measured 23 000 m^2 in area, a size that membrane roofs did not achieve again until the end of the 20th century. Although very few records remain, it is very likely that these Roman roofs built to provide shade were very sophisticated forms of construction. They were admired by contemporaries but not recorded because at that time they were associated wholly with engineering, not architecture. The pockets in the grandstands for the masts and pylons are the only remaining pieces of evidence for their existence. [5]
This knowledge of tensile surface structures was essentially preserved up until the middle of the 20th century. For example, although the *Handbuch der Architektur* (manual of architecture), an extensive encyclopaedia of building published around 1900, describes circus tents, at the same time it declares that "such temporary constructions certainly cannot be classed as belonging to the realm of architecture". [6] There were a few exceptions: the suspended roofs of the Russian engineer Vladimir Shukhov from the late 19th century or the fabric envelope to the "Pavillon des Temps Nouveaux" designed in 1937 by Le Corbusier for the World Exposition in Paris, but these had very little influence on the history of building and design in general.

The lightweight tensile surface structures of Frei Otto

All this changed in the middle of the 20th century. Frei Otto set up a small "four-point tent", as it was called, measuring 12.50 × 12.50 m at the German Horticulture Show in Kassel in 1955 which caused quite a stir because at this time nobody was familiar with the basic forms of tensile surface structures (Fig. A 15a). Although design, fabrication and erection took only six weeks, this simple roof over a music pavilion marked the start of a new era in membrane construction. This was the first ever demonstration of the principle of the opposing curvature of the prestressed membrane (see "Curvature", pp. 136–137). In addition to the music pavilion, Otto erected two other structures in Kassel: the group of three cushion-like "toadstools" (Fig. A 15b) and a corrugated tent roof, the "Falter" (butterflies), spanning over the vantage point at an intersection. All three structures were taken down at the end of the show. The success of these lightweight tent roofs led to a direct follow-up commission for the next German Horticulture Show in Cologne in 1957. Besides the entrance arch, a steel arch just 171 mm deep spanning 34 m and supporting a membrane which at the same time stabilised the arch against lateral overturning and buckling (Fig. A 17a), and the smaller "Humped Tent" (Fig. A 17c), it was primarily the star-shaped membrane over the central "Dance Pavilion" that caught the imagination of visitors (Fig. A 17b). The latter was formed by six masts and a membrane 1000 m^2 in area, which was made up of 12 identical segments arranged like a star with alternating high and low points around a central ring. Originally intended to be used for one

a

b A 16

a

b

c

A 17

summer only, the City of Cologne has re-erected the structure almost every year since then because of its popularity, which has meant that the membrane has had to be renewed several times. With its animated roof form, the balanced proportions and the precise design and construction, this small tent became not only one of the most influential lightweight structures but indeed one of the most important examples of German post-war architecture. It contrasts with the monumental edifices of the war years and the monotonous functionalism of the post-war period. It is a lightweight, temporary tent based on natural forms but at the same time indebted to technical progress. The designs of Frei Otto seemed to address the deep-rooted longing for a new type of building; there is no other explanation for the enormous influence that Frei Otto still exerts to this day.
His structures in Kassel and Cologne had already demonstrated all the forms of tensile surface structure. Encouraged by this successful beginning, he and others worked continuously to improve the constructional details, the materials and the form-finding methods in the following years. Over the decades it was not just the size of the structures that grew but also the range of possible applications.
Frei Otto gained international recognition with his free-form roofscape to the German Pavilion at EXPO 1967 in Montreal, which he designed together with Rolf Gutbrod (Fig. A 16). It was by far the largest roof he had realised so far – 8000 m^2. The loadbearing structure consisted of a net of 12 mm diameter steel ropes at a spacing of 50 cm. Constance-based Stromeyer & Co. fabricated the net in 9.50 m wide sections and shipped it to Montreal. Upon arrival on the site the various sections were fitted together on the ground and then lifted into the desired prestressed condition by raising the masts hydraulically. A membrane was suspended below the net to provide the actual weatherproof covering, attached to the steel ropes via thousands of clover leaf-shaped clamping discs.
The forces in the ropes had been calculated beforehand using elaborate measurement models at a scale of 1:75 at the University of Stuttgart's Institute of Lightweight Structures. A full-size trial building was also set up at the institute and is still in use today. Again, although originally only intended to be used for one summer, the German Pavilion in Montreal was retained for a further six years. The cable net became the model for the roofs for the Olympic structures in Munich in 1972.

Pneumatic structures

In the USA the development of building with membranes was essentially driven by the American armed forces' need for non-metallic protective enclosures for their sensitive radar systems. This led, on the one hand, to the GFRP radomes already described, but, on the other, to a different solution, an air-supported fabric envelope, which Cornell Aeronautical Laboratories presented to the world in Buffalo, New York, in 1946. Over the following two years, a team led by the young aerospace engineer Walter Bird designed and built the first pneumatic radome, hundreds of which had been set up across Canada and the USA by 1954 (Fig. A 18). This structure, originally developed for the military, was quickly adopted for civilian uses, e.g. tennis courts, swimming pools and exhibition halls (Fig. A 19). For Bird it was primarily the technical advantages of pneumatic structures for roofing medium-sized buildings that were important, but the great visionaries of this period saw in them a potential for designing new living spaces. Buckminster Fuller, for example, developed his idea of a climatic envelope over Manhattan in 1950, and Frei Otto, who published a much heeded systematic study of pneumatic structures in 1962, presented his ideas for a man-made settlement in Antarctica. Both were of the opinion that air-supported envelopes spanning 2000 m and even more would be technically possible. The background to such visions was supplied by Frei Otto's contribution to the "how shall we live" Congress held in 1967: "The classical forms of building will continue to be developed and will use more efficient forms to span ever larger areas whose possible boundaries must even today be measured in kilometres. Large spans permit the unrestricted and adaptable utilisation of the enclosed area, unhampered by the construction. It is possible, for example, to con-

A 15 German Horticulture Show, Kassel (D), 1955, Frei Otto
a Music pavilion in Karlsaue Park
b The "Three Toadstools", a seating area illuminated at night
A 16 a, b German Pavilion at the 1967 World Exposition in Montreal (CAN), Rolf Gutbrod and Frei Otto
A 17 German Horticulture Show, Cologne (D), 1957, Frei Otto
a Entrance arch
b "Dance Pavilion" with membrane roof
c "Humped Tent", view from the bank of the Rhine
A 18 Radome prototype, Walter Bird
A 19 Swimming pool enclosure, Walter Bird

A 18

A 19

struct large spatial grids made from variable three-dimensional nets that are not fixed in anyway, to tension these in the air and – why not? – accommodate housing units in them. The latest developments in building technology permit the realisation of development and intensification through synchronous change. The city in the sea or indeed on the moon, glasshouses in Antarctica and many other dreams are no longer utopian, but rather planning predictions." [7]
Frei Otto predicted that his plans for a town in Antarctica would be realised by the early 1980s; he had proved the feasibility of such a project together with Kenzo Tange and Ove Arup. However, the project never came to fruition.
The British avant-garde architects belonging to the Archigram group were also fascinated by pneumatic structures. They saw the structures as an opportunity to create flexible, adaptable, movable constructions – a total contrast to bourgeois architectural traditions.
The climax of the development of pneumatic structures could be seen at EXPO 1970 in Osaka: from movable canopies to inflated information pavilions and cushion roofs. The best-known pneumatic structure was probably the Fuji Pavilion of Yutaka Murata and Mamoru Kawaguchi (Fig. A 20). With its spectacular forms and colours, its link with pop art was undisguised. The pavilion comprised 16 arch-like tubes 4 m in diameter and 78 m long over a plan area 50 m in diameter. All the tubes were connected to a central fan which in the normal case created a pressure of 1000 Pa, but this could be increased to 2500 Pa during high winds. Another important structure was the USA Pavilion designed by the Davis, Brody & Ass. architectural practice in collaboration with the designers Chermayeff, Geismar, de Harak & Ass. and the engineer David H. Geiger. Its cable net-reinforced pneumatic construction would later become the model for many large single-storey sheds (Fig. A 21). The structure was oval in plan with axis dimensions of 142 and 83 m and a rise of just 6.10 m. It was the addition of a net of 32 wire ropes 48 mm in diameter that made the shallow curvature possible. The wire ropes were attached to a peripheral concrete compression ring, the weight of which prevented the roof from lifting. With a roof weight < 5 kg/m², only a small overpressure was needed. The exhibition area, sunk partly below the level of the surrounding site, was entered via air locks. This pavilion was one of the larger structures at EXPO 1970, but its significance was primarily due to its restrained and ingenious design.
Another first at EXPO 1970 was a roof with pneumatically prestressed polymers cushions; designed by Kenzo Tange and the engineers Yoshikatsu Tsuboi and Mamoru Kawaguchi, this form of construction has in the meantime become very important in architecture (Fig. A 22). The roof consisted of a steel space frame covered by square air-filled cushions each measuring 10.80 × 10.80 m. The pneumatically prestressed cushions were lightweight, transparent and not affected by the deformations and thermal movements of the large steel structure underneath, which measured 291 × 108 m. The internal overpressure was very low and could be increased to cope with strong winds. The upper membrane consisted of six plies of polyester foil, the lower membrane five. Pneumatically prestressed structures did not become as popular in the following years as had originally been anticipated because of the frequent technical problems during their long-term operation.

A 20

a

b
A 21

a

b
A 22

Cable nets and membrane roofs for sports stadiums
Roofs to large sports facilities have gradually become the domain of tensile surface structures over the years. Such amenities require long-span constructions that provide shade and protection from the rain, but otherwise do not usually have to comply with any other requirements with respect to sound or thermal insulation. Lightweight constructions are therefore able to exploit their full potential.

Anchored systems
The structures developed by Frei Otto were prestressed by tying back the lightweight roof surfaces via cables and masts to foundations in the ground. One highlight of this form of construction was the roof to the stadium for the 1972 Olympic Games in Munich. In terms of both its architectural concept and its constructional details, the roof designed by Günther Behnisch, Frei Otto and engineers from Leonhardt & Andrä (Jörg Schlaich) is modelled on the cable net of the German Pavilion for EXPO 1967 in Montreal, but on a much larger scale. Numerous studies and innovations – still relevant today – were necessary for the realisation: the covering of acrylic sheets (see Figs. E 5.16 and E 5.17, p. 218), ground anchors, new types of cable, fatigue-resistant clamps, anchorages and saddles of cast steel and, first and foremost, numerical form-finding methods (see "Form-finding", pp. 138–140) plus computer-assisted drawing and calculation programs, which were being used on a large construction project for the first time.
However, the construction of the cable net in Munich also revealed one great disadvantage of such structures: open roofscapes of this size require enormous tensile forces which in turn call for elaborate anchorages in the ground. In Munich the gravity foundations for the main cable are the size of small apartment block!

Spoked wheel systems
Another approach is to use constructions based on complete tension and compression rings which are therefore known as spoked wheel systems. These are particularly suitable for large sports grounds which are often circular or oval in plan.
Drawings dating from the 17th century showing reconstructions of ancient roofs over Roman arenas indicate suspension systems with a complete tension ring at the inner edge of the roof. The American engineer David H. Geiger developed this idea further for roofing over modern sports arenas. His first roof structure of this type was the gymnastics hall completed in 1986 ahead of the Olympic Games in Seoul (1988).
Such closed systems are preferred these days because, in contrast to the anchored systems, they need no large foundations to resist the tensile forces. One example of a spoked wheel system, which at the same time gives us an idea of the spatial effect of the covered arenas of ancient times, is the roof to the bullfighting arena in Saragossa, Spain, designed by the engineers Jörg Schlaich and Rudolf Bergermann and completed in 1990 (Fig. A 24). The primary structure consists of an outer compression ring 83 m in diameter and two inner tension rings, spaced apart by vertical props, each 36 m in diameter. Sixteen radial cables connect the tension and compression rings. The vertical propping at the inner tension rings stiffens and tensions the system. In the outer ring a compressive force ensues that is in equilibrium with the tensile forces in the inner rings. The compression ring is mounted on top of the grandstand which means the latter essentially carries only the vertical loads and elaborate anchorages for the tensile forces are unnecessary. A movable membrane provides a roof to the sand-covered arena in the middle. When open, the membrane is gathered beneath a central hub, a principle that Frei Otto had used as early as 1967 for the roof over the ruins of an abbey in Bad Hersfeld, Germany. The movable roof is closed by pulling it along the radial cables attached to the lower inner tension ring and then tensioned to prevent it flapping in the wind by splaying the central hub. As tensioning the central membrane requires considerably larger forces than the opening and closing operations, separate drives are provided for these two functions.
Schlaich and Bergermann took the design of the spoked wheel roof one step further for the conversion of Stuttgart's light athletics and football stadium in 1993 (Fig. A 23). Another form of construction would have been impossible because Stuttgart's mineral water stipulations prevented the use of guy ropes back to the ground – and hence the associated foundations. In contrast to the solution employed in Saragossa, this system, over an oval plan, consists of two compression rings, spaced apart by vertical props, and one inner tension ring. A total of 40 radial cables every approx. 20 m span between the inner tension ring, which consists of eight parallel cables each 79 mm in diameter, and the compression rings. The radial cables spanning up to 58 m divide the roof, a total area of 34 000 m², into 40 segments. Each individual membrane segment is itself supported by seven compression arches mounted on the lower radial cables. The arches lend the membrane sufficient curvature and reduce the unsupported spans so that a lightweight, light-permeable, PVC-coated polyester fabric can be used as the roof covering. This form of construction proved to be extremely efficient and became the prototype for numerous stadium roofs throughout the world designed by Schlaich and Bergermann and their partner Knut Göppert.

A 23

A 20 Exhibition pavilion of the Fuji company at the 1970 World Exposition in Osaka (J), Yukata Murata and Mamoru Kawaguchi
A 21 USA Pavilion at the 1970 World Exposition in Osaka (J), Davis, Brody & Ass. with David H. Geiger
a Aerial view
b Interior (overpressure)
A 22 Roof to Festival Plaza at the 1970 World Exposition in Osaka (J), Kenzo Tange, Yoshikatsu Tsuboi and Mamoru Kawaguchi
a Aerial view
b Close-up of polymer cushions
A 23 Roof to Gottlieb Daimler Stadium, Stuttgart (D), 1993, Schlaich, Bergermann & Partner
A 24 Bullfighting arena, Saragossa (E), 1990, Schlaich, Bergermann & Partner
a Aerial view
b Closing the roof over the central arena

a

b A 24

A 25

A 26

a

b A 27

Tensile surface structures in contemporary architecture
The roof in Stuttgart is representative of the change in notions of form. The coherent, large and gently sweeping surface of the roof in Munich was dissected into small segments in Stuttgart. This transition from the random roofscape embedded in its surroundings to an autonomous, optimally engineered, modular structure is typical of the architectonic configuration of tensile survace structures towards the end of the 20th century.
The way in which form is dependent on mechanical principles and the inherent potential to create highly efficient structures exerted a great fascination on architects and engineers in the final years of the 20th century. In some instances the logic of the form and the design is inflated by the architectural realisation, a fact that also manifests itself in an expressive display of the construction and its details. A good example of this late 20th century movement – so-called high-tech architecture – is the Inland Revenue Centre in Nottingham by Michael Hopkins dating from 1994 (Fig. A 28).
These days, architects are mostly searching for other forms – forms that are not determined by engineering and the physical laws of tensile structures. Building with woven fabrics and polymer foil should fit in with, not dominate, the overriding architectural concept. In the ideal case architects are able to achieve new forms and still do justice to the logic of the design and material. Examples of this are the Allianz Arena in Munich by the Swiss architects Herzog & de Meuron (Fig. D 1.18, p. 142), or the National Aquatics Centre ("Watercube") in Beijing by the Australian architects PTW, to name but two. Thomas Herzog is also exploring new paths with his project for the mountain rescue service in Bad Tölz (2008) (see "Training centre for mountain rescue service", pp. 260–261).

Materials in membrane architecture – from natural to synthetic fibre fabrics and polymer foil
It was not only cultural contexts and progress in the design and analysis of tensile surface structures that determined the development of building with membranes. Innovations in the materials themselves – and primarily the changeover from natural to synthetic fibres – played a decisive role. This fact is particularly evident in the development of pneumatic structures.
The idea for the pneumatic structure, and its constructional predecessor, was supposedly the first hot-air balloon, built by the Montgolfier brothers in 1783, and the hydrogen balloon flown by Jacques Charles just a short time later. The English researcher and engineer Frederick William Lanchester was certainly one of the first to transfer the idea of pneumatics to a building. His design for a field hospital supported by just a minimal overpressure without masts or suspension ropes was patented in 1917. However, this idea remained on the drawing board because no airtight fabrics were available at that time with which an economically viable hospital could have been built. It was not until the introduction of polymer-coated membranes in the mid-20th century that Walter Bird was able to take up Lanchester's ideas and build a great many pneumatic structures.
During the 1950s and 1960s experiments were carried out everywhere with a diverse range of synthetic fabrics made from polyamide (nylon, Perlon), polyester (Trevira, Dacron) or acrylic (Dralon) with coatings of synthetic rubber (Hypalon, neoprene), PVC or polyurethane.

Frei Otto used fabrics made from natural fibres for his first tensile surface structures. For example, the membrane over the music pavilion at the 1955 German Horticulture Show in Kassel was made from approx. 1 mm thick heavyweight cotton fabric and its 18 m span was much larger than the spans typical for tents up until that time (Fig. A 15a, p. 16). However, the disadvantages of natural fibres become evident when they are exposed to the weather and high stresses. Frei Otto, too, therefore soon began experimenting with synthetic fibres.
By the time of the 1957 German Horticulture Show in Cologne he was already using a PUR-coated glass fibre membrane for the entrance arch (Fig. A 17a, p. 17). However, this new material did not last long: although the glass fibre material was unaffected by UV radiation, it was affected by moisture, which permeated through the coating. The arch was therefore given a covering of tried-and-tested cotton fabric after just one season.
A polyamide fabric used for a tent at the 1957 "Interbau" building exhibition in Berlin did not last long either. After just six weeks the membrane developed a tear, the cause of which – as was later discovered – was dyeing with titanium oxide. Again, this synthetic fibre membrane had to be replaced by a dependable cotton fabric.

A 25 Fuller looking out of the top of his "Necklace Dome", Black Mountain College, Asheville (USA), 1949, Richard Buckminster Fuller
A 26 Union Tank Car Company, dome spanning 130 m, Baton Rouge (USA), 1958, Richard Buckminster Fuller
A 27 "Brass Rail" restaurant at the 1964 World Exposition in New York (USA)
a Exterior view
b Bird's-eye view of roof from inside
A 28 Inland Revenue Centre, Nottingham (UK), 1994, Michael Hopkins
A 29 Private house, Tokyo (J), 1996, FOBA

A 28

A 29

Frei Otto's first projects employing PVC-coated polyester fabric were the roof over the open-air theatre in Wunsiedel (1963), a convertible roof in Cannes (1965) and the German Pavilion in Montreal (1967). By 1970 this fabric had become established as a durable, flexible and cost-effective standard material for tensile structures (see "PVC-coated polyester fabric", p. 104).

Glass fibre fabric

Glass fibre fabric was used as an alternative to the UV-sensitive synthetic fibres from an early date. In doing so, various coatings were tried out. Besides the PUR coating already mentioned above in conjunction with the entrance arch to the 1957 German Horticulture Show in Cologne, a PVC coating was used on the American Pavilion at EXPO 1970 in Osaka (Fig. A 21, p. 18). This pioneering structure inspired a series of similar single-storey shed designs, such as the "Pontiac Silverdome" designed by the architect Don Davidson and the engineer David H. Geiger and built near Detroit in 1975. This was the first time a PTFE-coated glass fibre fabric was used, which by the end of the 20th century had become another high-quality and, in addition, virtually inflammable standard material for tensile surface structures. However, this air-supported membrane had to be replaced by a conventional supporting framework of steel beams after being damaged by snow in 1985 – symptomatic of the failure of very large pneumatic structures, so-called airdomes.

Polymer foil

The technique of extruding polymer film (often called foil) made from polyamide, polyethylene or PVC has been known since the 1940s. Walter Bird, Richard Buckminster Fuller, Kenzo Tange and others used transparent PVC foils. Their high resistance to gas diffusion makes them especially suitable for pneumatic structures. However, they achieve only low strengths, which means that they can only be used for unimportant components carrying low loads. The stronger, more durable and UV-permeable extruded ETFE foil did not become available until the mid-1970s. It was used initially to replace the glass in glasshouses and was not employed for building envelopes until after being used on a glasshouse in Arnheim in 1982, which paved the way for its use in architecture (see "Foil", pp. 94–99).

However, the new materials were used for other purposes only indirectly connected with building, e.g. the "treetop raft" of 1986 developed by the French architect Gilles Ebersolt in cooperation with the botanist Francis Hallé which allowed the treetops of tropical rainforests to be reached and studied directly for the first time. The structure of the PVC-coated polyester tubes, which are connected with aramid fibre nets to create a hexagon approx. 27 m across, forms a surface that can be used as a "floating" laboratory by up to six people. A hot-air balloon carries the raft to the respective study site. This example shows that structures made from synthetic materials can be ideal for highly specific applications, e.g. temporary, mobile structures for very specific sites.
Fabrics and polymer foils are also being used increasingly even though building specifications are becoming more and more demanding – frequently because of higher thermal insulation standards. Numerous innovations are improving their performance constantly. Those improvements include functional layers, e.g. low E coatings (an optical functional layer with a low emissivity), which was used for the first time at Bangkok's new airport (see "Passenger terminal complex, Suvarnabhumi International Airport", pp. 277–279), new translucent thermal insulation (see "Aerogels in tensile surface structures", pp. 220–221) and integral photovoltaics (see "Photovoltaics", pp. 122–123).
In many cases the use of these materials leads to very striking buildings, the design of which is determined by the material. Whereas there are many examples of large buildings where membranes have been used, membrane architecture has been employed rather less often for smaller projects. A small house in Tokyo provides one significant example, built on a site measuring just 4 × 21 m in 1996. The envelope consists to a large extent of a translucent PTFE-coated glass fibre fabric in double curvature, with the house "breathing light in the 24-hour rhythm of the city", according to the architects.

Structures with transparent and translucent envelopes

While many architects and engineers were still grappling with the idea of the industrially prefabricated housing unit, Buckminster Fuller was already turning to new areas. He had been experimenting with industrial manufacturing methods for vehicles and aircraft since the 1920s and later taught himself everything about the geometric studies of spheres. In the late 1940s he and his students at Black Mountain College, a tiny art school in North Carolina, built his first geodesic domes. He used transparent foil for the covering because it did not place any appreciable load on his delicate arrangement of rods nor did it impair the appearance (Fig. A 25). In his view, synthetic materials were not "synthetic"; he saw the structure of polymers as a further development of the principles of natural geometrical orders. [8] Finally, at the age of 58, he received his first proper commission: the roof to the Ford Rotunda (1953). Here he used a vinyl material to cover the lattice dome and therefore probably created the first structure with a transparent polymer envelope (Fig. A 26). Numerous geodesic domes followed as a result, including his most famous structure, the USA Pavilion at the 1967 World Exposition in Montreal, where the resolved, exposed structure of the dome had a lasting influence on the next generation of architects.
For this project Buckminster Fuller developed a two-layer space frame with a diameter of 76 m and a height of 61 m (Fig. A 33, p.23). It consisted of steel tubes, the outer layer of which formed a triangular grid, the inner layer a hexagonal one. Between the two layers he placed moulded elements of acrylic sheet with triangular awnings on the inside that could be moved to provide shade depending on the position of the sun. A computer program ensured that the shading elements tracked the sun and therefore only the minimum number of panels were closed, thus retaining the transparent and lightweight character of the dome. This dynamic coordination between interior climate and view in/out was Fuller's interpretation of what we now call a "smart" building envelope. Unfortunately, the structure was destroyed by fire during maintenance work in 1976.

A 30 Petrol station, Thun (CH), 1962, Heinz Isler
a Canopy during construction
b View of soffit
A 31 "Les échanges" pavilion at EXPO 64, Lausanne (CH), 1964, Heinz Hossdorf
A 32 Roof to Olympic Games stadium, Munich (D), 1972, Günther Behnisch, Frei Otto and the engineers of Leonhardt & Andrä (Jörg Schlaich)
A 33 USA Pavilion at the 1967 World Exposition in Montreal (CAN), Richard Buckminster Fuller
a Photograph taken against the sun
b Section of the dome viewed from inside
A 34 Studies of folded plate structures and space frames, Renzo Piano
a Movable roof for a sulphur processing plant, 1966
b, c Studies of space frames with polymer pyramids,1964/65

a

b

A 30

A 31

A 32

Other architects and engineers, too, discovered that translucent polymers could be used to provide a new design and construction element. One good example of this is the petrol station canopy in Thun, Switzerland, designed by the engineer Heinz Isler in 1960. Isler became famous through his concrete shells, for which he was using polymers for the moulds and the transparent rooflights with diameters of 5–8 m as early as the mid-1950s. He was therefore very familiar with this material. The canopy in Thun is in the form of a 50 cm thick sandwich element measuring 14 × 22 m on plan. It was built on the ground. Firstly, plies of glass fibre-reinforced polyester were laminated together to form the soffit, with a relatively low proportion of glass fibres (25 %) in order to achieve a good degree of translucency. Preformed boxes, open on one side, were placed on the soffit, with the open sides together, before the soffit had fully dried. The plies to create the top surface of the canopy were then laid on top of the closed top surfaces of the boxes (Fig. A 30a). The ensuing slab was then lifted as a whole into position on top of the eight fixed-base steel columns with their shallow column heads (Fig. A 30b). This simple structure achieved its effect through its translucency. But the roof became discoloured after a number of years and was finally painted white 10 years after was first built, which turned this special translucent structure into a standard petrol station canopy.
The Swiss engineer Heinz Hossdorf was another who experimented with translucent polymers and used these for the roof to the central exhibition area for EXPO 1964 in Lausanne, for instance (Fig. A 31). He placed 24 canopy-type elements (each 18 × 18 m) over a rectangular area measuring 108 × 72 m. Each canopy consisted of four identical hyperbolic paraboloids supported on a fixed-base tubular steel column and also braced back to the column. The areas between these canopies were closed off with triangular elements. A total of 192 elements with two basic forms were laminated by hand for this roof. The GFRP elements were only 3 mm thick and had a glass fibre content of just 30 % in order to achieve maximum light permeability.
The surfaces were lit from above, which meant that at night the whole structure was evenly illuminated. Steel frames and prestressing stabilised these large but very thin GFRP segments. A hydraulic system was used to pull the top of each column downwards and create the prestressed force. As with an umbrella, the segments are pushed outwards by the struts and tensioned. The prestressing principle makes it clear that this structure not only employs the language of tensile surface structures, it is also a very close relation in terms of its construction as well. It could have been realised in a very similar way with a fabric as well. After just three years this elegant structure was demolished and not one single canopy remained. [9]
The roofs to the 1972 Olympic Games facilities in Munich also played a part in spreading the use of transparent polymers (see "Cable nets

a

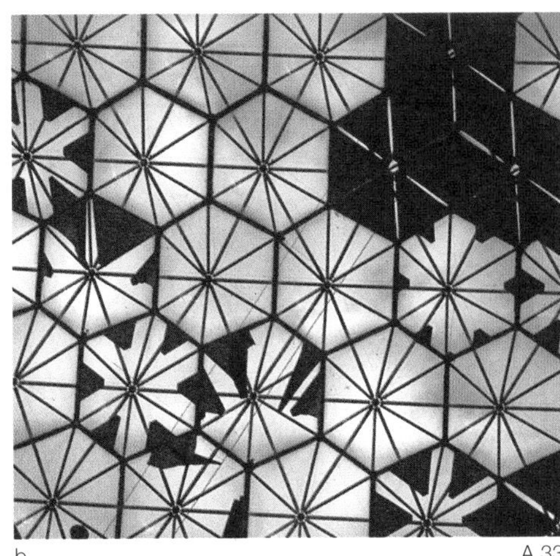
b

A 33

and membrane roofs for sports stadiums", p. 19). Initially, the architects led by Günther Behnisch discussed numerous alternatives for the covering to the cable net – from PVC-coated membranes like those used in Montreal to metal tiles or timber sheathing.
The television companies, however, wanted a light-permeable roof surface because during the previous football World Cup in 1970 in Mexico the stadium roofs had cast strong shadows on the pitches, and the television cameras could not compensate for the ensuing contrast. Various light-permeable foils and sheets were therefore investigated and it was discovered that only acrylic sheet satisfied the fire and durability requirements (Fig. A 32). Panels measuring 2 × 2 m were produced and then stretched to 3 × 3 m at a temperature of 150 °C. In the event of a fire the panels try to shrink at about 200 °C, but the aluminium frame prevents this. The ensuing stresses cause the panels to crack, which allows heat and smoke to escape upwards. An additive in the acrylic material prevents the spread of flame and the formation of dangerous molten droplets. The panels were fixed to the pretensioned cable net with an aperture of 75 cm. Approx. 14 cm wide black neoprene strips join the panels together in order to accommodate the movement of the cable net and the expansion and contraction of the panels. This is what gives the roof its visual character and the loadbearing cable net becomes less intrusive. Initially, the superimposition of neoprene strips and cables was considered undesirable, but in the meantime the image of the roof has become so characteristic that it will remain unchanged even though these days ETFE foil could be used to achieve a covering essentially free from joints. Panels almost identical in terms of material and construction were used when after about 25 years the acrylic panels had to be replaced due to embrittlement and discolouring. Like the original panels, soot particles were added to the majority of the new panels to give them a slight hue.

The Olympic facilities in Munich and the American EXPO pavilion in Montreal are pioneering and much admired structures that have inspired many architects to employ light-permeable polymers. Renzo Piano is mentioned here as an example. In the mid-1960s one of his tutors was the mathematician and engineer Zygmunt Stanisław Makowski, who alongside the architect and engineer Konrad Wachsmann and the mechanical engineer Max Mengeringhausen can be classed as one of the pioneers in the field of modern space frames. At the University of Surrey's "Plastic Research Unit" Makowski was also experimenting with folded plate structures and space frames made from moulded GFRP parts with pyramidal or hyperbolic paraboloid forms, which acted as the roof covering and at the same time helped to carry the loads (Fig. A 34). Influenced by this, Renzo Piano designed such structures for simple exhibition halls or warehouses in Italy. Although these first space frames were very straightforward in terms of their construction and design language, they nevertheless mark the start of Piano's involvement with materials, their properties, their processing and the ensuing architectural opportunities. He returned to the theme of the polymer pyramids for his IBM pavilion of 1982. This pavilion was designed to house a travelling exhibition visiting 20 European cities. A lightweight construction and simple assembly and dismantling were the main requirements of the design brief. The truss-like arches spanning 12 m consisted of just three materials: laminated birch wood for the top and bottom chords, transparent polycarbonate for the cross-bracing pyramids and aluminium for the connecting elements (Fig. A 35, p. 24).

Compared with the structures of the 1960s, the development of polymers was now becoming clear: initially used as a protective envelope to radar installations for functional reasons, then as roofs over industrial plants or pneumatically supported roofs over swimming pools, they were now becoming materials that could also satisfy high quality demands regarding appearance and feel. Finally, architects such as Richard Buckminster Fuller, Günther Behnisch or Renzo Piano began using polymers for the structure and design of outstanding buildings and thus helped them find their place in architecture.

a

b

c

A 34

Potential, trends and challenges

Synthetic materials have in the meantime become highly developed, tried-and-tested and efficient materials and offer the following advantages over conventional materials:

- Huge potential for lightweight structures due to high specific strengths
- Resistance to aggressive media
- Low thermal conductivity
- Diverse design options in terms of form and transparency
- Adjustability of material properties through additives
- Integration of functional and constructional components

Combined with or bonded to conventional materials, e.g. glass, wood-based products or metals, many new options are available which will be presented below.

Applications and potential

These days, synthetic materials come into their own mainly when special requirements regarding weight, durability, form, colour and translucency are relevant.

Polymers for lightweight construction

In architecture, a high specific strength, i.e. a favourable ratio of tensile strength to self-weight, is primarily important for membrane materials. A frequently used and vivid means of appreciating the specific strength is the so-called breaking length. This is the length at which a fibre suspended vertically will break under its own weight (see "Mechanical properties", pp. 48–49). For typical metallic materials such as aluminium or steel, this length is about 15–25 km, for natural fibres such as cotton or silk 40–50 km and for glass fibres up to 180 km.

As a comparison, the polyamide or polyester fibres currently in use achieve breaking lengths of about 100 km and carbon fibres about 250 km. Much longer breaking lengths of up to 400 km are possible with high-strength polyethylene fibres, and the latest materials based on nanotechnology ("carbon nano tubes") can theoretically achieve breaking lengths of up to 5000 km, but up until now such fibres have only been produced on a laboratory scale.

At the moment, high-strength fibres cannot be woven to form a fabric that can be used practically or economically for tensile surface structures. However, this shows that the development of efficient materials for such structures is by no means over.

Polymers for corrosion-resistant external components

The weathering resistance and durability of polymers are critical for external applications. In contrast to metals, many polymers are also resistant to acids and alkalis. They have therefore been used for many years in applications where such properties are crucial, e.g. covers to sewage treatment tanks, pipes and vessels

a

b

A 35

A 35 IBM Pavilion during the exhibition in Milan (I), 1984, Renzo Piano
a Interior view
b Exterior view
A 36 Fibre-optic sensors in carbon fibre-reinforced polymer
a Parallel with reinforcing fibres
b Perpendicular to reinforcing fibres

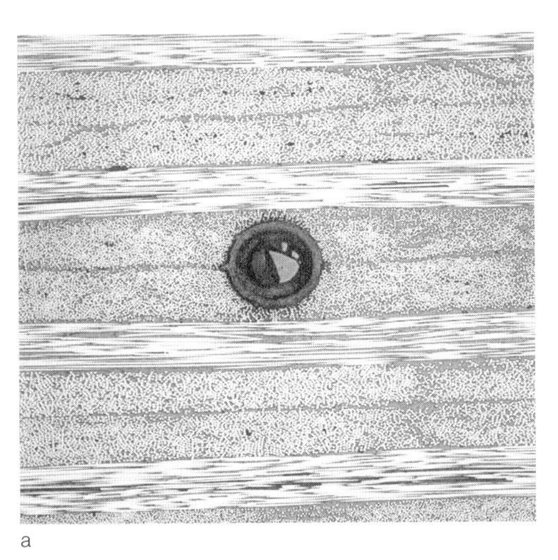
a

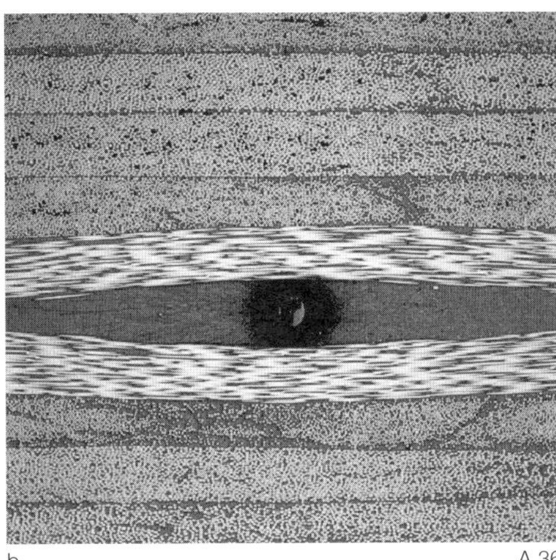
b A 36

in the chemicals industry, or walkways and platforms in offshore applications. And as our environmental conditions become more and more aggressive, so this resistance becomes increasingly important for other uses in the construction sector. For example, intensive research is being carried out into bridge decks made from glass fibre-reinforced polymers (GFRP). These are resistant to frost and de-icing salts which in combination with moisture are the main cause of corrosion damage and the inevitable repairs to reinforced and prestressed concrete bridges which are so costly and disruptive to traffic (see "Special semi-finished products for engineering applications", pp. 92–93).
In the early days of building with synthetic materials, UV light caused considerable damage to the materials because it attacked the bonds between the carbon atoms. In the meantime, however, stabilisers that absorb UV light and reflective coatings are used which provide reliable protection.

Polymers for the thermal envelope
The low thermal conductivity of polymers – very similar to that of timber and hence clearly below that of glass and concrete and much, much lower than that of all metals – is particularly interesting for the design of the building envelope. The thermal conductivity of a polymer can be reduced still further by foaming up the material, and the use of heavy gases enables polymers to achieve values even higher than that of stationary air. Appropriate foams made from polystyrene (PS) and polyurethane (PUR) are undergoing constant optimisation, especially with respect to their permeability to infrared radiation, their outgassing behaviour and greater porosity. Furthermore, phenolic resin foams with a very low thermal conductivity of only approx. 0.022 W/mK are currently at an advanced stage of development.
Thermoplastic materials, mostly PVC and polyamide, have been in use for some time as frames for facade glazing because they are ideal thermal breaks. Intensive research is currently being carried out into the use of GFRP for windows and facades because, apart from its low thermal conductivity, it can be used as a loadbearing material and is also durable. In addition, extruded (pultruded) GFRP sections with a glass fibre content of about 70 % exhibit a similar coefficient of expansion to glass itself. Consequently, it is possible to create a rigid adhesive bond between glazing and GFRP without the fear of causing significant restraint stresses as a result of disparate expansion/contraction behaviour. It is then no longer necessary to provide an elastic layer between the glass and its frame to compensate for the different behaviours (see "GFRP-glass composite", p. 164). Many manufacturers of windows and facades are currently working on such developments. The use of GFRP could result in slimmer frame widths compared with other materials, especially wood or PVC – from the architectural viewpoint a considerable bonus (see "Company headquarters", p. 244).

Geometry and moulding
In contrast to metal, glass, timber and other conventional building materials, many synthetic materials are suitable for moulding and shaping methods that enable the relatively simple production of components with complex shapes and hence open up new design options. This brings chances for design, but also risks because that theme of "doing justice to the material" so critical in architecture seems to become elusive. Apparently everything and anything is possible! That is especially true for forms of construction with rigid materials, but to a certain extent also pneumatic structures in which the cutting pattern allows the realisation of many ideas regarding form, even though the inherent logic does define a clear framework for the shaping.
The shaping options are, however, also important for many construction details, which without preformed gaskets, clips, built-in boxes and mountings made from polymers would become impossible (see "Building with semi-finished polymer products", pp. 160–173).

Translucency and transparency
The light permeability of materials is an important design element and in the case of synthetic materials can often be adjusted across a wide range (Fig. A 41, p. 27). Polymers are the only materials that allow the building of long-span but at the same time light-permeable structures. A light permeability of approx. 40 % can be achieved with PTFE fabrics for tensile surface structures, and with fibre-reinforced thermosetting polymers values of up to even 85 % are possible. Fluoropolymer foil in the thicknesses used in building can achieve a light transmission of up to approx. 95 %, and acrylic sheet yet higher values.

Trends and developments
Many of the possibilities that polymers offer are currently hardly exploited and are still at the development stage.

Adjusting the material properties
Traditionally, structures are assembled from a limited number of materials with defined properties. When building with polymers and membranes, it is first of all necessary to fully understand the basics in order to choose the right solution from the vast range of raw materials and semi-finished products. Diverse combinations of foils, fibres and coatings are possible for membranes. The same is true for fibre composites, where the reinforcing fibres, the formative synthetic material (matrix), fillers and additives can be varied, often very easily. In doing so, it is not only the technical properties, but also the visual and haptic qualities that can be specifically controlled. The selection and control of the material components represent new and demanding responsibilities for architects and engineers. Interesting visual effects can be achieved by adding thermochromic, phosphorescent or photochromic pigments. Research into and the use of such options for "smart" building envelopes, whose light permeability can be adapted to suit the outside temperature or UV radiation, are still at the early stages of development. The same applies to the integration of materials that store heat or moisture (e.g. phase change materials – PCM, see also p. 33). Combined with transparent polymers, this can result in interesting visual and building physics characteristics (see "Building physics and energy aspects", pp. 108–123), but these aspects are still currently undergoing investigation.

Polymers for exploiting solar energy

Polymers offer numerous options for the optimum passive and active use of solar energy. Radiation exchange plays a relatively major role in the majority of structures made from polymers and so the exact adjustment of the optical properties becomes crucial. This concerns transmission in the UV range for glasshouses and solar transmission for building envelopes, but also behaviour in the infrared range (reflection and absorption; see "Building physics and energy aspects", pp. 108–123, and "Shopping centre in Amadora", pp. 256–257). These properties can be adjusted by way of additive methods, i.e. the lamination of various materials, by exploiting nanostructures and microstructures, but also through special coating processes. Many of these optimisation processes represent major challenges for designers, especially in those cases where the material is exposed to the interior or indeed the exterior climate. In solar technology the first steps with respect to building integration for photovoltaics have already been taken for PC, PMMA, ETFE and glass/PTFE (see "Photovoltaics", pp. 122–123, and "Complex building envelopes", pp. 212–223). Polymers have long since been crucial in standard photovoltaic modules (e.g. as cover or backing sheets or as a substrate for flexible photovoltaic elements). Great things are expected to come from the development of polymer-based photovoltaic technology, which is currently grouped under the heading of "organic PV". This technology is expected to cut costs in the production of photovoltaics and make products easier to use in practice.

In the area of solar thermal systems, polymers already account for approx. 15 % of the components used. New developments are underway; these concern the absorber itself, but also supporting frameworks, connectors, cables and the insulating and covering materials.

Outlook – multi-functional elements made from polymers

The processing of synthetic materials often takes place at comparatively low temperatures and pressures, which is why it is possible to integrate functional elements. For example, it is relatively easy to incorporate light-channelling glass or polymer fibres for later lighting effects in fibre composites (Fig. A 40).

The integration of sensors for measuring temperature, stresses or damage is important in aerospace applications. Embedding these in the material protects them against external influences and enables the measurement of variables within the component itself and not only on its surface. The use of piezoceramics is very common in aircraft. These convert strains into electrical voltages to enable permanent monitoring of the mechanical actions within the component.

Fibre-optic sensors represent another form of technology that is currently being developed for aircraft; the first applications are undergoing trials. Even though the diameter of these fibres is much larger than that of the glass fibres used to reinforce the material itself, they are related and the two types are therefore easily combined. The sensor fibres are connected to a light source; a change in the wavelength of the light allows conclusions to be drawn regarding the stress and temperature in the component (Fig. A 36, p. 25).

The next step in the development is the use of actuators for the active control of component geometry. Piezoelectric or electrostrictive materials are used for the actuators, which in a reversal of the sensors convert an electrical voltage into an elongation. They are mostly integrated into the fibre-reinforced synthetic material in the form of thin plates just a few tenths of a millimetre thick. Piezoelectric actuators are currently being used primarily for high-frequency vibration damping functions. One typical example of this is controlling the vibrations of helicopter rotor blades. One future application could be active acoustic facades (Figs. A 37 and A 38). Research into other actuators is currently ongoing, e.g. shape memory materials, which are already being used in medical technology applications in the form of wires or fibres. These are metals or polymers that have different basic shapes at different temperatures, to which they always return upon cooling or heating. Consequently, with temperature control, large active elongation is possible at low frequencies, in contrast to piezoelectric materials. Polymer gels

Multi-functional materials for "smart" structures

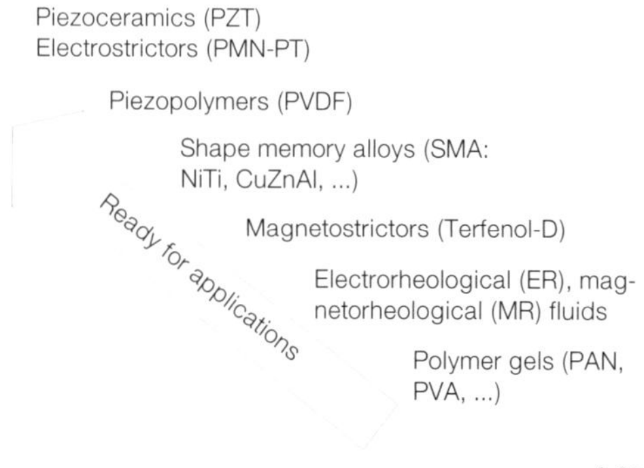

A 37

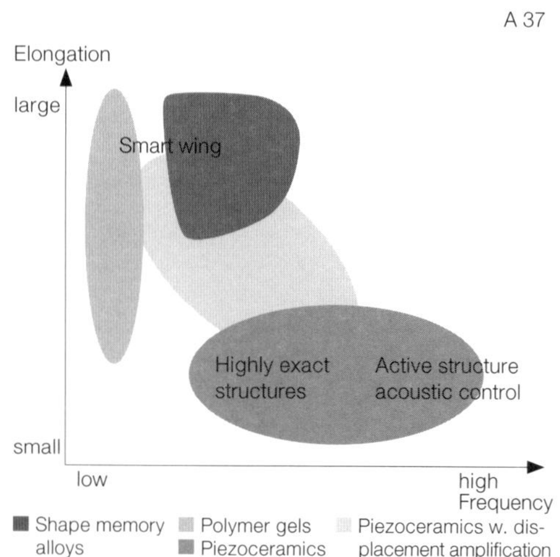

A 38

Building envelopes with flexible materials

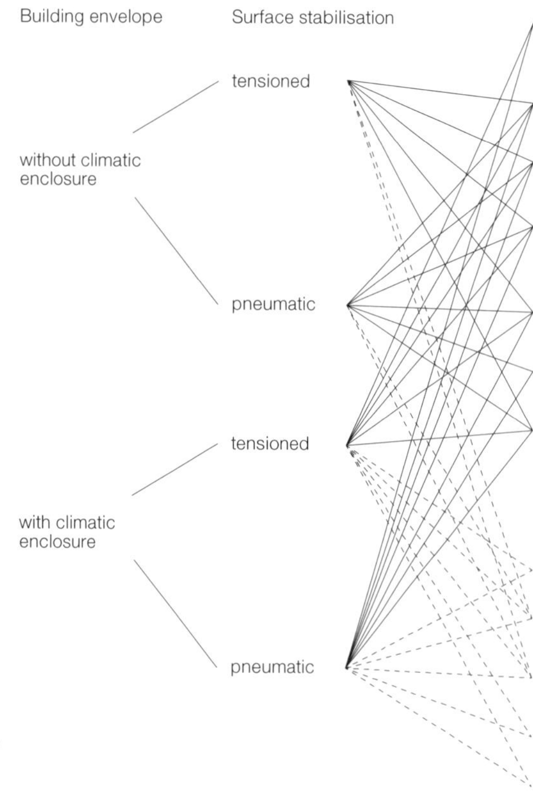

A 39

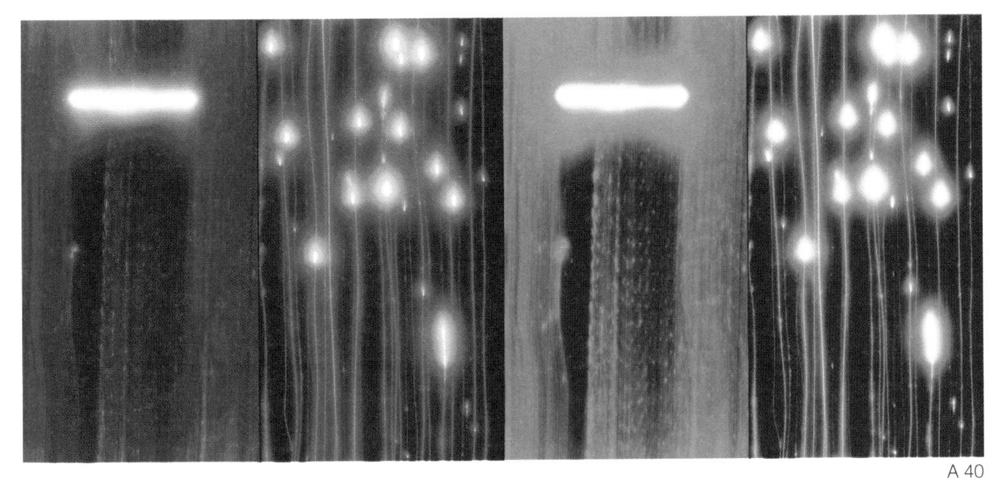
A 40

A 41

could also be suitable for actuators. These are carbon compounds that, in damp media, react by exchanging ions and changing their volume. One possible application could be "artificial muscles" for the active control of sunshading elements in facades. [10]

All these developments open up numerous opportunities, many of which have only been used very tentatively so far and are still being researched.

Challenges

However, there are also obstacles that prevent the widespread application of polymers in architecture.

Reaction to fire

Plastics are made from organic polymers or petroleum and are therefore combustible in principle even though this is hardly possible in practice for some fluoropolymers (PTFE and ETFE). Even the addition of flame retardants has so far not resulted in making polymers incombustible. Furthermore, although such additives reduce the flammability, they often increase the toxicity of the fumes given off. It is therefore often impossible to use polymers where the specification calls for inflammability or fire resistance. Solutions familiar from steelwork, e.g. cladding with mineral fibre boards or applying intumescent paint finishes, have proved to be unsuitable in trials. More research is required into the development of active and passive fire protection measures for materials and components made from synthetic materials. In the meantime, the first ceramic – and therefore incombustible – resin systems for fibre composites have been introduced, but not yet tested in practice.

Ecological aspects

Depending on the application, components made from synthetic materials score differently in ecological audits (see "Environmental impact of polymers", pp. 124–131). There is an urgent need for research into the problems that polymers cause at the end of their useful lives. This applies especially to fibre composites or membranes made from various, virtually inseparable and highly chemically resistant components. The growing awareness of the environment and more stringent legislation is making it more and more difficult to dispose of such products in landfill.

Natural fibres made from flax, hemp or ramie are currently being used as substitutes for glass fibres in the linings of vehicles and rolling stock, also in the furniture and leisure industries. However, these natural fibres are usually still embedded in a conventional petrochemical polymer, which limits the ecological advantages. Replacing petrochemical polymers by resins based on natural materials is even more difficult. Biopolymers such as polylactic acid (PLA), which is made from starch, are already being used in great quantities for containers, packagings and similar products. However, the development of natural polymers made from starch, sugar or vegetable oils that provide the high mechanical strengths and levels of durability required for buildings is still at a very early stage (see "Biopolymers", pp. 62–64). At the moment a number of automotive manufacturers are testing moulded parts made from iopolymers for vehicle bodies. To what extent biopolymers might be suitable for loadbearing or enclosing components in buildings, and thus be able to replace finite raw materials, is currently unclear and will be one of the key challenges for materials researchers in the coming years.

References:

[1] see also Genzel, Elke; Voigt, Pamela: Kunststoffbauten: Teil 1. Die Pioniere. Weimar, 2005
[2] ibid., p. 40ff.
[3] ibid., p. 134ff.
[4] Blundell Jones, Peter: Peter Hübner: Building as a Social Process. Stuttgart, 2007, p. 26
[5] Graefe, Rainer: Vela Erunt. Die Zeltdächer der römischen Theater und ähnlicher Anlagen. Mainz, 1979
[6] Schmitt, Eduard: Zirkus- und Hippodromgebäude. In: Handbuch der Architektur. Part 4, No. 6. Stuttgart, 1904
[7] ibid. [1], p. 167
[8] ibid. [1], p. 26
[9] Schlaich, Jörg: Das Olympiadach in München. Wie war das damals? Was hat es gebracht? In: Behnisch und Partner, Bauten 1952–1992. Stuttgart, 1992
[10] Grohmann, Boris A.; Wallmersperger, Thomas; Kröplin, Bernd-Helmut: Adaptive Strukturen und gekoppelte Mehrfeldprobleme. In: Stahlbau, vol. 69, No. 6, pp. 446–454

A 37 Multi-functional materials and their readiness for applications
A 38 Actuators for "smart" structures
A 39 Measures for increasing the efficiency of fabric building envelopes
A 40 Light-channelling fibres laminated into GFRP panels, itke/University of Stuttgart
A 41 Translucent GFRP sandwich panels illuminated with LEDs, "Syn Chron" art installation, 2004, Carsten Nicolai

Part B Materials

Fig. B Translucent facade panel made from glass fibre-reinforced polymer

Polymers

B 1.1

Polymers have been indispensable materials in everyday life, in industry and in medicine for many years. According to data provided by PlasticsEurope, an association of polymer manufacturers, a total of approx. 12.5 million tonnes of polymers was processed in Germany in 2007, and the construction industry accounted for approx. 25 % of that total – second only to the packagings sector (32.4 %) and therefore representing the second largest market for polymers (Fig. B 1.2). In comparison with other sectors, the construction industry uses more polymers with good strength properties (e.g. PVC-U, thermosets) because of the need for materials with good loadbearing and durability qualities. Up until now, the use of polymers in architecture has concentrated mainly on secondary items such as sheeting, insulation, paints or floor coverings. However, their use for loadbearing structures and building envelopes is growing in importance.

Polymers are synthetic materials made from organic molecules. Their synthesis involves assembling various individual molecules (monomers) to form macromolecules, the so-called polymers. The term polymer is also often used as a synonym for plastic. The vast number of monomers available and the various combination options results in more than 200 different polymers, whose properties can be further adapted with additives. Traditional materials such as steel, timber or concrete offer far fewer opportunities for varying their form, feel and strength. It is precisely the vast array of options that makes the subject of polymers seem totally incalculable and hard to grasp. But at the same time this is their decisive advantage. Whereas with traditional materials it is the material that determines the construction, with polymers the designer can choose or adapt the properties to suit the mechanical, visual or building physics requirements. Despite all the variations, however, there are some properties common to all polymers. These include, for example, their low self-weight, their good mouldability, their distinct time-related behaviour and – in principle – their combustibility because of the carbon compounds they contain.

Classification of polymers

We classify polymers according to the way in which the organic molecules are bonded together, which has an effect on their strength and melting characteristics (Fig. B 1.3). Polymers are divided into three groups according to the degree of cross-linking:

- Thermoplastics (or thermosoftening plastics)
- Elastomers
- Thermosets (or thermosetting plastics)

It is difficult to describe the typical characteristics of each of these three groups in general terms because the characteristic values exhibit such a wide scatter. The following descriptions should therefore be regarded more as tendencies.

In thermoplastics the molecules are not cross-linked. These polymers therefore exhibit relatively low strengths and generally a low heat resistance. They can be melted and remoulded again and again, which is a great advantage for industrial manufacture and recycling. The majority of everyday plastic articles in our homes and workplaces, and also packagings, are made from thermoplastics.

The molecules of elastomers are cross-linked and therefore these polymers cannot be melted again once they have been produced. The raw material for elastomers is tough crude rubber, which is made elastic by the cross-linking. Elastomers (colloquially referred to as rubber) are always processed prior to the cross-linking reaction. Their low strengths make them unsuitable as construction materials but they are frequently used as seals in joints or as bearing pads to ensure an even load transfer. Vehicle tyres represent one of the main applications for elastomers in everyday life.

Thermosets have densely cross-linked molecules and it is this fact that allows them to achieve higher strengths and better durability than other types of polymer. Thermosets cannot be melted down again and exhibit a relatively high heat resistance. Light switches and plugs are frequently made from thermosets.

B 1.1 Polymer granulate (PVC)
B 1.2 Polymer processing in Germany according to industrial sector (2007)
B 1.3 Classification of polymers according to their chemical structure
B 1.4 Production of polymers from petroleum

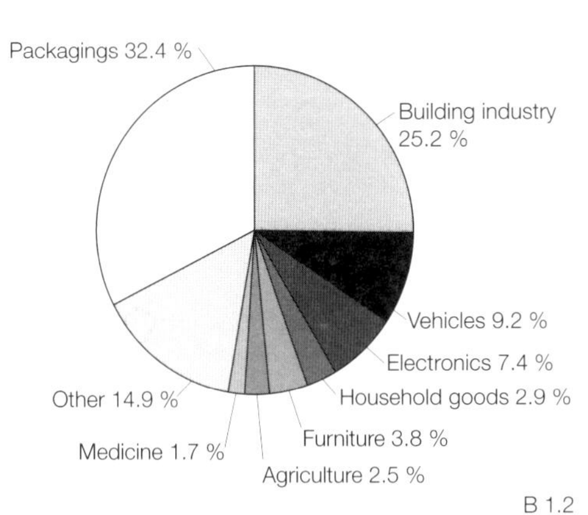

B 1.2

Polymers

Thermoplastics	Elastomers	Thermosets
• No cross-linking between molecular chains • Meltable and mouldable • Rather inferior mechanical properties	• Weak cross-linking between molecules • Cannot be melted again after cross-linking • Very high extensibility	• Strong cross-linking between molecules • Cannot be melted again after cross-linking • Very good mechanical properties

B 1.3

Hybrid forms made from the polymers of two of the above groups are also available, combining the favourable properties of both types. For example, thermoplastic elastomers (TPE) are very elastic but at the same time meltable. The molecular structures of some polymers, e.g. polyurethanes or silicones, can be varied to such an extent that they can be produced in the form of thermoplastics, elastomers or thermosets. In the case of the silicones, the presence of silicon in the polymer molecule results in a number of properties that differ from all other polymers. Silicones exhibit good high-temperature and weathering resistance and, in contrast to the majority of polymers, are incombustible.

Production of polymers

Practically all everyday polymers originate in petrochemical processes, i.e. they are based on petroleum (crude oil). The processing in the oil refinery involves initially heating the petroleum and dividing it into its constituents (fractions) according to their density. The naphtha fraction obtained as a result of this process, which accounts for approx. 10 % of the total output, is subsequently turned into polymers. All the other components, such as petrol, kerosene, heating oil or bitumen, are used for other purposes.
To produce polymers, the naphtha must first be broken down into smaller hydrocarbon molecules in the so-called cracking process. Cracking produces individual monomers such as ethylene, propylene or acetylene – the "building blocks" for the creation of polymers (Fig. B 1.4). It is these monomers that are assembled to form synthetic polymers.
It is also possible to use other raw materials, e.g. natural gas, coal or renewable substances, to obtain the monomers, but costs mean that such polymers are restricted to a less significant role at the moment (see "Natural fibre-reinforced plastics and biopolymers", pp. 60–65).

Polymer formation

The assembly of the individual monomers to form chains or networks takes place by way of three different reaction mechanisms: polymerisation, polycondensation and polyaddition.
The outcome of this chemical bonding is in each case a polymer, i.e. the plastic material. In polymerisation, the monomers are linked together to form polymers with the help of catalysts but without the reaction producing any by-products. Copolymerisation is a form of polymerisation in which different monomers are combined.
As the name suggests, polycondensation involves the production of water (condensate), in some cases hydrogen chloride, ammonia or alcohol, as part of the reaction. In most cases a phased reaction is used to join together two different types of molecular component, which results in a continuous condensate discharge. It is important to make sure that this by-product can escape unhindered and is properly drained away.
The third type of reaction is polyaddition. This is also a phased chemical reaction in which various molecular components are bonded together. The difference between this and polycondensation is primarily that, like polymerisation, the reaction does not produce any by-products.

Polymer manufacture

Polymers are manufactured in chemical plants, where fillers and additives are already mixed in as required, and output as semi-finished products

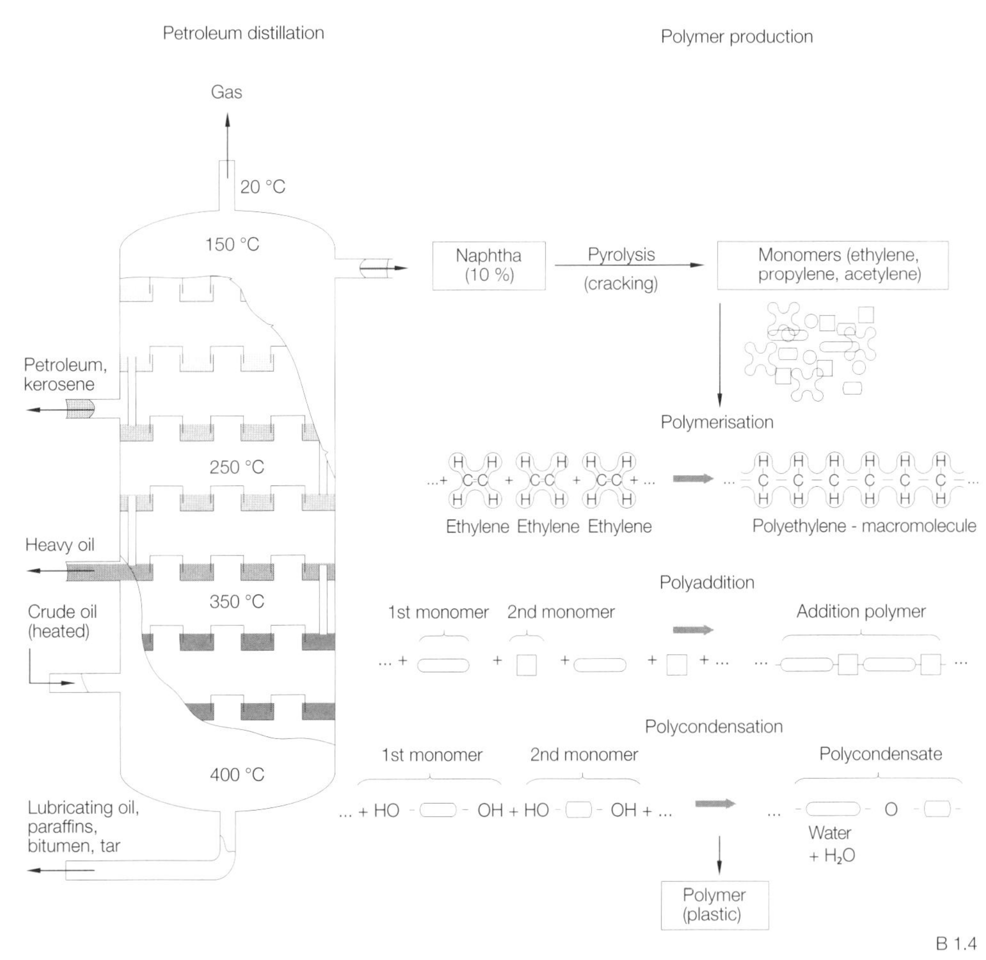

B 1.4

B 1.5

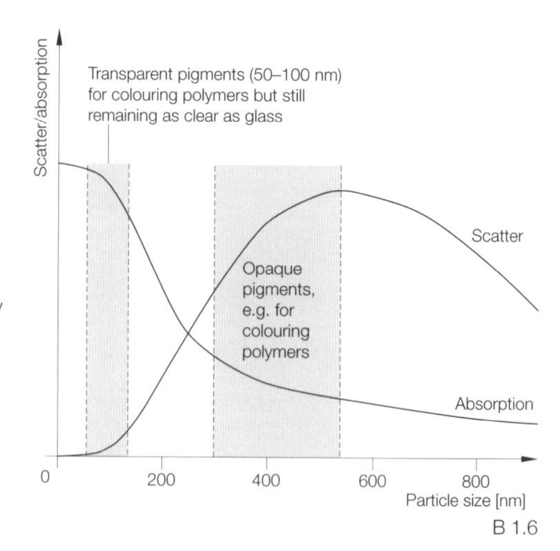

B 1.6

B 1.5 Fibre-reinforced polymer with thermopaints
B 1.6 Relationship between particle size and transparency for pigments
B 1.7 Fillers and their effects
B 1.8 Triple-wall polymer sheet with photochromic top coat
B 1.9 Plastic buttons with a mother-of-pearl effect
B 1.10 Polymer with special effect pigments
B 1.11 Carbon nano tubes (CNT) viewed under the microscope (approx. 100x magnification)

ready for further processing. The three groups of polymers differ in terms of the processing operations required and the primary products used.
Thermoplastics are available in granular or powder form, and although they already possess their final chemical composition, they must first be melted down in a processing plant and then moulded to form the final product. Elastomers are produced from crude rubber, which in contrast to the final product is not yet cross-linked. The crude rubber is first processed and moulded, and the vulcanisation is carried out afterwards. It is vulcanisation that achieves the cross-linking to create a polymer with the help of sulphur, pressure and a high temperature. Thermosets are initially produced in the form of a liquid primary product (synthetic resin) or a moulding compound, which again are not yet cross-linked. The chemical reaction takes place by adding a hardener during the final processing. The processing and treatment methods are described in detail in "Primary products" (pp. 68–75).

Fillers and additives

The properties of polymers are essentially influenced by the fillers and additives mixed with the basic material (Fig. B 1.7). Substances that improve the properties or are used as reactants are known as additives, whereas substances that serve only to extend the polymer, i.e. increase its overall "bulk", are known as fillers. Without appropriate additives, many polymers would be useless because it is the additives that allow the properties of a polymer to be matched to the requirements profile. The possibilities for modifying the properties of, for instance, PVC through the use of additives are especially pronounced. Although softer (plasticised) and harder (unplasticised) forms of PVC are identical in terms of their chemical make-up, the different amounts of plasticisers give rise to totally different materials with their own typical applications.
Additives change not only the properties but also the workability of a polymer, and this fact should be taken into account when designing a component or planning a processing operation. For example, an unsaturated polyester resin to which a flame retardant has been added to achieve a certain fire resistance takes much longer to process because of its higher viscosity. Various aspects are crucial when designing the composition of the polymer:

- Desired service life
- Exposure to weather and UV light
- Chemical resistance
- Final processing intended
- Desired colour and transparency
- Fire protection requirements
- Mechanical properties specification

Polymer manufacturers have many years of experience in the effects of additives and fillers and the various combination options and so the composition of the polymers should be left to them or at least agreed with them. Polymer processors therefore normally purchase polymers that have already been combined with additives and fillers. The following materials are in general use as fillers and additives:

- Cost-reducing fillers (e.g. kaolinite, chalk, or oil for elastomers)
- Colourants (dyes and pigments)
- Catalysts and reactants for controlling the chemical reaction
- Stabilisers for improving durability (e.g. when exposed to UV light)
- Plasticisers in thermoplastics to prevent brittleness
- Flame retardants (halogens, aluminium trihydrite or hydroxide)
- Thixotropic materials for improving the coating properties with thermosets

However, the plasticisers frequently required can dissolve out of the polymer and possibly be absorbed into the bodies of humans or animals via direct contact or through water – and the chemicals they contain, e.g. bisphenol A, are suspected of being harmful to health. The additives present in polymers are important for the recycling of thermoplastics. Recycling without a loss of quality is only possible when mixing identical polymers containing the same fillers and additives.

Colouring polymers

Numerous thermoplastics and thermosets are, in principle, transparent, and therefore there is wide scope for colouring them to achieve various degrees of translucency or opaqueness. A number of non-light-fast polymers is always coloured to make them opaque and optically brightened in order to guarantee a consistent appearance. The colourants used are divided into soluble dyes and insoluble pigments. The borderline between organic pigments and dyes is sometimes indistinct because owing to their polymer structures they may also be soluble in polymers.

Dyes

Dyes that are soluble in polymers are, like the polymers themselves, made mostly from organic compounds. They should be insoluble in water if fading during use is undesirable. In contrast to pigments, dyes produce a transparent colouring; the polymer itself remains as clear as glass. However, an opaque colouring is possible when combined with (white) pigments. Dyes exhibit a better heat resistance than pigments, which makes them ideal for colouring heat-resistant polymers.

Pigments

In contrast to dyes, pigments do not dissolve in the polymer, but instead are added in the form of tiny particles, as small as possible, shaped like needles, flakes or beads. A transparent or opaque finish is possible depending on the size of the particles (Fig. B 1.6): pigments with particle sizes of 50–100 nm scatter the incident light hardly at all, i.e. the polymer remains transparent; larger particles (300–550 nm), on the other hand, scatter the light to a much greater degree, and the material then appears opaque. Various substances can be used as pigments, and the most common are the relatively inexpensive metal oxides. The characteristic colour of a pigment depends on its chemical composition. Carbon black is an inorganic pigment that is inexpensive and widely used. Organic pigments are available in a wider range of colours than the metallic pigments, but are more expensive. They lend polymers a better shine, but have an inferior covering power.

+ to +++ Improvement in properties
- Reduction in properties

		Tensile strength	Compressive strength	Elastic modulus	Impact strength	Reduced shrinkage	Better heat resistance	Chemicals resistance	Economy
Spherical fillers	Sawdust	+			+	+			+
	Carbon black			+	+	+			
	Metal oxides			+	-	+	+		
	Calcium carbonate (chalk)		+	+	-+	+	+		++
	Kaolinite				-	+	+	+	+
	Silica			+	-	+			+
	Sand/quartz powder		+	+	-	+			++
Flake-like fillers	Graphite					+		+	+
	Talcum		+	+	-	+	+		+
	Mica	+		++	-+	+	+	+	+
Fibrous fillers and reinforcing materials	Polymer fibres				++				
	Carbon fibres	+++	+	+++	-	+	++		-
	Glass fibres	++	+	++	-+	+	++		+

B 1.7

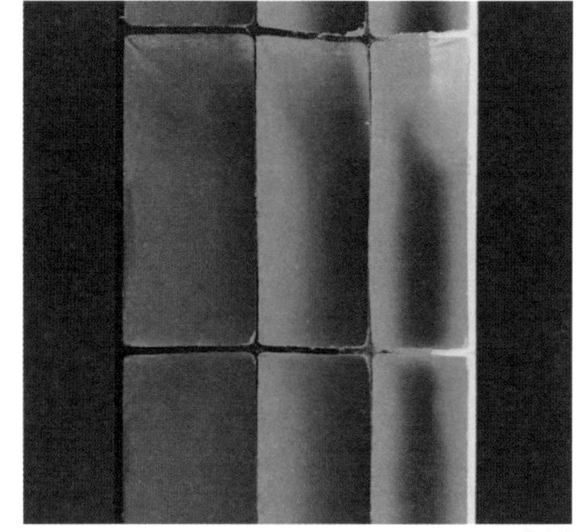

B 1.8

Special effect colourants
These include phosphorescent paints, optical brighteners, thermopaints, special effect pigments (Fig. B 1.10) or paints with a mother-of-pearl shine. They can be based on either dyes or pigments. Fluorescent and brightening paints (brighteners) convert UV light into visible light and lend the polymer or the synthetic fibre a particularly radiant, bright colouring. Thermopaints change their crystal structure as the temperature of the substrate or component changes, which alters their colour (Fig. B 1.5). This effect is reversible in principle, but after repeated cycles chemical processes can take place which render the process irreversible.
Inorganic special effect pigments are relatively large flakes which may even be visible to the naked eye. Their layered structure reflects the light and therefore produces a metallic effect in the colouring which changes depending on the viewing angle; glitter effects are also possible. The pigments themselves frequently consist of metal oxides, aluminium or copper. Special effect pigments are very common in (synthetic-based) paints for the automotive industry. Natural fish scales or, alternatively, lead carbonate are introduced into the polymer to create a mother-of-pearl shine, an effect that is used, for example, in plastic buttons or combs (Fig. B 1.9).

Additives with building physics and mechanical functions
Certain pigments are able to influence how heat is stored in or reflected from polymers. Micaceous pigments, for example, increase the reflective power of the polymer, i.e. they reflect a considerable proportion of the incident infrared light, but the polymer remains transparent for visible light. The energy transmittance through transparent polymers sheets in facades due to radiation can therefore be reduced. Thermochromic or photochromic additives first absorb energy and then re-emit it after a delay (Fig. B 1.8); thermopaints react to temperature differences, whereas photochromic additives absorb the radiation energy directly. However, these effects are in most cases not pronounced enough to make a contribution to building physics, which is why they are used primarily for decorative reasons.

Phase Change Materials (PCM)
Materials that store energy, so-called phase change materials (PCM), can regulate the temperature balance of building components. These materials are not polymers, but can be used to fill the voids of double- and triple-wall sheets or, in the form of microbeads, can be mixed directly into the polymer itself (see "Sandwich panels", p. 90). In contrast to thermochromic materials, PCMs do not undergo a chemical reaction, but rather a physical phase transition from solid to liquid. Furthermore, the presence of a "plateau temperature" at which the latent heat storage functions is also necessary – another difference between these and thermochromic materials. Once the temperature exceeds this limit, the PCM absorbs or releases a disproportionate amount of energy. In doing so, the material itself remains at the plateau temperature (within certain limits) even when energy is being absorbed or released at a constant level. PCMs are mostly paraffins or salt hydrates, which have transition temperatures that are easy to adjust to the ranges relevant to building physics.

Moisture-absorbing additives
The moisture absorption capacity of polymers is relatively low when compared with timber or natural fibres. It is possible, however, to add limited amounts of moisture-absorbing substances, so-called desiccants (getters), to the polymer matrix of a plastic. The spacers between panes of glass in double glazing, for instance, can be made of such a material, which then absorbs residual gases in the cavity such as water vapour.

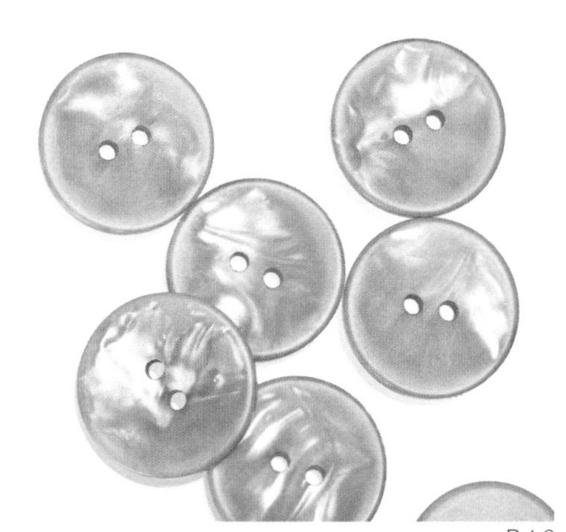

B 1.9

B 1.10

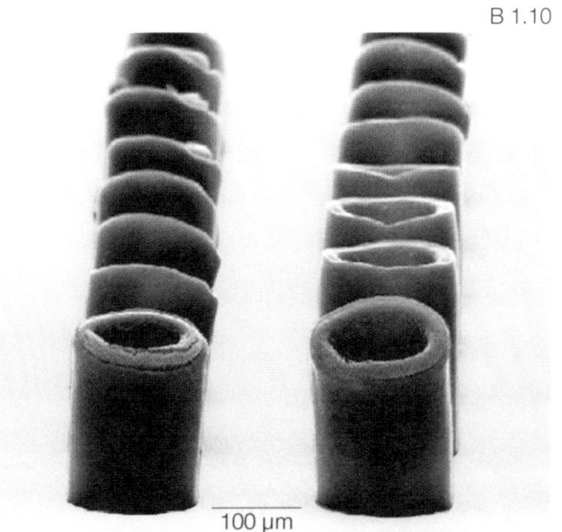

B 1.11

Carbon nano tubes
Carbon nano tubes (CNT) are tubular, cross-linked, electrically conductive carbon molecules with a strength exceeding that of high-strength carbon fibres. They can be mixed into the polymer in the form of small particles, which allows them to control a wide variety of mechanical properties (Fig. B 1.11, p. 33). For example, in fibre composites they substantially improve the adhesion between the fibres and the polymer matrix. The development of applications and investigations into the environmental impact of CNT are, however, still ongoing.

Fibres
The inclusion of fibres in the form of short pieces, long fibres or as textiles can bring about a considerable increase in the strength and the elastic modulus (elongation of material under stress) of a polymer. Glass fibre-reinforced polymer (GFRP) and carbon fibre-reinforced polymer (CFRP) are the most common forms of fibre-reinforced material. As the fibre content increases, so the polymer matrix starts to perform only shaping and protective functions, with the fibres governing the mechanical properties. Textile membranes can be regarded as the extreme case, with the polymer matrix providing merely a thin coating to the fibres.
The fibres that can be considered for architectural applications are described in detail in "Fibres" (pp. 48–53), and the semi-finished textile products in "Textiles". (pp. 69–72).

Properties of polymers

The properties of polymers are far more diverse than those of traditional materials such as timber, metals or concrete (Fig. B 1.19, p. 38). Fibre-reinforced polymers in particular exhibit a wide scatter in their strength, elastic modulus and elongation values (Fig. B 1.12).
The user must select a suitable polymer – optimised with additives if necessary – depending on the mechanical, chemical and processing requirements. It is therefore not only important to know which characteristics polymers exhibit, but also to what extent these characteristics can be varied.

Our perception of polymers

The sensorial qualities of a polymer determine our first impression of it. In contrast to other building materials, polymers vary considerably with respect to their look, feel or sound. And vice versa: their sensorial characteristics can also be helpful when trying to identify an unknown synthetic material.

Visual perception
The transparency of a material is its property of being pervious to radiation. It varies from material to material depending on the wavelength under consideration: a material transparent for visible light may be opaque for other wavelengths. Transparency with respect to visible light plays an important role in architectural design. On the other hand, transparency with respect to ultraviolet or infrared radiation is important as regards building physics (see "Light and heat radiation characteristics", pp. 113–116).
A component that presents no obstacle to a view through is described as transparent, but a component through which only a blurred view is possible is referred to as translucent, and a component that is totally impermeable to light is opaque (Fig. B 1.14).
The degree to which a component is transparent depends to a great extent on its dimensions. For example, it may be possible to supply one and the same material in the form of a highly transparent foil, a translucent sheet or even a completely opaque panel. Accordingly, the terms transparent, translucent and opaque are used colloquially to classify a property of a particular component, not normally a property of a material.
The transparency of polymers depends on the fillers added and their chemical structure, i.e. the arrangement of the molecules. In thermoplastics this structure ranges from completely irregular (amorphous) to more or less regular (semi-crystalline). The molecular structure is in the first place dependent on the polymer used, but can be affected by the production process. Semi-crystalline thermoplastics such as polyethylene (PE), polypropylene (PP) or polytetrafluoroethylene (PTFE) are either milky or even totally opaque in appearance, whereas amorphous thermoplastics are highly transparent, e.g.

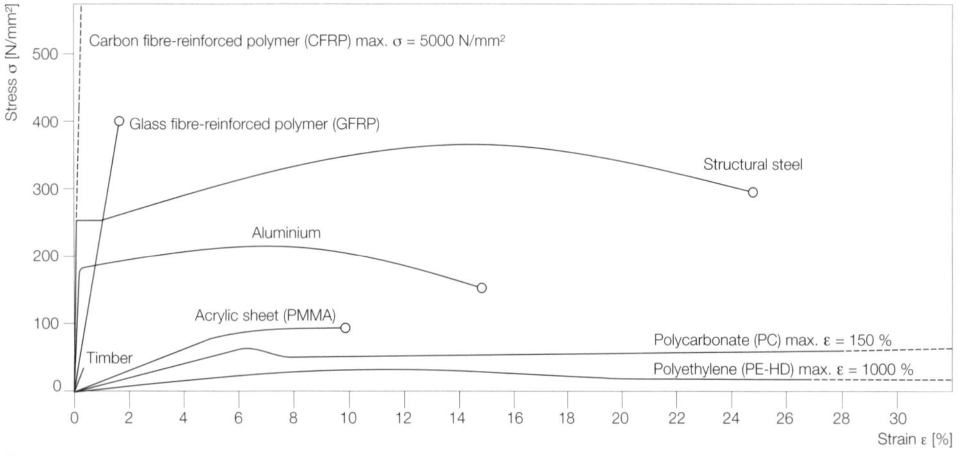

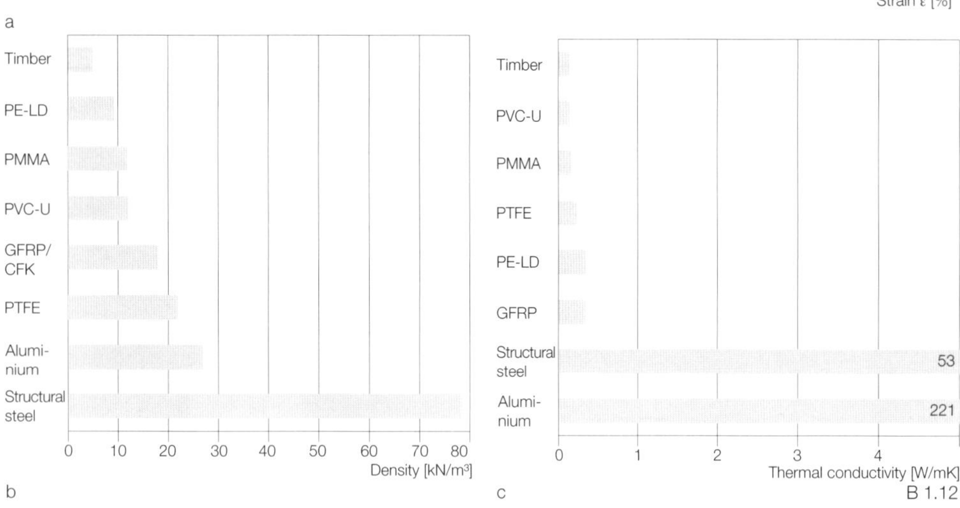

B 1.12

B 1.13

B 1.12 Typical polymers compared with traditional building materials
a Mechanical properties (stress-strain curves)
b Self-weight (density)
c Thermal conductivity
B 1.13 Yellowed plastic
B 1.14 Transparent, translucent and opaque polymers

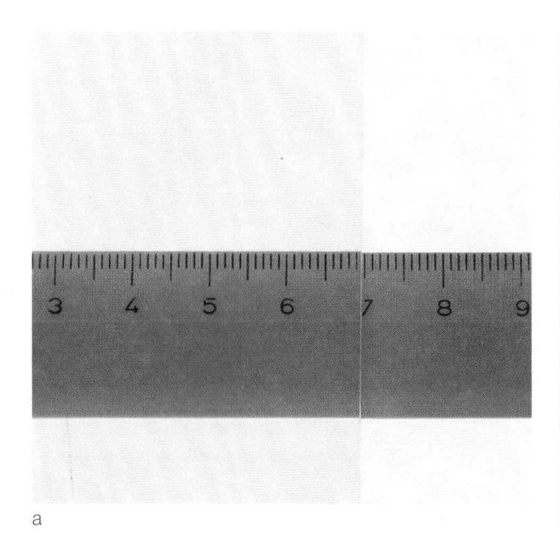

a

b

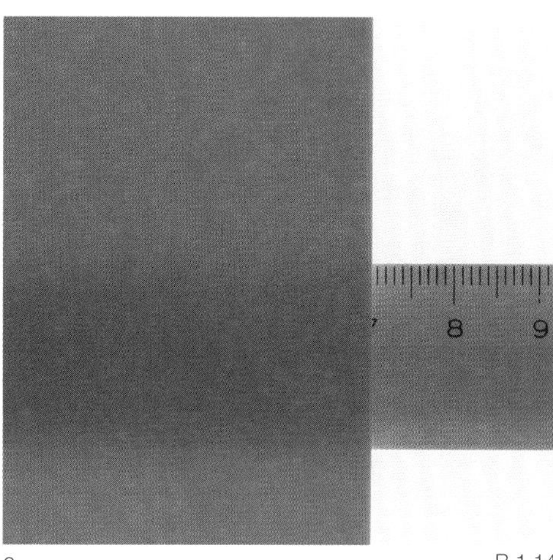

c

B 1.14

polyvinyl chloride (PVC), polystyrene (PS), polymethyl methacrylate (PMMA – acrylic sheet) and polycarbonate (PC).
In the case of thermosets, the dense cross-linking prevents the molecules from attaining a regular arrangement, which is why such polymers are normally transparent. In elastomers the molecules are only partly cross-linked, which would lead us to suspect that transparent elastomers would be possible in theory. However, the fillers used, such as carbon black and oil, rule out any transparency. Nevertheless, in order to produce a transparent, elastic material, it is possible to combine elastomers and thermoplastics chemically or physically (thermoplastic elastomers – TPE).
Permanent exposure to UV radiation can cause some transparent but non-light-fast polymers, e.g. PVC, to become "cloudy" over time, and thus lose their transparency. In the case of PVC, radiation breaks down the hydrogen chloride on the surface, which leads to yellowing (Fig. B 1.13).

Haptic perception
Polymers are mostly used without any additional coatings, so the quality of the surface of the material is particularly relevant. PE, PP, PTFE and cellulose acetate (CA) feel very "waxy" to the touch, which is generally regarded as a pleasant feeling – the handles of tools, for example, are therefore often made from CA. The scratch resistance of polymers also varies, with PE and plasticised PVC (PVC-P) being particularly sensitive to scratches, PMMA somewhat less so. The hardness of a material correlates to a certain extent with its scratch resistance, and the hardness is in turn dependent on the material's elastic modulus and yield stress, i.e. the mechanical stress at which the material starts to exhibit a permanent plastic deformation.

Acoustic perception
A specialist can identify a polymer by the sound it makes when it is struck, or by the crinkling sound of a polymer foil. For example, PVC-P, acrylonitrile-butadiene-styrene (ABS), PMMA, PA and CA sound rather dull, whereas other polymers tend to "clang", e.g. unplasticised PVC (PVC-U), PC or PS. The latter has a very characteristic "glassy" sound, especially when it breaks.

Mechanical properties
The tensile or compressive strength of a material describes the maximum stress the material can accommodate. In the case of polymers, the value of the tensile strength is frequently higher than that of the compressive strength. The elastic modulus describes the elongation of the material when subjected to a stress – a high elastic modulus corresponds to a low deformation. But the actual elongation of a component depends on the geometry of its cross-section. The combination of elastic modulus and cross-sectional geometry determines the stiffness of a component. The elastic moduli of polymers are often not constant, but instead decrease with the load, i.e. the deformations intensify disproportionately in relation to the increasing load (Fig. B 1.12a). In addition, both the elastic modulus and the strength of every polymer depends on the temperature – both values drop as the temperature of the component rises. For example, the tensile strength of polycarbonate at a component temperature of 100 °C is only two-thirds of that at room temperature.

Failure behaviour
The safety of a structure is not only dependent on the loads a material can carry, but also on the failure behaviour of that material. A brittle material fails abruptly once it reaches its breaking point, possibly resulting in sharp, dangerous fragments and splinters. We speak of brittle behaviour, also of low (notched) impact strength, or of glass-like behaviour. However, materials with a ductile or viscoelastic behaviour do not break at all in the ideal case. And subjected to an impact load, such a material can absorb some of the energy. Another advantage of a ductile material is that local overloads can be accommodated through plastic deformation. The material begins to "flow", i.e. the deformation increases while the stress remains more or less constant. This transfers loads to neighbouring areas. Polymers cover the whole range between brittle and viscoelastic, with certain additives (plasticisers) frequently being used to improve the material behaviour in the direction of the latter.
The failure behaviour of polymers can be divided into three categories: PE, PP, PA, PVC-P, PC, plasticised CA, PTFE and all elastomers exhibit ductile failures. The so-called strain (or stress) whitening is characterised by the conspicuous, white rupture in the material. The behaviour of unplasticised PVC (PVC-U) and the styrene copolymers (SB, ABS, ASA), which exhibit strain whitening, lies between that of ductile and brittle. PMMA, PS, the styrene copolymer SAN and all thermosets are glass-like in their behaviour and exhibit brittle failure. In terms of durability and reliability, brittle failure must be regarded as a negative characteristic. Polymers that are actually ductile can become brittle as a result of ageing and the associated degradation of the plasticiser they contain, and thus change their failure behaviour.

Hardness
The hardness of a material describes the degree to which its surface resists the penetration of a pointed object. Hardness depends on the elastic modulus and yield stress of the material. Various testing methods are employed in practice, the particular method depending on the hardness range of the material to be tested. All the tests use a bar with a conical or spherical tip that is pressed into the material; the resulting indentation depth is then measured. The "Shore A" method is used for soft elastomers, "Shore D" for harder elastomers and soft thermoplastics (DIN 53505). Harder thermoplastics and all thermosets are measured according to the "Rockwell" method (DIN EN ISO 6508-1) and fibre-reinforced polymers make use of the "Barcol" method (according to DIN EN 59).

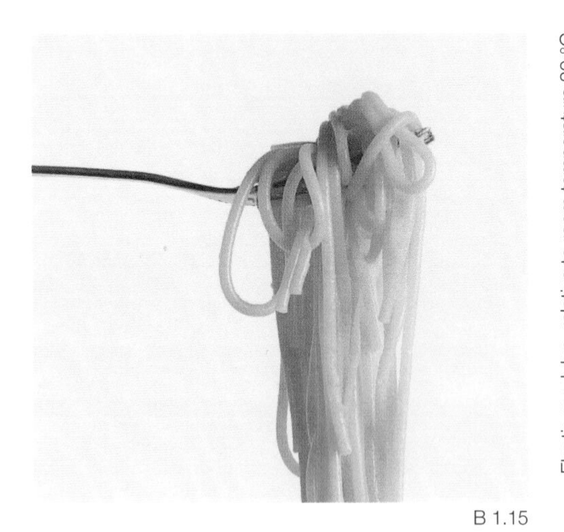

B 1.15

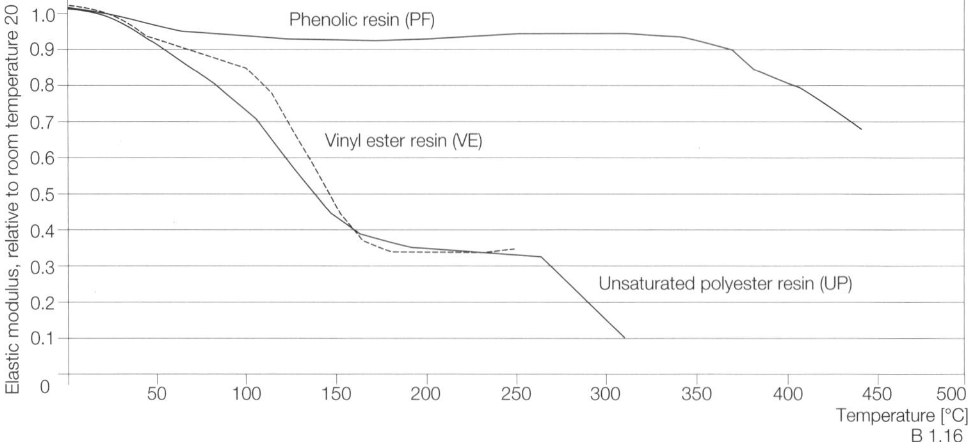

B 1.16

Creep, creep rupture strength and relaxation
One critical feature of polymers is their irreversible reaction to permanent mechanical actions. Subjected to a constant load, the individual molecular chains of the polymer slide past each other, which increases the deformations and can lead to delayed failure. The behaviour of the material is best illustrated by using spaghetti as a model (Fig. B 1.15). Individual strands (representing the molecular chains in this case) suspended from a fork will gradually work their way slowly downwards due to their self-weight. If the load is not excessive, then this sliding slows down because the individual strands of spaghetti stick to each other, and indeed the process finally comes to halt. Subjected to a high load, however, the individual molecular chains can snap – the material fails. This behaviour is therefore more pronounced in the non-cross-linked thermoplastics than in the thermosets with their dense cross-linking.
Creep is the steady increase in the plastic deformation of a material subjected to a constant load, which can be many times the original elastic deformation. Creep in polymers occurs mainly shortly after application of the load and continues until it reaches a maximum value. However, if the load exceeds a certain threshold, the deformations start to increase disproportionately after a longer period of loading until the material finally fails (creep rupture strength). The handles of a plastic shopping bag are a good example of this: at first they carry the (heavy) load, but become longer and longer and in the end do indeed tear after a few minutes. The duration of the action must therefore be taken into account in the calculations for plastic components (see "Calculations", pp. 150–154).
Relaxation basically describes the same mechanism as creep but in this case with respect to prestressed components whose strain is kept constant. The displacement of the molecules brings about a certain relieving of the stress in the material. This type of material behaviour is seen in, for example, prestressed membranes which – originally taut – lose this tensioning force over time (begin to sag) and may need to be retensioned (see "Compensation", p. 147). Higher temperatures can accelerate both creep and relaxation because the bonding forces between the molecular chains become weaker.

Thermal properties
The thermal expansion of polymers varies considerably; the values vary between 35 × 10^{-6}/K for phenolic resins (PF) and 250 × 10^{-6}/K for polyethylene (PE), which corresponds to an elongation of 35 and 250 mm respectively per 100 m length for a temperature change of 10 K. Compared with conventional building material such as timber (8 mm), steel (12 mm), glass (9 mm), aluminium (23 mm) or concrete (10 mm), it can be seen that polymers deform significantly as the temperature changes. Fixings for plastic components must therefore permit such expansion and contraction. Only fibre-reinforced polymers achieve values comparable with those of conventional building materials, i.e. between 0 and 35 mm (see "Building with semi-finished polymer products", pp. 160–173). Indeed, polymer fibres can even exhibit a negative coefficient of thermal expansion!

Behaviour at high temperatures
Some polymers suffer a drop in their elastic modulus and strength even at normal service temperatures (e.g. < 60 °C), although this effect is reversed upon cooling (Fig. B 1.16). Only as the temperature increases further does the polymer begin to soften and decompose, lose mass (Fig. B 1.17) and finally burn. [1]
The service temperature is that to which a material can be exposed without suffering any permanent damage and at which the strength and elastic modulus are not significantly reduced. Service temperatures are specified for short- and long-term actions. The so-called glass transition temperature (T_g), i.e. the temperature at which the polymer changes from a stiff to a viscoelastic state, is also frequently specified for thermoplastics. However, this temperature does not allow any conclusions to be drawn regarding the service temperature. The melting temperature of a thermoplastic indicates the temperature at which the polymer becomes completely fluid – a figure that is important for production.

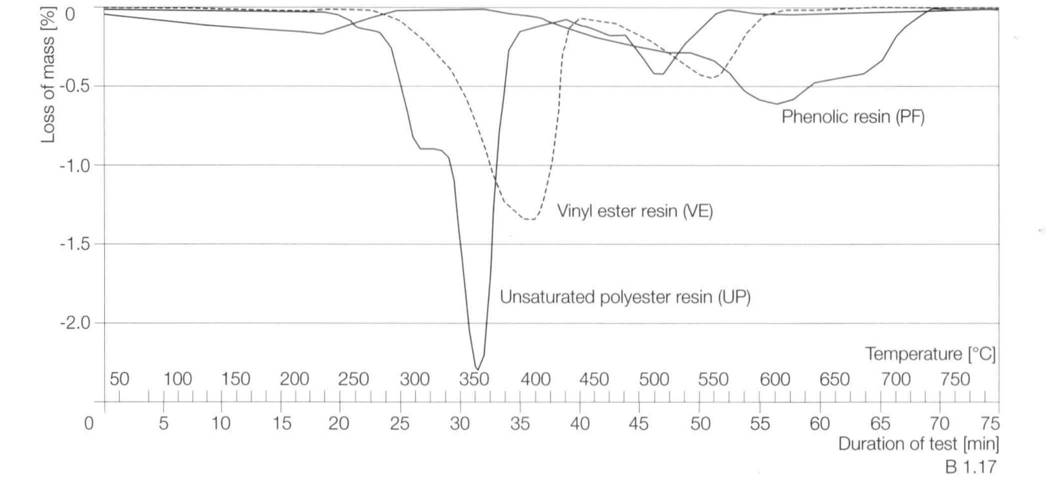

B 1.17

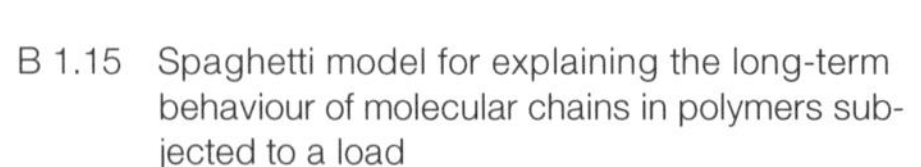

B 1.15 Spaghetti model for explaining the long-term behaviour of molecular chains in polymers subjected to a load
B 1.16 Change in the elastic modulus of thermosets exposed to fire
B 1.17 Loss of mass in thermosets exposed to fire
B 1.18 Properties of selected polymers

Type of polymer		Specification	Failure behaviour	Transparency	Density [g/cm³]	Service temperature long/short [°C]	Features	Trade names & synonyms	Chemical attack by			Tensile strength [N/mm²]	Elastic modulus [N/mm²]	Coeff. of linear thermal expansion 10^{-6}/K	Thermal conductivity [W/mK]
									acids	alkalis	weather				
Thermoplastics															
PVC	Polyvinyl chloride	U	strain whitening	transparent	1.46	65–70/75–90	Clanging sound		++	++	0	50–75	1000–3500	70–80	0.14–0.17
		P	ductile	transparent	1.27	50–55/55–65	Flexible like rubber, no sound		+	+	-	10–25	–	150–210	0.15
PE	Polyethylene	LD	ductile	translucent	0.92	60–75/80–90	Waxy feel, can be marked with fingernail		++	++	-	8–23	200–500	230–250	0.32–0.40
		HD	ductile	translucent	0.95	75–90/90–120			++	++	-	18–35	700–1400	120–200	0.38–0.51
PP	Polypropylene		ductile	translucent	0.90	100/140	Cannot be marked with fingernail		+	++	-	21–37	1100–1300	110–170	0.17–0.22
PS	Polystyrene		brittle	transparent	1.05	50–70/60–80	Sounds glassy		+	+	-	45–65	3200–3250	60–80	0.18
SB	Styrene butadiene		strain whitening	translucent	1.05	50–70/60–80	Not as brittle as PS		+	++	-	26–38	1800–2500	70	0.18
ABS	Acrylonitrile-butadiene-styrene		strain-whitening	translucent	1.05	75–85/85–100	Viscoelastic, dull sound, scratch-resistant	Abselex, Absinol	+	++	-	32–45	1300–2700	60–110	0.18
SAN	Styrene acrylonitrile		brittle	transparent	1.08	85/95	Viscoelastic	Luran	+	++	-	75	3600	80	0.18
ASA	Acrylate-styrene-acrylonitrile		strain whitening	translucent	1.04	70–75/85–90		Luran-S			-	32	1100–2600	80–110	0.18
PMMA	Polymethyl methacrylate		brittle	transparent	1.19	65–90/85–100	Clear as glass w/o colouring, dull sound	Acrylic sheet, Perspex	0	++	++	50–77	1600–3600	70–90	0.18
PC	Polycarbonate		ductile	transparent	1.20	135/160	Tough, clanging sound	Makrolon, Lexan	0	--	0	56–67	2100–2400	60–70	0.21
PET	Polyethylene terephthalate			transparent	1.37	100/200		Vivak, Mylar	+	+	0	47	3100	40–60	0.24
PA	Polyamide	6	ductile	translucent	1.13	80–100/140–180	Viscoelastic, dull sound, high damping	Nylon, Perlon	--	+	-	70–85	1400	60–100	0.29
		66	ductile	translucent	1.14	80–120/170–200			--	+	-	77–84	2000	70–100	0.23
PTFE	Polytetrafluoroethylene		ductile	opaque	2.17	250/300	Waxy feel		++	++	++	25–36	410	120–250	0.25
ETFE	Ethylene tetrafluoroethylene			foil transparent	1.75	150/220			++	++	++	35–54	1100	40	0.23
CA	Cellulose (tri) acetate		ductile	transparent	1.30	70/80	Pleasant feel, dull sound		--	-	-	38	2200	120	0.22
Elastomers (with fillers)															
	Natural rubber		ductile	opaque		70/90		rubber, latex	0	0	--	approx. 30.0			
	R rubber		ductile	opaque		100–130/120–130		neoprene, chloroprene, butyl, nitrile	-/+	0/+	--	approx. 20.0–25.0		variable	
	M rubber		ductile	opaque		120–170/150–200		Buna AP, Keltan	+	+	++	approx. 20.0			
	Q rubber		ductile	opaque		180/300		silicone	0/-	0/-	++	approx. 8.0			
Thermosets															
PF	Phenolic resin		brittle	translucent	1.30	110/140	Not light-fast, heat-resistant	Bakelite	-	-	+	20–60	1500–2500	35	0.35
		with sawdust	brittle	opaque	1.40	110/140			-	-	+	25	560–1200	10–50	0.35
		fibre-reinforced	brittle	opaque	2.00	110/140			-	-	+	variable	variable	variable	variable
UP	Unsaturated polyester resin		brittle	transparent	1.20	150/200		synthetic resin	0	0	+	40–70	3000–4200	80–150	0.7
		fibre-reinforced (GFRP))	brittle	translucent	1.80	150/200			0	0	+	80–240	7000–23000	9–30	0.25
EP	Epoxy resin		brittle	transparent	1.20	130/180	High strength		+	+	0	60–125	3000–6000	60	0.88
		fibre-reinforced (CFRP)	brittle	opaque	1.70	130/180						1350–2800	165000–300000	0,2	17.0
VE	Vinyl ester resin		brittle	transparent	1.20	130/180	Resistant to chemicals	Phen-acrylatharz	+	+	0	70–84	3400–3600	53–65	
PUR	Polyurethane		ductile	opaque	1.05	50–80/70–100	Versatile	PU	0	+	-	70–80	4000	10–20	0.58

++ excellent resistance. + good resistance. 0 some resistance. - little resistance. -- no resistance

transparent; foil transparent; translucent; opaque

B 1.18

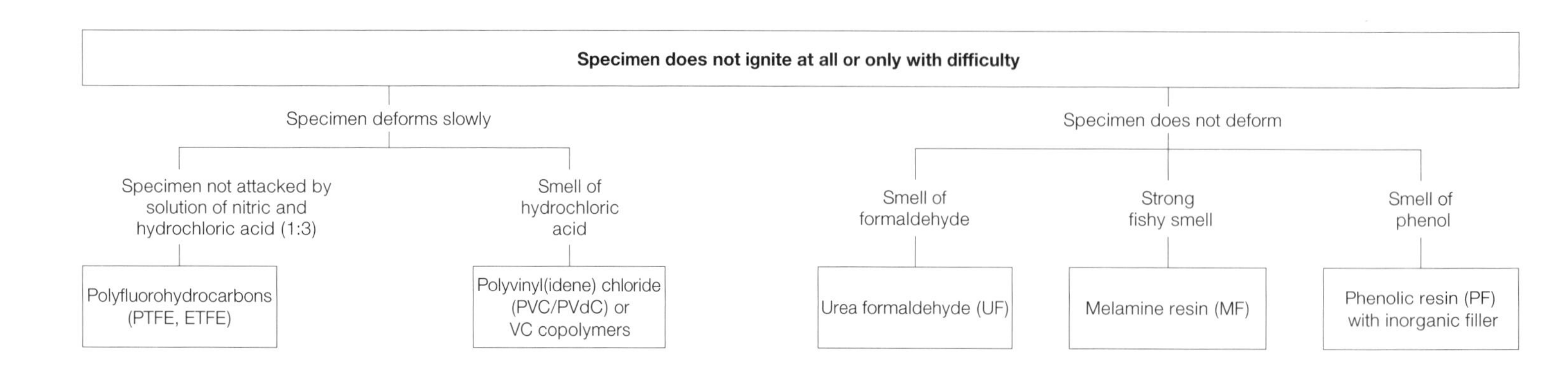
Specimen does not ignite at all or only with difficulty
Specimen deforms slowly
Specimen does not deform
Specimen not attacked by solution of nitric and hydrochloric acid (1:3)
Smell of hydrochloric acid
Smell of formaldehyde
Strong fishy smell
Smell of phenol
Polyfluorohydrocarbons (PTFE, ETFE)
Polyvinyl(idene) chloride (PVC/PVdC) or VC copolymers
Urea formaldehyde (UF)
Melamine resin (MF)
Phenolic resin (PF) with inorganic filler

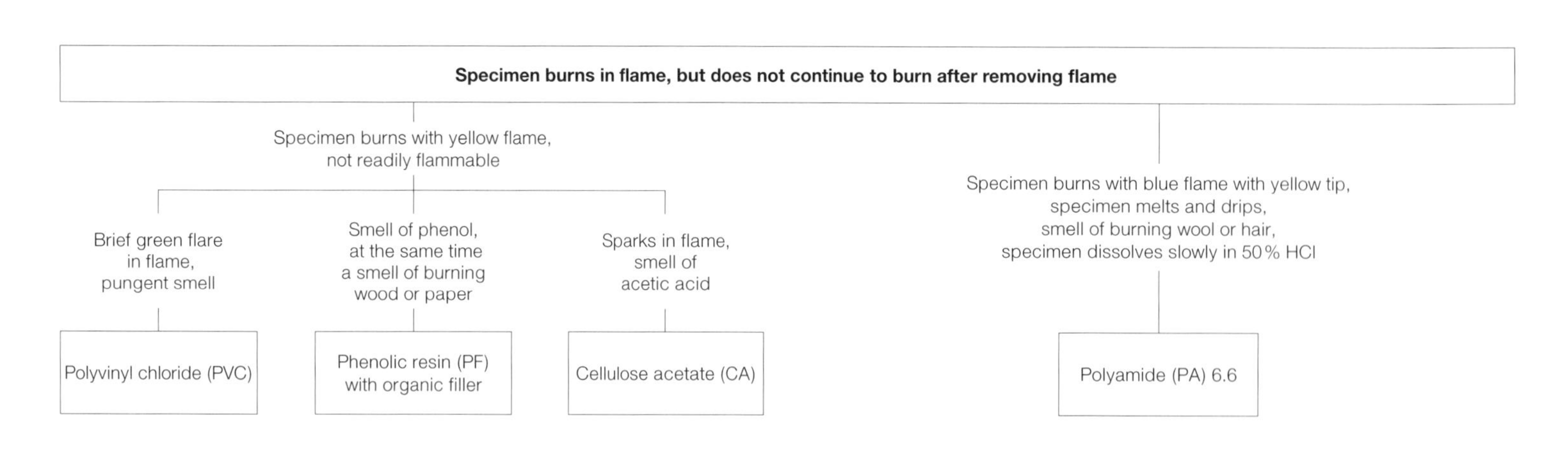
Specimen burns in flame, but does not continue to burn after removing flame
Specimen burns with yellow flame, not readily flammable
Specimen burns with blue flame with yellow tip, specimen melts and drips, smell of burning wool or hair, specimen dissolves slowly in 50% HCl
Brief green flare in flame, pungent smell
Smell of phenol, at the same time a smell of burning wood or paper
Sparks in flame, smell of acetic acid
Polyvinyl chloride (PVC)
Phenolic resin (PF) with organic filler
Cellulose acetate (CA)
Polyamide (PA) 6.6

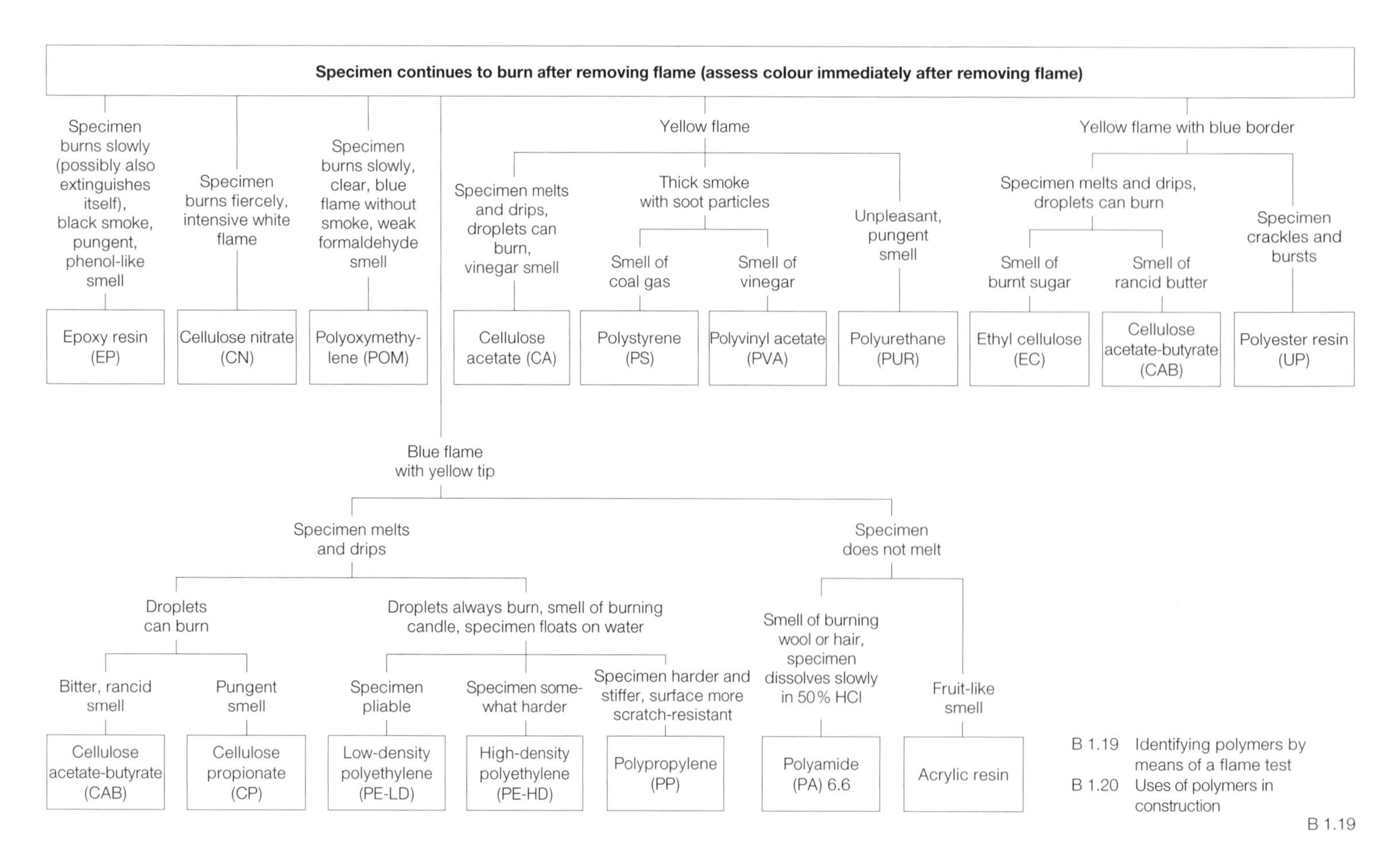
Specimen continues to burn after removing flame (assess colour immediately after removing flame)
Specimen burns slowly (possibly also extinguishes itself), black smoke, pungent, phenol-like smell
Specimen burns fiercely, intensive white flame
Specimen burns slowly, clear, blue flame without smoke, weak formaldehyde smell
Yellow flame
Yellow flame with blue border
Specimen melts and drips, droplets can burn, vinegar smell
Thick smoke with soot particles
Smell of coal gas
Smell of vinegar
Unpleasant, pungent smell
Specimen melts and drips, droplets can burn
Smell of burnt sugar
Smell of rancid butter
Specimen crackles and bursts
Epoxy resin (EP)
Cellulose nitrate (CN)
Polyoxymethylene (POM)
Cellulose acetate (CA)
Polystyrene (PS)
Polyvinyl acetate (PVA)
Polyurethane (PUR)
Ethyl cellulose (EC)
Cellulose acetate-butyrate (CAB)
Polyester resin (UP)
Blue flame with yellow tip
Specimen melts and drips
Specimen does not melt
Droplets can burn
Droplets always burn, smell of burning candle, specimen floats on water
Bitter, rancid smell
Pungent smell
Specimen pliable
Specimen somewhat harder
Specimen harder and stiffer, surface more scratch-resistant
Smell of burning wool or hair, specimen dissolves slowly in 50% HCl
Fruit-like smell
Cellulose acetate-butyrate (CAB)
Cellulose propionate (CP)
Low-density polyethylene (PE-LD)
High-density polyethylene (PE-HD)
Polypropylene (PP)
Polyamide (PA) 6.6
Acrylic resin

B 1.19 Identifying polymers by means of a flame test

B 1.20 Uses of polymers in construction

B 1.19

Combustibility
All polymers are essentially combustible, but each type of polymer displays its own particular reaction to fire. Furthermore, additives or fillers can influence a polymer's behaviour in fire. A flame test is therefore often necessary to identify a polymer (Fig. B 1.19). The crucial factor here is whether the polymer begins to burn when exposed to the flame of a Bunsen burner and whether it continues to burn or extinguishes itself after removing the flame. Moreover, the colour of the flame and the emission of fumes and smoke are also significant factors for identifying polymers. Also important for the building industry is whether a polymer forms hot droplets of material and what amount of smoke is to be expected (see "Reaction to fire and fire protection", pp. 119–120).

Durability and recycling
Polymers vary considerably in terms of their long-term durability. Whereas moisture does not cause any problems in most cases, the effects of the weather and various media can damage the material (Fig. B 1.18, p. 37), especially in conjunction with high temperatures. Synthetic fibres are particularly sensitive to these influences because of their large surface area (see "Polymer fibres", pp. 51–52).
Intensive UV radiation can attack the carbon bonds in polymers and thus destroy the molecular chains, and can also dissolve the plasticisers out of a polymer, which results in yellowing or embrittlement. Polymers react to UV exposure very differently depending on their molecular structure. Fluoropolymers (PTFE, ETFE) and silicone are permanently resistant, and acrylic sheet (PMMA), PET, PC, PVC-U and thermosets exhibit good resistance. Stabilisers can be added to other polymers to protect the molecular structure and make them more resistant to UV light. In principle, polymers can absorb moisture and water to a certain extent. However, the effects of moisture on polymers vary considerably. Whereas most polymers are water-resistant, in some materials the water can break down the chemical bonds and then attack the surface of the polymers (hydrolysis). Moisture and many media such as alkalis and acids do not have any negative effects on the mechanical properties of the majority of thermosets used in the building industry, however.
In contrast to other organic building materials, e.g. timber, most polymers are resistant to microorganisms. However, biodegradable polymers have been designed which can be decomposed by moisture or microbes in order to solve the waste problem of disposable packagings. There is a fundamental contradiction here between the desire for a durable building material on the one hand and fully ecologically neutral usage on the other (see "Natural fibre-reinforced polymers and biopolymers", pp. 60–65).

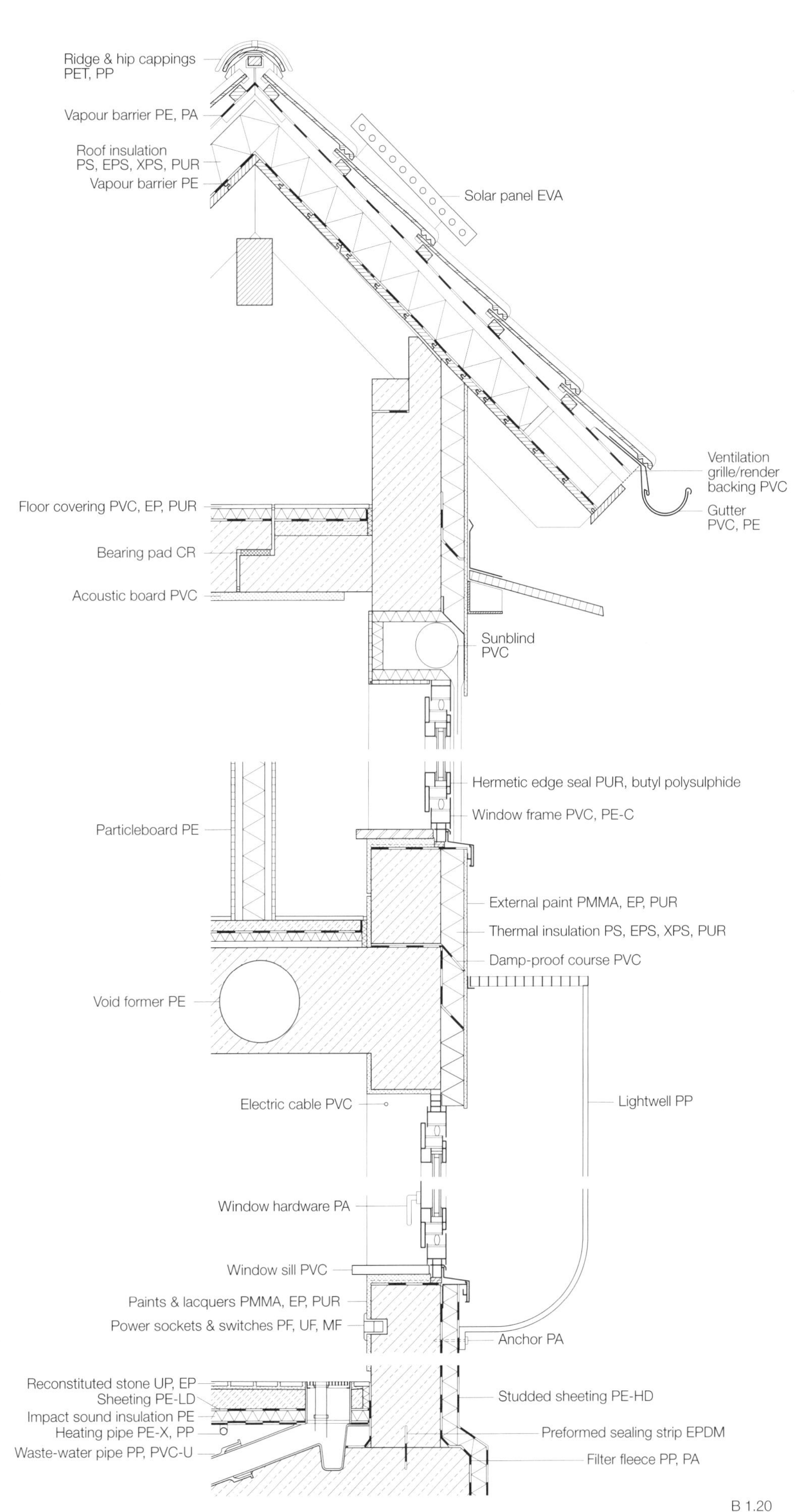

B 1.20

B 1.21 Properties of thermoplastics depending on temperature
a Amorphous polymers (PVC, PS, PMMA, PC), with range of application below glass transition temperature in hard elastic vitreous region, tending towards brittle failure behaviour
b Semi-crystalline thermoplastics (PE, PP, PTFE, ETFE), with range of application above glass transition temperature in soft elastic region, tending towards ductile failure behaviour
B 1.22 Blending of thermoplastics
B 1.23 Polyvinyl chloride (PVC)
B 1.24 Polyethylene (PE)
B 1.25 Polypropylene (PP)
B 1.26 Polystyrene (PS)

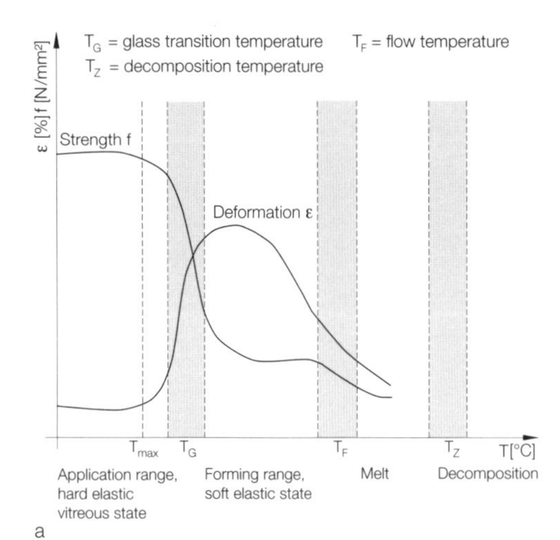

a

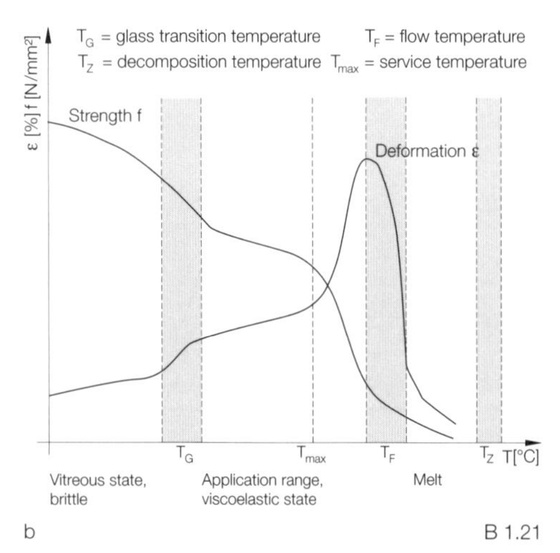

b

B 1.21

	PVC	PE-LD	PE-HD	PP	PS	ABS	SAN	PMMA	PC	PET	PA
PVC	++										
PE-LD	×	++									
PE-HD	×	×	++								
PP	×	×	×	++							
PS	×	×	×	×	++						
ABS	-	×	×	×	×	++					
SAN	+	×	×	×	×	++	++				
PMMA	++	×	×	×	-	++	++	++			
PC	--	×	×	×	×	+	+	++	++		
PET	×	×	×	×	--	--	×	×	++	++	
PA	×	×	×	×	--	×	×	×	×	--	++

+ to ++ blend well
× do not blend
- to -- can blend

B 1.22

Recycling
Only thermoplastics are worth considering for complete recycling because only these polymers can be melted down and remoulded. Besides ensuring that polymer waste streams are segregated for recycling, it is also important to make sure that the additives and fillers used in the polymers are identical or nearly so. In practice this can only be guaranteed by a materials life cycle controlled by the manufacturers, which requires a corresponding logistical input. One example of this is the materials life cycle for PVC window frames operated by European manufacturers. Thanks to the uniform composition of the polymers used, all the products covered by this life cycle can be mixed and recycled at the end of their (initial) useful lives – the recycling rate is almost 100 %.
If complete recycling is impossible, the waste can be processed to form products of lower quality (downcycling). Employing polymers waste as bulk fill materials, insulation, floor coverings and similar purposes is possible, but depending on the intended usage, segregated waste streams may again be necessary. However, for downcycling it is not necessary to ensure that all waste components contain identical fillers and additives.
The diversity of the polymer products used in the construction industry makes segregated waste streams almost impossible. In the automotive industry this problem is dealt with by using barcodes so that every individual synthetic material can be identified again at the end of a vehicle's useful life.

Thermoplastics

Thermoplastics (or thermosoftening plastics) consist of linear or branched molecular chains which do not form chemical bonds with each other, but instead are held together by weak physical forces. These so-called secondary valency forces are broken down when the material is heated. The molecular chains can then move and that means the polymer material becomes soft and mouldable (Fig. B 1.21). Thermoplastics exhibit a viscoelastic material behaviour and can be welded and recycled. They tend to have lower strength values than thermosets and generally a limited heat resistance. Owing to their higher viscosity, they are less suitable as substrates for fibre-reinforced polymers than thermosets.

Polymer compounds

Polymer blends are mixtures of various polymers which, however, do not react with each other, but instead are only physically mixed and interlinked by a so-called coupling agent. Mixing such materials together enables the properties of several basic materials to be combined to satisfy different specifications (Fig. B 1.22).
And it is not only possible to combine various thermoplastics – thermoplastics can also be mixed with elastomers. In the so-called thermoplastic elastomers (TPE), the two phases are either chemically bonded (block polymers) or simply purely physically mixed together (polymer blends). At service temperatures, TPEs exhibit the chemical properties of an elastomer, e.g. good extensibility, whereas at high temperatures, however, they behave like thermoplastics, e.g. are easily moulded and weldable. TPEs are mainly used to replace soft thermoplastics such as PVC-P where a higher elasticity is required, e.g. waterproof sheeting. Another advantage is that, unlike elastomers, they can be coloured; from opaque to high transparency, all nuances are possible.

Polyvinyl chloride (PVC)

▷ Window frames, pipes, rooflights, floor coverings, membrane coatings (Fig. B 1.23)

PVC is by far the most common synthetic material in use in the building industry. It has a higher strength and higher elastic modulus than the other thermoplastics. PVC is also widely used in the construction sector because of its good ageing resistance, excellent resistance to chemical substances and – compared with other thermoplastics – its good fire protection qualities. This transparent material is, however, not permanently light-fast, which is why it is frequently coloured to produce an opaque product. Its coefficient of thermal expansion and thermal conductivity are, for a thermoplastic, on the low side. In principle, PVC is brittle and therefore requires the addition of plasticisers.
We speak of plasticised or unplasticised PVC depending on the quantity of plasticisers and stabilisers added during production. Compared with unplasticised PVC-U, plasticised PVC-P exhibits a better viscosity, even at low temperatures, but does have a lower strength, lower elastic modulus and poorer weathering resistance. The plasticisers in PVC can diffuse out of the material and collect on the surface, which can cause problems when the surface is in contact with other polymers and adhesives. An alternative method of softening the brittle PVC is to form a blend of PVC and chlorinated high-density polyethylene (PE-HD). The polythene improves the viscosity of the PVC, which allows the quantity of plasticisers to be reduced.
PVC is usually supplied as a powder which is then melted for injection-moulding, extrusion and other processes. It is relatively cheap to produce and easy to work – welding, gluing and moulding can all be carried out without problems.

Polyvinyl butyral (PVB)

▷ Interlayers in panes of laminated glass

Foils made from high-molecular PVB are highly transparent and therefore ideal for bonding together panes of glass to form laminated glass. PVB foil is laid between the panes of glass and then subjected to high pressure and high temperature to bond the panes together. PVB belongs to the group of polyvinyl acetates, which are also frequently used for solvent-based adhesives.

Polyethylene (PE)

▷ Waterproof sheeting, water pipes, hollow-core slab formers, glass replacement in glasshouses, polymer fibres (Fig. B 1.24)

Polyethylene is an inexpensive, mass-produced polymer with a low self-weight. Without pigments, it has a milky white appearance and loses its transparency with increasing density. This polymer has a high extensibility and exhibits a very viscoelastic failure behaviour. Its gas permeability is higher than that of the majority of other polymers, but it can absorb only a limited amount of water. PE has very low strength and elastic modulus values, but its thermal conductivity is relatively high compared with other thermoplastics. It is not weather-resistant; sheeting made from low-density polyethylene (PE-LD) is quickly decomposed by UV radiation.
Two methods are used for producing polyethylene: polymerisation at high pressure results in a material with low density, low strength and low elastic modulus (PE-LD), whereas low-pressure polymerisation produces a polymer with a higher density and at the same time higher strength and higher elastic modulus (PE-HD).
In principle, PE's resistance to chemicals, the weather and UV light increases with its density. Adding carbon black stabilises the molecular structure and therefore increases the resistance to UV radiation. A cross-linked polyethylene (PE-X) can withstand higher service temperatures and has a better creep rupture strength.
The workability and weldability of PE is very good, especially for foils made from PE-LD. However, the non-polar structure makes it unsuitable for gluing because the adhesive cannot achieve the dipolar bonds necessary for the adhesive effect. Moulding is possible in principle, but is not easy to carry out because this material does not exhibit a distinctive thermoelastic zone.

Polyethylene ionomers

▷ Interlayers in panes of laminated glass, pipes

Ionomers can be obtained from various polymers. Those commonly used for the interlayers of laminated glass are based on polyethylene. Generally, ionomers consist of both ionised and non-ionised components. This results in the special properties that allow the material to adhere to other materials, which in the laminated glass application exceed the characteristic values of the PVB foils usually employed. Heat breaks down the bonds of the two components and the material becomes thermoplastically workable. Ionomer foils are as clear as glass and tough, and can be used in a thickness of just 12 µm.

Ethylene vinyl acetate (EVA)

▷ Waterproof sheeting, adhesive foils for solar modules

The addition of vinyl acetate increases the gas permeability of polyethylene and at the same time enhances its transparency. The elongation at failure and the notched impact strength are also substantially improved. Basically, EVA is processed in the same way as PE-LD, and the elasticity increases as the vinyl acetate content rises. EVA foil is used for embedding solar cells in panes of glass – heat is applied to bond them permanently to the glass.

Polypropylene (PP)

▷ Pipes, covers, containers (Fig. B 1.25)

Polypropylene is another mass-produced polymer, with properties similar to those of PE. However, its strength and heat resistance are somewhat higher, whereas its thermal conductivity is lower. PP can be reinforced with fibres to increase its strength even further. Like PE, it has a low density, lower than that of water. Untreated PP has a milky appearance and requires the addition of fillers to achieve the necessary durability and toughness required for construction applications, which usually make it opaque. Stabilisation to prevent damage by UV radiation is more involved than with PE and leads to poorer results – PP is therefore unsuitable for external applications.
The processing of PP is similar to that of PE: it is easily moulded and welded, but likewise difficult to glue.

Polystyrene (PS)

▷ Thermal insulation, impact sound insulation, sandwich panel core material (Fig. B 1.26)

PS is, like PE and PP, a cheap, mass-produced polymer with a relatively low density, but better mechanical properties. PS is dimensionally stable and has a low coefficient of thermal expansion and low thermal conductivity. The disadvantages are its brittle failure behaviour and its sensitivity to UV light, which can be optimised by stabilisers to a limited extent only. Although PS is highly transparent and has a shiny surface, it yellows quickly when exposed to direct sunlight, becomes brittle and has a tendency towards stress cracking. Therefore, PS is only suitable for internal applications. One good identifying feature of this polymer is its "glassy" ring when struck or the rustling sound of a PS foil.
PS is not only suitable for welding, but also for gluing – a marked contrast to PE and PP.
In the form of an expanded (EPS) or extruded (XPS) rigid foam it can be used for thermal insulation or as the core of sandwich panels made from fibre-reinforced polymers (see "Core materials", pp. 72–75).

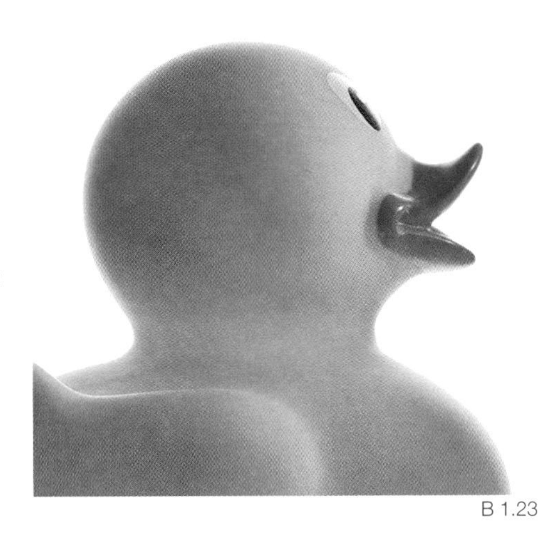

B 1.23

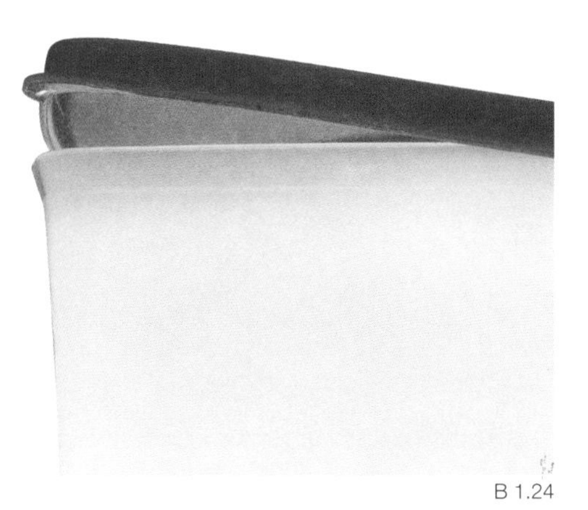

B 1.24

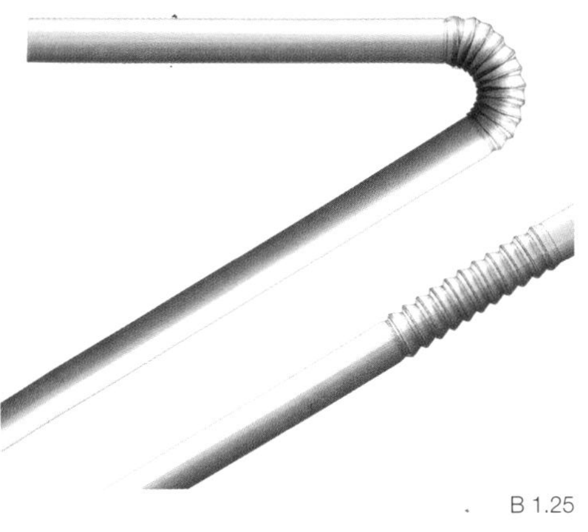

B 1.25

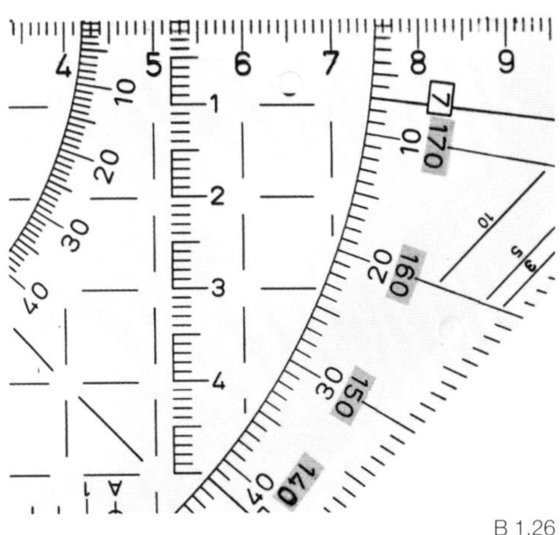

B 1.26

B 1.27

B 1.28

B 1.29

Styrene copolymers (SB, ABS, SAN, ASA)

▷ Furniture, seat shells, sanitary linings, external cladding (ASA only) (Fig. B 1.32)

Styrene copolymers have a similar chemical structure to polystyrene and essentially similar properties. Due to the chemical or physical combination of different monomers, it is possible to optimise the impact or weathering resistance (compared with polystyrene). Like PS, styrene copolymers have a shiny surface finish. Acrylate styrene acrylonitrile (ASA) in particular is also suitable for external applications – the higher polarity of its molecules gives it excellent weathering resistance.

Other thermoplastics or elastomers are frequently added to improve the impact resistance, scratch resistance or mechanical properties of the polymer in general and therefore make it more robust.

Polymethyl methacrylate (PMMA)

▷ Glazing, roofing, furniture

PMMA (acrylic sheet) is a typical building industry polymer which compared with other thermoplastics exhibits excellent mechanical properties and a superb shine. The light transmittance of a 3 mm thick sheet is approx. 92 % and is therefore better than mineral glass. Although this hard material is highly scratch-resistant when compared with other thermoplastics, it is more sensitive than glass or polycarbonate. PMMA is resistant to external influences, especially UV radiation. Its failure behaviour is relatively brittle when the material has not been modified by adding elastomers or fibres.

In contrast to many other thermoplastics, PMMA can be produced directly in the form of semi-finished products such as moulded sheets, sections or pipes. The cross-linking takes place directly in the mould. Like other thermoplastics, PMMA is first produced as a granulate and subsequently extruded to form, for example, sheets. The strength and elastic modulus of the semi-finished products are superior to those of the granulate.

Another advantage of PMMA is the simple hot working. After heating to approx. 130 °C (extruded PMMA) or 150 °C (moulded PMMA), it is easy to form and retains its shape after cooling (see "Forming", p. 172).

Polyester

Polyester is a generic term for a group of polymers, all of which have a comparatively high tensile strength and a high elastic modulus. In addition, they have – for polymers – a very high heat resistance, an excellent resistance to chemical influences and a good transparency. Polyesters are therefore especially interesting for external applications. The individual polymers of the polyester group are often classified under their group name. For example, the PET fibres important for membranes are simply called polyester fibres by manufacturers.

Polycarbonate (PC)

▷ Glazing (double- and triple-wall sheets), roofing, spandrel panels (Fig. B 1.28)

In terms of its properties, polycarbonate is similar to PMMA and is used for many of the same applications. The strength, elastic modulus and durability are similar for the two materials. However, UV stabilisers are required for PC that is to be used outside in order to prevent yellowing. PC is transparent, although its light transmittance is lower than that of PMMA.

One great advantage of PC is its high toughness, which is about 10 times that of PMMA. Typical applications are therefore constructions where impact loads are expected. The service temperature of PC, at up to 135 °C, is much higher than that of PMMA. Reinforcing PC with glass fibres improves its tensile strength considerably and also raises the service temperature to 145 °C. PC is shaped by first preheating it for several hours at 110 °C and then allowing it to dry. Afterwards, it is shaped at 180–210 °C by means of stretch forming, or by using compressed air or a vacuum process. The shaping process is therefore far more complicated than for PMMA.

Polyethylene terephthalate (PET)

▷ Fibres, high-strength foil (Fig. B 1.27)

PET has a higher degree of crystallisation than polycarbonate and hence a lower transparency. A better transparency can be achieved, however, by producing an amorphous structure, but that lowers the mechanical properties and the heat deflection temperature. Generally, PET shares the good properties of the other polyesters, such as high strength, high elastic modulus and excellent weathering resistance. But in contrast to PC, PET is also resistant to stress cracking. And just like PC, PET requires several hours of drying time prior to processing. It is the extrusion of high-strength foils that is most interesting for the building industry, also the so-called melt spinning to form high-strength threads and wires. As with the PET fibres, these fibres are also simply referred to as polyester fibres. They are very robust and absorb hardly any moisture, which is why they are important for membrane structures.

Glycol-modified PET (PET-G) has a higher impact strength, is ideal for deep drawing and is therefore frequently used in modelmaking.

Poly(p-phenylene ether), modified (PPE + PS)

▷ Window frames, solar collectors

The polyester PPE is processed exclusively blended with polystyrene in order to achieve an adequate heat resistance. PPE + PS has excellent mechanical properties and the dimensional stability of PPE + PS is particularly high. As with the other polyesters, this material is very weather-resistant and also self-extinguishing in a fire. One special feature is the easy further processing, e.g. the surface can be easily painted or printed.

Polyamide (PA), aramid

▷ Fibres, door hardware, thermal breaks in window frames, coated garden furniture (Fig. B 1.30)

Polyamides are semi-crystalline and therefore opaque. In the special form aramid there are aromatic rings in the molecular structure and this form is used almost exclusively for producing high-strength fibres. Polyamide and aramid have good mechanical properties, especially a high damping capacity and good abrasion resistance. Fibres made from these materials exhibit a very viscoelastic failure behaviour – they can absorb large amounts of impact energy. Polyamides also have a high heat deflection temperature and are resistant to chemical effects, but are less weather-resistant and light-fast, which means that stabilisers such as carbon black are indispensable for external applications. Polyamides absorb a comparatively large amount of moisture from their surroundings, which, on the one hand, reduces their strength, but, on the other, improves their viscoelastic properties.

Cellulose acetate (CA)

▷ Transparent thermal insulation, spectacle frames, tool handles (Fig. B 1.31)

Cellulose acetate is obtained from the chemical reaction between cellulose (from cotton or timber) and acetic acid. We distinguish between cellulose diacetate (CA) and cellulose triacetate (CTA) depending on the amount of acetic acid bonded. The latter is more difficult to process thermoplastically but has a better resistance to water and heat. The preferred processing methods for CA are injection moulding, extrusion, extrusion blow moulding and hot working.
CTA is primarily processed in a casting method to form hard foils, which owing to their good transparency can also be used for LCD screens. In contrast to the other polymers described here, cellulose (tri)acetate is not obtained from petroleum, but instead from renewable raw materials. It was in the 1920s that cellulose acetate replaced celluloid as an emulsion carrier for film strips because of its lower flammability.
CA is characterised by its good transparency, strength, surface hardness and shine, heat resistance, grip and low moisture absorptance. In addition, its high surface elasticity makes it highly resistant to scratches and its low electrostatic charge capacity results in dust-free surfaces. Another plus point is its high mechanical damping capacity, which is why cellulose acetate is ideal for the handles of tools, for instance. Also characteristic is the high heat radiation absorption, which makes both CA and CTA worth considering for transparent thermal insulation. This type of polymer can only be used in areas protected from the weather because there are no suitable additives available that ensure permanent effective protection against UV radiation and moisture.

Fluoropolymers

Fluoropolymers differ from the other thermoplastics in a number of ways. Their mechanical properties can be classed as low, which is why this group of materials is hardly suitable as a construction material – with the exception of pneumatically prestressed polymer cushions or PTFE fabrics. It is first and foremost the exceptional surface characteristics that make fluoropolymers very interesting materials for the building industry. The low surface roughness means that dust and dirt cannot adhere to the surface; these polymers are practically self-cleaning and therefore constitute an ideal coating material. Furthermore, this group of materials is extremely resistant to the weather and UV radiation and is also non-flammable. In addition, the service temperature range is unusually broad for thermoplastics: from -200 to +300 °C.

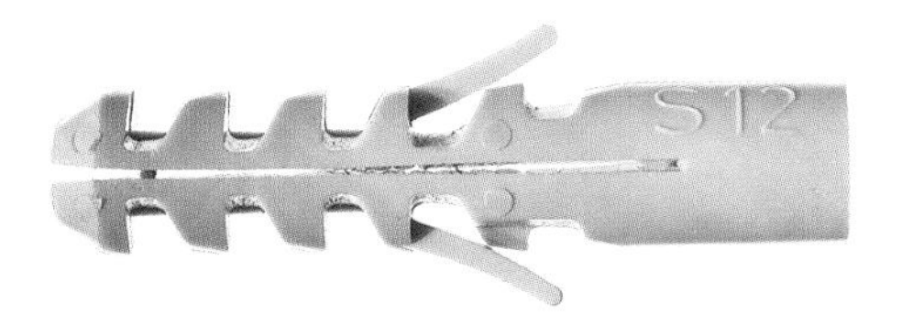

B 1.30

B 1.31

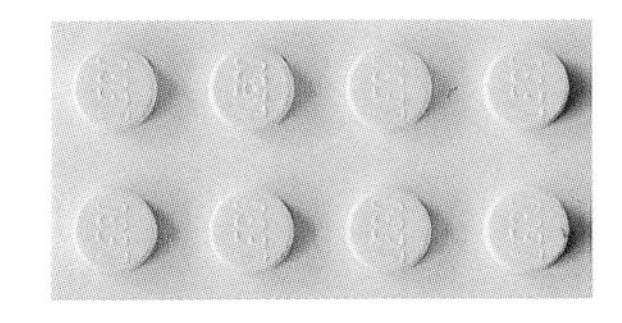

B 1.32

B 1.27 Polyethylene terephthalate (PET)
B 1.28 Polycarbonate (PC)
B 1.29 Polytetrafluoroethylene (PTFE)
B 1.30 Polyamide (PA)
B 1.31 Cellulose acetate (CA)
B 1.32 Acrylonitrile-butadiene-styrene (ABS)

B 1.33

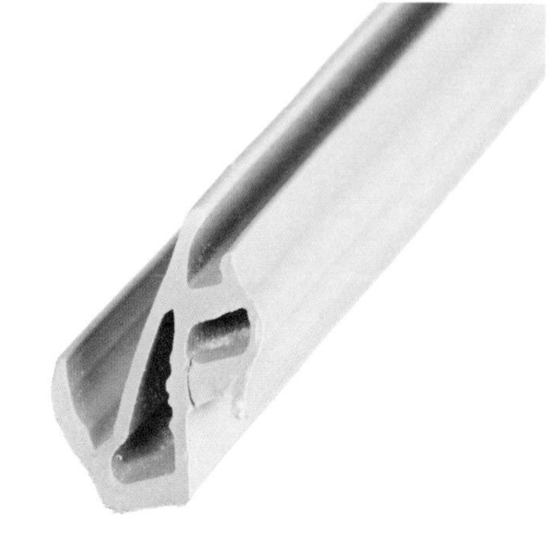

B 1.34

B 1.33 Natural rubber
B 1.34 Ethylene propylene diene monomer rubber (EPDM)
B 1.35 Styrene butadiene rubber (SBR)
B 1.36 Silicone rubber
B 1.37 Properties of elastomers depending on temperature, range of application lies above glass transition temperature in rubber-like elastic region, tending towards ductile failure behaviour
B 1.38 Comparison of common elastomers

Polytetrafluoroethylene (PTFE)
▷ Membrane coatings, sliding bearings, foil, PTFE fibres (Fig. B 1.29, p. 42)
In the construction industry the milky white PTFE is used for coating membranes in order to create a self-cleaning surface. Another application is the use of PTFE discs in low-friction sliding bearings for bridges. After production, PTFE cannot be remelted like other polymers, which prevents hot working. However, moulded parts and foils can be produced through sintering and extrusion.

Ethylene tetrafluoroethylene (ETFE)
▷ Foil
The chemical structure and properties of ETFE are basically similar to those of PTFE, but in contrast to the latter, ETFE is easy to work thermoplastically. The addition of ethylene also increases the strength and the elastic modulus. ETFE is more transparent than PTFE, which is why it is commonly employed for highly transparent and dirt-repellent foils. Glass fibres can be used to reinforce ETFE foil in order to meet high mechanical demands (e.g. for laboratory equipment).

Tetrafluoroethylene hexafluoropropylene vinylidene fluoride terpolymer (THV)
▷ Foil
This so-called terpolymer consists of three fluoropolymers. It is very easy to work thermoplastically and is used mainly for foil. Its light transmittance is outstanding – up to 97 % for a 100 μm foil. However, the maximum service temperature is well below that of ETFE.

Elastomers

At the moment about one-third of the elastomers produced worldwide are based on natural rubber, which is obtained from the sap of rubber plants – also known as latex. The remainder of the production is based on synthetic rubbers obtained from petroleum.
Natural rubbers have been known in South America for several hundred years and were later introduced into Europe. One use of the sticky compound is to waterproof textiles, e.g. the Mackintosh raincoat patented in 1823. Natural rubber first became important for technical applications after the invention of vulcanisation in 1839, a process that makes rubber permanently elastic. Synthetic rubbers appeared later, initially as replacements for natural rubber and then for special applications following further developments.
Elastomers (colloquially referred to as rubbers) are classed as an "intermediate polymer group" – between the non-cross-linked thermoplastics and the densely cross-linked thermosets – because of their molecular structure. In contrast to thermoplastics, elastomers cannot be resoftened once the molecular linking has been completed.

The raw material for an elastomer is known as crude rubber, irrespective of whether it is of natural or synthetic origin. The transition of the rubber from the liquid to the solid state is called coagulation. However, this is not a chemical reaction, merely a physical hardening. This firm raw material is very tough and high mechanical forces are needed to work it. First of all, the crude rubber is shredded, then mixed with fillers and moulded. If the material is too tough, the polymer chains must first be broken down by adding chemicals (mastication) prior to further processing. After that, the chemical cross-linking of the molecules (vulcanisation) can take place with the help of sulphur or sulphur-based compounds at high pressure and high temperature. The originally plastic, permanently deformable rubber is thus turned into elastic rubber, i.e. an elastomer.
The mechanical properties of elastomers remain relatively constant as the temperature rises within their range of use, although the service temperatures vary depending on the material (Fig. B 1.38). The minimum service temperature is characterised by embrittlement of the elastomer, the maximum temperature by the decomposition of the material (Fig. B 1.37). Owing to their high extensibility, they are not useful as construction materials, but are frequently used as loadbearing jointing materials or for waterproofing or sealing. Elastomers return to their original form even after severe elongation. The durability and elasticity of elastomers can be controlled by

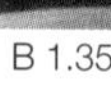

B 1.35

B 1.36

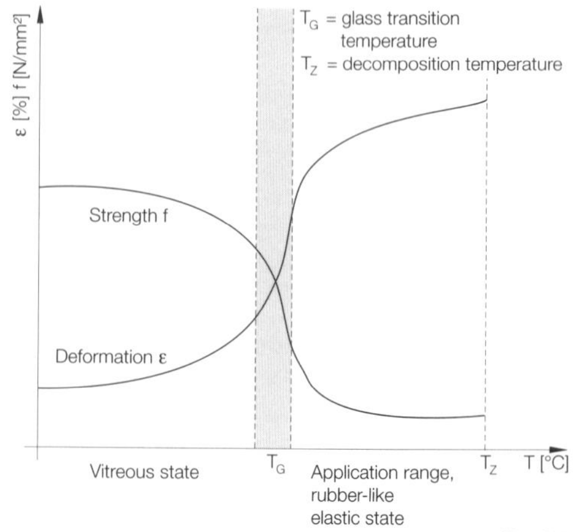

B 1.37

		Tensile strength	Elasticity	Wearing resistance	Weather & ozone resistance	Heat resistance	Flexibility at low temp.	Gas permeability	Long-term service temp. [°C][1]
Natural rubber	NR	++	++	o	--	--	++	-	100
R rubbers	SBR	+	-	+	--	-	+	-	110
	BR	--	++	++	--	--	++	-	100
	IIR	-	--	-	o	o	o	++	130
	CR	+	+	+	-	-	o	+	120
M rubbers	EPDM	o	o	-	++	+	+	o	140
	FKM	o	--	-	++	++	--	+	210
	EAM	o	--	-	++	+	-	+	170
Silicone rubber	MVQ	-	+	--	++	++	++	--	200
	FVMQ	-	o	--	++	+	+	--	180
Polyurethane rubber	AU	++	+	++	+	o	-	+	130

[1] approx. 1000 hours for optimum material   +, ++ good properties   o average properties   -, -- poor properties

B 1.38

adding active fillers which at the same time reinforce the material. The filler used for dark elastomers, e.g. vehicle tyres, is normally carbon black, for light-coloured products micro-dispersed silicic acid or oil. The weathering resistance of elastomers is generally good, but there is always the risk that air, or rather the oxygen in the air, could dissolve out the chemically bonded sulphur which then makes the elastomer crumbly, and causes it to age.
The elastomers relevant for the building industry are briefly described below. The various synthetic rubbers are divided into a number of groups according to their chemical composition and properties. The so-called R rubbers include – in addition to natural rubber (NR) – a number of synthetic elastomers with properties similar to those of natural rubber. R rubbers have comparatively high strengths, but a lower weathering resistance.
The synthetic M and Q rubbers (silicone elastomers) represent a contrast because they are highly weather-resistant but not as strong. There are also other groups that have been developed for specific applications.

Natural rubber (NR)
Natural rubber is based on vegetable rubber (latex) and belongs to the group of R rubbers. It still plays an important role because it has many positive properties that cannot be matched by synthetic rubbers (Fig. B 1.33). Its strength, extensibility and rebound resilience are excellent, the rise in temperature under dynamic loads very low. Two-thirds of the world's HGV tyres are therefore currently produced from natural rubber. For other applications, however, natural rubber is gradually being replaced by the specialised and frequently less expensive synthetic rubbers.
The sulphur required for vulcanisation improves the generally limited long-term durability and weathering resistance of natural rubber. Nevertheless, it is sensitive to UV radiation and ozone over the long-term, also petrol. These disadvantages can be problematic for construction applications because of the long service lives expected.

Styrene butadiene rubber (SBR)
▷ Floor coverings, electric cable sheathing, hoses, sealing gaskets, vehicle tyres (Fig. B 1.35)
SBR is one of the synthetic R rubbers, which are very similar to natural rubber. They have a limited service temperature range and relatively poor weather and ozone resistance. However, they are inexpensive and therefore frequently used in applications where they are not directly exposed to UV radiation.
In contrast to NR, SBR has a better resistance to abrasion and products can also be manufactured in lighter colours.

Ethylene propylene diene monomer rubber (EPDM)
▷ Waterproof sheeting, linings, expansion joint gaskets, floor coverings (Fig. B 1.34)
As with the group of M rubbers in general, EPDM tends to have inferior mechanical properties to those of the R rubbers, but exhibits outstanding ozone and weathering resistance plus a relatively high gas permeability. The heat resistance of the M rubbers is also higher than that of the R group. EPDM is important for applications in the building industry where direct exposure to the weather and UV radiation is to be expected. And another area where EPDM excels is for building components exposed to a combination of steam or water and high temperatures.

Silicone rubber (Q)
▷ Jointing materials, window and door gaskets (Fig. B 1.36)
Silicone rubber has a very high heat resistance, indeed can even be heated to more than 400 °C for a few minutes. It is also ideal for low-temperature applications. This type of Q rubber is very difficult to wet, i.e. it is also water-repellent and anti-adhesive. It also exhibits a much higher gas permeability than natural rubber.
Silicone rubber has a different chemical structure to the majority of synthetic materials. Its molecular chains are formed primarily from silicon atoms and carbon appears only – if at all – in side groups. It is this structure that makes the material incombustible and therefore suitable for applications with a very wide temperature range. Its weathering and ageing resistance are excellent and when exposed to UV light the molecular chains are much more stable than all other synthetic materials.

Polysulphide rubber (TM)
Polysulphide rubber can be processed in solid form or – in contrast to most other rubbers – also in liquid form. In the building industry, liquid TM can be used as a joint sealing compound. It then cures during the final processing by adding an oxidising agent or through the action of the moisture in the surrounding air.

Polyurethane rubber (AU or EU)
Polyurethane rubber is processed in a viscous state. Like all polyurethanes, it has good wearing and weathering resistance, excellent strength and good elasticity.

Casting polyurethane elastomers (PUR)
In the cross-linked state, casting polyurethane elastomers exhibit the typical properties of elastomers, but can be processed as a liquid resin prior to cross-linking. High wearing and abrasion resistance, good strength and weather resistance are the main advantages of these materials. Their good damping properties make them especially interesting for floor coverings in sports centres.

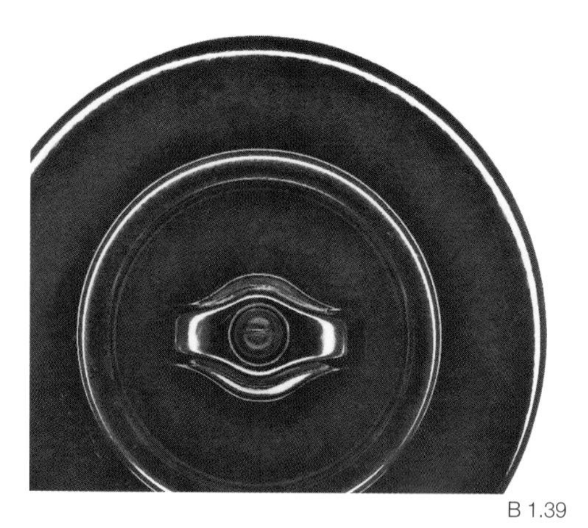
B 1.39

B 1.40

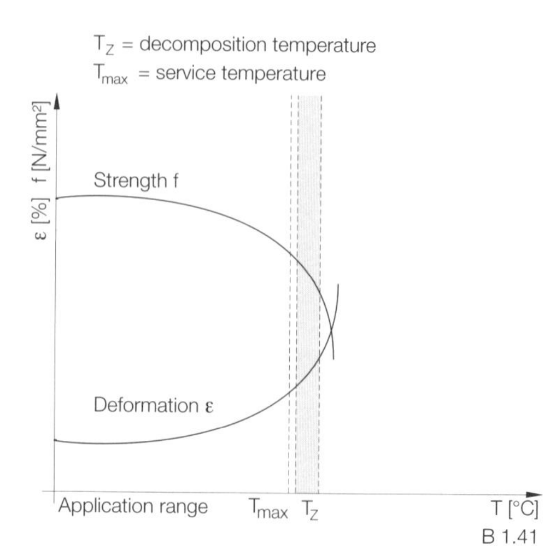

B 1.41

Thermosets

Thermosets (or thermosetting plastics) were first produced and processed on an industrial scale at the beginning of the 20th century, making them the oldest completely synthetic materials. Although thermosets account for only approx. 20 % of the output of the plastics industry as a whole and thus tend to play only a subsidiary role, their good mechanical properties and high chemical resistance mean they are widely used in the building industry. They are processed in the form of a liquid primary product (reactive resin) – a contrast to the other groups of polymers. The inclusion of fibres results in a high-quality compound thanks to the good surface wetting and it is this fact that makes them ideal for fibre-reinforced polymers. The chemical cross-linking reaction in the polymer first takes place at the processing stage.
The molecular chains of a thermoset form a dense, closely woven, three-dimensional network, which results in a hard, brittle microstructure. The dense network of molecules prevents the infiltration of solvents, which is why thermosets are highly resistant to chemicals. This molecular bond cannot be broken down by applying heat either, and so thermosets do not melt (Fig. B 1.41). The heat resistance of thermosets is higher than that of thermoplastics, but their strength and elastic modulus start to decrease noticeably even before a temperature of 100 °C has been reached (Fig. B 1.16, p. 36).
The structure and properties of thermosets vary much more than those of thermoplastics and elastomers, which is why they have to be specially designated after manufacture in order to be able to identify the exact chemical structure and properties, e.g. their suitability for external applications.

Primary products

The primary products for thermosets are moulding compounds or casting resins, which, like elastomers, are only cross-linked during the final processing. A moulding compound is a pourable or viscous mixture of resin plus hardener and filler. Merely heating these causes them to harden (one-part system). As all the components necessary for the chemical cross-linking are present in such moulding compounds, they even harden at room temperature after a certain length of time, which limits their shelf life. Casting resins, on the other hand, are pure liquid resins to which a hardener (catalyst) is added during the final processing, which results in a longer storage time for the primary product (two-part system). Casting resins are also commonly known as synthetic or reactive resins. The different primary products do not affect the chemical compositions of the final thermosets significantly, however.

Phenol formaldehyde, phenolic resins (PF)

▷ Power sockets, fibre-reinforced polymers meeting fire protection requirements, facade cladding, door linings (Fig. B 1.39)

The first PF polymers manufactured on an industrial scale, which became known under the trade name Bakelite, was developed as long ago as 1905 (see "From alchemy to chemistry", p. 10). Even today, PF materials still play an important role in the plastics industry, partly because of their low production costs. They are particularly useful for applications involving high service temperatures or where a better reaction to fire is important. In a fire, PF polymers give off less smoke and toxic fumes than other thermosets. PF polymers are opaque, have a natural yellowish brown colour and therefore are only suitable for dark-coloured products. These materials also tend to darken when exposed to light. Their mechanical properties are somewhat inferior to those of other thermosets.
PF polymers are created through the polycondensation of phenol and formaldehyde. The condensation process produces water as a by-product during the hardening and this must be drained away. PF materials are suitable for many different processing techniques, e.g. in the form of moulding compounds they can be injected into closed moulds, as a viscous resin (phenolic resin) poured into moulds, or used to produce fibre-reinforced materials. Foams made from phenolic resin achieve very good thermal insulation values. PF polymers are also frequently used for hardboard.

Aminoplastic resins (UF, MF)

▷ Power sockets, glues and adhesives, foams (Fig. B 1.40)

Aminoplastic resins such as urea formaldehyde (UF) or melamine formaldehyde (MF) are similar to the PF polymers in terms of their chemical structure and also their properties. They differ from these, however, in that they are light-fast, i.e. do not darken in sunlight, and are therefore ideal for light-coloured building components. UF is an aminoplastic resin with a special surface shine and a high degree of hardness. Its mechanical properties are comparable with those of the PF materials, shrinkage is lower and dimension stability is good. UF is therefore ideal for manufacturing dimensionally stable components. In addition, MF exhibits better weathering resistance.

Unsaturated polyester resin (UP)

▷ Sealing materials, glass fibre-reinforced polymer (GFRP) (Fig. B 1.42)

UP is transparent to pale yellow and its mechanical properties lie in the middle of the range for thermosets. Its good tenacity, even at low temperatures, is an advantage. But the comparatively large amount of shrinkage during curing, which fillers can only partly compensate for, proves to be a disadvantage. The degree of shrinkage depends on many factors, which is why it cannot be compensated for by shape alone. Owing to its low moisture absorption, UP resin is ideal for external applications. Its service temperature is much lower than that of PF polymers. It requires the addition of a flame retardant because it is not self-extinguishing. UP resin is mostly used for producing GFRP because it combines well with the glass fibres, is easily worked and is also relatively inexpensive. However, the transparency decreases as more and more fibres are added and therefore GFRP is mostly translucent to opaque. The raw material for the production of UP components is a solution of unsaturated polyester in a reactive solvent, usually styrene. Polyester resins cure after adding a catalyst and release heat during the reaction. A certain variation in the mixing ratio between resin and hardener is permissible without this having an effect on the material properties of the finished polymer. This is a con-

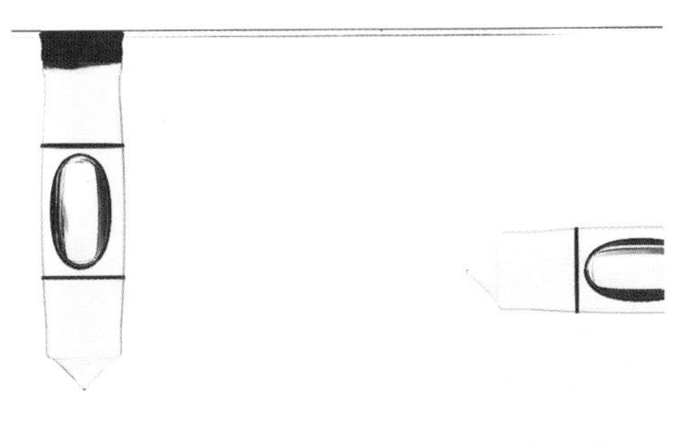
B 1.42

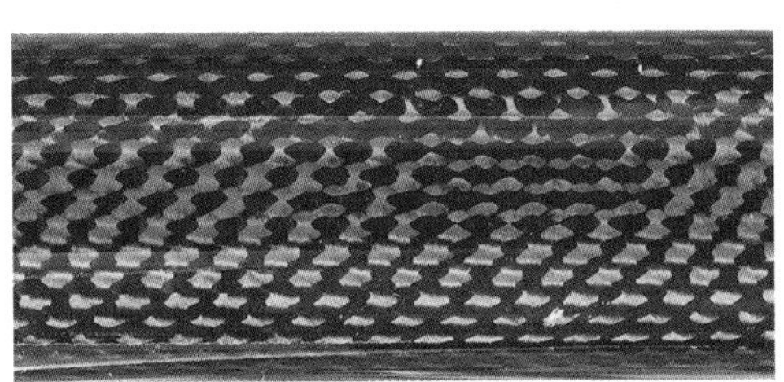
B 1.43

B 1.44

siderable advantage for manual processing. As with all thermosets, UP can be worked hot or cold; an accelerator must be added to enable curing to take place at room temperature. Following the actual hardening reaction, UP should be allowed to cure for several hours at a temperature of approx. 70 °C in order to achieve its full strength and chemical resistance. This procedure is known as annealing. The solvent styrene is the reason for the typical smell of UP components and can lead to irritation of mucous membranes and respiratory passages. Subsequent steam treatment can reduce the odour emissions and place the products in the category of physiologically harmless.

Epoxy resin (EP)

▷ Surface protection and coatings, adhesives, polymer concrete, carbon fibre-reinforced polymer (CFRP) (Fig. B 1.43)

Epoxy resin is characterised by its particularly high (adhesive) strength and chemical resistance. It hardly shrinks upon hardening and its moisture absorption is lower than that of UP, for example. Therefore, EP is ideal for heavily loaded components or adverse environmental conditions. Although EP resin is essentially clear with some natural colouring, it is not light-fast and therefore light colours are not to be recommended. However, protective coatings in the form of highly transparent PU gel coats plus optical brighteners enable the production of transparent, colourless components. EP is primarily used for high-performance fibre-reinforced components, mostly in combination with carbon fibres. The less expensive UP is usually sufficient for embedding glass fibres. Although EP is not readily flammable, it is not self-extinguishing, which is why it does not usually comply with specific fire protection requirements.
The production involves mixing the non-cross-linked EP with a hardener. In contrast to UP, the exothermic reaction mechanism requires that the recommended mixing ratio be adhered to exactly. Cold curing takes about 24 hours. Afterwards, the component must be allowed to cure further for several hours, which involves heating it successively to approx. 100 °C. The hardening time is generally longer than that required for UP materials. If, however, higher temperatures are used during the curing, then the hardening time can be reduced to a few minutes and this improves the mechanical properties, especially the heat resistance. Another difference between EP and polyester resins is that no unpleasant odours are given off during curing, although the hardeners and thinners used do represent a health risk. The casting resin must not be allowed to touch the skin during processing and protective goggles must be worn, but the finished material is physiologically harmless.
Epoxy resins are frequently used as adhesives or coatings. For such products, the addition of a silicate can improve the dimensional stability during processing and reduce the tendency to creep in the hardened state. These products are then known as epoxy resin mortars or polymer concrete depending on the mixing ratio.

Vinyl ester resin (VE)

▷ Fibre-reinforced polymers

Vinyl ester resin is similar to UP resin, but is tougher and exhibits better fibre wetting characteristics for fibre-reinforced polymers. VE is used, first and foremost, when a particular resistance to chemicals or a high impact or fatigue resistance is required. The mechanical properties are mostly better than those of UP, but are inferior to those of epoxy resin. Vinyl ester is relatively expensive and therefore it is used for special applications, primarily in the chemicals industry. It is obtained from EP via chemical reactions and its processing is similar to that of UP.

Polyurethane (PUR)

▷ In situ foam, rigid foam, lacquers and coatings (Fig. B 1.44)

Polyurethanes can be made from various components and therefore their properties can differ accordingly. The molecular chains vary between linear, or rather non-cross-linked, to densely cross-linked and therefore polyurethanes are allocated to different polymer groups. For example, soft PUR foam is an elastomer, whereas rigid PUR foams or PUR lacquers are thermosets, and thermoplastic polyurethane elastomers (TPU), which are used in damping elements or sports equipment, must be allocated to the thermoplastics because of their properties. In the building industry, however, is almost exclusively polyurethanes in the form of thermosets that are important as construction materials. Polyurethane can be processed as a casting resin with a hard or highly elastic characteristic. Its heat resistance lies in the range of the other thermosets. More usual is the process to form a rigid material for thermal insulation or sandwich panels. To do this, the polyurethane is foamed with various blowing agents (see "Foams", pp. 72–74). The lengths of the molecular chains control the properties of the material: long chains result in elastic foams, whereas short chains produce rigid foams.

References:

[1] Ludwig, Carsten: Glasfaserverstärkte Kunststoffe unter hoher thermischer und mechanischer Belastung. Dissertation. Stuttgart, 2009, pp. 156f.

B 1.39 Phenol formaldehyde, phenolic resin (PF)
B 1.40 Aminoplastic resin
B 1.41 Properties of thermosets depending on temperature, application range lies in vitreous region, brittle failure behaviour
B 1.42 Unsaturated polyester resin (UP)
B 1.43 Carbon fibre-reinforced epoxy resin (CFRP)
B 1.44 Polyurethane foam (PUR)

Fibres

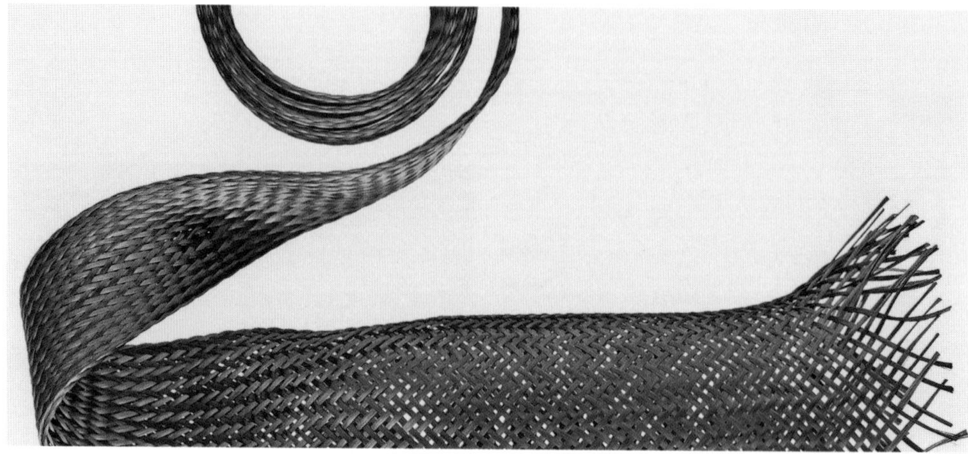

B 2.1

In relation to their length, fibres have a very small cross-section and therefore a distinct orientation. Whereas their natural "role models" such as wool actually occur in the form of fibres, synthetic materials must first be turned into fibres. Fibres are flexible, versatile in their use and processing and have a high strength. They have therefore a long history of use for the production of textiles. We generally distinguish between inorganic fibres (made from glass or carbon), polymer fibres (synthetic fibres), metal fibres and natural fibres (Fig. B 2.5). All man-made fibres are referred to as chemical or synthetic fibres. Synthetic fibres are generally preferred for architectural applications because only these fibres exhibit the strength and durability necessary for permanent structures. Apart from carbon fibres, all synthetic fibres are produced from solid materials by way of melting and stretching processes.

Properties and applications

Apart from glass and metal fibres, the majority of fibres, first and foremost the polymer fibres, consist of bundles of tiny fibres when viewed under the microscope (Fig. B 2.7). The diameters of synthetic fibres vary between 5 and 24 μm, whereas natural fibres can be up to 500 μm in diameter. Indeed, human hair is comparatively thick at 120 μm. The mass per unit length of the fibres is measured in dtex, where 1 dtex = 1 g per 10 km.

As the individual fibres (filaments) would be too fine for further processing, they are grouped into larger units immediately after production (Fig. B 2.4). A bundle of parallel fibres is known as a roving, whereas a twisted bundle of fibres is known as a yarn. The number of fibres per roving or yarn is specified in kilo (= 1000 fibre = 1 K). Rovings represent the typical raw material for processing into fibre-reinforced polymers (see "Fibres", p. 77), primarily by way of mechanised methods. Yarns, on the other hand, are used for making woven or knitted fabrics (see "Textiles", pp. 69–72). Their twist eases the processing and increases the effective strength of the fibre bundle because the individual filaments within the yarn are loaded more uniformly.

The actual production and further processing of the various fibres vary considerably and therefore the various operations are explained in more detail in the descriptions of the individual fibres. What the different processes have in common is that the individual fibres are wetted with a protective coating (called size or finish) immediately after production ready for the further processing. These substances reduce the buckling sensitivity and improve the adhesion among the fibres themselves or between the fibres and the polymer in the final fibre composite. We distinguish here between textile sizes for fibres that are further processed to form textiles, and bonding sizes for fibres that are to be embedded in polymer. Which material is suitable for the protective coating depends on the respective type of fibre.

Mechanical properties

Fibres have a much higher strength than their respective raw material. The melting and stretching processes during production align the internal structure of the fibre in the longitudinal direction and thus improve the strength of the material. In doing so, air inclusions are compressed, which reduces the negative effect that such flaws have on the strength in the longitudinal direction of the fibre. The strength of synthetic fibres increases as the diameter decreases (Fig. B 2.2). The more pronounced the longitudinal orientation of the microstructure in the fibre, the greater the decrease in the mechanical properties in the transverse direction. Fibres are frequently sensitive to transverse compression, especially carbon fibres.

The intended uses of the fibres lead to different requirements regarding, for example, strength, buckling sensitivity or low self-weight. If we consider tensile strength alone, then carbon fibres exhibit the highest values of all materials available for practical usage (Figs. B 2.3 and B 2.10, p. 50). They are, however, relatively sensitive to buckling.

The relationship between strength and self-weight is interesting when planning lightweight, loadbearing structures. The breaking length of a fibre is a good indicator for the choice of material (Fig. B 2.6). This value corresponds to the theoretical length a vertically suspended fibre could

B 2.1 Braided hose made from carbon fibres
B 2.2 Strength of a glass fibre in relation to the fibre diameter
B 2.3 Stress-strain diagrams for various fibres
B 2.4 Possible forms of processing an individual fibre (filament)
B 2.5 Classification of types of fibre
B 2.6 Breaking lengths of various fibres compared with natural silk from spiders
B 2.7 Glass, carbon and aramid fibres viewed under the microscope

reach before breaking under its own weight. Whereas conventional structural timber has a breaking length of only a little over 40 km, a polyethylene (PE) fibre could be up to 400 km long because of its low self-weight. The record for the longest theoretical breaking length is currently held by carbon nano tubes; however, this material is not yet available in the lengths necessary for the construction industry.

Applications in architecture

The properties of fibres are very much dependent on the raw material from which they are made and the respective production method. The strength and elastic modulus of some fibres can be specifically varied to suit the intended applications. Which properties of fibres can be optimised depends on the type of processing and the type of application.

Fibre-reinforced polymers

Fibres are further processed in many different ways to form fibre composites, where they form the reinforcement embedded in a polymer, the so-called matrix (see "Fibres", p. 77). Fibres with a minimum elongation, i.e. a high elastic modulus, are preferred for this; the tensile strength of the fibre is in most cases of secondary importance only. Glass and carbon fibres are the usual choices in practice, but in some sectors aramid or PE fibres are also in use. Other polymer fibres are not worth considering because of their low elastic modulus, which would lead to excessive deformations of the finished component. In addition, the thermosets normally used (see "Thermosets", pp. 46–47) can only accept a limited amount of elongation. The tensile strengths of soft fibres cannot be fully exploited because the polymer cracks before the tensile strength is reached, which leads to failure of the entire component. Metal fibres are ruled out because of their smooth surfaces, which do not allow an adequate bond to be achieved with the polymer.
If we compare glass and carbon fibres, then we discover that the tensile strengths of the fibres alone are roughly identical. However, the elastic modulus of carbon fibres is much higher than that of glass fibres. Therefore, owing to the limited extensibility of the plastic matrix, the strength of carbon fibre-reinforced polymer (CFRP) is higher than that of glass fibre-reinforced polymer (GFRP).
Natural fibres have been enjoying a renaissance in recent years. The fibres are hollow and that results in a low self-weight and hence lightweight constructions. However, natural fibres tend to absorb moisture and their mechanical properties exhibit severe scatter, which means they cannot be considered for loadbearing components at present. From the ecological viewpoint, however, we can expect to see more use being made of these fibres in the future. Their good acoustic and haptic properties make natural fibres potentially useful for cladding or interior applications (see "Natural fibres", pp. 61–62).

Textile membranes

In contrast to fibre composites, a certain extensibility, i.e. an elastic modulus that is not too high, is advantageous in membrane structures. The extensibility of a membrane increases the permissible tolerances in the cutting pattern – geometrical discrepancies can be compensated for to a certain degree by overstressing. Moreover, the prestress required in the membrane can be set more reliably. Polymer fibres made from PET or PTFE are used as well as glass fibres.
Fibres with a very high elastic modulus, e.g. carbon or metal fibres, are unsuitable for membrane structures. As soft fibres are preferred, textile membranes are coated exclusively with extensible polymers (see "Coatings", pp. 100– 103).

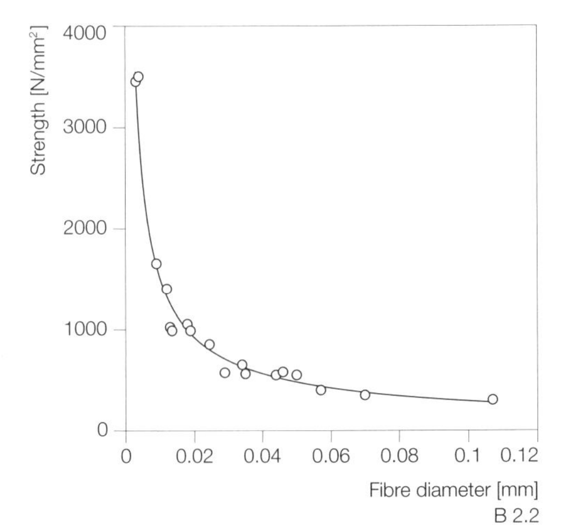

B 2.2

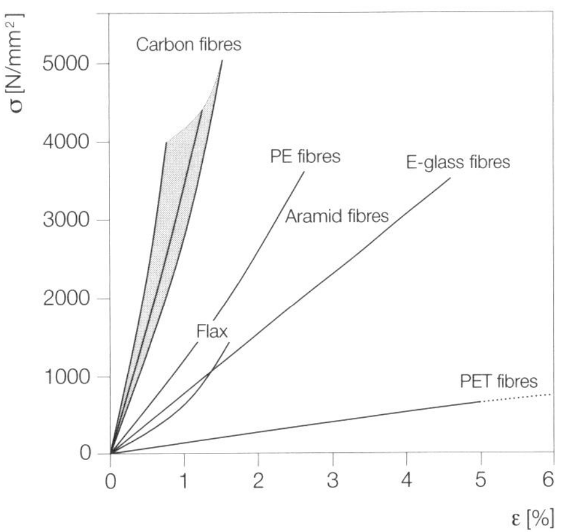

B 2.3

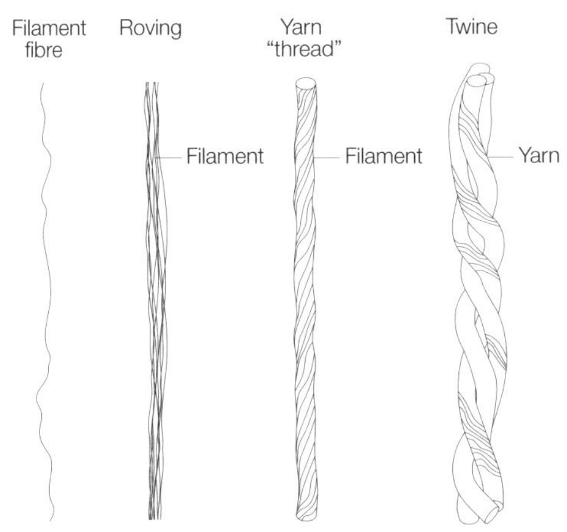

B 2.4

Natural fibres	Organic synthetic fibres (polymer fibres)
• Flax • Sisal • Hemp • Jute • Ramie • Banana • Asbestos[1]	• Polyethylene (PE) • Polyethylene terephthalate (PET) • Polyamide (PA) • Polyimide (PI) • Polyacrylonitrile (PAN) • Polytetrafluoroethylene (PTFE) • Aramid
Metal fibres	**Inorganic synthetic fibres**
• Steel • Aluminium • Copper	• Glass • Carbon • Basalt • Ceramic

[1] Harmful to health, banned in EU and Switzerland

B 2.5

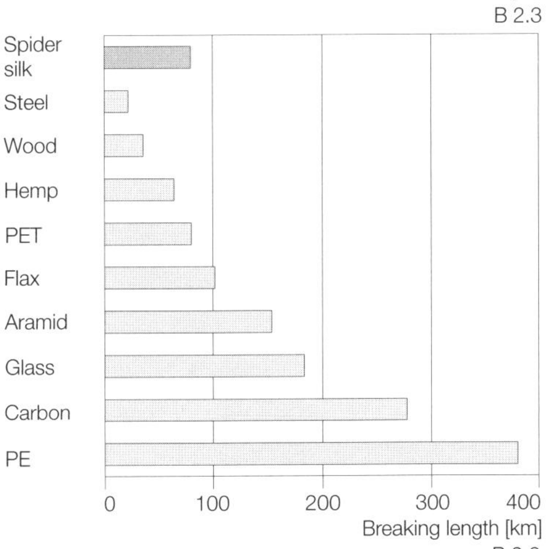

B 2.6

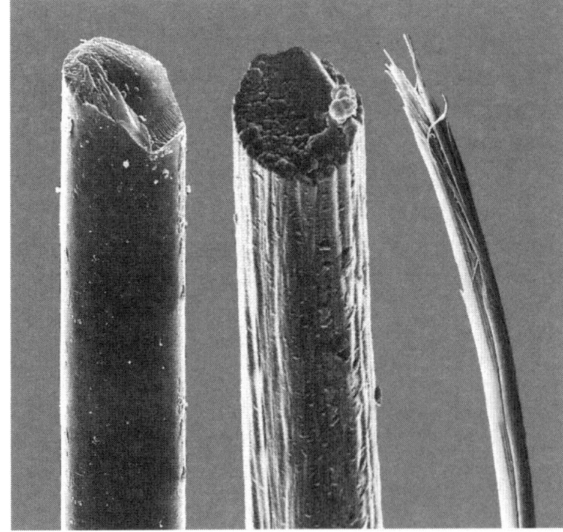
B 2.7

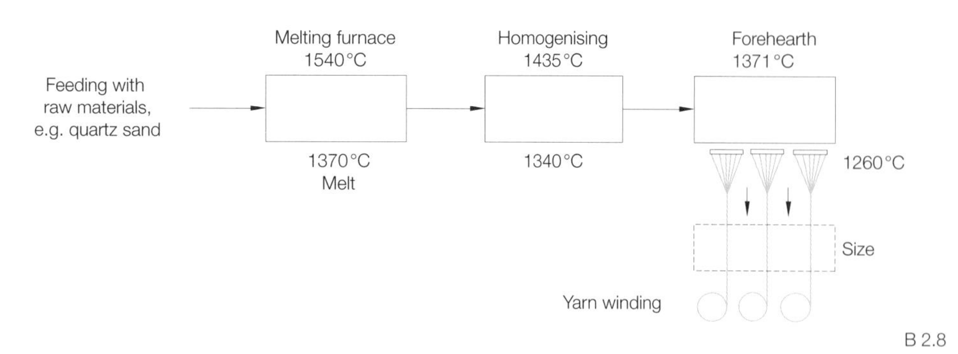

B 2.8

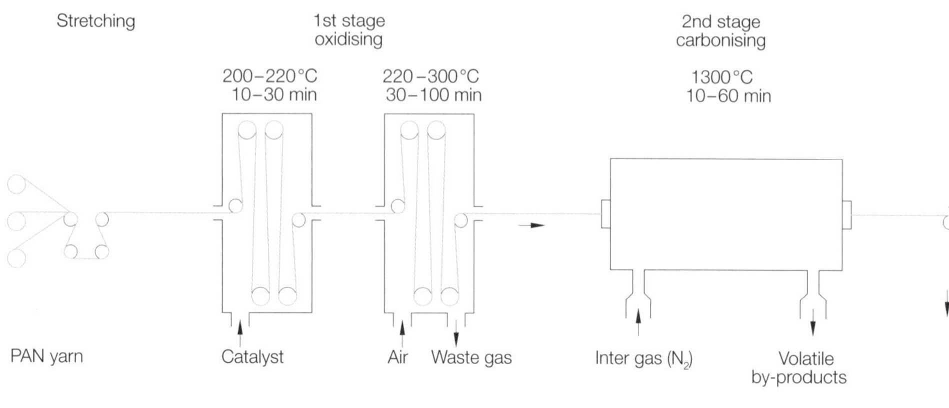

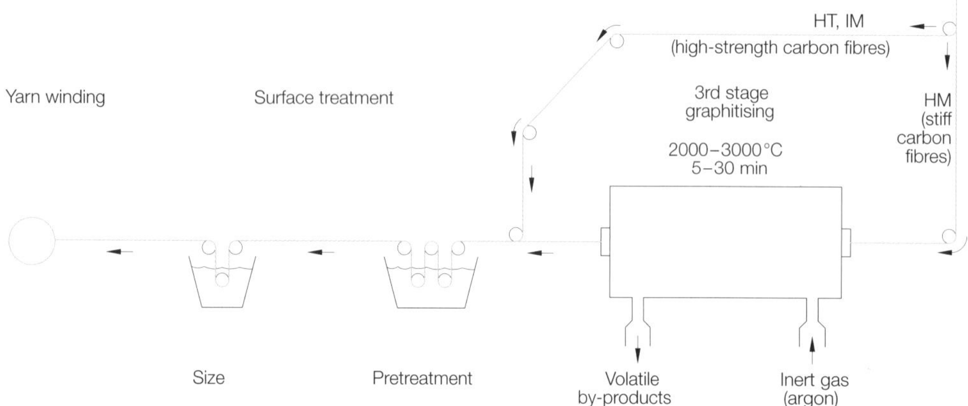

B 2.9

Property (in direction of fibre)	Specification	Tensile strength $[10^3/mm^2]$	Elastic modulus $[10^3/mm^2]$	Elongation at failure [%]	Density $[g/cm^3]$	Coeff. of thermal expansion $[10^{-6}/K]$	Thermal conductivity [W/mK]	Fibre diameter [μm]
Inorganic fibres								
Glass	E	3.4–3.5	72–77	3.3–4.8	2.52–2.60	5.00	1	9–24
	R/S	4.4–4.6	75–88	4.1–5.4	2.50–2.53	4.00	1	9–24
	AR	2.7	21–74	2.0–4.3	2.68–2.70		1	9–24
Carbon	HT	3–5	200–250	1.2–1.4	1.75–1.80	-1.00	17	7–9
	IM	4–5	250–350	1.1–1.9	1.73–1.80	-1.20		7–9
	HM	2–4	350–450	0.4–0.8	1.79–1.91	-1.30	115	7–9
Polymer fibres								
Aramid	IM	2.7	58	3.3	1.44	-2.00	0.04–0.05	12
	HM	2.4–2.7	120–146	1.5–2.4	1.44	-4.00	0.04–0.05	12
Polyester (PET)		1.1	10	22	1.38			
PA		0.9	5	20	1.16			
PE		2.7–3.6	89–116	10–45	0.97	-12.10		
Natural fibres								
Flax		0.8–1.5	60–80	1.2–1.6	1.40		0.04	5–38
Hemp		0.6–0.9	70	1.6	1.48		0.045	16–50

E: electric glass, R/S: high-strength glass, AR: alkali-resistant glass, HT: high tensile strength, IM: intermediate modulus, HM: high modulus

B 2.10

Inorganic fibres

Inorganic fibres are all those synthetic fibres that are not based on carbon compounds. However, carbon fibres made from pure carbon, and not a carbon compound, are also classed as inorganic fibres. Metal fibres are also inorganic but are usually treated as a separate group.
The properties of inorganic fibres are fundamentally different to those of organic polymer fibres. Inorganic fibres do not exhibit any creep, i.e. their elongation remains constant under long-term loading. In addition, they can be used at much higher service temperatures and they are definitely stiffer than organic fibres.

Glass fibres

▷ Glass-fibre membranes, glass fibre-reinforced polymers (GFRP) (Fig. B 2.11)

Glass is melted and drawn into thin threads in order to produce glass fibres. E-glass (E = electric) is the standard fibre produced. It contains no alkalis and is subject to attack in a basic environment; AR-glass (AR = alkaline-resistant) is therefore used for textile-reinforced concrete. Other types of fibre are available for special applications: C-glass (C = corrosion) with its good chemical resistance, or the high-strength R- and S-glass types (R = resistance, S = strength) with high heat and fatigue resistance.
E-glass consists of quartz sand (SiO_2), limestone ($CaCO_3$) and – in contrast to float glass – boric acid plus large quantities of aluminium oxide. In the melt spinning process, these raw materials are melted down in a furnace over several days, refined and finally forced through spinning nozzles. The viscous threads, still approx. 2 mm thick, are stretched to about 40 000 times their original length using a fast-rotating winding machine and in the process reduced to the desired diameter of 9–24 μm (Fig. B 2.8). As glass fibres are very sensitive to notches, like all fibres they are given a coating of size during production, or rather prior to weaving. The amorphous structure of glass fibres makes them isotropic, i.e. they exhibit identical properties in the longitudinal and transverse directions. Their tensile and compressive strength are therefore almost the same. The main differences between glass fibres and other common types of fibre is their uniform and approximately circular cross-section, also their loadbearing behaviour, which is linear-elastic up to a brittle failure. Their small diameter of just a few micrometres means that they are flexible, but in comparison with other fibres they tend to be rather sensitive to buckling.
Like all inorganic fibres, glass fibres exhibit very little creep. They absorb very little moisture, but nevertheless still tend to corrode when exposed directly to the weather and must therefore be coated or embedded in a polymer. One advantage of glass fibres is that they do not burn. Permanent temperatures up to 250 °C have no effect on the mechanical properties of the fibres. Glass fibres are transparent and have a greenish

tinge that only becomes noticeable as the thickness of the component increases. Loose glass fibres appear opaque and white because the incident light is reflected from their large surface area. These surface reflections can be suppressed by building the fibres into a transparent polymer; the composite material then becomes translucent. To achieve this, the glass fibres and the polymer must, however, exhibit similar refractive indexes.

Carbon fibres

▷ Carbon fibre-reinforced polymers (CFRP) (Fig. B 2.12)

Carbon fibres have a much higher elastic modulus than all other fibres. The mechanical properties can be varied much more easily than is the case with, for example, glass fibres. Carbon fibres can be produced in different forms:

- Standard modulus fibres (high tensile, HT) with high tensile strength
- High modulus (HM) fibres with high material stiffness
- Intermediate modulus (IM) fibres with moderate tensile strength and material stiffness

Carbon fibres exhibit anisotropic properties: stiffness and strength in particular are much lower transverse to the fibres than in the direction of the fibres. The coefficient of thermal expansion is negative along the length of the fibre, but positive in the transverse direction. Carbon fibres therefore shorten as they get warmer. They are brittle and sensitive to buckling, which is why their surfaces must be protected by a epoxy resin coating.
The advantages are good dynamic properties, low self-weight and very high corrosion resistance, and the fact that they exhibit no significant creep. Carbon substances are black and their crystalline structure means they are always opaque. Despite their good mechanical properties, up until now carbon fibres have only become established in the aerospace industry and a number of niche markets. The reason for this is the cost of their production. In the building industry they are used, for example, for heavily loaded bridge cables (see "Special semi-finished products for engineering applications", pp. 92–93).
Carbon substances occur in nature in crystalline form as graphite and diamond, but these natural materials cannot be processed to form fibres. Therefore, a polymer fibre is first produced, mostly polyacrylonitrile (PAN), from which all the elements it contains apart from the main one, carbon, are subsequently dissolved out and removed (Fig. B 2.9). This process is carried out by means of a multi-stage heat treatment with temperatures up to 3000 °C and simultaneous stretching of the fibres. The mechanical properties required can be obtained by adjusting the process temperature. The energy needed for heating is one reason for the high price of carbon fibres. Production methods using coaltar or mineral pitch are also available. Fibres with a high axial orientation are produced from a melt of these raw materials using a spinning method. The subsequent operations are similar to the method for PAN fibres.
Fibres made from carbon nano tubes (CNT) have a tensile strength many times that of normal carbon fibres. Up until now, however, it has not been possible to produce CNT fibres on a large scale, only as very short filaments.

Polymer fibres

Polymer fibres are made from synthetic materials and exhibit the typical properties of polymers: they are extensible, but tend to creep and are combustible. The fibre production process enables much better mechanical properties to be achieved than is the case with the respective polymer. Polymer fibres are lighter than inorganic fibres, generally tougher and also exhibit a lower elastic modulus in most cases. As a rule, the strengths lie below those of inorganic fibres. Polymer fibres are generally intensely anisotropic, with a much higher strength and elastic modulus in the longitudinal direction than in the transverse direction. Normally, polymer fibres are neither weather-resistant nor light-fast, and therefore always require a protective coating. Polymer fibres are typically produced using the melt spinning method. In this method, the polymer is melted under the exclusion of air, forced through spinning nozzles and generally hardened by cooling in air. In the wet spinning method, the hardening takes place in a liquid, in the so-called coagulating bath.
Apart from aramid and polyethylene fibres, polymer fibres are not used in fibre-reinforced composites but instead are used primarily as the basic material for membranes because this is where their flexibility and extensibility is critical. Fibres can be obtained from virtually every thermoplastic – polypropylene (PP; Fig. B 2.19, p. 53), polyimide (PI) and polyacrylonitrile (PAN) as well as those described below.

B 2.8 Method for producing glass fibres
B 2.9 Method for producing carbon fibres
B 2.10 Various properties in the direction of the fibre
B 2.11 Glass fibres
B 2.12 Carbon fibres
B 2.13 Aramid fibres

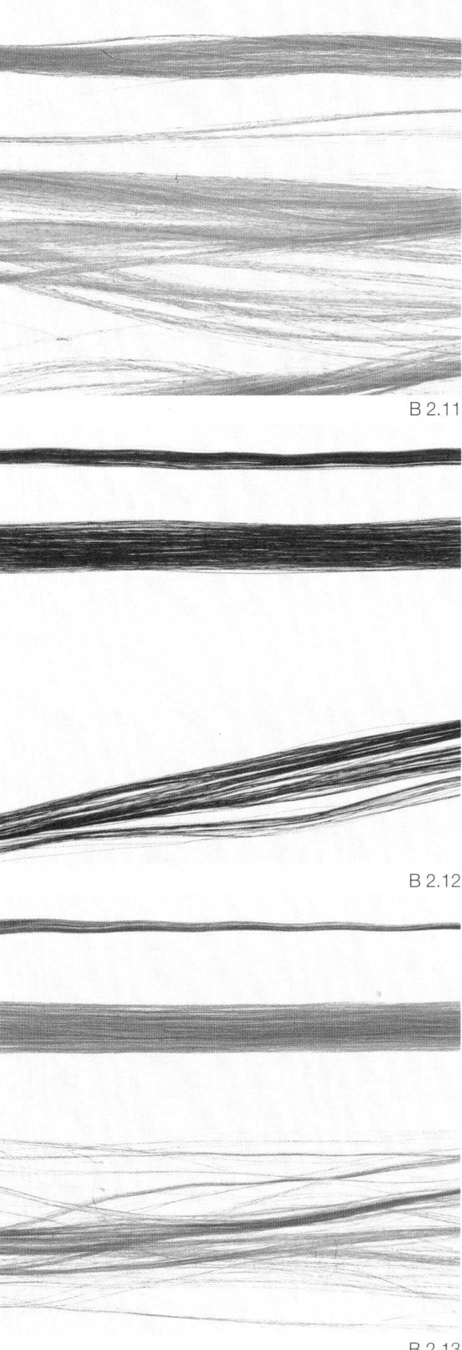

B 2.11

B 2.12

B 2.13

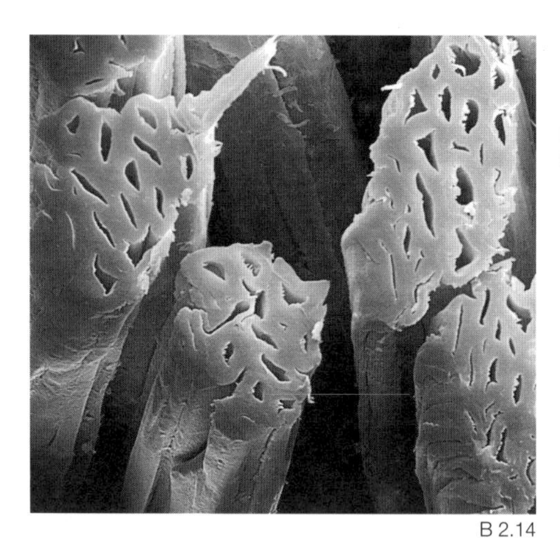
B 2.14

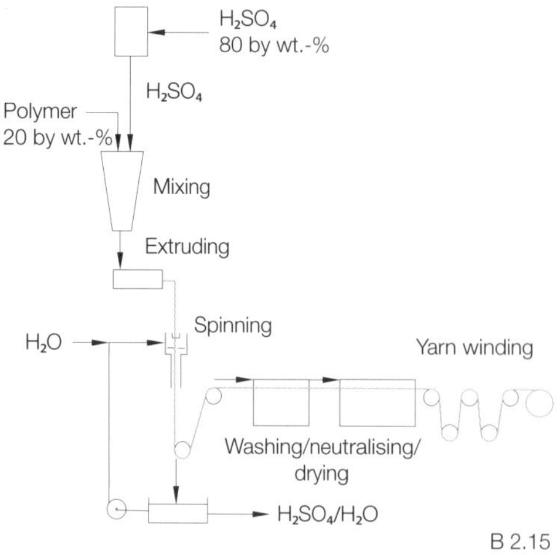

B 2.15

B 2.16

Aramid fibres

▷ Hauling ropes, aramid fibre-reinforced polymers (AFRP), safety helmets (Fig. B 2.13)

Aramid fibres are very lightweight fibres that consist of aromatic polyamides. As with all polymer fibres, the strength properties are intensely anisotropic, and apart from that the compressive strength of the fibres is much lower than the tensile strength. Aramid fibres are therefore ideal for ropes or fibre composites in tension, but less suitable for applications involving bending or compression. Their disadvantages are their tendency to absorb moisture and the relatively low resistance to heat and UV light. In contrast to glass and carbon fibres, composites employing aramid fibres are difficult to machine because the tough fibres cause high tool wear. Aramid fibres are therefore rarely used in the building industry. But their low weight and good impact resistance makes them ideal for safety helmets or bulletproof vests. Their characteristic failure behaviour enables them to absorb impact energy and thus cushion a blow. They are also sometimes combined with CFRP in order to increase their toughness or prevent the spreading of cracks (see "Preparing the polymer", pp. 68–69).

In contrast to other polymer fibres, aramid fibres cannot be produced by means of the melt spinning method because they do not exhibit a distinct melting behaviour. Aromatic polyamide is dissolved with an acid and spun to form fibres. Afterwards, the fibres are washed and dried under tension, which results in a fibre diameter of approx. 12 µm (Fig. B 2.15).

Polyethylene fibres (PE fibres)

▷ Ropes, polyethylene fibre-reinforced polymers (Fig. B 2.17)

Fibres made from polyethylene (PE) have a very low self-weight and even float on water. The fibre structure is anisotropic like all polymer fibres, which means that the mechanical properties in the direction of the fibre are much better than those perpendicular to the fibre. The thermal expansion in the longitudinal direction is negative and the compressive strength of PE fibres is practically zero. Therefore, these fibres can be used for tensile applications only, e.g. for ropes. Their impact strength is quite remarkable, similar to the aramid fibres. Like the raw material, polyethylene, itself, the fibres also exhibit a very low surface adhesion. Only with the help of a special coating is it possible to use PE fibres for composites.

The manufacture of high-performance PE fibres is carried out using the gel spinning method, which is similar to the production of aramid fibres. Here again, the polymer is first broken down in a solvent and then the solution is forced through a nozzle, cooled in a water bath, then stretched, dried and finally spun.

Polyamide fibres (PA fibres)

▷ Clothing, sports goods

Polyamide fibres, known as nylon, are characterised among the polymer fibres by their high strength, stiffness and toughness. The values depend on the crystalline microstructure and the water content of the polyamides. Fabrics employing polyamide fibres were used in the early days of membrane structures. The disadvantage here, however, is the severe elongation of the material when it absorbs moisture and the associated drop in the prestress. Polyamide fibres shrink if the temperature rises too severely. They exhibit a high resistance to chemicals, but the resistance to UV light is relatively low. These days, the flexibility and lightness of polyamide fibres makes them favourites for the clothing industry in particular, also for tents, spinnakers in sail-making, parachutes and paragliders. The fibres are produced using the melt spinning method and can be coloured in the spinning nozzle or further processed as a white material for later colouring.

Polyethylene terephthalate fibres (PET fibres), polyester fibres

▷ Polyester membranes, straps, ropes, sewing threads (Fig. B 2.18)

Fibres made from polyethylene terephthalate (PET) represent the most important raw material for textile membranes apart from glass fibres. It is mainly the semi-crystalline structure of these organic synthetic fibres that determines their mechanical properties. The fibres are highly flexible and have good compressive and tensile strengths, but their stability upon exposure to UV radiation is very low. Polyester membranes can therefore only be used with coatings (e.g. PVC). Owing to their flexibility and buckling resistance, these fibres are often used for ropes, belts or sewing threads. In the form of a fabric, these properties make PET fibres useful for temporary and convertible structures.

The fibres are obtained from polyethylene terephthalate using the melt spinning method. The resulting white material can be coloured with dispersion paints (see "Paints", p. 58). Various thermoplastics fall under the heading of polyester, and PET is the raw material most commonly used for the production of fibres. This is why PET fibres are often simply referred to by manufacturers as polyester fibres. Many manufacturers concerned with the production of membranes also use the abbreviation PES, which, however, is incorrect from the materials science viewpoint because PES already stands for the thermoplastic polyether sulphone.

Fibres made from aromatic polyesters

In a similar way to aramid (a special form of polyamide), polyester, too, can be provided with aromatic rings (Vectran). The resulting fibres have a high impact strength and a low self-weight. They are used, for example, in combination with carbon fibres for fibre-reinforced polymers in the aerospace industry.

Polytetrafluoroethylene fibres (PTFE fibres)

▷ PTFE membranes, sewing threads (Fig. B 2.16)

The strengths of PTFE fibres are somewhat lower than those of the other polymer fibres. But the tear propagation resistance of PTFE fabrics is comparatively high, i.e. once a tear appears in a PTFE membrane, complete tearing stops more readily than with other types of fibre. PTFE fibres show a strong tendency to creep under constant loading. The high flexibility and resistance to buckling are positive features, though. In membrane construction, PTFE fabrics are therefore preferred for convertible roofs. They are permanently resistant to chemicals and are classed as not readily flammable. Their good UV stability and the self-cleaning (anti-adhesive) surface means that even uncoated PTFE fabrics can be used for membrane structures. Their high light transmittance of up to 40 % is important for architectural design.

B 2.17

B 2.18

B 2.19

B 2.20

B 2.21

Owing to their high melting viscosity, PTFE fibres cannot be produced using the melt spinning method and their resistance to solvents makes them unsuitable for the wet spinning method. So special matrix and extrusion spinning methods have therefore been developed in which the extruded fibres achieve higher strengths and lower shrinkage rates.

Natural fibres

▷ Natural fibre-reinforced polymers (NFRP), loose materials for thermal insulation (Fig. B 2.20)

The large scatter of the mechanical properties and the moisture sensitivity of natural fibres has led to them playing only a subsidiary role in construction up until now. And as the growth process cannot be fully controlled, the diameters and tensile strengths of natural fibres vary. In future, however, we can expect to see such fibres being used more and more because of their ecological benefits. Asbestos, which was once used for fibre-cement products, is banned in the EU because of the carcinogenic risks and is therefore irrelevant these days.

We divide natural fibres into the following three groups:

- Mineral fibres (e.g. asbestos),
- Animal fibres (e.g. silk)
- Vegetable fibres (e.g. flax)

Only the vegetable fibres are relevant for the building industry and these will be discussed below.

Hemp and flax fibres in particular are characterised by good mechanical properties, which, however, are inferior to those of glass fibres. But they are more flexible and also tougher; composites with natural fibre reinforcement therefore break without causing splinters and sharp edges (see "Natural fibre-reinforced polymers", pp. 60–61). Lightweight components are possible because of the low self-weight of natural fibres. In addition, their hollow fibre structure (Fig. B 2.14) improves the sound insulation properties and is also responsible for the high water absorption. Fibres that are not dried prior to processing can lead to flaws in the fibre composite after the water has evaporated. Furthermore, natural fibres are not permanently weather-resistant and can also be decomposed by microbes.

Their production and processing requires less energy than similar products made from glass fibres. Vegetable fibres are also less expensive in the form of final products. Components reinforced with natural fibres can be disposed of with a zero carbon balance, at least in terms of the natural fibre content.

The cross-section of a natural fibre changes over its length and can lie between 20 and 500 µm depending on the fibre. Natural fibres have rough and uneven surfaces, which results in a good bond with the encasing polymer during further processing. Unlike synthetic fibres, natural fibres have a finite length. They are either processed to form fleeces and matting or spun into yarns which then form the raw material for producing fabrics. Tool wear during machining is less than that with glass or polymer fibres.

The heat resistance of natural fibres is low compared with glass fibres. A loss in strength is evident when the temperature remains at 180 °C or higher, and natural fibres disintegrate at temperatures of 200–250 °C. Natural fibres tend to function as wicks in a fire and therefore must be protected with a suitable flame retardant.

Metal fibres

▷ Fibre-reinforced concrete, metal fabrics, wire ropes (Fig. B 2.21)

Metal fibres in combination with polymers or as a membrane are only worth considering when electrical screening is necessary or a high ductility is required. In aircraft, for example, aluminium fibres are used to reinforce polymers. Their relatively large diameters and smooth surfaces mean that metal fibres are generally unsuitable for combining with polymers because it is not possible to generate an adequate bond between the two. In addition, most metals suffer from corrosion.

In the building industry, metal fibres are used primarily in fibre-reinforced concrete, where they help to minimise crack widths. These fibres have a varying cross-section or kinks, and it is this profiling that improves the bonding characteristics of what are actually smooth surfaces.

Metal wires and ropes

Metal wires and ropes are very important components in construction. To form ropes, individual wires are wound into larger cross-sections (stranding). Steel has a high elastic modulus and therefore steel ropes are comparatively stiff. However, the voids that ensue during the stranding make the rope susceptible to corrosion. Wires and ropes should therefore either be made from stainless steel or provided with some form of permanent protection. Safety barriers, insect screens, etc. can be made from wire meshes and metal fabrics. Owing to their high ductility, metal wires are ideal for absorbing impact loads.

B 2.14 Hollow fibre structure of a natural fibre (bast)
B 2.15 Method for producing aramid fibres
B 2.16 Sewing threads made from fluoropolymer fibres (PTFE fibres)
B 2.17 Rope made from polyethylene (PE) fibres
B 2.18 Rope made from polyester fibres (PET fibres)
B 2.19 Rope made from polypropylene (PP) fibres
B 2.20 Rope made from hemp fibres
B 2.21 Steel rope

Adhesives and coatings

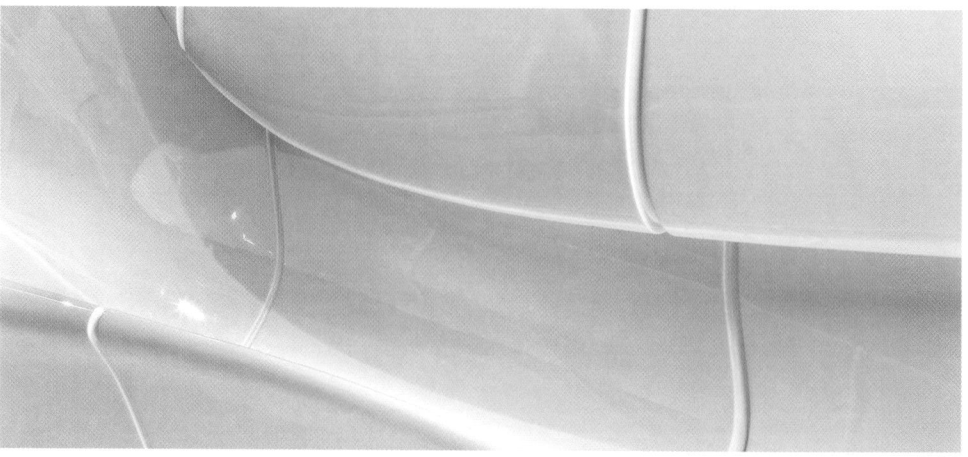

B 3.1

Most of the adhesives and coatings used these days are based on polymers and so they are important not only for polymer components. For example, synthetic materials play just as much a role in the corrosion protection products for steel beams as they do for the adhesive joints of loadbearing glass assemblies. The adhesives and coatings are based on various synthetic materials whose chemical structures are in most cases adjusted in such a way that they guarantee simple usage and good surface adhesion. Most materials are applied in thin layers and the chemical cross-linking reaction (curing) first takes place within the scope of the actual application. For this reason, many adhesives and coatings are in the form of two-part systems that react with each other upon being mixed just prior to use.

Adhesives

Adhesives can be used to create good loadbearing, long-lasting joints. Gluing is a method of jointing that is very frequently used for connecting semi-finished polymer products. The pin-type fasteners (nails, screws, bolts, etc.) so common in timber and steel construction lead to unsatisfactory results when used with polymers because so many polymers, especially fibre-reinforced types, are brittle (see "Means of connection", pp. 161–164). Only thermoplastics can be joined by welding, but this method of connection is only relevant for membrane structures (see "Welding", p. 106).

The fundamentals of adhesive joints

The surface of the component to which the adhesive is applied is known as the substrate. To achieve a good adhesive joint, the contact faces should be degreased, roughened and cleaned beforehand. Some systems require a primer to be applied first before applying the adhesive, which improves the bond between the adhesive and the substrate. The primer can be made from exactly the same substance as the adhesive, but will contain a lower quantity of fillers in order to improve the reactivity. Adhesives usually have a limited working time, i.e. the time between mixing and solidification (curing), the so-called pot life, which can make applying adhesive to larger joints somewhat troublesome. In some systems curing is controlled by external means, e.g. UV light.

Loadbearing effect

We distinguish between loadbearing and non-loadbearing adhesive joints depending on the particular application. The latter serve purely to retain a component in position and the loadbearing capacity does not have to be verified by calculation. Such joints are those, for example, for fixing waterproof sheeting or floor coverings in place. Loadbearing joints, on the other hand, are specifically designed to transfer loads. These structural joints must be able to accom-

Reactive adhesives (curing by way of chemical reaction)

- Acrylate adhesives
  - Cyanoacrylate adhesives
  - Radiation-curing adhesives
  - Methacrylate adhesives
- Polyurethane adhesives
  - Thermoplastic PUR adhesives
  - Thermoset PUR adhesives
- Epoxy resin adhesives
  - Epoxy resin adhesives
  - Viscous epoxy resin adhesives
  - Epoxy resin mortar
  - Polymer concrete
- Silicone adhesives
  - 1-part silicone adhesives
  - 2-part silicone adhesives

Non-reactive adhesives (curing by physical means)

- Hot-melt adhesives
- Dispersion/solvent-based adhesives
- Solvents

B 3.2

B 3.1 Paint finish on glass fibre-reinforced polymer (GFRP)
B 3.2 Selection of adhesives relevant for the building industry
B 3.3 Compatibility between substrate and adhesive
B 3.4 Weathering resistance of adhesives used for joining glass and GFRP (joint thickness = 2 mm) established in tests involving accelerated weathering

Adhesive joints between polymers	PVC-U	PVC-P	PP	PS	Polystyrene foam (EPS, XPS)	PC	PET	PMMA	PUR
PVC-U	2, 3, 4, **6**, 7, 8								
PVC-P	**6**, 7	**6**							
PP	**3**, 7	7	**3**, 7						
PS	2, 3, 4, **6**, 7, 8	**6**	**3**, 7	2, 3, 4, **5, 6,** 7, 8					
Polystyrene foam (EPS, XPS)	1, **6**, 7, 8	7	7	1, **6**, 7, 8	**1**, **6**, 7, **8**				
PC	2, 3, 4, **6**, 7, 8	**6**	**3,** 7	2, 3, 4, **5, 6,** 7, 8	1, **6**, 7, 8	2, 3, 4, **5, 6,** 7, 8			
PET	2, 3, 4, **6**, 7, 8	**6**	**3,** 7	2, 3, 4, **5, 6,** 7, 8	1, **6**, 7, 8	2, 3, 4, **5, 6,** 7, 8	2, 3, 4, **5, 6,** 7, 8		
PMMA	2, 3, 4, **6**, 7, 8	**6**	**3,** 7	2, 3, 4, **5, 6,** 7, 8	1, **6**, 7, 8	2, 3, 4, **5, 6,** 7, 8	2, 3, 4, **5, 6,** 7, 8	2, 3, 4, **5, 6,** 7, 8	
PUR	**2, 3,** 4, 6, 7, 8	**6**	3, 7	**2, 3,** 4, 6, 7, 8	1, **6**, 7, 8	**2, 3,** 4, 6, 7, 8	**2, 3,** 4, 6, 7, 8	**2, 3,** 4, 6, 7, 8	**2, 3,** 4, 6, 7, 8

1 Solvent-based adhesives ("all-purpose"): compatibility with solvent must be clarified
2 Two-part adhesives
3 Cyanoacrylate adhesive ("superglue")
4 Silicone
5 Solvents
6 Synthetic adhesives
7 Double-sided adhesive tapes
8 Construction adhesives
bold: preferred

B 3.3

modate forces from the primary loadbearing system and their load-carrying capacity must be verified by calculation when designing the joint. The reliability of the adhesive joint therefore becomes relevant to safety issues. Due attention must be given to the proper design and execution of such adhesive joints because the quality of the joint cannot be checked afterwards.

Selecting the adhesive
The following parameters must be taken into account when choosing an adhesive:
- The compatibility of the adhesive with the substrate (Fig. B 3.3)
- The bond between the adhesive and the surface of the substrate
- The permissible stresses in the adhesive
- The weathering resistance and long-term behaviour
- The elasticity of the adhesive

We distinguish between reactive adhesives, which cure by way of a chemical reaction (cross-linking) upon application, and non-reactive adhesives that cure by physical means and merely undergo a change of state upon application. The reactive adhesives, which include acrylate, polyurethane and epoxy resin materials, generally achieve higher strengths (Fig. B 3.2). In the case of the non-reactive adhesives, on the other hand, there is no chemical reaction with the surface of the substrate, instead only physical forces of attraction build up between the two. Solvents are frequently used and so the compatibility between the polymer and the adhesive should be checked in order to prevent damaging the material. Appropriate information can be found on the adhesive's packaging. Other substrates, such as steel or concrete, are not attacked by the adhesive, but with such materials it is the roughness of the surface that is critical for the choice of adhesive. The consistency of the adhesive during application is just as important as the stiffness of the adhesive once it has cured. Smooth surfaces (metals, non-reinforced polymers) can be joined with runny (low-viscosity) adhesives, whereas substrates with an uneven surface (concrete, fibre-reinforced polymers) need a thicker, viscous adhesive. The in situ tolerances must be compensated for by designing a thicker joint.

Weathering resistance
Tests carried out on adhesive joints between glass and GFRP (Fig. B 3.5, p. 56) have revealed that the weathering resistance of silicone adhesives is excellent, that of epoxy resin adhesives is good, but that of acrylate adhesives is unsatisfactory (Fig. B 3.4). Polyurethane adhesives are generally not UV-resistant and hence unsuitable for external applications. [1]
The weathering resistance of adhesives is generally investigated in climatic test chambers, where intense UV radiation plus moisture and temperature cycles simulate accelerated ageing, but also sometimes by way of spray tests. Comparing the results of artificial, accelerated weathering with those of natural ageing behaviour reveals very different performances for the individual adhesives. Tests in artificial conditions can therefore only indicate a tendency with respect to the durability of an adhesive joint because in the laboratory it is very difficult to simulate the actual UV load that occurs plus the temperature and moisture fluctuations and their interaction. On the other hand, weathering tests lasting several years are impossible to carry out during the planning phase, which is why the results of laboratory testing have to be used in practice (see "Accelerated weathering", p. 156).

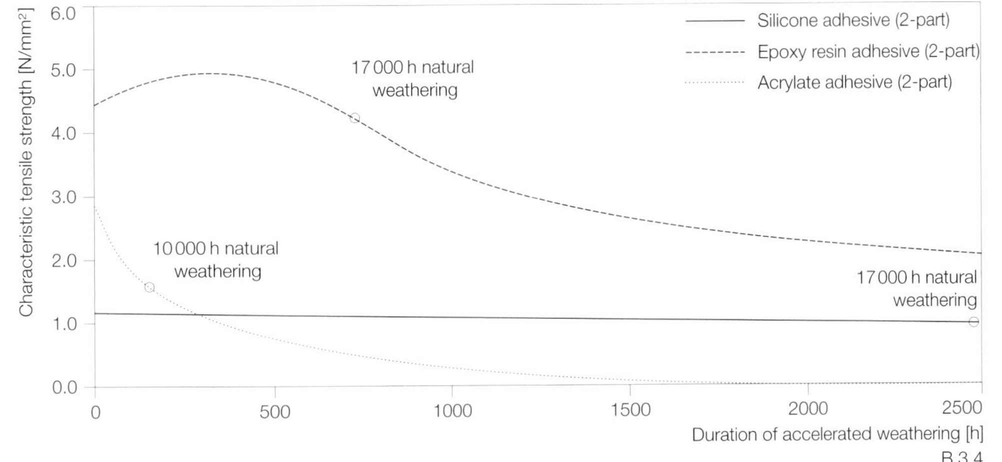

B 3.4

Acrylate adhesives
When using acrylate adhesives, a chemical cross-linking (see "Polymer formation", p. 31) similar to the production of thermoplastics takes place during the application of the adhesive. Catalysts such as moisture, oxygen or radiation (e.g. UV light) initiate the reaction process. After curing, the properties of the adhesive are the same as those of a thermoplastic. Acrylate adhesives are transparent (Fig. B 3.8, p. 57) but they can yellow under UV light. Their ageing behaviour depends on the particular product and the thickness of the adhesive joint. Most acrylate adhesives are one-part systems, but there are some two-part products.

Cyanoacrylate adhesives (one-part)
Commonly referred to as "superglues", cyanoacrylate adhesives are especially suited to stiff and very thin adhesive joints (e.g. joining two steel components or two identical polymers). Such a stiff adhesive joint is, however, less suitable for connecting disparate materials because the different rates of thermal expansion would cause high restraint stresses.
The cross-linking (curing) takes place during application as a result of certain factors, primarily the humidity of the air; a relative humidity between 30 and 70 % is ideal. A higher value or direct contact with water leads to an abrupt curing reaction and a joint with little strength. As the moisture required infiltrates via the surface, the thickness of the layer of adhesive should not exceed 0.2 mm. Cyanoacrylate adhesives

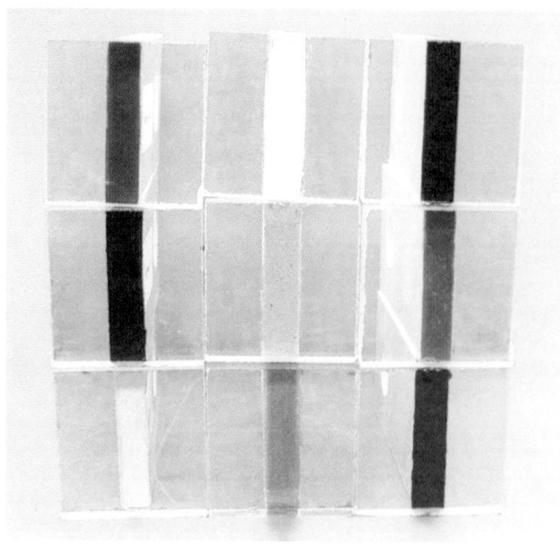

B 3.5

B 3.6

B 3.5 Specimens with various adhesives in joints between glass and GFRP
B 3.6 Two-part adhesive in twin cartridges with mixing tube and application gun
B 3.7 Epoxy resin adhesive
B 3.8 Acrylate resin
B 3.9 Silicone resin adhesive

must be stored in totally dry conditions because of the catalytic effect of moisture. The stabilisers used rule out adhesive joints in acidic environments, or at best they can be carried out only with great delays because the adhesive takes much longer to cure.
The maximum service temperatures are relatively low: 70–80°C for long-term effects and 100–110°C only briefly. Full wetting of the contact faces is not a problem because of the low viscosity. Compared with other adhesives, cyanoacrylate products cure very quickly. They are very good for joining a whole range of thermoplastics and elastomers such as PS, SBR, NBR, PMMA, PC and MF, and not quite so good for other materials such as EP, PF, PSU, PET and PVC-HD. The application of a primer beforehand is necessary for non-polar thermoplastics (PE, PP) because the molecular structure of the substrate does not offer sufficient bonding opportunities for the adhesive.

Light-curing adhesives (one-part)
For adhesives whose curing mechanism is initiated by radiation or light, it is easier to influence the time of the reaction than is the case with other acrylate adhesives. This can be very important when more time-consuming shaping work has to be carried out first with the liquid adhesive. In the case of adhesive joints over a large area, e.g. panes of glass, adequate working time (pot life) for applying the adhesive and adjusting the components is advantageous. Light-curing adhesives cure rapidly upon exposure to intensive radiation, usually artificial UV light (occasionally electron beams or visible light). However, the adhesive and the substrate must be accessible for the radiation treatment or transparent for UV light.

Methacrylate adhesives (two-part)
Methacrylate adhesives cure as a result of the reaction between their two components. The mixing ratio can be varied to some extent without altering the final properties of the adhesive significantly. Curing takes at least one hour and is therefore much slower than the one-part acrylate adhesives. These adhesives are mostly supplied in twin cartridges (Fig. B 3.6). Both components are squeezed out at the same time with a gun-type tool and mixed together in the application tube or nozzle immediately prior to being applied to the surface of the joint. Storing the components separately means that methacrylate adhesives have a longer shelf life than the one-part acrylate types. And in contrast to other acrylate adhesives, they can be set to be comparatively viscous upon application so that joint thicknesses of up to 3 mm are possible.

Polyurethane adhesives (one-part, two-part)
Polyurethane adhesives are very versatile products with high strengths. They adhere to the majority of surfaces and are frequently used for fixing flexible materials, e.g. floor coverings. Polyurethane adhesives are resistant to the effects of the weather and chemicals, but are not permanently resistant to UV light. In contrast to acrylate adhesives, they are based on the polyaddition of molecules (see "Polymer formation", p. 31). Depending on their structure once cured, they can be classed as thermoplastics or thermosets, with correspondingly variable properties. One-part systems cure with the help of the moisture in the air (humidity ≥ 40%). To do this, the substrate must also be suitably permeable to moisture. Such adhesives must therefore be stored in absolutely dry conditions in order to prevent curing before the actual application. There are also one-part systems available that cure upon applying heat. In contrast to the methacrylate adhesives, keeping to the exact mixing ratio is crucial for these two-part systems. If the composition deviates from the ratio specified, the components do not react fully and this has a negative effect on the strength of the final joint. In addition to these systems there are also polyurethane adhesives containing solvents which, however, must be allowed to escape during application.

Epoxy resin adhesives (two-part)
Epoxy resin adhesives are stiff, high-strength products that are useful for structural joints, e.g. between steel and concrete or between fibre-reinforced polymers (Fig. B 3.7). They are suitable for rough surfaces and therefore relatively versatile in their range of applications. Like polyurethane adhesives, these adhesives also cure by way of a polyaddition reaction. The cured adhesive is a thermoset and exhibits the typical properties of those polymers such as high strength, high elastic modulus and brittle failure behaviour. The addition of coarse-grained fillers enables adhesive joints several centimetres thick to be realised. Almost all epoxy resin adhesives are two-part systems and the mixing ratio must be adhered to exactly. Most of the products available are cold-curing systems, but heat treatment (annealing) can improve the mechanical properties considerably. Cured epoxy resin adhesives are very stiff and their tendency to creep is comparatively low. Adding thermoplastic or elastomeric components produces a hard but viscous epoxy resin adhesive with a less pronounced tendency towards brittle failure behaviour.

Epoxy resin mortar and polymer concrete
Epoxy resin adhesives are frequently mixed with non-reactive fillers. In the building industry, mortar or concrete mixes with a high proportion of quartz sand are commonly used in order to reduce the cost of materials and create a more viscous consistency to ease the workability. In polymer concrete the amount of epoxy resin adhesive is typically 10% by wt., in epoxy resin mortar 50%, which correspond to amounts between 20 and 80% by vol. As with the epoxy resin adhesive itself, these mouldable products are very stiff and exhibit brittle failure behaviour, and the strengths vary depending on the resin content. The surface adhesion is lower than that of a pure epoxy resin adhesive because of the fillers. Epoxy resin mortar is used, for instance, for attaching carbon fibre-reinforced (CFRP) lamellae to concrete components (see "Repairs with CFRP laminates", p. 92).

B 3.7

B 3.8

B 3.9

Silicone adhesives (one-part)

Silicone adhesives (Fig. B 3.9) are robust, durable products. Despite their rather low strength and low elastic modulus, their reliability makes silicone adhesives suitable for loadbearing joints, e.g. structural sealant glazing. They exhibit excellent weathering and heat resistance, are practically incombustible and are deformable and ductile, which means they can compensate for restraint stresses – sudden brittle failure is ruled out. This is particularly advantageous when materials with different coefficients of thermal expansion have to be joined together, e.g. aluminium and glass. On the other hand, this is the reason why shear-resistant connections with a high load-carrying capacity are not possible in practice.
The chemical structure of silicone adhesives corresponds to that of the elastomer silicone rubber (see "Silicone rubber", p. 45). They are generally supplied in the form of one-part systems. In these systems the curing process (vulcanisation) takes place at room temperature with the help of the moisture in the air. But the curing process is very slow in comparison with other adhesives, indeed in normal climatic conditions the curing process can take several days. The acidic vulcanising agents frequently used lead to the formation of acetic acid during usage – responsible for the noticeable smell. Two-part systems are employed where the humidity of the air is not adequate or a thick layer of adhesive is required. Silicone is viscous during application and ideal for sealing joints permanently as well as being used as an adhesive. In addition, special silicone adhesives are available with a higher thermal conductivity, which is achieved by mixing metal particles into the adhesive, for instance.

Non-reactive adhesives

In contrast to the reactive adhesives (curing by way of a chemical reaction), this group of adhesives relies on the creation of a physical bond instead of a cross-linking process. The strengths that can be achieved are therefore mostly below those of the reactive adhesives. However, their simpler handling makes them popular for non-loadbearing adhesive joints.
Different types are available which function in very different ways:

- Hot-melt adhesives are applied hot and cure upon cooling.
- Dispersion and solvent adhesives consist of polymers dissolved in water or solvent respectively. These cure when the water evaporates or the solvent volatilises. However, these "all-purpose adhesives", as they are called, achieve only low strengths. Furthermore, care should be taken to ensure that the solvent is compatible with the polymers to be joined (especially in the case of foams).
- In solvent welding the surfaces of the components to be joined are softened by a solvent and then pressed together. The solvent volatilises to produce a permanent connection.

Coatings

Most of the coatings used on an industrial scale are based on synthetic materials because these are easy to work and exhibit good resistance to environmental influences. Coating materials frequently consists of three components:

- Pigments or dyes
- Binders as surface protection and bonding agent
- Solvents (which volatilise after application)

Polymers themselves do not normally require any protective coatings on their surfaces. The material in conjunction with fillers can usually comply with the technical and visual requirements without the need for further surface finishes. During the production of fibre-reinforced polymers, a layer of pure polymer (a so-called gelcoat) is applied to the polymer in order to protect the fibres (see "Surface finish", p. 78). Additional paint or lacquer finishes are sometimes used on polymers as well for decorative reasons. And in order to achieve a coarser surface finish, e.g. for floor coverings, polymers are often finished with a coarse-grained material.

Classification of coatings

Coating materials are generally classified according to the binder they contain and, for example, designated as acrylic lacquers or silicone resin paints. However, as most of these products contain not just one single substance but rather several components that form a complex coating system, they are classified here with respect to their application or function. The respective basic ingredients for the individual coating systems are in some cases identical. For example, we distinguish paints and lacquers according to their binder content, but these two types of coating essentially consist of the same components. Paints have a higher pigment content and after application are generally diffusion-permeable. Lacquers, on the other hand, have a higher binder content and surfaces treated with lacquers are comparatively impermeable to water vapour and gases.

Coatings with protective functions

In addition to their decorative functions, coatings can also be used to protect the surfaces of materials susceptible to corrosion, e.g. metals, reinforced concrete or fibres. Such corrosion can be caused by water, UV radiation, carbon dioxide, dissolved de-icing salts or petrol.

Systems for protecting steel against corrosion

Steel is protected against moisture either by a covering of zinc (e.g. hot-dip galvanising), a polymer coating or a combination of the two (duplex coating). Most of the polymer coating systems for steel involve first applying a primer made from zinc dust and then a top coat of acrylic, alkyd, polyurethane or epoxy lacquer. A primer is unnecessary with high-build epoxy resin lacquers because the lacquer is usually applied in several coats.

B 3.10

Layer	Material
Substrate	Polymers, metals, etc.
Levelling layer	Filling compound, e.g. unsaturated polyester resin (UP), applied only in dabs
Primer	2-part polyurethane systems
Filling compound or undercoat	Unsaturated polyester resin (UP), acrylates, epoxy resin (EP)
Final coat	
Base coat	Cellulose-acetate-butyrate (CAB) with polyesters and acrylates, polyurethane (PUR) with pigments
Top coat	Acrylic lacquer, alkyd lacquer, epoxy lacquer (EP), polyurethane lacquer (PUR)

B 3.11

	Wet abrasion	Cleanability	Resistance to solvents	Resistance to alkalis	Resistance to acids	Resistance to petrol	Resistance to spirit
Paint, low binder content (dispersion paint)	-	--	--	--	--	--	--
Paint, high binder content (latex paint)	+	o	--	--	--	--	--
Acrylic lacquer, aqueous	++	o	--	--	--	--	--
Alkyd lacquer	++	+	+	--	o	+	++
Epoxy lacquer	++	++	++	++	++	++	++
Polyurethane lacquer	++	++	++	++	++	++	++

B 3.12

Systems for protecting concrete surfaces
Multi-part coating systems based on epoxy resin or polyurethane are used for protecting concrete components. These systems create a barrier to carbon dioxide and water and can also bridge over smaller cracks. The coating delays the neutralisation of the protective environment of the concrete (carbonation) which protects the reinforcement against corrosion. Horizontal concrete surfaces can be permanently protected against the effects of the weather in this way. At the same time, the coating protects the concrete against oils and petrol or increases of roughness of the surface, e.g. for floor coverings.

Floor finishes and road surfacing
The finishes to industrial floors, parking decks or bridges have to satisfy special requirements. Besides protecting the substrate of concrete, steel or fibre-reinforced polymer, the finish must provide a permanently coarse surface and be able to withstand high loads, e.g. vehicles. The advantages of polymer coatings over asphalt or concrete finishes are that they can be applied cold, usually exhibit a higher load-carrying capacity and also cure relatively quickly. This latter point shortens the time required for application and may well result in a shorter interruption to traffic or factory operations. The surface of the covering can be adjusted from very smooth to coarse to suit the specification.
Finishes based on epoxy resin or polyurethane are mixed with quartz sand in order to increase their stiffness and at the same time reduce the tendency to creep. Polymer concrete has a resin content of only 10 % by wt. Therefore, it cannot be used as a waterproof finish but can be applied in thicknesses of several centimetres.
Contrasting with this, a reactive resin has a higher resin content, can seal the surface and is applied in thicknesses of just a few millimetres. Reactive resins are approved as a road surfacing on steel bridges. As both polymer concrete and reactive resin finishes exhibit poor surface adhesion, a coat of primer (epoxy resin without fillers) is necessary between the substrate and the coating.
When using polymer floor finishes in public buildings such as schools or sports centres, low-emissions products must be selected. Coatings made from synthetic materials can emit harmful gases even many years after being installed and therefore the quantity of volatile substances is limited in Germany by the so-called AgBB scheme (health-related evaluation of emissions of VOC and SVOC from building products) for habitable rooms.

Composites
As fibres are generally not corrosion-resistant, they are either encased in a polymer (fibre-reinforced materials) or coated with synthetic materials (textile membranes). The PTFE fibres used for textile membranes can also be used uncoated in some instances, but product-specific coating methods based on PVC or PTFE are customary in most cases (see “Doctor blade method”, p. 101, and “Dip coating method”, p. 103). Special coatings can reduce the surface emissivity of membranes – the low E effect known from glazing (see “Selectivity and low E surfaces”, p. 116).

Coatings for fire protection
Fire protection coatings are based on dispersion paints or acrylic resins to which a blowing agent has been added. When the temperature rises above 200 °C, the blowing agent causes the so-called intumescent coating to swell to up to 120 times its original thickness. The foamed coating thus functions as a layer of thermal insulation between the fire and the component requiring protection. Intumescent coatings are used primarily on steel beams in order to increase their fire resistance.
Tests with beam sections made from glass fibre-reinforced polymer (GFRP) have revealed that their fire resistance cannot be improved significantly by adding a such a coating. The polymer loses a considerable amount of its strength and stiffness before the reaction temperature of the coating is reached and so the protective function begins too late in the event of a fire (Fig. B 3.10).

Decorative surface coatings
It is often the decorative effect of a coating that is the most important factor even when, for example, a lacquer also provides a protective function. Almost all the paints and lacquers used these days are based on synthetic materials. Polymer components themselves, however, are coated only in exceptional circumstances because the basic material can be produced in the colour required and with a smooth surface. Polymers and composites have a low elastic modulus and so the extensibility of the coating must be checked first (Fig. B 3.13)

Paints
Most paint finishes are dispersions, which include latex, the silicate or silicone resin paints and dispersion paints. These mixtures of two or more substances, which are not dissolved in each other, generally consist of pigments, binders and solvents (usually water or another organic solvent). The binders used are synthetic materials such as silicone resin or acrylates, but also slaked lime or potassium water glass. After applying the paint to the substrate, the solvent volatilises and the pigments and binders are deposited on the surface. In contrast to lacquers, dispersion paints are permeable to water vapour. Latex paints contain a relatively high proportion of binder and are therefore less permeable to water vapour. Dispersions can be applied with simple tools and are relatively inexpensive.

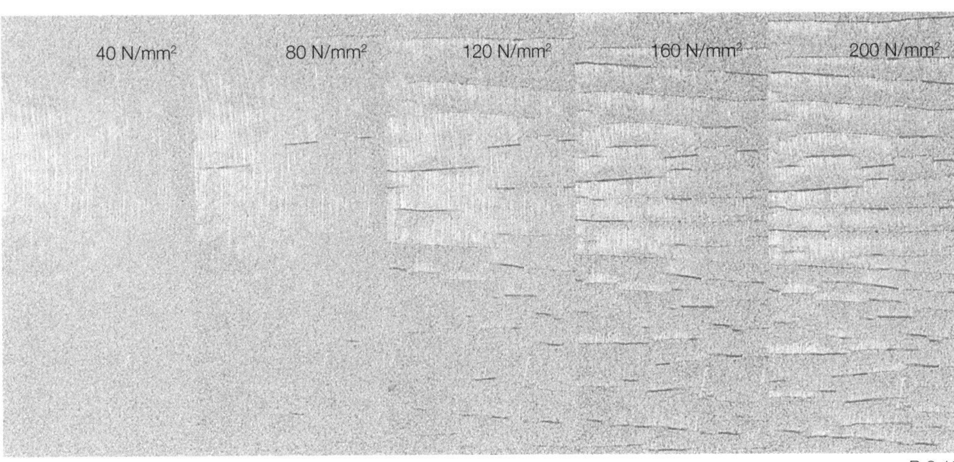

B 3.13

B 3.10 GFRP beam with fire-resistant coating
B 3.11 Typical coating structure of a lacquer system
B 3.12 Surface characteristics of lacquers and paints; in multi-layer systems the top coat determines the finish
+, ++ good characteristics
o average characteristics
-, -- poor characteristics
B 3.13 Crack growth in a paint finish applied to glass fibre-reinforced polymer (GFRP) due to increasing static load; illustration shown full size
B 3.14 Special-effect paint finishes
a Multi-colour effect
b Interference paint, appearance varies with viewing angle
c Aluminium look

Synthetic resin finishes

Synthetic resin finishes are based on dispersion paints to which a siliceous aggregate (quartz sand) has been added to improve the capacity for forming into various shapes. The addition of an aggregate lends the material a plastic, mouldable consistency. Despite their unfamiliar feel, such synthetic resin finishes are preferred in conjunction with external thermal insulation composite systems (ETICS) because they are more elastic and more waterproof than mineral renders.

Lacquer systems

Lacquer systems mostly consist of several components or coats that must be coordinated with each other (Fig. B 3.11). It is primarily the top coat that is responsible for the properties of the final surface, but the combination of the individual components also plays a part in the appearance and the characteristics of the coating.
It may be necessary to apply a levelling layer first in the form of a filling compound, e.g. of unsaturated polyester resin (UP), in order to achieve a flat final surface. With fibre-reinforced polymers in particular, such a layer will be able to compensate for most of the unevenness in a first step. Afterwards, a primer is applied to ensure a good bond between the substrate and the subsequent coats of lacquer. On polymers only a physical bond develops between the substrate and the primer, which is normally a two-part polyurethane product. In the next step minor unevenness is compensated for with a filling compound, which also fills any pores. Systems based on unsaturated polyester resin (UP), alkyd resin, acrylates or epoxy resin (EP) are used for this and can be sprayed on to the surface to achieve thicknesses of up to 0.1 mm. Alternatively, an undercoat can be used, applied with a brush or roller. Once it has dried, the layer of filling compound is rubbed down, baked or immediately given a final coat which determines both the appearance and the protective function.
Metallic lacquers are always applied in two coats – base coat and top coat. The base coat provides the desired effect, e.g. by way of metallic pigments (Fig. B 3.14); it must be processed with a solvent content of up to 80 % for paint technology reasons and therefore such coatings are poor from the environmental viewpoint. In recent years, however, there has been progress in the development of water-based lacquers. Base coats consist of cellulose acetate-butyrate (CAB) in combination with polyesters and acrylates, water-soluble systems contain polyurethane.
The transparent top coat protects the lacquer system against mechanical and chemical effects and consists of acrylic, epoxy, polyurethane or alkyd lacquers. The top coat is crucial for the technical properties of the final surface. Acrylic lacquers are more elastic, more diffusion-permeable and more resistant to UV light, but alkyd lacquers are easier to clean and more scratch-resistant, and epoxy and polyurethane lacquers have an excellent resistance to chemicals.

Coating methods

Paints are frequently applied with brushes or rollers, lacquers tend to be sprayed on. In dip coating the substrate is immersed in a tank of lacquer. Coil coating is suitable for large batches or large areas because this form of application consumes less paint than spraying. The even application with rolls results in a uniform appearance and a durable coating. Powder coating is possible on electrically conductive substrates, e.g. metals, and results in very consistent coating thicknesses. The lacquer particles are sprayed on to the surface and adhere because of the electric charge. Afterwards, they are heated in a furnace where the cross-linking (curing reaction) takes place. The coating methods used for membranes are explained in the section entitled "Textile Membranes" (p. 100).

References:

[1] Peters, Stefan: Kleben von GFK und Glas für baukonstruktive Anwendungen. Stuttgart, 2006, p. 123

a

b

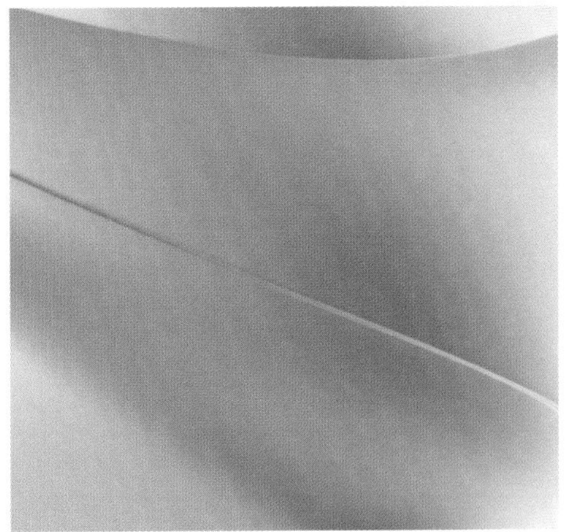
c

B 3.14

Natural fibre-reinforced polymers and biopolymers

Carmen Köhler

B 4.1

It is still early days for natural fibre-reinforced polymers and biopolymers in architecture. The first polymers, made from natural cellulose, appeared at the start of the 20th century (see "From alchemy to chemistry", p. 10) and only gradually did synthetic materials made from petroleum take their place. One hundred years later we are now aware of the finite nature of our planet's resources and a reversal of this process is now in progress.
In natural fibre-reinforced polymers (NFRP), natural vegetable fibres are encased in a petroleum-based polymer matrix. These reinforce the polymer and increase the proportion of renewable raw materials (RRM) in the composite, while reducing the weight of the component.
Biopolymers (or organic plastics) are synthetic materials essentially manufactured from vegetable substances – an approach that spares our finite resources. And natural-fibre reinforced biopolymers represents yet another group of materials for sustainable construction.

Natural fibre-reinforced polymers

"The car that grows in a field." [1] That was Henry Ford's slogan for the new car he presented to the public in 1941. During his presentation, Mr. Ford attacked the bodywork of his car with a hammer in order to demonstrate the excellent stability of the material used, which could handle 10 times the number of blows that the metals of the time could withstand, without suffering any visible damage. Furthermore, the hemp material used, made from phenolic resin, resulted in a car body that was about 30 % lighter than conventional car bodies. However, the cultivation of hemp had been practically banned in the USA since 1937 and so his prototype could not be developed further. Nevertheless, the "Hemp Car" was one of the first examples of the use of natural fibre-reinforced polymers, produced by embedding natural vegetable fibres in a petroleum-based polymer such as the thermoplastics polypropylene (PP) and polyethylene (PE), or the thermoset epoxy resin (EP). Elastomers are not used for natural fibre-reinforced polymers.

The properties of NFRPs using the example of vehicles
So far it has been the automotive industry that has made the main use of natural fibre-reinforced polymers. Such materials have been used in vehicles because of their light weight, primarily for interior components such as dashboards, door linings, parcel shelves, pillar linings or spare wheel compartments.
The hollow fibre structure of vegetable fibres makes them much lighter than glass fibres, for instance. Their favourable failure behaviour, without sharp edges or copious splinters, plus their good sound insulation values represent further technical advantages. Less wear on tools during processing and the affordable prices for such fibres are further crucial factors in their favour.
From the ecological viewpoint, the advantage of vegetable fibres is that they can increase the proportion of renewable raw materials in a building component to up to 90 % by wt. [2] In addition, the energy consumption of the semi-finished product from cultivation to production is lower, e.g. for a fleece based on natural fibres some 60 % lower than that for the production of a similar glass-fibre fleece. [3]
Natural fibre-reinforced polymers can only exhibit a better recycling behaviour, however, when the fibres are embedded in a thermoplastic matrix. Thermosets cannot be melted down and remoulded. Since the EU's directive covering end-of-life vehicles, which obliges manufacturers to take back their vehicles, came into force in 2000, the proportion of thermoplastic binders used in the production of interior components has risen to 65 % (position as of 2009). [4]
For automotive manufacturers, the processing of components made from thermoplastic composites is also beneficial from the economic viewpoint because the forming, the integration of fasteners and the attaching of decorative facings (lamination) can be carried out in one operation. This aspect can also be transferred to the building industry, where modular non-loadbearing partitions can be produced in a similar way. And without facings, there are diverse architectural design options for combining the appearance and feel of natural materials with the advantages of synthetic materials.

B 4.1 Honeycomb board made from cellulose impregnated with synthetic resin
B 4.2 Classification of natural vegetable fibres
B 4.3 Facade made from synthetic resin reinforced with lignin and cellulose fibres, EME Fusion Hotel, Seville (E), 2008, Juan Pedro Donaire
B 4.4 WPC facade, Finland Pavilion, World Expo, Shanghai (CN), 2010, Teemu Kurkela/JKMM Architects
B 4.5 Interior components made from natural fibres in a typical family saloon car

NFRPs in building

Natural fibre-reinforced polymers represent a new class of materials for the building industry and are therefore not yet in widespread use. Wood-plastic composites (WPC) represent one of the few examples of a thermoplastic reinforced with natural fibres that is being used in construction. These materials, with a wood flour content of up to 90 % by wt., a matrix of polypropylene (PP) and additives (pigments, UV stabilisers, etc.), can be used to produce sections and hollow-core cladding panels. Components made from WPCs exhibit better weathering resistance and better durability than timber. [5]
In Spain almond shells (waste from the foodstuffs industry), which consist mainly of lignin and cellulose, are crushed and mixed with a thermoset resin to form cast components (see "Lignin-bonded natural fibre composite", p. 64). During the curing process, microscopic pores form which provide good insulation against heat and cold. [6] Natural fibre-reinforced polymers are also used in applications where weight-savings, acoustics or safety are important for non-loadbearing components, e.g. trade show structures, loudspeaker cabinets, safety helmets, cases, abrasive belt backings or furniture.
One futuristic example of the use of natural fibre-reinforced polymers in architecture is the modular "Universal World House", which was developed in 2009 by the Bauhaus University, Weimar, for deployment in developing countries. All the structural components and the interior fitting-out elements are made from sandwich panels based on cellulose impregnated with a synthetic resin (Fig. B 4.1). These lightweight cellulose building boards are weather-resistant and can even be formed into wash-basins. [7]
Natural fibre-reinforced polymers can compete with polymers such as ABS, PP/glass fibre and to some extent also GFRP. Their disadvantage is their low impact strength, which, however, can be substantially improved by adding natural fibres with high extensibility, e.g. cotton fibres.

Natural fibres

Natural fibres can be divided into animal, vegetable and mineral fibres (see "Natural fibres", p. 53). Vegetable fibres are mainly used for natural fibre-reinforced polymers and it is these that will be considered on the following pages (Fig. B 4.2).

Vegetable fibres

Vegetable fibres are largely composed of cellulose in the form of chemical compounds with pectin, lignin and water. The percentages of the individual components vary according to the particular type of fibre. Cellulose is essentially responsible for the tensile strength and lignin functions as a compression-resistant matrix.
A high lignin content results in a high degree of lignification and hence stiffer, but at the same time more brittle, fibres.
Bast fibres (stalk fibres) such as hemp or flax are generally preferred because of their mechanical properties. The fibres are found in the outer part of the stalks of the plants, where they contribute to stability. These fibres are therefore characterised by a high fibre strength and low elongation at failure. The properties of the individual natural fibres are very different to the continuous synthetic fibres manufactured in controlled production processes. Natural growth processes result in finite lengths and the fibres are sensitive to heat. The mechanical properties of vegetable fibres start to decrease when subjected to a constant temperature of 180 °C or more, and the fibres are destroyed completely at temperatures above 200–250 °C.
Natural fibres that are not fully embedded in the polymer matrix tend to function as wicks and so a suitable flame retardant must be used. Natural fibres are hygroscopic, i.e. they absorb water vapour from their surroundings. The fibres should therefore be dried prior to processing in order to avoid flaws in the final composite material.
Flax is the most popular material for natural fibre reinforcement in the automotive industry. Short flax fibres are produced almost exclusively in Europe and are mostly by-products from the production of long fibres for the textiles industry. Since the repeal of the German ban on the growing of low-narcotic hemp species in 1996, the cultivation of hemp in Germany has experienced a revival. Hemp fibres are primarily used as a special cellulose for composites and insulating materials. [8]
The most important "exotic" natural fibres are jute fibres, which come mainly from India and Bangladesh, kenaf fibres from the stems of a malva plant that grows up to 4 m high in Africa and Asia, and sisal fibres, which are obtained from the leaves of agave plants in Africa and South America. Coconut fibres, mostly from southern Asia, are also used, mainly in vehicle seats. And abaca fibres from the Philippines were first used as an underbody covering in 2005. These hard fibres from the leaves of a banana species comply with the special quality demands placed on such an outer part of a vehicle's bodywork, i.e. stone impact, resistance to weather and moisture. [9]

Cultivation and obtaining the fibres

A period of about 3–4 months passes from the sowing to the harvesting of bast fibres. Flax plants reach a height of max. 1.20 m, but hemp can grow to a height of 3.50 m. After cutting, the bast fibre stalks are left in the fields for 2–4 weeks for retting, i.e. the breaking down of the cement-like substances between the fibre stalks by microorganisms. Afterwards, the straw is pressed into bales and transported to the fibre processing plant, where the broken particles of the woody interior of the plant stalk (shives), which occur during the production of bast fibres, plus other non-fibrous components are separated from the fibres mechanically. The bundles of fibres are separated into individual fibres and refined in various additional stages: cleaning, rolling, carding and unravelling.

Natural vegetable fibres	
Seed fibres	Cotton
	Kapok
Bast fibres	Linseed (flax)
	Hemp
	Jute
	Kenaf
Hard fibres	Agave
	Sisal
	Abaca
Fruit fibres	Coconut
Wood fibres	Spruce
	Pine

B 4.2

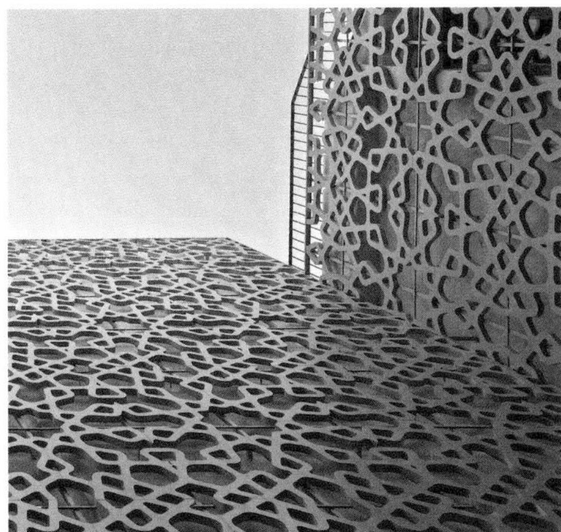

B 4.3

B 4.4

B 4.5

Basis	Biodegradable	Non-bio-degradable
Petroleum	Copolyesters Polycaprolactone (PCL)	Polypropylene (PP) Polyamide (PA 6) Epoxy resin (EP)
Blends	Thermoplastic starch (TPS) Cellulose blends	Epoxy resin made from RRM Polyamide (PA 6.10)
Natural substances	Polylactide (PLA) Polyhydroxybutyrate (PHB) Lignin	Cellulose acetate (CA) Polyamide (PA 10)

B 4.6

B 4.6 Biodegradability of petroleum- and bio-based plastics
B 4.7 Car seat cover made from heat-resistant polylactide (PLA) fibres
B 4.8 Fitting a natural fibre fabric into a die
B 4.9 Biopolymers made from renewable raw materials (RRM) – simplified schematic overview

B 4.7

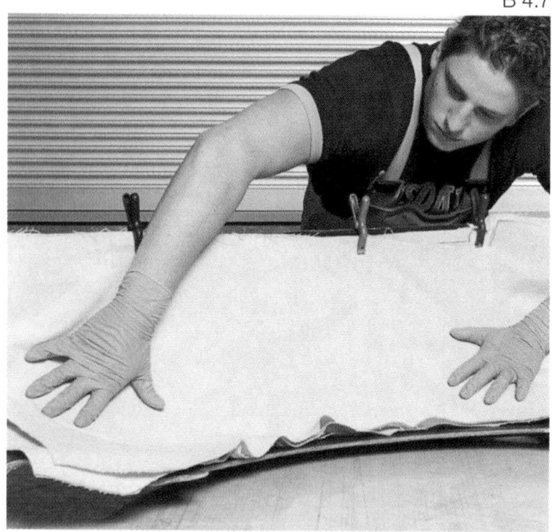

B 4.8

Integrating natural fibres into building components
Building components made from natural fibre-reinforced polymers are mainly produced from semi-finished products in the form of fleeces (non-wovens) (see "Primary products", p. 70). The 6–10 cm long natural and polypropylene fibres are mixed together, carded and hardened mechanically to form hybrid felts. Afterwards, this semi-finished product can be pressed into any shape in a die.
The use of a thermoset binder enables fleeces or felts made from 100% natural fibres to be sprayed with a resin system and afterwards pressed into shapes as required in a compression moulding process. Resins are liquid and so cannot be worked into the semi-finished fibre product. Components made from natural fibre-reinforced polymers are mainly produced by pressing methods. Further processes suitable for NFRPs are injection moulding or impact extruding, which also enable the realisation of more complex geometries.
Mixtures of natural fibres have proved worthwhile in practice. The best mechanical values for composites are achieved by mixing a rather finer fibre such as flax or jute with coarser fibres such as hemp or sisal. Vegetable fibres can also be spun into yarns and subsequently woven into industrial fabrics, which can be used for high-quality NFRP components with a thermoset matrix. This method of processing is, however, more costly.

The future for vegetable fibres
Great things are expected from the research into functional fibres made from cellulose. The natural polymer cellulose can be dissolved without modifying its chemistry and spun into continuous fibres. This means it is possible to develop bespoke fibres with reproducible properties. Depending on the additives used (e.g. soot particles or paraffins), the fibres can be made magnetic, thermoregulating or electrically conductive. Up until now, these fibres have been used only in functional clothing and jackets for motorcyclists [10]. However, textile heating systems or climate-regulating membranes can be produced which can then be incorporated in a textile facade.

Biopolymers

Biopolymers are synthetic materials that are essentially produced from renewable raw materials (RRM) such as starch or cellulose. Such materials are also known as bio-based or organic plastics. [11] The term "biopolymer" is, however, not always applied consistently. Biopolymers are also known as biodegradable plastics when their compostability to EN 13432 has been verified.
These polymers can be produced from petroleum or renewable raw materials. Their biological degradability depends not on the raw materials from which they are made, but rather on the chemical structure of the polymer. There are some petroleum-based polymers that can be composted, but bio-based polymers are in fact not generally biodegradable (Fig. B 4.6). Compostable biopolymers made from petroleum or renewable raw materials are preferably used for temporary applications such as packagings, catering articles or agricultural or horticultural purposes. They are also known as second-generation biopolymers.
The Japanese automotive industry has been replacing petroleum-based polymers by bio-based polymers for the building of vehicle dashboards since 1996. The reasons for this are the sparing of resources, environmentally efficient production and the easier disposal of biopolymers. As more and more fibre-reinforced polymers are being used in the building industry, users are also calling for not only the fibres, but also the matrix to be replaced by sustainable materials. With the help of photosynthesis, plants produce approx. 170 billion tonnes of biomass from sunlight and carbon dioxide every year in the form of cereals, grasses, etc., and some of these plants can be used as the raw materials for biopolymers. [12] The current production of biopolymers amounts to 0.4 million tonnes annually – accounting for only 0.01 % of the land available for agriculture globally. [13] In addition, waste materials from the agricultural, foodstuffs and cosmetics industries are available in almost unlimited quantities.

Biopolymers with long-lasting functionality
Second-generation biopolymers were developed as temporary polymers that can be composted. The focus for third-generation biopolymers is, however, maximising the content of renewable raw materials in conjunction with long-lasting functionality. The aim here is to develop biopolymers whose properties are comparable with conventional polymers and in doing so to close the material life cycle wherever possible. Bio-based plastics can be produced directly from natural biopolymers such as cellulose or starch through modification. However, it is also possible to produce monomers from renewable raw materials that are then polymerised to form a biopolymer (Fig. B 4.9).

Disposal of long-lasting biopolymers
The recycling of conventional thermoplastics (PET, PP, etc.) is associated with a downgrading in properties (downcycling effect). This disadvantage is even more pronounced with biopolymers because of their generally lower thermo-mechanical and chemical resistance. The disposal method preferred for long-lasting biopolymers is incineration, which results in almost zero-carbon energy production. What this means is that the incineration releases only as much carbon dioxide (CO_2) as the plant extracted from the atmosphere during its growth. The same quantity of CO_2 is produced if the biomass is allowed to rot naturally and be decomposed by microorganisms. Mind you, as plasticisers and additives are often added to non-petroleum-based biopolymers and CO_2 is given off during

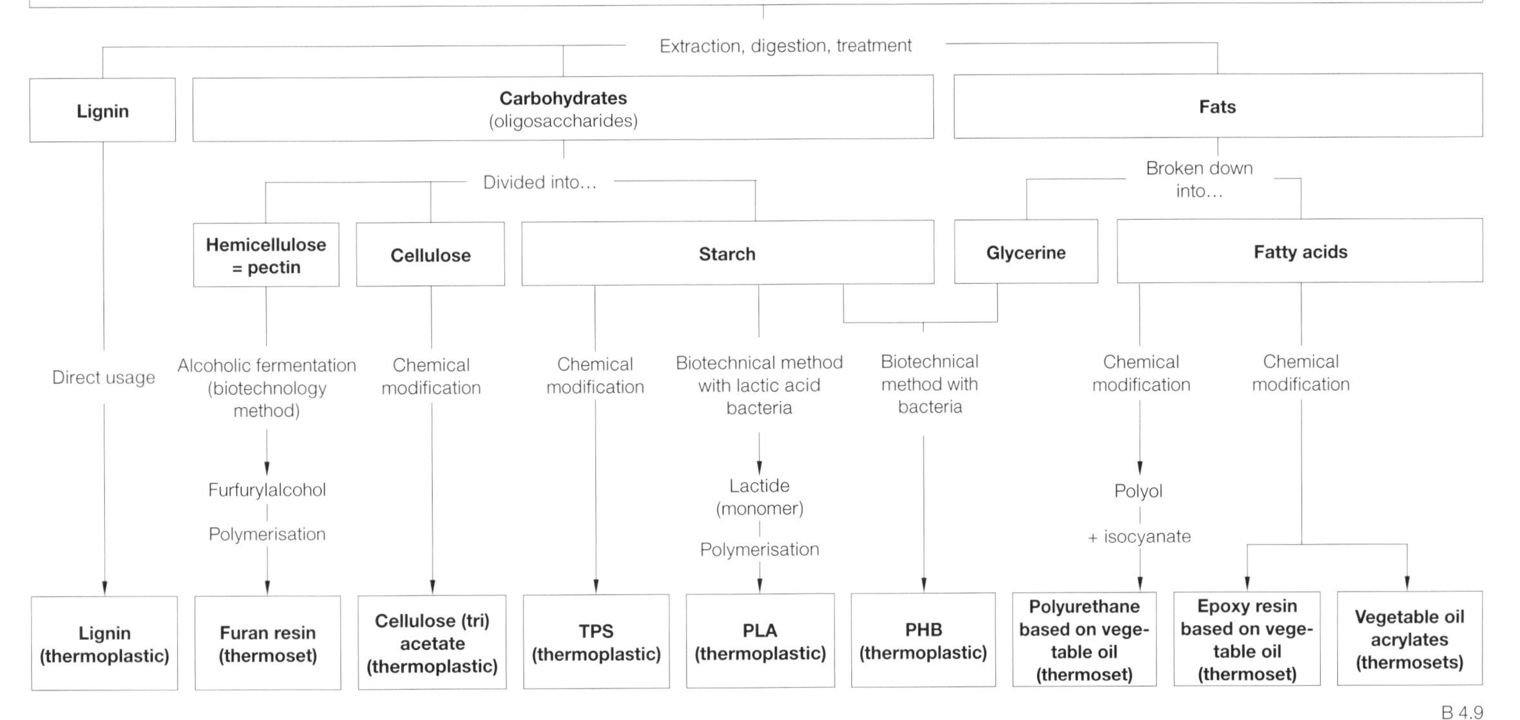

B 4.9

their production, processing and disposal, the carbon footprint is not exactly zero.
Some biopolymers, especially polylactides (PLA), can be broken down into their monomers, repolymerised and recycled without suffering a downgrading in any of their properties. This so-called chemical recycling is the subject of current research. The chemical resistance of the majority of biopolymers is inferior to that of conventional polymers and therefore it takes less energy to reduce them to their original monomers again.

Biopolymers – overview and examples
Biopolymers are classified just like conventional polymers – as thermoplastics, elastomers and thermosets – and can be processed and machined with the same machinery. The most common biopolymers are described below.

Thermoplastic starch (TPS)
▷ Packagings, catering articles
Thermoplastic starch (TPS) is currently the most common biopolymer (80 % market share). The water-soluble starch is mixed with a water-repellent, petroleum-based polymer and the plasticiser glycerine. TPS can replace typical plastic packaging materials. Applications in the building industry are possible, e.g. for insulation, but limited because of the material's approx. 4 % moisture absorption. [14]

Cellulose (tri)acetate (CA, CTA)
▷ Spectacle frames and lenses, tool handles, foils for TFT screens, transparent thermal insulation
Cellulose is present in all plants and is therefore the commonest naturally occurring biopolymer. It is insoluble in water, does not melt and must therefore be modified. The chemical reaction with acetic acid produces cellulose diacetate or triacetate (see "Cellulose acetate", p. 43). The maximum long-term service temperature is 80 °C. [15]
Cellulose acetate is scratch-resistant because of its high surface elasticity and is characterised by its shiny surface, grip and a light transmittance that is comparable with that of float glass. It resists the build-up of an electrostatic charge and that means dust-free surfaces. Additives can be mixed with cellulose acetate to reduce its flammability or make it weather-resistant. [16] [17]

Polylactide (PLA)
▷ Packagings, fibres for (functional) textiles, drinks bottles, housings for electrical equipment
The lactic acid polymer polylactide (PLA) is produced in a biotechnical process with the help of bacteria from starch or sugar. Compared with the modification of naturally occurring biopolymers (e.g. cellulose), this method of production offers the chance to tailor the chemical structure of the PLA, and therefore its properties, too. The properties of PLA are therefore certainly comparable with those of PP and PET. Polylactides are scratch-resistant, waterproof and transparent, and also exhibit good mechanical properties (Fig. B 4.11, p. 64), which can be further improved by increasing the degree of crystallisation. PLA materials are gas-permeable and ideal for printing, which makes them suitable for functional textiles as well as packagings. The service temperature of standard PLA is approx. 55 °C. It is possible, through careful selection of the fermentation bacteria, to mix together the lactic acid polymers with different degrees of crystallisation in a controlled way (stereo-complex). This results in a material with much improved properties which is already being used for microwave-safe containers, injection-moulded products for the automotive and electronics industries, ironable fabrics, and bottles for hot filling. [18]

Polyhydroxybutyrate (PHB)
▷ Packagings, equipment housings
It was in 1924 that scientists working at the Pasteur Institute in Paris discovered that bacteria produce polyhydroxybutyrate (PHB) from surplus nutrients, which they then store in their cells as reserves, similar to the way to humans and animals store fat. Potential starting substrates are starch, sugar, glycerine or palm oil. This biopolymer exhibits stable properties over a temperature range from -30 to +120 °C. PHB is a high-crystalline polymer with a smooth, shiny surface. It is resistant to UV radiation and is more waterproof than PLA. Other advantages are its suitability for printing and its low tendency to creep. Its properties can be varied quite considerably. The disadvantages are the high production costs, caused by the high capital outlay necessary for biotechnology production plants and the production of small quantities because of the low demand. Optimised methods of production will, however, cut the cost of this material in the long run. The brittleness of this polymer and its price can also be reduced by mixing together different types of polymer to create so-called blends.

B 4.10

B 4.11

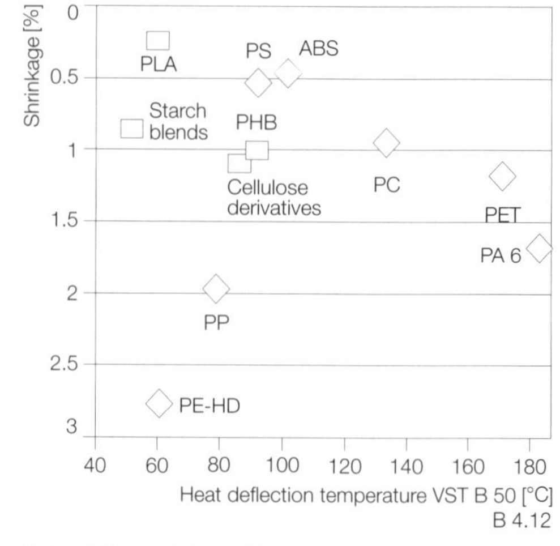

B 4.12

Biopolymers versus conventional polymers
The elastic moduli and the stiffnesses of thermoplastic biopolymers are similar to those of petroleum-based polymers. Indeed, the stiffness of polylactide is higher than that of conventional thermoplastics. Fig. B 4.11 shows the notched impact strength in relation to the elastic modulus. The notched impact strength indicates a material's resistance to impact-type actions. As the toughness increases, so the elastic modulus of a biopolymer decreases, just like a conventional polymer (see "Failure behaviour", p. 35). One advantage of thermoplastic biopolymers is their lower rate of shrinkage compared with conventional thermoplastics, a fact that is important in the production of high-precision components. Cellulose derivates, PHB and PLA stereo-complexes exhibit the maximum heat deflection temperatures. The heat deflection (or distortion) temperature is a measure of the heat resistance of a polymer subjected to a defined load. These temperatures are comparable with those of polystyrene or the industrial polymers acrylonitrile-butadiene-styrene (ABS).
Most thermoplastic biopolymers absorb more moisture than petroleum-based polymers. However, apart from thermoplastic starch, this absorption remains below 1 %. [19]
The development of long-lasting biopolymers is only just beginning and so far only a few findings regarding their long-term properties, e.g. creep, UV resistance and fatigue behaviour, have been published.

Natural fibre-reinforced biopolymers

Combining biopolymers with natural fibres results in improved mechanical and thermal properties.

Natural fibre-reinforced PLA (thermoplastic)
▷ Housings for electronics, vehicle interiors
By adding heat-absorbing metal hydroxides to a biocomposite and reinforcing the material with short kenaf fibres, a Japanese electronics group has been able to launch a virtually non-flammable mobile phone housing onto the market (Fig. B 4.13). Mineral flame retardants, especially aluminium and magnesium hydroxide, have been used to retain the sustainability aspect of the biocomposite. The processing time for the injection moulding of these mobile phone housings has also been shortened from five minutes to one minute.
In contrast to other polymers, PLA can be processed at temperatures above 160 °C. This means that the demoulding temperature is reached faster and the production time optimised with respect to the heat sensitivity of the natural fibres. In the "S-House", a demonstration project carried out by Vienna University of Technology, a prototype for a non-loadbearing partition made from natural fibre-reinforced biopolymers, several layers of fleece made from straw, flax and polylactide fibres were laid on top of each other and pressed together. [20] This sandwich panel has stable facing plies and a relatively soft but nevertheless compression-resistant core. The result is a component with integral sound insulation – modular partitions made from 100 % renewable raw materials with a low weight for quick and easy installation and repositioning.

Lignin-bonded natural fibre composite (thermoplastic)
▷ Loudspeaker cabinets, shoe heels, technical components (machinery), musical instruments, backing boards for high-quality wood veneers
Lignin is the second most common naturally occurring biopolymer and functions as the stabilising matrix between the cellulose fibres in all vegetable fibres and in wood. It impregnates the moisture capillaries in plants and is therefore more waterproof than wood. This biopolymer is dark brown in colour, absorbs UV light almost totally and is difficult to decompose both biologically and chemically. In conjunction with natural fibres, it combines the positive properties of naturally grown wood with the unrestricted mouldability of thermoplastics. It is therefore also known as liquid wood. [21] The use of lignin, a constituent of wood, lends the composite similar mechanical and thermal properties to those of wood, e.g. with regard to the coefficient of thermal expansion. It is therefore suitable as a connecting element in timber construction. Lignin rots slower than wood when affected by moisture.

Natural fibre-reinforced bioresins (thermosets)
Fatty acids from vegetable oils can be converted into thermoset bioresins by means of chemical reactions. The substances used for curing are mostly non-bio-based. Components obtained from renewable raw materials are still undergoing development and not yet ready for the market.
Compared with conventional thermosets, e.g. phenolic or unsaturated polyester resins (UP), the thermoset bioresins are somewhat less stiff and absorb less moisture. In the case of bio-based reactive resins based on vegetable oils (e.g. linseed oil), it is the hydrophobic, i.e. water-repellent, nature of the oil used that is mainly responsible for this characteristic. In addition, a significantly higher UV resistance has been verified for these resins, which is attributable to the different chemical structures that both resins form during the curing phrase. Nevertheless, after they have cured, both systems belong to the polyesters from the chemistry viewpoint. The maximum permissible temperature for these resins is 180 °C.
The addition of zero-halogen flame retardants improves the non-flammability without impairing the ecological features. Prices for bioresin systems are comparable with those for conventional resins. Combined with hemp and flax fabrics, it has been possible to build various bodywork prototypes that could replace glass fibre-reinforced polymers for external applications; for example, a "nudge bar" has now successfully completed a 12-month on-the-road test on a bus in service in the northern German town of Braunschweig.
Corrugated cardboard plus hemp and flax fabrics form the constructional elements of a designer chair conceived as a prototype (Fig. B 4.14). The bioresin based on linseed oil is injected with the help of a vacuum infusion (see "Resin infusion and vacuum methods", pp. 79–80). Decorative facings are unnecessary because the untreated surface is an integral part of the design concept.
In the building industry, the use of a similar method to produce a modular partition is conceivable. The injection of the binder could be controlled in a vacuum so that the quantity of resin decreases towards the inside of the com-

ponent. This would result in a material with stiff facing plies and internal insulation satisfying both thermal and acoustic requirements. The acoustic efficiency of natural fibres could be exploited because of low quantity of resin in the middle. The facing plies could be structured differently to suit haptic and visual requirements.

A vision of the future of building

Japanese vehicle manufacturers are using polylactide (PLA) reinforced with kenaf or abaca fibres for the bodies of various prototypes. Vehicles are exposed to the weather, temperature changes and mechanical actions. The facades of buildings are subjected to similar conditions. Up until now, studies have proved that polylactide has a high resistance to UV radiation. Textile sunshading systems made from PLA are due to be launched onto the market very soon.[22] Biopolymer cladding for facades and biopolymer linings for partitions will follow shortly after. The permeability with regard to oxygen, carbon dioxide and water vapour could result in the development of moisture-regulating and gas-permeable facades. The advantages of biopolymers over components made from the natural biocomposite wood are mainly to be found in the mouldability and the options for integrating functions.
In other areas of technology the potential integration of various components, and hence the possibility of creating multi-functional elements, is already being exploited. One electronics group is producing mobile phone prototypes made from biopolymers with the shape memory effect. The mobile phone can be bent and worn on the wrist. Applying heat enables the original, "memorised" shape to be reinstated. Used on facades or sunshading elements, "smart" systems could be created that change their geometry automatically at defined temperatures and without consuming any energy.
Biopolymers enable not only technological innovations, but also totally new conceptual approaches. For instance, it is possible to develop buildings that biodegrade after a defined period of use. In the immediate future this could be useful for emergency accommodation in disaster regions or for buildings in nature conservation areas. After usage, the construction made of biocomposites would present nutrients for bacteria which would then decompose the structure directly in situ, turning it into humus.
Bio-based material systems offer the potential for creating multi-functional high-performance materials without consuming finite resources in doing so. Even though such materials are currently still expensive and their durability needs to be improved, bio-based material systems present us with amazing opportunities.

References:

[1] http://www.hanfplantage.de/hemp-car-das-auto-das-auf-dem-acker-waechst-06-07-2009, 20 Aug 2010
[2] http://www.hero-hessen.de/stoffliche-nutzung/holz-kunststoff-verbundwerkstoffe/index.html, 11 Jun 2010
[3] http://media.daimler.com/dcmedia/0-921-646299-1-813756-1-0-0-0-0-1-11694-614316-0-1-0-0-0-0-0.html?TS=1292875098156, 21 Oct 2009
[4] http://www.biowerkstoffe.info/verbundwerkstoffe/verarbeitung/formpressen/, 25 Aug 2010
[5] http://www.kosche.de/homekovalex/index.php?option=com_content&task=view&id=37&Itemid=68, 29 Oct 2009
[6] http://www.duralmond.com/htm/celosias/a_medida_ENGLISH.html, 29 Oct 2009
[7] http://www.kunststofforum.de/information/news_swisscell-paneele-erobern-afrika_5886, 29 Oct 2009
[8] http://www.fnr-server.de/ftp/pdf/literatur/pdf_227-brosch_NFRP_2008.pdf; p. 14, 11 Jun 2010
[9] ibid. [3]
[10] http://www.smartfiber.de/index.php?option=com_content&view=article&id=7&Itemid=29&lang=en, 24 Aug 2010
[11] http://www.european-bioplastics.org/index.php?id=126, 19 Oct 2009
[12] http://wip-kunststoffe.de/uploads/File/naturfasercompounds08/07_Seliger.pdf, 10 Jun 2010
[13] Endres, Hans-Josef; Siebert-Raths, Andrea: Technische Biopolymere: Rahmenbedingungen, Marktsituation, Herstellung, Aufbau und Eigenschaften. Munich, 2009, p. 32
[14] ibid., p. 217, Fig. 5.48
[15] Domininghaus, Hans et al.: Kunststoffe. Eigenschaften und Anwendungen. Berlin, 2008, p. 1322
[16] ibid. [13], pp. 199f.
[17] ibid. [15], pp. 1319f.
[18] http://www.teijin.co.jp/english/news/2007/ebd070912.html, 18 Sept 2009
[19] ibid. [12], p. 217, Fig. 5.48
[20] Wimmer, Robert et al.: Grundlagenforschung für die Entwicklung von Produktprototypen aus Naturstoff-gebundenen Vliesen. Pub. by Federal Ministry for Transport, Innovation & Technology. Vienna, 2007, pp. 27ff.
[21] http://www.tecnaro.de/deutsch/grundsaetze.htm?section=arboform, 29 Oct 2009
[22] Witthuhn, Barbara: Ein T-Shirt aus Zucker. In: Berliner Zeitung, 25 Oct 2005.

B 4.13

B 4.10 Shoe heel made from a lignin-bonded natural fibre composite
B 4.11 Impact strength plotted against elastic modulus for various biopolymers and conventional polymers
B 4.12 Shrinkage plotted against heat deflection temperature for various biopolymers and conventional polymers
B 4.13 Mobile telephone housing made from keraf fibre-reinforced polylactide
B 4.14 Lounge Chair "AufjedenFalz" made from hemp, flax, fig tree bark and bioresin; mehrwerk designlabor, Enrico Wilde
B 4.15 Design study for a car body made from natural fibre-reinforced polylactide (PLA)

B 4.14

B 4.15

Part C Semi-finished products

Fig. C Temporary terminal building, Vienna (A), 2005, Itten + Brechbühl, Baumschlager Eberle P.ARC

Primary products

C 1.1

The manufacture of polymer or membrane semi-finished products usually makes use of standardised primary products generally purchased as finished items by the final processors. A whole range of primary products, in the form of pre-mixed polymer blends, standard textiles or core materials, is therefore available to the designer, and these can be processed to form an even greater range of diverse final products (Fig. C 1.3). Textiles, for example, can be used for both membranes and fibre-reinforced polymers.

Preparing the polymer

Polymers are treated and refined with additives in various operations between their synthesis in the reaction vessel and the final processing. The mixture is known as a compound. The steps in the process chain differ for the three types of polymer – thermoplastics, elastomers and thermosets. The specific technological requirements result from the respective properties with regard to molecular structure and reaction to heat (see "Classification of polymers", p. 30). Thermoplastics can be melted and remelted an infinite number of times – the polymer reaction has already taken place in the manufacture of the material. In contrast to this, the cross-linking in elastomers and thermosets cannot take place before the processing, and so these materials cannot be reshaped again afterwards.

The treatment of the basic material up to the point of forming a processable polymer is usually carried out by the polymer supplier, but in some cases by the final processor. To do this, the polymer, or rather the primary product, is crushed or blended and then mixed with additives and fillers. Blending in the dry state is known as mixing, in the plastic state homogenising. The additives are frequently indispensable for the workability of the polymer, and can also have a considerable influence on properties such as colour, reaction to fire, strength or the price of the material (see "Fillers and additives", pp. 32–34).

Thermoplastics

In most cases the synthesis of thermoplastics in the chemicals plant results in products in powder form. They are enriched with additives and fillers prior to processing and mainly marketed in the form of granulates. Only in the case of PVC do larger final processors (> 350 t per year) purchase the polymer in powder form and process it themselves. This approach is usually more economical for PVC because its properties can be considerably adjusted by adding appropriate additives and fillers and therefore it is possible to create a compound that is exactly right for each particular product.

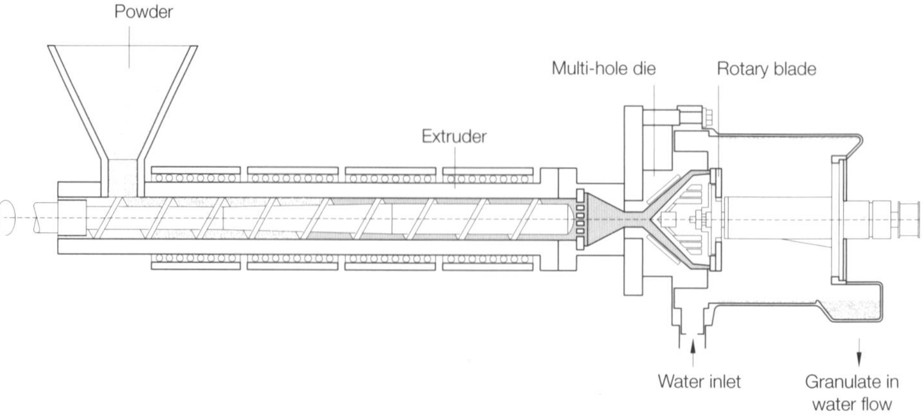

C 1.2

C 1.1 Blended fabric made from carbon and aramid fibres
C 1.2 Granulation of thermoplastics
C 1.3 Methods of processing polymers and the resulting semi-finished products

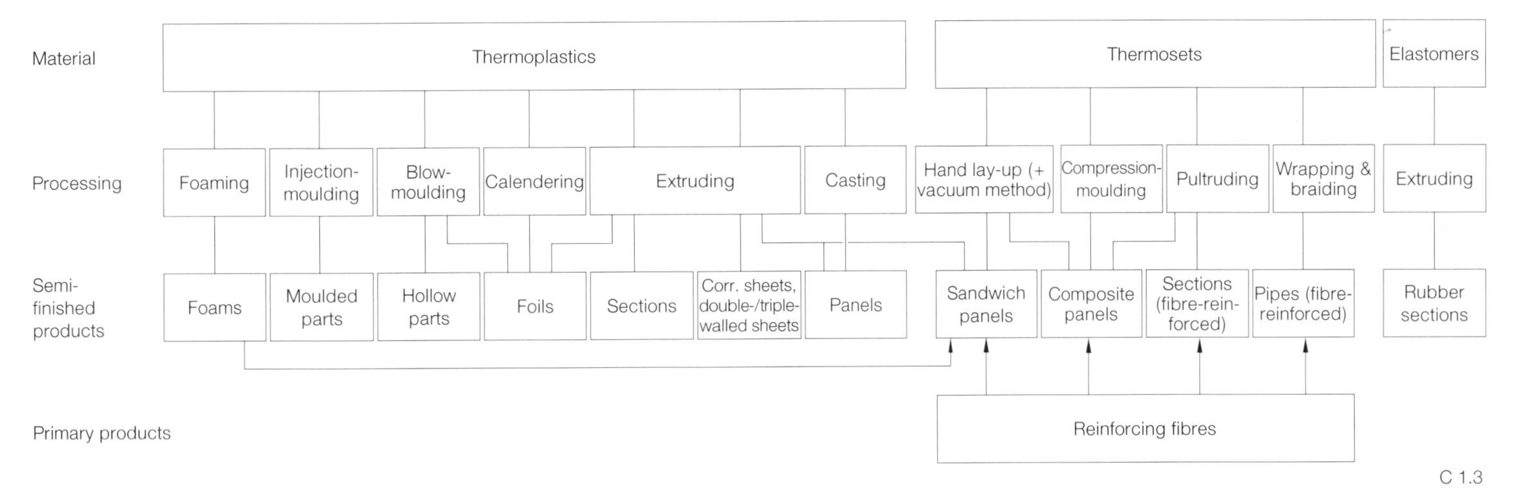

C 1.3

Blending
Good blending of the components is crucial to the final properties of the polymer. For this reason, recycled thermoplastics can in some circumstances achieve better properties because the polymer is mixed yet again in the recycling process. Besides continuous blending (e.g. in a screw mixer), there are numerous discontinuous methods (e.g. in a mixing drum) that can be employed, especially when processing smaller quantities. Afterwards, the compound is melted down and homogenised. The softened material can then be processed directly or granulated for later processing.

Granulation
Thermoplastics that are not prepared by the final processor or are to be processed later are produced as granulates that can be easily stored and transported.
Granulation takes place immediately after plastifying the polymer compound in an extruder. In this process, the melt is forced through dies, cut into pellets a few millimetres long by a rotary blade and cooled with water (Fig. C 1.2). The result is bead- or lens-shaped grains, also cylindrical grains when using cold granulation. The granulate (Fig. B 1.1, p. 30) is dried prior to storage; further drying directly prior to final processing is necessary for some polymers, e.g. PC, PA and PMMA.

Final processing
The processing options for thermoplastics vary considerably depending on the geometry of the semi-finished product to be produced. What all the processes have in common is that the polymer granulate is first melted down and homogenised in a screw mixer before being fed into the mould. When producing foil, the melt is calendered or extruded (see "Production of foil", pp. 94–96). When coating membranes, the thermoplastic is applied to the textile in the form of thin coats (see "Coatings", pp. 101–103). Solid sheets, sections and random geometries can be produced by moulding, injection moulding, pressing or extruding (see "Extrusion", p. 83, and "Moulded items", pp. 91–92). Core materials or insulating layers made from polymers are foamed (see "Production", p. 74).

Elastomers
Crude rubber, the raw material for elastomers, is supplied by manufacturers in the form of bales or sheets, which are then processed to form the final material by the final processor. Robust crushing machines are essential because crude rubber is very tough. First of all, the viscosity of the material is reduced in masticators or mills, which eases the homogeneous blending with fillers and additives. Carbon black or silicic acid (silica) are important additives for elastomers. Rubbers are processed immediately after blending. The customary methods (extrusion, calendering, pressing or injection-moulding) are similar to those used for thermoplastics.
Elastomers cannot be melted again after the polymer reaction and so the cross-linking (vulcanisation) takes place after the forming processes (see "Elastomers", pp. 44–45). High temperatures are always necessary and in some cases overpressure of up to 200 bar as well. Cold cross-linked systems are used for special applications; however, these require much longer curing times.

Thermosets
Thermosets are purchased by the final processors in the form of liquid reactive resins, less often as premixed moulding compounds. As with the elastomers, the cross-linking reaction first takes place during the forming processes because, like elastomers, thermosets cannot be remelted or reshaped once they have cured. The as yet non-cross-linked resins are supplied in reactive solvents (e.g. styrene); the shelf life of the container is often less than 12 months. Fillers and additives, e.g. flame retardant, generally will have already been mixed in by the polymer producer. Prior to processing, a hardener, followed by an accelerator, is added to the resin. Curing then takes place at room temperature or a higher temperature. During this, the gel time, i.e. the time between adding the hardener and the onset of the curing reaction, limits the maximum possible workability time of the resin.
Besides reactive resins, there are also primary products to which the hardener has already been added, e.g. impregnated fabrics (prepregs) or runny compounds. The shelf life of such a semi-finished product is much shorter than that of a reactive resin. The curing reaction is triggered during the processing by a higher temperature.
Thermosets are primarily used for fibre-reinforced polymers. The semi-finished products are compression-moulded, manually laminated, pultruded, wrapped or braided (see "Production", pp. 79–81). Less common, however, is the use of thermosets as casting resins or moulding compounds.

Textiles

Textiles are semi-finished products made from woven fibres. They are important primary products for membrane fabrication and fibre-reinforced polymers because loose fibres cannot be processed as a rule. Only in exceptional cases are filaments or bundles of fibres (rovings, yarns) used directly for reinforcing a synthetic material. Besides the traditional woven fabrics, a huge variety of different textiles is now available for specific applications. Figs. C 1.5–1.9 (pp. 70–71) provide an overview of the standard textiles and corresponding forms of weave for these materials.

Basic terminology
The standard fibres and their corresponding forms of processing are described in the chapter entitled "Fibres" (pp. 48–53). A single fibre is known as a filament. A roving is a bundle of parallel filaments and a yarn, or thread, consists of twisted filaments. A twine is made from several twisted yarns.

Woven fabrics

Woven fabrics are produced from systems of threads crossing at right-angles. The warp threads run parallel to the longitudinal direction of the fabric (they are fixed to the weaving loom) and the weft threads are interwoven perpendicular to these with shuttles or a jet of air. The weft threads generally undulate, i.e. pass above and below the warp threads. When the material is loaded this leads to different strains in the textile in the warp and weft directions, depending on the type of weave.
Different arrangements of raised warp threads during the weft insertion (floating) produce different types of weave that exert a considerable influence on the mechanical properties. The three main types of weave are plain, twill and satin weave. The smallest repetitive unit of a weave is known as the rapport.

Types of weave

Plain weave (also known as calico or linen weave) is the simplest and tightest type of weave. Here, the warp threads lie alternately above and below the weft threads (Figs. C 1.5a and C 1.6). Plain weave exhibits good dimensional stability and can be cut anywhere without fraying. Hopsack weave (also known as mat, Panama or Celtic weave) is a special form of plain weave in which two or three parallel warp and weft threads are woven together.
Twill weave (also known as croisé weave) is the result of an unequal rhythm in which the weft thread passes once above and then at least twice below the warp thread (Figs. C 1.5b and C 1.7). Shifting the change by one step per course produces a diagonal rib. Twill weave is stronger and stiffer than plain weave because the strain in the warp direction is lower. In addition, the suppleness, the so-called drapeability, is better (Fig. C 1.4 b).
In satin weave (also known as atlas weave), the weft threads initially pass beneath a warp thread and subsequently above more than two warp threads (Figs. C 1.5c and C 1.8). After each course, the change is shifted accordingly by at least two steps. This type of weave is characterised by its excellent drapeability (Fig. C 1.4c). In fibre-reinforced polymers it is therefore used for components with tight radii in order to achieve smooth surfaces.

Non-crimp fabrics

In contrast to a woven fabric, the layers of fibres in a non-crimp fabric are laid on top of each other and not interwoven (Figs. C 1.5d and C 1.9). The fibres are fixed in position only by means of additional, thin sewing threads.
Using a non-crimp fabric instead of a woven fabric for a fibre composite improves the mechanical strength of the finished component because the fibres are not integrated in an undulating form. Another advantage is that the orientation of the fibres can be relatively easily adapted to the loading directions because they do not necessarily need to be at right-angles to each other, and instead can be incorporated at any angles. It is also possible to build a non-crimp fabric with not just two, but several layers, one above the other. One use of non-crimp fabric is as the reinforcement in textile-reinforced concrete.

Complex mats

Complex mats are being used more and more, especially for machine-made fibre composites. Additional, random fibres are laid on a multilayer non-crimp fabric and again fixed in place with sewing threads. These short pieces of fibre have a very fine structure; attached to the outside of a component, this results in a very consistent, smooth surface. Core materials can be integrated into the non-crimp fabric during production if required.

Braids

Impact resistance is often important for fibre composites, which is why braided textiles are used (Figs. C 1.5e and B 2.1, p. 48). The crisscrossing fibres result in a greater friction force upon fracture and hence the desired impact resistance. Braiding is frequently used as the fibre reinforcement for pipes, too. The angle between the fibres can be adjusted and adapted to suit the loads.

Chopped strand mats and fleeces

Chopped strand mats are made from a random arrangement of pieces of fibre that are bonded together (Fig. C 1.11, pp. 72). When the mat comes into contact with the resin during processing, the bond is loosened and the fibres adapt perfectly to the shape of the component. The composite achieves consistent properties within its plane without any dominant direction. Such composites are used, for example, for vessels, moulded parts or covers that only need to satisfy low mechanical requirements. Chopped strand mats can be draped easily over curved shapes in further processing. Fine mats, known as fleeces or non-woven fabrics, are used as the outermost plies in fibre composites in order to achieve smooth surfaces. Sandwich components with a core of fleece are also available (see "Core fleeces and spacer fabrics", p. 75).

Knitted fabrics

Knitted fabrics are produced by forming loops or stitches. The manufacturing process is essentially similar to knitting by hand. As these textiles do not have a dominant direction, their suitability as a reinforcement for polymers is limited. They are primarily used as backing

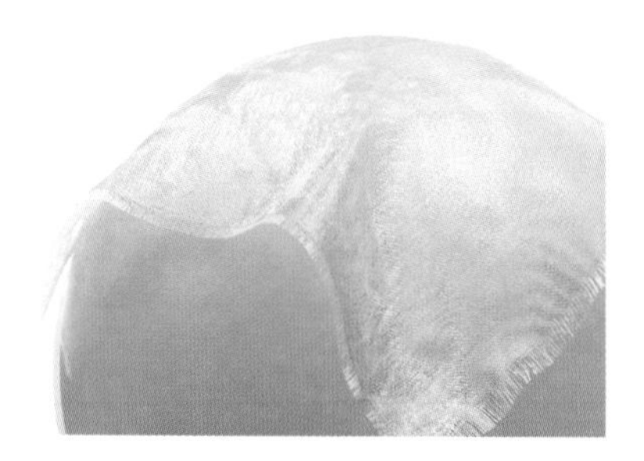

a

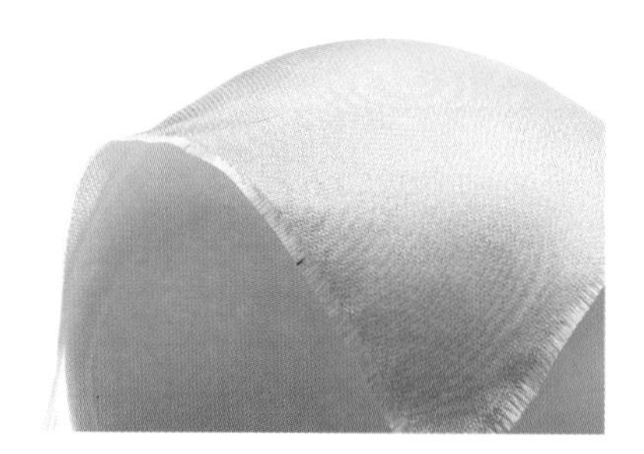

b

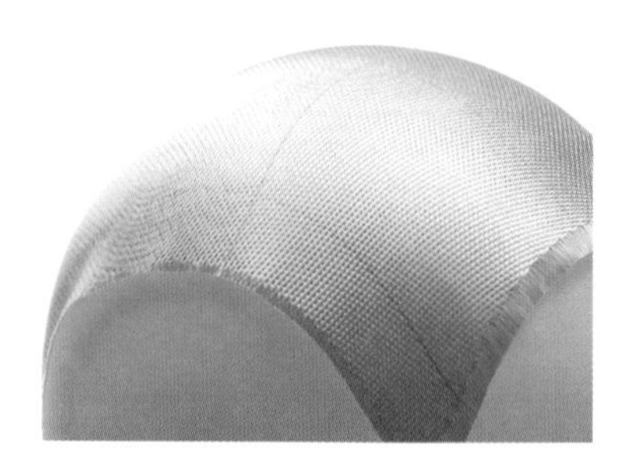

c

C 1.4

a

b

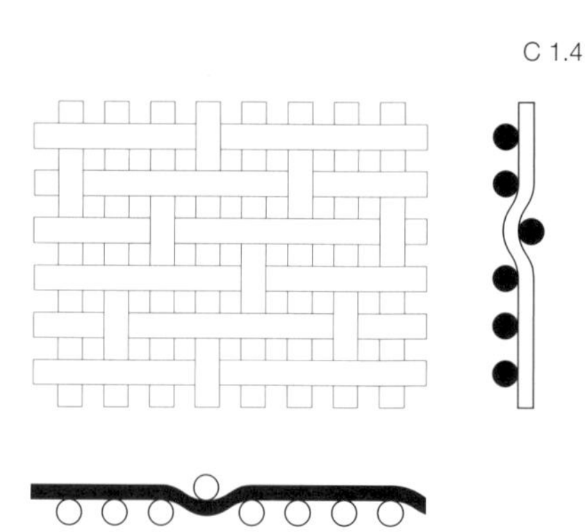

c

materials for other reinforcing fibres or for fixing such fibres. Their very good drapeability makes them suitable for uses involving very small radii.

Peel-ply fabrics

Peel-ply fabrics are not used for reinforcing polymers, but instead for producing a rough surface. Such a surface is desirable when further plies are to be attached to a fibre-reinforced polymer at a later stage of production, or for bonding a further lamination. Peel-ply fabrics are attached to a fibre-reinforced polymer as the final ply, but are removed again (peeled off, hence the name) before the polymer has fully cured, which results in a ragged, rough surface (see Fig. E 2.23, p. 180).

Selection

When selecting a suitable textile, it is primarily the loadbearing behaviour that is crucial as well as manufacturing aspects. The loadbearing behaviour is determined by the orientation of the fibres, their waviness (undulations) and the weight per unit area (g/m²).

Textiles for membranes

Pure woven fabrics or composites made from woven fabrics and several layers of coating are used for textile membranes. Other types of textile, e.g. non-crimp fabric, do not play a role here.
Plain weave is generally used for lightweight membrane types and uncoated fabrics. Hopsack weave is employed for thicker, coated fabrics because the reduced waviness (undulation) of the threads results in a material with lower creep under high loads and because of the reduced disparity in the stiffnesses in the warp and weft directions. An even stiffness distribution throughout a fabric is advantageous and so coated membrane materials in which the weft threads are pretensioned during the weaving process are also available. The pretensioning distributes the undulations equally between the warp and weft threads, which leads to equal stiffness in both directions.

Textiles for fibre-reinforced polymers

Textiles are employed for reinforcing planar, thin-wall components made from fibre-reinforced polymers. With manual types of production in particular, this substantially reduces the work required compared with the direct processing of the fibres. The use of standardised textiles results in better control of the orientation of the fibres in the component. It is also possible to combine different types of fibre, e.g. carbon and aramid fibres (Fig. C 1.1, p. 68).
The most common textiles for fibre composites are woven fabrics, non-crimp fabrics, complex mats, braids, chopped strand mats and fleeces. However, the textile structure is only required for the processing because afterwards the fibres are sufficiently fixed in place by the polymer. Chopped strand mats lose their bonding strength upon contact with the polymer and therefore the individual pieces of fibre can be better adapted to the final form of the component (Fig. C 1.11, p. 72). In the case of woven fabrics, the undulation of the fibres has a negative effect on the strength properties of the finished component. For this reason, non-crimp fabrics made from layered, non-undulating fibre plies are being increasingly used as the reinforcement in fibre-reinforced polymers (Fig. C 1.10, p. 72). When using pultrusion, a method of manufacture that is frequently employed, the fibre reinforcement does not consist of textiles, but rather mostly of parallel bundles of fibres (rovings). However, additional textiles are laid over the entire surface in this case.

C 1.4 Drapeability of woven fabrics:
a Plain weave
b Twill weave
c Satin weave
C 1.5 Various textiles (undulations of threads in warp and weft directions omitted for clarity):
a Plain weave
b Twill weave
c Satin weave
d Non-crimp fabric, with sewing threads
e Braid
C 1.6 Plain weave
C 1.7 Twill weave
C 1.8 Satin weave
C 1.9 Non-crimp fabric

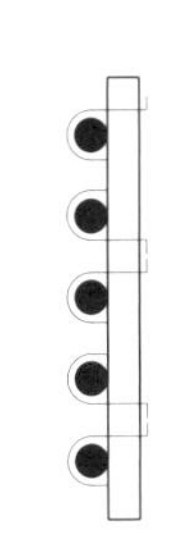

d

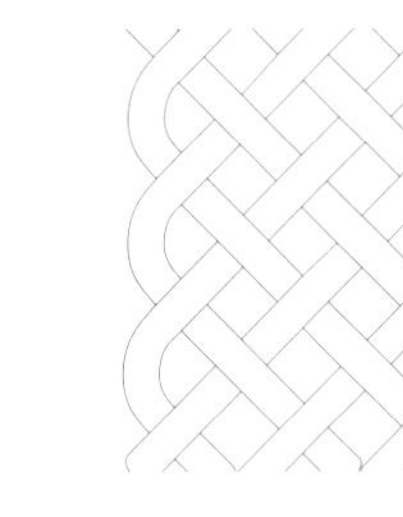

e

C 1.5

C 1.6

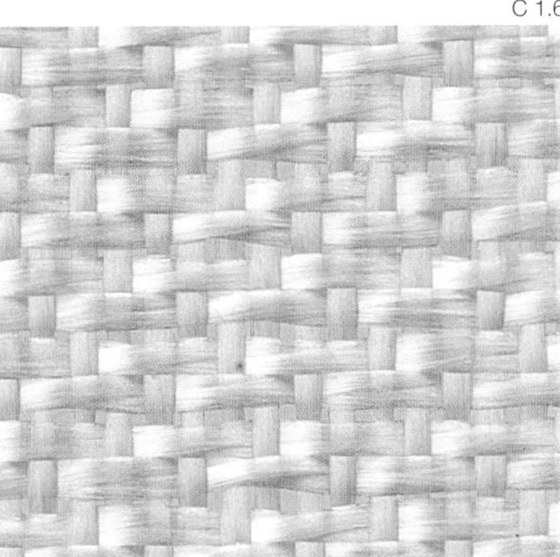

C 1.7

C 1.8

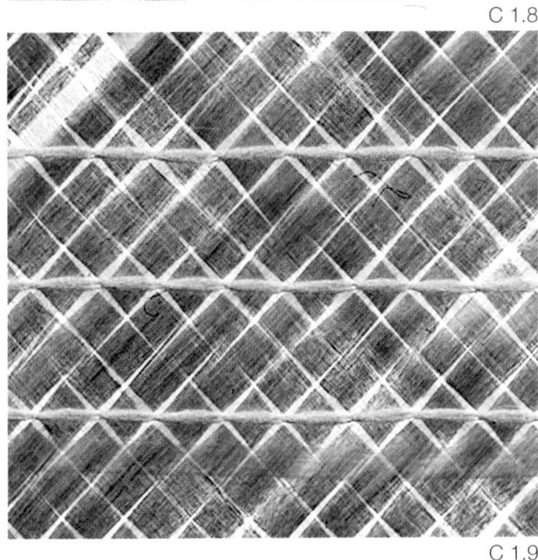

C 1.9

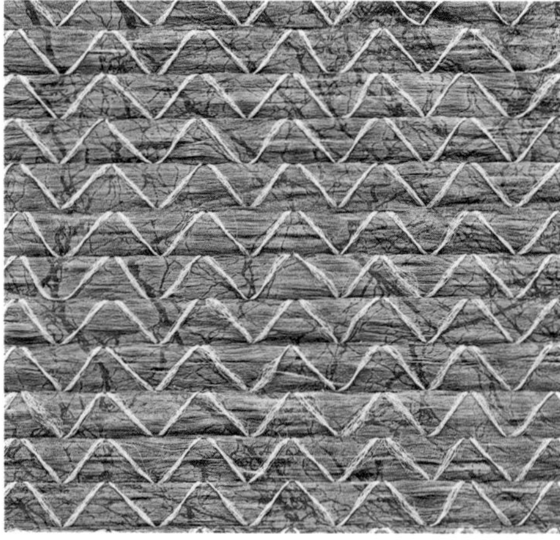

C 1.10

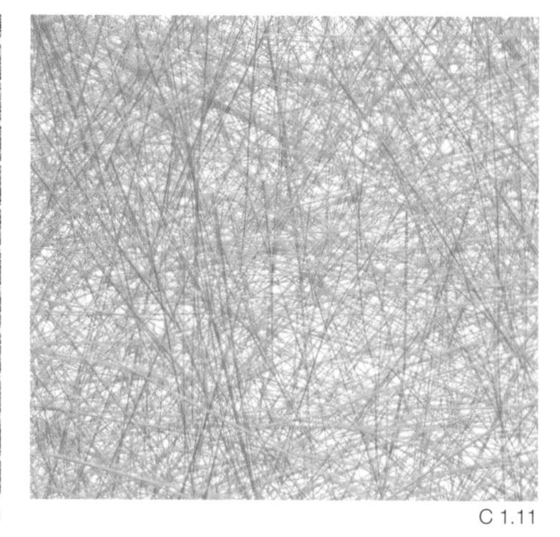

C 1.11

C 1.10 Non-crimp fabric made from carbon fibres
C 1.11 Chopped strand mat
C 1.12 Systematic classification of core materials
C 1.13 Construction of a sandwich panel
C 1.14 Scanning electron microscope images of foam cells
a Open cells
b Closed cells
C 1.15 Forms of supply and applications for polymer foams

Core materials

Core materials are lightweight materials that are used for composite components (e.g. translucent thermal insulation) but primarily for sandwich elements. These consist of a comparatively thick but lightweight core, loadbearing facing plies and intermediate plies, usually adhesives, that can transfer the loads (Fig. C 1.13). The core transfers the shear between the facing plies and at the same time can function as thermal insulation. The lower self-weight of sandwich elements enables economic forms of construction and longer spans than are possible with solid components.
In the following, it is the cores of sandwich elements made from fibre-reinforced polymers that are discussed in detail. These elements consist of textiles as facing plies which are impregnated with a liquid polymer (resin) and laminated layer by layer onto the core. In this case additional, intermediate plies (e.g. of adhesive) are unnecessary. The production methods used result in maximum laminate thicknesses for facing plies made from fibre-reinforced polymers, which limits the spans that can be achieved with solid panels. In this respect, sandwich elements can achieve significant improvements in the loadcarrying capacity (see "Sandwich elements", p. 177 and "Details for sandwich elements", pp. 182–184).
Sandwich elements made from polymer foams generally exhibit the best building physics and mechanical properties. They are preferred by architects when the sandwich element does not have to be translucent. Three-dimensional modelling of polymer foams is possible, but expensive. Hollow structures with honeycomb cores are usually more economical, but have poorer thermal insulation properties and are more difficult to work. The poor drapeability is another disadvantage and the forming possibilities for three-dimensional honeycomb cores are limited. However, combined with transparent facing plies, light-permeable components are possible. Balsa wood is another material used for cores in addition to foams and honeycomb structures, and fleeces and spacer fabrics are employed for thin sandwich layers. Fig. C 1.12 provides an overview of various core materials. Sandwich elements require local reinforcement with steel, aluminium or polymer sections in order to carry loads at supports or connections because the core materials usually have only relatively low strengths. Designing sandwich structures in the best way for the respective materials is explained in the chapter entitled "Building with free-form polymers" (pp. 174–187).
Sandwich elements, like other composite components, cannot be easily recycled because, once joined, it is often difficult if not impossible to separate the core from the facing plies.

Foams

On the microscopic level, foams either have interconnected open cells (Fig. C 1.14a) or closed cells with continuous, enclosing walls (Fig. C 1.14b), depending on the raw material and the method of production. There are also hybrid forms that have open-cell conglomerates of closed-cell foam particles, so-called particle foams. The pore content of integral skin foams, on the other hand, varies within the component, usually decreasing towards the outside where it forms a closed surface that can be used as the facing plies of an integrated sandwich panel. This also protects the hollow structure against the infiltration of fluids.
Foams can be made from diverse materials. For reasons of cost and better workability, most foams used in architecture are made from polymers. However, metal, ceramic or glass foams can be used where service temperatures must comply with certain requirements.

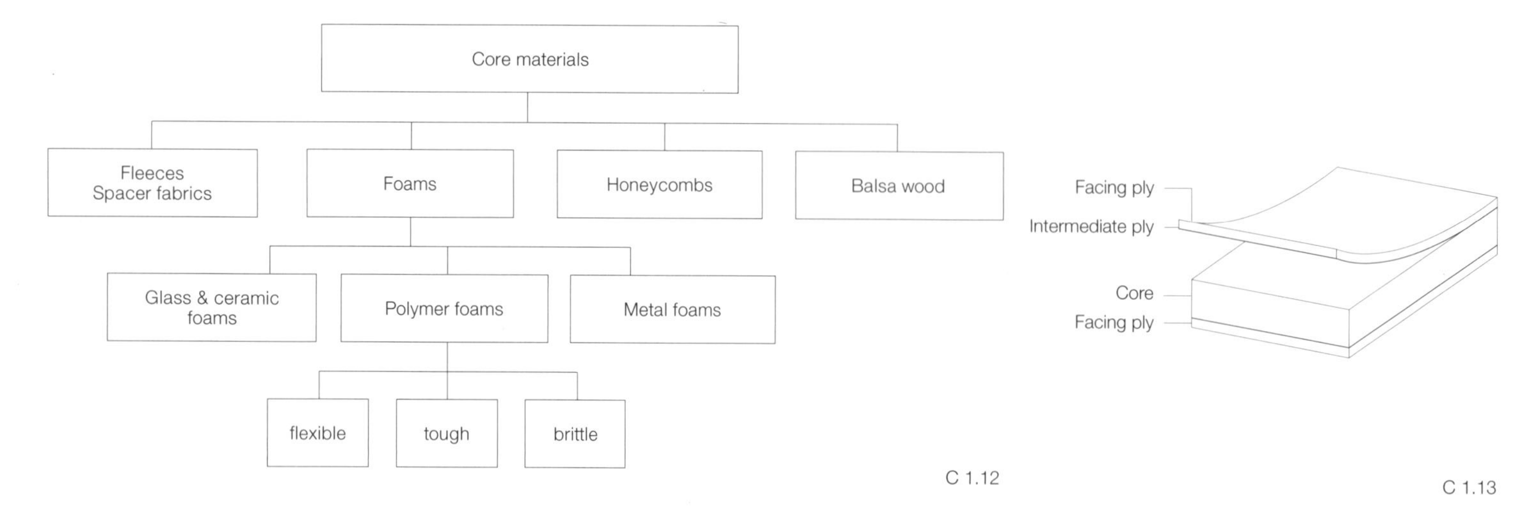

C 1.12

C 1.13

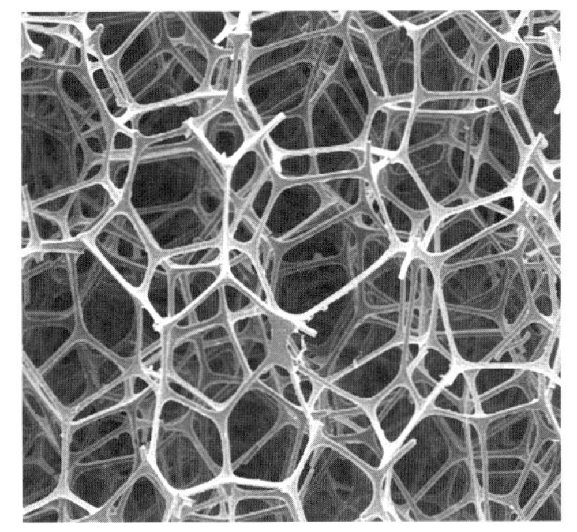

a

b

C 1.14

Polymer foams

We generally distinguish between flexible, tough, and brittle polymer foams. All types can be used for insulating layers, but only tough foams are worth considering as the cores of loadbearing sandwich elements. Flexible foams are too unstable for sandwich components and brittle foams are too sensitive to damage to be suitable as structural components. The choice of a suitable foam is frequently based on a compromise between strength, thermal performance and cost.

Open- or closed-cell foams have different properties which give them different advantages depending on the particular application. For instance, closed-cell systems should be preferred for the cores of fibre-reinforced polymers because they do not absorb the liquid resin during the processing. Foam made from tough PVC-U is particularly suitable for this. On the other hand, open-cell systems are necessary for vacuum insulation panels because the air has to be evacuated from the hollow pores (see "Vacuum insulated systems", pp. 111–112). When exposed to the weather or contact with stationary water, integral skin foams or closed-cell systems are beneficial. Figs. C 1.15 and C 1.16 (p. 74) provide an overview of the properties, forms of supply and applications for foams.

Production

Foams can be made from virtually all polymers. The foam structure is achieved with a blowing agent that is mixed into the polymer and, upon the application of heat, forms gases, or separates these out, at a defined temperature. Only in special cases is air mixed in mechanically. Physical blowing agents expand upon reaching the boiling point of a gas (e.g. carbon dioxide) and it is this increase in volume that forms the cells or pores. Relatively low processing temperatures are adequate for physical blowing agents; the foam produced is light in weight with a very regular structure. Chemical blowing agents, on the other hand, require higher temperatures. They rely on reaction processes to separate out the gases and produce denser foams. Chemical blowing agents are used for integral skin foams.

Polymer	Class	Density [kg/m³]	Form of supply	Cells	Applications
PE	flexible	25–40	Sheets, blocks, moulded items	closed	Cushioning, packaging (particle foam)
PE-LD	flexible	10–35	Sheets	closed	Thermal & impact sound insulation
	flexible	200	Structured foam boards	closed	Impact sound insulation
PP	flexible	10–35	Sheets		Thermal & impact sound insulation
	flexible	20–90	Moulded items, sheets		Energy absorbers in cars (bumpers, seats, roof lining – textile-covered), filling foam behind facing plies, in-mould skinning
	flexible	100–500	Foils, suitable for deep-drawing	closed	Meat packaging, meal trays, cutlery, bungs
	flexible	500–700	Structured foam foils & tapes		Packaging tapes, insulating foils
EVAC-X	flexible	40–260	Coiled	closed	Insulated clothing, rubber-like
PS	tough	10–30	Blocks, moulded items		Thermal insulation, packaging (particle foam)
	tough	>20	Extruded sheets & tapes with/without skin	closed	Frost protection for pipes, roads & railways
	tough	60–200		closed	Cardboard packaging, paper coating
	tough	60–200	Hot-formed foils		Egg-boxes, meal trays, disposable cutlery
	tough	approx. 60	Sheets, milled (felted)		Impact sound insulation
	tough		Sheets	closed	Road sub-bases (for increasing load-carrying capacity)
	tough	400–500	Sheets, sections	closed	Interior fitting-out with surface texture, decorative panels
	tough	20–25	Moulded items (lost foam), also PS/PMMA copolymer		Models for lost-foam casting, e.g. lightweight metal cylinders, casting foam technology
PS/PP-E	flexible/tough		Sheets, moulded items		As for PS but better thermal stability, car linings, lightweight cycle helmets
PVC-U	tough	40–130	Panels & blocks	closed	Core material for sandwich panels, liquid gas insulation, life-rafts, etc.
	tough	500–700	Extruded sheets, suit. for hot-forming, d = 2–20 mm		Building material, linings & cladding
PVC-P	flexible	50–150	Panels & blocks	closed	Exercise mats, attenuation of machine vibration
	flexible	70–130	Panels & blocks	open	Sound insulation, gas-permeable foam cores
	flexible	250	Rolls		Backing to floor coverings
MF	flexible	approx. 10	Sheets	open	Sound absorbers, heat shields, decorative panels, preformed insulation for pipes & vessels
PMI	tough	30–300	Panels, d = 1.65 mm	closed	Structural components in aircraft construction, core material for sandwich panels
UP	brittle		Lightweight elements	hybrid	Reactive resin foamed concrete
PUR	flexible/tough	30–300	Blocks, sheets, moulded items	hybrid	Furniture, mattresses, vehicle interiors, preformed insulation
PF	brittle	40–100	Sheets		Insulating material

C 1.15

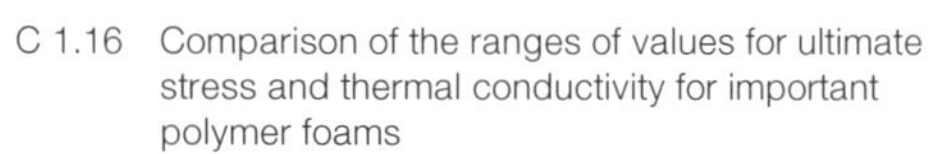

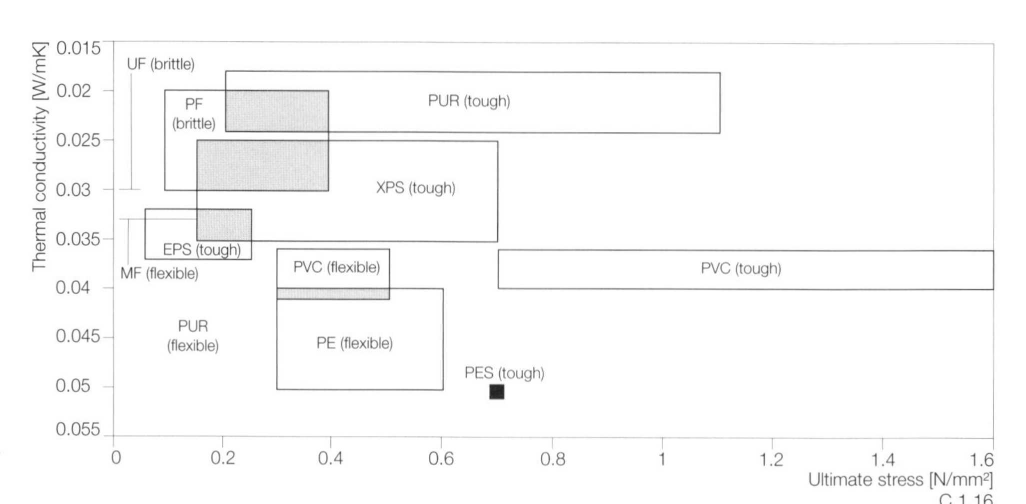

C 1.16

C 1.16 Comparison of the ranges of values for ultimate stress and thermal conductivity for important polymer foams
C 1.17 Aramid honeycomb core
C 1.18 Structured core fleece
C 1.19 Non-structured core fleece
C 1.20 Spacer fabric prior to impregnation with polymer
C 1.21 Balsa wood

Foam boards are produced continuously in slabstock plants. For sandwich panels, it is also quite common to foam up the core directly between the rigid facing plies. In discontinuous methods, the blowing agent is sprayed onto the mould beforehand.
Integral skin foams are produced using a pressurised method with very careful control of the mould temperature. This causes the pores to collapse thus increasing the density at the boundaries of the material. Integral skin foam components must be given their final form during the production, reworking is impossible. Thermosets are the most suitable polymers for producing integral skin foams.
Alternatively, a non-pressurised two-coat method can be used to apply a polymer without a blowing agent to the boundary zone first of all, followed by a polymer containing a blowing agent.

Gases that harm the climate
Chlorofluorocarbons (CFC) were frequently used as physical blowing agents in the past but are now banned because of the damage they cause to the ozone layer. Chemical blowing agents release water vapour, nitrogen, carbon monoxide or ammonia. These gases also harm the climate, albeit to a lesser degree than CFCs. Just like with floor coverings (see "Floor finishes and road surfacing", p. 58), when these foams are used in interiors there is always a health risk because of the gases that are emitted over time.

Polystyrene foams (EPS, XPS)
Polystyrene foams are tough and exhibit relatively good thermal insulation properties, but have a rather low load-carrying capacity. The common particle foam made from expanded polystyrene (EPS) is given a white colour. It is primarily used for insulation applications where there can be no direct contact with water. By contrast, extruded polystyrene foams (XPS) have a finer pore structure and are supplied in various colours depending on the particular manufacturer (green, pink, blue). XPS is heavier than EPS and waterproof because of its closed-cell structure. The mechanical values of XPS are higher than those of EPS, but the insulating values and the specific heat capacity of EPS are marginally better. Both types of foam have benefits depending on the mechanical and geometrical specifications. And both types of foam can also be used as the core in a sandwich component made from fibre-reinforced polymer. Although their mechanical values are relatively low, they are very cheap.

Polyurethane foams (PUR)
Polyurethane can be used as the raw material for foams with very diverse properties. Both soft elastomeric foams and also tough rigid foams with excellent loadbearing properties can be produced. PUR foams exhibit good adhesive properties and adhere to facing plies or surface finishes when they are foamed directly against these, without any need for further materials. They also have very good thermal insulation properties. When embedded in fibre-reinforced polymers, rigid PUR foam boards tend to absorb resin. But as polyurethane represents a good compromise between strength and economy, it is widely used for mould-making and as a sandwich material. It is easy to shape with CNC milling machines.
Elastic PUR foam is commonly used in the building industry for retrofitted seals with a good thermal performance, e.g. around windows, but it cannot perform a loadbearing function.

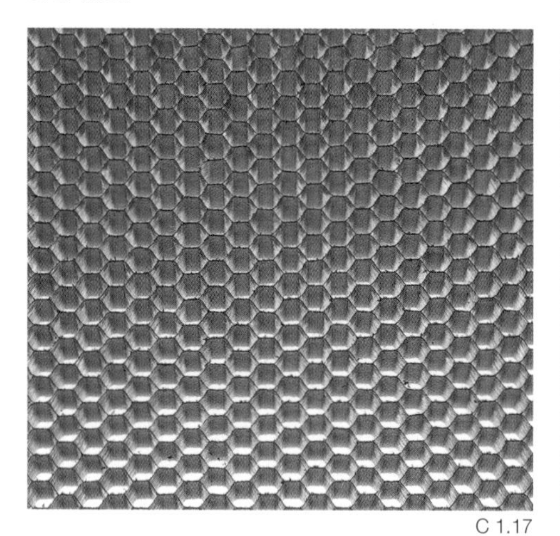
C 1.17

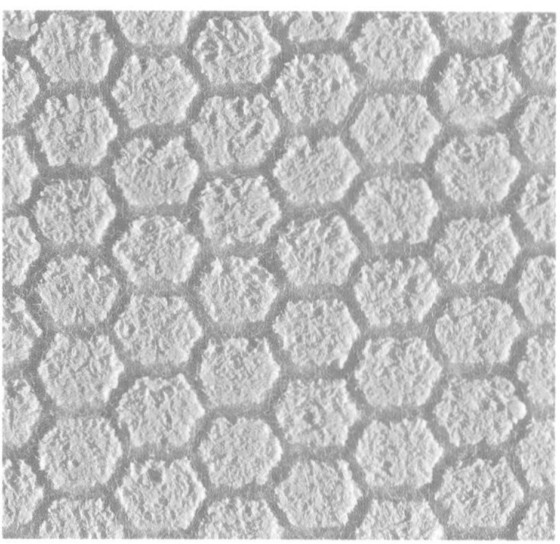
C 1.18

C 1.19

Polyvinyl chloride foams (PVC)
PVC foams can also be produced in flexible or tough versions. The mechanical properties of rigid PVC foam are better than those of the other polymer foams. As PVC foam absorbs hardly any resin, it is ideal for use as a core material in fibre-reinforced polymer products. The high production costs, however, mean that PVC foam is used as a core only where high demands are placed on the load-carrying capacity. Its thermal insulation properties are poorer than those of PUR foams.

Honeycomb cores
Sandwich elements with honeycomb cores are particularly light in weight and are frequently less expensive than foams. Honeycomb cores are used for fibre-reinforced polymers and also for translucent thermal insulation. Very high load-carrying capacities are possible depending on the particular system. The air-filled voids of honeycomb cores are much larger than those of foams and so they cannot be used as thermal insulation.
Aluminium, aramid paper impregnated with phenolic resin, thermoplastics such as PP or PET, or glass fibre-reinforced polymers are among the materials suitable for creating the honeycomb structures. The facing plies are bonded or laminated directly to the honeycomb core to produce a sandwich element. In some cases the honeycomb is produced with a fleece covering to simplify the attachment of the facing plies. The drapeability of honeycomb cores is limited, which is why they are primarily used for flat or only gently curved sandwich panels. They are normally produced in thicknesses of between 1.5 and 90 mm.

Aramid honeycomb cores
Honeycomb cores made from aramid paper are currently very popular for boats and light aircraft (Fig. C 1.17). This core material is especially flexible and relatively inexpensive. The aramid honeycombs are supplied as sheets measuring approx. 1.20 × 2.40 m and with thicknesses starting at 1.5 mm. The standard type is hexagonal in section, but oval structures with improved drapeability are also available. The facing plies are frequently made from polymers reinforced with glass or carbon fibres and are laminated directly over the honeycomb core. The resin in the fibre-reinforced polymer bonds the facing plies to the aramid core, consequently a sufficiently generous amount of resin should be allowed for in the design.

Thermoplastic capillary honeycomb cores
Honeycombs made from thermoplastics such as PP or PET generally have a circular cross-section. They are both elastic and impact-resistant and are therefore highly suitable for absorbing shocks or reducing vibration. Thermoplastic facing plies can be attached directly to the honeycomb by hot-plate welding (e.g. for translucent thermal insulation). With facing plies made from fibre-reinforced polymers, aluminium or glass, a layer of fleece is first applied to the capillary structure to improve the bond.

Core fleeces and spacer fabrics
Prefabricated cores and spacer fabrics can be used for producing thinner sandwich panels with thicknesses ranging from a few millimetres to a few centimetres. Such cores are inexpensive and require little effort to integrate them into sandwich structures. Strength and transparency vary considerably depending on the particular system.

Spacer fabrics
Spacer fabrics (Fig. C 1.20) are made from two facing plies of a glass-fibre cloth linked by perpendicular threads. During lamination, the spacer fabric is impregnated with resin and pressed together. Afterwards, the threads re-erect themselves automatically to create a sandwich-type laminate between 3 and 23 mm thick with improved flexural stiffness. In the final condition, the layers of cloth fully impregnated with resin function as loadbearing facing plies, whereas the intermediate layer, only partially impregnated with resin, serves as the core of the sandwich element. Special resin formulations have to be used in order to prevent an accumulation of styrene in the core, which would have a negative effect on the curing of the polymer. Owing to the exclusive use of glass fibres and the thin facing plies, it is possible to produce laminates with a good degree of transparency.

Core fleeces
Perforated fleece materials made from polyester fibres and hollow microspheres are used for producing especially thin sandwich structures up to a thickness of about 6 mm (Figs. C 1.18 and C 1.19). During laminating, the perforations are filled with the resin, which creates a good bond with the facing plies. Laminates with core fleeces split less easily than sandwich components with a foam core. The use of hollow microspheres means that not the whole of the fleece is impregnated, which reduces the overall weight of the component.

Balsa wood
Balsa wood (Fig. C 1.21) has a density between 100 and 200 kg/m^3 and therefore lies in the middle of the range of rigid foam products. Its sensitivity to moisture can be a problem in some applications because it swells and rots. The mechanical properties of balsa wood lie below those of rigid foams and so the latter are usually preferred as core materials where a certain load-carrying capacity must be achieved. However, balsa wood is still indispensable in modelmaking because of its low cost and easy workability.

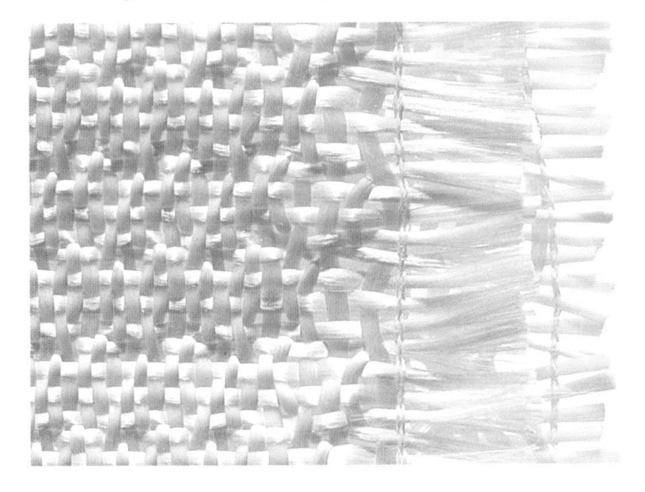
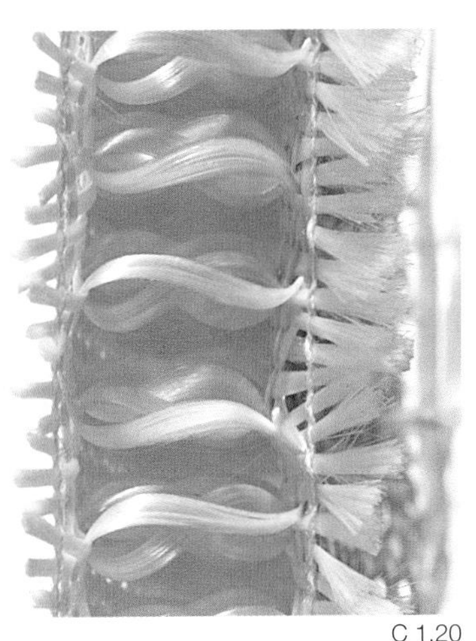
C 1.20

C 1.21

Fibre-reinforced polymers

C 2.1

Fibre-reinforced polymers play an important role in architectural applications because in contrast to unreinforced polymers they can be used to produce large-format components and longer spans. Semi-finished products (see "Semi-finished polymer products", pp. 82–93) and free-form designs are therefore possible (see "Building with free-form polymers", pp. 174–187). These composites consist of various fibre materials and polymers. In some cases the polymer is in the form of facing plies on either side of a core material.
The customary abbreviations or designations used are as follows:

- Glass fibre-reinforced polymer (GFRP)
- Carbon fibre-reinforced polymer (CFRP)
- Laminate – layered composite made from fibres and polymer
- Resin – thermoset prior to curing (also reactive or casting resin)
- Matrix – shaping and bonding substance (resin or polymer) in the final state

Constituents

The optical and mechanical properties of fibre-reinforced polymers are determined by the interaction of their constituents. The fibres increase the load-carrying capacity and stiffness of the polymer and hence are essentially responsible for those properties in the finished composite material. The polymer, on the other hand, does not perform any loadbearing functions as such, but rather stabilises and protects the fibres.

Polymers

The polymer matrix defines the shape of the composite component and protects the fibres against UV radiation and aggressive media such as moisture or chemicals. At the same time, the polymer forms the surface and therefore determines the degree of transparency, the colour and feel of the fibre composite. Normally, the semi-finished products are not coated again after production. As with all synthetic materials, various additives and fillers are added to the fibre composite material to control or adjust the properties of the final material. For example, flame retardants are added to comply with fire protection requirements, and in pultruded semi-finished products in particular, mineral fillers are needed to reduce shrinkage processes (see "Fillers and additives", pp. 32 – 34).

Conventional resin systems

Thermosets are used almost without exception for fibre composite components. The low viscosity of the resin prior to the curing reaction ensures that the surfaces of the fibres are well wetted. Moreover, thermosets are more resistant to environmental influences than thermoplastics. Unsaturated polyester resin (UP), epoxy resin (EP), vinyl ester resin (VE) and phenolic resin (PF) are in widespread use in the building industry (see "Thermosets", pp. 46–47). UP is

a

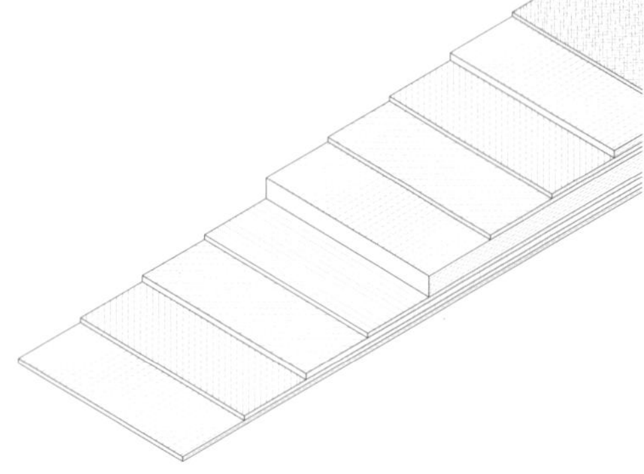

b

C 2.2

C 2.1 Factory production of fibre-reinforced polymers (pultrusion)
C 2.2 Example of fibre plies in a pultruded section
a Test specimen (polymer matrix burned off)
b Schematic view
C 2.3 Properties of various fibre composites (guidance values)

Material	Specification		Density [kg/dm³]	Tensile strength, longitudinal [N/mm²]	Elastic modulus, longitudinal [N/mm²]	Tensile strength, transverse [N/mm²]	Elastic modulus, transverse [N/mm²]	Coefficient of thermal expansion [10⁻⁶/K]	Thermal conductivity [W/mK]
Glass fibre-reinforced polymers (GFRP)	Pultruded laminate	GFRP-P E23	1.8	240	23000	50	7000	9.0/30.0[1]	
	Chopped fibres laminate	GFRP-M	1.5	80	7000	80	7000	30.0	0.25
	Hybrid laminate	GFRP-MW	1.6	120	12000	120	12000	25.0	
	Wrapped laminate	GFRP-FM/FMU	1.6	160	15000	50	8000	15.0/30.0[1]	
Carbon fibre-reinforced polymers[3] (CFRP)	High tenacity	CFRP-HT	1.6	2800	165000	0	–		
	Intermediate modulus	CFRP-IM	1.6	2800	210000	0	–	0.2[2]	17.0
	High modulus	CFRP-HM	1.6	1350	300000	0	–		

[1] Parallel with/perpendicular to direction of fibres
[2] Parallel with direction of fibres
[3] Fibres aligned exclusively in longitudinal direction of component = unidirectional

Chopped fibres laminate: planar laminate with reinforcement exclusively in the form of chopped fibres
Hybrid laminate: planar laminate with chopped fibres reinforcement and non-crimp or woven fabrics
Wrapped laminate: planar laminate with characteristic dominant direction

C 2.3

suitable for all standard applications and especially for glass fibre-reinforced polymers, EP for high-strength components and for carbon fibre-reinforced polymers, VE where high resistance to chemicals is required, and PF for demanding fire protection requirements. A ceramic matrix can also be used, but this results in a comparatively low strength.

Fibres

Which particular method of processing the fibres is suitable for the production of which particular semi-finished product depends on the method of manufacture and the mechanical properties required.

Long fibres

Long fibres (rovings or continuous fibres) are bundles of fibres that have not undergone any further treatment. They provide linear reinforcement with a high fibre content and ensure a composite with good mechanical properties. Long fibres are primarily used for machine-based production methods such as pultruding, wrapping or braiding. For manual methods, long fibres are too awkward to handle, which is why textiles are preferred.

Short fibres

Short fibres (discontinuous fibres) lie in random directions in the polymer. However, to improve handling, short fibres are frequently processed in the form of chopped strand mats (see "Chopped strand mats and fleeces", p. 70). The temporary fixing of the fibres (sizing) is broken down upon contact with the liquid resin, which allows the fibres to adapt to the shape of the component. Fleeces are very fine fibre mats made from short fibres which are specified for the surfaces of laminates. It is also possible to mix short fibres directly into the liquid resin to produce a moulding compound for compression- or injection-moulding methods. Chopped strand mats and fleeces are found in all planar fibre composite components.

Textiles

Textiles are arranged in plies, one above the other, in a composite to create a planar reinforcing material. The proportions of fibres used and hence the mechanical properties that can be achieved are lower than those of materials with long-fibre reinforcement. Besides the traditional woven fabrics, it is also possible to use non-crimp fabrics, in which the fibres are not woven together but simply laid on top of each other. The fibres in non-crimp fabrics do not undulate and this enables composite components with higher strengths. Complex mats contain additional short fibres laid on the surface of a non-crimp fabrics. The chapter entitled "Primary products" (pp. 68–75) contains an overview of the textiles available. Textile reinforcing products are easier to handle in manual methods of manufacture and are used where fibres need to be aligned in several directions.

Common fibres in the building industry

The building industry tends to prefer glass fibres because of their high strength and relatively low price. The expensive carbon fibres are used less often although they achieve much better mechanical properties than GFRP. Aramid fibre-reinforced polymers are less common in architectural applications because their toughness makes them difficult to process and causes considerable tool wear. Natural fibres have so far not exhibited the moisture resistance necessary for components exposed to the weather. Therefore, only the properties of GFRP and CFRP are described and compared in this chapter.

Properties of fibre-reinforced polymers

Although machine-made GFRP components can achieve the strength of structural steel, their elastic modulus is at best only one-tenth that of steel. This is why it is not easy to achieve long spans. CFRP, on the other hand, has a similar elastic modulus to that of steel and at the same time a much higher strength (Fig. C 2.3).

Interaction between fibres and matrix

The strength of the composite component depends on the interaction between the fibres and the polymer matrix. A fracture in a laminate is generally caused by cracks in the matrix, which are in turn caused by the maximum admissible strain in the polymer being exceeded. Using a polymer with a high maximum permissible strain therefore increases the strength of the entire composite component.
The adhesion between the fibres and the polymer is also crucial for the load-carrying capacity of the component. Flaws reduce the adhesion between the fibres and the matrix and this means the strength is always lower than that of the unreinforced polymer. Subjected to shear or lateral tension (e.g. in adhesive joints), the individual plies can become detached from each other (delamination). Recently, however, attempts have been made to improve the adhesion of the matrix by adding carbon nano tubes (see "Carbon nano tubes", p. 34).

Arrangement of fibres

Components loaded primarily in the longitudinal direction require mainly long fibres (rovings) so that all the fibres are aligned in one direction – unidirectional (UD) fibre reinforcement. However, GFRP sections can also be reinforced by textiles positioned in the boundary zones, which increases the shear capacity, the bearing capacity of bolted and screwed connections and the shear strength of adhesive joints. In the form of thin strips such as CFRP laminates, on the other hand, exclusively unidirectional reinforcement is generally sufficient because the reinforcement is not loaded in the transverse direction. The strength perpendicular to the laminate is low because carbon fibres exhibit poor strength when subjected to lateral compression.

Fibre lay-up

The fibres in the composite component are usually arranged in several layers with alternating fibre orientations; Fig. C 2.2b shows the fibre geometry of a pultruded section by way of an example, and Fig. C 2.2a the remainder of a test specimen from which the surrounding polymer has been burned away in order to reveal a total of 13 individual plies. The middle, solid ply of unidirectional rovings is in this case comparatively thick, and bonded between several textiles with different fibre alignments. Whereas the function of the central rovings is primarily load-bearing, the outer textiles improve the shear

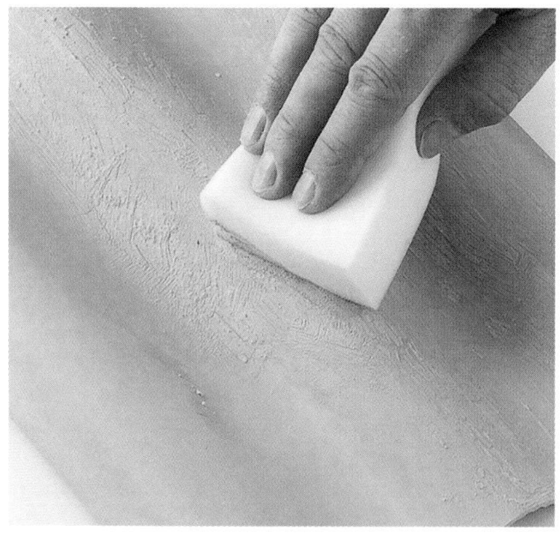
a

b

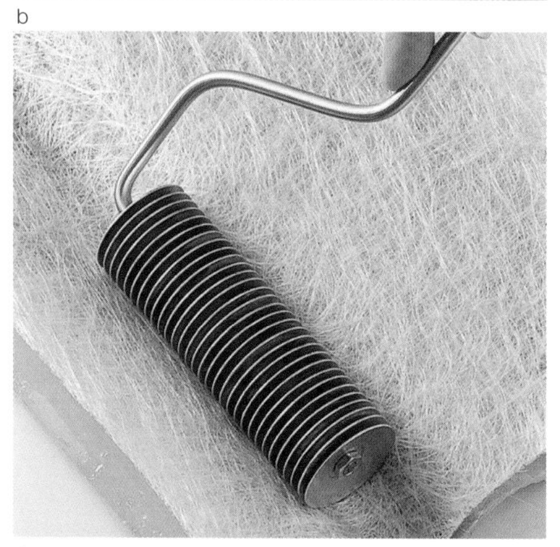
c

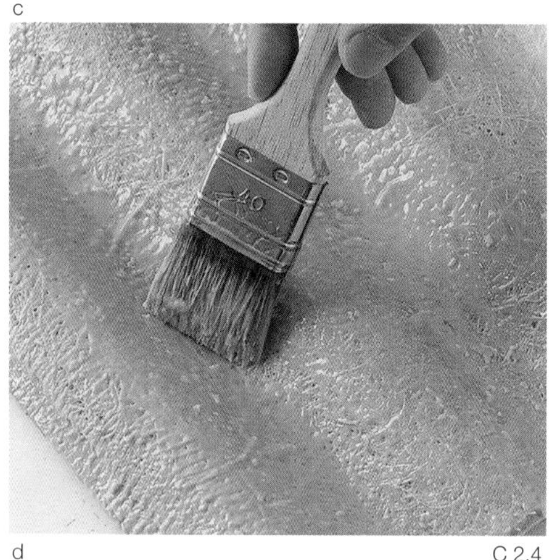
d C 2.4

capacity and the bearing capacity of bolted and screwed connections. The outermost ply is a fine layer of fleece which ensures a smooth surface. The plies are not assembled one by one during production, but rather prefabricated in the form of non-crimp fabric or complex mats (see "Non-crimp fabrics", p. 70).

Reaction to fire and high temperatures
It is the type of resin used and the additives that determine the service temperatures of fibre composites and how they react to fire. Basically, the fibre composites commonly used in the building industry are flammable (class B2 to DIN 4102-1). If a component must comply with class B1 (not readily flammable), then phenolic resin (PF) will have to be used or an unsaturated polyester resin (UP) filled with a flame retardant. Under certain conditions it is even possible to achieve class A2 (incombustible component containing combustible materials) when a ceramic matrix is used. It should be noted that a "filled" polyester resin makes the processing more difficult and permits the addition of only a small quantity of fibres. Epoxy resin (EP) is unsuitable where a certain fire resistance is important.

Surface finish
The surface finish of a fibre-reinforced polymer is of course critical for the appearance of the semi-finished product, but also for its durability. There should be no fibres on the surface because these can absorb water and hence corrode. A layer of pure resin must therefore be applied to protect the loadbearing laminate. In hand lay-up this is the so-called gelcoat, which is applied to the mould as the first non-fibre ply or sprayed onto the finished component afterwards. In the case of pultruded or compression-moulded components, a fine fleece is attached, which protects the inner fibrous plies against media such as water, chemicals or UV radiation.
Blisters can form directly below the gelcoat if water is able to infiltrate into the laminate via small cracks. Such damage should be repaired by removing all unsound surface material and reapplying the gelcoat. Impacts or excessive loads on the component can cause such damage.

Processing
Standard woodworking machinery can be used to process GFRP and CFRP semi-finished products. However, hardened saw blades and drills, e.g. diamond-tipped, should be preferred because otherwise the tools wear too quickly. The best results are achieved with water jet cutting. Although the dust from machining operations is not dangerous, it can irritate the skin, which is why the use of dust extraction or water sprays (to bind the dust) is recommended (see "Health and safety advice", p. 157). The thermosets normally used cannot be welded; jointing is in most cases by way of bolts, screws or adhesives (see "Means of connections", pp. 161–164).

Recycling
Generally, composite materials cannot be recycled because full and proper reuse means separating the components. Furthermore, thermosets are generally used for GFRP and CFRP and these cannot be melted down again, so it is impossible to separate the constituents. The only alternatives are downcycling to a low-grade filling material, or incineration for energy generation (see "Reuse", pp. 130–131).

Production

Various methods can be used for producing GFRP and CFRP semi-finished products depending on the cross-sectional geometry and the size of the batch. Manual laminating is good for small batches or one-offs, also large components and complicated geometries. The manual resin infusion or vacuum method was developed to optimise the quality of the laminate and the reproducibility. Automated and hence less expensive methods such as compression-moulding, pultruding, wrapping and braiding are suitable for large batches and smaller components.

Hand lay-up
Components with irregular shapes in small batches, but also elements that owing to their large dimensions cannot be produced with automated plant, can be made using the hand lay-up technique (Fig. C 2.5). A mould is required for shaping the component. Simple geometries can be achieved with sheet metal or wood, but more complex one-off items normally make use of moulds made from rigid polyurethane foam. However, the number of reuses of such foam moulds is low because the foam is often damaged during the first demoulding operation. Moulds made from fibre-reinforced polymers are better for large batches because they last much longer (see "Mouldmaking", pp. 184–187).
The surfaces of the mould are ground and coated with a release agent to ease demoulding. In a rigid foam mould, the release agent also prevents the resin being absorbed into the foam. If the foam is to remain in the component as a core material, then a release agent is undesirable because it prevents a good bond between the foam and the next ply of material. The first stage in laminating is applying the gelcoat, a coat of non-fibrous pure resin < 1 mm thick, to the mould (Fig. C 2.4a). Special resins are used for this which exhibit a good hardness and impact resistance and to which a thixotropic agent has been added to make the resin less runny. This top coat protects the surface of the laminate.
Afterwards, textiles or fleeces are added, impregnated with liquid resin and pressed down with a roller to ensure good contact with the layer below and to remove all air bubbles (Figs. C 2.4b and c). The first ply is usually a fine fleece to ensure a good surface finish.

Chopped strand mats are used without exception for components requiring only a low load-bearing capacity, whereas woven fabrics and, preferably, non-crimp fabrics are used for load-bearing components. This process is repeated until the desired laminate thickness is achieved. The face in contact with the mould has a smooth surface, the inside face is rough.

Production quality
It is difficult to achieve the specified fibre alignment exactly during the manual lamination of components with irregular shapes. The maximum fibre content that can be achieved is 45% by vol. because the diverse textiles cannot be fitted together more densely. This proportion drops when the resin has been thickened through the addition of a flame retardant. The quality of the components produced heavily depends on the skill of the persons carrying out the work. Various techniques can be employed to reduce the number of flaws and air bubbles and increase the density of the laminate. These involve curing the laminate under pressure generated in various ways. Hollow components, for example, are compacted with an internal pressure hose, a method that results in a very dense laminate with a high fibre content and generates only minimal tooling costs.
Excess resin and air inclusions are frequently removed by applying a vacuum, which of course improves the density of the final laminate. To do this, the laminate is covered by a porous release film and a breather or bleeder cloth and the whole enclosed in a vacuum bag sealed along the edges with a special tape.

Resin infusion and vacuum methods
The resin infusion (or induction) and vacuum methods are further developments of hand lay-up method designed to achieve a more consistent laminate structure, fewer air inclusions and a smooth surface on both sides (Fig. C 2.6). In contrast to hand lay-up, in this method the resin is not applied before, but rather after all the fibrous plies have been laid in position dry. Prior to applying the resin, the laminate is enclosed airtight in a porous release film and breather cloth.
In the resin infusion method, the air is evacuated at one point and at the same time resin is forced in under pressure on the opposite side. This method is also known as resin transfer moulding (RTM).
In the vacuum method, the resin is sucked into the cloth by the low pressure. This method is also known as vacuum-assisted resin transfer moulding (VARTM). It takes longer than the resin infusion method but achieves better results.
Curing in an autoclave, a heated pressure vessel in which the temperature and pressure cycles can be controlled exactly and reproducibly, results in products with a very high quality. Components are cured at pressures of 2–25 bar and temperatures of approx. 180°C. The hydrostatic pressure acting on all sides enables lightweight moulds to be used, even for com-

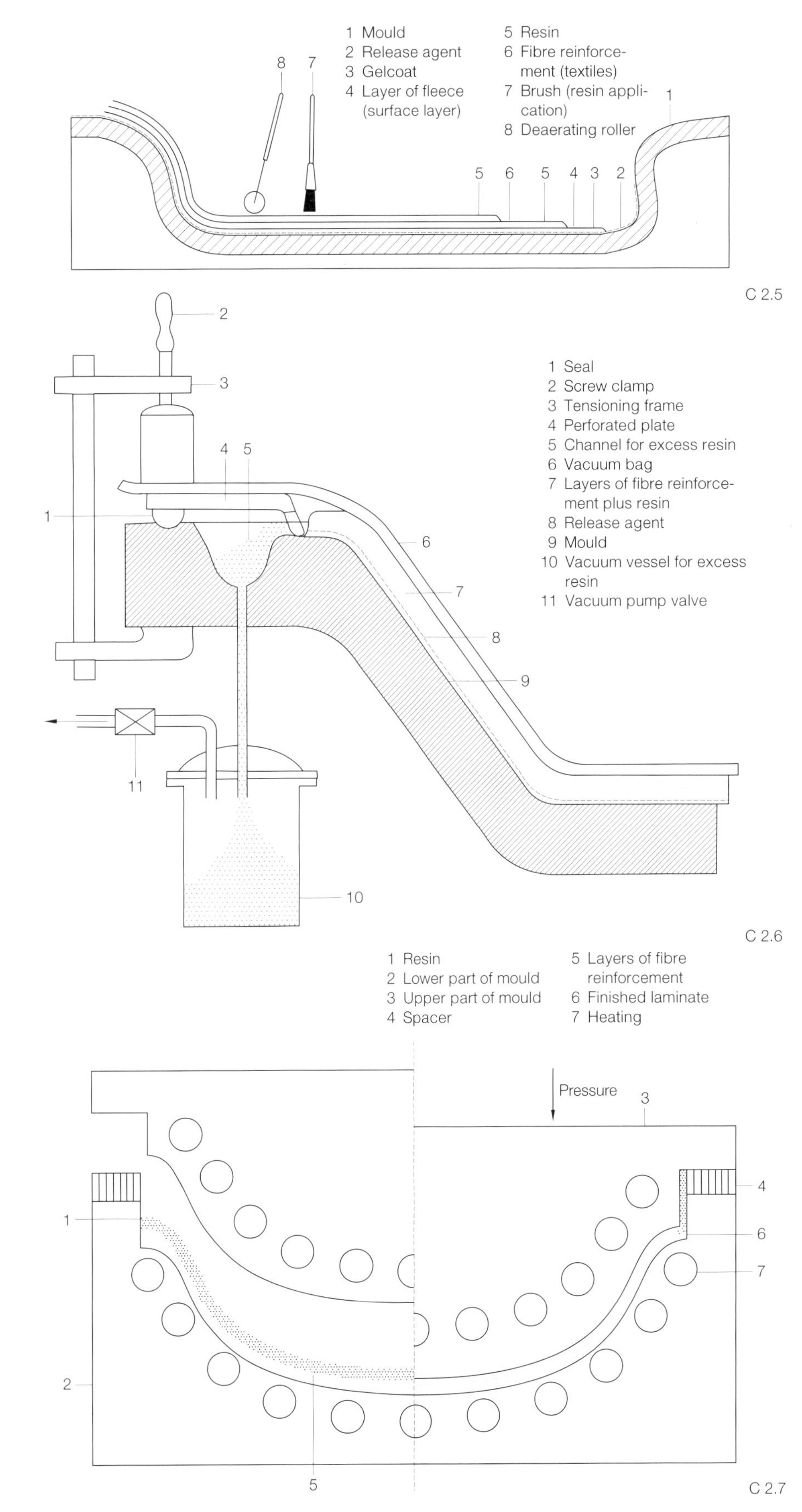

C 2.4 The steps in manual laminating
a Applying the release agent to the mould
b Applying the layer of pure resin (gelcoat), waiting until it hardens
c Laying the fibre reinforcement, pressing into place and eliminating air bubbles with a roller
d Applying the liquid resin and further fibre reinforcement layer by layer

C 2.5 Manual laminating
C 2.6 Resin infusion and vacuum methods
C 2.7 Compression- and transfer-moulding methods

plex and large structures. High-performance components for the aerospace industry are produced in autoclaves.

Compression- and transfer-moulding methods
The automated manufacture of moulded items made from fibre-reinforced polymers requires a relatively high initial investment in tools and moulds needed for the compression- and transfer-moulding methods that can be used (Fig. C 2.7, p. 79). Such methods are therefore primarily useful for the industrial manufacture of large series. The moulding typically takes place in a two-part metal mould, although moulds made from synthetic resin may be used for compression-moulding. The best fibre content that can be achieved is only approx. 50 % by vol. Components that must comply with more demanding specifications are produced by transfer-moulding with steel or aluminium moulds. Fibre contents of up to 65 % by vol. are possible with this method.

Pre-impregnated textiles
Both compression- and transfer-moulding techniques can be based on fluid as well as on prefabricated semi-finished products, so-called prepregs. Prepregs (short for pre-impregnated fibres) are reinforcing fibres already impregnated with resin which cure under high pressure at high temperature. The fibre impregnation process is therefore separate from that of the actual moulding process. The prepregs are prepared on machines to achieve a consistent wetting of the fibres with the resin, which is what enables a high-quality fibre composite to be produced. Prepregs reinforced with short fibres, so-called sheet moulding compounds (SMC), are semi-finished products used for the industrial production of large series. They are reinforced with glass fibres 25–50 mm long. UP resins are typically used, but occasionally VE for components that are to be subjected to higher loads. The resin compound and the fibres are packed between polymer carrier foils and further processed to form endless rolls of material. This leathery material is cut to size and moulded in two-part, heated steel moulds under high pressure (30–140 bar). The most important applications are large batches of control cabinets, hoods and covers, vehicle components (e.g. tailgates, oil sumps) and other moulded items. As such automated methods are economical only for large series, they have so far played no role in architectural applications.

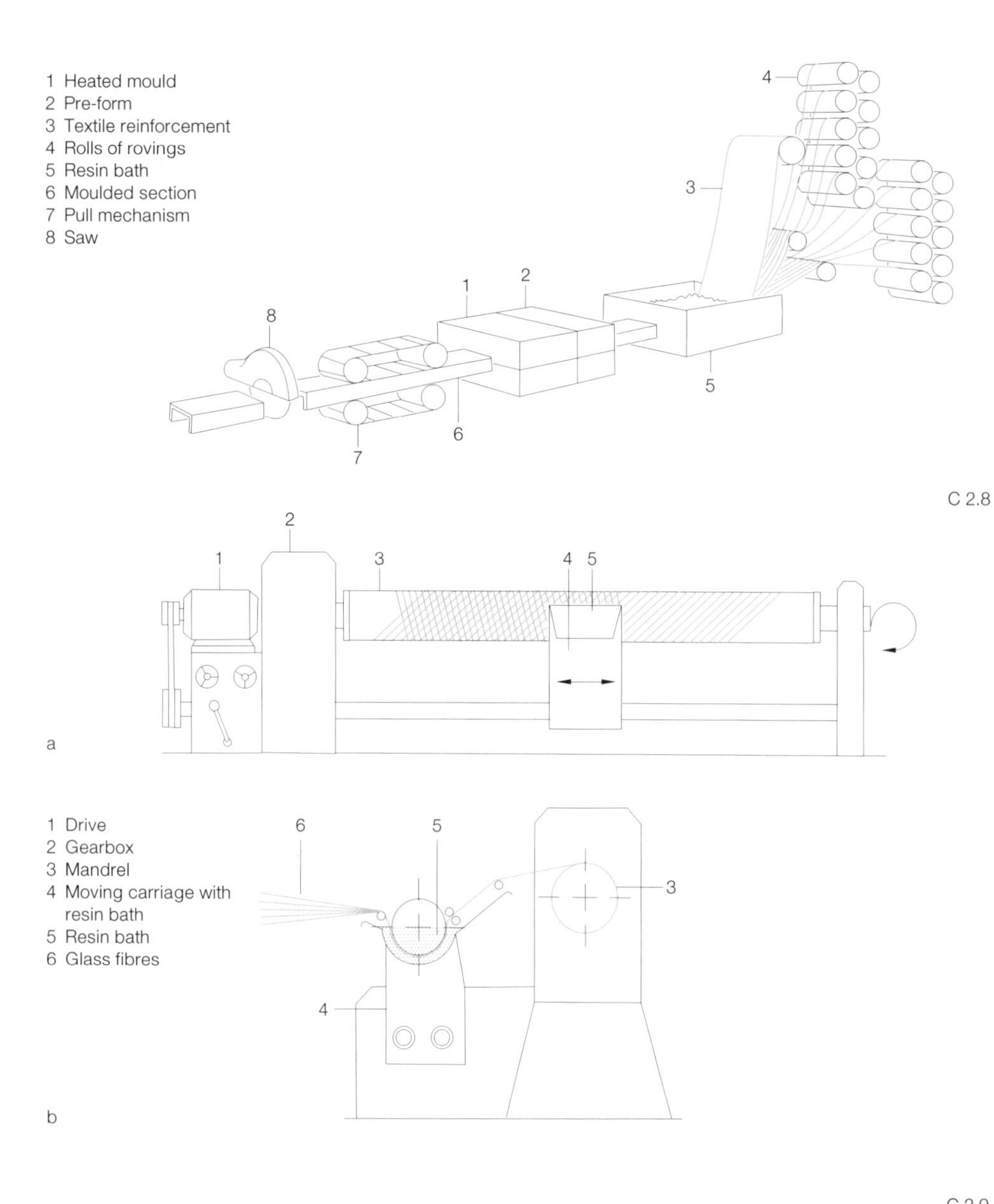

C 2.8

C 2.9

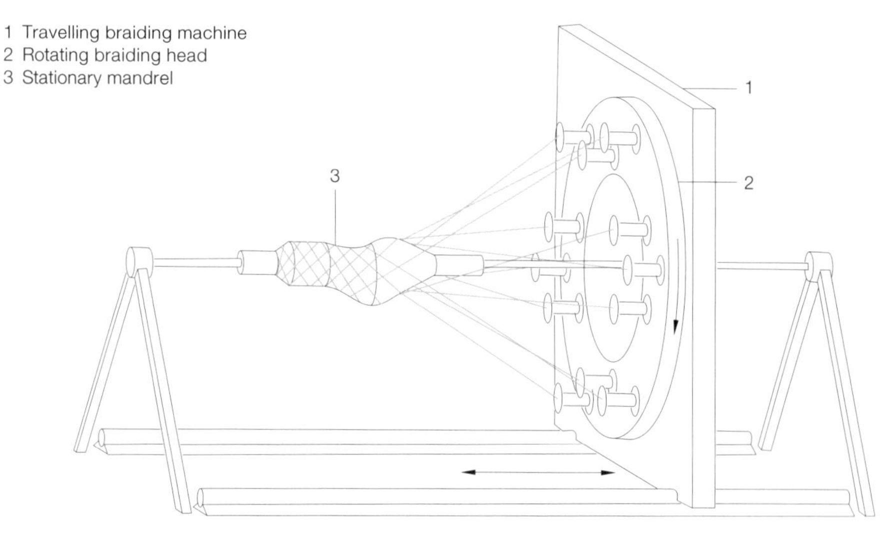

C 2.10

C 2.8 Pultrusion
C 2.9 Composite wrapping
a Wrapping the fibres
b Impregnating the fibres with polymer
C 2.10 Braiding
C 2.11 Braiding a hose with a mandrel
C 2.12 Fibre spraying

Pultrusion

Pultrusion (Fig. C 2.8) is currently particularly significant for semi-finished products in the building industry because it represents a relatively simple way of producing sections and sheets with a high fibre content and a low scatter of the mechanical properties. The method involves pulling long fibres (rovings) impregnated with resin through a heated mould where the polymer cures within a few minutes at a high temperature. Alternatively, it is also possible to pull dry fibres through the mould and inject the resin directly. The rovings can be joined by textiles to reinforce the surfaces of the products; their positions are controlled by rollers. The reinforcement in the form of unidirectional rovings in the longitudinal direction is essentially responsible for the flexural strength. The nature of the pultrusion method means that the mechanical properties perpendicular to the pultruding direction are much lower, and are primarily influenced by the textiles. Complex mats (non-crimp fabrics) made from layers of long fibres with a covering of short fibres) are frequently specified for the surfaces. The long fibres increase the loadbearing capacity in the longitudinal and transverse directions, the short fibres ensure a more consistent surface finish.
A fibre content of 70 % by vol. can be achieved with pultrusion. UP is generally used as the matrix, occasionally VE or PF, and normally EP for carbon fibre-reinforced sections. The manufacturing tolerances of the industrial process are good, but the shrinkage of the thermoset matrix upon curing and inaccuracies in the positioning of the fibres means that the tolerances are poorer than those of metal sections. In principle it is possible to produce virtually any cross-sectional form by means of pultrusion, but the dimensions of the sections are limited by the plant, generally to wall thicknesses between 0.5 and 100 mm and maximum overall dimensions of 650–1250 mm.
Ribs or other profiling transverse to the pultruding direction are impossible. Pultruded sections are normally straight, although curved sections have become possible more recently. [1]
The standard sections stocked by most manufacturers are essentially similar to those familiar from structural steelwork (Fig. C 3.7, p. 84). However, more and more complex geometries for special applications are gradually appearing, e.g. pultruded window frame sections or bridge decks. Pultrusion requires comparatively elaborate and expensive tooling, and setting up the plant is very time-consuming, all of which means that custom sections are worthwhile only for larger quantities (usually at least 1000 production metres).

Wrapping

Also known as filament winding, this is a production method for pipes, vessels, tanks and other rotationally symmetrical hollow components (Fig. C 2.9). The high level of mechanisation in this method enables the fibres to be arranged exactly, reproducibly and with a high density.

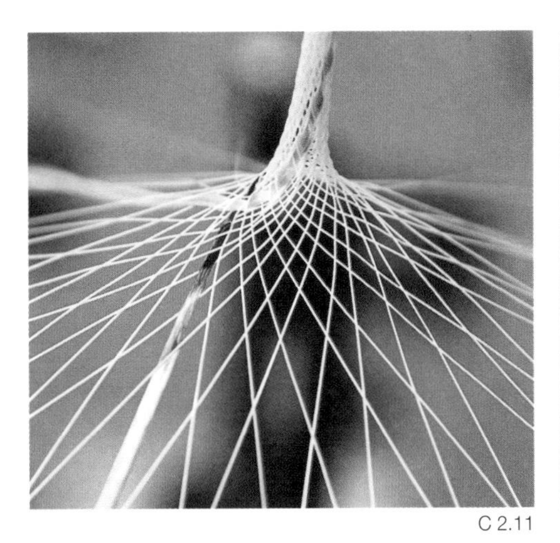

C 2.11

In composite wrapping, pretensioned rovings are wound around a rotating mandrel; mats or woven fabrics can be also be used. The fibres can be wound wet, i.e. impregnated with resin, or dry. In the latter case, they are subsequently impregnated with resin using the infusion method (see above). The fibre reinforcement of the laminate is controlled by the rotary speed of the mandrel and the speed of winding the fibres. One-off mandrels made from a soluble substance or, for larger series, reusable mandrels made from steel or aluminium are used depending on the batch size and the geometry of the component. To ease demoulding, mandrels are often slightly conical in shape, or made from folding segments. For pipes with thin walls, the fibres are installed at an angle of approx. 15–75° to the longitudinal direction, which makes the pipe more resistant to dents in service. It is not possible to apply the fibres at an angle of 0°.

Braiding

The braiding method, which is similar to wrapping, requires elaborate, expensive machinery and is mainly used for highly stressed components in the aerospace industry. In this method, a large number of fibres from a braider are wound, one over the other, onto a mandrel (Figs. C 2.10 and C 2.11). Either the mandrel or the rotating braiding head is fixed, the other part then moves and can lay the fibres continuously over the length of the component. The overlapping fibres can be used to create very complex components with varying cross-sections. In addition, different types of fibre (e.g. glass and carbon fibres) can be combined and the arrangement of the fibres adapted to suit the intended loads.
In contrast to wrapping, it is possible to attach fibres parallel with the longitudinal direction of the component (0° alignment). The resin is applied after braiding using the infusion or injection method. Pipes with braided reinforcement can also be pultruded. The criss-crossing fibres and the ensuing friction between them give braided components a high impact resistance.

C 2.12

Fibre spraying

This is an inexpensive method for the manual fabrication of large laminates with a complex geometry but low demands regarding loadbearing capacity (Fig. C 2.12). The method involves installing a roving in a spray gun which also chops the fibre into small pieces. These short fibres and a resin with a short reaction time are sprayed onto the mould at the same time. Air bubbles are subsequently pressed out with a grooved roller like with hand lay-up. The thickness of the laminate varies considerably with this method, and it is not possible to control the orientation of the fibres either. However, the advantage of this method is the minimum amount of work necessary and the option of being able to laminate vertical surfaces or membranes.

References:
[1] www.thomas-technik.de/pdf/Radius_Pultrusion.pdf, 19 Aug 2010

Semi-finished polymer products

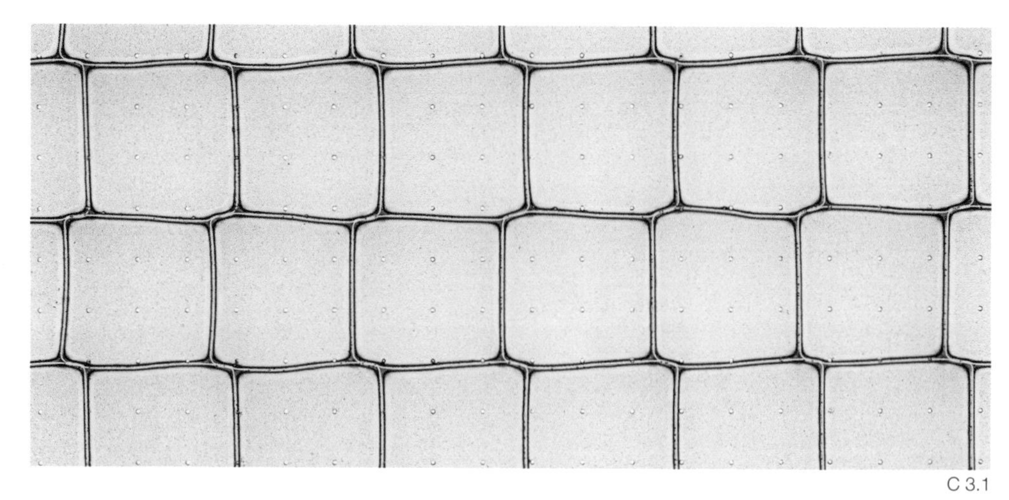

C 3.1

We can classify semi-finished polymer products according to their geometry: linear sections, planar products and three-dimensional moulded items (Fig. C 3.6). In addition, we can also distinguish them according to their functions: planar products are laid side-by-side over large areas, whereas sections or moulded items are installed as individual components. Apart from a few exceptions, semi-finished polymer products are made either from thermoplastics (without fibre reinforcement) or thermosets (with fibre reinforcement).

Sections

Sections are prismatic, linear components with a constant cross-section. The range of section geometries extends from tubes to H-sections and complex cross-sections (Fig. C 3.4). In rare cases, e.g. conical tubes, a cross-section that tapers or curves over its length are also possible. In terms of the spans and cross-sectional forms feasible and the recycling options, there are considerable differences between thermoplastics and fibre-reinforced polymers.

Sections made from thermoplastics
Sections made from unreinforced thermoplastics are used for hoods and covers, for decorative purposes and for interior applications. They do not achieve the strengths normally required for loadbearing building components. For external applications such as sunshades, window frames or screens, unplasticised polyvinyl chloride (PVC-U) is the number one choice because it is inexpensive and durable. It can also be used to produce transparent sections which, however, are not suitable for permanent use outdoors because they yellow over the years. Better for such applications are tubes and sections made from acrylic sheet (polymethyl methacrylate, PMMA, Fig. C 3.5) or polycarbonate (PC) because these materials remain light-fast for many years. Many different thermoplastics can be considered for linings or furniture. The choice of a suitable material is governed by its feel, scratch resistance, strength or colouring options.

Window frame sections
Frames made from PVC-U enjoy a larger market share than wood and aluminium. So far, other materials such as polypropylene (PP), acrylate-styrene-acrylonitrile (ASA), polyurethane (PUR) or glass fibre-reinforced polymers (GFRP) have played only minor roles. Owing to the large quantities produced, this semi-finished polymer product in particular is frequently the focus of attention in public discussions concerning the environmental effects of plastics in architecture (see "Environmental impact of polymers", pp. 124–131). Although PVC window frames are indeed everyday items in the housebuilding market, their bulky forms and poor visual and

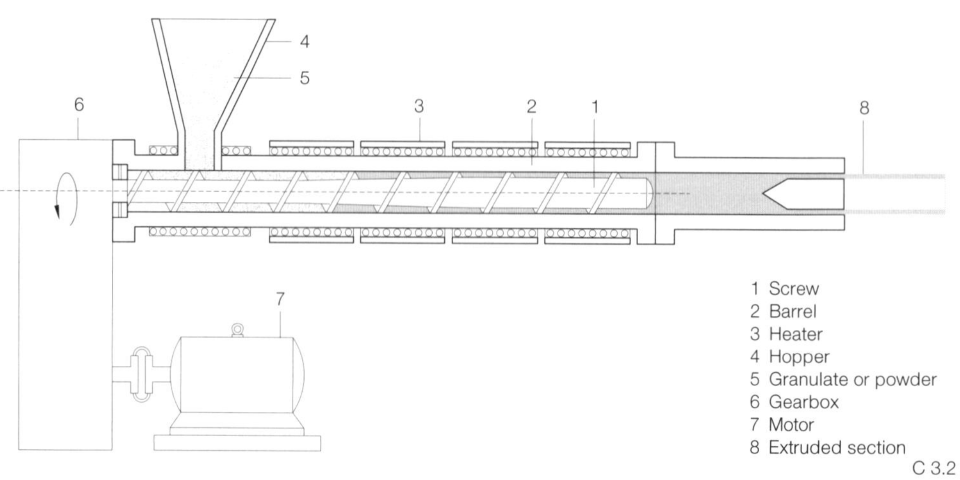

1 Screw
2 Barrel
3 Heater
4 Hopper
5 Granulate or powder
6 Gearbox
7 Motor
8 Extruded section

C 3.2

C 3.1 Sandwich panel made from polycarbonate (PC)
C 3.2 Extrusion of sections
C 3.3 Window frame section made from PVC

C 3.4 Section made from glass fibre-reinforced polymer
C 3.5 Tubes made from acrylic sheet (PMMA)
C 3.6 Overview of semi-finished polymer products

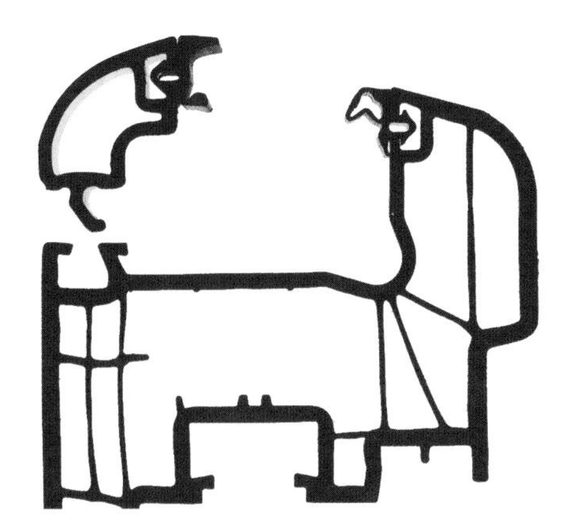

C 3.3

C 3.4

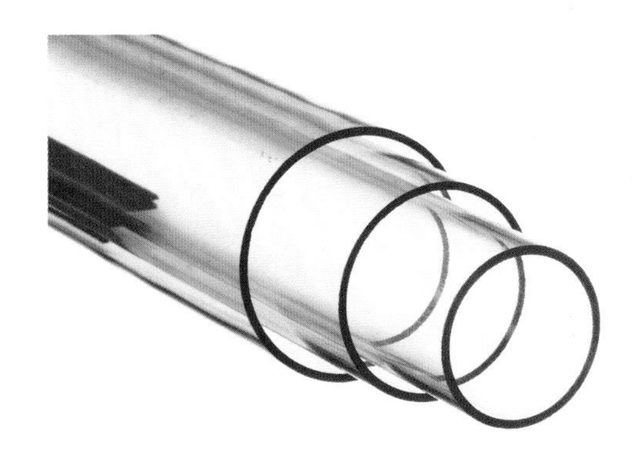

C 3.5

haptic qualities frequently make them unsatisfactory elements from the architectural viewpoint.
The cross-sectional forms of window frames have undergone continual development over the past decades, aimed at improving their thermal insulation and loadbearing characteristics. Modern PVC window frames (Fig. C 3.3) have a multitude of chambers separated by thin webs. Metal bars are incorporated in the sections at certain points to improve the load-carrying capacity. However, PVC sections are unsuitable for frames with longer spans because the unreinforced polymer lacks the necessary stiffness. Developing and fabricating new cross-sections for a particular construction project is very expensive compared to the actual cost per unit. The designer therefore has little scope for developing new window frame sections and must make use of the semi-finished products already available on the market.
Window frame sections are produced by continuous extrusion and sold by the metre. The sections are normally coloured white. One fact that has a positive effect on the economy and recyclability of PVC window frames is that, after extrusion, the semi-finished product needs no further finishing or coating except perhaps the application of a decorative foil or sheet of aluminium if required.
The preformed rubber seals made from EPDM are either black or grey in colour depending on the filler used. They are integrated into the section immediately after extruding the PVC. Afterwards, the sections are cut to length and shipped to the window manufacturers, who carry out the further fabrication work. The use of the thermoplastic PVC means that the sections are easy to cut and work, and they can also be welded together to form mitred corners. Attaching the window hardware also takes place during the final processing.

Production of thermoplastic sections
Sections made from thermoplastics such as PVC or PMMA are usually extruded and so the component can be cut to any (transportable) length. Injection-moulding is another method suitable for shorter components (see "Injection-moulding", p. 91).

Extrusion
Extrusion represents a very economic method of production for large quantities of thermoplastic components because it is a continuous method. All the polymers that are worth considering for thermoplastic sections and planar products are suitable for extrusion. The minimum feasible wall thicknesses of the sections vary depending on the viscosity of the polymer; for example, the webs of PMMA products are thicker than those of PC or PVC. The cross-sections can be configured as required by installing suitable dies, and it is also easy to combine different polymers by using co-extrusion or hollow chambers. However, the formed item (extrusion) must be prismatic, i.e. exhibit a constant cross-section over its entire length.
In the extrusion process (Fig. C 3.2), the polymer granulate, or in the case of PVC the powder, is fed into the extruder. The thermoplastic is already polymerised and contains all the necessary fillers and additives. The granulate is forced through the extruder by a screw, at the same time being compressed and melted together. The polymer melt is thoroughly mixed in the channels of the screw and gradually builds up the pressure required for the actual extrusion process. The melt is finally pressed through the die at the end of the extruder. In doing so, alignment units or negative pressure control and align the cross-sectional form. The temperature gradient in the extruder and the alignment of the cross-section have to be set up differently depending on the polymer used and depend on the experience of the manufacturer. A certain amount of experience is essential to ensure the production of an undistorted, consistent cross-section. A polymer that is too runny would collapse again after being formed, whereas with a melt that is too viscous it will not be possible to achieve the thin walls required. The extrusion is subsequently cooled and cut to length.
The combination of two or more extruders (co-extrusion) enables the production of semi-finished

Semi-finished polymer products made from thermoplastics

Sections

made from thermoplastics
- Acrylic sheet sections (PMMA)
- PVC-U sections
  - window frame sections
  - transparent sections

made from fibre-reinforced polymers
- Simple structural sections
  - GFRP sections
  - CFRP laminates
  - CFRP-GFRP composite beams
- Integrated sections
  - window frame sections
  - complex cross-sections
  - modular systems

Planar products

made from thermoplastics
- Acrylic sheets (PMMA)
- Polycarbonate (PC)
  - sheets
  - twin-/multi-wall sheets
  - sandwich panels
  - modified polyester (PET, PET-G)
- other thermoplastics (PVC, PS, SAN)

Composite products
- Fibre-reinforced polymers (GFRP, CFRP)
  - sheets
  - sandwich panels
  - planks
  - grids, gratings
- Laminates and wood-based board products
- Wood-plastic composites
- Mineral boards made from PMMA/PC and aluminium hydroxide (ATH)

Moulded items

made from thermoplastics and fibre-reinforced polymers
- Furniture and interior fitting-out
- Building services
  - switches
  - wall anchors

C 3.6

products made from different polymers or one polymer with different additives (e.g. colourants). This could be a transparent twin-wall sheet with a coloured facing, for instance. However, the design and fabrication of the die requires considerable input, which is why new cross-sections are only worthwhile when at least several thousand production metres are required.

Sections made from fibre-reinforced polymers
Sections made from fibre-reinforced polymers are primarily suited to loadbearing applications. Apart from a few exceptions, the building industry prefers glass fibres for the reinforcement because they are relatively inexpensive and durable. Carbon fibres, on the other hand, are only economically viable for heavily loaded components such as ropes or reinforcing laminates. Natural or aramid fibres are currently hardly used at all.

Arrangement of fibre reinforcement
The fibre reinforcement in pultruded sections is primarily in the form of long fibres (rovings) (see "Properties and applications", pp. 48–49) integrated in the longitudinal direction of the component. Additional textiles and fleeces are incorporated in the surfaces of the sections (Fig. C 3.8). Whereas the rovings determine the load-carrying capacity in the longitudinal direction, the outer layers improve the shear capacity and the appearance. In custom sections there may be more textile reinforcement than fibres if a high loadbearing capacity is necessary in the transverse direction.

Dimensions of sections
Wall thicknesses between 1.5 and 100 mm are possible, depending on the particular manufacturer. Thicknesses > 15 mm can be problematic, however, because the heat of reaction during production cannot dissipate and that can lead to cracking due to restraint.
The internal corners of pultruded sections should have a radius of at least 5.0 mm, but not less than the thickness of the wall. Currently, overall dimensions of up to 1250 x 650 mm are possible, but this depends on the manufacturer. In theory there is no limit to the length of a component because the sections are produced continuously. However, the sections are generally stocked in lengths of 6 m.
Pultrudred sections are always prismatic, i.e. have a constant cross-section over their entire length. They are generally straight, but curved sections can now also be produced. [1] It is possible to include cable ducts, core materials or longitudinal ribs, but transverse ribs are impossible.

Simple cross-sectional geometries
The cross-sections marketed by the various manufacturers are very similar to those of structural steelwork (Figs. C 3.7a–f, h, i). The axial force and bending capacities of these beams are comparable with those of steel sections. However, the much lower elastic modulus results in much larger deformations. Structures made from these sections can therefore suffer from stability problems. The I-sections in particular must be continuously supported in order to prevent lateral buckling of the compression flange. Furthermore, the low loadbearing capacity of screwed and bolted joints is another disadvantage. Structures made from these sections are discussed in the chapter entitled "Building with semi-finished polymer products" (pp. 160–173).

CFRP sections
Owing to their high price, sections made from carbon fibre-reinforced polymers (CFRP) are only produced in small sizes and only used for heavily loaded components. Such applications include, for example, strengthening laminates for concrete refurbishment projects (see "Repairs with CFRP laminates", p. 92) or pipes made from braided CFRP.

C 3.7

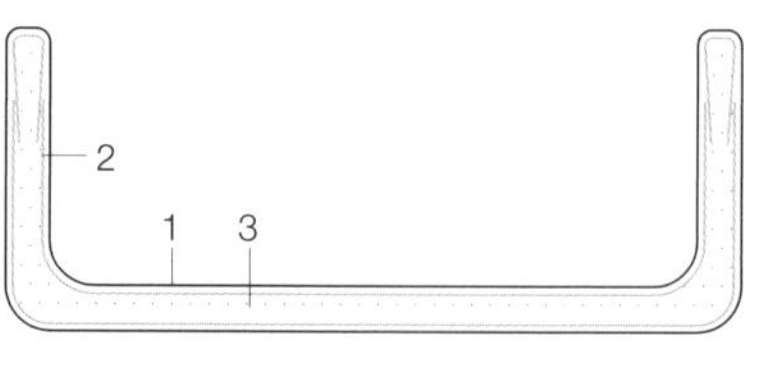

C 3.8

C 3.7 A selection of pultruded sections made from fibre-reinforced polymers
a Flat
b Square hollow
c Equal leg angle
d I-section
e Tube
f Channel
g Handrail
h T-section
i Unequal leg angle
j Plank
k Window frame
l Panel
m 45° connector
n 3-way connector
o Rail
p Coupler
q, r Bridge deck
s CFRP-GFRP composite beam

C 3.8 Make-up of pultruded sections (schematic)
1 Pultruded section made from fibre-reinforced polymer
2 Textile reinforcement, e.g. overlapping complex mats
3 Long fibres (rovings)

C 3.9 Profiled solid acrylic sheet (PMMA)
C 3.10 Twin-wall acrylic sheet (PMMA)
C 3.11 Corrugated acrylic sheet (PMMA) with textured surface

C 3.9

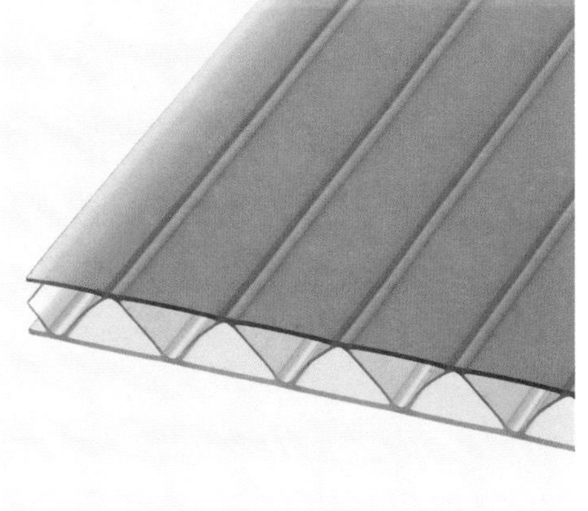

C 3.10

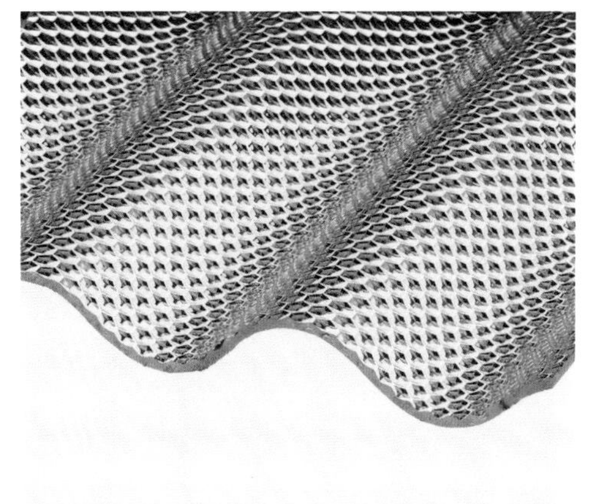

C 3.11

CFRP-GFRP composite beams
These composite beams were developed to reduce the deformations of GFRP beams (Fig. C 3.7s). The flange, which is primarily responsible for the bending capacity of the beam, is reinforced with unidirectional carbon fibres. The webs and the textile reinforcement on the surface are made from the less costly glass-fibre products. The result is the optimised use of the materials and a higher loadbearing capacity.

Complex cross-sectional geometries
Designs inspired by the sections used in structural steelwork usually result in a very high consumption of materials and structures that do not make the best use of those materials. For this reason, the development of cross-sectional geometries has continued in recent years, and this has resulted in semi-finished products to suit specific applications (Figs. C 3.7g, j, k). The potential design freedoms can therefore be exploited to the full in terms of both the form of the cross-section and the combination of materials. Other functions are becoming the focus of attention, not just load-carrying capacity. For example, in the case of window frame sections it is not just loadbearing aspects that are important these days, but also thermal insulation, a factor that is taken into account through the inclusion of voids (Fig. C 3.7k). In addition, the shoulder against which the pane of glass is fitted is also integrated in order to simplify final assembly. Multi-chamber sections permit a better use of the material. Such complex cross-sectional forms would be impossible in steel. The advantages of fibre-reinforced polymers are specifically exploited here.

Modular systems
Modular systems were developed to overcome the limited dimensions possible with pultruded cross-sections. It is therefore possible to fabricate large panels or cladding by combining smaller elements (Figs. C 3.7l–r). The modules can be fitted or glued together; even bridge decks can be constructed in this way (see "Special semi-finished products for engineering applications", pp. 92–93). There are also elements available that can be simply clipped together to speed up assembly.

Production of fibre-reinforced sections
Pultrusion is the most important method of manufacture for fibre-reinforced sections. However, wrapping or braiding are used for pipes, tubes and other hollow sections (see "Production", pp. 78–81)

Series production
Designers are always faced with the problem that new cross-sections can only be produced economically when a certain minimum quantity is ordered. This minimum quantity starts at approx. 1000 production metres for large cross-sections, but can be as much as 10 000 metres for small cross-sections. It is therefore impossible to develop new cross-sections for every construction project, and the products already available must be specified in most cases. However, the production of custom parts may be worthwhile for larger projects.

Planar products

Sheets, panels and boards are certainly among the most important semi-finished polymer products for architectural applications. A wide range of products is available to the designer and these semi-finished goods often fulfil several functions and include tongue and groove joints or thermal insulation, for instance. However, not all the semi-finished products described below are stocked as standard by the manufacturers and sometimes components with the particular properties required must be specially ordered. In particular, the very wide range of thicknesses, colours and qualities possible with fibre-reinforced polymers such as GFRP mean that "making for stock" it is not a sensible approach for most manufacturers.
Planar semi-finished polymer products are used for facades, roofing, furniture and interior fitting-out, also spandrel panels, linings, sanitary facilities and worktops.
We essentially divide planar semi-finished polymer products into thermoplastic, usually transparent, products and composite products (Fig. C 3.6, p. 83). The former are made from various thermoplastics (e.g. acrylic sheet and polycarbonate) in different geometries. The material properties of these semi-finished products are very similar. However, the properties of composite products made from polymers and fibres or mineral aggregates exhibit a much wider scatter depending on the particular constituents of the product. These semi-finished products can be in the form of fibre-reinforced polymers such as GFRP and CFRP, laminates, wood-plastic composites or mineral boards. In terms of their geometry, fibre-reinforced components can be further subdivided into solid boards and sandwich panels, also grids and planks.

Planar products made from thermoplastics
Typical applications for such thermoplastic products are balcony canopies, bus shelters, greenhouses or industrial buildings. In recent years we have seen more and more facades clad entirely in, usually, transparent polymer materials, sometimes in combination with integral lighting or thermal storage materials. The polymer sheets and panels available on the market vary considerably in terms of the materials and cross-sections used. By far the most common are those made from acrylic sheet (PMMA) and polycarbonate (PC). Special applications often make use of sheets and panels made from glycol-modified polyethylene terephthalate (PET-G), polystyrene (PS), PVC and styrene acrylonitrile (SAN). All these products exhibit a good transparency, but can also be produced in coloured, milky or opaque variations. Solid, profiled and hollow geometries are available. Great progress has been made in recent years regarding the UV stability and notched impact strength of polymers. The outcome of this is that durable materials suitable for external applications are now available as well. PMMA in particular remains light-fast for many years, but other polymers may require the addition of stabilisers to achieve adequate light-fastness.

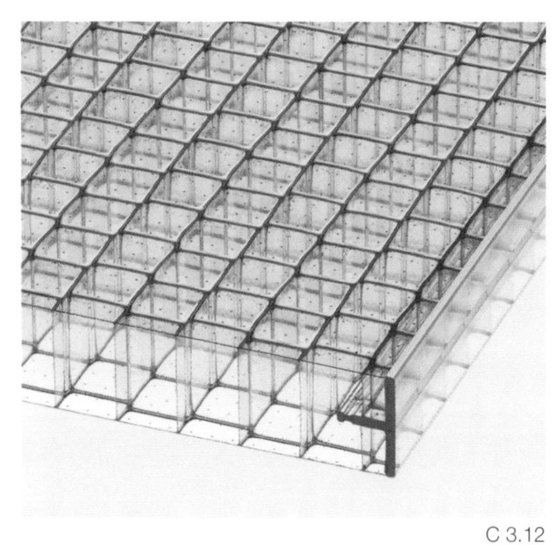
C 3.12

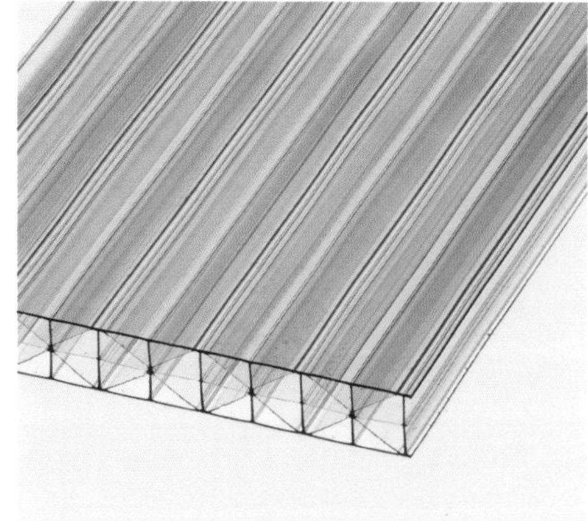
C 3.13

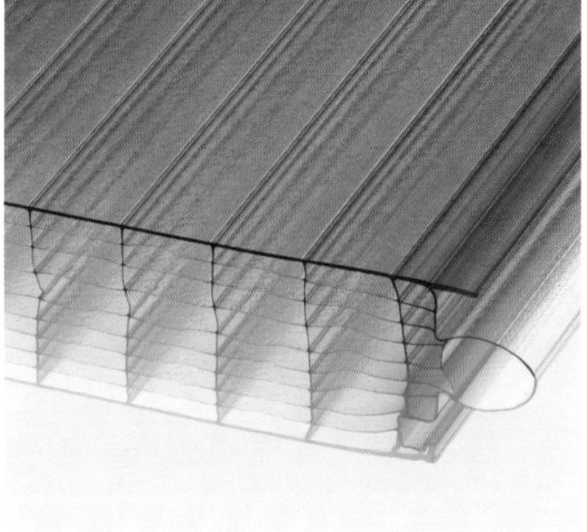
C 3.14

Applications
Planar polymer products have an advantage over glass when a low self-weight is necessary or single or double curvature panels are required. Curvature is achieved either by hot-forming during manufacture or by forcing the product into a curved shape during installation, which is possible to a certain degree. Furthermore, planar polymer products have a far more diverse design potential than glass. Polymer products are frequently used when the brittleness of glass is a problem or glass cannot provide adequate protection against impact loads. Polycarbonate products in particular are ideal for safety and security applications (e.g. spandrel panels or protective enclosures) because of their good ductility. In addition, it is possible to integrate clip-fit or bent-up edges into the products to simplify installation (Figs. C 3.14 and C 3.15). But the disadvantage is the scratch resistance of the thermoplastics in general use, which varies from material to material. Special polishes can be used to make scratched surfaces appear like new, but each type of material generally needs its own particular polish.

Thermal behaviour
The high coefficients of thermal expansion of transparent polymer sheets and panels must be taken into account during the design. For example, a facade panel 2 m long can expand and contract by 10 mm as a result of temperature fluctuations. Holes for fasteners or clamp fixings must therefore permit sufficient deformation in order to avoid damage caused by thermal loads.

Mechanical properties
Polymer sheets and panels are not simply substitutes for glass because the two materials are entirely different when it comes to their processing and applications. The tensile, or rather bending, strengths of panels made from PMMA or PC are relatively similar to those of glass, with the polymers having slightly better values. The self-weight of glass is, however, more than twice that of those polymers, but the elastic modulus of glass is 25–30 times higher (Fig. C 3.18).
If we compare, by way of an example, solid pieces of glass and PMMA or PC with the same thickness, then the permissible spans of the polymer products are only about one-third that of glass because of their deformation. The polymer products must be three times the thickness of the glass in order to achieve the same span. Polymer sheets and panels are therefore frequently in the form of hollow products with two, three or more walls in order to save weight and at the same time increase their stiffness.

Thermal insulation
The thermal conductivity of PMMA and PC is only about 20 % that of glass, which is a great advantage in ensuring that a facade design achieves the desired thermal performance. Unfortunately, unlike glass, polymers are not gastight and so it is not possible to fill the cavities with noble gases to improve the thermal insulation (see "Transparent thermal insulation", pp. 112–113).

Acrylic sheet (PMMA)
Products made from acrylic sheet (see "Polymethyl methacrylate", p. 42) have been used for architectural applications since the 1960s. This material is primarily used for solid products (Fig. C 3.9, p. 85), but also for twin-wall sheets (Fig. C 3.10, p. 85), tubes or other profiles (Fig. C 3.11, p. 85). The webs must be thicker than those of polycarbonate products. PMMA is a thermoplastic that can be shaped upon the application of heat. It has a higher light transmittance than glass and can also be produced in coloured, satinised or opaque versions. As it is permeable for UV light, it is also ideal for greenhouses (see Fig. C 6.32, p. 116); however, sheets providing protection against UV light are also available. Compared with other polymers, PMMA is very durable and light-fast, and does not discolour or become cloudy as a result of long exposure to UV radiation. Products with reduced flammability are available for special applications. PMMA is more brittle than polycarbonate, but the splinters and fragments that form upon breakage are not sharp. Its inferior hardness makes it more susceptible to scratches than polycarbonate.
Solid sheets are either moulded or extruded. Moulded PMMA has a higher strength and is easier to shape. Furthermore, the service temperatures are higher and its behaviour in fire is better than that of extruded material. PMMA products are produced in thicknesses from 1.5 to 120 mm as standard, with a maximum size of approx. 2 × 3 m for solid sheets. Profiled twin-wall sheets can only be extruded.
The semi-finished products can be worked with standard woodworking tools but the material tends to develop stress cracks. All corners and notches should therefore be rounded if possible. Fig. C 3.17 shows the manufacture of a facade element that is being cut from a moulded solid sheet on a CNC milling machine. Specially ground high-speed tools and saws should be used for drilling, cutting and milling work, otherwise the PMMA material can tear or melt locally. The semi-finished products can be very effectively joined with acrylate adhesives and when the work is carried out carefully, the joints are virtually invisible.
Solid acrylic sheet can be deep-drawn at a temperature of 150 °C (extruded) or 160 °C (moulded) (see "Forming", p. 172). Neither the strength nor the transparency is impaired even in the case of repeated reshaping, which makes PMMA ideal for recycling.

Polycarbonate (PC)
In terms of its optical and mechanical properties, polycarbonate (see "Polycarbonate", p. 42) is similar to acrylic sheet. Products made from PC are used when enhanced heat resistance or a ductile failure behaviour is required. The high notched impact strength of the material – also at low temperatures – is a decisive reason for using PC where safety and security are critical. In contrast to acrylic sheet, polycarbonate is not usually produced in solid forms, but rather as hollow products (Fig. C 3.14). The low viscosity of the material during processing is an advantage, which permits very thin walls. Typical PC sheets have between two and six levels of orthogonal voids, which gives them a better loadbearing capacity and stiffness than solid sheets and also improves the thermal insulation effect. Sheets with x-shaped webs have appeared in recent years which improve the thermal insulation properties even further (Fig. C 3.13). The optical quality and transparency of PC are somewhat inferior to those of PMMA.

The permissible service temperatures are higher than those of acrylic sheet and the behaviour in fire is usually better; not readily flammable PC sheets are available as standard. PC exhibits good durability but additives are necessary where long-lasting light-fastness is a requirement. Products with UV protection on the outer face should be used for external applications. For a polymer the scratch resistance of polycarbonate is good.
Hollow PC sheets (twin-wall, multi-wall, etc.) are extruded (see "Extrusion", p. 83). Co-extrusion can be used to add a coloured PC sheet to a twin- or multi-wall product, or to provide a UV-resistant coating or apply a water-repellent surface texture.
Polycarbonate can be worked with conventional tools and such work is less problematic than with acrylic sheet because PC is less brittle and less sensitive to stress cracking. Silicone or solvent adhesives can be used for adhesive joints. Shaping polycarbonate is more complicated than acrylic sheet because the material first has to be dried at a temperature of approx. 110 °C and the forming temperature, at 180–210 °C, is relatively high. The material cools quickly and so the mould itself must be heated.

Sandwich panels made from polycarbonate (PC)

The polycarbonate interlayer of so-called drawn-core sandwich panels (Figs. C 3.12 and C 3.16) is not extruded, but rather laid as a sheet between two heated moulds and drawn by these into a three-dimensional structure. Afterwards, facings of PC or PMMA are attached by laminating or welding.

Sheets made from polyethylene terephthalate (PET)

Transparent sheets also make use of other polyesters that essentially exhibit similar material properties to those of polycarbonate, which also belongs to the polyester group (see "Polyester", p. 42). Amorphous PET and the glycol-modified copolyester PET-G can be formed at much lower temperatures than their raw materials and are also permanently transparent. These materials add solid sheets with a ductile behaviour and good hot-forming characteristics to the range of semi-finished polycarbonate products. The transparency of PET and PET-G does not suffer even after several forming processes. Both modifications are only suitable for considerably lower service temperatures (approx. 65 °C) than polycarbonate and are also less ductile.

Solid sheets made from amorphous PET and the copolyester PET-G are extruded. Working the materials is similar to that of polycarbonate. Hot-forming is especially quick and reliable with PETG; no pre-drying is necessary and the forming temperature is 100–160 °C. Amorphous PET can also be formed, but must be cooled quickly to preserve the transparency.

Other thermoplastics

Other thermoplastics can be used for semi-finished sheet and panel products required for subsidiary components or special applications. Products made from polyvinyl chloride (PVC), polystyrene (PS) or styrene acrylonitrile (SAN) are generally less durable and less light-fast, but mostly cheaper than the polymers described above. These materials require the addition of a stabiliser to protect against UV radiation if they are to be used outside, and polystyrene in particular has very limited suitability for external applications. The strengths and stiffnesses of PS and SAN are, however, comparable with the above materials.
Less important components such as roof coverings over industrial sheds or temporary structures can make use of, for example, corrugated sheets made from transparent PVC, which represent a cheaper alternative. However, the permanent exposure to UV radiation causes the material to lose its transparency and become matt.
Solid sheets made from PS and SAN are easy to shape and are therefore suitable for interior fitting-out purposes, e.g. sanitary applications.

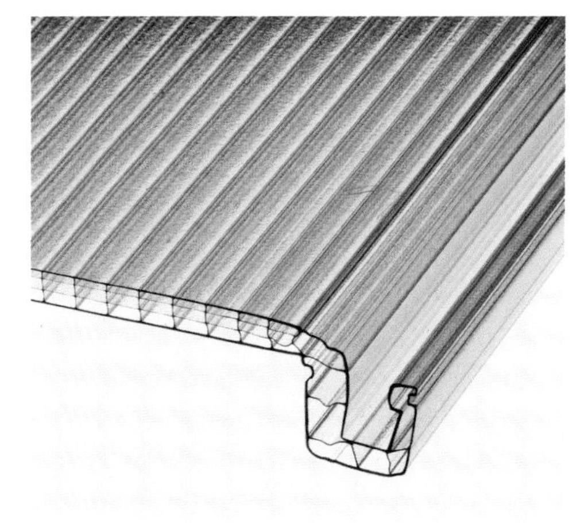

C 3.15

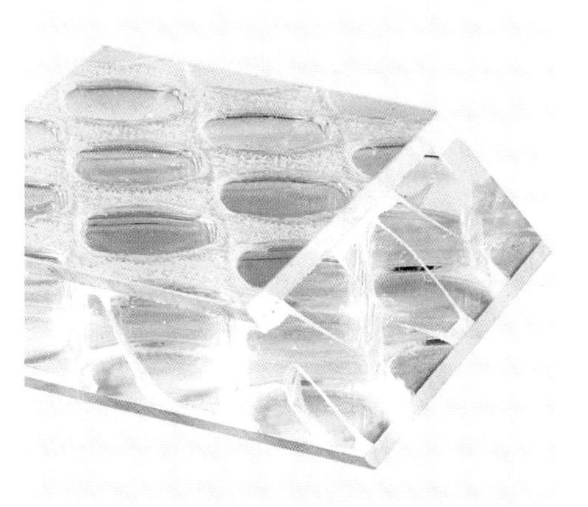

C 3.16

C 3.17

Material	Density $[g/cm^3]$	Tensile strength $[N/mm^2]$	Elastic modulus $[N/mm^2]$	Coefficient of thermal expansion $[10^{-6}/K]$	Thermal conductivity [W/mK]
Acrylic sheet (PMMA)	1.19	50–77	1600–3600	70–90	0.18
Polycarbonate (PC)	1.20	56–67	2100–2400	60–70	0.21
Float glass	2.50	45	70000	9	1.00

C 3.18

C 3.12 Sandwich panel made from polycarbonate (PC)
C 3.13 Twin-wall sheet made from polycarbonate (PC) with x-type webs for optimum thermal performance
C 3.14 Multi-wall sheet made from polycarbonate (PC) integral clip-in fixing
C 3.15 Multi-wall sheet made from polycarbonate (PC) with integral bent edge
C 3.16 Core-drawn sandwich panel made from polycarbonate (PC)
C 3.17 Machining a moulded PMMA panel with a CNC milling machine
C 3.18 Properties of acrylic sheet and polycarbonate compared to float glass

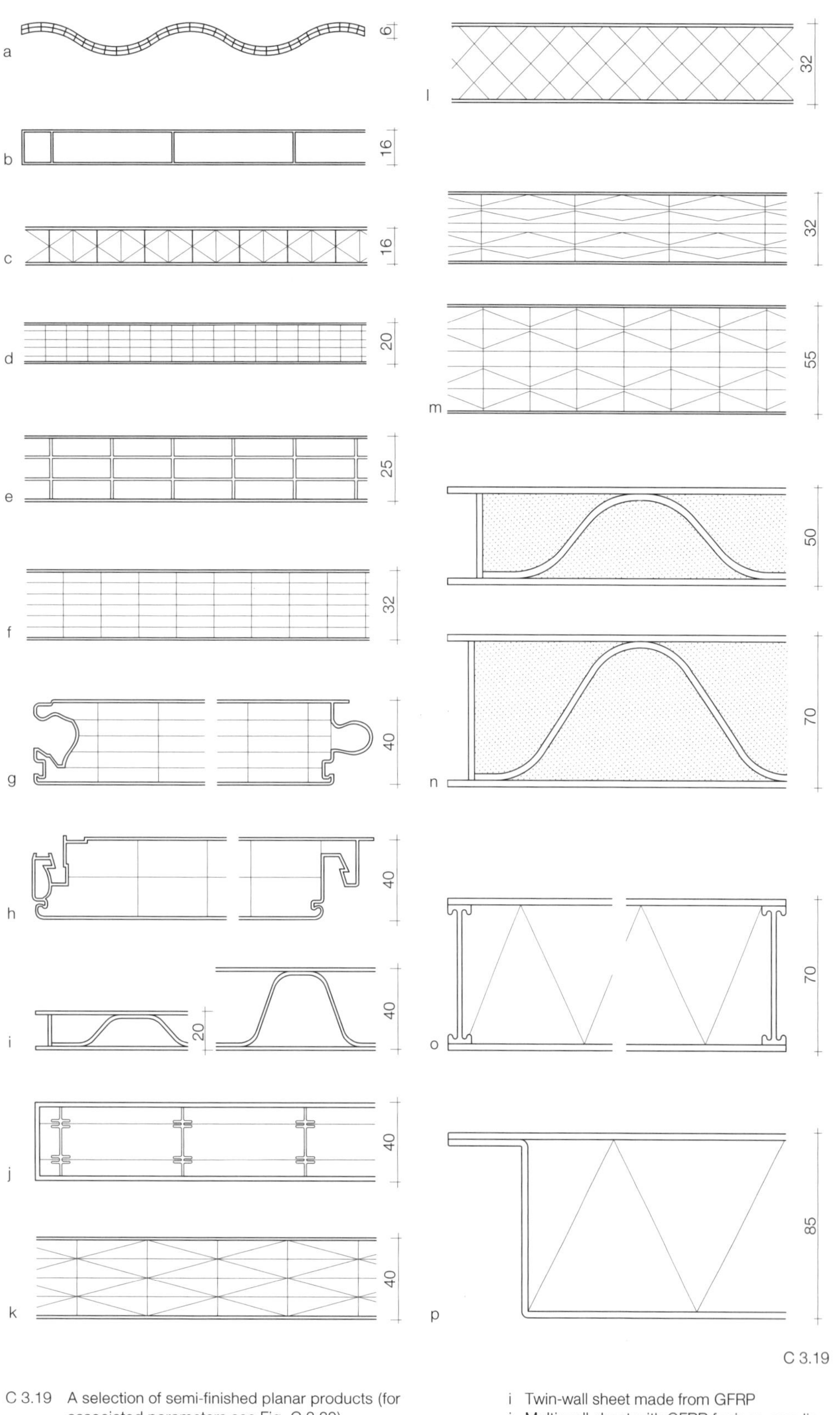

C 3.19 A selection of semi-finished planar products (for associated parameters see Fig. C 3.20)
a Twin-wall corrugated sheet (PC)
b Twin-wall sheet with thick walls (PMMA)
c Twin-wall sheet with thin x-type webs (PC)
d Multi-wall sheet with thin webs (PC)
e Multi-wall sheet with thin webs (PMMA)
f Multi-wall sheet with thin webs (PC)
g Multi-wall sheet with integral clip-in fixings (PC)
h Multi-wall sheet with integral clip-in fixings (PVC + PMMA)
i Twin-wall sheet made from GFRP
j Multi-wall sheet with GFRP facings, acrylic sheet webs and foil inlays
k–m Special multi-wall sheets for thermal insulation (PC)
n Twin-wall sheets made from GFRP, with aerogel filling
o, p Sandwich panels with GFRP facings and internal insulation

C 3.20 Various parameters for semi-finished planar products

Production of unreinforced planar products
Sheets, boards and panels made from unreinforced polymers are either moulded or extruded.

Moulding
Thermoplastics can generally only be moulded in the non-cross-linked state because only then are they sufficiently runny. Moulding is frequently used, first and foremost for PMMA planar products. [2] "In situ polymerisation" involves filling the monomers and initiators of the polymer into a mould and then initiating the reaction mechanism by applying heat. Moulding the acrylic sheet between two parallel panes of glass results in an excellent surface quality. Moulded PMMA has a higher strength and better heat resistance than extruded material.

Extrusion
Profiled semi-finished products and twin- or multi-wall sheets are extruded. The manufacturing process corresponds to that used for producing thermoplastic sections (see "Extrusion", p. 83). Twin- or multi-wall sheets with different colours are co-extruded.

Composite planar products
Where the mechanical or haptic properties of polymers are unsuitable for the intended application, it is possible to combine the polymers with other materials or fibres to form a composite material. The following improvements are therefore possible:

- Higher load-carrying capacity and reduced deformations
- Better thermal insulation properties
- Enhanced surface hardness (scratch resistance)
- Wider range of design options

Combining the polymer with fibres, paper, wood, foam or mineral aggregates usually means that the resulting composite product is opaque. Only the combination of glass fibres and a polymer can result in a product that is translucent up to a certain thickness (Fig. C 3.19n–p); fully transparent composite sheets or panels are, however, not possible. A printed foil can be inserted which then shimmers through the polymer and remains visible.

Fibre-reinforced polymers (GFRP and CFRP)
The principal properties and production of GFRP and CFRP have been described in the chapter entitled "Fibre-reinforced polymers" (pp. 76–81).
Thermosets (resins) are generally used for planar-type semi-finished products because these create a consistent bond with the fibres. The less expensive glass fibres are normally used for the reinforcement.
The loadbearing capacity or the thermal insulation properties can be improved by producing fibre-reinforced sheets in the form of sandwich components with a lightweight core or as planks with strengthening ribs. Grids and gratings, on the other hand, are used when a planar

Material	Manufacturer	Product name	Cross-section (Fig. C 3.19)	Thicknesses available [mm]	max. width [mm]	max. length [mm]	Weight [kg/m²]	U-value[1] [W/m²K]	Energy transmittance[1] g-value [%]	Light trancemittance[1] [%]	Sound reduction index[1] R'_w [db (A)]	Building materials class (DIN 4102-1)
Solid products												
PMMA	Evonik Röhm	Plexiglas XT, extruded, UV-permeable		1.5–25	2050	3050	4.8	5.4	85	92	26	B2
	Evonik Röhm	Plexiglas GS, moulded, UV-permeable		2–160	2050	3050	4.8	5.4	85	92	26	B2
PC	Bayer Sheet Europe	Makrolon GP, impact-resistant, colourless		0.75–15	2050	3050	4.9			87		B1
PET-G	Simona	Simollux, unbreakable, can be deep-drawn without pre-drying		1–15	2050	3050	5.1			90		B1
PET	Thyssen Schulte	Nudec PET-UV, graffiti-proof, stiffer than PET-G, UV protection		4	2050	3050	5.3			89		B1
PVC	Simona	Simona PVC-Glas-SX transparent, enhanced impact resistance, unsuitable for use outdoors		0.8–15	1500	3000	5.3	5.1		84		B1
GFRP	Fiberline	Pultruded GFRP, flat sheets, opaque		1.5–25	500	6000	5.6	5.5				B2
GFRP	Lamilux	Lamilux plan, translucent or coloured		0.8–5	3200	12000	5.6	5.5				B2
Mineral board	DuPont	Corian		4–19	930	3658	6.8					B1
Mineral board	LG Chem Europe	Hi-Macs		4–12	910	3680	6.8	5.6				B1
Corrugated products												
PMMA	Evonik Röhm	Plexiglas resist farblos C struktur 76/18, enhanced impact resistance, textured finish		3	1045	4000	4.0			88		B2
PC	Bayer Sheet Europe	Makrolon onda multi longlife 2/177-51, corrugated twin-wall sheet, rigid, UV protection		5	1097	7000	2.0	3.7	78	77		B2
PVC	Solvay	Ondex, Sollux, 76/18, lightweight, inexpensive, simple processing		1.2	988	6000	2.0			80		B1
GFRP	Scobalit	Various corrugated and trapezoidal forms matching the opaque sections of other manufacturers		0.9	3000	2000	20			89		B2
Twin-/multi-wall products												
PMMA	Evonik Röhm	Plexiglas Alltop, colourless, UV-permeable, NO DROP coating	b	16	1200	7000	5.0	2.5	91	82	22	B2
PMMA	Evonik Röhm	Plexiglas Heatstop, opal or blue, NO DROP coating, reflects IR radiation, impermeable to UV radiation	e	16/32	1230	7000	5.7	1.6	30	40	24	B2
PC	Brett Martin	Marlon CST, corrugated twin-wall sheet	a	6	1152		2.0	3.3		79		
PC	Bayer Sheet Europe	Makrolon multi UV 3X/16-25, colourless, impermeable to UV radiation	c	16	2100	15000	2.5	2.0	62	66	18	B2
PC	Bayer Sheet Europe	Makrolon multi UV 6/20-20, colourless, impermeable to UV radiation	d	20	2100	14000	3.1	1.7	57	58	21	B2
PC	Brett Martin	Sevenwall (Seven), Marlon ST, multi-wall sheet	f	32	2100		3.6	1.3		64		
PC	Rodeca	PC 2540-6, opal anti-glare, tongue and groove joints, two-tone colouring possible	g	40	500	11000	4.2	1.2	45	45	22	B2, B1
PC	Bayer Sheet Europe	Makrolon multi UV 5M/40-20, impermeable to UV radiation	k	40	1230	6000	4.2	1.0	47	47	19	B2
PC	Brett Martin	Marlon, XX wall, diagonal webs	l	32/35	2100		3.8	1.4		64		
PC	Brett Martin	Marlon, Tenwall, complex web configuration	m	32/55			3.6	1.1		54		
PC	Rodeca	Multi-function panels		10	630			2.9				
PVC	Rodeca	PVC 2340-3, with co-extruded acrylic UV protective layer	h	40	300	11000	5.5	1.7		67	21	B1
GFRP	Scobalit	Light elements, rigidity ensured by diagonal webs	i	20/40	2400	8000	5.3	2.6		78	20	B2, B1
GFRP	Butzbach	Varioplan plus, colour: Brillant, clear material, crystal structure, 3 colours		40	486	15000	11.0	2.6	42	78	25	B2
GFRP	Butzbach	Varioplan plus, colour: Brillant, with 2 intermediate foils	j	40	486	15000	11.0	1.2	42	63	27	B2
GFRP	Scobalit	Scobatherm Nanogel translucent, aerogel granulate filling, F 30	n	50/70	1.25	0	12.0	0.4	26	23	27	B1
GFRP	JET	Grillodur, 2-leaf, natural colour, GFRP sheet bonded to aluminium section, suitable for foot traffic		70	2000	5600	8.0	1.6	69	77	25	B2
GFRP	JET	Grillodur, with spun glass inlay, enhanced sound and thermal insulation, light-scattering	o	70	1200	8000	10.0	0.6	46	51	34	B2
GFRP	Scobalit	Scobatherm Monifex, filling material: folded foils made from vegetable cellulose	p	85	935	3000	5.7	0.6	48	39	28	B1
GFRP	Fiberline	Facade planks, translucent		40	500	6000	8.2					B1

[1] These values were calculated for a sheet thickness of 4 mm in the case of solid sheets, for the twin-/multi-wall sheets the lower thickness was used.

C 3.20

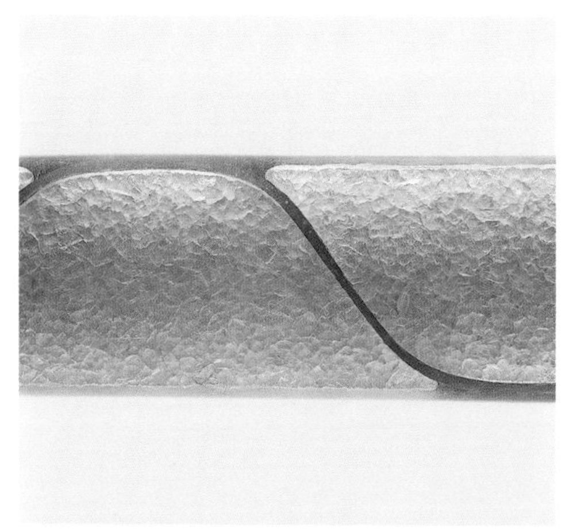
C 3.21

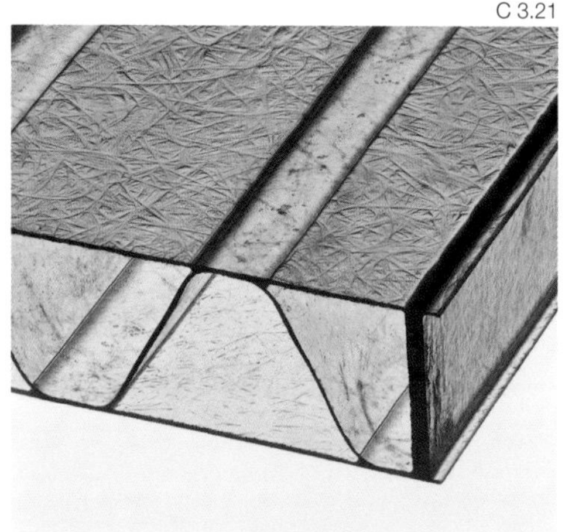
C 3.22

C 3.23

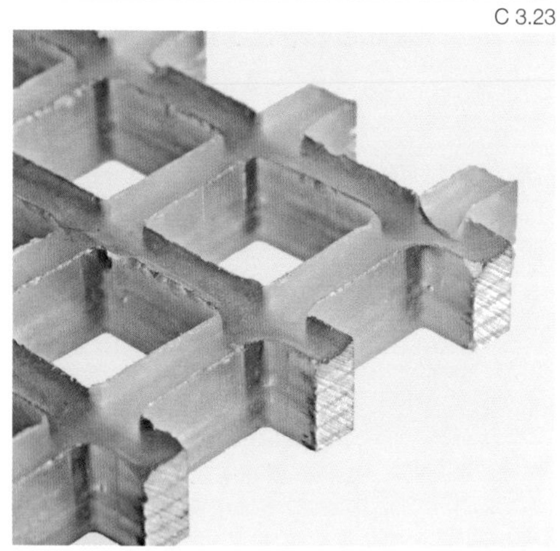
C 3.24

product with an open structure is required (e.g. open-grid flooring).

Sandwich panels
Planar products subjected to bending exhibit the highest stresses in their extreme fibres (i.e. at the surfaces) and are little utilised in the core zone. Solid GFRP or CFRP products with a density of up to 2.0 g/cm^3 are relatively heavy compared to other polymers and, furthermore, the production of laminates > 15 mm thick requires extensive technological input. These boundary conditions put considerable constraints on the spans that can be achieved. In sandwich panels the core, which is understressed, is replaced by a lighter material with a lower loadbearing capacity so that the entire sandwich element can be made much thicker but still solid. Typical core materials are foams, honeycomb structures or spacer fabrics (see "Core materials", pp. 72–75).
Sandwich panels are used when a planar element with a high stiffness is necessary, e.g. shells in compression, long spans or panels with point loads as in bridge-building.
Moreover, lightweight core layers have a low thermal conductivity. It is also possible to fill hollow GFRP elements with materials having good thermal insulation or thermal mass (Figs. C 3.21 and C 3.26).

Planks
Planks are planar products provided with strengthening ribs on one side. Their production is much simpler than that of sandwich panels because they are made of only one material. The webs are mostly parallel and so automated production by way of pultrusion is possible. A further development of the plank is the twin-wall transparent plank with closed voids. However, the webs are approx. 2 mm thick at least because of the fibre reinforcement.
Planks and twin-wall planks can be used as facade cladding (Fig. C 3.23) or for the surfacing to walkways. This form of construction does not bring any significant improvement in the thermal insulation properties, however.

Grids
Grids or gratings, which do not have a closed structure, represent special types of planar products. Long fibres (rovings) are laid in the mould and are therefore integrated into the synthetic resin. The individual ribs are upright, which increases the load-carrying capacity. Grids, however, cannot be manufactured in a continuous process, and are instead produced in large moulds. Typical applications include, for example, floors and walkways in industrial plants or balustrade infill panels (Fig. C 3.24).

Laminates and wood-based board products
Besides the use of fibres for reinforcement, thermosets are also processed in combination with other materials such as wood or paper. Synthetic resins such as melamine formaldehyde (MF), urea formaldehyde (UF) or phenol formaldehyde (PF) are mainly used. These tend to be rather brittle and their strengths are lower than those of the polymers normally used for fibre composites. However, combined with wood-based products and paper, they achieve very good results. In addition, wood and paper can absorb the moisture that ensues with these resins during the curing reaction (polycondensation). Moulding compounds made from wood chippings and phenolic resin have been processed on an industrial scale since the start of the 20th century. Fibreboard made from thin wood veneers plus a synthetic resin binder achieves a higher strength, but in this case the synthetic binder plays only a subsidiary role. Compared to solid timber, wood-based board products are comparatively weather-resistant and achieve high strengths for wood-based products. Moulding compounds and fibreboard with a synthetic resin binder are used for furniture, but also for industrial applications.
All laminates and wood-based board products are pressed during the curing reaction in order to prevent the formation of air bubbles and voids. Curved components can be produced with appropriate moulds, as well as flat boards. Printed papers are frequently included for decorative purposes. These are impregnated with melamine resin and pressed to form laminates. Owing to the use of phenolic or aminoplastic resins, laminates are usually brittle, a fact that must be taken into account during their processing.

Wood-plastic composites (WPC)
In contrast to the familiar phenolic resin moulding compounds, in a wood plastic composite wood fibres and sawdust are mixed into the thermoplastic matrix, usually of polypropylene (PP) or polyethylene (PE). The proportion of wood substances frequently lies between 50 and 80 % by wt. In contrast to natural wood, WPC components can be formed into any shape and are waterproof. [3] On the other hand, the bonded wood is not resistant to microbes and has limited heat resistance. One use of WPCs is as hollow facade cladding panels (Fig. C 3.25). They are produced by extrusion or compression- or injection-moulding.
For details of other polymers reinforced with natural fibres, please refer to the chapter entitled "Natural fibre-reinforced polymers and biopolymers" (pp. 60–65).

Mineral boards
Mineral boards are composites made from thermoplastics such as acrylic sheet (PMMA) or polycarbonate (PC) plus mineral aggregates. Traditionally, mineral boards are used in sanitary facilities or as worktops in kitchens, but are being increasingly used for other interior fitting-out purposes or as facade cladding. The colourants and aggregates chosen determine their appearance. The mineral aggregate lends the material a surface hardness that is very hard for a synthetic material and a correspondingly high elastic modulus. Additional coatings are

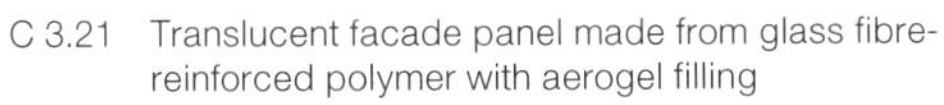

C 3.21 Translucent facade panel made from glass fibre-reinforced polymer with aerogel filling
C 3.22 Transparent twin-wall sheet made from glass fibre-reinforced polymer
C 3.23 Facade plank made from translucent glass fibre-reinforced polymer
C 3.24 Grid made from glass fibre-reinforced polymer
C 3.25 Wood-plastic composite panel
C 3.26 Composite panel with honeycomb core made from cellulose
C 3.27 Injection-moulding plant

C 3.25

C 3.26

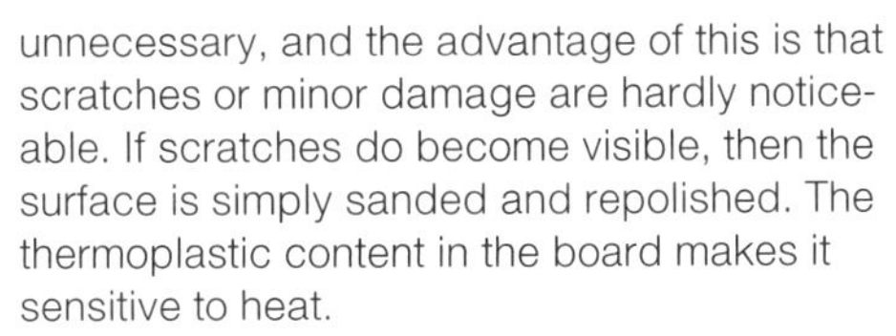

unnecessary, and the advantage of this is that scratches or minor damage are hardly noticeable. If scratches do become visible, then the surface is simply sanded and repolished. The thermoplastic content in the board makes it sensitive to heat.
The aggregates account for up to 90% by wt. (or 80% by vol.) of the composite, which is why the name *mineral* board has become established. Aluminium hydroxide (ATH) is a typical aggregate, at the same time a common flame retardant, which lends the mineral board product a certain fire-retardant property. The viscous mixture of polymer, aggregates and additives is moulded to form boards that are struck off at the desired thickness and then rolled.
Mineral boards can be recycled in principle, but recycling is not carried out on a wide scale at the moment. One of the reasons for this is the diverse dyes and fillers currently used by manufacturers.
The semi-finished products can be butt-jointed, glued or welded together, which enables large areas to be covered without visible joints. Thermoplastics are used and so the boards can be hot-formed during processing. The typical solution, for reasons of cost, is to produce thin boards up to 10 mm thick and bond these to standard particleboard. Thicker boards can be fixed to a supporting framework via threaded sockets integrated into the boards (see "Sheets", pp. 168–171). [4]

Moulded items

Moulded items or parts are semi-finished products with a three-dimensional geometry. In contrast to sections and planar products, they are individually designed to suit the intended application. Ideally, a moulded item will not need any further processing after production and can be used directly. Injection-moulded parts made from thermoplastics represent the most important group here. In addition, fibre-reinforced polymers can be laminated to create three-dimensional items.
Where a building or project exceeds a certain size, it can prove economic to design new moulded items. The design of moulded parts to suit the materials used depends on many factors. The relevant design rules are described in detail in the chapter entitled "Building with free-form polymers" (pp. 174–187).

Thermoplastic moulded items

Everyday artefacts and many technical components are frequently made from polymers in the form of semi-finished three-dimensional products. In the building industry, injection- or blow-moulded semi-finished products are primarily used for interior fitting-out and building services applications because these methods only allow the production of small elements with a relatively low loadbearing capacity. Light switches, wall anchors and furniture are just a few examples of the vast range of injection-moulded items available.
Many different functions can be integrated into moulded parts and almost any regular or irregular shape is possible. The design options that polymers offer in general can be fully exploited and fully realised with moulded parts. Injection-moulding is an economic method of production for large series and supplies high-quality results.

Production of thermoplastic moulded items
Generally speaking, injection-moulding is the commonest type of production in the polymer industry. [5] Blow-moulding is used for thin-wall hollow artefacts and essentially corresponds to the extrusion blow-moulding used for foils (see "Extrusion", p. 95). In addition, moulded parts can be produced from flat sheets and panels by hot-forming (see "Hot-forming", p. 172).

Injection-moulding
Injection-moulding can be used to produce parts with very good surface finishes and good dimensional stability. Further processing is not usually necessary.
The injection-moulding machine (Fig. C 3.27) is made up of injection and clamping units plus the mould itself, with the injection unit not unlike an extruder in terms of its overall configuration (see C 3.2, p. 82).
The polymer granulate or powder is drawn into the channels of the screw where it is homogenised and plasticised by the application of heat. The screw is pushed forward horizontally for the injection stage and therefore functions like a piston, forcing the plasticised polymer through the nozzle into the mould. The clamping unit supplies the counter-pressure and enables the mould to be opened after the injection stage to release the moulded part. In the mould itself, the plasticised polymer is fed through channels (gates), which should be arranged concentrically around the component in order to ensure an even distribution of the injected material.

1 Clamping unit
2 Injection unit (extruder)
3 Machine bed
4 Mould
5 Drive
6 Granulate or powder

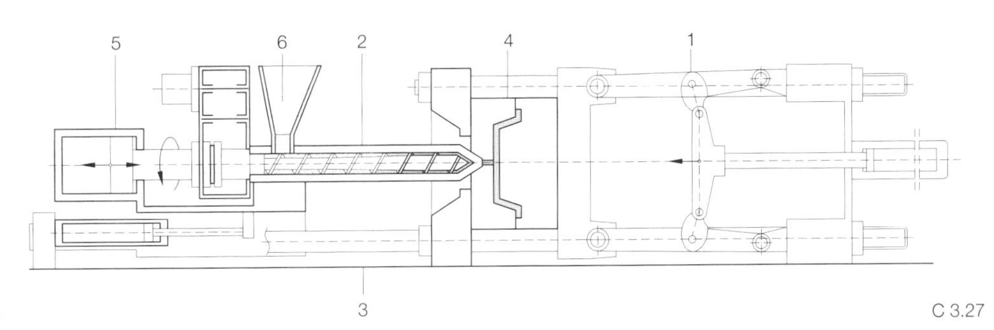

C 3.27

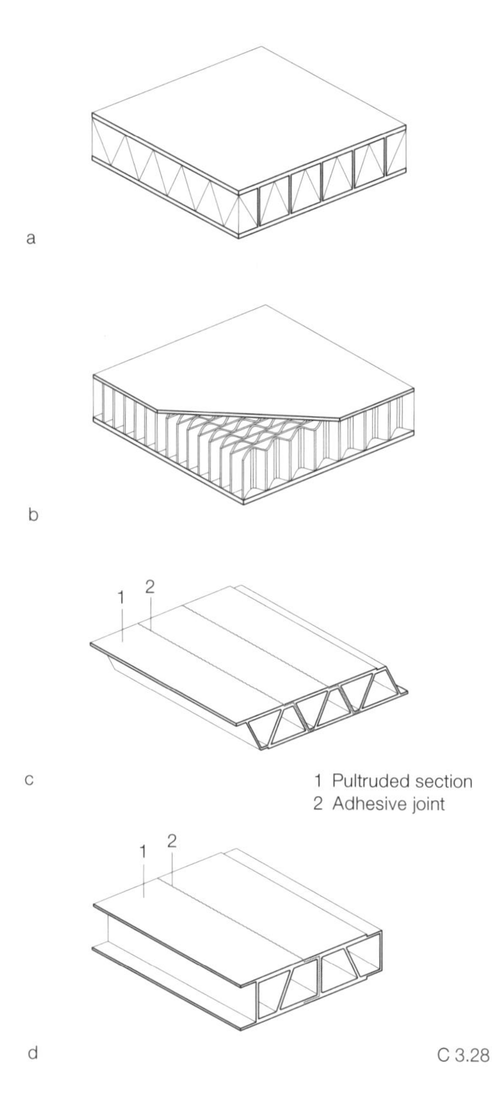

C 3.28

C 3.28 Various bridge deck configurations
a Sandwich bridge deck with rigid foam core
b Sandwich bridge deck with honeycomb core
c, d Bridge decks made from pultruded sections bonded together

C 3.29 Component strengthened with strips of CFRP laminate

C 3.30 Road bridge with GFRP deck, Friedberg (D), 2008, Knippers Helbig
a Erection
b View of edge of deck

C 3.29

Sources of errors in injection-moulding
The wall thicknesses of injection-moulded parts should all be the same in order to avoid thermal stresses. Excessively thick walls cause accumulations of mass which can lead to trapped air bubbles (pinholes). Corners should be rounded so that they can cool uniformly. In addition, injection-moulding can result in weld lines where plasticised polymer flows together from two directions or around an opening and does not fuse together properly. Openings in parts should therefore be avoided if at all possible.

Special injection-moulding methods
Short fibres can be mixed into the polymer to comply with particular loadbearing requirements. The orientation of the fibres results from the direction of flow of the polymer melt during the production.
Reinforced reaction injection moulding (e.g. for PUR integral skin foam) employs a different technique to that of injection-moulding. In this method the blowing agent incorporated in the foam formulation supplies the pressure required to fill the mould. The pressure of the foam or a special surface treatment eliminates the air pores on the surfaces and the result is an integral skin foam with a solid surface and a cellular core.

Example: the Panton chair
The well-known Panton chair is produced fully automatically from polypropylene (PP) reinforced with short fibres using the injection-moulding method. After the first series of chairs was produced at great cost from pressed GFRP in the 1960s, it was possible to reduce the price considerably by switching to automated production. Rigid PUR foam and the styrene copolymer ASA were used for the chair in the intervening years but were dropped because of the considerable amount of further work required and the poor ageing resistance. The chair is today made from PP but with a matt surface finish because of the material's low scratch resistance. This flowing chair form with its rounded corners is very comfortable and at the same time reduces the stress concentrations in the polymer material. This design shows, on the one hand, the options for polymers and, on the other, how to employ a form that results in consistent utilisation of the material. [6]

Fibre-reinforced moulded items

Free-form components made from fibre-reinforced polymers are in most instances one-offs intended for specific projects. However, certain semi-finished products such as hoods and covers for sewage treatment plants, rooflights or linings are manufactured in large numbers. For reasons of cost, glass fibres are used almost exclusively as the reinforcement. The irregular forms are frequently shell-shaped because the favourable loadbearing effect of a curved shape also enables longer spans to be realised with GFRP. The deformation problem, which occurs with sections or planar products, can be avoided by choosing a suitable geometry.

Production of fibre-reinforced moulded items
One-offs or small series rely on manual techniques such as laminating, resin infusion or fibre spraying. Compression- or injection-moulding can be used for large batches. The methods of production are described in the chapter entitled "Fibre-reinforced polymers" (pp. 78–81).

Special semi-finished products for engineering applications

Harsh environmental conditions such as direct exposure to the weather, de-icing salts dissolved in water plus dynamic loads and wide temperature fluctuations lead to material corrosion and fatigue in conventional building materials. Reinforced concrete bridges often have to be fully refurbished after just 25 years. Fibre composites can be used for repairs but also in new bridges. It has been shown, however, that loadbearing structures built entirely of fibre-reinforced polymers are not economic as a rule. Such "all-composite solutions" will therefore remain the exception for the foreseeable future.

Repairs with CFRP laminates

Laminates or strips made from carbon fibre-reinforced polymer (CFRP) have been used since the mid-1990s for strengthening damaged reinforced concrete loadbearing structures (Fig. C 3.29). They are bonded to the surface and supplement or replace the corroded steel reinforcement. They can also be used to upgrade the loadbearing capacities of existing structures and therefore improve the factors of safety for imposed or seismic loads. In these cases CFRP laminates can also be attached to masonry components or timber beams. The relatively expensive laminates are only attached locally where their high tensile strength can be fully utilised.
The CFRP laminates are produced in widths between 50 and 120 mm and in thicknesses of 1.2 and 1.4 mm using the pultrusion method. In doing so, the carbon fibres are aligned exclusively in the longitudinal direction (unidirectional) – resulting in a laminate with a high stiffness and tensile strength in the longitudinal direction. Their low weight and flexibility make them very easy to handle on the building site. Wider CFRP strips with unidirectional or textile reinforcement are also produced. In contrast to GFRP products, high-quality epoxy resin (EP) is used exclusively for CFRP components. CFRP laminates are bonded to the reinforced concrete or masonry construction with an epoxy resin mortar (see "Epoxy resin mortar and polymer concrete", p. 56), with the bonding process for reinforced concrete frequently being carried out in conjunction with prestressing in order to make use of the high strength of the laminates more effectively and more economically. This approach minimises cracking in the concrete and reduces the deformations of the loadbearing structure.

External prestressing tendons
The latest developments focus on the use of CFRP laminates as external prestressing tendons for traditional or "low-tower" cable-stayed bridges (so-called extradosed bridges). [7] The anchorages for the CFRP laminates, which are sensitive to transverse compression, and the change in direction (harping) at the intermediate supports represent particular challenges.

GFRP bridge decks
Glass fibre-reinforced polymers are used for road bridge decks because they resist corrosion and fatigue better than conventional materials. The planar products are combined with a primary loadbearing structure of steel or reinforced concrete. Steel-GFRP composite construction has been used widely, first and foremost in the USA, since the mid-1990s. The USA's Federal Highway Administration (FHWA) lists about 70 bridges that have been built with a deck made from GFRP (position as of 2009). [8] GFRP decks are frequently used to replace existing conventional decks during refurbishment work. The damaged decks of composite or steel bridges have been replaced by GFRP decks in many projects; the abutments and main bridge beams are retained.
The possibility to being able to prefabricate lightweight planar products in larger dimensions and transport these to the building site enables bridges to be quickly refurbished and reopened to traffic. One key advantage is that, unlike reinforced concrete, the semi-finished products plus the adhesives and coatings required do not need any long curing times. Several road bridges with GFRP decks have also been built in South Korea recently, including Noolcha Bridge in Busan with a length of 300 m and a width of 35 m. When it was completed in 2007 it was the largest structure in the world built from a fibre-reinforced polymer. [9]

Product forms
Sandwich panels or combined, pultruded sections are used for bridge decks. Sandwich panels carry loads in both directions with the same stiffness, which is why they are ideal for carrying the wheel loads of vehicles (Figs. C 3.28a and b). However, the manual production process results in more generous tolerances than is the case with pultruded sections. The construction details at junctions, joints and connections are also more complicated. Pultruded planar products (Figs. C 3.28c and d) consist of a succession of prismatic sections bonded together. Most of the fibre reinforcement is aligned in the longitudinal direction of the component. Jointing is carried out either in situ or beforehand, in the factory, to form units that are nevertheless transportable. The pultruded bridge deck sections typically span 2–3 m between the main girders. The GFRP deck is either clamped, connected via headed studs or bonded to the main girders.

Example of a steel-GFRP composite bridge
The bridge deck panels made from pultruded GFRP for the steel-GFRP composite bridge in Friedberg north of Frankfurt am Main are bonded to the steel beams with an epoxy resin mortar. The bridge superstructure, including cantilevering footpaths and cycle tracks, bridge parapets, railings and road surfacing, was completely prefabricated in an empty warehouse beforehand, which reduced the work on site to a minimum. The integrated form of construction as a frame eliminates all components that might need servicing, e.g. elastomeric bearings or carriageway expansion joints.
The hollow GFRP sections were closed off at the ends to protect against animals and vermin (Fig. C 3.30b), but the cross-sections of the pultruded bars remain visible in the finished structure.
The road surfacing of polymer concrete (see "Epoxy resin mortar and polymer concrete", p. 56) ensures a rough surface and the uniform distribution of point loads.

References:
[1] http://www.thomas-technik.de/pdf/Radius_Pultrusion.pdf, 19 Aug 2010
[2] Domininghaus, Hans: Die Kunststoffe und ihre Eigenschaften. Berlin/Heidelberg, 2005
[3] http://www.kosche.de/homekovalex/index, 19 Aug 2010
[4] http://www2.dupont.com/Corian/de_DE/assets/downloads/documentation/corian_cladding_de.pdf, 11 Feb 2010
[5] Schwarz, Otto; Ebeling, Friedrich Wolfhard; Furth, Brigitte: Kunststoffverarbeitung. Würzburg, 2002
[6] Remmele, Mathias: Aus einem Guss: Die Entwicklung des Panton-Stuhls.
In: deutsche bauzeitung 4/2006, pp. 27ff.
[7] Knippers, Jan; Hwash, Mohamed: Umgelenkte Lamellen aus kohlenfaserverstärktem Kunststoff für freistehende Spannglieder im Konstruktiven Ingenieurbau. In: Beton- und Stahlbetonbau 10/2008, pp. 68ff.
[8] http://www.fhwa.dot.gov/Bridge/FRP/, 19 Aug 2010
[9] Lee, Sung Woo; Kee-Jeung, Hong: Experiencing More Composite-Deck Bridges and Developing Innovative Profile of Snap-Fit Connection. In: COBRAE Conference – Benefits of Composites in Civil Engineering. Stuttgart, 2007

a

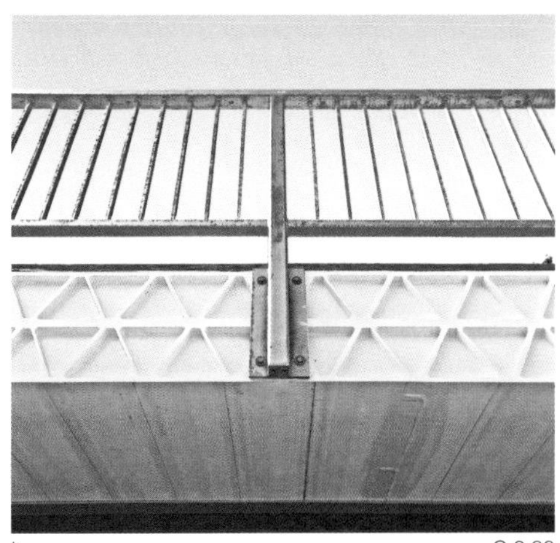
b

C 3.30

Foil

C 4.1

Strictly speaking, the term foil should be reserved for very thin metals. However, it has become established in the building industry for a homogeneous polymer material that is very thin relative to its surface area. In the building industry, foil made from single or composite polymers is used not only for temporary and transport purposes, but primarily for the following functions:

- For waterproofing against precipitation in roofs and facades
- For waterproofing against moisture and hydrostatic pressure in the soil
- For improving the airtightness of building envelopes (to reduce ventilation heat losses)
- As a vapour barrier or vapour check
- As thermal insulation
- For improving the solar control and thermal performance properties of glazing
- For improving the thermal insulation effect of insulating glass units
- In the fabrication of laminated safety glass
- For improving room acoustics with the help of so-called acoustic foil (see "Acoustic foil", p. 118)
- For coating interior surfaces (furniture, built-in items, partitions, floor coverings, etc.)

A detailed presentation of the polymers that can be used and their properties for all the above applications would exceed the scope of this book. This chapter will therefore essentially concentrate on the uses of foil in construction, and the chapter entitled "Building physics and energy aspects" (pp. 108–123) will investigate applications that concern, for example, appearance or acoustics, in conjunction with other materials.

Foil used in construction must satisfy demanding specifications regarding strength, weather resistance, UV stability, surface quality and weldability – properties that are currently offered by very few products only. Therefore, foil made from ethylene tetrafluoroethylene (ETFE) is used almost exclusively for external applications these days. One potential alternative is tetrafluoroethylene hexafluoropropylene vinylidene fluoride (THV), although so far its inferior material properties (primarily its poor soiling behaviour) have led to this material being used on only very few occasions. PVC foil, on the other hand, is used for interior applications and temporary structures (e.g. trade fair stands), and PE foil is well established as an alternative to glass for greenhouses.
In principle we distinguish between different types of foil depending on the configuration of the material:

- Single-ply foil made from one material
- Two-ply foil made from two layers of the same material
- Composite foil made from two or more plies of different materials

Production of foil

A foil web is the wide strip of material produced which is then wound up into a reel (Fig. C 4.5, p. 96). Reels can contain more than 1000 m of material depending on the type of foil and its thickness. The properties of the foil can be different in the longitudinal and transverse directions depending on the production process.

In the first place we distinguish between two different methods of manufacturing polymer foil: moulding and thermoplastic processing. In moulding, a solvent is added to the basic granulate before this blend is moulded to form a foil. The solvents used have a negative effect on the properties of the final foil and so this method is hardly used these days. In thermoplastic processing, the polymer is processed to form a melt without the addition of any solvent. This type of production can be further subdivided into calendering and two forms of extrusion.

Calendering

In the calendering process the raw material, in powder form, is melted down and compacted by applying heat and pressure and then rolled out to form a thin foil in a so-called calender (from the French *calandre* = roller), a series of heated and polished rolls, and finally cooled via "chill" rolls. This method is particularly suitable for producing PVC foil, but calendering can be used for producing foils from polymers such as PE, PP, ABS and other thermoplastics. The surface of the foil can be structured, e.g. embossed, directly in the calendering process.

C 4.1 ETFE foil in various thicknesses (from top to bottom: clear 250 µm, clear 200 µm, white 200 µm)
C 4.2 Properties of loadbearing foils for construction applications

Extrusion
In this method the granulate is melted, mixed, homogenised and transported in a heated metal barrel containing the rotating plasticising screw. This process generates a very high pressure directly in front of the end of the screw which forces the material through a die (see "Extrusion", p. 83). We can subdivide extrusion into two types depending on the die geometry.

Extruding flat foils with a wide-slot die
The use of a die in the form of a wide slot plus downstream "chill" rolls results in a high-quality foil with an excellent surface finish that also complies with high optical requirements (Figs. C 4.3a and C 4.5, p. 96). The manufacturing process is, however, relatively slow. In order to prevent variations in thickness or optical deficiencies such as streaks or waves when producing transparent foil (e.g. ETFE), it is important to ensure that the temperature and the flow rate at the outlet remain very consistent. That in turn requires a considerable investment in the extruder and the dies and, first and foremost, also limits the width of the foil that can be produced in this way. For example, the maximum width of ETFE foil that can be supplied is currently approx. 1.55 m.

Extruding tubular foils with an annular die
An annular die with a mandrel in the middle initially forms the melt into a tube as it leaves the extruder. Air blown in via the mandrel subsequently expands the tube to three or four times its original size. This tube is then carefully cooled and wound up to form reels of "lay-flat" tubular foil or slit open and rolled up as flat foil (Fig. C 4.3b, p. 96). Such foils have an essentially homogenous strength in the longitudinal and transverse directions. This method of production, which generates flat foil from a three-dimensional mould, achieves a high throughput and comparatively large reel widths exceeding 3 m in some cases. Such foil cannot satisfy high optical standards, however. Blown ETFE foil is therefore not used very often in the building industry, except perhaps as a roofing material for greenhouses.

	ETFE foil	THV foil	PE foil	PVC-P foil
Polymer	copolymer of ethylene tetrafluoroethylene	terpolymer of tetrafluoroethylene hexafluoropropylene vinylidene fluoride	polyethylene	polyvinyl chloride
Typical applications	architecture	architecture (as laminate)	greenhouses	interior
Density [g/cm³] (DIN 53479)	1.75	1.98	0.95	1.16–1.35[1]
Standard thicknesses [µm]	12–300	150–500	180–200	70–220
Tensile strength [N/mm²] (DIN EN ISO 527-1)	40 or measured according to DIN 53354 approx. 400 N/50 mm	> 24	approx. 24	10–25[1]
Elongation at rupture [% of length] (DIN EN ISO 527-1)	> 300	> 500	> 400	170–400[1]
Tear propagation resistance [N/mm] at 23 °C longitudinal/transverse (DIN 53363)	> 300/> 300	> 100/> 100 for 200 µm thk.	no data available	no data available
Elastic modulus [N/mm²] (DIN 53457)	800–1000 N	> 50	no data available	no data available[1]
Formability	high	higher than ETFE foil	no data available	high[1]
Long-term stability	very good UV resistance	very good UV resistance	poor UV resistance, approx. 4–5 years (Central Europe) after modification	poor UV resistance
Melting point	260–270 °C	115–125 °C	no data available	no data available
Service temperature range [°C]	-200 bis +150	-50 bis +80	-25 to +80	no data available
Reaction to fire	not readily flammable	not readily flammable	flammable to highly flammable	not readily flammable
Sensitivity to soiling	very low	low	high	high
Light transmittance [%]	> 90	80–93	80–90	up to 90
Remarks	milky at flexed edges	–	higher UV resistance (> 5 years) through co-extrusion with EVA	–
Variations available	transparent, dyed white, various colours, printing possible	transparent	transparent, dyed white	white as standard, other colours

[1] Depends on type and quantity of plasticiser

C 4.2

C 4.3 Foil extrusion
a Extrusion of flat foil
b Extrusion of tubular foil (blown foil)
C 4.4 Flat foil extrusion plant
C 4.5 Reel of ETFE foil
C 4.6 Clear ETFE foil
C 4.7 Coloured ETFE foil
C 4.8 a–c Various printed ETFE foils

1 Metering
2 Granulate
3 Melting
4 Filter
5 Smoothing
6 Cooling
7 Forming
8 Thickness measurement
9 Reel of foil
10 Extruder
11 Air
12 Wide-slot die
13 Air ring
14 Nip rolls
15 Cutting to length

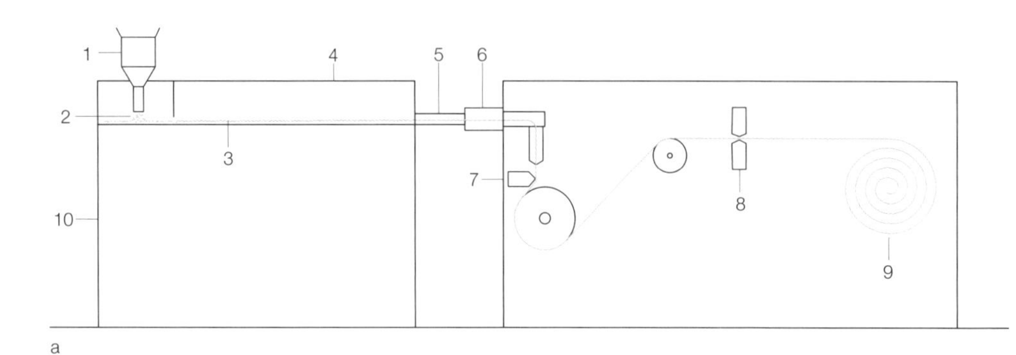

a

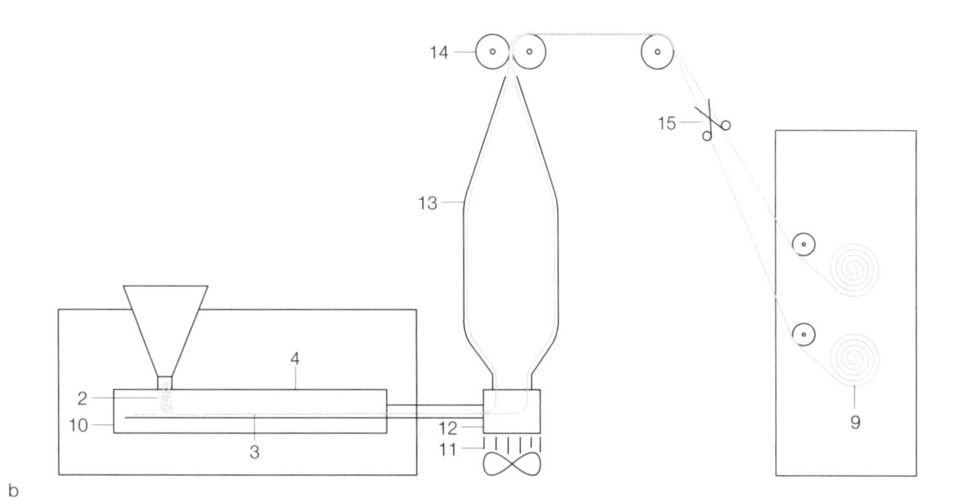

b

C 4.3

C 4.4

C 4.5

Production quality

Flaws that can occur during the production of foils have a negative effect on their usefulness. Such flaws can be local impurities or blemishes, e.g. holes, or more extensive problems such as wavy edges, creases, streaks or thicknesses outside the permissible tolerances. Optimum extruding, rolling or blowing speeds can help to reduce such problems.

Additives

It is also possible to include diverse additives when manufacturing foil – added either during the production of the polymer itself, or during the production of the foil. Such additives include, for example, lubricants or antiblocking agents for optimising the further processing, also antistatic agents, antioxidants and UV absorbers or stabilisers. Pigments are used almost exclusively for colouring foil because the chemical polymer properties make many dyes unsuitable. The addition of pigments colours the entire foil material. The most important white pigment is titanium oxide, which is also used for the production of ETFE foil, for instance (see "Fillers and additives", pp. 32–34).

Further processing options

Foil can be perforated, formed (e.g. embossed, microstructured), printed, coated or laminated in further processing stages. The types of processing possible depend on the particular polymer. Specific pretreatment stages are necessary in some cases in order to increase the polarity (surface energy) of ETFE, which is actually non-polar. The mechanical properties of certain polymer foils can be considerably improved by stretching. To do this, the extruded foil is passed over rolls, the speeds of which increase between machine inlet and outlet, which results in the polymer being stretched in the longitudinal direction. This process can be repeated for the other direction, and then we speak of biaxially stretched material (normal for PP and PET foil, for example).

Semi-finished products and forms of supply

Proper storage and transport is important for reels of high-quality foil that must comply with demanding optical specifications. Ideally, they should be stored and transported on reels that are supported at their ends (see Fig. C 4.5) so that the foil itself is not in contact with any surfaces. Such handling avoids pressure marks and creases in larger and hence heavy reels. The polymer foils used most often for building applications are briefly described below.

ETFE foil

One of the foil materials employed most frequently in the building industry for loadbearing enclosing components is the copolymer ETFE. Since it was launched onto the market in 1970, ETFE has remained one of the most stable chemical compounds known and is therefore

ideal for use in environments where the material is exposed to a diverse range of aggressive actions (acids, alkalis, UV radiation, etc).
Like its chemical relation polytetrafluoroethylene (PTFE), ETFE exhibits an excellent long-lasting soiling behaviour, is very resistant to environmental influences, is also heat- and weather-resistant and boasts long-term UV stability. ETFE foil hardly absorbs short-wave UV radiation, and so the material neither yellows nor becomes brittle. Its mechanical properties are also advantageous. With all these benefits, it is hardly surprising that ETFE is ideal for membrane and tensile structures and is by far the most popular foil material for such applications. Owing to its very high light transmittance and the high permeability in the UV range so important to plant growth, which at the same time limits bacteria growth, the material is frequently used for building envelopes in zoos, greenhouses and other biotopes, and swimming pools. The properties of transparent, pure ETFE foil remain very constant within the production process. Where very large quantities of foil are required, combining different batches from various manufacturers in the same project presents no problems.

Colouring, printing and coating

The addition of pigments enables ETFE foil to be produced in white or other colours. However, the range of colours is limited and depends on the particular manufacturer. White foil, which achieves a very diffuse scattering of the incoming light, is produced in this way (Fig. C 4.7). Provided large quantities are required, the degree of transmittance of a white ETFE foil can be controlled within certain limits through the amount of titanium dioxide added. However, the white pigmentation reduces the radiation transmittance in the UV range considerably. ETFE can also be printed, but the anti-adhesive surface of ETFE means that pretreatment is necessary if the ink applied is to adhere to the material. All manufacturers have their own specific types of pretreatment and printing configurations. A rotogravure printing technique is used and that means many different motifs and patterns are possible. Dots with varying degrees of coverage have become standard (Fig. C 4.8a,b). Where large quantities are required, the repetitive pattern itself and hence the degree of coverage can be varied virtually without any restrictions (Fig. C 4.8c). In addition, the degree of transmittance of the ink itself can be controlled within certain limits. White or silver are the colours used most often because in the majority of architectural applications reflection (of light and heat) is just as important as light transmittance. An unprinted border of sufficient width (30–50 mm) should always be left for welded joints, or printing must be subsequently removed from this zone by mechanical or chemical means. Metallic, ceramic or organic (wet method) coatings can be applied to foils in special plants using techniques such as sputtering, for example. However, these coating methods are still at an early stage of development when it comes to ETFE foil (Figs. C 6.28 and C 6.29, p. 115).
The difficulty with printing is achieving sufficient adhesion between the extremely thin coating layer and the ETFE – realised through matching the materials carefully and through pretreatment. In addition, the functional layers on both sides are often at risk of corrosion and must be permanently protected by suitable techniques. The total make-up must be able to withstand the actions during processing and erection and accommodate the inevitable strains induced in the material during long-term usage.
Laminating foils one on top of the other protects printed motifs and coatings. ETFE foil laminates have a layer of pure ETFE on the outside and can therefore be processed just like single-ply ETFE.

Mechanical properties of ETFE foil

The most important mechanical parameters of foil materials are their tensile strength, elongation at rupture, tear propagation resistance and elastic modulus (Fig. C 4.2, p. 95; see also "Mechanical properties", p. 105). Especially important for ETFE foil is the way these values depend on the duration of loading and the ambient temperature.
ETFE foil is almost isotropic in its behaviour, virtually linear-elastic up to a certain point for short-term loads. Fig. C 4.9 (p. 98) shows the strength/elongation relationship for the typical range of thicknesses (100–300 μm) in which the tearing resistance is > 40 N/mm². The approximately linear-elastic zone, in which the material exhibits its maximum stiffness, extends up to an elongation of approx. 10 %. The tensile strength at this elongation can be used in structural analyses. Afterwards, the curve flattens off noticeably, indicating increased strain and plastic deformation. The force that can be accommodated increases up to failure.
The curve shifts depending on the stress state, the stiffness changes depending on whether the material has been prestressed in one direction (monoaxial) or two (biaxial).
Fig. C 4.10 (p. 98) shows the stress–strain diagrams for samples of material with monoaxial and biaxial pretension; the stiffness of the monoaxial specimen is much lower than that of the biaxial version.
In addition to the duration of loading, the temperature of the surroundings also has a considerable influence on the stiffness of the material as well as its relaxation and creep behaviour. Fig. C 4.12a shows the different cyclic loads on a specimen in the longitudinal and transverse directions. At approx. -25 °C the strains always revert to zero even after several loading cycles (Fig. C 4.12b, p. 98). The material begins to creep significantly even at a temperature of just +35 °C, a fact that is revealed by the shift in the strain curve, which indicates a residual strain after each loading cycle (Fig. C 4.12c, p. 98). When designing the details for a structure, this phenomenon must be taken into account, especially with moderate and higher temperatures, e.g. between an air-filled cushion and the supporting construction or with regard to tensioning systems for single-ply designs. The same applies for choosing the magnitude of tensioning when using ETFE in building envelopes exposed to high temperatures or severe temperature fluctuations. As ETFE starts to lose strength at a temperature of +70 °C, the material tends to be more suitable for longer spans in colder or temperate climate zones.

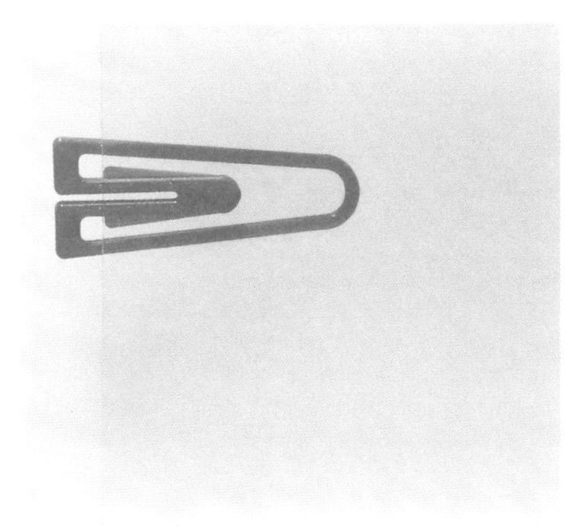

C 4.6

C 4.7

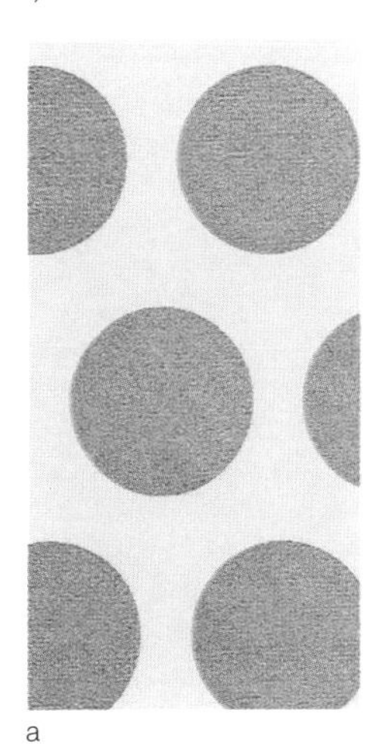

a

b

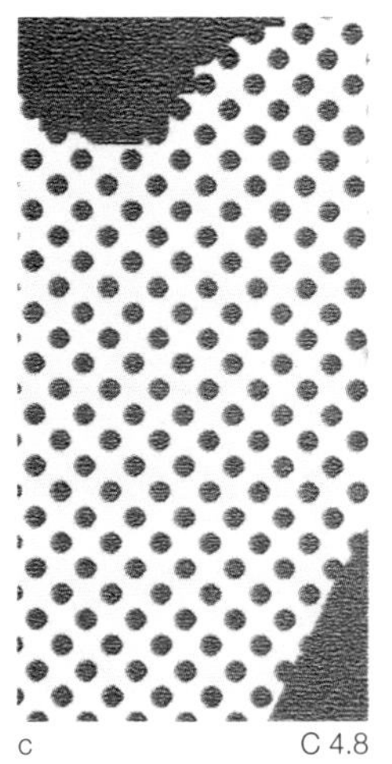

c C 4.8

Fatigue strength tests involve subjecting the material to a constant, high stress over a longer period of time and measuring the strain. Such tests reveal that the creep of the material drops again after approx. 1000 hours regardless of the magnitude of the load (Fig. C 4.10). ETFE also exhibits a high tear propagation resistance, good impact strength and a high resistance to flex cracking.

Fabrication of ETFE foil

The typical fabrication steps such as cutting to size and welding are described in the chapter entitled "Fabrication" (pp. 106–107). The aspects discussed here are therefore those specific to foil.

Welding is used to join together pieces of ETFE foil. This involves applying heat (approx. 280°C) and pressure to an approx. 10–15 mm overlap between two foil sections, either in 15–30 s cycles or at a rate of approx. 3 m/min in a continuous operation (Figs. C 4.13 to C 4.15). A width of 6–10 mm is standard for the weld seam itself. In contrast to a number of other synthetic materials, no additional materials or chemical substances are required for the welded connection.

Straight seams (see "Welded seams", p. 198) or uncut large sections can be welded together in fast cycles with welding beams. Curved edges are welded with roller devices. Laser welding methods are currently undergoing trials. It is hoped that laser welding will enable the width of the weld seam to be reduced to approx. 3–4 mm and the speed of welding to be increased considerably. This would make even complicated irregular seams possible which could then open up other applications for ETFE foil (e.g. complex absorber or heat exchanger geometries).

Fabrication also includes the installation of the air valves required for pneumatic cushions, possibly also rainwater overflow systems (Fig. E 3.16, p. 194). Keders (see below) are preferably welded on as part of the prefabrication work, and EPDM/polymer clamping bars (see "Details", pp. 190–191) usually attached in the factory.

C 4.9 Typical strength–elongation diagram for ETFE foil
1 Approximately linear-elastic zone
2 Tensile strength at 10% elongation
3 Yield strength
4 Ultimate tensile strength

C 4.10 Stiffness of ETFE foil subjected to monoaxial and biaxial stress

C 4.11 Fatigue strength tests carried out on biaxially and anisotropically prestressed ETFE foil subjected to various stresses

C 4.12 a Biaxial tensile tests with incremental load increases for various temperatures [1]
b Stress–strain curve from biaxial tensile test at -25°C
c Stress–strain curve from biaxial tensile test at +35°C

C 4.13 Continuous welding of an ETFE foil

C 4.14 Continuous welding of a printed ETFE foil

C 4.15 Profiled weld seam

C 4.16 PP keder welded into the edge of a foil

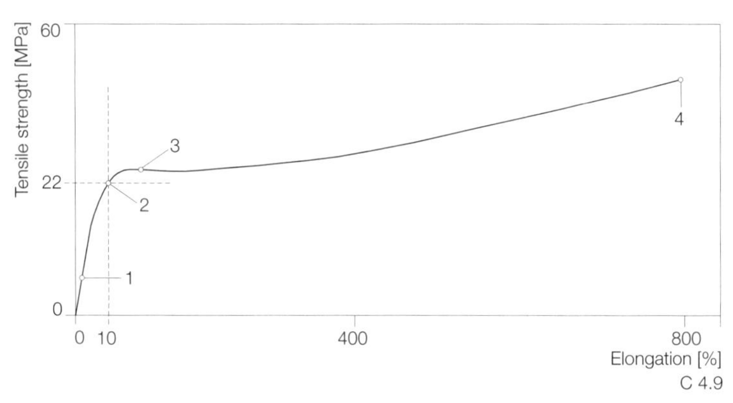

C 4.9

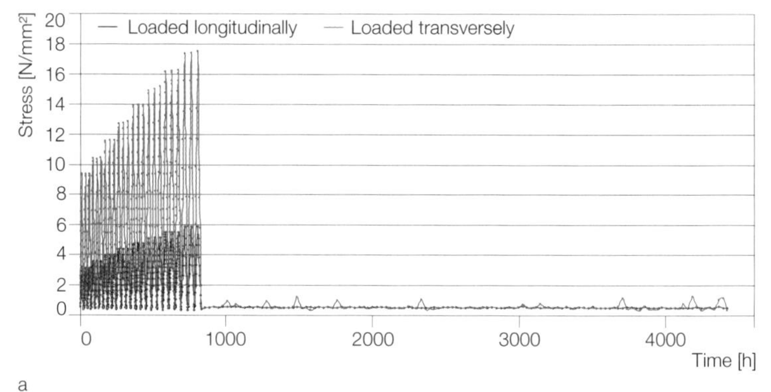

a

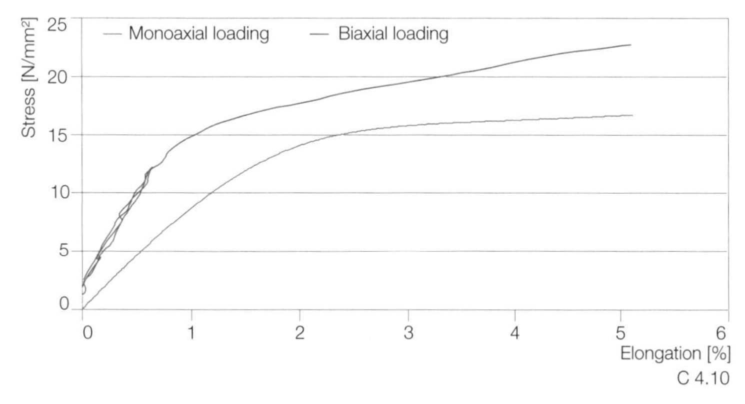

C 4.10

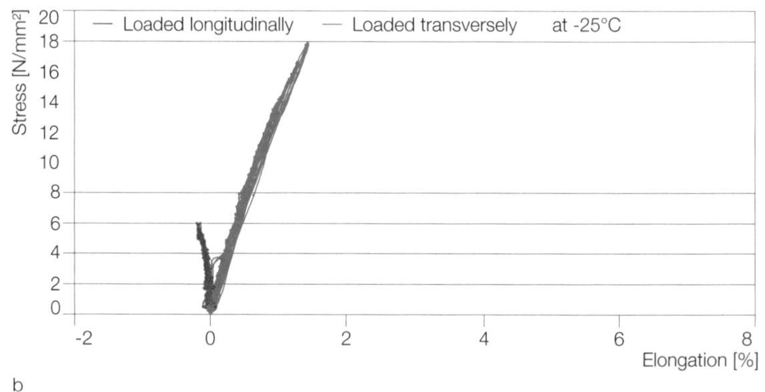

b

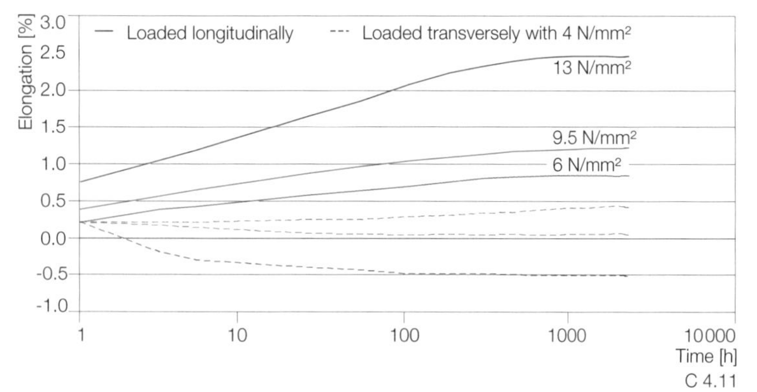

C 4.11

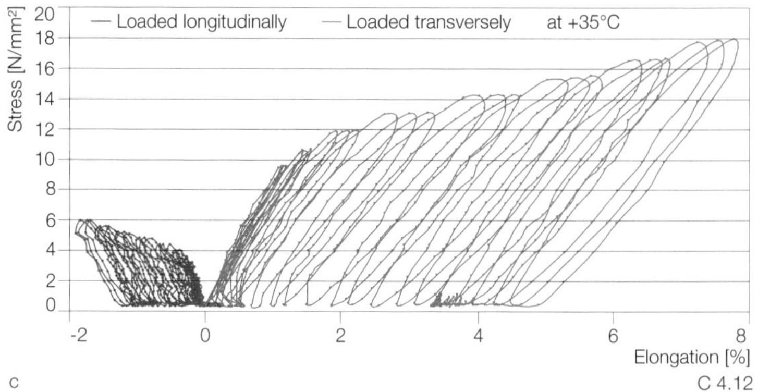

c

C 4.12

PVC foil
Polyvinyl chloride foil is made from PVC containing plasticiser (PVC-P) and has comparatively low UV and heat resistance. Its low strength, the high strains in the material and an unfavourable soiling behaviour all contribute to limiting its use for building applications. However, this material is inexpensive and therefore it is often used internally, e.g. as a surface finish and for furniture and trade fair stands. It can be joined by welding or adhesives.

PE foil
Polyethylene foil is extremely cheap and available in various thicknesses, which are used for many applications on construction sites. Its low price and high light transmittance make it a favourite for greenhouses even though it is not very durable. PE foil is not UV-resistant and so a suitable formulation must be employed, which increases its service life to a few years for external applications, depending on the actual level of UV radiation. This low-budget material is also frequently employed for temporary structures. For example, the "bubble" of the "Mobile Action Space" project (p. 252) is made from a translucent, fibre-reinforced PE foil.

PTFE foil
Foil made from polytetrafluoroethylene (PTFE) is self-cleaning, stable in UV light and very resistant to chemical substances and mould growth. It is produced in thicknesses from 0.025 to 6 mm and widths up to 1.5 m by means of a peeling method not unlike that used for producing wood veneers: a rigid, wide blade slices off the foil web from a rotating cylinder of solid material. PTFE foil normally has a milky white appearance but can be produced in other colours as well. It has a lower strength and lower formability than ETFE foil and so it can only be used for construction projects when laminated to glass cloth (see "PTFE-coated glass-fibre cloth", p. 104). For other applications, PTFE foil can be produced etched on one side or as a self-adhesive material (with acrylic or silicone adhesives). Typical applications outside the building industry include reusable baking foil, conveyor belts and screw thread sealing tapes. It is also very important as a separating layer in the welding of polymers. It prevents material adhering to the welding mirrors, the hot metal surfaces required when welding the corner joints of PVC window frames.

THV foil
The properties of the fluoropolymer THV (tetrafluoroethylene hexafluoropropylene vinylidene fluoride) are similar to those of ETFE. Foils made from this material are likewise highly transparent, very durable and not readily flammable. Compared with ETFE, they are more elastic, easier to work and can be joined using high-frequency welding (see "Fabrication", pp. 106–107). But they are inferior in terms of their optical properties and especially their soiling behaviour. THV has a lower tearing resistance than ETFE and so it can only be used for bridging over small spans, e.g. for filling the apertures of cable nets. THV is sometimes used as a coating for high-quality polyester membranes (see "Semi-finished products and forms of supply", pp. 103–105).

Keders

The edges of cushions, rigid edges to membranes and flexible clamping bar joints and edges are joined by so-called keders (beading) to form structural, interlocking connections between flexible membranes and stiff keder rails or clamping bars (see "Edges", pp. 190–191, and "Clamping and keder details", pp. 197–198). Keders can be made from polypropylene (PP, Fig. C 4.16), PVC monofilaments or polyurethane (PUR). In order to ensure that the keder does not deform under load to such an extent that it slips out of its rail, it should exhibit a Shore hardness of at least SH 50 (see "Hardness", p. 35). Steel ropes or round aluminium sections can be used for the keders in tensile structures. Ropes made from polymers are generally unsuitable because of their relatively flexible construction.
As with lightweight types of membrane, keders can also be welded into strips along the edges of a foil.

References:
[1] Saxe, Klaus; Homm, Thomas (University of Duisburg-Essen): Mechanische Eigenschaften von ETFE-Folien für vorgespannte Strukturen. Contribution to Techtextil Symposium, 12 Jun 2007

C 4.13

C 4.14

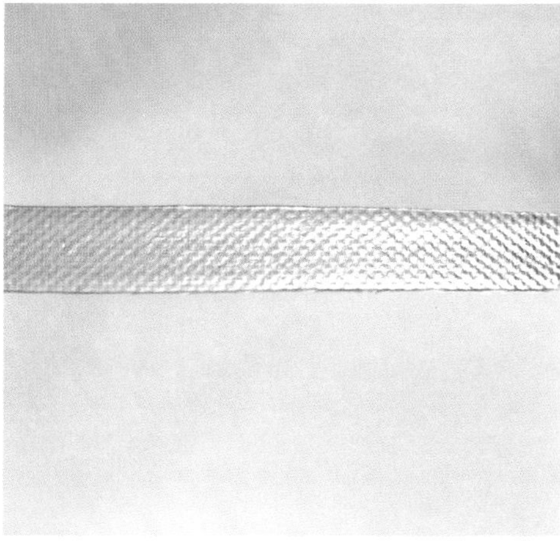
C 4.15

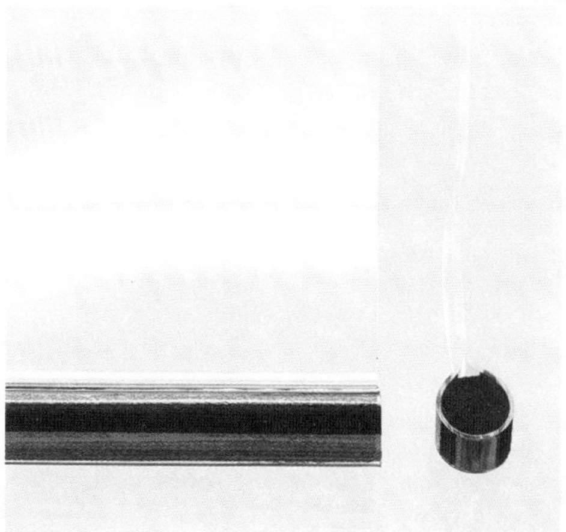
C 4.16

Textile membranes

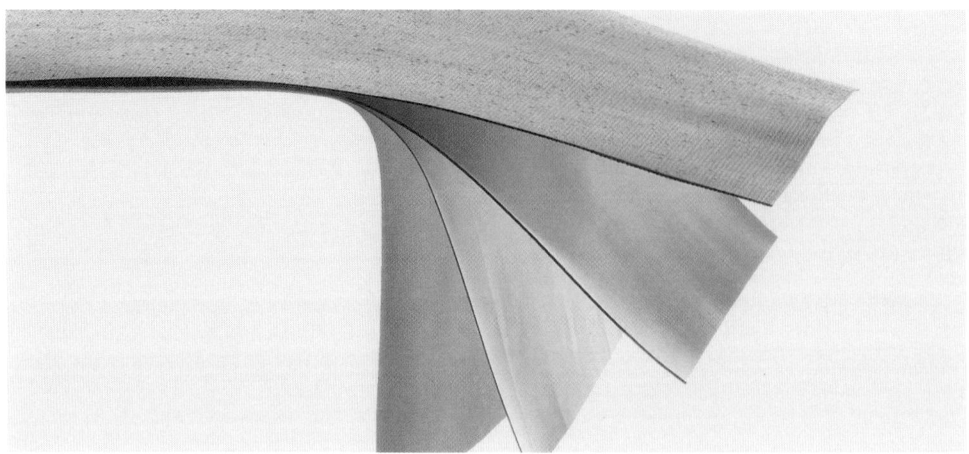

C 5.1

The term membrane is derived from the Latin word *membrana* (= skin). It describes a flexible material that is very thin relative to its surface area. In biology this term stands for a thin layer of skin with a separating or boundary function. In the building industry textiles in the form of coated and uncoated woven fabrics and also polymer foils or thin sheet metals can all be classed as membranes. This chapter deals with the engineering textiles relevant for tensile surface structures. As membranes perform both loadbearing and enclosing functions, their surface characteristics are just as important as the tensile strength and elasticity of the material used. The mechanical properties are primarily influenced by the thread material used and the type of weave, whereas coatings provide a protective, waterproofing function and produce the desired surface finish.

The membranes typically used in construction projects are composites of woven fabrics and several layers of a coating substance. Uncoated, i.e. open woven fabrics with coated fibres, are sometimes used in certain cases, e.g. convertible membrane structures with high demands placed on flexibility.
Uncoated woven fabrics and nets can also be used for sunshades and room acoustics purposes.

Requirements profile for membrane materials

Very diverse requirements are placed on membrane materials for mechanically prestressed structures (Fig. C 5.3). Currently, there are no materials on the market that satisfy all demands completely. So the criteria must be weighted accordingly depending on application and location. For example, whereas very high strength and good long-term behaviour are crucial for the roof to a large sports stadium, lightness, foldability and flex cracking resistance are the deciding factors for convertible membrane designs. The qualities of three typical membrane materials satisfying different specifications are compared with each other in Fig. C 5.2; the best material currently available in each class is given a value of 100%. From this diagram it is clear that none of the products can cover all requirements equally. Criteria such as flex cracking resistance and light transmittance must be assessed separately for each project. The cost of a material must not be considered in isolation, either, because the choice of material always has an effect on the fabrication and construction costs specific to a project and at the same time must be coordinated with the expectations regarding the durability of the material.

Coatings

The most important function of a membrane coating is to protect the woven fabric against moisture, UV radiation, fire and attack by microbes or fungi; its quality is therefore crucial to the service life of the material. However, the coating to a membrane not only protects the fabric and hence improves its durability, but also influences the mechanical properties. Fixing the geometry of the woven fabric increases, in particular, its shear stiffness and also improves the tear propagation resistance in some instances. Coated membrane materials are therefore similar to composite materials (see "Fibre-reinforced polymers", pp. 76–81). Thermoplastic coatings enable individual pieces of membrane material to be welded together. And membranes can be coloured either by adding pigments to the coating or printing on the coating itself.
The woven fabric must be pretreated before applying coatings, normally on both sides. The coatings used for all customary fabrics made from synthetic organic and inorganic fibres (polyester, PTFE, glass; see "Fibres", pp. 48–53) are made from thermoplastics (PVC, PTFE and other fluoropolymers). Exceptions are silicone rubber, which belongs to the elastomers group, and silicone resin, which is a thermoset. Generally speaking, coatings have an influence on the following properties:

- Strain and shear stiffness
- Weldability
- UV protection of the fabric
- Watertightness
- Reaction to fire

C 5.1 Four membrane materials with similar strengths but very different flexibilities; from top to bottom: PTFE/glass, polyester-PVC, coated PTFE fabric, uncoated PTFE fabric
C 5.2 Comparison of three typical membrane materials (best value in each case taken as 100%)
C 5.3 The properties required of membrane materials
C 5.4 The make-up of a polyester-PVC membrane
C 5.5 Plants for coating membranes
a Doctor blade plant
b Dip coating plant

- Light transmittance
- Light reflectance
- Scattering the incoming light
- Soiling behaviour
- Colouring
- Heat radiation

Various methods are used to apply coatings to fabrics, and these are described below.

Doctor blade method

The doctor blade method is generally used for PVC and silicone coatings (Fig. C 5.5a). The premixed, viscous coating paste (plastisol) for PVC-coated polyester membranes (polyester-PVC) consists of PVC powder dispersed in a plasticiser. Additives such as heat and light stabilisers, fungicides, bactericides and pigments are mixed in as required. This paste-like compound is spread over the woven fabric and the excess scraped off with fixed doctor blades. This operation is generally repeated several times: the first step is the application of a bond enhancer and the actual coating itself is applied in the second and, if necessary, third steps. Afterwards, the PVC and the plasticiser are chemically bonded in a gelation oven at a temperature of about 180 °C. A coating on both sides is normal and so the whole procedure is repeated for the other side, unless the work is being carried out a vertical coating plant in which case both sides are coated at the same time. Finally, top coats are applied with rollers or by spraying. A top coat prevents the plasticiser from escaping under the action of UV radiation and also optimises the surface with respect to abrasion and soiling behaviour (Fig. C 5.4).

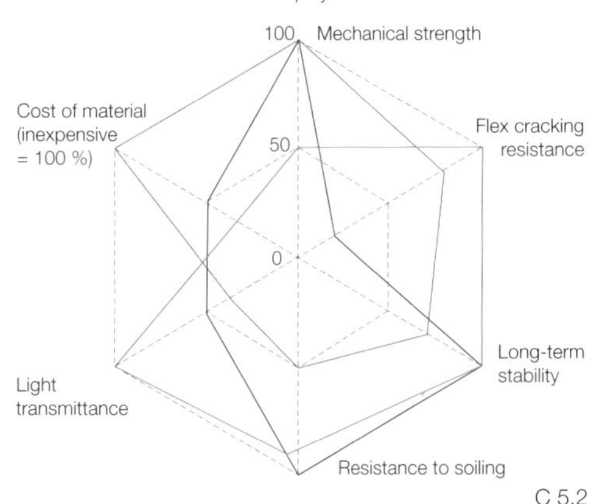

C 5.2

Mechanical strength	• High tensile strength • High tear propagation resistance • Similar stiffnesses in warp and weft directions	• High elongation at rupture • Low creep under high long-term loading • Good formability
Flex cracking resistance	• Foldability (mobile or convertible designs)	• No fibre breakage under compressive stresses
Protection against the effects of the weather	• Resistant to chemical and biological influences	• Stable in UV light
Surface characteristics	• Weldable • Self-cleaning, anti-adhesive surface	• Suitable for coatings • Aesthetically appealing feel and colour
Fire protection	• Not readily flammable or better • No burning droplets	• Minimum fume and smoke development (toxicity)
Light transmittance	• Desired transmittance	• Desired reflection
Economy	• Low raw materials costs • Low fabrication costs	• Low material-related design and construction costs • Long life expectancy

C 5.3

1 Untreated fabric
2 Bond enhancer
3 Coating
4 Top coat
5 Untreated fabric
6 Bond enhancer scraped off with air knife
7 Gelation oven
8 "Chill" rolls
9 Top coat scraped off with knife-over-roll
10 Gelation oven
11 Coated fabric
12 Dipping tank
13 Scraping off
14 Drying
15 Pre-sintering
16 Sintering

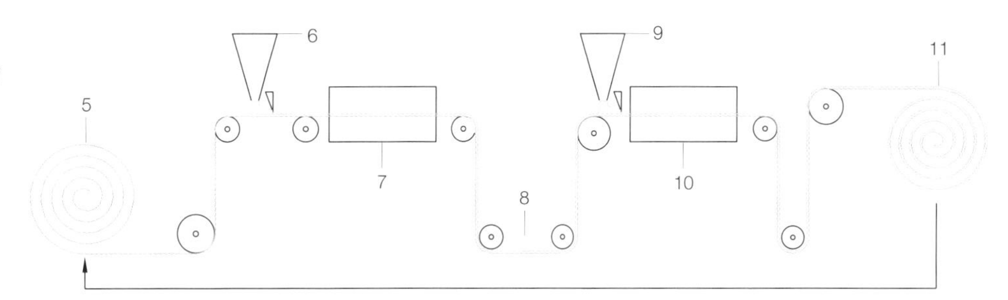

a

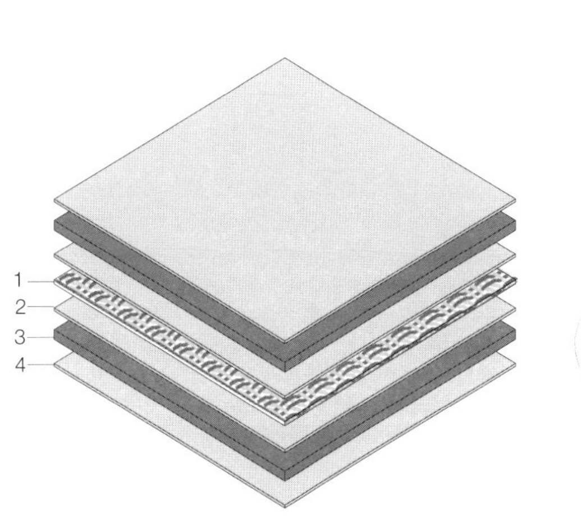

C 5.4

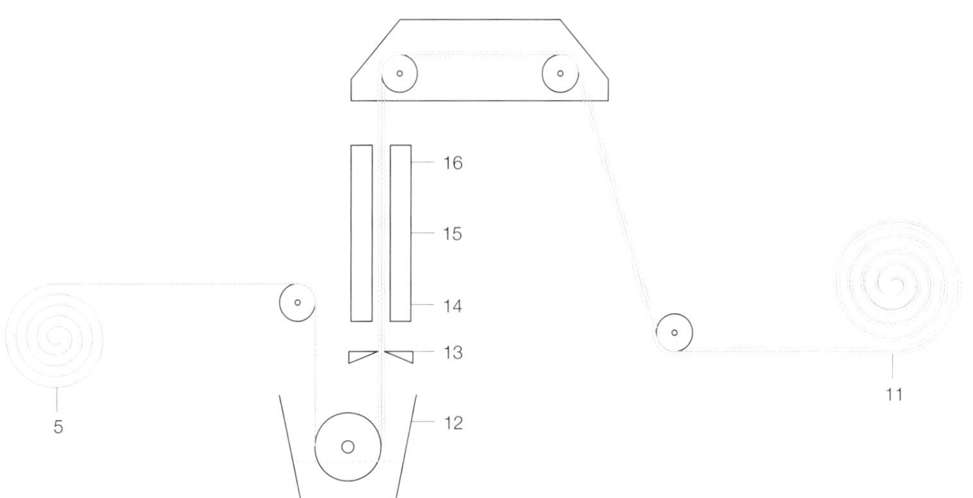

b

C 5.5

	PVC-coated polyester fabric	THV-coated polyester fabric	PTFE-coated glass-fibre fabric	Silicone-coated glass-fibre fabric	PDFE-laminated glass-fibre mesh	Coated PTFE fabric	Uncoated PTFE fabric
Applications, special features	Diverse applications, very cheap standard material	High-quality surface, very high light transmittance	For permanent structures, high-quality standard material	For permanent structures, high light transmittance	For permanent structures, high light transmittance with high strength	For permanent and mobile structures, high light transmittance	For permanent and mobile structures, high light transmittance, low rainproofing quality
Jointing methods	High-frequency and impulse welding	High-frequency and impulse welding	Impulse welding with intermediate foil	Vulcanising (bonding) or stitching and gluing (combination seam)	Impulse welding with intermediate foil	High-frequency welding	Stitching
Long-term stability	Good UV stability with sufficiently thick coating, good chemical resistance	No data available	Very good UV stability, very good chemical resistance	Good UV stability, good chemical resistance	Good UV stability, very good chemical resistance	Very good UV stability, very good chemical resistance	Very good UV stability, very good chemical resistance
Sensitivity to flex cracking	Highly resistant to flex cracking, suitable for convertible systems	Resists flex cracking, suitable for convertible systems	Highly sensitive to flex cracking, unsuitable for convertible systems	Low sensitivity to flex cracking	Highly sensitive to flex cracking, unsuitable for convertible systems	Highly resistant to flex cracking, suitable for convertible systems	Highly resistant to flex cracking, ideal for convertible systems
Sensitivity to soiling	Vulnerable to soiling, better with top coat, e.g. fluoride lacquer	Good soiling behaviour	Very good soiling behaviour, self-cleaning	Vulnerable to soiling	Self-cleaning, but dust and dirt can collect owing to rough surface	Good soiling behaviour	Good soiling behaviour
Light transmittance	5–15% Greying causes a rise in solar absorption	15–23%	8–20%	25–30%	43–46%	20–40%	35%
Environmental impact (coating and fabric considered separately, separation generally still difficult, first recycling systems still being established)	PVC degrades and forms chlorine/hydrochloric acid, collect and return network exists; polyester can be melted down or reused as short fibres	THV decomposes at high temperatures	Environmentally friendly disposal of glass fibres, PTFE does not degrade but decomposes at high temperatures and produces fluorine	Environmentally friendly disposal of glass fibres, silicone can be recycled	Environmentally friendly disposal of glass fibres, PTFE does not degrade but decomposes at high temperatures and produces fluorine	Waste streams must be kept separate, PTFE does not degrade but decomposes at high temperatures and produces fluorine	Waste streams must be kept separate, PTFE does not degrade but decomposes at high temperatures and produces fluorine
Reaction to fire (building materials class to DIN 4102)	B1	B1	A2 (types I and II) B1 (types III and IV)	B1	B1	B1 S1–d0 (EN 13501)	B1 S1–d0 (EN 13501)
Standard colours	White as standard, other colours available	White as standard	White as standard, limited selection of colours	White and silver as standard, other colours	Colourless	White as standard	Some coloured yarns available
Weight per unit area[1] to DIN 55352 [g/m²]	Type I: 750 Type II: 900 Type III: 1100 Type IV: 1300 Type V: 1450	Type I: 1150 Type II: 1200	Type I: 800 Type II: 900 Type III: 1200 Type IV: 1500	Type 0: 200 Type I: 340 Type III: 685 Type IV: 1100	1050	1080	320 530
Tensile strength[1] (warp/weft) to DIN 53354 [N/50 mm]	Type I: 3000/3000 Type II: 4200/4000 Type III: 5800/5400 Type IV: 7500/6500 Type V: 10 000/9000	Type I: 3500/3000 Type II: 5000/4500	Type I: 3500/3500 Type II: 5000/4500 Type III: 7000/6000 Type IV: 8000/7000	Type 0: 2500/1750 Type I: 3000/3000 Type III: 5000/5000 Type IV: 8000/8000	4500/4000	4000/4000	2000/2050 4000/3700
Tear propagation resistance[1] (warp/weft) to DIN 53363 [N]	Type I: 300/300 Type II: 500/500 Type III: 850/800 Type IV: 1200/1200 Type V: 1800/1800	Type I: 700/700 Type II: 600/600	Type I: 300/300 Type II: 350/350 Type III: 500/500 Type IV: 500/500	Type 0: 350/400 Type II: 300/300 Type III: 400/400 Type IV: 500/500	250/250	798/752	365/330 669/550
Service life	15–20	No data available	> 25	> 20	> 25	> 25	> 30
Cost of raw materials[2]	15–45%	60–140%	50–150%	110–180%	100–180%	100–140%	120–170%
Examples	Fig. D 1.1, p. 134; Figs. D 1.14–D 1.17, p. 141; Fig. E 4.50, p. 210		Examples 17–22, pp. 262–281	Fig. D 1.21, p. 142		Figs. D 1.32 & D 1.33, p. 147; example 23, pp. 282–285	Fig. D 1.37, p. 149; Fig. E 4.1, p. 196; Fig. E 4.51, p. 210

[1] Mean values [2] Compared with the average price for PTFE/glass (100%)

C 5.6

Dip coating method

Dip coating is used primarily for PTFE coatings, but in some instances also for PVC coatings on wide-mesh fabrics (Fig. C 5.5b, p. 101).
To coat glass-fibre materials with PTFE (PTFE/glass), the fabric is immersed in a dispersion of PTFE particles and thus coated on both sides. Raising the temperature incrementally during the drying and sintering stages causes the water to evaporate, the wetting agent for reducing the interfacial surface tension to decompose and, finally, the PTFE particles to sinter at approx. 330 °C. The process is repeated several times in order to achieve the coating thicknesses necessary. PTFE coatings can only be applied to woven fabrics with a very high melting point because of the high sintering temperatures; coating a polyester fabric with PTFE is therefore impossible.

Low E coatings

So-called low E (low emissivity) coatings lower the heat radiation effect considerably and are currently being offered for various membrane materials, e.g. PTFE/glass, (Fig. C 5.15, p. 107). How such coatings work is described in the chapter entitled "Selectivity and low E surfaces" (p. 116).

Semi-finished products and forms of supply

The textile backing and the coating are made from different materials and so both are mentioned when designating the membrane material. Common combinations of woven fabric and coating are (Fig. C 5.6):

- Polyester fabric with PVC or THV coating
- Glass-fibre fabric with PTFE or silicone coating or with laminated PTFE foil
- PTFE fabric with fluoropolymer coating (also available uncoated)

At present, PTFE/glass and polyester-PVC are the most common membrane materials with the largest shares of the market.

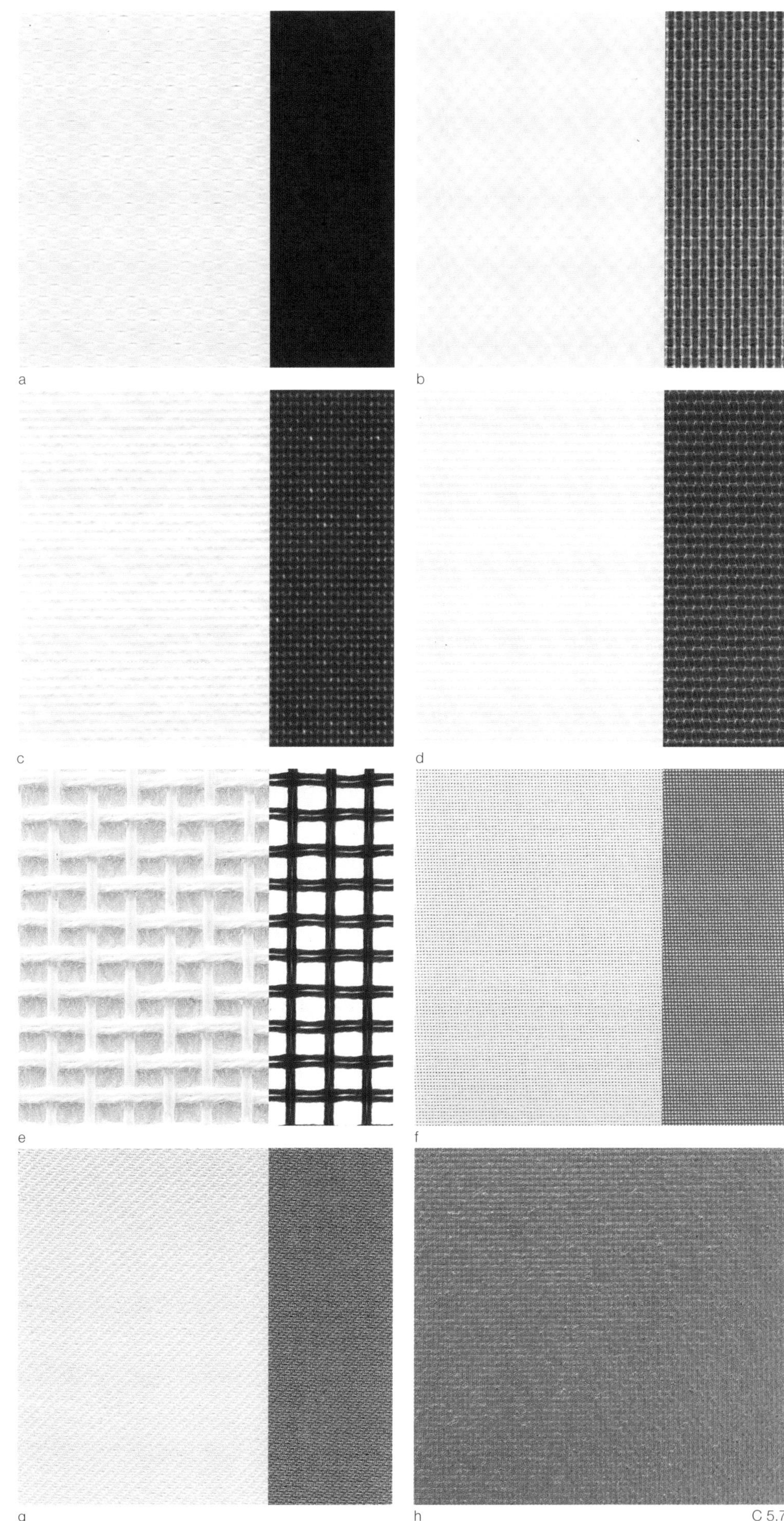

C 5.6 The properties of standard textile membrane materials
C 5.7 Coated and uncoated fabrics, in each case photographed in direct light and – to enable a qualitative comparison of the light transmittance – lit from behind
a PVC-coated polyester fabric
b THV-coated polyester fabric
c PTFE-coated glass-fibre fabric
d Silicone-coated glass-fibre fabric
e PTFE-laminated glass-fibre mesh
f Coated PTFE fabric
g Uncoated PTFE fabric
h Coating for reducing emissivity (low E coating) applied to a PTFE/glass membrane (photographed in direct light only)

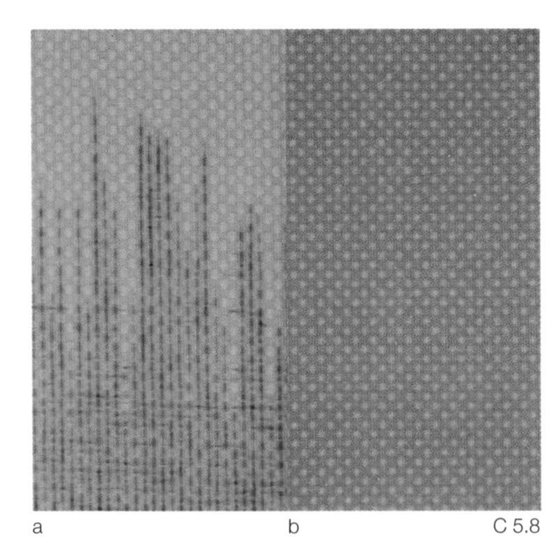

a b C 5.8

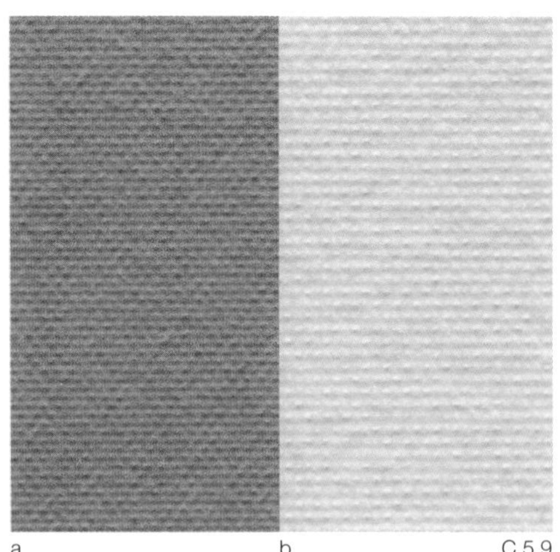

a b C 5.9

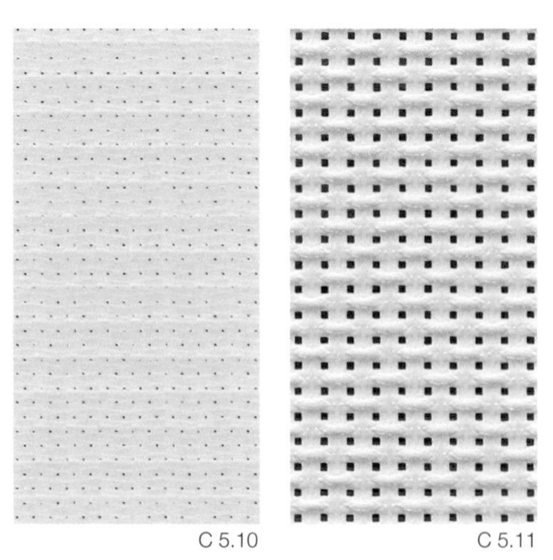

C 5.10 C 5.11

PVC-coated polyester fabric

Polyester-PVC (Fig. C 5.7a, p. 103) is widely used for tensile structures. Its high mechanical strength and flex cracking resistance make it a favourite for both permanent membrane roofs and convertible designs. Owing to the low cost of its raw materials and production, polyester-PVC is one of the least expensive membrane materials available on the market. It is also very widely used in a similar form for other applications (e.g. HGV tarpaulins). Polyester-PVC membranes are enhanced for construction uses in order to improve their long-term behaviour. It is especially important to coat the fibres with a so-called low-wick substance in order to prevent moisture being absorbed and dust and dirt particles adhering at exposed edges (Fig. C 5.8). The polyester fabric consists mainly of the synthetic polymer polyethylene terephthalate (PET); the abbreviation PES often used is the internationally agreed designation for polyester fibres (see "PET fibres", p. 52).
In the past, the rapid ageing of the material due to embrittlement of the coating had a serious negative effect on the image of tensile surface structures. Today, the loss of the UV and heat stabilisers, also the plasticiser, can sometimes be slowed down by sealing the material with acrylate and PVDF (polyvinylidene fluoride) lacquers or PVF (polyvinyl fluoride) laminates. These top coats made from fluoride lacquer also create a smooth, anti-adhesive finish that helps to prevent dust and dirt clinging to the surface. However, as these materials have a much higher melting point than PVC coatings, it is sometimes necessary to roughen the surface prior to welding. Fig. C 5.4 (p. 101) illustrates the typical make-up of a polyester-PVC membrane.

THV-coated polyester fabric

Polyester fabric coated with the polymer tetrafluoroethylene hexafluoropropylene vinylidene fluoride (THV) is a relative newcomer to the market (Fig. C 5.7b, p. 103). THV is a fluoropolymer that, in the form of a foil, is used as an alternative to ETFE (see "THV foil", p. 99). The main advantages of a THV over a PVC coating are its better weathering resistance and the self-cleaning effect of the surface plus its much better light transmittance and UV resistance. The mechanical properties are comparable with those of polyester-PVC types I and II. One disadvantage is sometimes its relatively high weight per unit area (when compared with its strength). Experience regarding its long-term behaviour in practice is not yet available.

PTFE-coated glass-fibre fabric

Glass-fibre fabric coated with polytetrafluoroethylene (PTFE, better known as Teflon; see "PTFE foil", p. 99; Fig. C 5.7c, p. 103) is regarded as one of the most durable membrane materials because the coating is self-cleaning and very resistant to chemical substances and mould growth. Lightweight versions (types I and II) with a relatively thin coating are incombustible (DIN 4102 building materials class A2), heavier types are classed only as not readily flammable because of the thicker coating (DIN 4102 class B1). Newly coated material is initially beige in colour when shipped due to the decomposition of the wetting agent in the coating, but fades after erection due to the action of UV radiation (sunlight) (Fig. C 5.9). This process takes approx. 2–3 months in Northern Europe, a correspondingly shorter time in regions with higher levels of solar radiation. Factory-prebleaching is possible but very expensive, and also reduces the strength of the material. The PTFE coating is generally given a top coat in order to improve the anti-adhesive characteristic and weldability. A thermoplastic fluoropolymer foil, e.g. made from perfluoroalkoxy (PFA), perfluoroethylene propylene (FEP) or tetrafluoroethylene-perfluoro methyl vinyl ether (MFA), is applied to the seam to improve the weldability for impulse welding (see "Hot-plate and impulse welding", p. 106).

Silicone-coated glass-fibre cloth (glass-silicone)

Owing to its high light transmittance, its good mechanical properties and its flex cracking resistance, when compared with PTFE/glass, glass-silicone (Fig. C 5.7d, p. 103; see also "Glass fibres", p. 50) represents an interesting alternative to the customary membrane materials. The flexibility of the silicone coating makes the material easier to handle than PTFE/glass. And its light transmittance is three times higher than that of polyester-PVC; even coloured material still exhibits a very high light transmittance. And the chemical resistance of silicone helps to make this material very resistant to ageing processes. One disadvantage is the sticky surface of silicone rubbers and their tendency to attract a static electric charge, which can quickly lead to soiling. Newly developed top coats can improve the cleaning behaviour. Another disadvantage is that materials coated with silicone cannot be welded because they do not have a distinct melting point. Joints between pieces of material must be vulcanised or glued – expensive and complex processes (see "Gluing", p. 107). Although pure silicone is incombustible, the membrane material can only be classed as not readily flammable (DIN 4102 class B1) because of the additives in the coating and the top coats.

PTFE-laminated glass-fibre mesh

In this material a PTFE foil is laminated directly onto a wide-mesh glass-fibre backing net (Fig. C 5.7e, p. 103). The open mesh results in a very high light transmittance of up to 65 %. But the limited stretchability and formability of the material are disadvantages that make erection and prestressing very difficult. PTFE laminate is essentially self-cleaning, but dust and dirt can still collect on the uneven surface. Impulse welding can be used for joints on the surface. However, the material's low flexibility mean that it is difficult to fold over and form, for example, loops or pockets for integrating edge ropes or keders. One solution to this is to provide welded strips made from conventional PTFE/glass along the edges.

C 5.8 Polyester-PVC strips dipped in coloured ink
a without coating
b with fibres coated to minimise the wick effect (low-wick coating)
C 5.9 PTFE/glass membrane
a Directly after production
b Faded after exposure to UV light
C 5.10 Acoustic fabric with microperforations
C 5.11 PVC-coated polyester net as sunshading membrane
C 5.12 Qualitative comparison of the elongation at rupture of customary membrane materials in thicknesses with similar strengths; uniaxial tensile test at room temperature; the absolute values can vary considerably depending on manufacturer and batch.

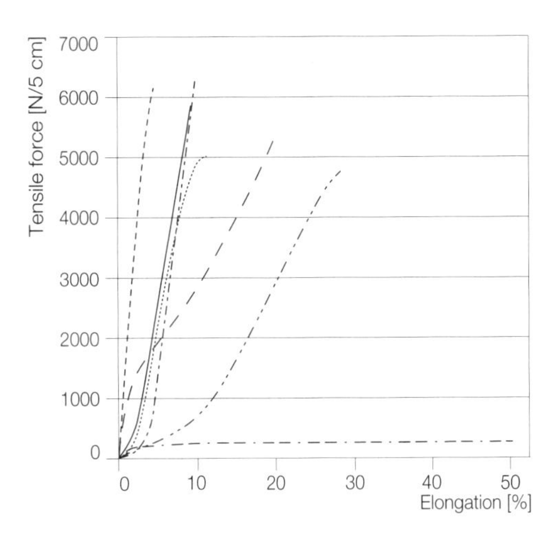

C 5.12

Coated and uncoated PTFE fabric

Uncoated PTFE fabric is frequently used for high-quality convertible membrane roofs with little need for watertightness (Fig. C 5.7g, p. 103; see "PTFE fibres", p. 52). It is characterised by extremely its high flex cracking resistance, light weight, high light transmittance and anti-adhesive surface (very favourable soiling behaviour). Fabrics in various colours are possible by colouring the PTFE fibres. Lightweight PTFE fabric with a very dense weave plus coated fibres can achieve a watertightness equal to max. 20 cm head of water. With coarser fabrics, however, this figure drops considerably and water incident on one side of the fabric passes through to cause a mist of very fine droplets on the other side. Applying a thin fluoropolymer coating using the dip coating method can increase the head of water to max. 300 cm while retaining the character of the fabric. Open PTFE fabric cannot be welded, only stitched; special adhesives can increase the watertightness of stitched seams. Owing to the tendency of PTFE to creep significantly when subjected to permanent loads, the pretensioning values chosen should be kept low and the spans limited if high snow loads are expected. Thermoplastic fluoropolymer coatings, which are applied to the fabric in a special extrusion method, were developed in order to achieve weldable, fully watertight PTFE fabrics. The material then scatters the incoming light in a similar way to ETFE foil. Coated in this way, PTFE fabrics can now combine their high-quality properties with the demands normally made on customary membrane materials.

PVC- or PTFE-coated aramid fabric

Aramid fabric, which can be coated with PVC or PTFE, is used as alternative to polyester and glass-fibre fabrics when a high tensile strength is required. Such membrane materials have been used only very occasionally hitherto and are only manufactured to order. PVC-coated aramid fabrics can achieve tensile strengths of, for example, up to 24 000 N/5 cm for a weight per unit area of approx. 2 kg/m^2 (as a comparison: polyester type V = 10 000 N/5 cm). The disadvantages are the high price and the very low UV resistance. The coating adheres poorly to the aramid fibres and has to be opaque for this reason, and therefore these materials are only available in opaque versions.

Coated and uncoated wide-mesh fabrics and nets

Besides the traditional use of membranes as loadbearing and enclosing structures, open fabrics and nets can be used internally as acoustic membranes (Fig. C 5.10; see also "Acoustic foil", p. 118), sunshades (Fig. C 5.11), room dividers or suspended ceilings, also in daylighting concepts (Fig. C 6.36, p. 117). Numerous requirements such as high strength and weathering resistance are irrelevant for indoor applications.
Various uncoated, incombustible glass cloths, not readily flammable polyester fabrics and, for example, PVC-coated wide-mesh polyester nets or uncoated PTFE nets are also available. Some nets and impregnated monofilament fabrics can be welded if they are coated.
A huge range of net and fabric products is available on the market which, however, will not be dealt with in detail here.

Mechanical properties

Tensile strength, tear propagation resistance, elongation at rupture and strain stiffness are the mechanical properties that describe a membrane. These properties differ in the warp and weft directions depending on the type of weave (see "Woven fabrics", p. 70). In the case of convertible and temporary tensile surface structures, the flex cracking resistance of the fibres and the flexibility of the membrane material are extremely important for guaranteeing successful assembly and dismantling, or gathering (convertible roofs).

Tensile strength

The tensile strength is typically determined using 5 cm wide strips in uniaxial tensile tests. The values in the weft direction are often somewhat lower than those in the warp direction. As the thickness of the membrane is negligible when compared with the width of the strip used in the test, the tensile strength is specified in the form of force per length (e.g. N/5 cm). Classifying the membrane materials in types according to increasing tensile strength was originally introduced for polyester-PVC membranes but in the meantime is also used for most of the other membrane materials. The classification is as follows:

Type I: ±3000 N/5 cm
Type II: ±4000 N/5 cm
Type III: ±5000 N/5 cm
Type IV: ±7000 N/5 cm
Type V: ±9000 N/5 cm

Tear propagation resistance

The tear propagation resistance specifies the maximum force that a torn membrane can still just carry. In a standard test, the value is either determined uniaxially using a specimen with a lateral incision or biaxially on a specimen with an incision in the middle. The tear propagation resistance should be as high as possible in order to prevent the entire tensile surface structure collapsing as a result of a local failure.

Elongation at rupture

The elongation at rupture is the percentage elongation at failure of a specimen subjected to uniaxial tension. The lower the elongation at rupture, the more likely it is that the material will fail abruptly (brittle failure). A higher value indicates a more ductile behaviour – noticeable deformations give warning of the impending failure of the material (Fig. C 5.12).

Strain stiffness

The strain stiffness of a fabric in the warp and weft directions is determined in a biaxial tensile test. Several incisions are made on all four sides of a specimen of the material. The individual strips are then clamped separately and guarantee the homogeneous transfer of the stresses. Force and elongation are measured over a period of time. The fabric is stretched to the prestressing level and then loaded in several cycles depending on the loads expected in the project or at the location, alternating in the warp and weft directions. The residual elongation that remains at the end of the test, which lasts several hours at prestressing level, is used as the compensation value for the fabrication of the membrane (see "Compensation", p. 148). Fig. C 5.13 shows the assessment of a typical

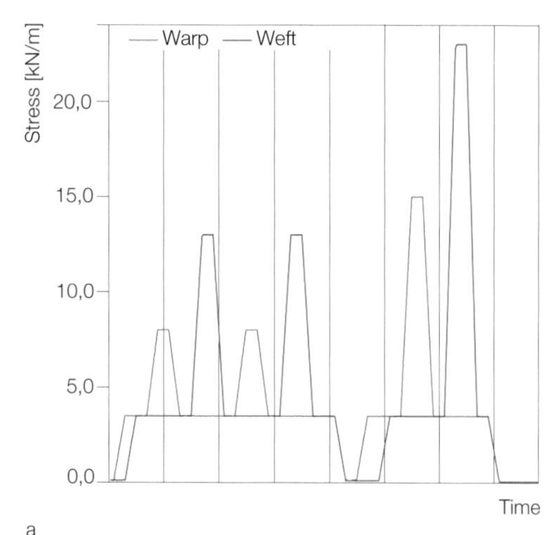

a

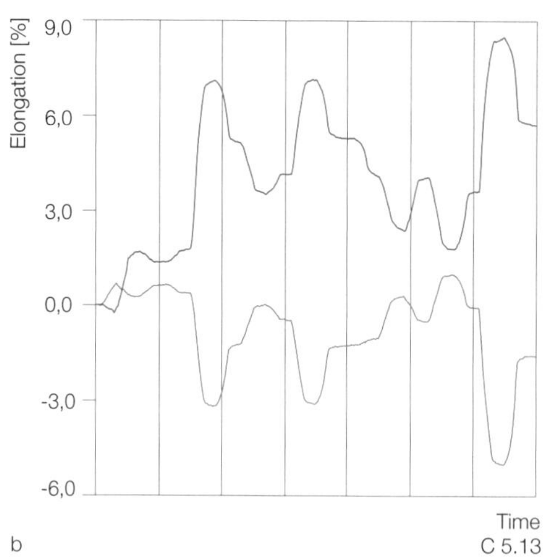

b

C 5.13

biaxial test for a type IV PTFE/glass membrane. In this case an isotropic prestress of 3 kN/m was initially applied to the specimen, i.e. the same pretension in the warp and weft directions, and subsequently increased alternately in the warp and weft directions. It is obvious from the graphs that the strain differs in the two directions. This effect can be less pronounced in other materials. Nowadays, special methods of manufacture for polyester-PVC membranes result in equal stiffness characteristics in the warp and weft directions.

Fabrication

The steps in the fabrication of textile membrane and foil designs are to a large extent very similar and so this section deals with the fabrication of foils. Specific steps that apply only to ETFE foil are described in more detail on p. 98.

The fabrication of a membrane for covering a large area assembled from individual webs of material is carried out in several stages:

- Preparing the cutting pattern, e.g. with a cutting plotter
- Welding the individual sections together
- Welding or folding over the edges, incorporating keders or sewing on belts
- Fitting components integrated into the membrane when there are edge belts
- Attaching corner fittings if applicable
- Folding or rolling and packaging, e.g. in protective foil, ready for shipping

Cutting pattern

A three-dimensional, curved membrane surface must be assembled from individual webs of material. The edge of each web must be concave on the outside when mechanical prestressing is to be used, convex for pneumatic prestressing (see "Cutting pattern", p. 147). It is normal these days for the curved pieces of the cutting pattern to be cut to size directly from the roll of material with a computer-controlled cutting plotter on a vacuum table. The cutting plotter is able to cut curved as well as straight lines. Laser cutters are unsuitable because of the high temperatures used. The aim is always to minimise the amount of waste when calculating the cutting pattern and positioning the pattern on the unrolled material. For some materials, fabricators and manufacturers have set up a direct return system for waste, which is then recycled and reused. The coating first has to be separated from the fibres in the case of polyester-PVC membrane waste, but ETFE foil waste can be melted down again directly.

Welding

Thermoplastic coatings can be fused together through a combination of heat and pressure – a process known as welding. The heat required for this is provided by high-frequency radiation, heating elements or electric impulses.
Once the weld seam has cooled sufficiently while applying constant pressure, it can reach about 90 % of the strength of the parent material depending on the particular material and the welding process. The strength depends on the contact pressure, the shape of the contact elements (smooth, serrated), the welding temperature and the pressure application time. Typical seam widths lie between 50 and 100 mm. The fabricator prepares specimens for carrying out uniaxial tests perpendicular to the weld seams to check their strength (see "Testing and approval", p. 154).

High-frequency welding
Also called radiofrequency (RF) welding, this type of welding can be used for thermoplastics with a polar molecular structure (e.g. PVC). High-frequency electromagnetic waves excite certain molecular groups in the coating, which causes them to vibrate, heat up and join the molecules together. The advantage of this method is its speed.

Hot-plate and impulse welding
PTFE-coated materials that cannot be joined using high-frequency welding can nevertheless still be welded by applying the necessary heat directly (hot-plate welding). The two opposing platens of a press at a temperature of approx. 340 °C join together the membrane coating with an intermediate foil made from a thermoplastic fluoropolymer. Applying a pressure of about 50 N/cm^2 for 40 s and allowing the connection to cool down slowly while still under pressure enables the weld seam to reach strengths of up to 90 % of that of the parent material.
Impulse welding is a special form of hot-plate welding in which electrical impulses in thin metal bars raise the temperature through resistance heating. The rapid cooling of the thin metal bars while still applying the contact pressure results in a faster processing speed.

Welding on site
Welding work on site is usually necessary for larger membrane structures, mostly for finishing clamped joints and open corner details. Occasionally, however, even prefabricated membrane sections are laid out and joined in situ. It must be guaranteed, however, that the necessary weld seam strengths can be achieved on the building site.
A heat gun (called a hot-air welder) plus a roller for pressing the surfaces together are usually sufficient for polyester-PVC membranes. However, PTFE/glass membranes require a special manual welding device because of the high pressure and temperature necessary (Fig. C 5.14).

Gluing

The joining of polyester-PVC membranes with special adhesives is well known from industrial applications. However, the seam strengths achieved are much lower than those of welded seams and so this method of jointing is not used for highly stressed tensile surface structures. Only glass-silicone membranes are, however, just occasionally still glued together because this material cannot be welded. Silicone can be vulcanised by attaching adhesive silicone strips at the position of the joint. The two pieces of material are joined together with a heating press which operates at a temperature of about 200 °C and applies a pressure of 15 N/cm² for 30–60 s. A cross-linking reaction takes place between the adhesive and the silicone bonds to join the two pieces firmly together.
Two-part adhesives can be used as an alternative. First of all, a solvent is applied to both sides of the joint separately in order to break down the cross-linking between the molecules in the silicone coating. The surfaces prepared in this way can then be bonded together with a cross-linking adhesive.
A combination seam, consisting of adhesive plus stitching with PTFE threads plus an adhesive silicone tape (for waterproofing) is sometimes used to produce a stronger seam. A seam strength equal to 65–80 % that of the parent material can be reached in this way.

Stitching

The high production speeds and high strengths of welded seams have led to stitched seams these days being restricted to non-weldable membrane materials (e.g. PTFE cloth or glass-silicone). Large tables (Fig. C 5.15) or sewing machines sunk into the floor are normally employed to handle the (usually) very large areas of material that have to be stitched together. The disadvantages are the lack of a waterproof joint and the high production costs. Special adhesives can be used to seal the stitched seams of open PTFE fabrics. Typical stitched seams and edge details with stitching plus the attachment of belts by stitching are described in the chapter entitled "Building with textile membranes" (pp. 196–211).

Assembling and packaging

Once it has been fully fabricated, the membrane is folded together or rolled up in the factory ready for dispatch (Fig. C 5.16). Foils or textiles are laid between the layers of the membrane in order to protect the material against damage during transport and erection on site. Care should be taken to avoid damaging membrane materials that are sensitive to flex cracking, e.g. PTFE/glass, during folding because this leads to failure of the material (see "Manufacturing quality and erection", p. 156/157). This problem can be avoided by laying foam tubes in the folds, for example. To ensure trouble-free erection, the corners must be labelled prior to packaging and unfolding instructions included with each shipment so that the membrane is moved around as little as possible on the building site.

Webbing belts

Webbing belts are used in tensile surface structures for various reasons, e.g. in convertible structures because of their foldability. For small and medium-sized membrane constructions in particular, they can be attached to the border of a flexible membrane to strengthen the edge. Belts stitched into the surface of the material can be used to form hips and valleys (see "Mechanically prestressed surfaces", p. 140). On larger membrane structures with steel perimeter ropes, especially in conjunction with polyester-PVC membranes, belts can accommodate tangential forces at the corners (see "Corner details with cable connections", pp. 207–209). One major use of belts is during the erection of tensile surface structures, where they are used for guying and temporary stabilisation of masts and booms. In the form of ratchet tie-downs, they are frequently used for tensioning the edges of membranes.
Most webbing belts are made from polyester fibres (Fig. C 5.17), sometimes polyamide fibres, and occasionally aramid fibres where a very high tensile strength is required. They are produced in webbing weaving mills on so-called needle looms, which can achieve very fast weaving speeds by inserting the weft yarn from both sides. Plain or twill weave are typically used for belts (see "Types of weave", p. 70). Depending on requirements, the yarns can be impregnated with water-repellent or flame-retardant substances or fungicides prior to weaving. Customary belt cross-sections lie between 20 × 2 mm and 200 × 15 mm and achieve ultimate breaking strengths of approx. 200 kN. Polyester webbing belts are not UV-resistant and therefore must be protected against exposure to direct sunlight, e.g. by incorporating them in pockets made from the material of the membrane.

C 5.13 Biaxial tests on a PTFE/glass type IV membrane
a Various stress levels
b Associated elongation
C 5.14 Manual welding device
C 5.15 Industrial sewing machine
C 5.16 Folding a fabricated membrane ready for shipping
C 5.17 Webbing belts made from polyester fibres

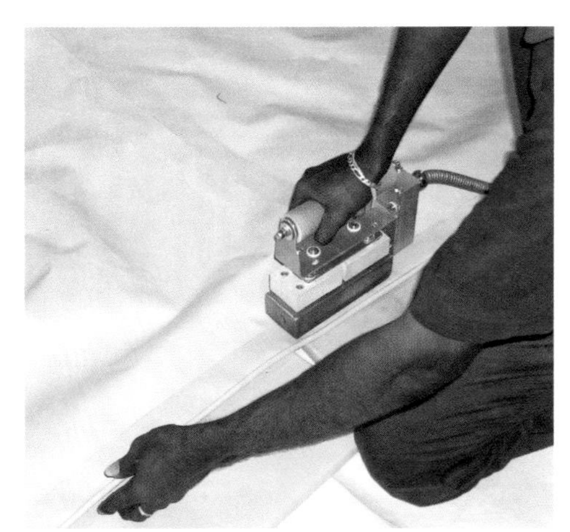
C 5.14

C 5.15

C 5.16

C 5.17

Building physics and energy aspects

C 6.1

Whether polymers are suitable for a construction application, and especially in the building envelope, calls for an assessment that goes beyond just considering the factors purely specific to their materials, fabrication and design. It must be remembered that building physics contexts and principles, which affect all the materials described in this book to the same extent, are also important. Fig. C 6.4 provides an overview of the characteristics and aspects relevant in this context.
The focus in this chapter is on individual materials and individual products, whereas the chapter entitled "Complex building envelopes" (pp. 212–223) looks at combinations of materials and their interaction within the building envelope. However, in some areas it is difficult to draw a precise borderline between these two, especially when considering fire protection, sound insulation and room acoustics, but also the subject of integrating active solar energy systems, for example.

Thermal insulation characteristics

The primary function of a thermal insulation material is to suppress the flow of heat as comprehensively as possible. As polymers play a major role in insulating systems (e.g. as insulating foams or as thermal break materials separating metal components), it is important to grasp the main principles in order to understand the functions properly. The terminology for the subject of thermal performance is regulated and described in detail in DIN 4108 parts 1–3 and DIN EN ISO 7345.

Heat transfer
Heat transfer is a form of energy flow that always takes place from a warmer, and hence higher-energy, side to a colder side. For any layer in a component, the quantity of energy transferred per unit of time depends on the temperature difference between the two sides of the layer, the distance covered by the energy (= thickness of layer) and the thermal conductivity of the material(s) forming that layer.

Heat is transported by three different mechanisms:
- Conduction (through gases λ_g and through solids λ_s)
- Convection λ_v
- Radiation λ_r

The proportions of these three mechanisms (Fig. C 6.2) in the total energy transfer depend on the temperature of the material and the material itself, as well as other factors. The quantity of heat Q as an energy form is specified in joules (J). The heat flow Φ is defined as the quantity of heat transferred per unit of time.

Conduction
Conduction is the primary means of heat transfer in solid bodies and fluids at rest. It takes place by way of the thermal vibration of molecules in a lattice and also by way of free electrons, although to distinguish conduction from convection, the material as an energy medium does not actually move itself. In porous insulating materials conduction takes place via the gases in the pores and, in the form of conduction through solids, via the pore skeleton.

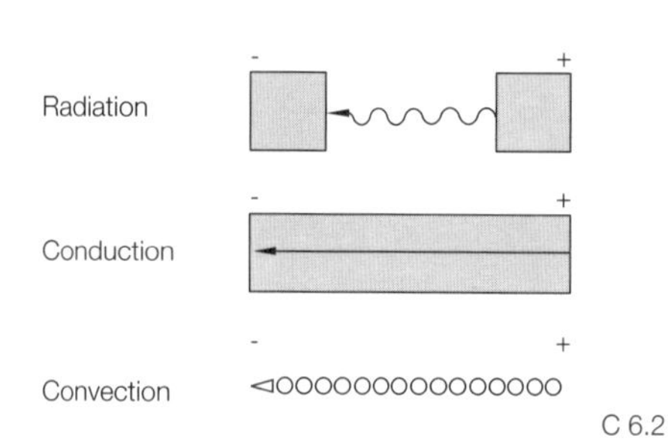

C 6.2

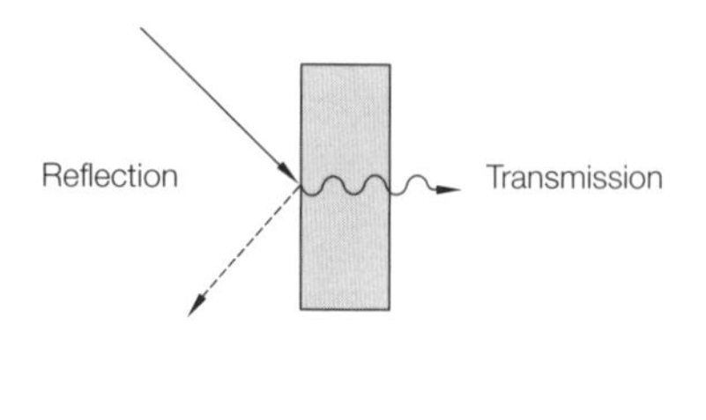

C 6.3

C 6.1 Unilever group headquarters, Hamburg (D), 2009, Behnisch Architekten
C 6.2 The basic principles of heat transfer
C 6.3 The transport of radiation energy (e.g. heat radiation)
C 6.4 Building physics aspects

Convection
Convection transports heat through the flow processes of larger numbers of moving particles. We distinguish between free (or natural) convection, which occurs as a result of natural buoyancy, i.e. density differences caused by temperature differences, and forced convection, which is caused by external effects such as the wind or fans. Free convection is also effective within non-hermetic insulating materials because in this case the air in the material forms a coherent system and the associated temperature gradient leads to thermally induced flow processes. Gases that themselves also transport energy via their mass diffuse through materials as a result of a pressure gradient, diffusion always taking place from the place of higher pressure to the place of lower pressure. In the context of thermal insulation materials, it is the transport of water vapour that is especially important because water vapour can absorb a considerable amount of energy owing to its specific heat capacity. In addition, absorbed moisture generally leads to a reduction in the thermal insulation effect because water exhibits a comparatively high thermal conductivity.

Radiation
Every body at a temperature above that of absolute zero (0 K) emits heat radiation in a range of frequencies specific to this temperature region. The warmer the body, the shorter is the wavelength of the radiation emitted. The radiation energy incident on a surface can be reflected, absorbed or transmitted, with all of these mechanisms adding up to a total of 100% because no energy can be lost (Fig. C 6.3). Heat radiation requires a heat transfer that takes place through an exchange of electromagnetic radiation energy between the surfaces of two bodies at different temperatures and separated by a medium (e.g. gas or air) that is permeable to the range of frequencies concerned (Fig. C 6.5). According to the Stefan-Boltzmann law, the following total radiation power ΔP_S emitted is as follows:

$$\Delta P_S = A \cdot \varepsilon_1 \cdot \varepsilon_2 \cdot \sigma \cdot (T_1^4 - T_2^4)$$

σ Stefan-Boltzmann constant, 5.67×10^{-8} [W/(m²K⁴)]
A Area of opposing surfaces [m²]
T_1, T_2 Surface temperatures ($T_1 > T_2$)
ε_1, ε_2 Surface emissivities, which take into account the radiation capacity of the respective surfaces

An ideal (theoretical) black-body radiator has an emissivity ε of 1 (= 100%). Real surfaces are grey, i.e. less intensive radiators where $0 < \varepsilon < 1$. The absorptance of a surface corresponds to the emissivity in the same range of wavelengths and therefore good radiators, for instance, also absorb well in this frequency range of the spectrum.
The difference in temperature between the opposing boundary surfaces plays a special role for transporting heat energy by way of radiation

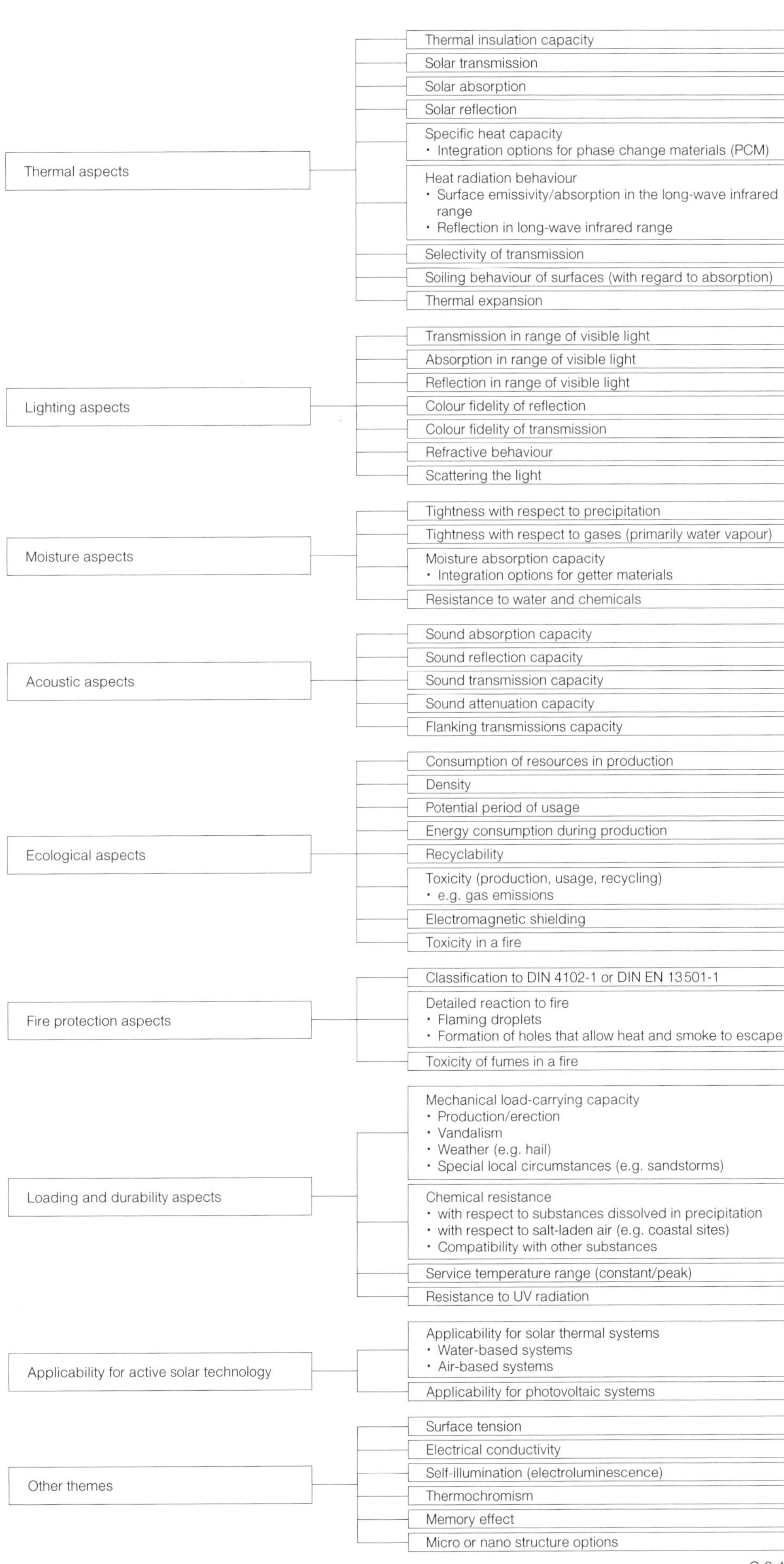

C 6.4

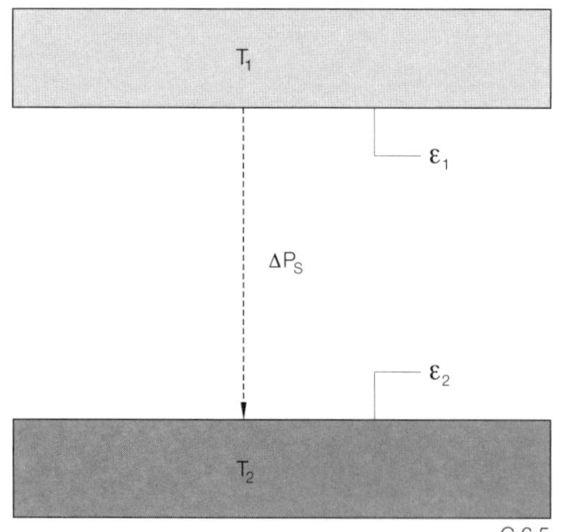

C 6.5

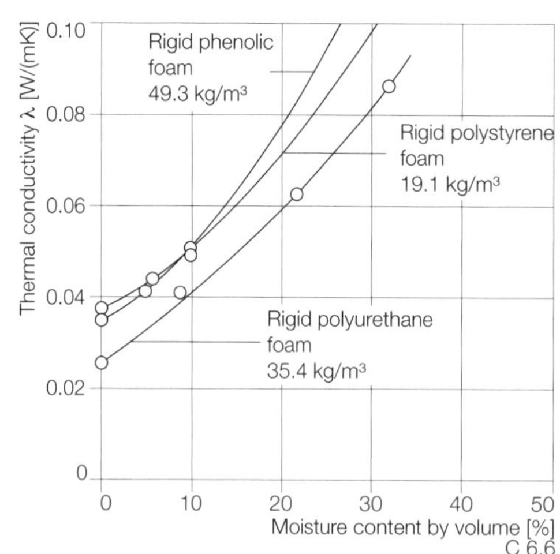

C 6.6

C 6.7

because this difference is included in the result as a quantity to the power of four. In interiors with a highly radiation-permeable enclosure overhead (e.g. glass roof), this leads to considerable radiation heat losses on clear nights (an extremely cold boundary surface), especially in summer. So heat losses can be reduced via a material's specific surface emissivity, which is an effect that has been exploited for many years in the form of low E coatings (= low emissivity) on insulating glazing. This is also possible with polymers and membranes by using appropriate coatings or by modifying the polymer structure.

Thermal conductivity

Only in homogeneous and isotropic materials does heat transfer take place exclusively via conduction. In all other materials, other heat transfer mechanisms are also involved. Nevertheless, we speak of thermal conductivity but mean the total effect of the individual effective mechanisms. In the building industry, the magnitude of the thermal conductivity is relevant not only for solid materials, but also for gaseous substances (e.g. argon in the cavities of insulating glass units) and liquids, e.g. water (Fig. C 6.8). In building contexts, the basis for calculating the heat flow through components is usually assumed to be the characteristic value λ_R taken from a standard or an approval document, which also takes into account a certain residual moisture content and the ageing behaviour of the insulating material.

The relationship between the heat transfer paths and the total energy transport is specific to the particular material. In porous materials this results in an equivalent thermal conductivity due to...

- conduction via the solid skeleton,
- conduction via the stationary gas,
- convection of the gas and/or gas-solid interaction, and
- radiation between the boundary walls and the solid particles themselves.

To what extent heat transfer takes place within a material depends on the following (and other) factors:

- Specific density ρ
- Structure of the material
- Moisture content (Fig. C 6.6)
- Nature, magnitude and distribution of pores
- Air pressure
- Temperature of the material

The thermal conductivity of stationary, dry air is approx. 0.026 W/mK and thus much lower than that of the majority of solid materials. Therefore, conventional insulating materials are based on the principle of containing a maximum quantity of stationary air. In addition, the insulating effect increases when the stationary air is surrounded by a skeleton of material that itself exhibits a low thermal conductivity and whose proportion by volume is minimised.

Furthermore, this skeleton must suppress convection within the voids and reduce the radiation permeability because stationary air cannot prevent either of these mechanisms. In practice optimised materials such as lightweight polymer foams or fibre mats achieve thermal conductivities that approach that of stationary air. The proportion of gas by volume in such materials is generally much greater than 90 %.

Heat storage

In principle, the specific heat capacity of a material is approximately proportional to its density, with the exception of water, which has an exceptionally high specific heat capacity. Consequently, the majority of polymers can store heat to only a very limited extent. This applies to membrane structures above all because their mass per unit area is very low.

Therefore, the integration of latent heat storage media (phase change materials, PCM, e.g. based on paraffins or salt hydrates) in membranes is the subject of ongoing research. Such technology is already available in the marketplace in the form of functional clothing. For building applications, however, the quantity that can be integrated, the durability and the fire safety aspects still represent major challenges.

		W/mK at 20 °C
Material	Copper	305
	Aluminium	221
	Iron	80
	Stainless steel	15
	Normal-weight concrete	2.1
	Masonry	0.2–1.3
	Window glass	0.8
	Timber	0.13–0.2
	Polymers (solid)	0.16–0.4
	Polymer foams	> 0.021
	Vacuum insulation systems	> 0.002
	Ice (at 0 °C)	2.2
Liquid	Water	0.60
	Alcohol	0.17

C 6.8

Material	Consumption by the building industry in 2001 in Germany [m³]	in Europe [m³]
Mineral fibres	16254000	64804000
Expanded polystyrene foam (EPS)	9550000	28396000
PUR/polyisocyanurate	1600000	5864800
Extruded polystyrene foam (XPS)	1100000	3900900
Perlite	260000	655370
Foamed glass	130000	296160
Vermiculite	44000	71820

C 6.9

C 6.5 The transport of radiation energy
C 6.6 Relationship between thermal conductivity and moisture content
C 6.7 Polystyrene foam with embedded infrared opacifier
C 6.8 Thermal conductivity of various materials and systems (selection)
C 6.9 Consumption of various insulating materials (selection) by the building industry for the year 2001
C 6.10 Thermal conductivity of various insulating materials and insulating systems
C 6.11 Thermal conductivities of selected gases
C 6.12 Make-up of a vacuum insulation panel (schematic)
C 6.13 Typical make-up of a metallised barrier foil
C 6.14 Thermal conductivity (measured values, not characteristic values) of various core materials depending on the pressure in the cell gas

Heat transfer in a porous insulating material
The total heat transfer (λ) in a porous insulating material is made up of conduction through solids (λ_s), conduction through gases (λ_g), heat radiation (λ_r), convection (λ_v) and coupling effects (λ_c), in other words:

$$\lambda = \lambda_s + \lambda_g + \lambda_r + \lambda_v + \lambda_c$$

The individual values depend on the following factors:

- λ Structure, density, pressure on material
- λ_g Type of gas, porosity, structure and size of pores
- λ_r Density, particle size, temperature
- λ_v Type of gas, porosity, structure and, above all, size of pores
- λ_c λ_s and λ_g

The absorption of moisture means that water becomes stored in the structure of the insulating material. The thermal conductivity therefore rises due to the relatively high thermal conductivity of water (0.60 W/mK). The structure of the solid at molecular level also has an influence on the thermal conductivity. Flaws in the lattice, foreign matter inclusions, low symmetry or disruptions in the crystalline lattice, also hairline cracks and pores lead to a diminished thermal conductivity.

Strategies for optimising a porous insulating material
The details given above allow us to deduce the following optimisation strategies for porous insulating materials with respect to the individual heat transfer mechanisms:

- Minimising the conduction through the solid λ_s by choosing a material with a low specific thermal conductivity, i.e. as far as possible a dry, non-crystalline structure with point-like material transitions and minimum density.
- Reducing the conduction through the gas λ_g by choosing a gas with low conductive properties (e.g. the heavy gases in polyurethane foams) and a skeleton of material with maximum porosity but minimum pore size. Microporous materials such as aerogels or fumed silica can thus reach thermal conductivities which, at approx. 0.018 W/mK, are already well below that of stationary air.
- Minimising the heat radiation λ_r through the even distribution of a high-density material that is impermeable to infrared radiation (a so-called opacifier) throughout the skeleton of insulating material, e.g. polystyrene foams optimised through the addition of a opacifier (Fig. C 6.7)

As the conduction through the gas accounts for a relatively high proportion of the total heat transfer, an effective strategy is to choose a gas with a low conductivity which remains, as far as possible, permanently in the pores (Fig. C 6.11). But reducing the quantity of gas, i.e. evacuating the pores, is much more effective.

Vacuum insulation systems
The function of a typical vacuum insulation system is based on the optimisation principles given above (Fig. C 6.12). In practice, polymers are used for both the gastight enclosing material and for the core material itself. Although up until now no polymer has been discovered that exhibits a gastightness equal to that of glass or metals, by combining and modifying polymers it is possible to produce suitable so-called barrier foils. In order to satisfy the various requirements in an optimum way, multi-ply systems are generally used in which every ply performs a specific function, e.g. loadbearing or protective (PA, PET), barrier or sealing layer (PE, PP). Polymer foils or polymer composite foils are frequently used for the hermetic edge seals to vacuum insulation systems because it is much easier to form the gastight joints (weld seams) using polymers than it is using metals and especially glass.

Gas	λ_g [W/mK]
Hydrogen (H_2)	0.175
Helium (He)	0.143
Air, nitrogen (N_2), oxygen (O_2)	0.026
Argon (Ar)	0.016
Pentane (C_5H_{12})	0.013
Krypton (Kr)	0.0095
Trichlorofluoromethane (R11)	0.0085
(Vacuum)	(0)

C 6.11

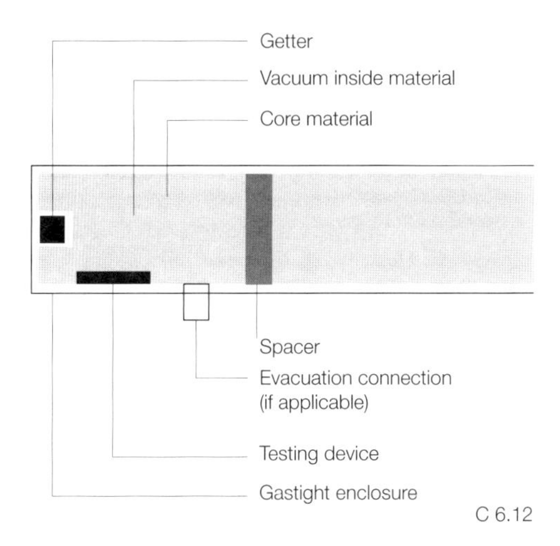

C 6.12

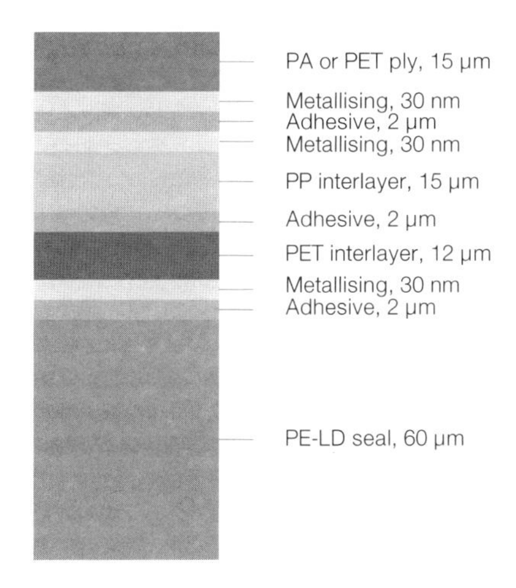

C 6.13

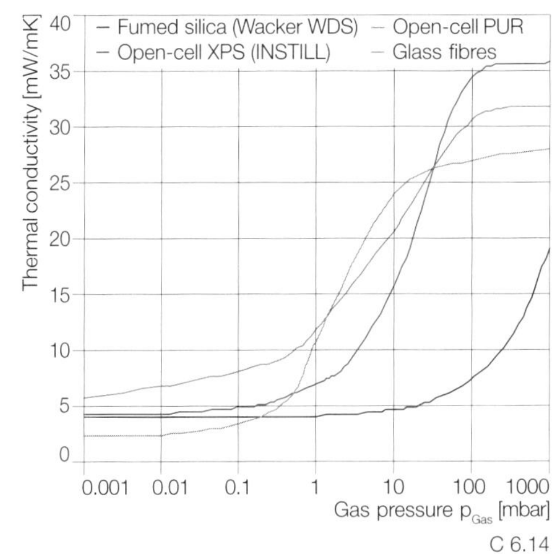

C 6.14

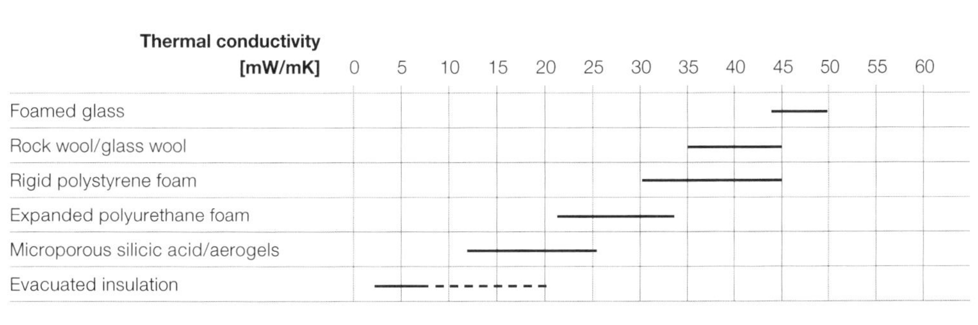

C 6.10

The main requirements for the core material are a low thermal conductivity for a minimum vacuum and at the same time adequate stability to resist the atmospheric pressure. A completely open-cell structure is also essential because otherwise it is impossible to reduce the number of gas molecules trapped in the pores. An adequate compressive strength is required not only to ensure the mechanical stability of the system (atmospheric pressure = approx. 10.3 t/m²), but indeed is also linked directly with the thermal conductivity of the core material, which generally rises approximately linearly with increasing density. Fig. C 6.14 (p. 111) reveals that although special open-cell polymer foams represent one option for vacuum insulation systems, up until now they have been unsuitable for building applications because of the very high demands placed on the vacuum and the ensuing short service life of the system. Starting with the same internal pressure, i.e. the pressure in the vacuum insulation system directly after production, the thermal conductivity rises relatively quickly over the life of the panel because of the inevitable ventilation. However, as systems based on such polymer foams are comparatively inexpensive, they are used for applications where a longer service life is not relevant, e.g. for extremely lightweight and highly efficient containers for transporting blood supplies.
The core material mostly used for vacuum insulation systems in the construction industry is microporous fumed (or pyrogenic) silica (reinforced with fibres and mixed with an infrared opacifier), and in future we can expect to see the use of perlite as well.

Sandwich elements, foil insulation

One key area for the use of various organic foam insulating materials (Fig. C 6.10, p. 111) is sandwich elements. In this case the process of filling a mould with foam, e.g. polyurethane foam, is exploited to create a bone-like component structure in which two outer leaves are joined together by a shear-resistant foam skeleton (Fig. C 6.15). This makes the component extremely rigid in relation to its weight. The disadvantage is that this process produces a composite component that is extremely difficult to separate into its constituent materials when it comes to be recycled at the end of its life.
There are other ways of using polymers to limit the heat transfer in components, besides foams and vacuum insulation systems. One option is foil insulation (Fig. C 6.16), which in most instances consists of several layers of air-filled pockets separated by metallised foil interlayers. The thermal conductivities of such products, measured according to the standard conditions, tends to be high. But the interlayers also reflect a large proportion of the heat radiation so these products could be particularly suitable for applications in which the radiation heat losses are disproportionately high.

Transparent thermal insulation

Transparent or translucent thermal insulation (TTI) is a material or component that functions as thermal insulation and at the same time allows sunlight for natural illumination and solar radiation for assisting the heating system to infiltrate through to the interior. In most cases TTI consists of vertical absorbent honeycomb or capillary structures made from PMMA or PC, which on the outside are covered with a transparent protective layer made from glass or polymer. The combustibility and maximum service temperature of the TTI material must comply with the constructional or legislative requirements. The customary applications for TTI are "solar wall heating systems", solar-heated thermal insulation or daylighting systems.
TTI materials are divided into organic and inorganic types. The latter include, first and foremost, silica aerogels, i.e. silicon compounds with pore sizes from 10 to 100 nm and a pore volume exceeding 80% (Fig. C 6.17). Current aerogel materials are available in opaque to translucent versions, are incombustible, can be directly recycled, resist temperatures up to 600 °C, are UV-resistant and hydrophobic and offer long-term stability. They are therefore especially suitable for building applications. They have a density of 90–100 kg/m³ and an internal surface area of 600–800 m²/g, and their thermal conductivity, at 0.018 W/mK, is below that of stationary air (approx. 0.024 W/mK).

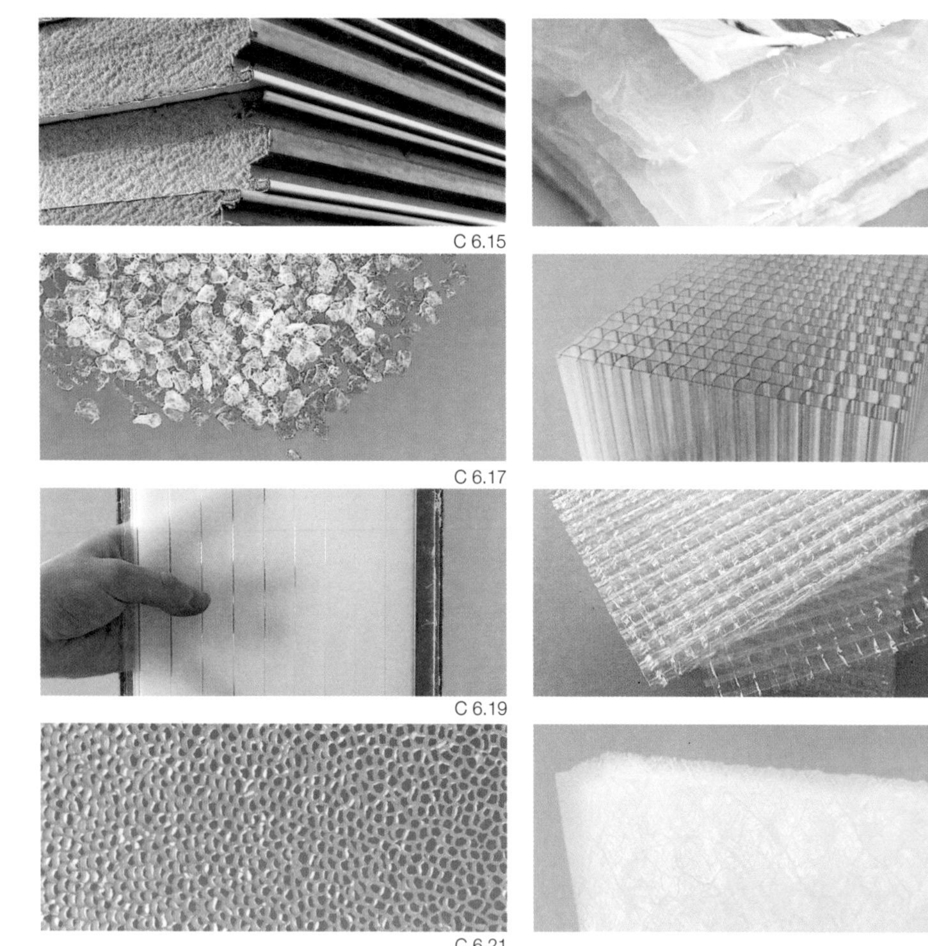

C 6.15 Sandwich element (sheet metal, PUR foam)
C 6.16 Foil insulation
C 6.17 Translucent aerogel granulate
C 6.18 Polymer honeycomb structure for transparent thermal insulation (TTI)
C 6.19 PC twin-wall sheet filled with translucent aerogel granulate
C 6.20 Thermal insulation made from several plies of cellulose diacetate (CA)
C 6.21 Transparent thermal insulation (TTI) in the form of a capillary tube structure
C 6.22 Glass-fibre spun fabric made from glass fibres plus synthetic resin, assigned to DIN 4102 class B1 and used in membrane applications, for example.
C 6.23 Overview of transparent/translucent thermal insulation (TTI) materials

Aerogels are supplied in the form of powders, granulates and monolithic blocks; the powder is suitable for opaque applications only but the granulates can also be used for translucent products, and using a monolithic aerogel results in an almost completely transparent thermal insulation component. However, this latter product is currently very difficult to obtain, complicated to produce and therefore very expensive. That was originally the situation for the production of any form of aerogel because the supercritical drying necessary was a very important stage in the manufacture.
It was not until the 1990s that the method of producing the granulate could be simplified to such an extent that it seemed like the way was paved for the widespread use of this group of materials. Aerogel granulates can now be produced in a continuous process and – in contrast to the products of the first generation – are hydrophobic and much less expensive. There are now numerous products on the market incorporating aerogel granulate as a translucent insulating material, e.g. PC twin-wall sheets (Fig. C 6.19), GFRP panels, lightweight building elements (e.g. for rooflights), etc. By now, this insulating material is also being used in combination with membrane materials (foils and textiles) (see "Aerogels in tensile surface structures", pp. 220–221).
There is also a group of organic, light-permeable products in addition to the group of inorganic TTI materials. Those products include honeycomb-like structures with various geometries (e.g. capillary, cellular or slotted structures) made from various materials such as polymers based on polymethyl methacrylate (PMMA), polycarbonate (PC), cellulose acetate (CA) and cellulose triacetate (CTA), also amorphous, transparent copolymers based on cyclic olefins and ethylene. Here, the material, the amount of material per unit volume and the three-dimensional geometry of the structure influence the light transmittance and energy parameters such as thermal resistance and g-value.

Light and heat radiation characteristics

Visible light is in physical terms electromagnetic radiation in a range of frequencies that can be perceived by the human eye. Those frequencies have wavelengths between approx. 380 and 780 nm. All materials emit a specific spectrum depending on their temperature (see "Radiation", pp. 109–110). Consequently, even the sun with a surface temperature of approx. 5778 K emits electromagnetic radiation with a spectral intensity distribution specific to this very high temperature. [1] Individual components of the light are filtered and attenuated on their way to the earth, e.g. by the atmosphere, and vary depending on local circumstances and according to daily and seasonal cycles. The radiation that reaches the earth's surface can be described by the solar spectrum (Fig. C 6.27, p. 114) – wavelengths between approx. 300 and 2500 nm, i.e. there are ranges either side of visible light: short-wave ultraviolet (UV) light and long-wave near infrared (NIR) light. The solar NIR light should not be confused with the heat radiation that is emitted by the materials of building components with customary exterior or interior temperatures. This heat (or thermal) radiation therefore takes place in a frequency range with much longer wavelengths which is further removed from visible light and is therefore also designated far infrared (FIR) (Fig. C 6.27, p. 114).

Material type/make-up	Thickness [mm]	Manufacturer (example)	Product name	U-value [W/m²K]	Thermal conductivity [W/mK]	Light transmittance, direct [%]	Light transmittance, diffuse [%]	g-value, vertical [%] approx.	g-value, diffuse [%]	Remarks
PC multi-wall sheets										
Sheet/air space/sheet	64	Bayer Sheet Europe		0.8		48		49	40	
Aerogel										
Aerogel granulate	25	Cabot	Nanogel	0.7		53		52		Hydrophobic
Aerogel-filled polyester twin-wall sheets	50	Scobalit	Scobatherm	0.41	0.022			25		
Aerogel-filled PC multi-wall sheets	25	Roda	Lexan Thermoclear	0.91		47				
Aerogel-filled coated PC multi-wall sheets	25	Roda	Lexan Thermoclear IR	0.91		34				Solar transmission 20%
Aerogel-filled insulating glass (30 mm filling)	38	Okalux	Okagel	0.6		52		52		
Cellulose honeycomb										
Glass/air space/cellulose honeycomb 30 mm backing sheet	98	gap-solar	gap – facade panel	0.74		0		14	9	Opaque system
Tough. safety glass + honeycomb + tough. safety glass + noble gas + tough. safety glass	50	gap-solar	gap – special effect panel	0.92		44	< 2	28	11	Honeycomb inlay casts shadows w. sun high in sky
Capillary inlay sheet (PMMA)										
Tough. safety glass capillary sheet, 40 mm (noble gas)/tough. safety glass	49	Okalux	KAPILUX-TWD	0.7		72		62	49	
Profiled glass with capillary inlay sheet, 40 mm	70	Glasfabrik Lamberts	Linit-TWD	1.2		35		36		
Prismatic sheet, PCM										
Glass + prismatic sheet + glass + noble gas + glass + PCM + glass	78	GlassX	GLASSXcrystal	0.48			1–4	48	29	TTI, overheating protection, thermal storage in one unit
Cellulose diacetate										
Multi-ply cellulose diacetate as thermal insulation material	10–60	Isoflex	Moniflex		0.057					B1 material to DIN 4102
Polymer honeycomb										
Glass + honeycomb (150 mm) + glass	158	Wacotech	TIMax CA	0.4		83	45	48		Honeycomb 20–150 mm
Glass-fibre spun fabric										
Glass + spun fabric (60 mm) + glass	68	Wacotech	TIMax GL	1.05		23	16	24		

C 6.23

C 6.24 Total transmission using the example of a double-leaf membrane design.
The total transmission through both leaves is as follows: $T_1 = 15\,\%$, $T_2 = 10\,\%$, $R_1 = 60\,\%$, $R_2 = 70\,\%$
$T_m = (T_1 \cdot T_2) / (1 - R_1 \cdot R_2) = 2{,}6\,\%$

C 6.25 The double curvature of membranes means that the angle-dependent transmittance and reflectance characteristics play an important role. Various effects are often visible from one viewing point, e.g. reflections of different strengths, but sometimes also changes of colour in the transmission.

C 6.26 Emissivity ε of selected materials

C 6.27 The greenhouse effect

C 6.28 ETFE with selective low E coating, laboratory specimen

C 6.29 ETFE with low E coating (opaque), laboratory specimen

C 6.30 Selective coating on PMMA

C 6.31 Radiation values for various materials

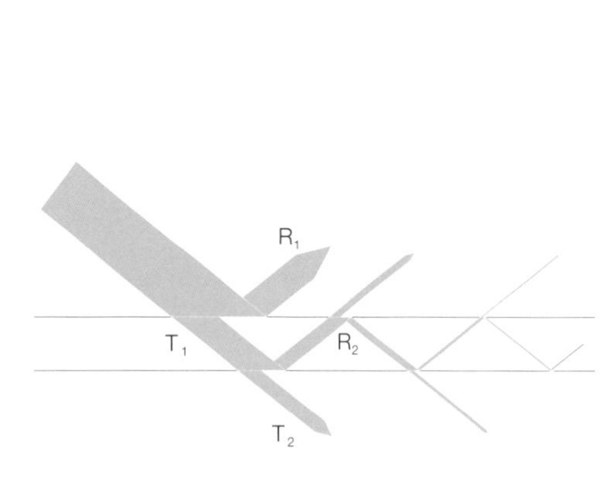

C 6.24

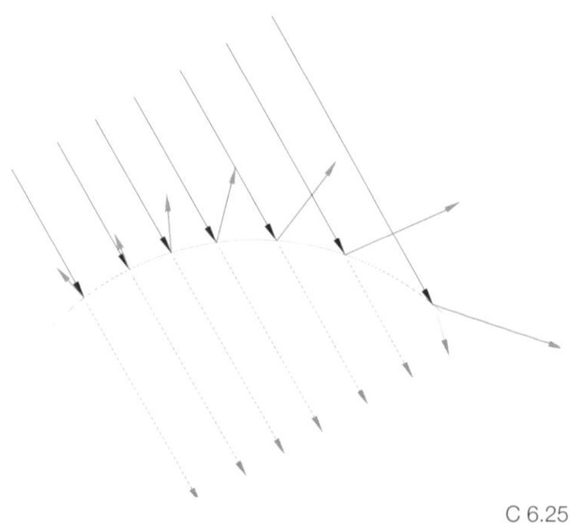

C 6.25

The intensity of the solar radiation and hence the energy it transports (corresponding to the area below the yellow line) is made up of the following components:

- approx. 5 % UV radiation
- approx. 45 % visible light
- approx. 50 % IR heat radiation

The radiation incident on a building component can be reflected, transmitted or absorbed to different degrees in the various frequency ranges depending on the properties of the material. And according to the law of conservation of energy, these effects must add up to 100 % (Fig. C 6.3, p. 108):

$$R + T + A = 1$$

The heterogeneous frequency-related reflectance causes materials to appear to the human eye in various colours, or to appear transparent in the case of light-permeable materials. Evolution has conditioned the human eye to perceive the sum of the intensity distribution of solar radiation in the visible range as neutral, white light. Reflectance, transmittance and absorptance are properties specific to a material and a surface, and are mostly specified in relation to the whole solar spectrum or just the visible part (e.g. for transmittance in the form of T_{sol} or T_{vis}). In addition, these properties depend on the angle of incidence and their intensity fluctuates considerably depending on the material. This is particularly relevant for the curved surfaces so common to membrane structures because the human eye perceives ever-changing angles of incidence, possibly with, for example, changes of colour in the transmission, irrespective of the sun's trajectory. Furthermore, in the case of reflectance and transmittance we must also consider direct and scattered components plus different refraction behaviour depending on the properties of the material and its surfaces. The appearance of buildings with ETFE facades in particular is considerably affected by this. In addition, this affects the total energy transmittance value, especially in the case of multi-layer applications, because multiple reflection effects take place between the individual plies. In principle, this applies to all light-permeable materials, but is especially relevant in tensile surface structures.

Greenhouse effect

Electromagnetic radiation absorbed by a material is converted into heat energy. This raises the temperature of the material affected and its heat radiation emission spectrum shifts accordingly. This relationship allows us to explain the so-called greenhouse effect:
Solar radiation penetrates a building material that is essentially transparent for the solar spectrum, e.g. glass or foil (Fig. C 6.27, green line) and strikes a material that absorbs the radiation energy to a large extent (e.g. an interior floor surface). This causes the material to heat up

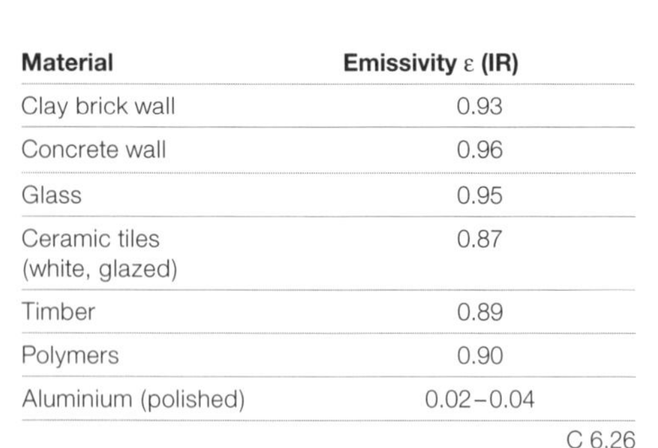

Material	Emissivity ε (IR)
Clay brick wall	0.93
Concrete wall	0.96
Glass	0.95
Ceramic tiles (white, glazed)	0.87
Timber	0.89
Polymers	0.90
Aluminium (polished)	0.02–0.04

C 6.26

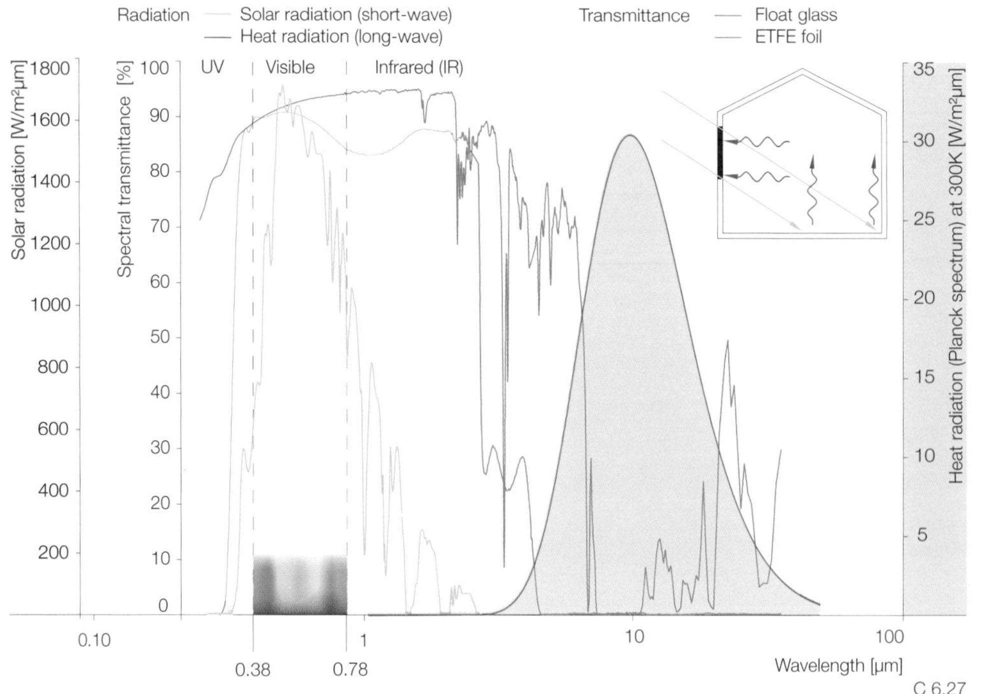

C 6.27

C 6.28

C 6.29

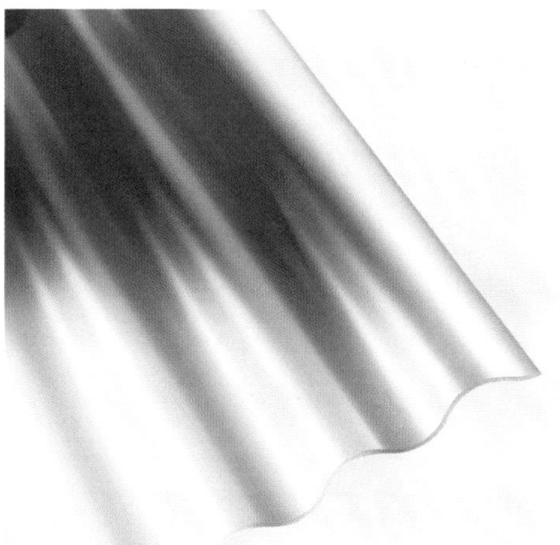
C 6.30

and emit heat radiation as a consequence. However, as the temperature, compared to that of the sun, is much lower (e.g. 40 °C instead of > 5000 °C), the maximum radiation is way beyond the visible range, in the so-called far infrared with wavelengths between 10 and 20 µm. The red line in Fig. C 6.27 indicates the emission spectrum. The heat radiation of the heated surface generally cannot leave the room again through the transparent building material through which the solar radiation originally entered because this material is not transparent for the long-wave far infrared radiation (Fig. C 6.27, green and blue lines). This is true for glass and the majority of polymers, but not for PE foil, for instance. The outcome is that interiors with such enclosing transparent surfaces are constantly heated by incoming solar radiation. This phenomenon can be intentionally exploited in the form of passive solar energy gains. This is how solar thermal collectors and greenhouses work. The light and heat radiation characteristics of translucent and transparent polymers vary considerably, i.e. with respect to their frequency-related transmission and absorption capacities. Furthermore, these characteristics can be further influenced by modifying the polymer structure, by surface treatments (e.g. nano structures) and by employing diverse coating technologies. The angles of reflection can also be adjusted. Fig. C 6.32 (p. 116) compares typical polymer materials and also glass.

Another important aspect for the building industry is the stability of the light radiation characteristics of a material in practice. For example, a decisive criterion for selection could be that polytetrafluoroethylene (PTFE) retains its very high solar reflectance through the self-cleaning effect of its surface over many decades of use (see "Passenger terminal complex, Suvarnabhumi International Airport, Bangkok", pp. 277–279).

In other situations it may be necessary to heat the interior air intentionally and hence create a flow of air by using a highly absorbent (black), open mesh fabric, e.g. to back up the natural ventilation of buildings in hot regions.

When choosing a material to cover a greenhouse, the visible and IR ranges are of course important, but also the UV range and the so-called PAR (photosynthetically active radiation) spectrum, i.e. that the portion of sunlight that is relevant for photosynthesis (approx. 400–700 nm). Polymers can generally be used – in the form of foil they are much thinner than glass and have correspondingly higher solar transmittance values (T_{sol} up to 97 %). In the short-wave UV range in particular, it is possible to achieve considerably higher transmittance values with polymer materials such as ETFE foil (Figs. C 6.31 and C 6.32a, p. 116).

Designation	Solar transmittance	Solar reflectance	Visual transmittance	Visual reflectance	UV transmittance	UV reflectance	Normal thermal emissivity $\varepsilon(T)$ at T = 300 K
Float glass, standard, 3 mm	0.87	0.08	0.90	0.08	0.66	0.08	0.90
Polymer sheets							
PC sheet, 8 mm	0.76	0.09	0.86	0.10	0.00	0.06	0.94
PC multi-wall sheet, 16 mm	0.53	0.35	0.58	0.39	0.00	0.17	0.94
PMMA solid sheet, 8 mm	0.80	0.07	0.92	0.08	0.01	0.04	0.96
PMMA twin-wall sheet, lattice, 16 mm	0.51	0.10	0.56	0.11	0.00	0.04	0.96
GFRP sheet, solid, natural colour	0.36	0.14	0.37	0.18	0.00	0.06	0.95
Woven fabrics							
Polyester-PVC	0.09	0.78	0.07	0.88	0.00	0.10	0.95
Polyester-THV	0.25	0.58	0.25	0.66	0.03	0.17	0.97
Silicone coated glass-fibre fabric	0.20	0.66	0.22	0.72	0.01	0.15	0.95
PVDF fabric	0.80	0.14	0.80	0.15	0.78	0.17	0.81
PTFE/glass-PF type II (bleached)	0.15	0.78	0.15	0.82	0.03	0.63	0.95
PTFE-laminated glass-fibre fabric (bleached)	0.47	0.40	0.47	0.45	0.30	0.42	0.89
PTFE fabric	0.41	0.51	0.38	0.59	0.12	0.09	0.95
Foils							
ETFE, 200 µm, with approx. 65 % silver printing	0.57	0.30	0.57	0.30	0.52	0.34	0.61
ETFE, 200 µm, clear	0.93	0.06	0.92	0.07	0.86	0.12	0.83
ETFE, 250 µm, white	0.44	0.48	0.37	0.62	0.01	0.07	0.90
PE foil, standard, with UV stabiliser, 200 µm	0.88	0.09	0.88	0.10	0.82	0.11	0.60

all measured values ± 0.02

C 6.31

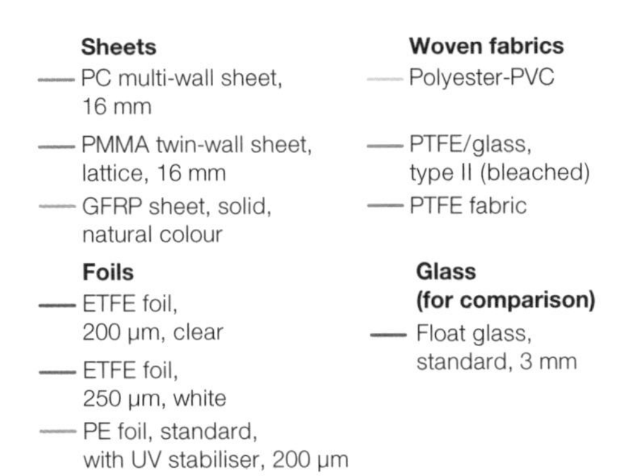

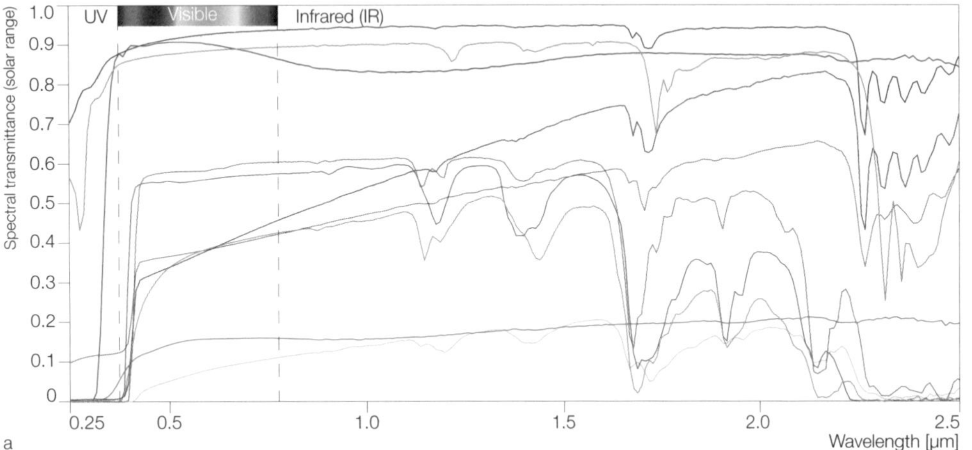

a

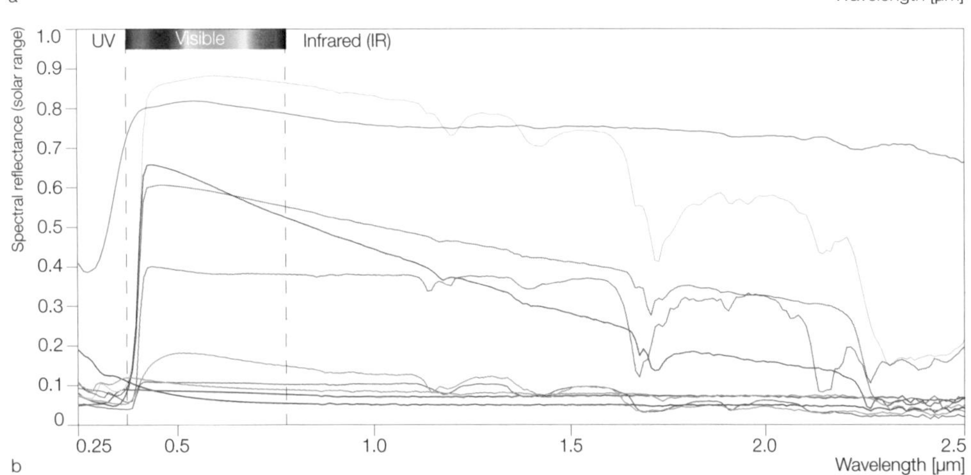

b

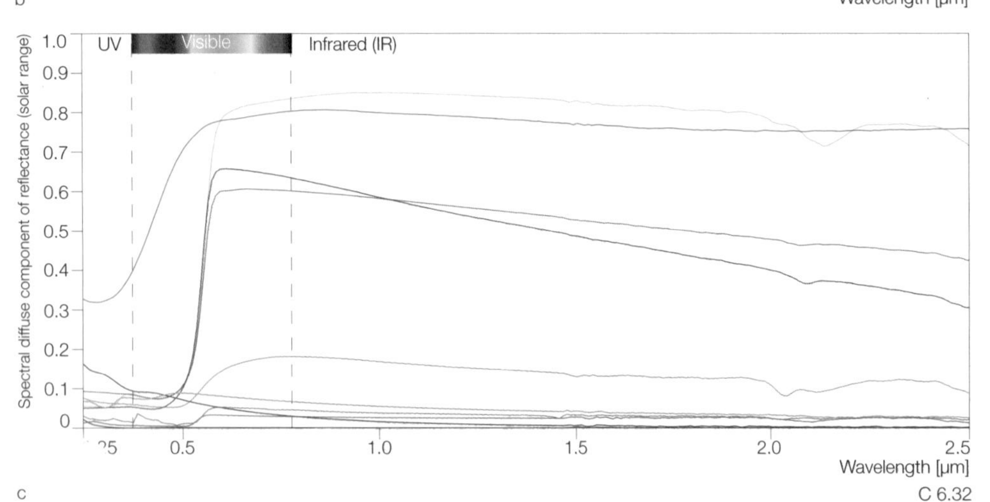

c

C 6.32

C 6.32 Optical measurements of various polymer and membrane materials in the range of solar radiation (0.25–2.5 μm wavelength)
a Spectral transmittance (solar range)
b Spectral reflectance (solar range)
c Spectral diffuse component of reflectance (solar range)

C 6.33 Specific water vapour diffusion resistance index for selected materials

C 6.34 Light-redirecting grid made from a highly reflective coated polymer

C 6.35 Licht-redirecting louvres in the cavity of an insulating glass unit

C 6.36 PUR-coated glass-fibre fabric for scattering daylight; university library, Berlin (D), 2005, Foster & Partners

Material	Water vapour diffusion resistance index μ
Clay brick wall	5–25
Concrete wall	70–150
Timber	40
PU thermal insulation	30–100
Bitumen	2–20000
PVC foil	20–50000
PE foil	100000

C 6.33

Selectivity and low E surfaces

Selectivity is the ratio between transmittance in the visible spectrum and the solar spectrum. Put simply, the aim of using selective materials is to allow a large amount of visible light to pass through a building component but at the same time to filter out – or, ideally, reflect – the high-energy radiation in the near infrared range. This can be achieved with many materials by including effective additional filter layers or by modifying the polymer structure (Figs. C 6.28 and C 6.30, p. 115). In the case of glass we even speak of "solar-control" glazing.

Another effective measure for optimising the heat radiation characteristics is to modify the reflectance in the far infrared range. Achieving a high reflectance (with correspondingly lower absorptance) in this frequency range of the spectrum, which is critical for interior temperatures, results physically in a likewise low surface emissivity ε. Such coating treatments are then known as low E coatings.

This technology has long since been used for insulating glass; the heat losses from the interior are reduced by the lower heat radiation on the outside of the inner pane of glass (which has a low E coating).

This development is starting to be used with polymers and membranes (Figs. C 6.28 and C 6.29, p. 115; see also "Passenger terminal complex, Suvarnabhumi International Airport, Bangkok", pp. 277–279, and "Shopping centre, Amadora", pp. 256–257) and we can expect to see many more applications for these types of modified materials in the future (see "Complex building envelopes", pp. 212–223).

Transparency and light

The permanent precision of optimised glass in terms of transparency and a view through is hardly possible with polymers. In terms of modifications, formability and production methods, however, polymers offer far more possibilities. This is shown very clearly by the examples of applications in other, very demanding sectors (e.g. military, aerospace) and also applies to the building industry. Systems to channel and redirect the incoming daylight (diffuse/direct, 2D and 3D structures) plus shading systems are in most cases only possible with polymers (Figs. C 6.34, C 6.35 and E 5.26c, p. 223).

Moisture characteristics

Moisture characteristics are of interest to the construction industry on two counts: firstly, the gastightness of a material, for water vapour especially, and secondly, the moisture absorption capacity. Compared with glass and metals of a thickness that can be regarded as gastight, all polymers are to some extent permeable for gases like water vapour. The water vapour diffusion resistance Z of a layer of material is calculated for a reference temperature of 10°C according to DIN 4108-3 as follows:

$$Z = 1.5 \cdot 106 \cdot \mu \cdot d \ [(m^2 hPa)/kg]$$

μ Water vapour diffusion resistance index specific to material (Fig. C 6.33)
d Thickness of layer [m]

The product $s_d = \mu \cdot d$ is designated the (water vapour) diffusion-equivalent air layer thickness and is classified as follows:
$s_d \leq 0.5$ diffusion-permeable
$0.5 < s_d < 1500$ diffusion-retardant
$s_d \geq 1500$ diffusion-tight

Polymers on their own are generally unsuitable for applications requiring very high gastightness, e.g. glazing or vacuum insulation systems. But by combining various polymers and coatings, especially in conjunction with metals and oxides, it is possible to achieve a high gastightness (e.g. for barrier foil; Fig. C 6.13, p. 111).

In building envelopes made from polymers and membranes, their share of the weight of the envelope and their moisture absorption properties are comparatively low, i.e. these components cannot make an effective contribution to buffering moisture. This fact must be taken into account when planning the building and its HVAC services and compensated for elsewhere if necessary. In principle, however, it is possible to integrate absorbent substances, so-called getter materials (e.g. silica gels, zeolites or other adsorbents), in the polymer matrix to a limited extent. This is especially interesting for applications in which residual gases, e.g. water vapour, have to be absorbed in enclosed volumes, as is the case, for example, in the spacers of insulating glass units. The getter material buffers, up to its saturation point, the residual water vapour that remains in the cavity between the panes after manufacture and also the water vapour in the air that infiltrates via the minimal leaks in the hermetic edge seal – up to the saturation point of the getter material. Therefore, this water vapour cannot condensate on the glass when the temperature drops below the dew point, and so the service life of the product is prolonged.

Sound insulation and room acoustics

Polymers play a major role in sound insulation and room acoustics and are employed for diverse measures associated with these fields (Fig. C 6.39, p. 119). The various applications make use of polymers, and especially polymer foams, for decoupling, deadening, attenuating and absorbing purposes, also for configuring the reflection characteristics.
In buildings, sound is important as both an external condition and an internal requirement (sound insulation, room acoustics) because the source of the sound can be on either side of the building envelope. So there are three areas to consider: noise immissions (noise from outside), noise emissions (sound from inside) and room acoustics (noise level in a room, audibility of speech, suitability for other uses, e.g. music). When it comes to the building envelope, the information given in DIN 4109 "Sound insulation in buildings" and, first and foremost, VDI Directive 2719 "Sound isolation of windows and their auxiliary equipment" are the most important works of reference in Germany. The VDI Directive specifies six sound insulation classes based on the exterior noise level which must comply with sound reduction index values between 30 and 50 dB depending on the use of the building. Other requirements apply where the exterior noise level exceeds 70 dB.
In air, sound waves propagate approximately spherically from their source (airborne sound). Once a solid material has been excited, e.g. through mechanical actions (footsteps on a floor), sound waves propagate through the mass of the building components (structure-borne sound), which in turn can excite a layer of air on the other side of the component – the vibrations are thus re-propagated in the form of airborne sound.
Sound waves can travel long distances by means of structure-borne propagation. Where the solid components of a building are coupled together, i.e. rigidly connected with each other (e.g. a waste-water pipe cast directly into a solid wall), sound may well be able to propagate throughout an entire building in this way. We speak of flanking transmissions when the propagation of the sound is not direct, but rather via indirect routes. Insulation against structure-borne sound places especially high demands on the planning team and calls for a high standard of workmanship on site because sound propagates through even the smallest of (unintentional) acoustic bridges. The solution here is to be found in acoustic decoupling, i.e. all connections between relevant components (e.g. between the floor covering and the structural floor underneath, or between the sanitary installation and the wall) are in a "soft" form so that vibrations cannot be transmitted directly.
One possible strategy against airborne sound propagation is to increase the mass of the separating components, making them as heavy as possible and thus more inert from the sound transmission point of view. This means using a material with a maximum density which is not easily excited by the incident sound waves in the air. Another important measure for insulating against the propagation of airborne sound is to seal all joints, gaps and cracks as effectively as possible.

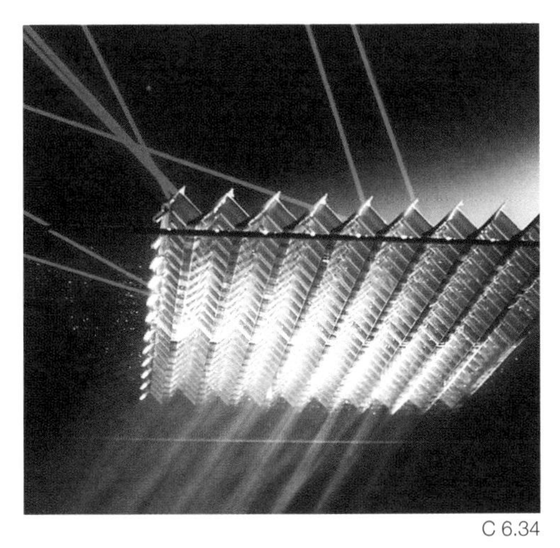
C 6.34

C 6.35

C 6.36

C 6.37

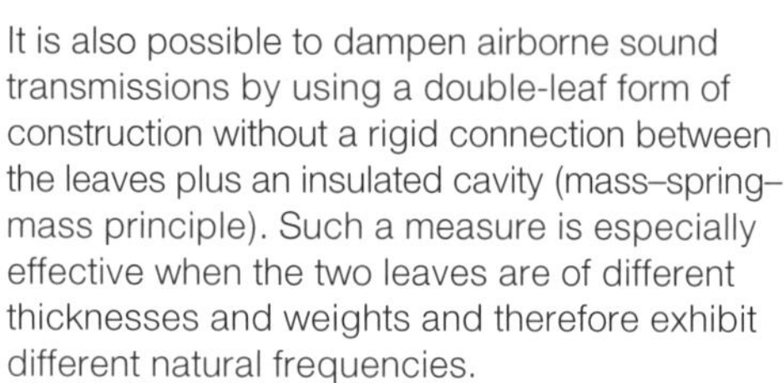

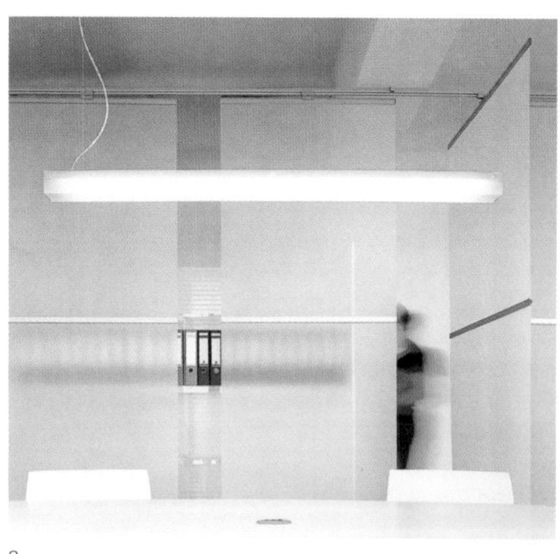

a

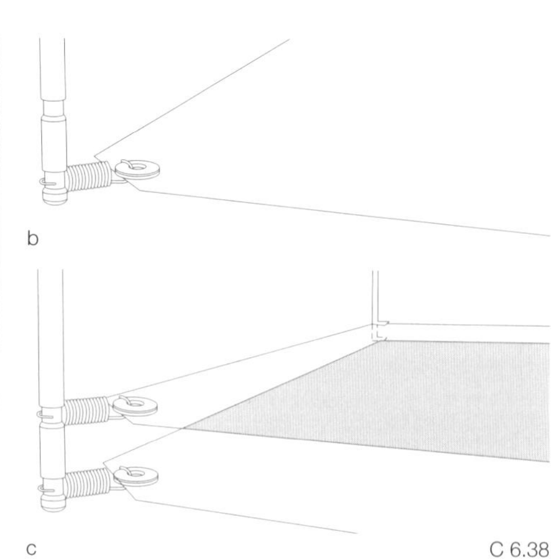

b

c

C 6.38

It is also possible to dampen airborne sound transmissions by using a double-leaf form of construction without a rigid connection between the leaves plus an insulated cavity (mass–spring–mass principle). Such a measure is especially effective when the two leaves are of different thicknesses and weights and therefore exhibit different natural frequencies.

Polymer and membrane structures

Polymer and, principally, membrane structures have an extremely small mass; for membranes this lies between only approx. 0.1 and 1.5 kg/m^2, for instance. This makes it difficult to achieve adequate insulation against the propagation of sound. One option is to integrate heavyweight intermediate layers. In the case of the building envelope to the airport passenger terminal in Bangkok (see pp. 277–279), an intermediate layer of polycarbonate sheets (7.2 kg/m^2) was incorporated and this helped to achieve a sound reduction index R'_w of 35 dB.

Designs with air-filled cushions pose a special problem: raindrops falling on the uppermost layer act like a drumstick hitting a drum, causing the cushions to vibrate. This is particularly noticeable with foil materials, whereas coated textiles tend to dampen the noise somewhat because of their surface characteristics and their greater inhomogeneity. Although in practice this drumming effect is only annoying during heavy rainfall, which is generally of short duration, this form of construction is nevertheless unsuitable for acoustically sensitive uses. Outer layers that interrupt the rainfall, e.g. fine nets, can reduce the noise level but have a negative effect on the view through the material and cleaning. And when ice and heavy snowfall is to be expected, such additional nets are unlikely to be viable from the technical viewpoint.

Room acoustics

Sound waves are always reflected to some degree by all the surfaces enclosing a room and the objects in the room. The non-reflected component is absorbed and/or transmitted depending on the material and form of construction. The sound absorption coefficient α specifies how much sound is absorbed. A value of $\alpha = 0$ means that the incident sound energy is completely reflected, and no reflections means that the incident sound energy has been completely absorbed, i.e. $\alpha = 1$. With a high sound absorption coefficient, an absorbent, usually soft, material absorbs the sound energy to a large extent and converts it into internal heat. This diminishes the reflected component in particular. In a highly reverberant room, for example, an absorbent lining on the ceiling can reduce the reverberation time significantly and thus improve the audibility of speech.

These processes do not take place uniformly over the entire frequency spectrum, but instead tend to display a rather non-uniform intensity distribution. The sound absorption coefficient is therefore measured for various frequencies. The rule of thumb is: the thicker the absorbent material, the better it is at absorbing low frequencies as well.

The relationships described above are also valid for multiple reflections and their reverberation times. A differentiated assessment of the frequency-dependent reflection and absorption processes is critical for the room acoustics situation (e.g. suitability for performances of music, audibility of speech). The smoother and harder the surfaces, the less distorted and more complete are the reflections. It is primarily the frequency-related uniformity of the reflections and a reverberation time adapted to the intended use that are crucial for good room acoustics. Diverse measures can be employed to achieve this goal, which are based on optimising/activating the surfaces of the room and in some cases installing additional elements:

- Perforated surfaces with suitable backing layers
- Layers of insulation in ceilings (open- and closed-cell materials)
- Components in the form of baffles, sound absorbers (e.g. with microperforations), screens, etc.

Acoustic foil

Specially developed acoustic foils, available in transparent, translucent and printed variations, are available for improving room acoustics. The effectiveness of these foils is based on microperforations, with diameters between 0.2 and 0.8 mm. Around the edges of these perforations, the ensuing friction converts the sound energy into heat, which in turn reduces reverberation times and noise levels (Fig. C 6.38a). Providing two layers of such a material increases the sound-absorbent effect further (Fig. C 6.38c). Owing to their very low weight (and the "invisibility" of the transparent variation), acoustic foils are suitable for retrofitting in existing buildings. These acoustic foils with their microperforations can also be used in conjunction with thermo-active floors because they do not impair the function of such floors. Using a printed foil with a reflective silver design, e.g. below a flat glass roof, results in a further benefit because the foil with its microperforations has a positive effect on the interior climate thanks to the reflection of long-wave heat radiation and the associated reduction in heat losses.

The products on the market are:

- UV-stabilised or UV-stable,
- not readily flammable (DIN 4102 building materials class B1 or B2),
- chlorine-resistant, and
- electrostatically neutral.

Room acoustics and membrane structures

When assessing and optimising the room acoustics qualities of foil and membrane structures, it must be remembered that due to their very low mass and the flexible nature of their structures and surfaces, airborne sound is transmitted directly and hardly reflected, especially in the low-frequency range. The materials used for pneumatic structures are airtight on the inside and so it is not possible to integrate additional absorbent materials at this point. So, as the building envelope is often unavailable in such situations, measures to improve the room acoustics must frequently be realised on the inside. With prestressed, multi-layer designs, on the other hand, the quality of the inner layer can also be designed and fabricated to meet acoustic criteria.

Weather-resistant, coated spacer fabrics represent another option for improving the sound insulation. These are attached to a membrane backing and support a second layer at a certain distance (currently up to 500 mm). The ensuing cavity can be filled with sand, for example, and

Measure			
Sound insulation	Sound insulation/sound attenuation	Profiled foams (e.g. with studs)	Flexible PUR foam PE foam (closed-cell)
	Attenuating structure-borne sound/damping drumming	Heavyweight foil	e.g. elastomer-modified heavyweight bitumen sheet
	Edge absorber/low-pitch absorber	Foam	Flexible, open-cell melamine foam
Improving room acoustics	Low-pitch absorber		
	Broadband absorber	High sound absorption capacity over a wide range of frequencies (porous absorber)	Flexible, open-cell melamine resin foam, flexible PUR foam
	Baffles (self-supporting sound-absorbing element)	High sound absorption capacity over a wide range of frequencies (porous absorber)	Flexible, open-cell melamine resin foam, flexible PUR foam
	Sound-absorbing fascia panels		Foil with microperforations/open fabric
	Demountable partitions		Foil with microperforations/open fabric
	Roller blinds		Foil with microperforations/open fabric

C 6.39

with even just a minimal thickness and weight it is possible to achieve a sound insulating effect, e.g. approx. 35 dB for 20 mm.

Reaction to fire and fire protection

Standards and directives play a decisive role in ensuring that planned construction measures are approved, but in practice almost always leave room for interpretation. Besides the feasibility of a design concept from the constructional viewpoint, it is usually necessary to prove the suitability of the building products to be used, especially with respect to their ageing behaviour and safety. For the latter, reaction to fire is one critical aspect. Considering a fire incident must be viewed as relevant to all tasks in building, although it is not always the fire that is so dangerous, but rather its consequences (e.g. extremely irrational sociopsychological behaviour patterns of the persons affected which can be triggered by a fire during an event attended by large numbers of people).
Fire protection aims at preventing or delaying the spread of fire, maintaining the load-carrying capacity of the structure for a certain period of time and, first and foremost, protecting the lives and health of the users of a building. This is why there are countless statutory and technical regulations and directives on diverse levels, e.g. in the building regulations of the federal states, in directives from TÜV, DIN, VDE, etc., which cover the choice of building materials, their properties and corresponding forms of construction plus protective measures.

Fire protection aspects represent a considerable obstacle to the further spread of polymers for building applications in general and for building envelopes in particular. A number of synthetic materials have through the catastrophic consequences of their use attained a sad notoriety with respect to their behaviour in fire, e.g. the widely used polyvinyl chloride (PVC) and polystyrene foams involved in the fire at Düsseldorf Airport in 1996.

The first fire protection and materials-related level of consideration is the classification of the materials or products to be used into building materials classes in line with current standards. In Germany that standard is DIN 4102-1:

A Incombustible materials
- A1 without organic constituents, no verification required
- A2 with organic constituents, verification required

B Combustible materials
- B1 not readily flammable
- B2 flammable
- B3 highly flammable

Considering the course of a fire, it should be noted that classes B2 and B3 cannot be regarded as self-extinguishing, i.e. a fire involving these materials can keep itself going. According to cl. 17 para. 2 of Germany's Model Building Code (MBO), highly flammable materials (B 3) may not be used at all if they still remain highly flammable in the installed condition.

Building authority requirement	Additional requirements		European class to DIN EN 13501-1		DIN 4102-1 class
	No smoke	No flaming droplets			
Incombustible	•	•	A1		A1
Minimum requirement	•	•	A2	s1, d0	A2
Not readily flammable	•	•	B, C	s1, d0	B1
		•	A2 A2, B, C	s2, d0 s3, d0	
	•		A2, B, C A2, B, C	s1, d1 s1, d2	
Minimum requirement			A2, B, C	s3, d2	
Flammable		•	D	s1, d0 s2, d0 s3, d0	B2
			E		
			D	s1, d2 s2, d2 s3, d2	
Minimum requirement			E	d2	
Highly flammable			F		B3

C 6.40

C 6.37 Sound absorber made from fabric-covered foam
C 6.38 Foil with microperforations for improving the room acoustics
a Sliding element
b Single layer
c Double layer
C 6.39 Polymers in sound insulation and room acoustics applications
C 6.40 Comparison of the DIN 4102-1 and DIN EN 13501-1 classes

Since 2010, DIN 4102 has been replaced by the European standard DIN EN 13501 parts 1 and 2 and the draft standard E DIN EN 1634-1. The European classification contains seven classes (A1, A2, B, C, D, E and F) plus uniform methods of testing.
The characteristic feature is now the time taken for the building material to burn completely (flashover). This point may not be reached at all for classes A1, A2 and B, whereas it is reached after a time of between 10 and 2 min. for classes C, D and E. In addition, further sub-classes for smoke development (s1, s2 and s3) and flaming droplets (d0, d1 and d2) have been introduced (Fig. C 6.40, p. 119). These classes must now be specified on the product packaging. Proof of the allocation of a building material or building product to a building materials class is carried out with the help of fire tests.

In the case of polymers, it is not only the actual basic material that is critical for the reaction to fire, but more often than not the semi-finished product or final construction product subsequently made from that material. The additional layers, coatings and treatments, but also polymer modifications and possibly the combination with other materials to form composites, have a significant influence on the properties relevant to fire protection. During the planning work it is therefore not sensible to rely on general statements regarding the fire protection classification of a certain type of polymer, but instead to find out about and verify the fire safety aspects of the intended products with the help of the approval documentation.

Despite diverse modification options, only very few types of polymer are non-flammable. This property is indeed desirable for many applications, but in the end not always the compelling and sole requirement. The issues are much more involved and need to be considered separately in each individual case. Often compensatory measures are possible which permit an alternative to the non-flammable building materials called for by standards and legislation.

Whether a material or product may be used at a certain point in a building depends on the fire protection classification and also other, sometimes decisive, factors and properties. As part of this appraisal it is important to determine the following points, for example:

- The temperatures of the melting point and the flammability point.
- Whether the material or product produces flaming droplets (although even droplets that are just hot and not flaming can still represent a serious problem).
- Whether the material "retracts" in the event of a fire and leaves holes, for example, which can allow heat and smoke to escape to the outside (similar to the function of an automatic heat and smoke vent).
- Which combustion products ensue and to what extent these are toxic.
- Whether the polymer is installed exposed or concealed, and hence, in the latter case, cannot be visually inspected.
- Which parts of the building components lose their structural functions at which temperatures and what consequences are to be expected.

Considering this last point, the extremely low mass of polymers can in some instances be critical in a positive way. For example, in the event of a fire an ETFE cushion roof loses its structural function at a relatively low temperature and the foil splits as a result, but this allows heat and smoke to escape from the interior quickly. Furthermore, owing to its very low weight, the ETFE foil of such a roof does not count as a relevant fire load, and the foil does not produce any flaming droplets, either. A fire brigade would evaluate such a fire scenario as relatively positive!

The constructional boundary conditions, e.g. where can toxic fumes spread to in the event of a fire, which temperatures are necessary in the occupied internal zones in order for a fire to start at the point concerned (distance from fire loads) and how the situation should then be assessed for the rescue of persons (fire scenario), must be considered when choosing materials and products.

Further aspects at building level that can be exploited in advance by employing compensatory measures are, for instance, limiting the number of users (e.g. by regulating visitor flows), increasing and improving the escape options, or adapting the building services (e.g. controlled fresh and exhaust air, fire detection and sprinkler installations).
These aspects, which in some cases can cause considerable additional costs, are not regulated by National Technical Approvals. Therefore, decisions regarding the choice of materials and forms of construction should be taken as early as possible by an interdisciplinary team that includes the approving authority and fire safety specialists.

Optimising the reaction to fire
There are several well-known methods that can be used to improve the behaviour of polymers in fire. These involve modifications during manufacture or further processing.

Incorporating flame retardants
Flame retardants can be applied either to the polymer structure or the surface of the material. They reduce the combustibility or mitigate the consequences of combustion. Their effect is based on the formation of an encapsulating layer of ash, a chemically generated sealed surface, physical cooling or the oxidation of combustible gases.

Optimising the mass proportions in composites
In a composite material consisting of various basic materials, it is the ratio of the combustible to the incombustible mass components that is crucial for the fire protection classification. This is the case with PTFE-coated glass-fibre fabric, for example; this is why the fire protection characteristics of this group of materials varies considerably depending on the proportion of the fibres with respect to the coating.

Fire protection for polymers in building services
Besides the issue of structural fire protection, it is also necessary to consider the sound and thermal insulation (and the latter includes both hot and cold systems) required for pipes and ducts. Lagging around cold pipework has to satisfy particularly high demands because in contrast to "normal" thermal insulation it is also essential to protect against saturation caused by condensation. In this case satisfying fire protection stipulations and normal processing criteria are joined by the need for closed-cell structures and a very high water vapour diffusion resistance. Owing to these special requirements, the use of incombustible insulating materials is limited when it comes to lagging for cold pipework and so combustible polymers have to be used. These may not produce any droplets, especially flaming droplets, must be self-extinguishing and may not cause a fire to spread through wall or floor penetrations, i.e. penetrations with insulated pipes or ducts may not impair the fire resistance of the components.

Incineration as subsequent usage
Although the reaction to fire of polymers is so disadvantageous for their use in construction applications, it does, however, lead to a fourth option after the end of their useful lives: incineration for energy generation. (The other three options are reuse and the recycling of their constituents or raw materials.) Polymers usually contain a very high proportion of carbon compounds and therefore have a comparatively high calorific value. If a certain polymer is therefore unsuitable for the other three end-of-life options, then incineration, taking into account economical and ecological criteria, is a reasonable alternative.

C 6.41 Relationship between wetting contact angle and surface tension
C 6.42 Water droplets on an ETFE foil
a without "No Drop" coating
b with "No Drop" coating
C 6.43 Electroluminescent (EL) foil
a not activated/voltage not applied
b in light-emitting state after applying a high-frequency a.c. voltage

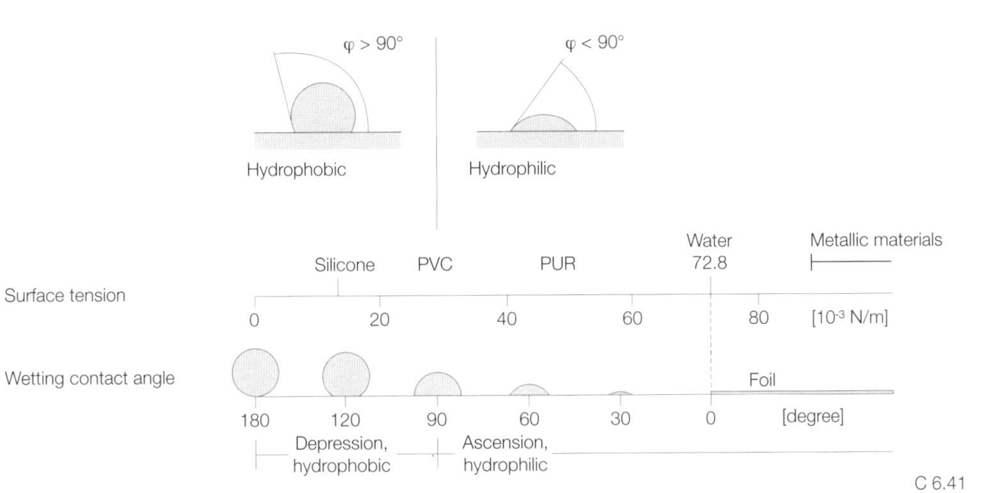

C 6.41

a

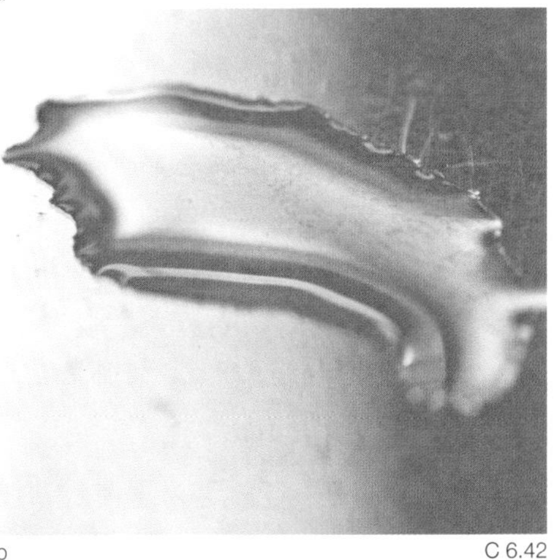

b C 6.42

Further characteristics

There are other aspects – in addition to the building physics and energy aspects already discussed – that are relevant to the choice of polymers and their use in the building envelope.

Loading and durability aspects

Properties such as abrasion resistance, elasticity (e.g. resistance to hail), mechanical load-carrying capacity and flex cracking resistance (e.g. for movable assemblies), mechanical surface resilience (e.g. due to regular sandstorms) plus UV and weathering resistance, including hydrolysis and alkali resistance, may well be relevant when deciding whether a polymer or membrane material is suitable for an external application taking into account the anticipated service life. A sufficiently concrete statement regarding durability for applications in the building envelope is only possible when the respective local external conditions are known, and these can vary considerably.

Soiling behaviour

The soiling behaviour of a material's surfaces represents an important criterion for maintaining a pleasing appearance and for the cost of cleaning. And owing to the often very large uniform surfaces of membrane structures in particular, this aspect should not be neglected. The fluoropolymer-based materials often used here (e.g. ETFE, PTFE and also PVDF to a certain extent) are far superior to glass in terms of soiling. Although particles of dust and dirt do remain on these membrane surfaces, they do not adhere properly. Consequently, such particles are washed away almost completely by regular rainfall and the original appearance remains intact for many years – also because precipitation or UV radiation does not cause any significant chemical changes in the surfaces.
Basically, the cost of cleaning the surface of a material goes hand in hand with its soiling behaviour. However, the constructional details are very important, too, because poor design can lead to accumulations of dust and dirt and unsightly streaks.

Modifying the surface tension

There are several polymer and foil materials available with a modified surface tension (e.g. PMMA and ETFE); these are marketed under the name "No Drop". The aim of this modification is to ensure that condensation does not drip from individual points on the surface, but rather drains away as a coherent film of water (Fig. C 6.42). This is especially important for greenhouses because dripping water can cause blemishes on lettuces, for instance, which makes them impossible to sell. How long this modified surface tension treatment lasts depends on the particular product. So far, however, the solutions available have not proved to be durable and must be reapplied regularly (e.g. with special sprays) to maintain the effect, which means the areas of foil must be accessible.

Electroluminescence

Electroluminescent (EL) foils are active light sources, so-called Lambert emitters, i.e. the luminance of the radiation emitted by the surface is identical from all sides. The light occupies a very narrow band of frequencies, is almost monochromatic, absolutely uniform and visible over a long distance (Fig. C 6.43). The lack of infrared emissions means that the radiation does not cause the source to heat up. EL foils with a light-emitting layer based on a metallic semiconductor phenomenon can be laminated to polymer sheets, panels or foils.
The typical make-up of an EL foil comprises a protective foil, a transparent electrode, pigment and insulation, a second electrode and another protective foil for the other side. Varying the doping of the luminescent pigment zinc sulphide allows a colour range from blue to yellow (approx. 480–580 nm) to be produced. Doping substances can be mixed to produce other colours (e.g. white). One disadvantage of using zinc sulphide as a pigment is its very high hygroscopicity. The protective foil on both sides must therefore be made from an efficient water-repellent material, e.g. polychlorotrifluoroethylene (PCTFE). Another pigment is already available in which the zinc sulphide molecules are microencapsulated and therefore protected. However, the greater spacing of the molecules means that the luminance suffers and is not quite so

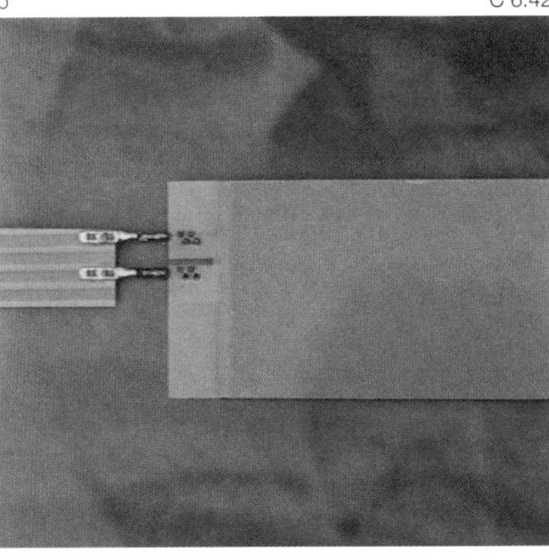

a

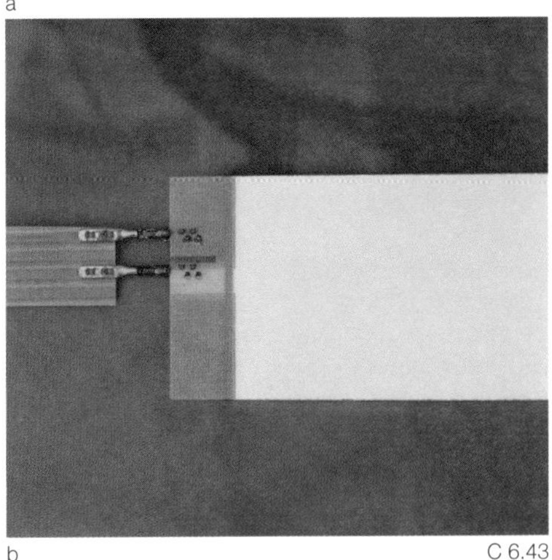

b C 6.43

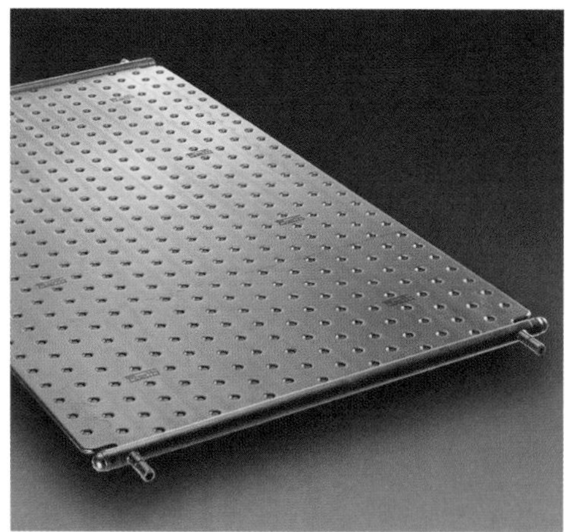

C 6.44

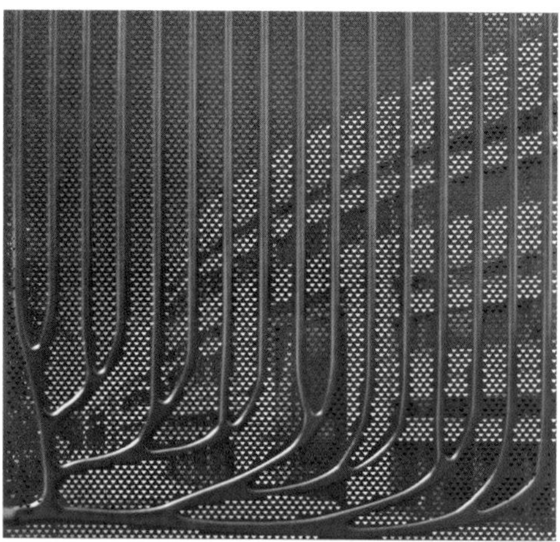

C 6.45

C 6.46

homogeneous. Such EL foils are extremely thin, highly flexible and inexpensive, and can also be cut. It is no longer essential to laminate them onto other materials, although this does prolong their service life. Polylaminates are sufficient for a protective foil in this case.
EL foils are well-known from military and aircraft applications and as the backlighting to liquid crystal (LC) displays. However, their potential applications in the building industry are numerous and diverse and EL foils are already in widespread use in some areas, e.g. as self-illuminated signs, as safety and emergency lighting for steps in cinemas, or in interior design.

Polymers in the active use of renewable energies

The active generation of energy by way of systems that are directly integrated into the building is becoming more and more important. The potential is theoretically huge, given the enormous areas available in the shape of facade and roof surfaces. Such active systems exploit solar energy (solar thermal and photovoltaic systems), wind energy, ambient heat (diverse types of heat exchanger) or also radiation towards the cold night sky for the renewable provision of cooling energy.

Solar thermal systems

Polymers can be used in solar thermal systems as a substitute for the glass covers or as a material for the absorber and the housing. Replacing the glass and metal by polymer materials can result in significant cost-savings. However, the requirements with respect to mechanical and optical properties and durability are high. Polymers are already widely used in unglazed collectors (no covers), often called "swimming pool collectors" (Fig. C 6.44). Optimising the geometry to compensate for the low thermal conductivity of the polymer is vital here. Current developments focus on the following aspects:

- Optimum absorption of solar radiation
- Reducing heat radiation losses
- New materials that optimise the thermal conductivity and specific heat capacity

In addition, thermomechanical stresses and the deformations they cause through expansion and contraction must be taken into account.

The optimisation of flow characteristics and permeable absorber structures for building-integrated applications are other areas currently being investigated (Fig. C 6.45). One of the aspects being studied within the scope of ongoing development projects is the stabilisation of the polymer structure against UV radiation by adding so-called nano fillers such as carbon nano tubes, which should simultaneously increase the thermal conductivity. Different types of foil as a replacement for covers made from "solar glass" (low-iron glass with optimised reflective behaviour) have been under investigation for a long time with the aim of saving weight and money. Foil can be used to optimise so-called lunar collectors, which provide renewable cooling energy: the convective heating of the absorber, which is used to dissipate heat into the cold night sky, can be reduced by covering it with a special foil (e.g. PE foil) with a high transmittance in the far infrared range.
In the future it may also be possible to use foil to construct switchable solar thermal collectors. Fitting a foil temporarily over the absorber can deactivate the thermal insulation effect and the high surface emissivity of the foil causes the aforementioned lunar collector effect. Fitting the foil and thus switching off the thermal insulation effect can also be used to reduce the stagnation temperature of the collector.

Photovoltaics

Polymers are used in photovoltaics for various functions. Experiments in which crystalline solar cells are applied to polymers, primarily PMMA and PC, have been carried out since the 1990s (Fig. C 6.46). Besides their use as bonding interlayers (glass/solar cell and solar cell/backing panel), mostly made from EVA (ethylene vinyl acetate), polymers are today also employed as covers and substrates for solar cells. Combining polymers with thin-film solar cells results in flexible modules that enable totally new applications (Figs. C 6.48 to C 6.51). PV modules can therefore be integrated into foil and membrane constructions without the need for additional supports – either attached to the foil or membrane with mechanical fasteners, inserted into custom pockets in the material or laminated to the surface of the material.
Up until now, the PV elements themselves have represented a high cost factor, calling for them to be applied to long-lasting substrate materials in order not to endanger the payback period for such an investment. Hardwearing and durable fluoropolymer-based materials such as ETFE foil and PTFE/glass are the main focus of interest for such applications. PV modules attached to membranes can be integrated into roofs or facades without the need for additional supporting frameworks. In such cases they not only supply electricity, but ensure indispensable shade for the interior (Fig. C 6.48), which limits solar gains in the summer, thus cutting cooling loads and energy consumption.
Fig. C 6.47 shows the different ways in which PV modules can be integrated into ETFE foil by laminating, and therefore must be taken into account during fabrication and in the cutting pattern (left), and how modules can be attached to textile materials (right). Forecasting the yield for membrane-integrated photovoltaics is far more complex than with conventional applications: the geometries of the different roof or facade structures are unique to every project and require new module sizes and layouts every time. The orientation of the individual photovoltaic elements with respect to the sun can vary within a project, indeed, vary within a module itself. The form of the membranes – governed by the geometry of the building, the supporting structure and the loads – is also crucial for the geometry of the PV installation. Moreover, complex three-dimensional forms complicate the appraisal of shading effects.
Further PV technologies are currently undergoing development, e.g. photovoltaics based on organic materials, which in future may possibly permit greater integration into textile materials (Fig. C 6.51).

C 6.44 Unglazed collector ("swimming pool collector")
C 6.45 Photomontage of a light-permeable thermal polymer absorber, Fraunhofer Institute for Solar Energy Systems (ISE)
C 6.46 PV module with polymer sheets as substrate (PC or PMMA)
C 6.47 Methods of production for PV modules for use with ETFE foil and woven fabrics
C 6.48 Flexible PV module (a-Si) integrated into the top layer of an ETFE foil cushion
C 6.49 "GROW", a prototype of a combination of thin-film PV and piezoelectric generators, embedded in an ETFE foil
C 6.50 Laboratory specimen of a flexible PV module (a-Si) applied to PTFE/glass
C 6.51 Prototype of a thin-film PV strip in a textile material

Wind power

The rotor blades of large wind turbines represent another major application for fibre-reinforced polymer composites, alongside aircraft and ships. And in the construction sector, such polymers could in future open up new applications in the field of building-integrated micro wind turbines. The first tests and studies are in progress.

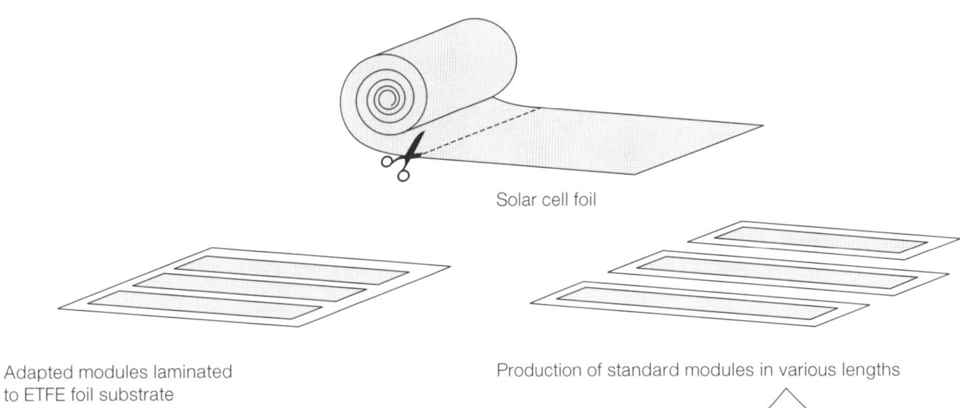

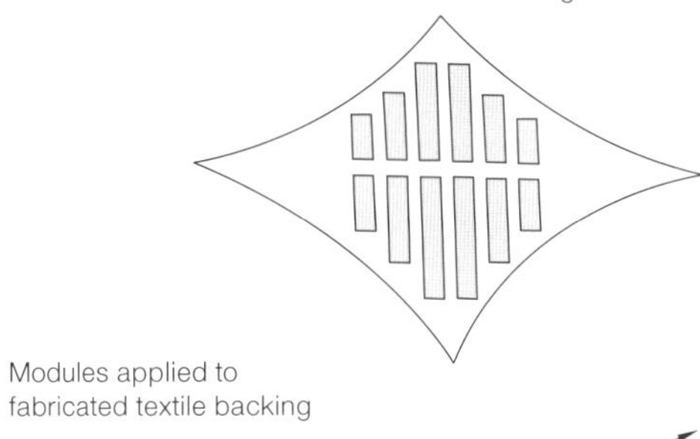

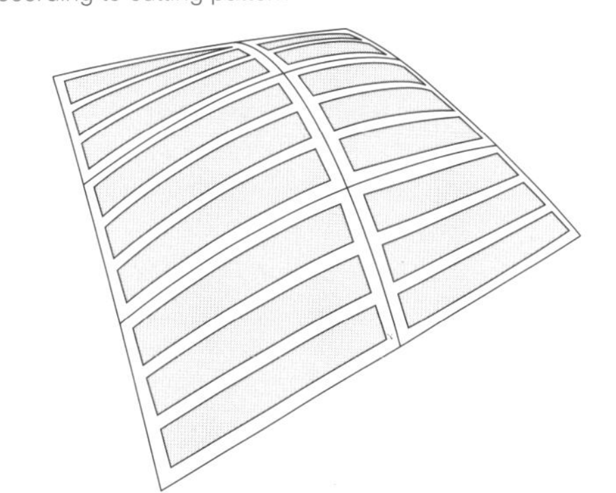

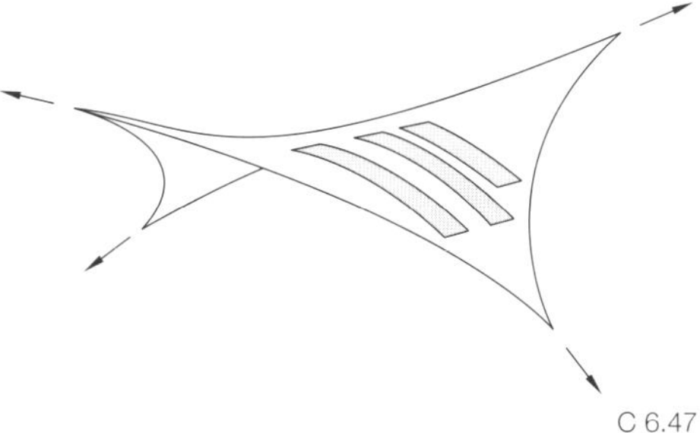

C 6.47

C 6.48

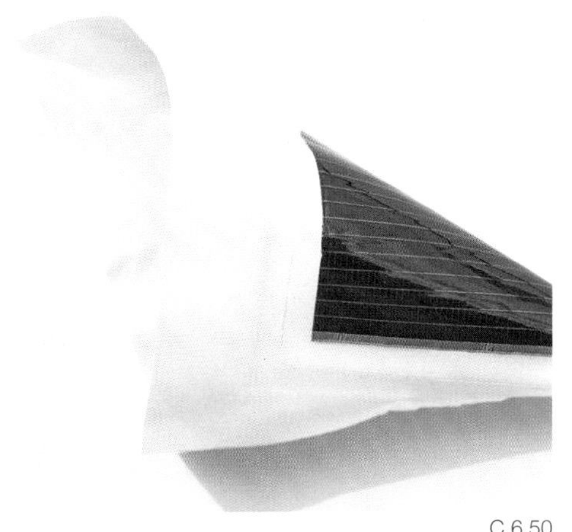

C 6.50

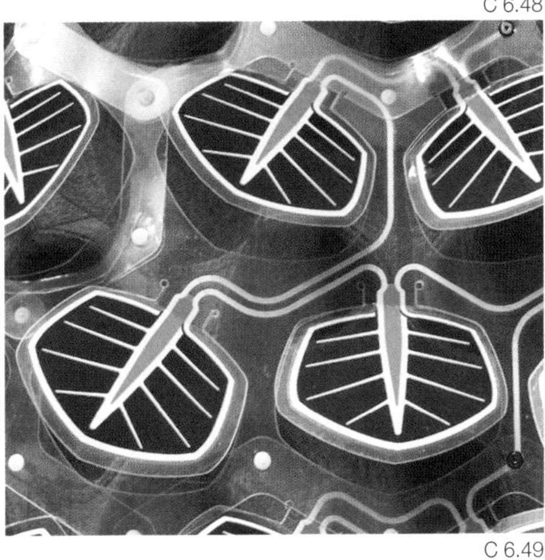

C 6.49

C 6.51

References:
[1] Williams, David R.: Sun Fact Sheet, Greenbelt 2004 (http://nssdc.gsfc.nasa.gov/planetary/factsheet/sunfact.html, 16 Aug 2010)

Environmental impact of polymers

Joost Hartwig, Martin Zeumer

C 7.1

There is a growing demand for ever-increasing efficiency in the operation of buildings. Associated with this is an ever greater focus on the energy consumption and environmental impact of the production and disposal of the materials used. In the light of the dwindling reserves of our planet's resources, the effects of planning decisions extend further and further into the future. Whereas other branches of industry have already experienced significant increases in efficiency, this development has not really been evident in the building sector: efficiency in the use of materials and rationalisation are lacking, the recycling rate is low.
The plastics industry is playing a leading role here. For example, we have already seen some increases in efficiency in the use of the enormous amounts of energy needed for the production of polymers. Nevertheless, or perhaps for this very reason, polymers offer plenty of scope for a two-sided discussion. On the one hand, polymers contain a high amount of primary energy compared to their mass, and emissions from the materials can represent dangers for the environment and users. On the other, they have a potential for generating savings through forms of construction that utilise materials efficiently. The use of polymer products can substantially reduce the amount of operating energy required, with additives enabling individual adaptation to the specific circumstances of a project.
Life cycle assessments can be used here as a key evaluation criterion in the objectification of the discussion on plastics.

Life cycle assessment

The life cycle assessment (LCA) approach has been around since the late 20th century and provides a good foundation for a transparent evaluation of the complex environmental impacts of products and processes. The effects can thus be evaluated from many different angles relevant to planning.
An LCA analyses the life of a product, which can have one or more functions. To do this, we consider the stages in that life such as obtaining the raw materials, production, processing and transport, also use, reuse and disposal if applicable. We distinguish between "cradle-to-grave" assessments that investigate the entire life cycle of a product, and "cradle-to-gate" assessments that consider only the life of a product up to the time it leaves the factory. DIN EN ISO 14040 describes the LCA method. There are four parts to an LCA: definition of goal and scope, inventory analysis, impact assessment and interpretation (Fig. C 7.2).

Definition of goal and scope

First of all, we describe the product and its function (functional unit) to be evaluated. Specifying the system boundaries defines which processes are to be included in the LCA of the product and which are to be left out. In the ideal case the inputs and outputs of the product system are elementary streams – indivisible substances, i.e. chemical elements and compounds that are obtained from nature (inputs) and elements that are returned to nature (outputs). The boundaries of the assessment of the product system, so-called cut-off criteria, are typically set at 1 % of the mass of the material, embodied energy and environmental relevance. [1] In doing so, the total of the mass of the material neglected may not exceed 5 %. [2] Ecologically critical substances (e.g. plasticisers in polymers) must always be investigated.

Inventory analysis

The inventory analysis embraces and quantifies the material and energy conversion processes relevant to the product system, taking into account the system boundaries and the cut-off criteria. Energy, raw materials and operating resources inputs as well as products, joint products (product systems with more than one final product) plus waste and emissions affecting air, water and soil must all be considered.

Impact assessment

The impact assessment determines what influence the results of the inventory analysis might have on defined potential environmental impacts. To do this, the results of the inventory analysis are linked to impact categories, each of which describes one potential environmental impact (e.g. climate change) and is specified by means of a so-called material equivalent

C 7.1 Perceiving the environment in the "Mobile Action Space", Berlin (D), 2009, raumlabor berlin
C 7.2 The sequence and phases of a life cycle assessment (LCA)
C 7.3 Product category rules (PCR), position as of Aug 2010
C 7.4 Examples of environmental or environmental declaration labels

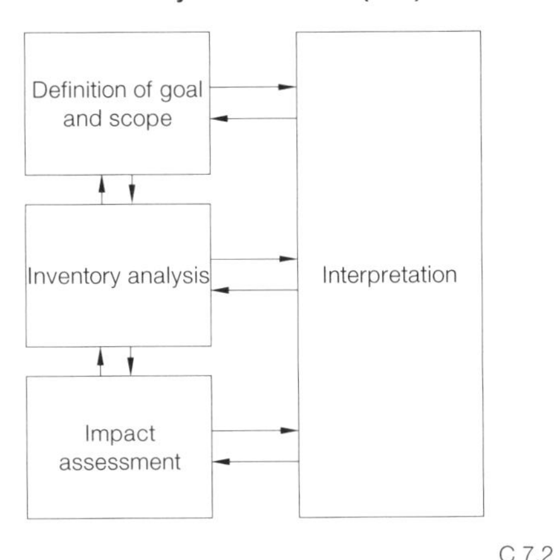

C 7.2

Product category rules (PCR)

Construction metals	Calcium silicate masonry
Structural steels	Lightweight concrete
Concrete roof tiles	Lightweight aggregates
Clay roof tiles	Metal pipes
Dispersion adhesives and undercoats	Mineral insulating materials
Wall anchors made from polymers and metal	Premixed mineral mortar
Fibre-cement	Mineral boards
Floor coverings	Aerated concrete
Gypsum boards	Foamed plastics
Glass reinforcing mesh	Laminates
Glass-fibre wall and ceiling finishes	Solid timber products
Wood-based products	External thermal insulation composite systems
Wood-cement composites	Clay brickwork

Institut Bauen und Umwelt e.V.

C 7.4

(e.g. CO_2 contribution to climate change).
All the materials flows in the inventory analysis that contribute to an impact category are converted into the respective material equivalent and collated with the help of defined factors. This approach allows us to describe a high number of emissions with little potential environmental impact. Which potential environmental impacts are to be depicted is, however, not regulated by universally applicable guidelines. The impact categories relevant for the environmental impact of a product must therefore be selected in each individual case. For buildings, it is usual to consider the following impact categories:

- Climate change potential (CCP, formerly global warming potential, GWP 100) [kg CO_2 equiv]
  Climate change potential describes the contribution of a material to the anthropogenic greenhouse effect.
- Ozone depletion potential in the stratosphere (ODP) [kg R 11 equiv]
  Ozone depletion is the reduction in the ozone layer, especially over the Antarctic (polar ozone hole) but also affecting other parts of the planet. The destruction of the ozone layer is primarily caused by halogenised hydrocarbons, e.g. chlorofluorocarbons (CFCs).
- Acidification potential (AP) [kg SO_2 equiv]
  Acidification is caused mainly by emissions from the combustion of sulphurous fossil fuels such as coal and oil, which form acids when they come into contact with water, and nitrogen oxides, which are also released during combustion processes.
- Photochemical ozone creation potential (POCP) [kg C_2H_4 equiv]
  The emissions that contribute to photochemical ozone creation are primarily those from vehicles (nitrogen oxides, hydrocarbons) and industry (hydrocarbons).
- Eutrophication potential (EP) [kg PO_4 equiv]
  It is mainly phosphorus and nitrogen, from fertilisers or household or industrial waste water, for example, that contribute to eutrophication (= overfertilisation).
- Primary energy intensity (PEI) [MJ]
  The primary energy intensity of a building material describes the energy media (resources) required for the production, use and disposal of that material. We distinguish here between non-renewable (e.g. petroleum, natural gas, coal, uranium) and renewable primary energies (e.g. electricity generated by wind power). In contrast to the other impact categories, which are output-related, i.e. consider environmental impact due to emissions from the materials or use thereof, PEI is an input-related impact category, i.e. an environmental impact caused by the consumption of limited resources (in this case energy sources).

Interpretation
The interpretation is carried out on the basis of the results of the inventory analysis and the impact assessment from which conclusions can be drawn and recommendations for the use of the product derived and summarised in a report. The report and the LCA on which it is based can be scrutinised by an independent group of experts. This is absolutely essential if comparative statements, e.g. with respect to rival products, are to be made or the results are to be made public.

Sources of LCA data for construction products
Compiling a product LCA is a time-consuming process that is generally carried out for the product manufacturer by a specialist company. The data records are normally prepared and collated for various, publicly accessible data sources where they are available to the planning team in a standardised form.
The ecological characteristics of a product are communicated in the form of environmental designations or declarations. And it is not only the building industry that has introduced various quality symbols and labelling systems (Fig. C 7.4). The ISO 14020 family of standards distinguishes between three different types of labelling system. The participation in such a labelling system is voluntary for the manufacturers, but in some instances is subject to considerable regulations.

Environmental labelling type I
This category covers the so-called eco-labels that are awarded to products within a particular product category which exhibit a particularly good environmental performance. To be awarded an eco-label, a product must comply with specified limiting values in order to be assessed as clearly more environmentally friendly than the average for that particular product category. The limiting values are regularly revised so that only a certain percentage of products in a category can be issued with the "best in class" label. Compliance with the limiting values is verified by measurements confirmed by independent institutes. One well-known type I label is the "Der Blaue Engel" (blue angel). Other examples are the FSC (Forest Stewardship Council) label for timber products and the EU's "Flower".

Environmental labelling type II
This category covers manufacturers' self-declared environmental claims for their products, sometimes referred to as "green claims". The declarations must take into account the restrictions given in DIN 14021 but are not checked by independent institutes.

Environmental labelling type III
This category covers environmental product declarations (EPD) in which the environmental impacts of products are described systematically and in detail. The information includes all the potential environmental impacts of a product without actually carrying out an assessment. Instead, an EPD provides potential users of a product with a basis for making decisions based on their own criteria. The starting point is a product LCA, but further indicators specific to the product (e.g. contamination of the interior air) are also included. In this form of declaration it is not the individual results of measurements that are checked by independent institutes, but rather conformity with the product category rules (PCR) drawn up to ensure an equivalent description within that product category (Fig. C 7.3, p. 125). In Germany EPDs are coordinated by the Institute Construction & Environment (IBU) and the Federal Ministry of Transport, Building & Urban Development (BMVBS). The

C 7.5 Primary energy spans of individual materials groups per mass of material [kg]
C 7.6 Primary energy comparison of components (according to values from the Ökobau.dat database, cradle-to-grave, production and disposal, Germany, 2009)
a Comparison of steel and GFRP beams in bending for identical deformations and bending moment capacities
b Comparison of horizontal, transparent roof coverings made from insulated glass and PC twin-wall sheets for identical load-carrying capacities and U-values
C 7.7 Life cycle assessment (LCA) values for polymer products according to functional unit

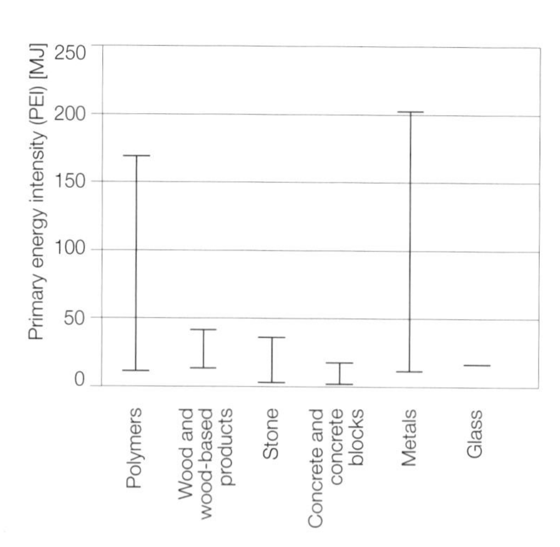

C 7.5

Identical deformation

		Steel beam IPE 200 g = 0.224 kN/m²	GFRP beam, pultruded IPE 360 g = 0.227 kN/m²
PEI non-renew.	[MJ]	421.30	1038.62
CCP	[kg CO_2 equiv]	47.98	161.17
ODP	[kg R11 equiv]	$1.32 \cdot 10^{-6}$	$2.36 \cdot 10^{-6}$
AP	[kg SO_2 equiv]	0.14	3.18
EP	[kg PO_4 equiv]	0.0135	0.0427
POCP	[kg C_2H_4 equiv]	0.0214	0.0906

Identical bending moment capacity

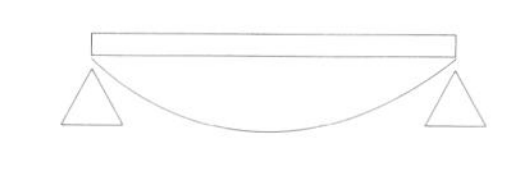

a

		Steel beam IPE 360 g = 0.571 kN/m	GFRP beam, pultruded IPE 360 g = 0.227 kN/m
PEI non-renew.	[MJ]	1073.94	1038.62
CCP	[kg CO_2 equiv]	122.31	161.17
ODP	[kg R11 equiv]	$3.35 \cdot 10^{-6}$	$2.36 \cdot 10^{-6}$
AP	[kg SO_2 equiv]	0.356	3.18
EP	[kg PO_4 equiv]	0.0343	0.0427
POCP	[kg C_2H_4 equiv]	0.0545	0.0906

Identical load-carrying capacity

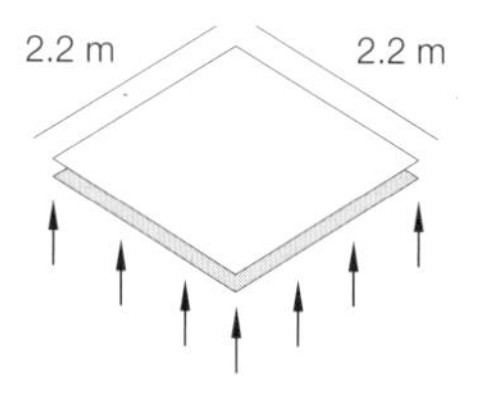

		Insulating glass g = 0.20 kN/m²	PC double-wall sheet g = 0.028 kN/m²
PEI non-renew.	[MJ]	432.00	431.20
CCP	[kg CO_2 equiv]	37.50	21.98
ODP	[kg R11 equiv]	$0.838 \cdot 10^{-6}$	$1.40 \cdot 10^{-6}$
AP	[kg SO_2 equiv]	0.16	0.04
EP	[kg PO_4 equiv]	0.0200	0.0048
POCP	[kg C_2H_4 equiv]	0.01	0.01

Identical U-value (1.3 W/m²K)

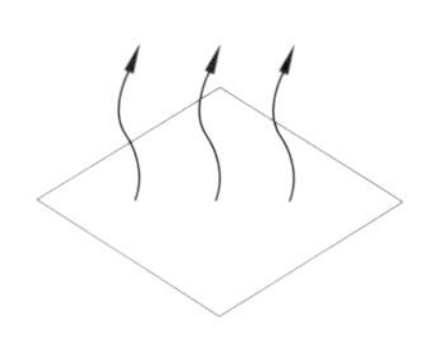

b

		Insulating glass g = 0.20 kN/m²	PC double-wall sheet g = 0.034 kN/m²
PEI non-renew.	[MJ]	432.00	523.60
CCP	[kg CO_2 equiv]	37.50	26.69
ODP	[kg R11 equiv]	$0.838 \cdot 10^{-6}$	$1.70 \cdot 10^{-6}$
AP	[kg SO_2 equiv]	0.1620	0.0047
EP	[kg PO_4 equiv]	0.0244	0.0058
POCP	[kg C_2H_4 equiv]	0.0108	0.0068

PEI non-renew.: primary energy intensity from non-renewable energy sources; CCP: climate change potential (formally global warming potential, GWP); ODP: ozone depletion potential; AP: acidification potential; EP: eutrophication potential; POCP: photochemical ozone creation potential

C 7.6

IBU supervises the preparation of PCRs for individual product categories and designates these. [3]

Databases

The Internet provides access to various databases containing a huge number of LCA data records. The Ökobau.dat database was published by the BMVBS within the scope of the development of the quality label of the German Sustainable Building Council (DGNB) and is specifically aimed at LCAs for buildings. The database is based on concrete product LCA data provided by individual manufacturers, where this is available, or on averaged data records for individual product categories. As more and more specific EPDs become available, so these will replace the averaged data records. So far, the database contains about 800 data records and is therefore the most comprehensive freely accessible database in Germany. Ökobau.dat can be reached via the website of the BMVBS. The connection with the IBU guarantees that the data records are constantly updated.
The European Union publishes data records at the inventory analysis level plus background information to product LCAs on its own website via the European Platform on Life Cycle Assessment (ELCD). Even though the database is regularly updated, it should be remembered when using the data that some data records could be more than 10 years old and may be affected by disparate regional reference variables (Germany, Europe), which can lead to significant differences in the results.
The publicly accessible databases are complemented by data prepared by commercial providers. Those providers can also prepare LCAs for products not included in the public databases. Such approaches will, however, remain the exception in the planning process, for reasons of cost alone.

The data situation for polymers

The plastics industry published eco-profiles for a whole series of primary and final products made from various polymers as long ago as the mid-1990s via its trade association Plastics Europe. The eco-profiles were produced, like the LCAs, based on the stipulations of DIN EN ISO 14040. They make use of averaged data records at inventory analysis level prepared with the help of the respective manufacturers. The data records are available via the EU's ELCD database. The data is currently being updated and changed to the EPD format.

	Thickness	Weight	Primary energy intensity (non-renew.)	Primary energy intensity (renew.)	Climate change potential (CCP)	Ozone depletion potential (ODP)	Acidification potential (AP)	Eutrophication potential (EP)	Photochemical ozone creation potential	Service life
Solid sheets (1 m²)	[mm]	[kg]	[MJ]	[MJ]	[kg CO_2 equiv]	[kg R11 equiv]	[kg SO_2 equiv]	[kg PO_4 equiv]	[kg C_2H_4 equiv]	[a]
PVC	10	12.2	961.36	15.62	42.21	$3.25 \cdot 10^{-6}$	0.0760	0.00754	0.02050	30–50
UP	10	20.0	1820.00	17.00	89.80	$3.42 \cdot 10^{-6}$	0.1620	0.02600	0.02340	32–50
PC	10	12.0	1848.00	28.92	94.20	$6.01 \cdot 10^{-6}$	0.1656	0.02040	0.02388	33–50
PMMA (extruded)	10	11.9	1654.10	18.09	79.73	$3.83 \cdot 10^{-6}$	0.2106	0.01880	0.03987	34–50
Glass	10	25.0	350.00	2.00	22.00	$7.08 \cdot 10^{-7}$	0.1602	0.02250	0.01325	35–50
Twin-/multi-wall sheets (1 m²)	**U-value [W/m²K]**									
PVC (d =16 mm)	2.7	2.8	220.64	3.58	9.69	$7.45 \cdot 10^{-7}$	0.0174	0.00173	0.00470	30–50
PC (d =16 mm)	2.4	2.8	431.20	6.75	21.98	$1.40 \cdot 10^{-6}$	0.0386	0.00476	0.00557	30–50
PMMA (extruded, d =16 mm)	2.5	5.0	695.00	7.60	33.50	$1.61 \cdot 10^{-6}$	0.0885	0.00790	0.01675	30–50
Profiled glass (double-leaf, d =16 mm)	2.8	36.4	509.60	2.91	32.03	$1.03 \cdot 10^{-6}$	0.2333	0.03276	0.01929	40–70
Insulating boards (1 m²)	**U-value [W/m²K]**									
XPS (d = 14 cm)	0.25	3.5	404.74	3.51	13.12	$7.55 \cdot 10^{-7}$	0.0293	0.00298	0.01287	25–45
EPS (d = 14 cm)	0.25	2.1	191.66	0.90	6.41	$1.97 \cdot 10^{-7}$	0.0136	0.00147	0.00220	25–45
PUR (d = 10 cm)	0.25	3.0	304.00	4.93	14.73	$2.41 \cdot 10^{-7}$	0.0467	0.00479	0.00780	25–45
Wood fibreboard (d = 16 cm)	0.24	22.4	717.47	582.56	2.24	$7.24 \cdot 10^{-7}$	0.0970	0.01319	0.01044	25–45
Waterproofing sheets (1 m²)	**Area [m²]**									
PE roofing felt (textile-reinforced)	1	0.14	12.99	0.21	0.65	$2.18 \cdot 10^{-8}$	0.0017	0.00020	0.00034	n.a.
PP roofing felt	1	0.13	11.23	0.16	0.44	$1.30 \cdot 10^{-8}$	0.0011	0.00015	0.00015	n.a.
PVC roofing felt with glass-fibre fleece (d = 1.8 mm)	1	2.30	226.55	5.08	13.55	$4.00 \cdot 10^{-7}$	0.0455	0.00453	0.00644	20–40
EVA roofing felt (d = 1.5 mm)	1	1.87	184.38	1.71	6.55	$3.50 \cdot 10^{-7}$	0.0114	0.00106	0.00337	30
EPDM roofing felt (d = 1.1 mm)	1	1.40	162.40	1.00	6.16	$1.75 \cdot 10^{-7}$	0.0104	0.00112	0.00342	50
Bitumen roofing felt (d = 4 mm)	1	4.70	165.91	0.69	2.27	$1.13 \cdot 10^{-7}$	0.0097	0.00084	0.00146	20–40
Pipes (per m)	**Diameter (DN)**									
PVC waste-water pipe	100 mm	1.620	109.19	1.63	5.83	n.e.	0.0251	0.00212	0.00211	35
PE waste-water pipe	100 mm	1.430	136.71	1.52	4.34	$3.12 \cdot 10^{-7}$	0.0085	0.00077	0.00159	35
PP waste-water pipe	100 mm	0.938	85.55	0.82	2.68	$1.68 \cdot 10^{-7}$	0.0052	0.00047	0.00088	35
S.S. waste-water pipe	100 mm	2.850	193.52	24.11	14.43	$1.22 \cdot 10^{-6}$	0.0804	0.03734	0.00476	40
PVC drinking-water pipe	1"	0.220	14.83	0.22	0.79	n.e.	0.0034	0.00029	0.00029	25–40
PE drinking-water pipe	1"	0.167	15.97	0.18	0.51	$3.64 \cdot 10^{-8}$	0.0010	0.00009	0.00019	25–40
PP drinking-water pipe	1"	0.246	22.44	0.22	0.70	$4.40 \cdot 10^{-8}$	0.0014	0.00012	0.00023	26–40
Copper pipe	1"	0.756	21.47	1.23	1.48	$1.85 \cdot 10^{-7}$	0.0078	0.00076	0.00059	27–40
Floor coverings (1 m²)	**Area [m²]**									
PVC	1		111.00	1.83	5.48	$4.17 \cdot 10^{-7}$	0.0201	0.00155	0.00393	15–25
Linoleum	1		89.90	57.90	0.74	$6.43 \cdot 10^{-7}$	0.0532	0.01050	0.00280	15–25
Disposal										
Burning of polymers in waste incineration plant.	–	1	-27.00	0.40	0.81	$-6.50 \cdot 10^{-8}$	0.0010	0.00010	0.00010	–

Life cycle assessments for functional units according to values from the Ökobau.dat database (cradle-to-gate, Germany, 2009); additional disposal data records for own calculations.

C 7.7

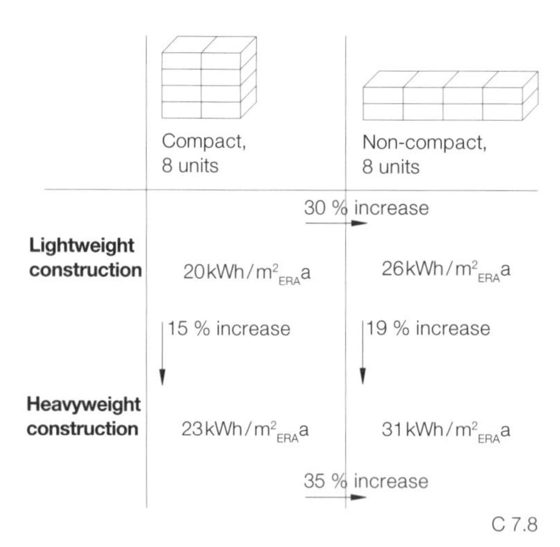

Compact,
8 units
Non-compact,
8 units
30 % increase
Lightweight construction
20 kWh/m^2_{ERA}a
26 kWh/m^2_{ERA}a
15 % increase
19 % increase
Heavyweight construction
23 kWh/m^2_{ERA}a
31 kWh/m^2_{ERA}a
35 % increase

C 7.8

C 7.8 Comparison of the grey energy content of lightweight timber structures and heavyweight masonry and concrete structures for compact and non-compact forms of construction, ERA = energy reference area

C 7.9 Constructional optimisation of a loadbearing system for a building envelope; "Oval", Baseler Platz, Frankfurt am Main (D), 2004, Albert Speer & Partner

C 7.10 Facade outer leaf; Unilever group headquarters, Hamburg (D), 2009, Behnisch Architekten

C 7.11 Waste disposal agency offices and operations building, Remscheid (D), 2006, Architektur Contor Müller Schlüter
a LCA for facade
b Constructional optimisation of building envelope through the use of twin-wall sheets

C 7.9

C 7.10

Comparison with LCA data

A comparison via the mass or the volume is generally not meaningful because of the different physical properties of products. More interesting for architects and engineers, within the scope of a holistic planning approach, is to compare forms of construction that are equivalent in terms of their building physics but can be decidedly different in terms of their environmental impact. Such a comparison must be carried out in a similar way to the LCA method described in DIN EN ISO 14040 and be based on a functional unit, e.g. 1 m^2 of external wall with the same U-value, or a pipe 1 m long. Fig. C 7.7 (p. 127) contains the LCAs for various polymers according to their applications and functional units. Textiles for membrane construction have been deliberately omitted because no reliable LCAs are currently available in the public domain (position as of May 2010).

LCAs and sustainability certification

In architecture the building is the ultimate functional unit. In order to assess this total performance, worldwide assessment systems with country-specific priorities for indicating the sustainability of buildings have been under development since the early 1990s. The most widely used systems are LEED (Leadership in Energy and Environmental Design) from the USA and BREEAM (Building Research Establishment Environmental Assessment Method) from the UK. The environmental impacts of building materials are included in the assessment in every system, but sometimes in different ways.
The quality label of the German Sustainable Building Council (DGNB), which was developed in 2007–2008, is one of the first methods to prescribe a certification system that looks at the entire life cycle of a building and also includes a type of building LCA. The basis for this building LCA in the German system are the EPDs of the individual construction products. The environmental impact of a whole building, and hence also the LCAs of construction products, is thus becoming a focus of attention for planners, users and investors.

The influence of the LCA in the life cycle of a polymer

In relation to their weight, polymers exert a high environmental impact when compared with many other typical building materials (Fig. C 7.5, p. 126). However, these values are put into perspective when they are related to a functional unit (Fig. C 7.7, p. 127).
A comparison between glass and polymer in a facade (reference size 1 m^2) reveals that a facade of twin-wall sheets can have a much lower environmental impact than a facade of glass (Fig. C 7.6, p. 126). The main reason for this is the different masses of the materials. Such comparisons, however, are not always absolute when we consider the actual characteristics of the materials, e.g. view out, view through. At the same time, they can draw attention to the need for engineering and architecture that does justice to the materials. Polymers can achieve a similar performance to many other materials, but with a lower weight, and this has a positive effect on the respective LCA.
According to surveys on the subject of environmental impact, the number one objective in the planning of a building seems to be the minimisation of material (Fig. C 7.8). [4] This can be achieved, however, in different ways, through parameters such as intelligent construction, integration of functions or adapting the performance of the polymer. It is necessary, in every project, to reappraise and choose the assessment framework to suit the loadbearing structure and the functional performance.

Intelligent construction

Intelligent construction is based on a technical and constructional assessment of the building task. The following aspects are just some that then need our attention:
- Loadbearing system
- Materials of the loadbearing system
- Jointing methods
- Dead loads

The architectural minimisation of material can be reached via these aspects on various levels.

Product systems optimised for construction

First of all, a product optimised specifically for a particular building task can be used. The example of a facade of twin-wall sheets (sheets clamped along their edges to linear metal supports) can be used to explain the relationships. The sheet is responsible for, at a rough estimate, 40 % of the environmental impact of the functional unit (Germany) and therefore as a product normally governs the LCA. If the polymer sheet itself can perform a structural function and thus obviate the need for any further supporting members, then this reduces the environmental impact of the functional unit. As a rule, this also applies when the thickness of the sheet has to be increased to cope with the structural function. This is particularly beneficial for surfaces that extend over several storeys and is limited technically by the maximum permissible unsupported span for that type of sheet.
An optimisation level for the environmental impact is created by the constructional requirements for connection and fixing details. A design that enables a large area to be covered with a minimum number of details reduces the grey (or embodied) energy in the material. For example, twin-wall sheets spanning in just one direction reduce the amount of material required in the construction and hence the environmental impact. At the building component level, this complex theme can be demonstrated by taking window frames as an example. Windows with wooden and polymer frames exhibit a much lower thermal transmittance than those with metal frames. And compared with wooden frames, the advantages of polymer frames are to be found in the

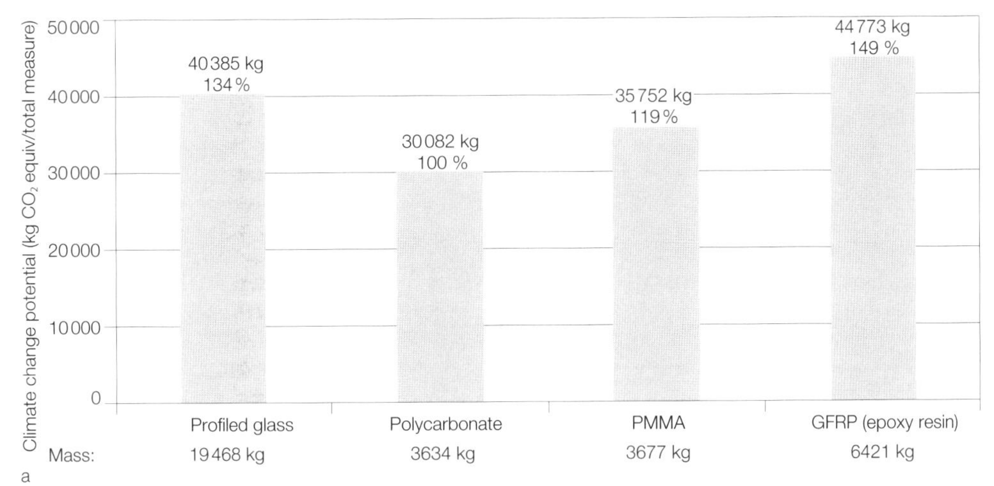

a

b C 7.11

easy workability of the material and the low material content, which leads to a high cost efficiency. As a wooden frame is, however, stiffer, it is sometimes possible to use narrower frame members, which in turn can result in the more efficient use of solar energy for passive heating purposes. In the end, it is therefore the total area of glazing in the window, assuming frames with identical U_f values, that becomes one of the most meaningful parameters for the designer. Materials with a chemical function also become important in this context where they constitute part of the building fabric. They can help to increase the storage capacity of the building (e.g. by way of latent heat storage) or change the vapour diffusion behaviour (e.g. smart foils). This can result in, for example, a facade design in which individual layers become totally unnecessary and that can often reduce the environmental impact.

Loadbearing systems designed to save materials
A standard product is generally overdesigned by its manufacturer because it is intended to cover diverse applications for a wide market. The alternative is a tailor-made loadbearing system that saves materials and has already been optimised for its task during the planning phase. In the polymers sector, foil structures can reach the limits of optimisation in terms of the efficiency of the material. With foil weights of 170 g/m², it is possible to achieve a thermal break between interior and exterior with material contents less than 0.5 kg/m². In such situations it is usually the supporting framework necessary that governs the LCA rather than the membrane itself.
The question that must be asked in the context of such optimisation is: Are we really reducing the environmental impact or only postponing it? We can use the Olympic Stadium in Munich to illustrate this point. The apparently lightweight architecture is only possible because of the massive foundations, which govern the LCA for the structure. Only through skilfully selected designs in which the forces are "short-circuited" can such an effect be realised as a "lightweight" construction with, as a result, a low environmental impact (Fig. C 7.9). This effect is relevant for different scales, e.g. at building component level: if we investigate the environmental impact of a particular roof design, we might find out that it is no longer the functional layer itself, but more likely the details (junctions, edges, rainwater drainage, etc.) that are the critical factors in the LCA. [5] And this is also true at the materials level because the properties of polymers themselves, through the use of different raw materials, can be changed to suit projects, adapted to suit technical requirements. For example, the addition of fibres does indeed produce a stiffer polymer, but at the same time creates a composite material whose reusability is limited because it is difficult to separate out the individual constituents at a later date. The situation is similar for specific coatings that are applied to increase UV stability, for instance.

Integration of functions
Polymers are ideal for "multitasking", i.e. carrying out various functional tasks simultaneously with just one component. The two main applications for such an approach are functional surfaces and facades. In a facade, polymers have an effect on, for example, humidity, thermal balance, lighting or energy generation. According to research, a low level of technology in a building, i.e. minimal building services compared with the size of the building, tends to reduce the environmental impact and running costs. [6] The use of technology (e.g. solar-tracking sunshading louvres) is therefore generally less effective in terms of energy consumption and environmental impact than a solution involving the building fabric itself (e.g. overhangs that cast shadows).
The example of the offices and operations building of the waste disposal agency responsible for Remscheid, Germany, proves that the use of a product system optimised for the particular design plus a "multitasking" approach can increase the advantage in terms of use of resources by a factor of 10 and hence achieve a reduction in costs of up to 50 % (Fig. C 7.11). The exact level of savings is based on the dimensions of the facade, its support and connection points and the supporting structure required. [7] Such a design becomes particularly efficient in terms of materials usage when the facade renders additional insulation unnecessary, i.e. when intelligent construction and integrated functions go hand in hand. Economic and ecological benefits are then combined.

Optimised functional performance
As the operating phase of a building (taken as 50 years) accounts for about 75 % [8] of the total LCA, improved functional performance leads directly to a marked reduction in the environmental impact of a building. Needing less energy to run the building might therefore be more effective than the savings realised through other measures.
When used for insulation and energy generation in a building envelope, transparent and translucent polymers have an especially positive effect on the overall LCA. In this situation, the facade has the task of, on the one hand, tapping additional energy sources for the building (e.g. as a microclimatic envelope or an air collector, or by providing process heat to back up the building services) and, on the other, generating this flow of energy to suit the needs of the building and its users (e.g. via selective reflection, sunshading or anti-glare systems) (Fig. C 7.10). With polymers in the facade (like with glazing) it is therefore the g- and U-values that need to be adapted. The minimum U-values given in the 2009 edition of Germany's Energy Conservation Act should be regarded as high for transparent and translucent polymer products and membranes in particular. On the other hand, polymers generally offer good g-values, which means that the higher passive solar energy gains can reduce the energy consumption. As this raises the risk of overheating in the building, advantageous in the end are those forms of polymer construction that can be regulated to suit users' needs or whose energy can be released into the environment again if necessary. Membranes and foils in pneumatic structures must be investigated particularly carefully because this is where an appropriate U-value can only be achieved through the permanent use of energy (e.g. for mechanical plant to dry the air and maintain the pressure). This means that the technical performance of the material (e.g. dimensional stability) only becomes possible through a permanent, technical input as part of the operation of the building (see "Air supplies",

pp. 192–193). Compared with the annual transmission heat losses of the component, this energy requirement can easily account for 10%. On the other hand, the solar heat gains through the component must be included in the balance as a positive factor. However, the lower environmental impact due to the material does not always outweigh the additional environmental impact of the operation. In energy terms, there would seem to be a limit to optimisation, where a further decrease in material is no longer sensible because the environmental impact is no longer reduced, simply postponed (Fig. C 7.12). From the energy viewpoint, designs that require mechanical plant are therefore more suited to structures with short life cycles (Fig. C 7.1, p. 124). In the case of longer life cycles, solar-active membranes can function as an integral, energy-generating component and thus cut the energy consumption markedly (Fig. C 7.13).
There is no universally applicable definition of how such an integrated material performance can be indicated in the LCA, for instance. In the end, the design team must employ static or dynamic computer simulations to check whether and when an optimum situation is reached for the building's life cycle. One decisive advantage of polymers is their essentially closed industrial production cycle. So-called customised mass production enables an adapted design without significant additional material consumption (e.g. through wastage). Projects are processed in digital form these days and this can function as a new type of communication interface between designers and manufacturers, which calls for a creative planning approach.

PEI, non-renewable [GJ]
60
50
40
30
20
10
0
Twin-wall sheet, no plant
Design w. mech. plant for maintaining air pressure & drying air
Fan power 3W/m²
Fan power 0.4W/m²
15
30
45
Time [a]

C 7.12

C 7.13

Health aspects

The use of polymers can result in health risks, especially in conjunction with functional surfaces. The transmission of harmful substances from polymers can take place in two ways:
Firstly, there is the chance that polymers emit harmful substances into the surrounding air which are then inhaled by persons. Volatile organic compounds (VOC) must be mentioned at this point. The chemicals of this group can escape from a material over a long period of time. Safety for the planner is only possible in the shape of the specific tests that depend on the product category and lead to type I environmental labelling, e.g. "Der Blaue Engel", EMICODE, EU "Flower". Product-related type III EPDs must also include such information.
Secondly, the direct absorption of harmful substances from polymers has been discussed recently. For example, the use of bisphenol A (BPA), a chemical with an oestrogenic effect, has been banned voluntarily by manufacturers of baby pacifiers in the USA and Canada, whereas the EU has relaxed the limiting values for bisphenol A. The evaluation of the health risks or otherwise of products changes with the status of research. Such unverified risk potential should also be included in a type III EPD.

Materials in long-term use

Polymers generally exhibit a moderate durability, which depends on the nature of the application, the environmental influences and the particular polymer. The prediction for the service life of a membrane is currently 25–30 years [9], but it seems that fluoropolymers can last even longer. Facades made from twin-wall sheets can be used for 30–50 years, and windows with polymer frames can be expected to last 40–60 years. The shorter the service life, i.e. the poorer the durability, the more important it is to recoup the embodied energy in the material's life cycle. The increased use of non-composite polymers will lead to better recyclability. The designer can therefore exert a positive influence on the LCA by choosing a "reversible" form of construction.

End-of-life options for polymers

Although only about 4% of the petroleum extracted from the earth is used for manufacturing polymers, dwindling resources will ensure that the production of polymers will in future depend more and more on reusing existing primary products. There are four ways of dealing with polymers that have reached the end of their (first) useful lives (Fig. C 7.14):
- Reuse
- Recycling the material
- Recycling the raw materials (monomers, gases, oils)
- Incineration

Reuse

Generally, reusing a product is the best solution from the environmental viewpoint. Incineration should be avoided if at all possible because the resource is then lost forever. The theoretical recyclability and its practical realisation therefore play an especially important role when it comes to polymers. Architects can thus determine the options for the reuses and/or recycling of polymers through foresight in their designs and choices of materials.

Recycling the material

This is the treatment of scrap polymers to form new polymer products made from recycled material. The polymer chains remain intact and are used to produce a new product; the polymer is formed anew. Therefore, only thermoplastics can be recycled in this way. They are first crushed, sorted and washed. Afterwards, the crushed material is dried, melted and processed to form a new granulate. In thermosets and elastomers the polymers are irreversibly cross-linked. In the sense of recycling the material, these materials can only be crushed and used as a bulk fill product (particle recycling). Polymer waste cannot be completely separated into uncontaminated waste streams and always contain fillers and additives. The recycled material thus obtained generally has a lower quality than the original polymer. In addition, the structure of the polymer is changed during the recycling process; the polymer chains are shortened.

When manufacturing products from 100% recycled polymers, changes to the properties of the component start to appear after just three processing cycles, and after five cycles significant damage appears that affects all the constituents (polymer chains, stabilisers, colourants, flame retardants, etc.) of the compound. Recycled material is therefore not normally used exclusively, but rather mixed with new polymer material. However, even this affects the quality of the new product, which is why the proportion of recycled material cannot be increased beyond a certain limit. In injection-moulding, for instance, the amount of recycled material is limited to 5% in order to maintain the quality of the polymer product. [10]
Owing to the modified properties of the recycled material, this type of recycling is actually downcycling. Only a few polymers, e.g. polyethylene terephthalate (PET), can be recycled without experiencing a loss in quality.
Product developments have a major influence on the prerequisites for recycling the polymer material. The following factors enable or ease this type of recycling and should be considered in the planning of a building:

- Reducing the diversity of polymers in the building. Using a large number of different polymers leads to increased work and costs during the sorting of the polymer waste.
- Using reversible compounds wherever possible which enable the polymer constituents to be readily exchanged (design for recycling, DfR).
- Using essentially compatible polymers, e.g. polycarbonate (PC) and acrylonitrile-butadiene-styrene (ABS), for indivisible forms of construction.
- Ensuring accurate documentation and/or labelling of the polymers. This can be marked directly on the component according to the stipulations of DIN 11469 (recycling code). Furthermore, special markers in the polymer (e.g. fluorescent dyes) ease the sorting of waste streams.
- Avoiding painting.

Recycling the raw materials
This is the chemical decomposition of the macromolecules and the reuse of the fragments in new synthesis processes.

Monomer recycling
In monomer recycling the polymers are broken down into their basic chemical constituents (depolymerisation). These monomers can always be repolymerised afterwards with the help of catalysts. Thermal depolymerisation can be used for acrylic resins (e.g. PMMA). This process is not influenced by additives (e.g. pigments) or soiling. In the case of PMMA, the MMA monomers obtained can be used again for other compounds such as casting resins.
The monomers of some polymers (e.g. PUR) are modified during depolymerisation, which leads to new polymerised products with other properties. In the case of PUR, monomer recycling cannot be used to produce a flexible foam from waste flexible foam. A prerequisite for monomer recycling is sorted waste streams. Problematic for high-quality polymers is guaranteeing a sufficient amount of waste for setting up an economically viable recycling system.

Petrochemical recycling
Owing to their chemical relationship with petroleum, polymer waste can be employed as a raw material in petrochemical processes and hence contribute to saving that valuable resource oil. The polymers are cleaned, crushed and subsequently fed directly into the petroleum stream. The waste should not contain any heavy metals and at worst only traces of chlorine if damage to the plant (e.g. corrosion) is to be avoided. This is not always the case when the waste contains large amounts of PVC (e.g. packaging waste). Petrochemical recycling is particularly suitable for small-format, soiled products with different configurations or compositions where sorting in order to reuse the materials directly is impossible or too costly.

Incineration
Polymer waste can be burned in a waste incineration plant. The energy stored in the polymer is then released and used for producing heat and generating electricity. In this case the polymer waste replaces other energy media and therefore can reduce the consumption of fossil, non-renewable energy sources. Owing to the production processes used, polymers have a similar (high) calorific value to that of petroleum or natural gas. Although incineration makes use of this embodied energy, instead of just disposing of the polymers in landfill, the waste is then no longer available for any other use. This end-of-life option should therefore always be regarded as the last alternative.

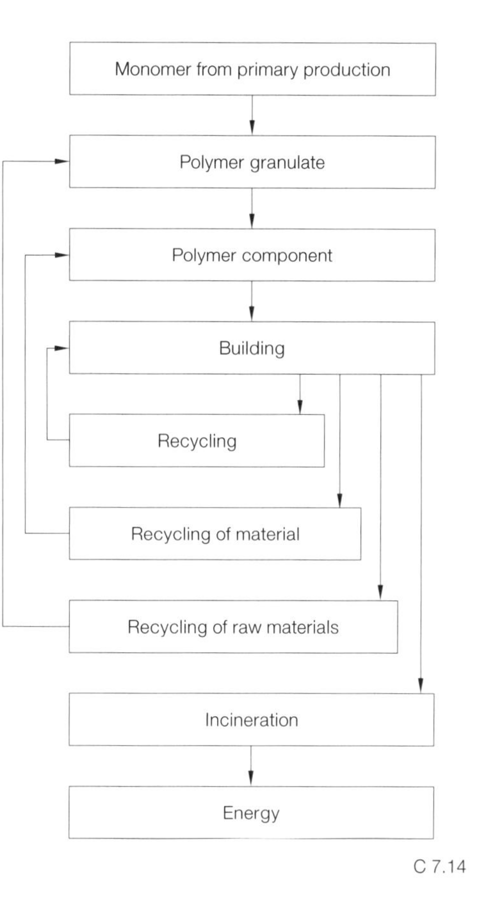

C 7.14

C 7.12 Primary energy consumption development for pneumatic structures with air pressure maintained by mechanical plant compared with a system without mechanical plant
C 7.13 Sunshading system in the form of a three-ply foil, light transmittance 5–50% (manufacturer's data)
C 7.14 Recycling options for polymers depending on type of recycling

References:
[1] Köpfler, Walter; Grahl, Birgit: Ökobilanzierung. Ein Leitfaden für Ausbildung und Beruf. Weinheim, 2009, p. 30
[2] Institute Construction & Environment (IBU): Leitfaden für die Formulierung der Anforderungen an die Produktkategorien der AUB Deklarationen (Typ III), 2006
[3] http://www.bau-umwelt.de, 20 Aug 2010
[4] Preisig, Hansruedi: Massiv- oder Leichtbauweise? In: TEC21, No. 42/2002, p. 17
[5] Hegger, Manfred, et al.: Construction Materials Manual. Munich, 2006, p. 101
[6] Sigg, René; Kälin, Werner; Plattner, Hugo: LUKRETIA – Lebenszyklus – Ressourcen – Technisierung. In: 14th Swiss Status Seminar, Energie- und Umweltforschung im Bauwesen, Zurich, 2006, p. 390
[7] Müller, Michael, et al.: Research report: Ökologische/Ökonomische Bewertung zweier Fassadenkonzepte – Glasfassade versus Kunststofffassade. Remscheid, 2007, pp. 68ff.
[8] http://www.dgnb.de, 20 Aug 2010
[9] LeCuyer, Annette: ETFE – Technology and Design. Basel/Boston/Berlin, 2009, p. 35
[10] Hellerich, Walter; Harsch, Günther; Haenle, Siegfried: Werkstoffführer Kunststoffe. Munich, 2004, p. 54

Part D Planning and form-finding

Fig. D Close-up view of soap bubbles

Loadbearing structure and form

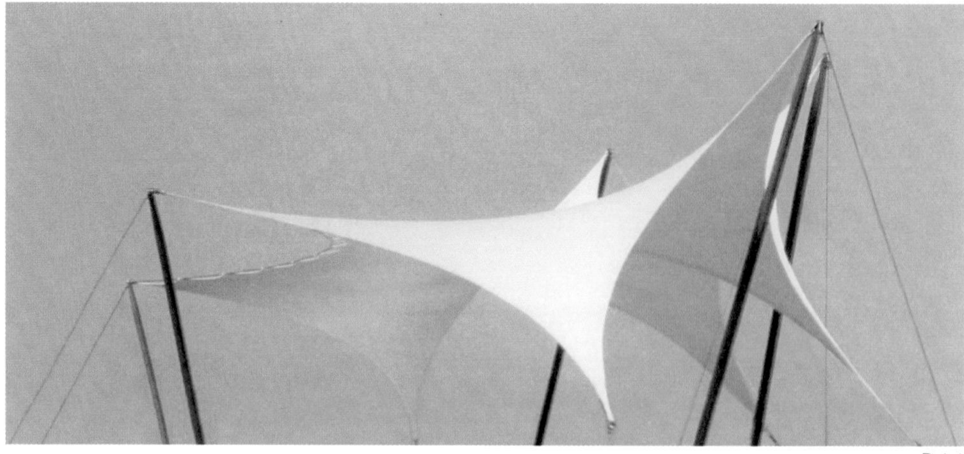

D 1.1

D 1.1 Membrane sail as a form-active structure; Saudi Arabia, 1990, Rasch + Bradatsch
D 1.2 Gridshell made from GFRP tubes, created by bending straight bars; research project, Ecole des Ponts ParisTech
D 1.3 GFRP arches in a bending-active structure; research pavilion, Institute of Building Structures & Structural design (ITKE), University of Stuttgart
D 1.4 Types of loadbearing structure
1 Beam
2 Grillage
3 Slab
4 Sandwich slab
5 Tied arch, made by bending straight bars
6 Gridshell, made by bending straight bars
7 Shell with curved folds, made by bending flat plates
8 Truss
9 Spatial frame
10 Folded plate
11 Shell
12 Arch
13 Lattice shell as inverted catenary arch (thrust line)
14 Inverted catenary arch (thrust line)
15 Cable
16 Cable net
17 Membrane structure

Owing to their low density but at the same time high strength, polymers embody the potential for creating lightweight structures. Besides the low weights of the materials themselves, the good weathering resistance and low thermal conductivity of the majority of polymers makes them suitable for lightweight systems in which the elements of the construction can be both loadbearing structure and enclosing envelope at the same time. Being able to design an efficient loadbearing geometry (lightweight structure) is extremely important if we are to exploit this potential to the full. Loadbearing structures are efficient when they develop a high load-carrying capacity and a high stiffness with as little material as possible while still transferring the loads safely to the supports. The efficiency of a loadbearing structure depends on the following factors:

- Global form = geometry
- Arrangement of loadbearing elements = topology
- Character of loadbearing elements = cross-section and material

Fig. D 1.4 shows different types of loadbearing structure categorised according to the way they carry the loads and their efficiency. The efficiency of the loadbearing structure increases here from the simple beam in bending to the plate, shell and membrane structures in tension, which are the focus of attention in this chapter.

Structural systems

In this chapter structural systems are subdivided into the following categories on the basis of various load-carrying principles [1]:

- Section-active structures
  - Beam
  - Frame
  - Grillage
  - Plate carrying out-of-plane loads
- Vector-active structures
  - Truss
  - Plane and curved trusses
  - Spatial framework
- Surface-active structures
  - Shell
  - Plate carrying in-plane loads
  - Folded plate
- Form-active structures
  - Cable structure
  - Membrane structure
  - Inverted catenary arch and shell
- Hybrid structures
  - Superimposition and/or coupling of section- and form-active structures (e.g. trussed beam)
  - Superimposition of vector- and surface-active structures (e.g. gridshell)

Section-active structures

Loadbearing structures that carry external loads primarily by way of bending moments are referred to as section-active systems because the bending moment is defined as an internal action effect imposed on a section through the structural member. Such loadbearing systems account for the majority of everyday loadbearing structures. Owing to the linear progression of the strain between the extreme fibres of the section, a large part of the central area of the cross-section of a beam, grillage or floor plate in bending plays only a small part in carrying the loads. More efficient are sandwich types of construction in which stiff facing, i.e. outer, plies carry the bending moments and a lightweight core, which provides a shear-resistant connection between the facing plies, carries the shear forces. With a two-dimensional structure subjected to bending (plate carrying out-of-plane loads), the surface geometry of the area can therefore be defined in any way.

Bending-active structures
One special form of the section-active structure is the curved structure whose geometry and system stiffness are realised through the elastic deformation of the loadbearing element. The principle of such bending-active structures are geometries based on elastic deformation. For example, gridshells are based on a planar lattice of linear members bent into a double-curvature shell form (Fig. D 1.2), or shell forms created by curved folds lying within the plane of the material. The advantage of this principle lies in being able to produce forms with complex curvature from simple straight or planar components.

D 1.2

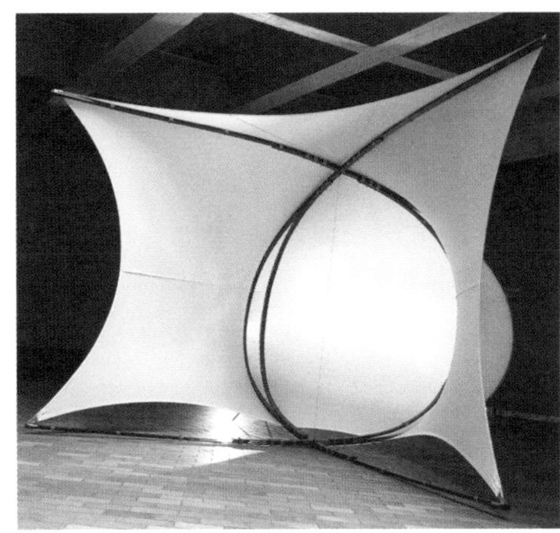
D 1.3

Thin components help because they permit very small bending radii and at the same time restrict the induced bending stresses to a low level with adequate reserves of strength. The necessary stiffness is achieved by joining together several bending elements and their induced bending stresses (Fig. D 1.3).

Vector-active structures
Joining together straight members to form a planar framework or grillages to form a spatial framework can increase the efficiency of a loadbearing system because the bending moments are resolved into tensile and compressive forces. The forces carried by the straight members, following the force vectors, are exclusively in the form of normal (i.e. axial) forces. Connecting the straight members to form a triangulated framework with articulated (i.e. pinned or hinged) joints (nodes) produces a stable structural system in which every component is loaded in either tension or compression. Each member's cross-sectional area can therefore be matched to the respective magnitude of the force. Compared with a structure in bending, this type of loadbearing structure uses the cross-section of the component to the full and therefore results in a favourable relationship between the loads to be carried and the self-weight of the construction.

Surface-active structures
Plate and shell structures that carry external loads via a combination of axial tension, compression and shear stresses without significant bending components are designated surface-active structures. Aligning the surface along the flow of forces makes it possible to activate purely axial states of stress in the surface. This is true for axially loaded plates and for folded plates, whose inclined plane elements resolve the external loads into axial force components. Curved surface-active structures, i.e. shells, are especially efficient when, with appropriate supports, loads acting perpendicular to the surface can also be carried by way of tension and compression without any bending. However, in the case of shell structures loaded primarily in compression, the risk of a stability failure (global or local buckling) means it is not possible to exploit the thickness of the component to the full.

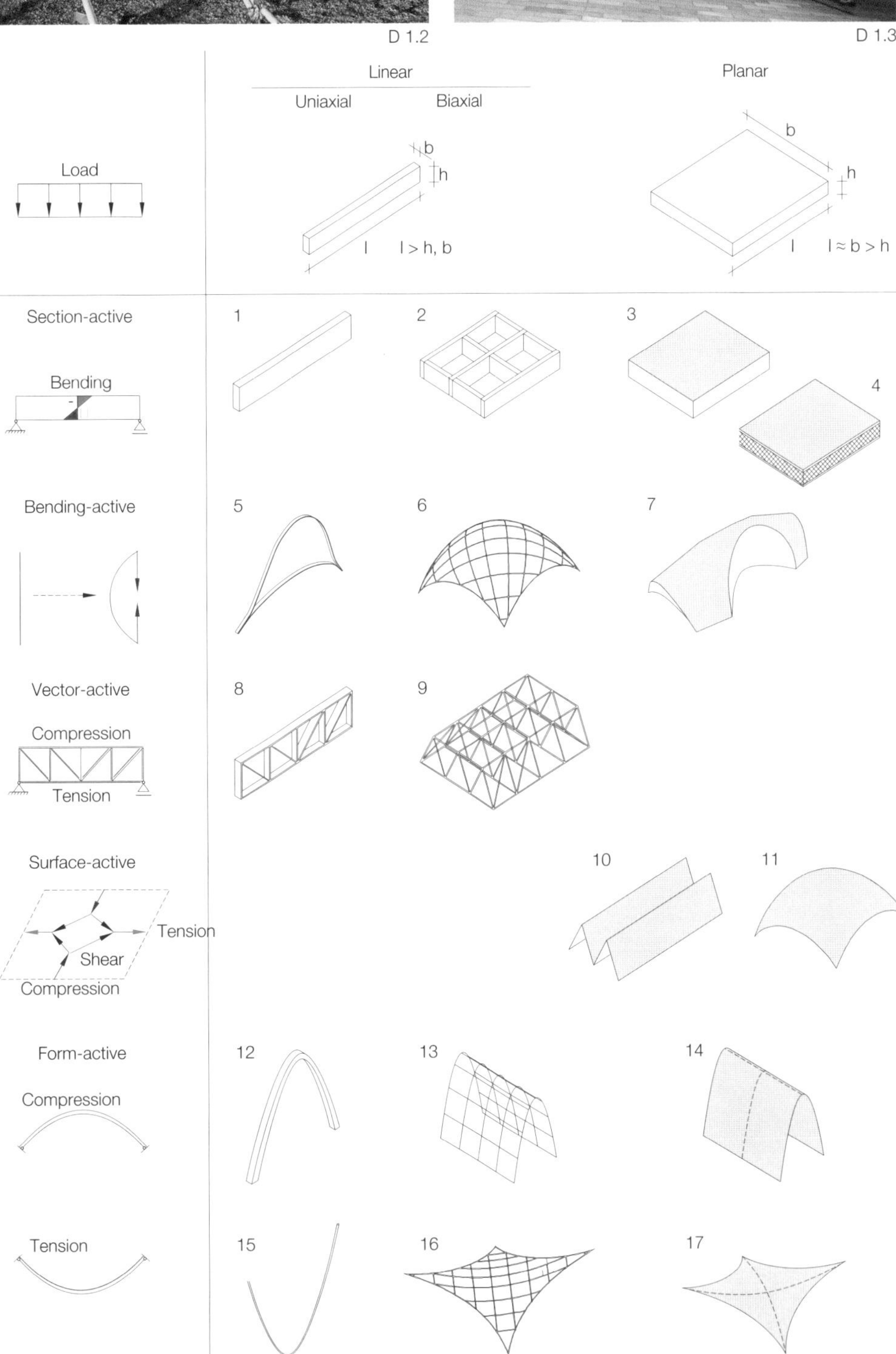

D 1.4

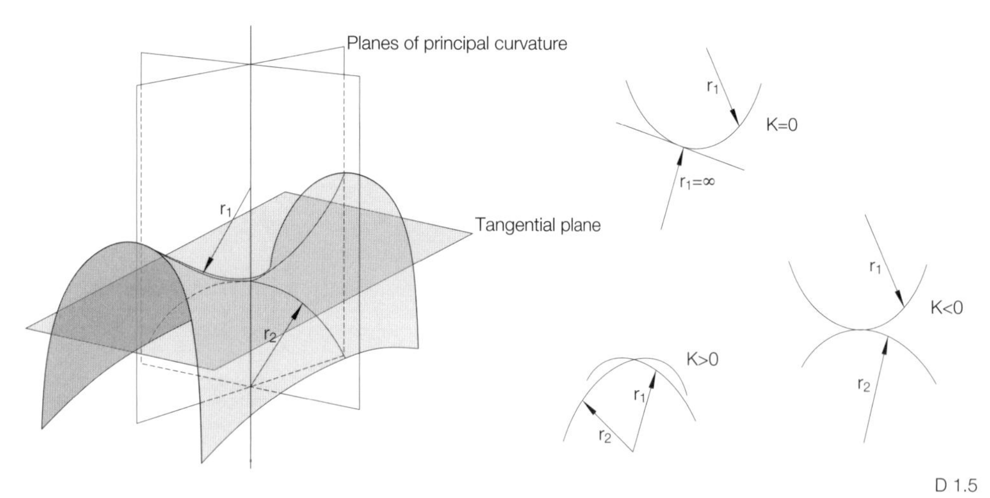

D 1.5 Principal curvatures r_1 and r_2, and Gaussian curvature K of curved surfaces
D 1.6 The principles for forming curved surfaces

Form-active structures

The characteristic feature of form-active structures is that they carry external loads either by way of pure tension (cables, membranes) or pure compression (arches) without shear forces or bending moments. In order to achieve this, it is necessary to match the geometry of the loadbearing structure to the flow of forces. With varying external actions (e.g. wind or snow), the geometry must be able to change as well (i.e. deform). Form-active structures in tension are among the most efficient loadbearing systems because failure by buckling is impossible. We therefore speak of lightweight tensile surface structures in this context. The basic principles for the design of such tensile surface structures are explained in more detail below.

Polymers in structural systems

Most section- and vector-active structures made from polymers are comprised of interconnected semi-finished products and are therefore not so very different from conventional steel or timber loadbearing structures. Linear members made from pultruded fibre-reinforced polymers can, for example, be produced with cross-sectional forms similar to those of typical steel sections (see "Sections made from fibre-reinforced polymers", pp. 84–85), and they are used by structural engineers in a similar way. The important thing here is to ensure that the connections between the semi-finished products and with other components are designed to suit the material (see "Connections for fibre-reinforced polymers", pp. 152–153, and "Building with free-form polymers", pp. 174–187). It should also be remembered that polymers and fibre-reinforced polymers have a lower elastic modulus than steel. Larger cross-sections must therefore be chosen in order to limit the deformations, which may well cancel out the original weight advantage.
However, the low stiffness in conjunction with the high strength can be exploited by using fibre-reinforced polymers for bending-active structures. Figs. D 1.2 and D 1.3 (p. 135) show prototypes of such structures. The bars used are actually produced as straight elements and are subsequently forced into their curved form. A system in equilibrium is created by joining together pairs of arches bent to various radii. Owing to the comparatively low elastic modulus of GFRP, however, the ensuing restraint stresses are only minimal. The residual elasticity is used for prestressing the membrane.
Free-form polymer elements covering large areas in the form of surface-active structures are mostly designed as components with an integral form in which further functions can be integrated. The form can be adapted ideally to the structural requirements through the double curvature of the thin-wall moulded components.

The use of polymers in sandwich designs has also proven to be especially efficient. Both the structural engineering and building physics demands placed on a building envelope can be satisfied with fibre-reinforced polymer laminates for the facing plies and a lightweight core material (Fig. E 2.36, p. 184).
Up until now, loadbearing polymers have been used in construction primarily in conjunction with form-active tensile surface structures. Only polymer-coated synthetic or glass-fibre fabrics exhibit the strength and durability necessary for such long-span membrane structures. Especially important in this context – besides the low density and high weathering resistance – is the elasticity of the material (see "Textile membranes", p. 49). The lower the stiffness, the greater the elongation must be when introducing the prestress. Only a sufficient amount of elongation guarantees that small changes in geometry and relaxation of the material do not lead to a significant decrease in the prestress. This requirement is satisfied by many polymers especially because of their high elongation at rupture coupled with high strength.

Geometry of lightweight surface structures

Lightweight surface structures are form- or surface-active loadbearing systems that carry external loads primarily by way of tensile and compressive stresses in the tangential direction (axial). One important factor for the loadbearing behaviour of lightweight surface structures is the curvature of the surface.

Curvature

The curvature of a surface can be described by two different parameters: principal curvature and Gaussian curvature.

Principal curvature

The principal curvatures of a surface describe the magnitude and direction of the minimum and maximum curvatures at one point on a surface. These result from the intersection of planes with the curved surface. The intersecting planes are perpendicular to the tangential plane at the point considered and are arranged so that the lines of intersection exhibit minimum or maximum radii of curvature (r_1, r_2) (Fig. D 1.5). The principal curvatures (k_1 and k_2) correspond to the inverse values of the radii of curvature ($k_i = 1/r_i$). The direction of curvature is indicated by the +/- signs of the radii; positive curvature, curving towards the observer, is designated convex, negative curvature, curving away from the observer, is concave.

Gaussian curvature

Gaussian curvature K is a measure of the curvature of a surface; again, the +/- signs indicate the nature of the curvature, which is the product of the two principal curvatures k_1 and k_2.

$$K = k_1 \cdot k_2 = \frac{1}{r_1} \cdot \frac{1}{r_2}$$

For surfaces in single curvature, one of the radii of curvature tends towards infinity; the Gaussian curvature is therefore zero. Such surfaces are developable, i.e. they can be unrolled onto a plane, e.g. the surfaces of cylinders or cones. We distinguish between positive and negative Gaussian curvature for surfaces in double curvature. The curvature is positive ($K > 0$) when the

centres of the radii of the two principal curvatures are located on the same side of the surface, also referred to as synclastic curvature. This type of curvature applies to domes and pneumatically prestressed membranes, for instance.
The Gaussian curvature is negative (K < 0) when the centres of the radii of the two principal curvatures are located on different sides of the surface and therefore one of the radii is negative. In this case the curvature can be called anticlastic. This is the situation with, for example, saddle-shaped surfaces in mechanically prestressed membranes.

Designing the form

The surface curvature necessary for carrying the load axially can be generated through various geometrical and physical approaches. In principle, we can distinguish between free, geometrical and structural optimisation methods (Fig. D 1.6).

Free-form surfaces

Free-form surfaces can also be referred to as random or irregular surfaces and are those surfaces that do not conform to any physical or geometrical laws. So-called non-uniform rational B-splines (NURBS) allow free forms to be described mathematically.
A NURBS surface or curve is calculated via its order, control points and a knot vector. Altering any of these parameters enables the form to be adjusted virtually *ad infinitum*. This type of graphical data processing using splines, whose control points are not located on the curve itself, is attributed to the French engineer Pierre Etienne Bézier. Any free form can be represented with the help of the Bézier splines. This approach originally intended for the design of car bodies and ships is today also used for designing free-form surfaces in architecture.

Geometrical surfaces

Surfaces with a simple geometrical definition have advantages in fabrication and erection because geometrical laws such as defined curvature, developability or the option of covering a surface with flat squares or rectangles are guaranteed. A geometrical surface is created by a generator and a directrix. If such a surface is defined by a polynomial, we speak of an algebraic surface. Surfaces of revolution, translation surfaces and ruled surfaces are examples of geometrical surfaces and are described below.

Surface of revolution

A surface of revolution is created by rotating a curve (the generatrix) about a straight line in its plane (the axis). If the generatrix is concave with respect to the axis, the result is a synclastic form, or dome, whereas a generatrix convex with respect to the axis produces an anticlastic form, or saddle-shaped surface.

Translation surface

A translation surface is created through the parallel translation of a generatrix along a directrix. The planes of the group of generatrix lines must also be parallel with each other. If the Gaussian curvature of the two curves is positive, the result is a synclastic form, or dome; if it is negative, then an anticlastic form, or saddle-shaped surface is created. The advantage of stretching the surface between identical, parallel-translated curves is that translation surfaces can be covered with planar squares or rectangles (e.g. panes of glass).

Ruled surface

A ruled surface is created through the movement of a straight line in space along curves of any form. Ruled surfaces in single curvature are generated from one group of straight lines, double-curvature surfaces from two groups of straight lines. Every point on the surface is intercepted by a straight line that lies within the ruled surface. Some surfaces of revolution and translation surfaces can also be described as ruled surfaces. These include the hyperboloid and the hyperbolic paraboloid. Double-curvature geometries that can be described as ruled surfaces can also be realised with straight components.

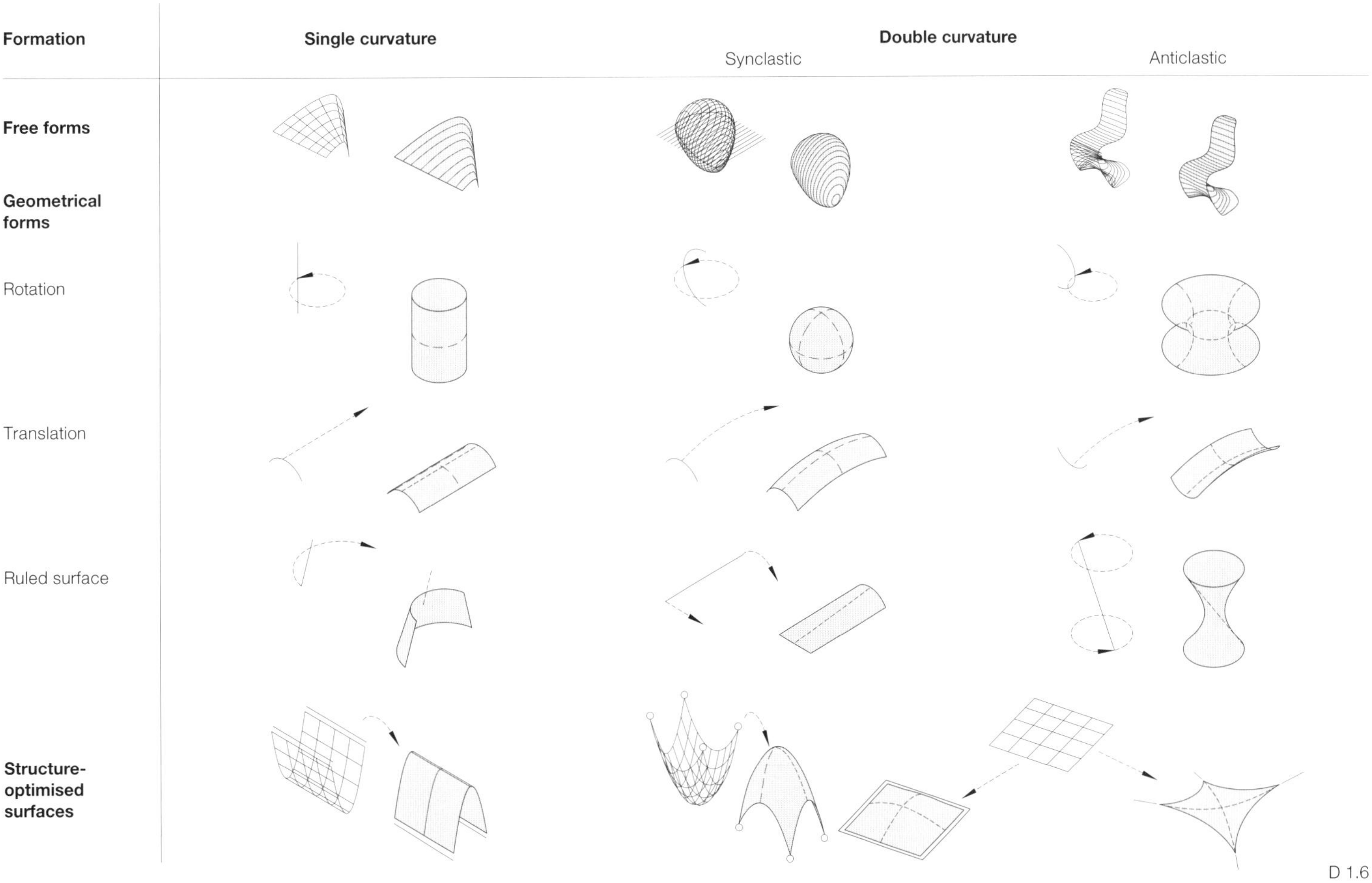

Formation	Single curvature	Double curvature – Synclastic	Double curvature – Anticlastic
Free forms			
Geometrical forms			
Rotation			
Translation			
Ruled surface			
Structure-optimised surfaces			

D 1.6

Structure-optimised surfaces

External loads do not necessarily lead to pure tensile or compressive states of stress in curved surfaces. For this reason, the aim of the structural optimisation of surface structures is to devise geometries for defined loads and support conditions which result, preferably, in pure membrane states of stress and hence efficient loadbearing systems. Form-finding is the term used to describe the search for a structure geometry that achieves a state of equilibrium for a given stress condition taking into account defined boundary conditions and, if applicable, external loads. The planning and design of surface structures with an optimised form is therefore considerably different to that of conventional forms of design because the development of the form is closely associated with the analysis of the loadbearing structure.

One widely used method for optimising the geometry of a shell in compression is the catenary form, actually the inversion of a catenary loaded purely in tension (a rope or chain suspended between two points) to generate a form loaded exclusively in compression. The catenary form can either be designed as a self-weight form or optimised for particular external loads by attaching weights. This approach can be used with chains for linear structures, arches, or suspended nets and clots for surface structures. However, it should be noted that an arch can only be optimised for one loading case, usually self-weight, and loads distributed differently lead to bending stresses. A shell in double curvature with appropriate support conditions is also able to carry uniformly distributed loads via a membrane state of stress even in the case of deviations from the pure catenary form.

The difficulty of such an approach is its realisation in practice because the ensuing complex form first has to be produced in an original mould in the factory or as formwork on site with a loadbearing supporting construction in order to create the final shell.

Tensile surface structures

The special characteristics of tensile surface structures represent the chief content of this chapter. The typical structural forms and aspects of their realisation in practice are demonstrated as well as the special form-finding methods.

Form-finding

Form optimisation methods are employed to determine the geometry of tensile surface structures. The aim of this form-finding process is to achieve a form that is in equilibrium with the given distribution of stresses, i.e. prestress in the surface, within the geometrical boundary conditions. In the case of air-supported, i.e. pneumatically prestressed, surfaces, the pressure difference between inside and outside in the form of a uniformly distributed load perpendicular to the surface also has to be included in the form-finding calculations.

Experimental form-finding

It was during the 1950s that Frei Otto developed the engineering principles for building with membranes (see "Development of tensile surface structures", pp. 16–21). The form-finding methods of those days were purely experimental. Physical models made from stretched rubber, fabrics, nets and soap films (Figs. D 1.7 and D 1.8) were used to create forms that were in equilibrium. Photogrammetry or other analogue methods of measurement could be used to transfer the ensuing surface geometries to the planning process. The approach with soap film has a special status because the film has zero stiffness and therefore assumes a homogeneous and isotropic stress condition, which means that the stresses at every point are identical in every direction. The outcome of this is that the resulting forms have minimal surface areas. A minimal surface describes the surface with the smallest area within an enclosing boundary; the values of the two principal curvatures are identical at every point on the surface. Strictly speaking, a minimal surface cannot be achieved in practice because the self-weight of the membrane is not considered in the form-finding process. However, the low weight of membrane struc-

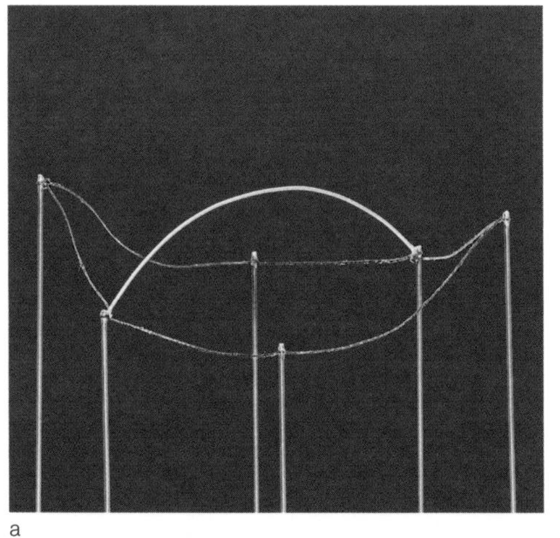
a

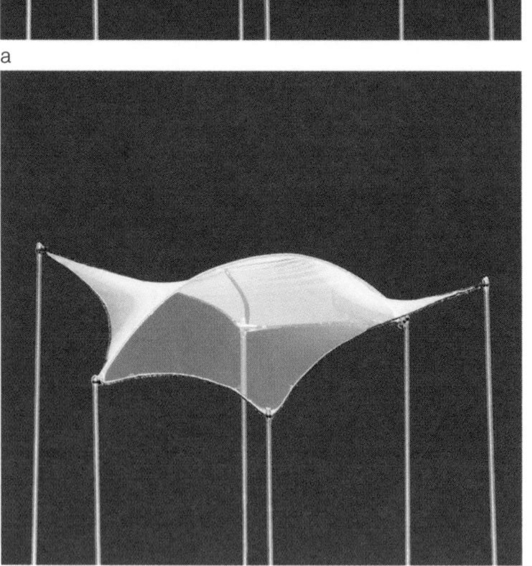
b D 1.7

a

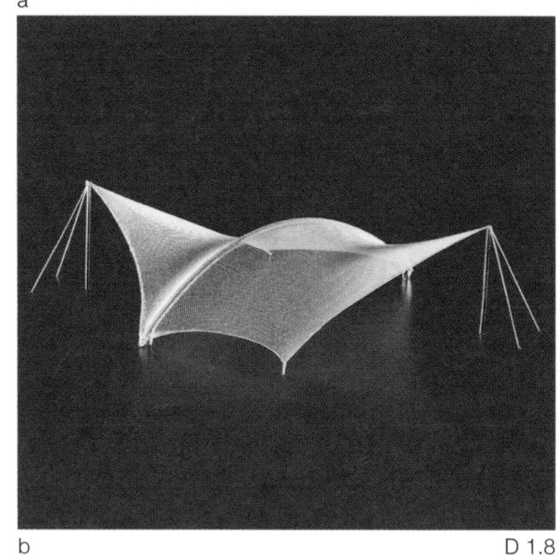
b D 1.8

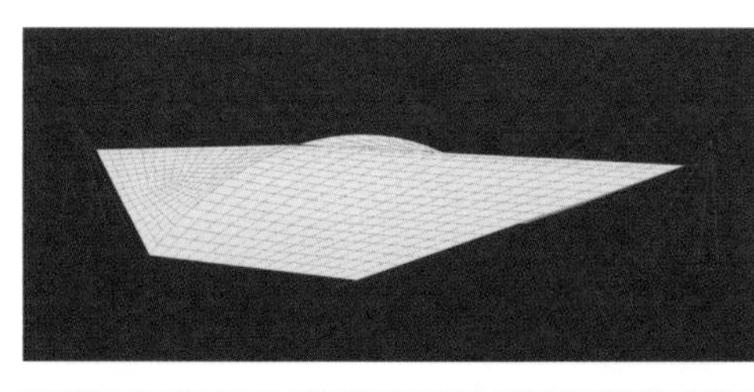

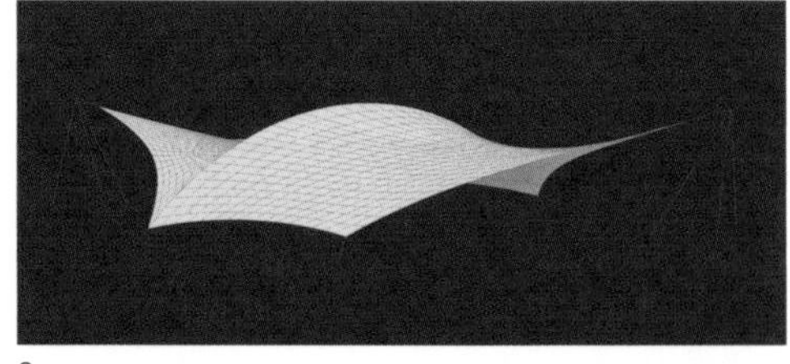
a

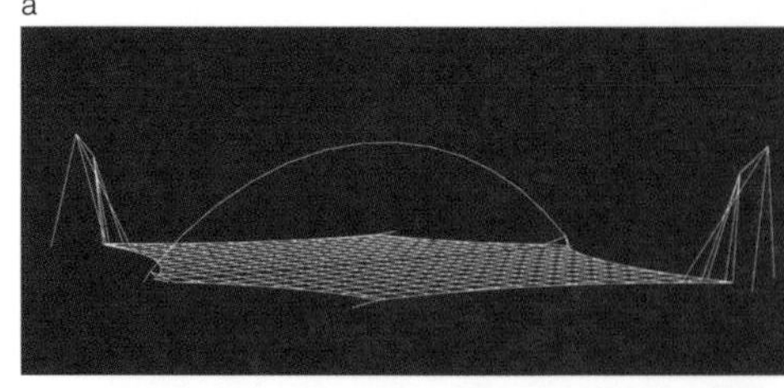

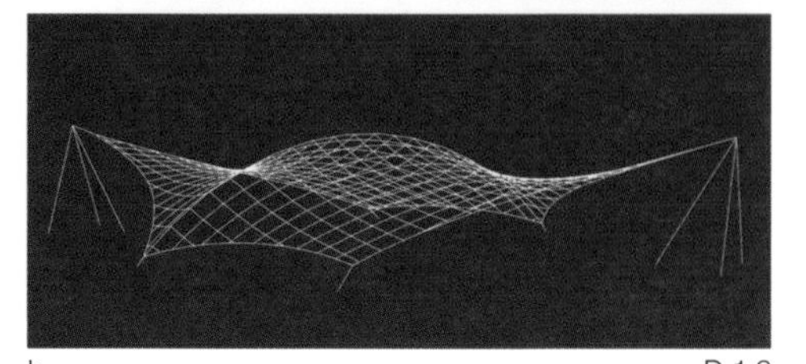
b D 1.9

tures means that the minimal surface approach is a reasonable starting point for a form-finding process.
Models made from fabric or tensioned nets have in the meantime given way to the numerical methods of form-finding commonly used these days, although the fabric model is still a favourite for developing concepts and for presentation purposes. It is easy to make from simple materials and is generally helpful in the early stages of form-finding. Highly elastic materials in particular, e.g. nylon or Perlon, are suitable for high-quality presentation models (Fig. D 1.8). The material is stretched gently and evenly over the support points (tubes, dressmaking pins or similar items). The perimeter members are then applied directly to the material using thin strips of adhesive, offset slightly inwards. This gives the edge a certain stiffness and prevents it from fraying. Excess material is then cut away and the corners are pulled into their final positions.

Numerical form-finding
These days, the final form-finding work for tensile surface structures is almost always carried out with the help of numerical methods, which are characterised by their high precision, flexibility and speed. Furthermore, the digital models produced are easily integrated into the subsequent structural analysis and computer-assisted design and fabrication processes. This type of form-finding is not dependent on the stiffness of the material and the absolute magnitude of the prestress. As a result, only geometrical parameters and the distribution of the prestress are specified. Typical numerical form-finding methods used these days are the finite element method, force density method and dynamic relaxation.

Finite element method (FEM)
In the finite element model the entire structure is subdivided (discretised) into elements joined together by nodes. The specific properties of typical linear or planar elements are represented by spring models. By considering the stress, distortion and displacement variables in the elements and complying with the condition that displacements of adjacent elements must be identical at their common nodes, it is possible to calculate the forces and deformations of the structure approximately. A state of stress equilibrium in special membrane elements ignoring the elastic stiffness is calculated for membrane form-finding tasks. When prescribing an isotropic prestress, this method ist also referred to as a soap film analogy.

Force density method (FDM)
The force density method was specifically developed for calculating pretensioned cable net designs. When used for form-finding, it is based on the equilibrium of forces at the nodes of the mesh. By summarising the force/length quotients to form the so-called force density, the conditional equations become linear and the system in equilibrium can therefore be calculated directly. A further development of the force density method enables the meshes to be linked directly to triangular elements and thus permit the structural analysis of membrane surfaces (Fig. D 1.9b).

Dynamic relaxation
In the dynamic relaxation a discretionary initial mesh composed of springs is prestressed, thus inducing osciallations. An artificially generated decay process enables the equilibrium form to be found for the mesh by means of viscoelastic or kinetic damping. This means that the original, actually static problem is converted into a dynamic problem.

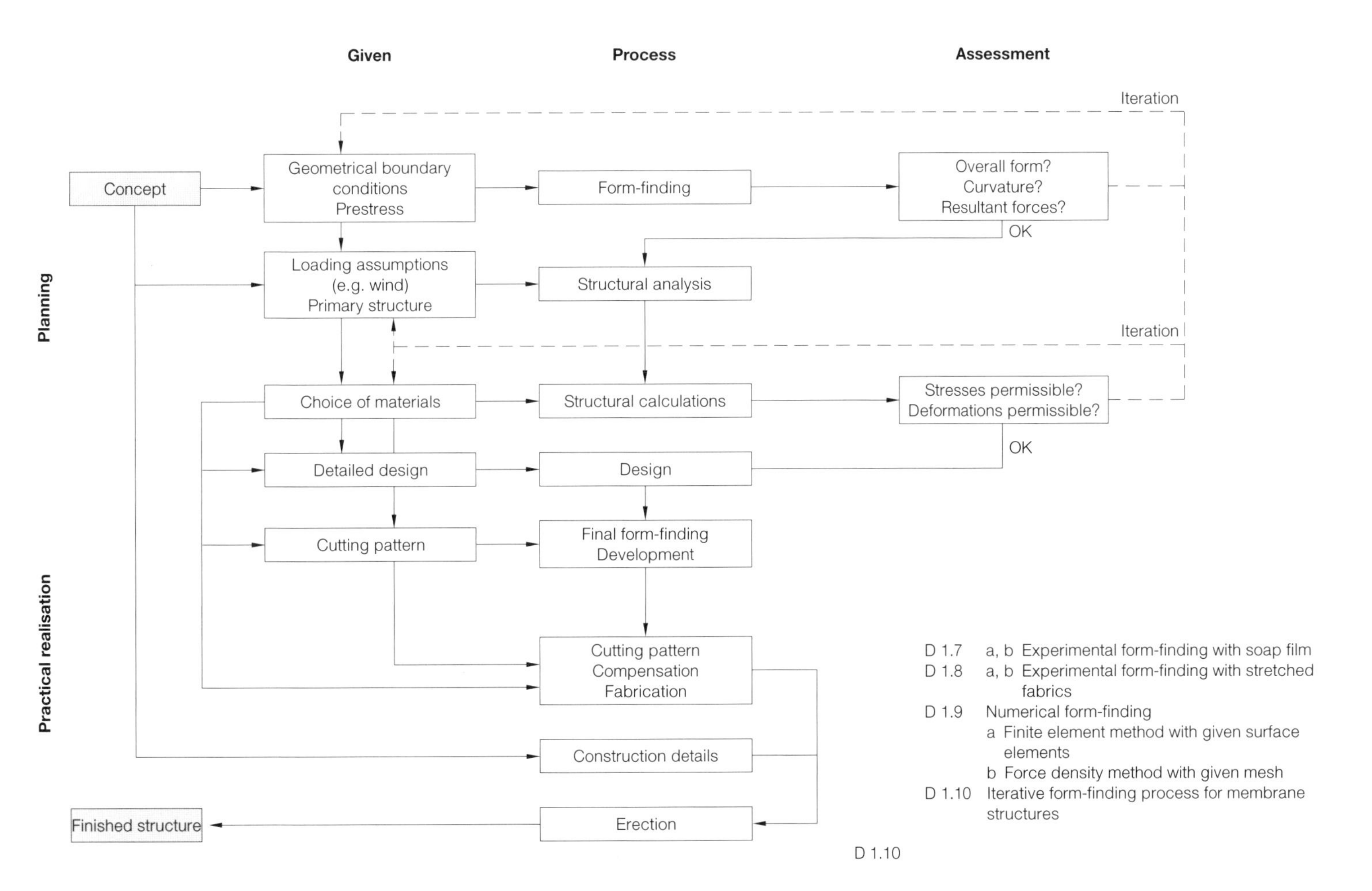

D 1.10

D 1.7 a, b Experimental form-finding with soap film
D 1.8 a, b Experimental form-finding with stretched fabrics
D 1.9 Numerical form-finding
a Finite element method with given surface elements
b Force density method with given mesh
D 1.10 Iterative form-finding process for membrane structures

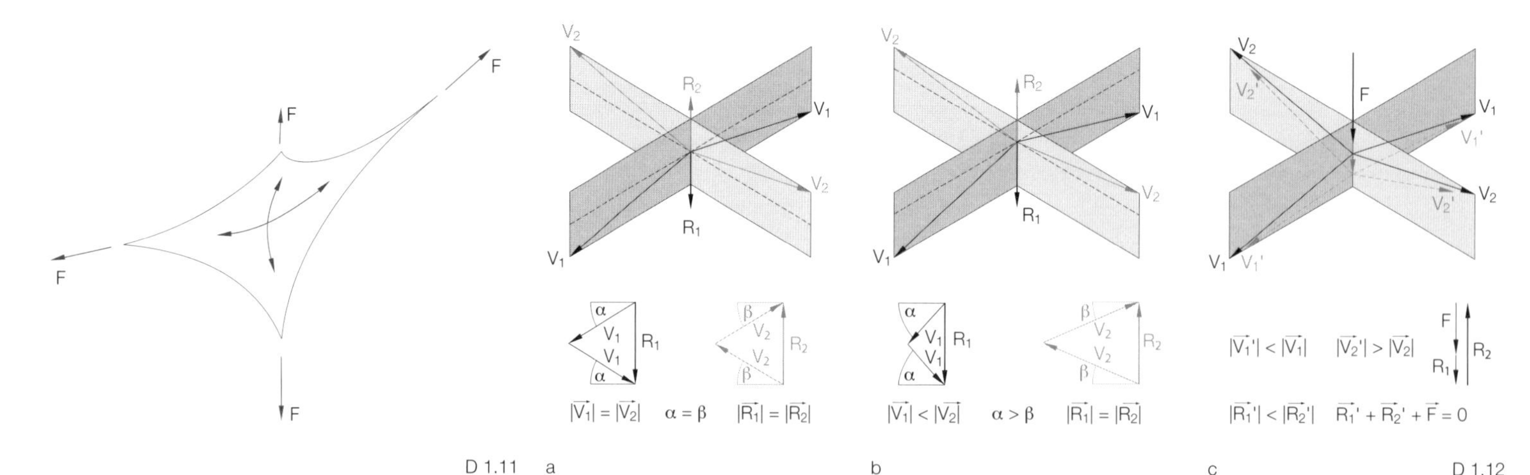

D 1.11   a   b   c   D 1.12

Form-finding process
Despite the often user-friendly software suites available, the close relationships between material, form and loadbearing behaviour plus the consequences for fabrication and erection call for a great deal of experience and interdisciplinary knowledge in all these areas in order to achieve a successful design. The result, which can be influenced by changing the boundary conditions and the magnitude of the prestress, must satisfy the requirements imposed by geometry, loadbearing behaviour, materials and form of construction. This turns form-finding into a complex iterative procedure that continues right through the planning (Fig. D 1.10, p. 139). Following the first form-finding step, in which the boundary conditions are defined, it is normally necessary to carry out further form-finding steps in the subsequent planning process. The geometry of the mesh used for the form-finding work, which at the start of the planning phase is generally still based on the system lines of the loadbearing structure, must track the boundary and support points as more and more detail is added to the design. Accordingly, the final form-finding for the cutting pattern for the material of the surface is usually not carried out until all the dimensions of the loadbearing structure have been specified and the detailed design work has been completed.

Loadbearing behaviour
The stiffness of a tensile surface or membrane structure is influenced by the geometry, i.e. in particular by the curvature of the surface, the prestress and the stiffness of the material. We speak of geometrical stiffness that is dependent on the surface curvature and prestress and elastic stiffness that are dependent on the properties of the material.
The most important geometrical variable in a tensile surface structure is the curvature of the surface. Only with sufficient double curvature is a membrane able to carry external loads safely. A limited amount of curvature requires high prestress values to be assumed in the calculations in order to limit the deformations of the membrane surface subjected to external loads. Wind-induced high-frequency flutter in particular can damage the material and the supporting construction and therefore must be prevented by applying an appropriate prestress. Also very dangerous are horizontal, level areas in which water can collect (ponding). A pool of water that grows as more and more water flows into it brings with it the risk that this heavy load will cause sudden failure of the material. During the design of a membrane structure it is therefore important to ensure that water can always drain away, even when rainfall is accompanied by high winds.
A prestress is applied to generate a state of constant tensile stress and therefore increase the stiffness of the membrane surface. We distinguish between mechanical and pneumatic prestressing. The former is generated by applying loads, e.g. by displacing the supports (Fig. D 1.12), the latter by creating a pressure difference between the top and bottom surfaces of the membrane, which as a uniformly distributed load causes a tangential force in the membrane (Fig. D 1.23, p. 143).

Mechanically prestressed surfaces
A membrane structure consists of flexible, prestressed surface elements and flexible, prestressed, or stiff perimeter elements. The three-dimensional arrangement of the perimeter elements in space and, possibly, further supporting elements in the surface creates a membrane form in double curvature. Such a membrane prestressed mechanically is stabilised by a state of equilibrium between the opposing sagging and hogging curvatures (Fig. D 1.11). Fig. D 1.12 shows this basic principle in a simplified form by way of two intersecting cables (wire ropes). The resulting vertical forces R_1 and R_2 at the intersection must be identical but of opposite sign in order to remain in equilibrium. In the associated force diagrams it can be seen that the intersection rises and therefore changes the angle of the force when the pretension in one of the cables is increased (Fig. D 1.12b). As a result, the ensuing vertical force R_2 and the opposing force R_1 remain identical in magnitude. The equilibrium condition is therefore also satisfied for anisotropic (i.e. different in two directions) prestresses. Introducing an external load F causes the system to deform due to the change in the angle and the membrane forces change from V_1 and V_2 to V_1' and V_2', producing a resultant R_2 opposing the external force (Fig. D 1.12c). The geometry adapts to the loads acting perpendicular to the surface until a new state of equilibrium is reached. Consequently, external loads can only be carried through deformations in the membrane surface; linked with this is an intense interaction between form and loadbearing behaviour.
It is the task of the designer to define the geometrical boundary conditions in such a way that the form-finding leads to an equilibrium form that is sensible in terms of both its construction and aesthetics. From the functional viewpoint, the deformations caused by external loads should be reduced to such an extent that the limits of serviceability are not exceeded and, for example, the membrane does not flutter when subjected to wind loads.

The complex geometrical diversity of membrane structures can be reduced to four basic types:
- Saddle and sail surfaces
- Surfaces with elements forming ridges and valleys
- Surfaces supported with high or low points
- Surfaces supported by arches

Saddle and sail surfaces
A sail surface must be stretched between at least four non-planar (i.e. not lying in the same plane) fixed points in space in order to produce a surface in double curvature (Fig. D 1.11). Curved, flexible cables or belts or straight, stiff perimeter elements can be designed to tension the edges of the sail surface (Figs. D 1.13a and c). Saddle surfaces with a least one rigid edge can be stretched over a triangular plan form when the stiff edge is curved perpendicular to the surface (Fig. D 1.13d,). Such surfaces also ensue when ridge or valley cables divide the surface into triangular zones (Fig. D 1.13g).

D 1.11 Basic principle for the mechanical prestressing of a surface

D 1.12 a–c States of equilibrium for a mechanically prestressed membrane using the example of two intersecting cables

D 1.13 Mechanically prestressed surfaces
- a Four-point sail with flexible edges
- b Four-point sail with rigid edges
- c Five-point sail with flexible edges and sail batten
- d Triangular surface with rigid arch along one edge
- e Sail with alternating ridge and valley cables
- f Sail with ridge cable and planar flexible edges
- g Undulating star with alternating ridge and valley cables
- h High-point surface with eye loop and ridge cables
- i Low-point surface with stiff ring
- j High-point surface with cable loop supported at two points
- k High-point surface with cable eye loop
- l High-point with "hump"
- m Arch-supported surface with arches along two edges
- n Arch-supported surface with inner arch stabilised by membrane
- o Addition of arch-supported surfaces
- p Arch along edge stabilised by outer flexible edge

D 1.14 Undulating star; "Dance Pavilion", Cologne (D), refurbishment, 2001, Rasch + Bradatsch

D 1.15 Surface with parallel elements forming ridges and valleys; movable membrane roof, City Hall, Vienna (A), 2000, Silja Tillner, Schlaich, Bergermann & Partner (structural engineering)

D 1.16 Low-point surface with individual supports; convertible umbrella canopies, Wasseralfingen Palace (D), 1994, Rasch + Bradatsch

D 1.17 Arch-supported surface; Poruklu Marina (TR), 2008, Lightweight Structures Group (LWSG), studio LD

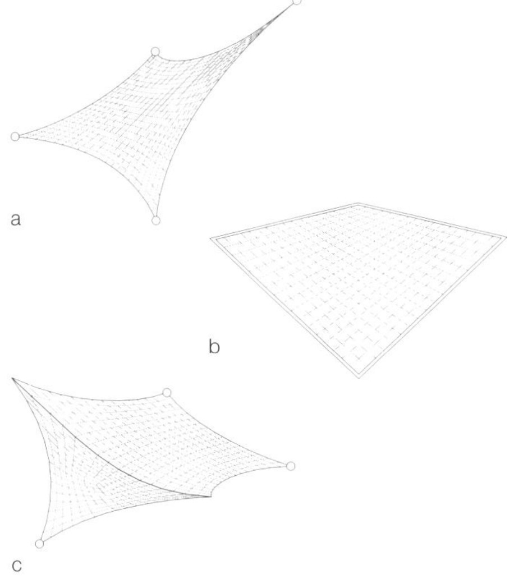

a b c

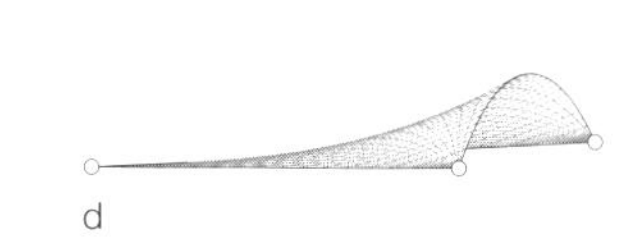

d

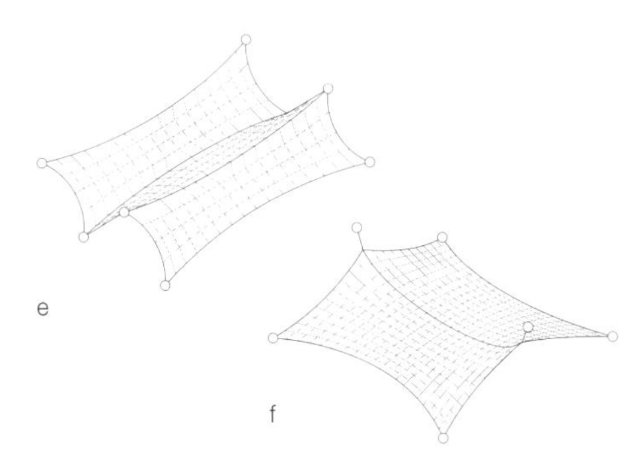

e f

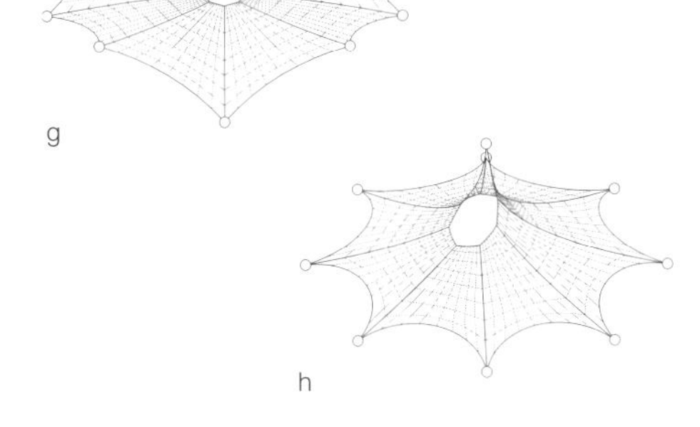

g h

i j k l

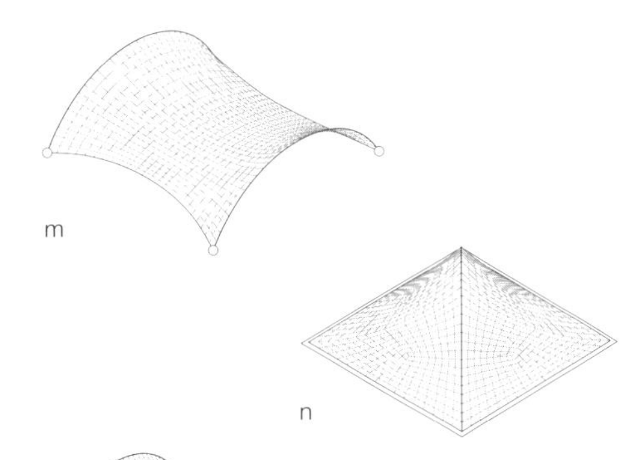

m n

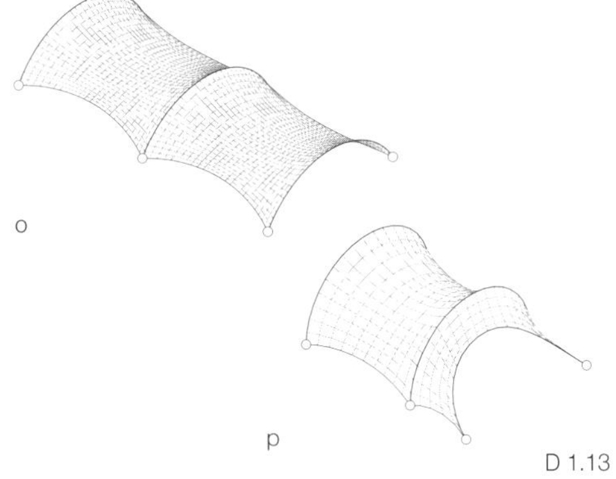

o p

D 1.13

D 1.14

D 1.15

D 1.16

D 1.17

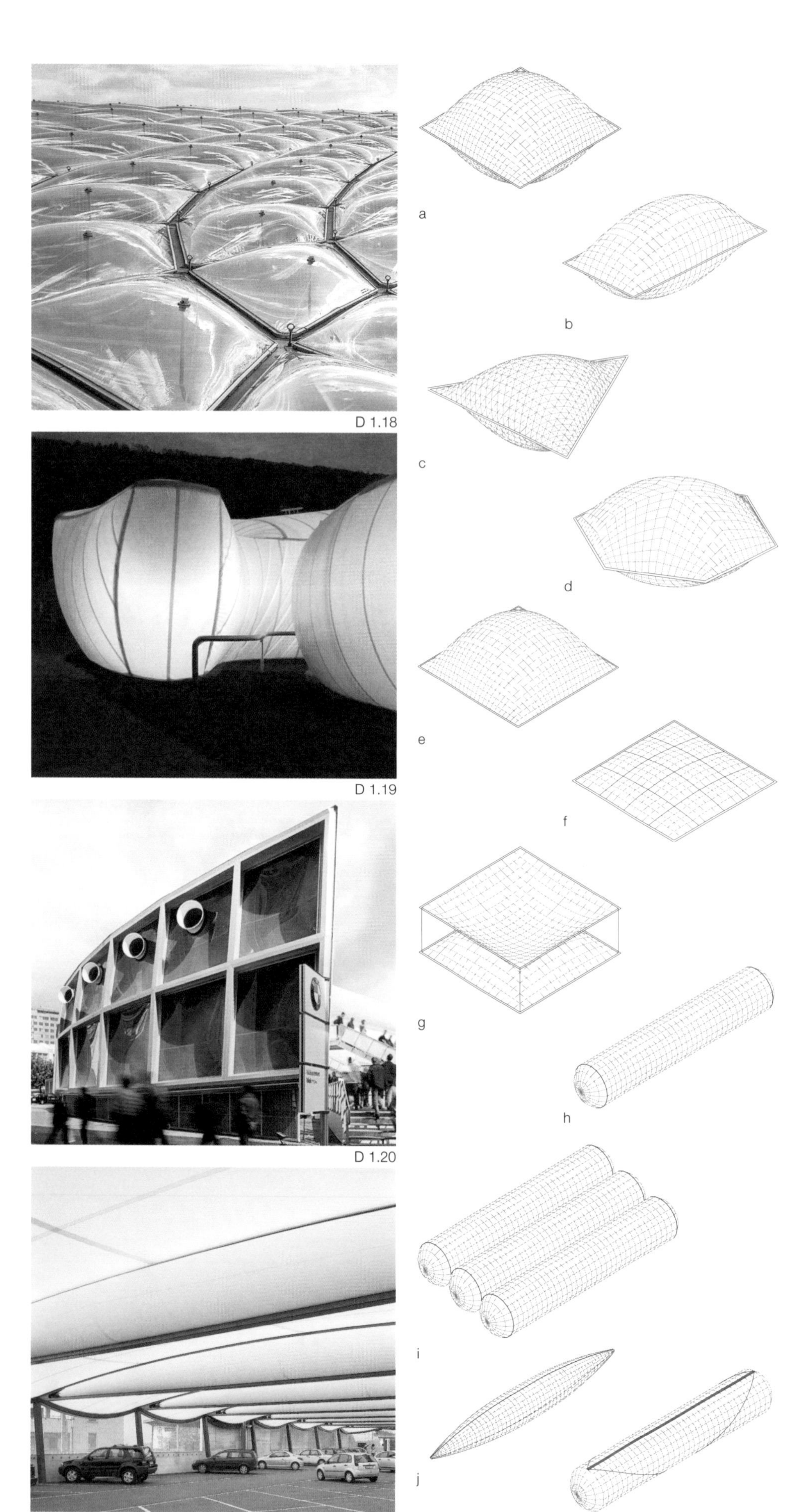

D 1.18

D 1.19

D 1.20

D 1.21

D 1.22

Surfaces with elements forming ridges and valleys
The elements forming the ridges and valleys are usually cables or belts incorporated in the surface. A ridge cable pulls the surface upwards so that it drops away from the cable at 90° to the direction of tension in the cable; a valley cable pulls the surface downwards so that it rises at 90° to the direction of tension in the cable. The use of such linear elements enables plane surfaces to be transformed into anticlastic surfaces or the curvature of anticlastic surfaces to be altered (Figs. D 1.13e–h, p. 141). Ridge and valley cables can be incorporated singly or as arrangements with alternating parallel (Figs. D 1.13e and f, p. 141) and radial (Figs. D 1.13g and h, p. 141) cables. For the membrane continuum, a ridge or valley cable acts like a flexible edge at which two surfaces join. The surface is therefore divided into smaller zones.
Ridge and valley cables are frequently used in combination with sails and surfaces supported with high or low points. They raise or lower the surface geometry and can prevent extreme necking in the formation of funnel-like or cylindrical surfaces (Fig. D 1.29, p. 145). On large surfaces ridge and valley cables can increase the stiffness and load-carrying capacity.

Surfaces supported by high or low points
Where a surface is raised or pulled down locally, we speak of high and low points respectively. Singularities, i.e. the raising of a surface at a single point, are not possible because the stresses in the material at the very peak would be infinitely high. The high or low point must therefore be truncated before the actual peak and held in place by a stiff ring (Fig. D 1.13i, p. 141) or a "hump" (Fig. D 1.13l, p. 141), or suspended from a cable (Figs. D 1.13j and k, p. 141). A stiff ring or a loop of cable acts like a closed internal edge. A loop of cable can be in circular, oval or rosette form. A cable forms a so-called eye loop when it is anchored at one point. Several cables can be arranged around the high or low point to form a rosette, or two cables anchored at two an eyelet shape.

Surfaces supported by arches
When a surface is supported by a linear, curving element, then this arch can accommodate the compression and uplift forces in the surface. Perimeter arches carrying loads on one side (Fig. D 1.13m, p. 141) are also subjected to severe bending perpendicular to the plane of the arch. The bending loads decrease when the membrane continues over the arch (Figs. D 1.13o and p, p. 141). With a symmetrical load the aim should be to place the plane of the arch in the bisector of the angle of the membrane surface passing over the arch. Where this is the case, the membrane can restrain the arch against buckling and the latter can therefore be designed as a very delicate, minimal structure (Fig. D 1.13n, p. 141). A surface with adequate geometrical and elastic stiffness is the prerequisite for this. An arch not stabilised by a membrane must be secured against lateral buckling.

Free corners
Incorporating elastic bars (sail battens) in the membrane surface enables free corners to be created which are stabilised solely by the bar in turn restrained by the surface without the need for any guy cables or supports. Owing to its elasticity, such a bar essentially adapts to the curvature of the surface, but can carry compressive forces because it is restrained against buckling by the membrane (Fig. D 1.13c, p. 141).

Pneumatically prestressed surfaces
Rigid perimeter members restrain the surface in the case of pneumatic designs. A difference in pressure between the inside and outside results in a uniformly distributed load that causes a membrane state of stress. Pneumatically prestressed surfaces – apart from those with acute-angled corners (Fig. D 1.22c) – generate synclastic forms. Where the internal pressure is greater than the atmospheric pressure, a cushion-type form curving outwards is the outcome, in the opposite situation an inward-curving form (Figs. D 1.22a and g respectively).
In most pneumatically prestressed designs the membrane stresses are resisted by rigid perimeter members so that – in contrast to many mechanically prestressed designs – no large tensioning forces have to be transferred to the subsoil. The limited stiffness of pneumatic cushions means that, unlike surfaces with mechanical prestressing, they cannot replace any ties in the loadbearing structure and therefore cannot contribute to the stiffness of the system. Such cushions therefore serve only as covering or enclosing elements, are not part of the loadbearing structure. Their low weight, long spans and comparatively generous tolerances for deformations make cushions a good choice for constructing building envelopes.
The load on the membrane is a result of the difference between the internal and external pressures plus the wind pressure/suction, and snow loads if applicable. Assuming that the air is incompressible (constant volume), it is true to say that any downward loads such as snow or wind pressure relieve the upper membrane of the cushion, while the tensile force in the lower membrane increases (Fig. D 1.24). The internal overpressure should therefore be specified to be greater than the anticipated external loads so that the upper membrane does not become slack. This situation is reversed in the case of suction loads, e.g. due to wind. However, the fan regulating the pressure cannot react quickly enough to changing conditions and so the deformation of the cushion caused by gusts of wind can lead to severe pressure fluctuations in the cushion (because according to the Boyle-Mariotte law the product of pressure and volume is always constant). These pressure fluctuations must be taken into account when designing the cushion membrane. Another difference between pneumatically and mechanically prestressed surfaces is that in the former the prestress in the surface is dependent on the geometry or, more precisely, the curvature of the surface. The tangential surface tension is proportional to the pressure difference between inside and outside and the radius of curvature of the surface (see "Pneumatically prestressed surfaces", p. 147).
We distinguish between air-inflated structures, i.e. cushion- and tube-like designs in which an enclosed volume is subjected to a partial vacuum or overpressure, and air-supported structures in which the entire interior is maintained at an overpressure.

Cushions
The main span of a cushion made from a typical material (e.g. ETFE foil) is limited to a few metres. To overcome this limitation, groups of cushions are added to a primary structure to form a building envelope (Figs. D 1.18 and D 1.22a–d). The geometry of each individual cushion depends on the layout of the primary structure framing the cushions. As pneumatic forms are always trying to attain the shape of a spherical cap, at least approximately, surfaces with opposite curvature occur in cushions bounded by frames with sharp corners (Fig. D 1.25). High stresses and wrinkles occur in these local, anticlastic zones which must be considered when designing the stiff edges around the cushions. The recommendation is to avoid corners with acute angles in order to guarantee the durability of the design. The curvature of the cushion (height difference between high and low points)

D 1.18 ETFE cushions; Allianz Arena, Munich (D), 2005, Herzog & de Meuron
D 1.19 Air-supported building; Biel Expo (CH), 2002, formTL
D 1.20 Negative pressure cushions; Dynaform BMW Pavillon, IAA, Frankfurt am Main (D), 2001, Franken Architekten
D 1.21 Tensairity beams; multi-storey car park, Montreux (CH), 2004, Luscher Architectes
D 1.22 Pneumatically prestressed surfaces
a Square cushion
b Rectangular cushion
c Triangular cushion
d Hexagonal cushion
e Air-supported building
f Air-supported surface with reinforcing cables
g Negative pressure cushion
h Tube
i Addition of tubes
j Tensairity beam with stiff top and bottom chords
k Tensairity beam with stiff top chord and cable bottom chord
D 1.23 Basic principle for the pneumatic prestressing of a surface
D 1.24 How an air-filled cushion carries the load
D 1.25 Pneumatically prestressed surfaces based on various plan forms compared with a spherical cap

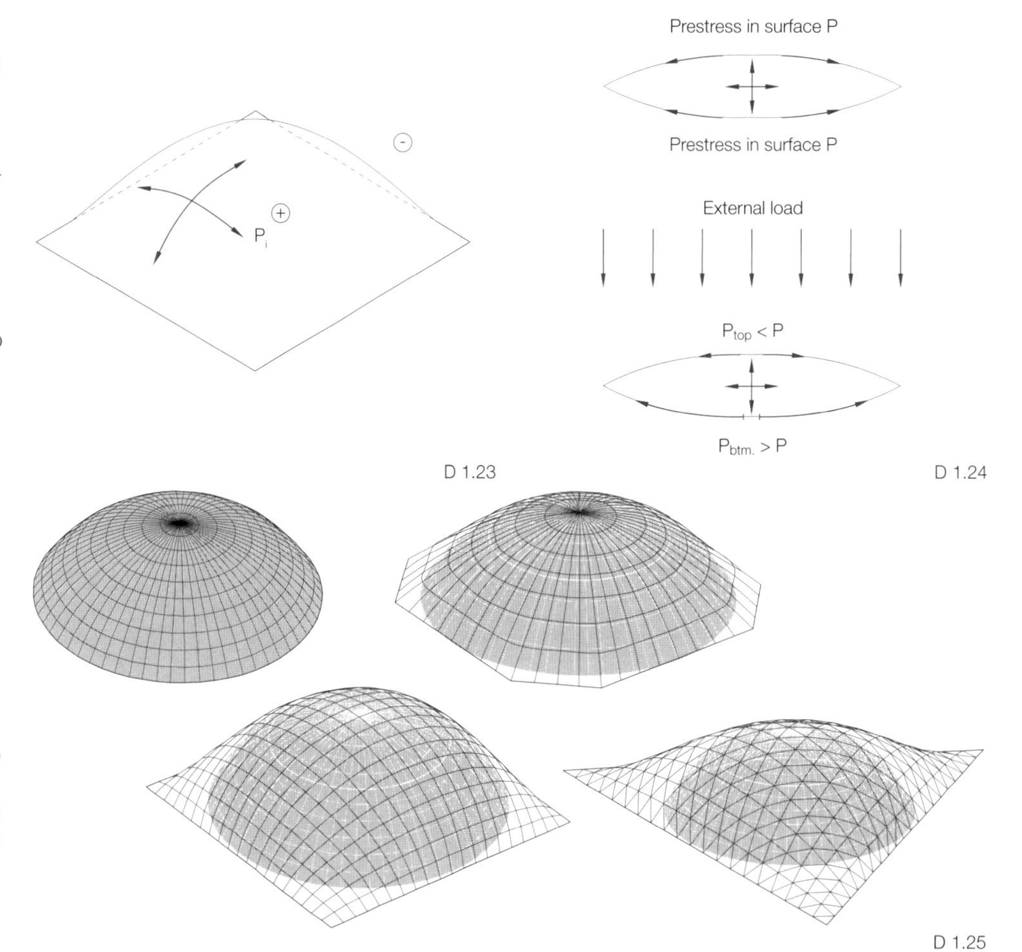

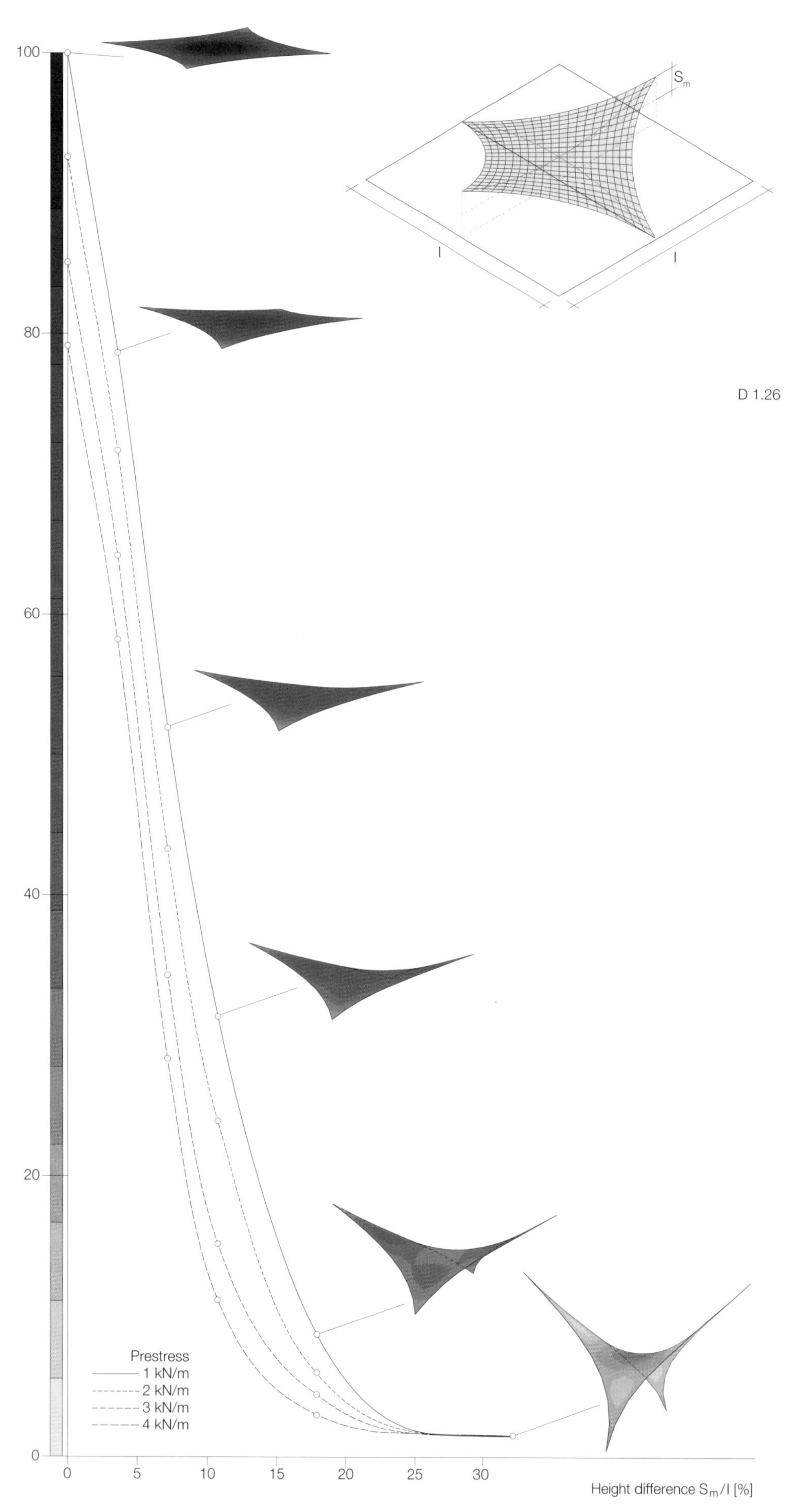

D 1.26

D 1.27

should also be adapted in order to be able to handle higher snow or wind loads where necessary.

Tubes

Tube-like air-filled elements are either used singly or in groups to form a combination of primary structure and building envelope (Figs. D 1.22h and i, p. 142). Used singly, they can also be employed as "smart" loadbearing elements whose stiffness can be adapted via the internal pressure to suit the loading. By using an appropriate cutting pattern with a shortened internal radius it is also possible to produce curved tubes.

Tensairity

In terms of the way it works, a Tensairity system can be considered as a trussed framework made up of thin bars and cables in which an air-filled tube acts as a stabilising element. The tube holds the compression and tension members of the structure apart and thus creates a structural depth. At the same time, it stabilises the compression member against buckling. The tension members can either be in the form of cables in tension forming a spiral around the tube (Fig. D 1.22k, p. 142) or in the form of a steel section forming a complete bottom chord (Figs. D 1.21 and D 1.22j, p. 142; Fig. E 3.19, p. 195).

Air-supported building

In contrast to cushion and tube systems, in an air-supported building, or air house, the entire interior is itself the air-filled structure (Figs. D 1.19 and D 1.22e, p. 142). Air-supported buildings can therefore only be entered and left via air locks. Owing to the large radius of curvature, a pressure only about 0.2 mbar (25 mm head of water) above that of the surrounding air is enough to support and stabilise an airtight membrane. Such a pressure does not cause any discomfort within the interior.
Comparing all design principles, pneumatic structures in the form of air-supported buildings are among the lightest. Strengthened with a cable net, it is possible to achieve spans of more than 200 m. However, owing to the high cost of energy for maintaining the internal pressure and a number of spectacular failures caused by snow loads and storms, this type of construction has not become widespread for such large structures. But for shorter spans, e.g. temporary roofs over tennis courts or venues for events, air-supported buildings are frequently specified because of their lightness, flexibility and very compact transport dimensions.

Defining the boundary conditions

All the methods employed in form-finding for tensile surface structures with membranes presume knowledge of the relationships between geometry, loadbearing behaviour and practical realisation.

Mechanically prestressed surfaces

The curvature of the edge cables and the directions and positions of guy cables and support points are critical for mechanically prestressed membrane structures. The geometrical, structural engineering and constructional significance of these parameters is explained in more detail below.

Fixed points

A fixed point is generally a support point for a mechanically prestressed membrane at which the tensile stresses are transferred to the subsoil either directly or indirectly via columns, guy cables, booms, etc. The architectural boundary conditions normally dictate the geometrical positions of the fixed points. Where there are no additional elements such as high points, arches, ridges or valleys, then an adequate but shallow difference in height between the fixed points should be chosen. This difference in height is equal to the sag of a cable s_c or a membrane surface s_m between its support points. In the case of membrane surfaces with isotropic prestressing, the maximum difference in height occurs at the point at which hogging and sagging principal curvatures meet, i.e. at half the height between the high and low points (Fig. D 1.26). Fig. D 1.27 compares the curvature-dependent deformations of various four-point membranes with the same material properties, prestressing, spans and wind loads (constant load per unit area perpendicular to surface). The deformation under wind load is greatest for a flat sail and for reference purposes this is regarded as 100%. With a difference in height fm/l of about 10%, the deformation is only 30 % of that of the flat sail, and the geometrical stiffness hardly increases beyond a difference of 25%. Deformations can be reduced by increasing the prestress, but only up to a certain point. Consequently, a higher prestress must be chosen for a shallow curvature, which, however, leads to high support reactions and stresses in the membrane and edge cables.

Curvature of edge cables

As the local membrane stresses predominantly act at 90° to the edge of the membrane, flexible membrane edges describe a circular arc approximately. It is therefore also possible to specify the relationship between the stress in the surface P [kN/m], the force in the edge cable F [kN] and the radius of curvature of the edge cable r [m] approximately using the two-dimensional hoop stress formula F = r · P. This formula makes it clear that the force in the edge cable depends only on the stress in the surface and the radius of curvature, not the span. Nevertheless, the span is indirectly significant because for reasons

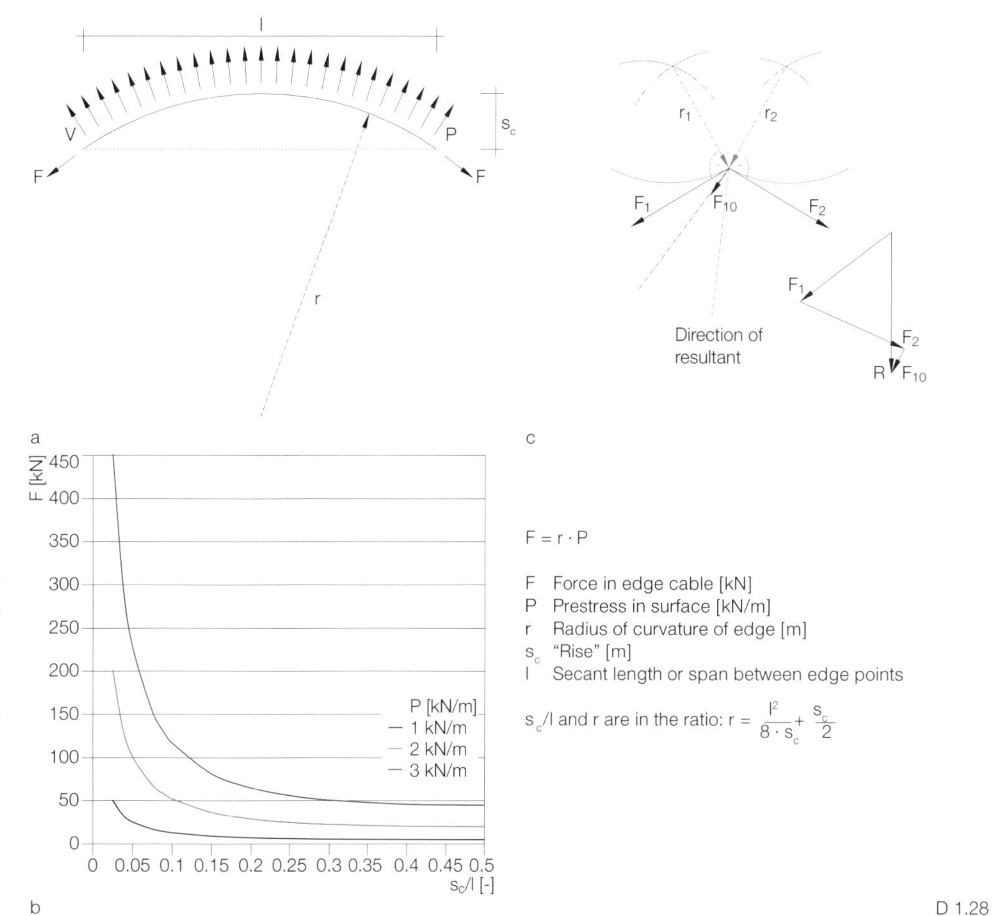

$F = r \cdot P$

F Force in edge cable [kN]
P Prestress in surface [kN/m]
r Radius of curvature of edge [m]
s_c "Rise" [m]
l Secant length or span between edge points

s_c/l and r are in the ratio: $r = \frac{l^2}{8 \cdot s_c} + \frac{s_c}{2}$

D 1.28

D 1.26 Relationship between the sag of a surface (difference in height between high and low points), span and difference between heights of corners

D 1.27 Comparison of the curvature-dependent deformations of various four-point sails with the same material properties, prestresses, spans and wind loads. The deformation of the flat membrane under wind loads is taken as the reference point (100%).

D 1.28 Relationship between surface prestress P, force in edge cable F and curvature of edge cable r for mechanically prestressed membranes with flexible edges (approximation)
a Edge cable geometry, definition of parameters
b How the force in the cable depends on geometry and pretension
c Forces at the head of a mast, shown on plan

D 1.29 How anisotropic prestress and ridge cables influence the curvature of the surface

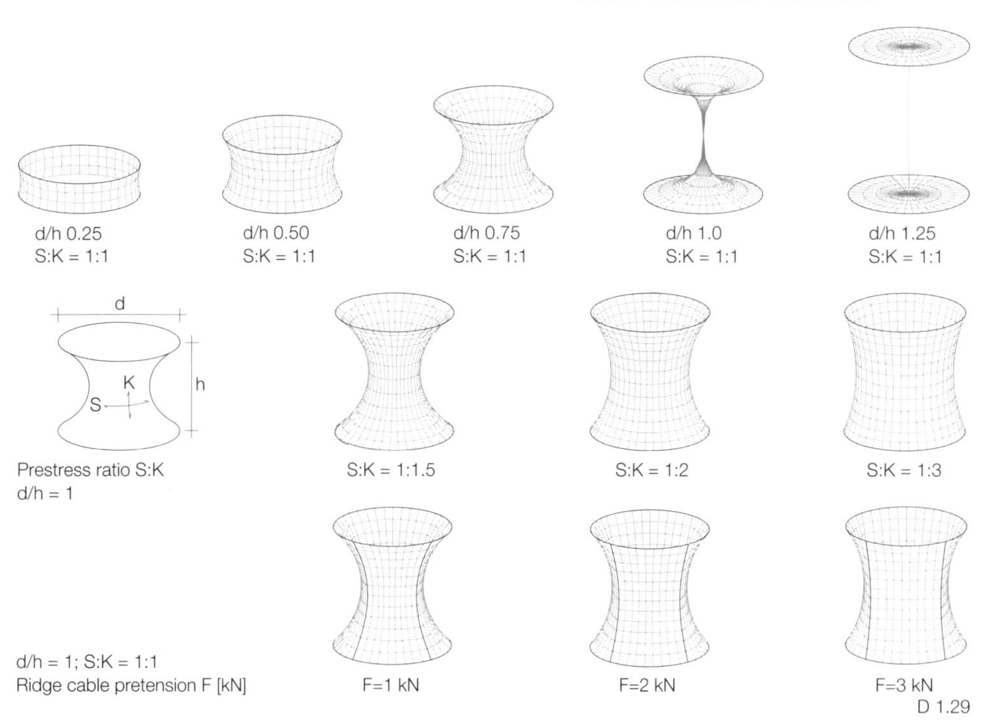

D 1.29

of geometry and construction, the radius of curvature normally increases with the span. If a membrane is to cover as large an area as possible, then the edge cables should be tensioned to the maximum possible and economically viable extent. With very long spans it can prove worthwhile to design the edges as scalloped, with the membrane connected to a polygonal, pretensioned cable in a series of small arcs. In geometry terms, the resulting minimum radius for an edge cable is half the span. Fig. D 1.28b (p. 145) shows the relationship between the "rise" of an edge cable and the force for three different pretensions. It can be seen that the force in the edge cable increases considerably below a rise of $s_c/l < 10\%$. At the same time, the force drops only minimally where $s_c/l > 20\%$. From this we can deduce that a sensible rise for an edge cable is approx. 10%.
Where the pretension and the radius of the edge cable are fixed, then it is possible to determine not only the magnitude but also the direction of the force in the cable at the support. The direction is given by the tangent of the edge cable arc at the point of support. If several cables meet at one point, adding together the force vectors produces the resultant support reaction. In Fig. D 1.28c (p. 145) the edge cable vectors F_1 and F_2 and the ridge cable vector F_{10} of a funnel-type membrane are added together. Such simple preliminary considerations enable the direction of the support reactions to be estimated and hence the arrangement of loadbearing members, e.g. masts and guy cables, to be optimised. In doing so, however, it is important to remember that the magnitudes of the forces and hence the magnitudes and directions of the resultants vary with varying loads (e.g. wind), which means that masts require two guy cables.

Curvature of the surface

Specifying the edge points in space means that the curvature of the surface can only be influenced within certain limits. A curvature given by the edge points and isotropic prestressing (i.e. equal in both directions) will frequently have to be adjusted for functional or structural reasons. For example, it may be necessary to reduce the sag of a membrane in order to achieve the internal clearance required or to avoid ponding. Ridge and valley cables, also anisotropic prestressing (different in the warp and weft directions), can be used to adjust the curvature of the surface. These options are best demonstrated using the example of the curved surface of a cylinder. The curvature must be limited for high-point and cylinder surfaces because these can collapse to a minimum stress. Fig. D 1.29 (p. 145) shows that the diameter of the isotropically prestressed membrane forming the surface of the cylinder decreases to such an extent beyond a certain height h that it collapses into two separate surfaces. In such cases further measures such as the introduction of ridge or valley cables or changing the prestressing ratios must be considered. Fig. D 1.29 (p. 145) shows the options for influencing the "necking" of a cylinder with a diameter (d) and height (h) ratio of 1:1.
It may be worthwhile optimising the curvature of the surface for relevant loading cases from the structural as well as the geometrical viewpoint. An attempt is often made to introduce more stiffness into the sagging curvature in order to prevent ponding and large deformations under snow loads. With a dominant wind suction loading case, the stresses in the membrane can be reduced by choosing a smaller radius of curvature for the vertical curvature.

Ridge and valley cables are frequently used in conjunction with isotropically prestressed membranes. They increase the stiffness of the membrane surface and hence reduce the deformations of and stresses in the membrane. At the same time, they divide the area into zones, which limits creep deformation in larger roof structures and is often desirable from the erection viewpoint, too. With high-point forms, ridge cables are also frequently used as retaining cables for the masts in the event of membrane failure. The constructional details of ridge and valley cables are often complicated if they are not located at joints between membrane sections or as stitched-on belts. Separate tension cables can slip on the membrane and so additional welded pockets for the cables will be necessary in most cases. Isotropic stress conditions are advantageous for the long-term behaviour of a membrane structure. With a markedly anisotropically prestressed membrane, the creep behaviour of many membrane materials can lead to more severe creep in the zones with higher stresses and hence the originally anisotropically prestressed membrane gradually approximating to an evenly stressed surface due to stress redistributions. In such a situation there is theoretically too much material available for an evenly stressed form, which can lead to wrinkles.
In the end, adjusting the prestress and using ridge and/or valley cables, taking into account the aforementioned criteria sensibly, is up to the judgement of the designer. Accordingly, an optimum solution for any specific project can only be found by considering form, material properties, loading assumptions and the desired appearance.

Prestressing values

The minimum value of the prestressing depends on the geometrical and elastic stiffness of the membrane. Forms with shallower curvature must be prestressed to a greater extent than forms with more pronounced curvature. Further, it is important to guarantee that every fibre in the material is adequately stretched in order to create an evenly prestressed, wrinkle-free surface whose prestress is not completely cancelled out under the action of external loads. At the same time, in order to have sufficient loadbearing reserves for external loads and to avoid excessive support reactions, a certain level of prestressing should not be exceeded. In practice, the magnitude of the prestress is customarily chosen so that it is retained over as large an area as possible when the membrane is loaded and the deformations due to wind pressure or snow loads do not lead to noticeable depressions in the surface in which water could collect. Typical values for the prestress lie between 1 and 5 kN/m.

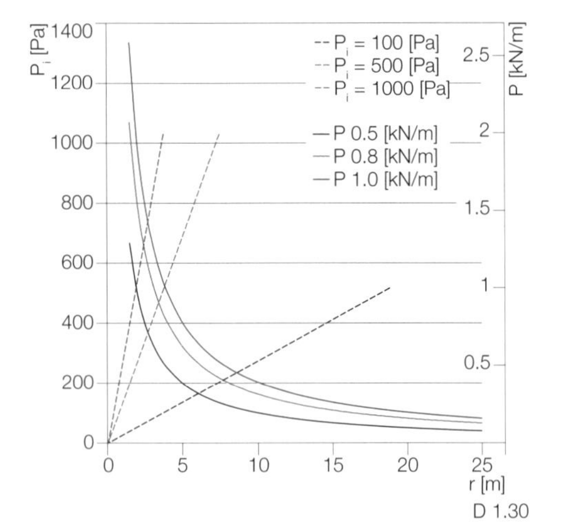

D 1.30

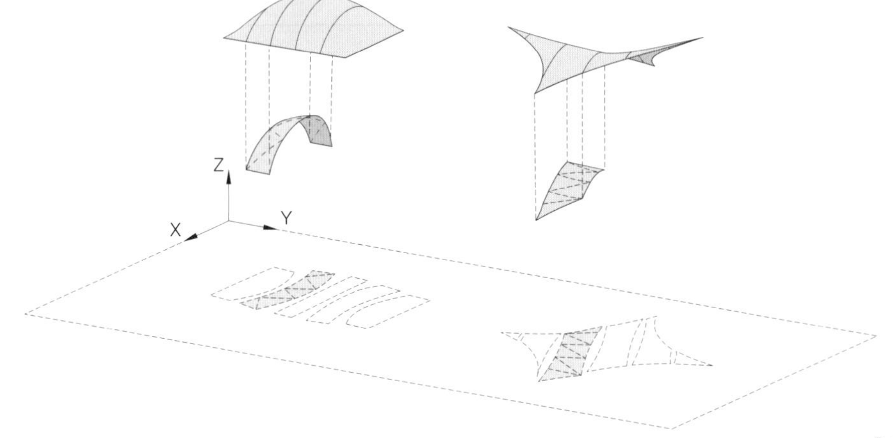

D 1.31

Pneumatically prestressed surfaces
In principle, for pneumatically prestressed surfaces there is a relationship between the curvature of the surface and the level of pressure necessary for the supporting effect. This relationship can again be illustrated by the hoop stress formula, which approximates to $P = 0.5 \cdot P_i \cdot r$ for a three-dimensional spherical cap. From this formula we can see that a larger radius of curvature r [m] requires a lower internal pressure in order to generate the same prestress P [kN/m], as is the case with relatively highly curved, smaller designs. This is familiar from everyday life – just compare the level of pressure P [Pa] in the tyre of a racing bicycle (7–10 bar) with that in a car tyre (approx. 2 bar), for instance.
In contrast to mechanically prestressed surfaces, the degree of pneumatic prestressing can be regulated by controlling the internal pressure. The overpressure necessary in cushions made from foils and membranes is therefore also dependent on the volume and the structural requirements. It should be set higher than the load expected from snow or wind and is normally in the region of 100–1000 Pa (10 000 Pa = 1 bar = 10 kN/m²); this is comparatively low but must be maintained. In some structural concepts the pressure is adjusted to suit different loading cases; for example, the internal pressure is doubled during heavy snowfall only and therefore does not have to be maintained at that level for the whole year. Fig. D 1.30 shows the relationships between prestress P, internal pressure P_i and radius of curvature r for three given prestressing values (solid lines) and also for three given internal pressures P_i (dotted lines). In the former case it becomes clear that the overpressure for a radius of curvature < 5 m must rise steeply in order to maintain a typical tension in the membrane. But if a minimum internal pressure has to be maintained because of external loads, then the stress in the membrane rises in proportion to the curvature.

Practical realisation
The result of every form-finding process is a three-dimensional, geometrical form for a prestressed membrane structure. To form the membrane surface, flat, unstretched webs of material have to be cut and joined together in such a way that the form in the constructed condition achieves the planned double-curvature geometry and the intended level of prestress. A membrane surface can also be constructed without the need for complicated cutting patterns with curved edges, and instead simply through the uneven overlapping of webs of membrane material or the use of open fabrics, the mesh of which can distort severely. As a rule, however, the curvature of the surface is achieved by curving the edges of the webs of material. An anticlastic double curvature is produced by removing material from the centre of the web and, vice versa, synclastic double curvature by adding material to the centre of the web. ETFE cushions represent a special case: their form is achieved through the elastic and plastic deformation of the foil material as well as the use of a cutting pattern. The final shape of the cushion is therefore not established until after a few loading cycles. A cutting pattern should still be used, however, where considerable curvature is required and if wrinkles at the corners are to be avoided.

Cutting pattern
Groups of radial or parallel geodesic lines are plotted on the surface of the membrane in order to determine the cutting pattern. A geodesic line describes the shortest distance between two points on a surface spanning between those points. The three-dimensional form is divided into strips along these lines which, for example, have been developed by triangulation into flat strips of material. Care should be taken here to ensure that the maximum distance between two cutting lines does not exceed the width of the web available (including an allowance for the seam) in the chosen membrane material. The distortion of the strips when they are transferred to two dimensions depends on the degree of curvature and the width of the web; the strips should therefore be kept relatively narrow in zones with significant curvature.
Ideally, the cutting pattern should follow the principal curvatures and the primary load-carrying direction. The increased stiffness parallel to the seam results in a maximum stiffness for the surface and hence small deformations when external loads are applied. The cutting lines on the web should therefore also run in the stiff, warp direction wherever possible. The recommendation here is to agree the exact layout of the webs with all those involved in the design because the seams will remain clearly visible, especially when lit from behind, and are therefore important factors in the final appearance (Figs. D 1.32 and D 1.33). It is mainly the seams that reveal the curvature of the surface through the diffuse light on the underside of the membrane. Laying the webs, for example, parallel with one of the principal curvatures enables the double curvature of the surface to be emphasized visually. At the same time, the direction of the cut must be closely coordinated with the prestressing direction during erection in order to guarantee that the material stretches and is not distorted diagonally.
Figs. D 1.34a–h (p. 148) show various typical cutting patterns for the four basic forms and the direction of the warp threads (K). A typical cutting pattern along the principal curvatures is shown in Fig. D 1.34a. Here, the stiffer direction, due to the warp threads and welded seams, is the sagging curvature, with snow loads being carried with a reduced risk of ponding.
In the case of sail surfaces it is also important to avoid tensioning warp threads exactly between two corners and therefore forming an unwanted ridge that overstresses the material. If for this reason the cutting lines are rotated through 45° with respect to the principal curvatures, then the low shear stiffness of the membrane material results in a very flexible surface. One compromise is a design turned through 22.5°, as shown in Fig. D 1.34b.
Surfaces with high or low points are typically cut radially (Fig. D 1.34e). However, webs tapering to a point means considerable wastage.
Fig. D 1.34f shows an alternative with less waste. Arch membranes are usually cut at 90° to the stiff perimeter arches (Figs. D 1.34g and h), although with very shallow designs the cuts can be parallel with the arches.

D 1.32

D 1.30 Relationship between internal pressure, radius of curvature and prestress in surface for pneumatically prestressed membranes (approximation):

$$P = 0.5 \cdot P_i \cdot r$$

P Prestress in surface [kN/m]
P_i Internal pressure [Pa; 1 Pa = 1 N/m²]
r Idealised radius of curvature of a spherical cap [m]

D 1.31 Transferring three-dimensional surfaces to two-dimensional cutting patterns for pneumatically and mechanically prestressed surfaces
D 1.32 Visible welded seams at night; Norwegian Pavilion, Shanghai Expo (CN), 2010, Helen & Hard/Melvær & Lien/Sweco Goener; Knippers Helbig/studioLD (membrane structure)
D 1.33 Norwegian Pavilion, high point with visible welded seams seen against the light

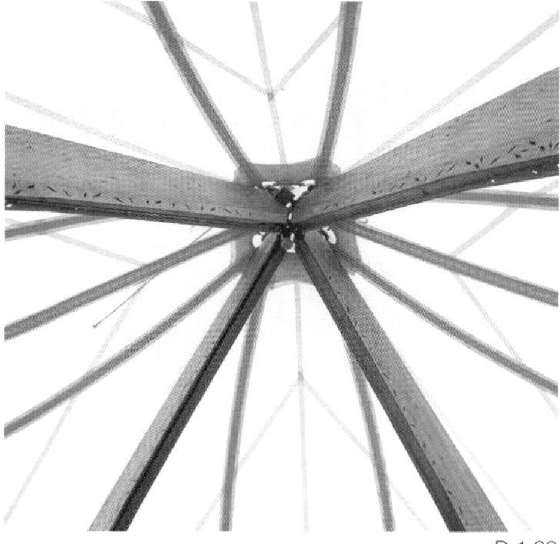
D 1.33

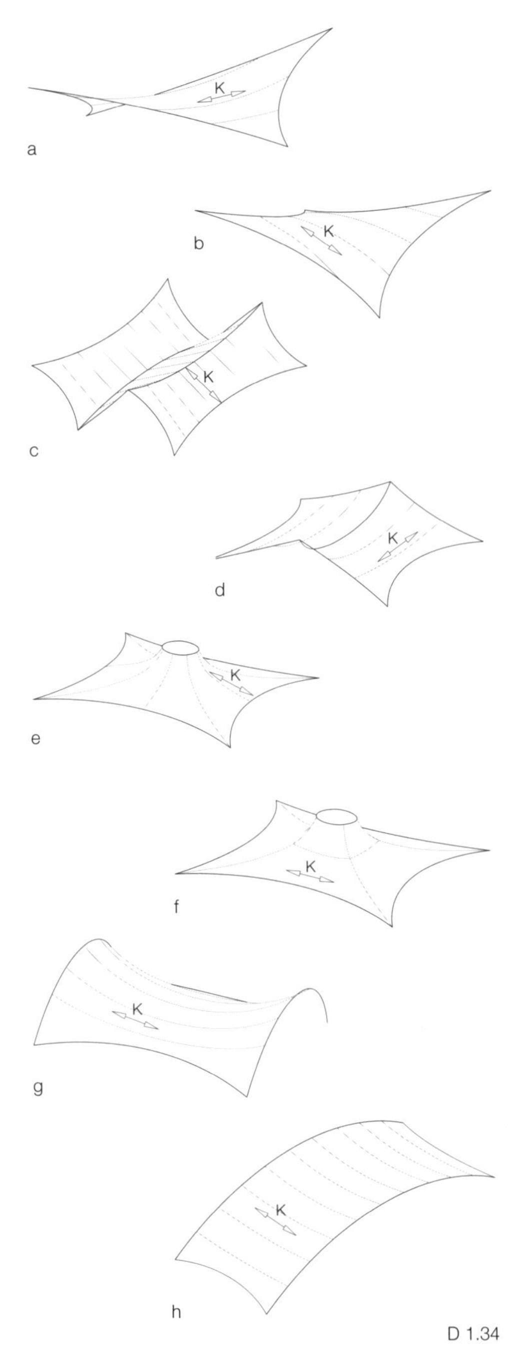

D 1.34 Typical cutting pattern layouts for the basic forms of mechanically prestressed membranes

D 1.35 Basic principles of mechanical prestressing
a Displacement of the corners by raking the masts at flexible edges
b Rotating a rigid edge
c Parallel displacement of a rigid edge
d Displacement of the corner and/or high points of flexible edges

D 1.36 Basic principles of convertible membrane structures
a Rolling
b Parallel gathering
c Circular gathering
d Central gathering

D 1.37 Funnel-shaped canopy, 10 x 10 m, Stuttgart (D), 1990, Rasch + Bradatsch

D 1.38 Convertible, centre-gathered membrane roof; tennis stadium, Rotherbaum, Hamburg (D), 1997, Schweger + Partner/Werner Sobek Ingenieure

Summing up, we can say that the orientation of the cutting lines depends on the following criteria:

- Directions of principal curvatures (minimising distortion)
- Erection sequence, introducing the prestress
- Positions of corners
- Shear stiffness of membrane material
- Architectural design
- Economic aspects (minimising wastage)

Compensation

The strips of membrane material transferred to two dimensions are reduced in size by the amount of elongation caused by the prestressing. This process is known as compensation. Accordingly, it is the anticipation of the elastic elongation in the cutting pattern in order to achieve the desired geometry in the prestressed state. The compensation value for a membrane material is determined from a biaxial tensile test in which a sample of the material is subjected to several typical loading cycles (see "Strain stiffness", p. 105). The elongation of the material is measured to enable a compensation value to be specified. This can differ in the warp and weft directions by several percentage points depending on the particular material. In a material such as PTFE/glass, for example, it can be the case that the warp threads actually shorten when subjected to biaxial prestress (Fig. C 5.13b, p. 106). This requires a negative compensation value, which is normally neglected in practice because the value is very small. New tests must be carried out for every batch of the material. The compensation value must therefore be recalculated not only for every project because of its specific prestressing and loading figures, but also for every different batch of material within a project. Increased stiffnesses, e.g. at the corners, can be taken into account through so-called decompensation, i.e. by reducing the compensation value.

The planning and fabrication steps such as transferring to two dimensions, cutting pattern and compensation simplify the ideal double-curvature geometry of the membrane structure. It is possible that the prestressed state originally planned can then no longer be achieved exactly. Inaccurate calculations and errors in workmanship can lead to wrinkles and erection problems, overstressed zones and, as a result, damage to the membrane.

One particular challenge is adapting the compensation values for belt-membrane edges because two different stiffnesses must be taken into account. Also relevant is the fact that the belt shortens with every stitch as it is sewn on – a value that can reach 1–2 % in total. In order to ensure that in the final condition the edge belt actually attains the prestress specified by the form-finding, both the different compensation values of belt and membrane and also the shortening due to the stitching must be taken into account.

Erection

A detailed erection plan with a carefully thought-out prestressing concept is indispensable for the successful realisation of a membrane structure. The actual plan will depend very much on the particular project but is generally affected by the following factors :

- Design (geometry, prefabrication)
- Local boundary conditions (accessibility)
- Material (prestressing rate, prestressing stages, prestressing distance)
- Cutting pattern (direction of span)
- Weather (safety)

Introducing the prestress can be carried out in principle by displacing or folding rigid edges or by pulling at individual points or by tying back flexible edges. These basic principles are can be illustrated by way of the four basic forms: rolling (a) as well as parallel (b), central (c) and circular gathering (d), as shown in Fig. D 1.35. A guyed mast should be positioned such that, if possible, it bisects the angle between the membrane and the guy cable. Furthermore, the angle between the cable and the mast should not be too small because otherwise the guy cable attracts very high forces. The edge and corner details should include appropriate connection options for temporary tensioning elements or equipment in order to introduce the prestress (see "Building with textile membranes", pp. 196–211).

The prestress is introduced successively over a longer period of time, which depends on the particular membrane material. The incremental increase in the prestress up to the desired level that can be retained over the long-term is necessary because of relaxation in the tension over time due to the creep of the material. This process can last several weeks in the case of materials such as PTFE/glass membranes.

The level of the prestress is controlled either geometrically via the target geometry of the positions of fixed points or the lengths of guy cables, or by measuring the force in the tensioning equipment. The prestress in the surface can be tested afterwards with special devices which measure the oscillation behaviour or the tensile resistance of the surface and must be calibrated for the particular material in a laboratory test.

Convertible membrane structures

Convertible or adaptable designs serve as loadbearing structures and are at the same time mechanisms permitting a reversible change in their form. Convertibility is desirable when a roof has to be opened and closed, for example. Potential weather conditions may dictate this requirement, e.g. temporary protection against sunshine or rain.

Owing to the lightness and flexibility of the majority of membrane materials, membrane structures are ideal for temporary and convertible designs. We distinguish between gathering and rolling mechanisms where membrane designs are concerned. The suitability of rolling mechanisms for mechanically prestressed membrane surfaces is limited because the double-curvature form cannot usually be rolled up without wrinkles; gathering mechanisms are therefore more popular. These days, many sports stadiums are roofed over with a membrane that is gathered in the middle (Figs. D 1.36d and D 1.38). In most cases the membrane rolls over rigid rails or wire cables. These should be designed in such a way that the travelling direction coincides with the prestressing direction, so the edge points move away from each other during the travel and transfer the prestress to the surface. Such systems can therefore only be gathered from the periphery to the middle. Gathering in the opposite direction only works when the inner edge points are splayed apart vertically (e.g. flying mast). When opening and closing such a roof, large distances must be covered at high speeds but with minimal forces, whereas the prestressing requires comparatively large forces applied over small tensioning distances. These two steps, opening the roof and tensioning the membrane, are therefore usually carried out by separate systems.

In a system in which the membrane is gathered in parallel folds (Fig. D 1.36b), the prestressing at 90° to the direction of travel can generally be preserved. Such systems have been derived from the traditional Spanish awning (*toldo*) and are initially tensioned through their self-weight only. In order to activate a mechanical prestressing, a *toldo* can be stabilised with alternating ridge and valley cables (Fig. D 1.15, p. 141).

Apart from systems using cables, membranes can also be gathered by means of folding mechanisms (Fig. D 1.37). Fibre-reinforced polymers are ideal for the movable parts of such designs because of their low self-weight. These days, such kinematic mechanisms are calculated with the help of elaborate computer simulations because of the numerous kinematic degrees of freedom.

References:

[1] Engel, Heino: Tragsysteme – Structure Systems. Ostfildern-Ruit, 1999, p. 41

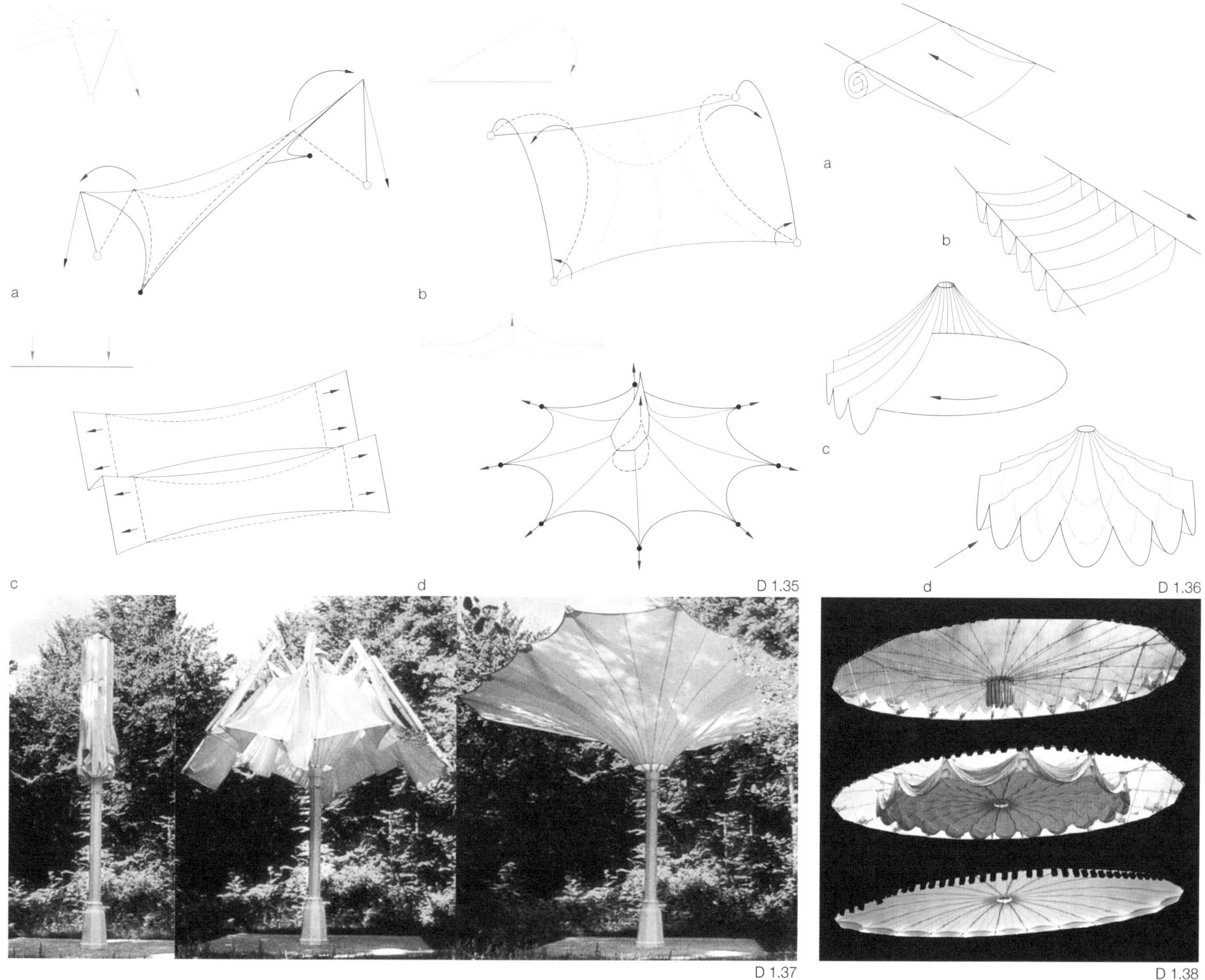

D 1.35

D 1.36

D 1.37

D 1.38

Detailed design aspects

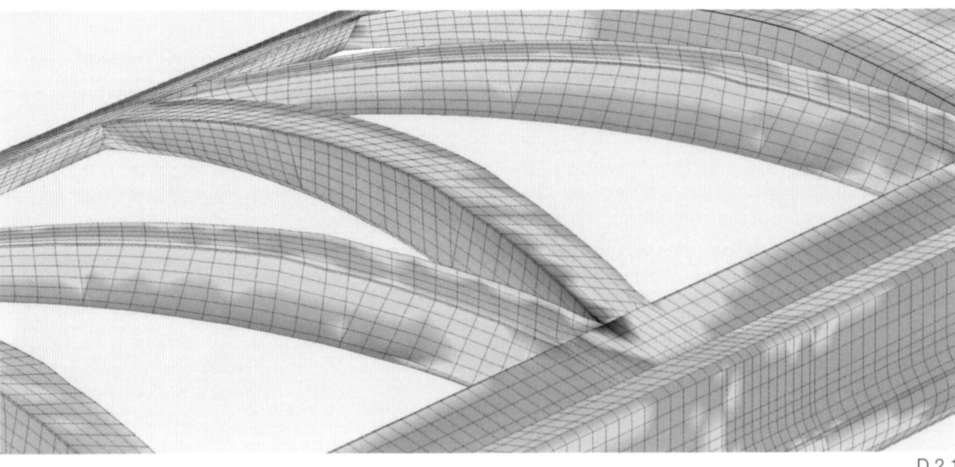

D 2.1

Once the form of a loadbearing structure has been fixed and suitable materials or semi-finished products have been selected, the next step is the vital one of sizing the loadbearing elements to ensure a design best suited to the materials and to enable the detailed design work to begin. This stage of the work involves determining the dimensions of the loadbearing members and also examining the feasibility with respect to the specific boundary conditions of the project. The series of tests required for most applications represent another crucial aspect here because it is normally necessary to check the properties of the polymers or membranes that have been specified prior to commencing work on site. The limitations with respect to processing and quality demands can then be taken into account in preliminary decisions regarding the construction details and the sequence of work on site.

Calculations

The first step is to determine the cross-sections required for the loadbearing polymer and membrane elements and to size the connections. Certain aspects related to the material must be taken into account here. On the one hand, duration of loading, temperature and environmental media have a direct influence on the strength and elastic modulus of synthetic materials and polymer fibres. On the other hand, it is also important to consider the interaction between the fibres and the polymer when using textile membranes and fibre-reinforced polymers because, in contrast to other materials, the behaviour of components with integral fibres is highly dependent on direction. The properties of the material and the distribution of stresses in the component vary depending on the orientation and quantity of the fibres.
Only the characteristics related to the materials which need to be considered when analysing loadbearing structures made from polymers or membranes are considered in the following, together with a brief overview of the most important parameters. The reader should refer to the appropriate standards and recommendations for full information on the structural calculations necessary.

Orientation of fibres

The load-carrying capacity and the distribution of stresses in fibre-reinforced polymers and textile membranes are defined by the types and quantities of the fibres used, their processing forms and orientation. It is the orientation of the fibres that determines the stiffness, or rather the elastic modulus, of a component and hence the alignment of the flow of forces. For example, a greater stiffness can be expected in the longitudinal direction of the fibres.
Semi-finished textile products are always used in a composite form, i.e. given a thermoplastic coating or embedded in a thermosetting resin. The two components function together and perform different structural tasks. Overstretching of the protective polymer must be avoided under load because it can tear, exposing the fibres to the weather.

Fibre-reinforced polymers

Laminates made from fibres and thermosets consist of several plies in which the fibres are arranged in parallel in one direction. The tensile and compressive stresses in the direction of the fibres are resisted by the fibres, whereas the surrounding polymer serves merely as a stabilising medium (Figs. D 2.2a and b). However, transverse loads and shear stresses are carried by the polymer directly (Figs. D 2.2c–e). These latter actions are usually critical because the adhesion between polymer and fibres and the load-carrying capacity of the polymer itself are comparatively low. Delamination of the component, i.e. the loss of the bond between the individual plies, is possible under shear loads.

Textile membranes

The stiffness of a textile membrane material also depends on the direction. Maximum stiffness is generally reserved for the warp direction. The stiffness values in the weft direction are somewhat lower because the weft threads undulate above and below the warp threads as a consequence of the manufacturing process. The shear stiffness of a membrane material depends on its coating, which is generally very low and can be neglected in the case of uncoated fabrics (Fig. D 2.3).

D 2.1 Numerical model of a roof structure made from a fibre-reinforced polymer
D 2.2 Loadbearing behaviour of fibre-reinforced polymers
a Rupture due to tension in the direction of the fibres
b Rupture due to compression in the direction of the fibres
c Inter-fibre failure as a result of shear and lateral tension
d Inter-fibre failure as a result of lateral tension
e Inter-fibre failure as a result of lateral compression
D 2.3 Anisotropic stress–strain behaviour of textile membranes
a Loaded in the warp direction
b Loaded in the weft direction
c Loaded at 45°
d Positions of test specimens cut from the textile membrane
D 2.4 How the duration of loading influences the mechanical properties of polymers
1 Wind, snow ($H \leq 1000$ m), imposed load in places of assembly, traffic on access roads
2 Snow ($H \geq 1000$ m), imposed load in residential and office buildings, traffic on public roads
3 Imposed load in factories, traffic on trunk roads
4 Self-weight
D 2.5 How media classes influence the mechanical properties of thermosets
1 Interior climate
2 Natural weathering
3 Severe UV exposure
D 2.6 How the ambient temperature influences the mechanical properties of polymers

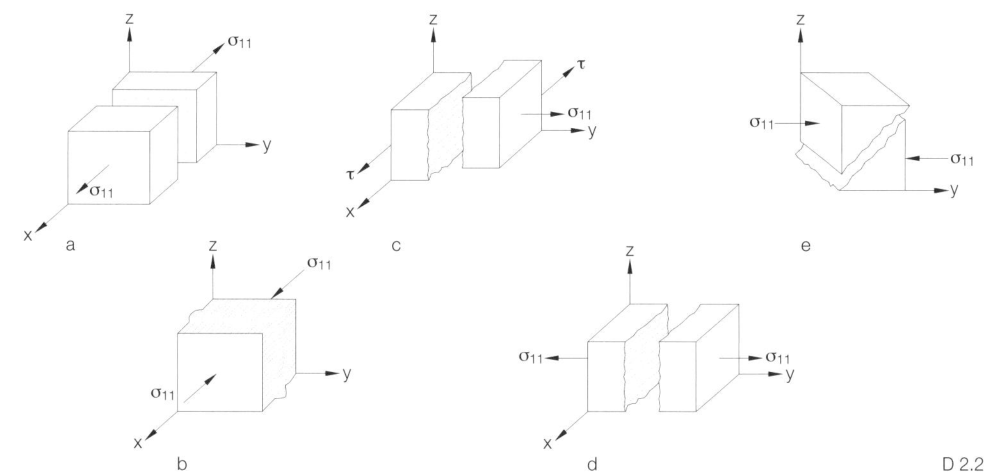

D 2.2

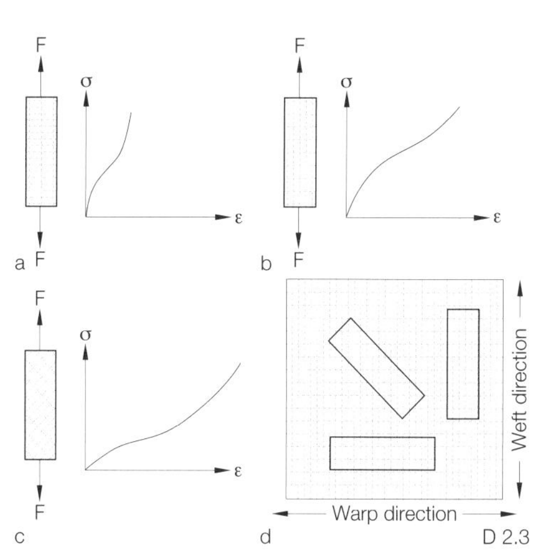

D 2.3

Generally speaking, assessing the stiffness of a membrane for a structural analysis by using a constant elastic modulus is difficult because the stiffness values are very different for uniaxial and biaxial states of stress. Furthermore, the state of stress is dependent on the loading history and the magnitude and duration of external loads acting on the structure. It has been demonstrated, however, that when analysing membrane structures with sufficient geometrical stiffness, the elastic modulus has only a limited influence on the stresses in the membrane. But when calculating deformations, e.g. to check the possibility of ponding for the wind pressure loading case, the elastic modulus is indeed significant.

Factors affecting mechanical parameters

The behaviour of polymers and polymer fibres (synthetic fibres) generally varies over time, i.e. deformations increase (creep) or a prestressed component is relieved (relaxation) in the case of long-term loads (see "Creep, creep rupture strength and relaxation", p. 36). In addition, the strengths of polymers and polymer fibres are lower for permanent loads than they are for brief loads (creep rupture strength). Another aspect is their temperature-dependent behaviour: both the elastic modulus and the strength of a polymer or polymer fibre drop as the ambient temperature rises. Moreover, the mechanical parameters are influenced by damaging media such as water, salt solutions or UV radiation.

Therefore, in contrast to materials such as steel, the period of use and the ambient conditions must be estimated as part of the design procedure. These criteria are incorporated directly in the calculations for the components by way of reduction factors.

Design concept for polymers

How loading conditions such as duration of loading, temperature or environmental media influence the mechanical parameters of polymers and fibre-reinforced polymers is estimated quantitatively via the material safety factor and three further influencing factors:

$$f_d = \frac{f_k}{\gamma_M \cdot A_1 \cdot A_2 \cdot A_3} \quad [1]$$

f_d Design value for strength
f_k Characteristic strength, taken from calculations or tests for short-term loading at room temperature
γ_M Safety factor for polymer or fibre-reinforced polymer
A_1 Influencing factor "duration of loading" (Fig. D 2.4)
A_2 Influencing factor "media class" (Fig. D 2.5)
A_3 Influencing factor "service temperature" (Fig. D 2.6)

The safety factor for unreinforced and manually produced fibre-reinforced polymers is γ_M = 1.5 and for industrially produced materials γ_M = 1.2.

Safety factors for the loads must also be included in the calculations.

Duration of loading

It is not only the magnitude of the loading that is critical, but first and foremost its duration. For example, wind loads occur relatively frequently, but a gust of wind lasts for only a few seconds. If all the gusts of wind over the lifetime of a structure are added together, the result is a relatively short duration and hence a minor influence on the creep rupture strength. However, factors such as self-weight, dead loads and prestressing act constantly on the component throughout its period of use and therefore have a much more significant effect on reducing the mechanical parameters.
The higher the fibre content of a fibre-reinforced polymer, the less pronounced is its behaviour over time because the glass and carbon fibres normally used do not exhibit creep.
Fibre composites exhibit different values for loads parallel with and perpendicular to the direction of the fibres (Fig. D 2.4). Tension in the direction of the fibres is carried almost exclusively by the fibres themselves, which means that the influence of creep is low in this situation. But with loads perpendicular to the fibres or shear forces, it is mainly the polymer that resists the actions and this increases the component's tendency to creep. Compressive forces in the direction of the fibres also lead to high stresses in the polymer because it stabilises the fibres against local buckling.

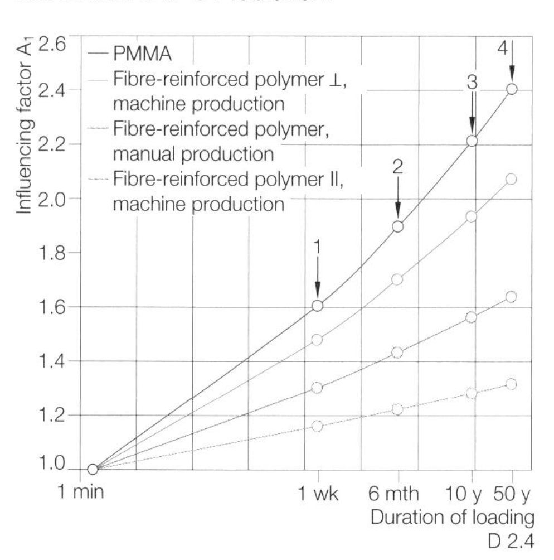

D 2.4

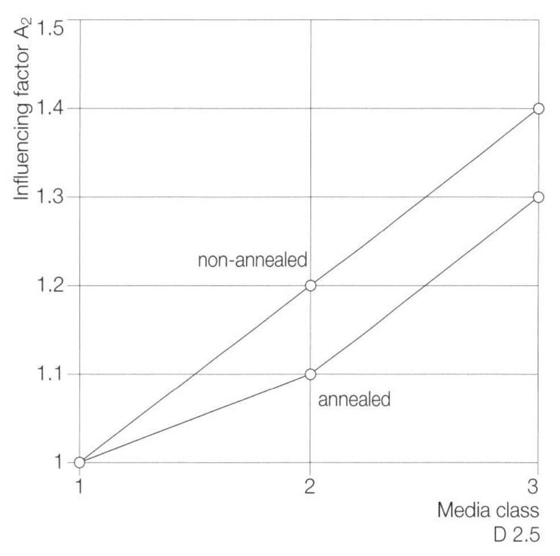

D 2.5

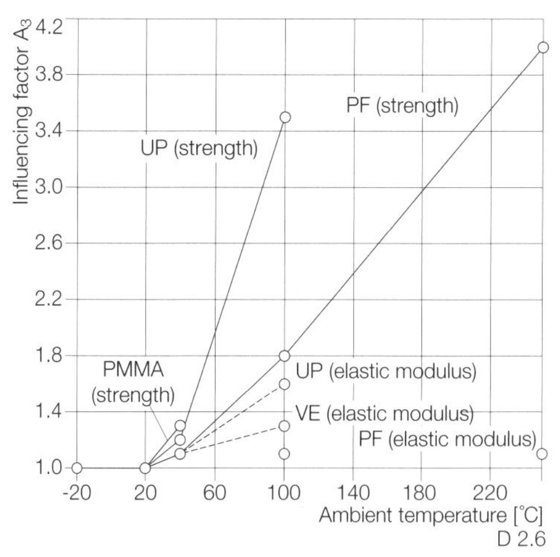

D 2.6

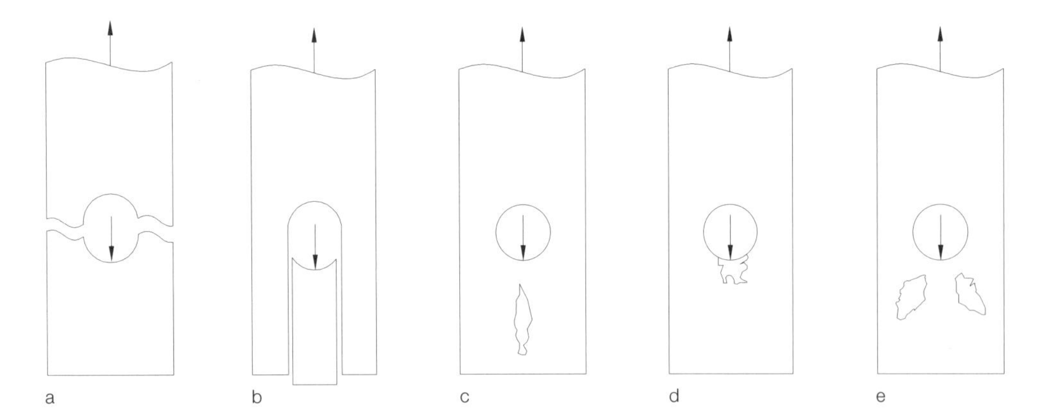

D 2.7

Influence of environmental media
First of all, it is imperative to clarify to what extent a polymer is suitable or otherwise for an application in a certain environment. The thermosets traditionally used for fibre-reinforced polymers are comparatively durable, although constant exposure to the weather can lead to a decline in their mechanical parameters. As polymers react differently to moisture, water or chemicals, the ambient conditions are described by way of "media classes" depending on the potential for causing damage (Fig. D 2.5, p. 151). The heat treatment of fibre-reinforced polymers (annealing) has a positive effect on their resistance to various media. For example, glass fibre-reinforced polymers should be annealed for a maximum of eight days after production for one hour per millimetre laminate thickness at a temperature of 50–100 °C (depending on the resin used).
The embedded fibres themselves exhibit very disparate characteristics: whereas carbon fibres generally exhibit a high chemical resistance, glass fibres can resist acidic media but suffer in alkaline media, especially when the ambient temperature is high at the same time.

Temperature
A polymer loses its load-carrying ability when its maximum service temperature is exceeded. But the strength and elastic modulus of a polymer start to fall even at temperatures well below such a limit. This decrease is reversible as long as the service temperature has not yet been exceeded. The extent to which values of parameters decrease can be estimated quantatively within the scope of the design procedure (Fig. D 2.6, p. 151). It is the compressive strength that suffers especially as a result of high temperatures because the polymer gradually softens and is then at risk of buckling. Whole components or even just certain zones reinforced with longitudinal fibres (rovings) can accommodate tensile forces well above the limits of the application because the polymer in the zones with such fibres does not perform any primary loadbearing function.

Connections for fibre-reinforced polymers
When building with semi-finished polymer products it is mostly the connections that are the critical points in the design. In particular, the bolted or glued loadbearing connections typically used for fibre-reinforced polymers can handle only low forces. Local concentrations of stresses occur in the component and, furthermore, fibre-reinforced polymers can accommodate only comparatively low shear stresses. Bolts can tear through the material, adhesive joints can suffer delamination. The preferred connections for loadbearing components made from fibre-reinforced polymers are described below. The information also applies to unreinforced polymers in principle.

Bolted connections
Detachable connections are generally in the form of bolted connections in shear. The forces that can be transferred via a bolted joint are much lower than the load-carrying capacity of the gross cross-sectional area because the fibre reinforcement in the fibre composite is essentially aligned in one direction and there is a lack of plastic redistribution of stresses. The maximum load-carrying capacity is determined by the potential failure mechanisms (Fig. D 2.7). Besides the tensile failure of the net cross-section (a) or a bearing failure (b) (Fig. D 2.8), the cross-section can also fail as a result of excessive local stress peaks, e.g. tensile splitting (c), local overstresses (d) or diagonal strut (e) failures. Failure mechanism (b) usually governs in fibre-reinforced polymers. A much simplified calculation for the load-carrying capacity of a bolted connection between pultruded fibre-reinforced polymer components, depending on the shear strength of the laminate, is as follows: [2]

$$F_R = 2 \cdot \left(e_1 - \frac{d_0}{2}\right) \cdot t \cdot f_\tau$$

where:
$e_1 \geq 3.5\ d_0$ and $b \geq 4.0\ d_0$

F_R Admissible shear force
t Thickness of laminate
d_0 Diameter of hole

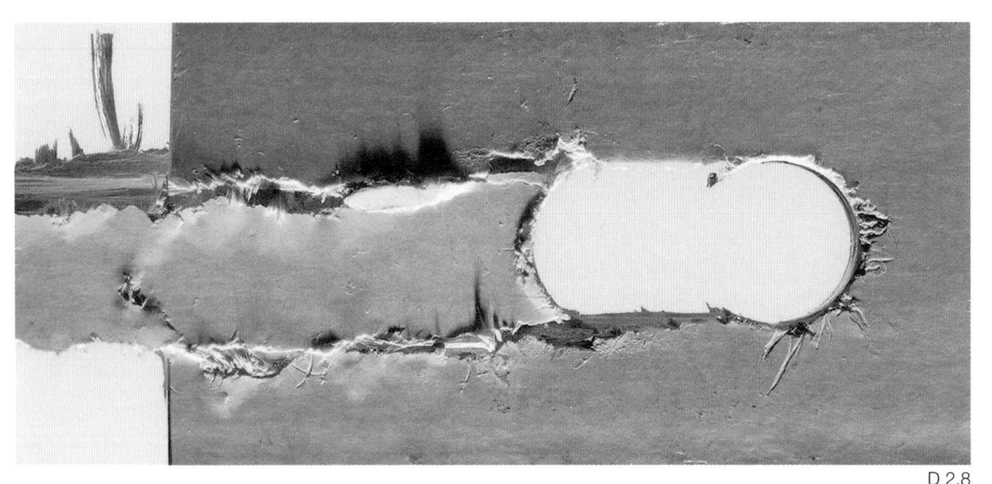

D 2.8

D 2.7 Failure mechanisms for bolted connections
a Tensile failure of the remaining cross-section
b Bearing failure
c Splitting as a result of lateral tensile stresses
d Local overstressing
e Failure of the diagonal struts
D 2.8 Bolted joint in longitudinally fibre-reinforced polymer – bearing failure
D 2.9 How the length of an adhesive joint influences the distribution of the shear stresses
a–c Stress distribution with increasing length of adhesive joint
d Failure mechanism: adhesive starts to peel apart at the edges first
e The stress at the edge hardly decreases with increasing length; the force that can be transmitted therefore hardly increases, either.
D 2.10 Adhesive joint in longitudinally fibre-reinforced polymer – failure in component

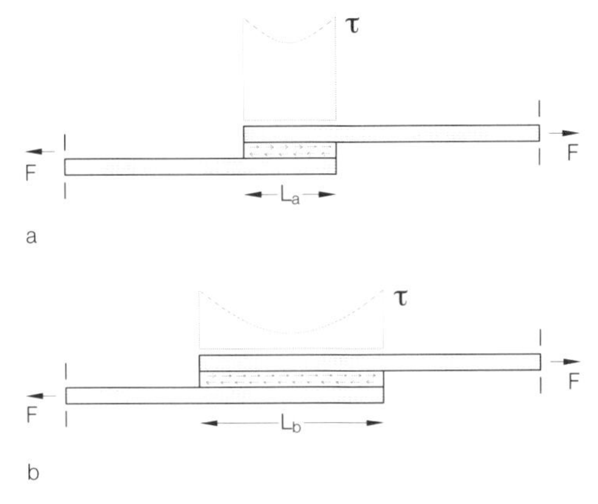

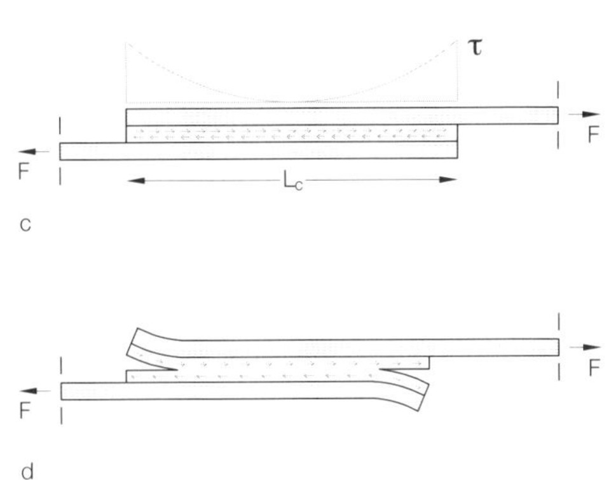

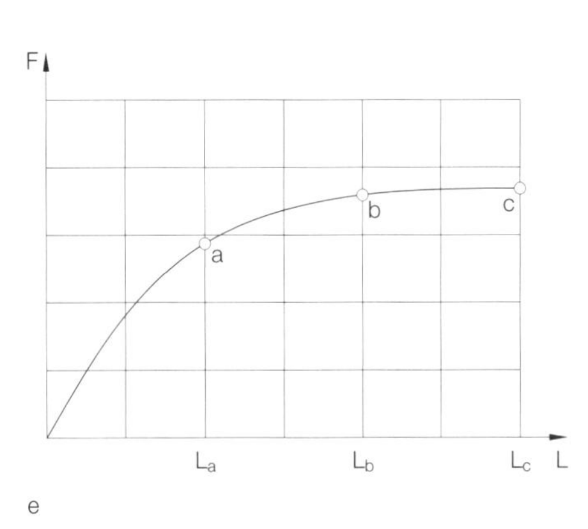

D 2.9

e_1 Edge distance in direction of force
b Width of laminate
f_τ Admissible shear stress in direction of force (determined in tests or taken from manufacturer's data)

The admissible shear stress of a pultruded cross-section is approx. $f_\tau = 25$ N/mm². With $e_1 = 3.5 \cdot d_0$ and $b = 4.0 \cdot d_0$, this results in an admissible shear force of $F_R = 150$ N/mm² $\cdot\, t \cdot d_0$. Assuming a bolt with a diameter of 10 mm and a pultruded GFRP component with 10 mm wall thickness, this corresponds to a force of 15 kN. This value must be reduced by the safety and other factors.

Glued connections
Gluing is a method of jointing that is very much suited to polymers and fibre-reinforced polymers which guarantees a load transfer over a certain area. In principle, a glued connection can fail by one of the following three mechanisms:
- Cohesive failure of the adhesive (failure of the adhesive substance)
- Adhesive failure between glue and component (loss of adhesion between the two materials)
- Failure of the component in shear (failure of the material or delamination of the fibre composite; Fig. D 2.10)

What all three failure mechanisms have in common is that besides the mechanical properties of the adhesive, it is also the dimensions of the connected components, or the internal structure of the fibre composite, that are critical for the distribution of stresses in the adhesive joint. Local stress concentrations cause the adhesive joint to fail first, and the crack propagates over the entire adhesive joint. Increasing the length of the adhesive joint in the direction of the force, and thus increasing the area of the adhesive, hardly improves the load-carrying capacity because it is the peak stresses at the start and end of the joint that determine the load-carrying capacity, and only relatively low stresses prevail in the middle zone (Fig. D 2.9).
The load-carrying capacity of the connection is also determined by the characteristics of the mating surfaces. The theoretical analysis of the load-carrying capacity of a glued joint therefore depends on many influencing factors and can only be carried out for the component as a whole. Various adhesives can be used for glued joints in building (see "Adhesives", pp. 54–57). In connections between components made from fibre-reinforced polymers it is not generally the adhesive joint itself that fails, but rather the adhesion between the individual plies of the composite component because of the low interlaminar shear strength in the components themselves. The interaction relationship given below has been confirmed in several series of tests. It describes the relationship between the utilisation of the shear and axial stress capabilities at one point of the glued surface. [3]

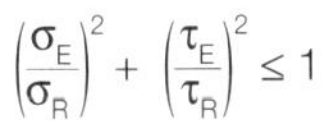

$$\left(\frac{\sigma_E}{\sigma_R}\right)^2 + \left(\frac{\tau_E}{\tau_R}\right)^2 \leq 1$$

σ_E Tensile stress acting perpendicular to adhesive joint
σ_R Admissible tensile stress perpendicular to adhesive joint
τ_E Shear stress acting parallel with adhesive joint
τ_R Admissible shear stress parallel with adhesive joint

Stresses of approx. $\sigma_R = 1.0$ N/mm² and $\tau_R = 8.0$ N/mm² are possible with common pultruded sections, which with an adhesive joint measuring 4 × 5 cm on plan equates to a shear force of 16 kN. As with bolted connections, the admissible stresses must be reduced by the safety and other factors.

Design concept for textile membranes
As the majority of textile membranes are made from synthetic fibres (in some cases with a polymer coating), the methods of analysis are similar to those already described for polymer designs. In addition to the duration of loading, temperature and other ambient conditions, it is also necessary to take into account production- and design-related influences such as details at seams or edges.
The following factors have an influence on the strengths of membranes and foils:
- Magnitude and duration of loads
- Ambient temperature and fluctuations thereof
- Age
- Seam details
- Creep behaviour of fibres and coatings
- Production methods and the ensuing tolerances
- Environmental influences

How these factors affect the strength depends on the material used, the design of the seams between sections of material, the size of the structure and the intended period of use. Consequently, it is difficult to define a unified design method that is right for all membrane materials and types of construction. Various methods are in use in Europe, North America and Japan, and these include different values for the various in-

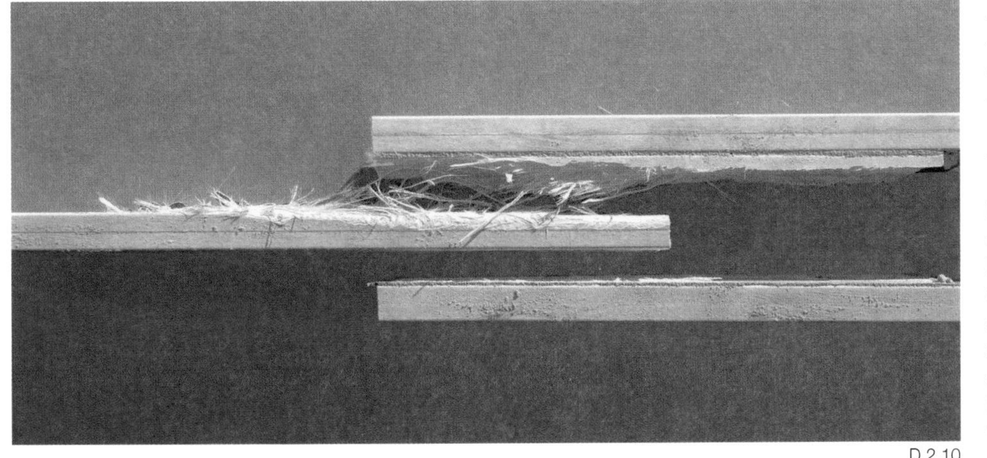

D 2.10

fluencing factors which are combined to form one safety factor for different loading cases. As a rule, these values are 3–4 for short-term loads (e.g. wind) and 5–7 for long-term loads (e.g. prestress). Despite the different design methods, there is reasonable agreement between the safety factors that have been determined.

There is no regulated design concept for foils and membranes in Germany. The only standard available is DIN 4134 "Air-supported structures; structural design, construction and operation". This document cannot be used directly for foil cushions or mechanically prestressed membranes, but does form the basis for a modern design method employing reduction factors. The method was developed at the Institute of Plastics Processing, RWTH Aachen University, and is based on data obtained empirically from tests on the customary membrane materials PTFE/glass and polyester-PVC. Here, the dissertation by Jörg Minte still forms an important basis for the procedure and the determination of the reduction factors. These factors decrease the permissible stresses and increase the applied loads. The permissible stresses f_d are calculated as follows:

$$f_d = \frac{f_k}{\gamma_m \cdot A_i} \text{ [N/5 cm]}$$

f_d Design value for stress [N/50 mm]
f_k Uniaxial tensile strength to DIN EN ISO 1421 [N/5 cm]
γ_m Safety factor (1.4 for surfaces, 1.5 for connections)
A_i Combination of reduction factors depending on application and loading case

The uniaxial tensile strength is measured on a strip 5 cm wide, the individual reduction factors are based on tests. The following classification is used:

$A_0 = 1.0–1.2$
Reduction factor for taking into account the influence of multi-axial (biaxial) stress states that reduce the strength with respect to that for a uniaxial condition.

$A_1 = 1.6–1.7$
Reduction factor for taking into account the influence of long-term loading effects that reduce the strength.

$A_2 = 1.1–1.2$
Reduction factor for environmental effects (media, radiation, etc.) that reduce the strength.

$A_3 = 1.1–1.25$
Reduction factor for high temperatures.

The following safety factors are proposed for the applied loads in typical loading combinations:

Permanent load:	$1.0 \cdot G + 1.3 \cdot P$
Winter storm:	$1.0 \cdot G + 1.1 \cdot P + 1.6 \cdot W$
Summer storm:	$1.0 \cdot G + 1.1 \cdot P + 0.7 \cdot W$
Maximum snow:	$1.0 \cdot G + 1.1 \cdot P + 1.5 \cdot S$

P Prestress
G Self-weight
W Wind load
S Snow load

In order to take proper account of unforeseen stress peaks during erection, the designer is advised to check a loading case with an increased prestress, e.g. erection: $1.0 \cdot G + 2 \cdot P$.

Testing and approval

Some products, such as textile membranes, foil or acrylic or polycarbonate sheets, were specially developed and tested for building applications. Frequently, however, the manufacturers involved in the production of components made from polymers do not work exclusively for the building industry. On the one hand, therefore, the suitability of the products for particular applications must be confirmed by testing and, on the other hand, the manufacturers must become involved in the procedures specific to the building industry.
There are no membranes or polymers on the market that are universally approved and standardised as building materials. In many cases it is therefore necessary to carry out tests on such materials in advance of their use in order to ascertain whether a material is suitable for the intended application and the products supplied by a manufacturer comply with the technical specification.
The actual approval procedures vary considerably from country to country. In some instances it is up to the discretion of the client to decide what demands are being placed on components and how these are to be tested; in other cases an official approval from a certain authority must be obtained or the engineer responsible for checking the structural calculations will ask for appropriate proof. Approval is not usually required for non-loadbearing components where failure represents no danger to users.
In Germany all loadbearing components made from polymers must be approved. Such an approval can be in the form of a general approval for a product (National Technical Approval, abZ) or a limited approval that is obtained during the scope of and applies to just one construction project (Individual Approval, ZiE). The latter is issued by the senior building authority in the federal state in which the project is located. Application for an approval is requested informally from the appropriate authority by the client or the client's representative. The authority then either agrees to the expert proposed by the client or will itself propose an expert to be responsible for the approval. Following successful tests, an Individual Approval (ZiE) can be granted.
A National Technical Approval (abZ) for products produced in series is issued by the German Institute of Building Technology (Deutsches Institut für Bautechnik, DIBt) based in Berlin. The boundary conditions for this approval procedure are more general, not related to any particular project. The application procedure and the tests and calculations required are considerably more comprehensive than those required for an Individual Approval. A number of approvals for CFRP laminates for strengthening building components have already been issued in Germany and one approval for pultruded GFRP sections is in preparation. National Technical Approvals also stipulate boundary conditions with which an application must comply, e.g. restricted to non-dynamic loads, compulsory additional products such as adhesives,

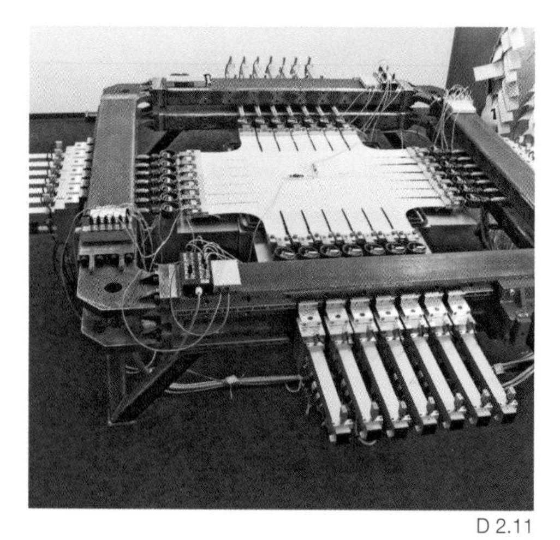
D 2.11

D 2.12

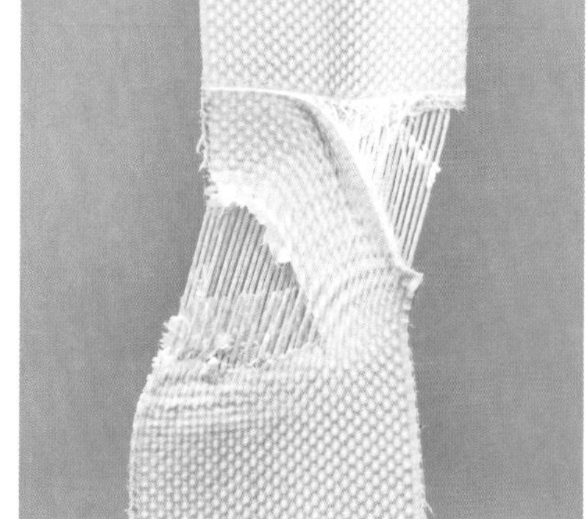
D 2.13

Test series	Size of specimen[1] [mm]	Quantity	Standard
Tensile strength	250 × 25 × t	5	DIN EN ISO 527
Bending strength	300 × 30 × t	5	DIN EN ISO 14125
Compressive strength	125 × 25 × t	5	DIN EN ISO 14126
Interlaminar shear strength	200 × 25 × t	10	DIN EN ISO 14130
Shear strength	250 × 25 × t	5	DIN EN ISO 14129
Strength of connections	variable	3	none
Storage underwater	300 × 100 × t	5	none
Freeze-thaw cycles	300 × 100 × t	5	DIN EN 1367-1
Temperature, dynamic	1000 × 100 × t	5	DIN EN ISO 899
Accelerated weathering	130 × 45 × t	5	DIN EN ISO 4892
Dynamic load	300 × 100 × t	5	DIN 53442
Fire test	250 × 90 × t	2 × 3[2]	DIN EN 13501-1, EN ISO 11925-2, EN 13823, EN ISO 1716, EN ISO 1182

[1] Recommended values, depending on thickness of laminate (t)
[2] For EN ISO 11925-2a only

D 2.14

Test	Standard international	Standard national
Tensile strength	EN ISO 1421	DIN 53354
Elongation at rupture	EN ISO 1421	
Tear propagation resistance	EN ISO 4674-2	DIN 53363
Creep Relaxation	EN ISO 899-1	
Adhesion of coating	EN ISO 2411	DIN 53357

D 2.15

working procedures, etc. Where these conditions are satisfied, the approved product can be used without the need for any further approval or testing.

Membranes

An Individual Approval (ZiE) is required for any structure employing a membrane or foil. To obtain this, a series of tests is carried out on material produced specifically for the particular construction project. Tests are performed to ascertain the uniaxial tensile strengths of the material itself and the seams in the warp and weft directions, possibly supplemented by biaxial tests (see "Strain stiffness", p. 105).
The biaxial state of stress in a membrane has a considerable influence on its stiffness and strength. Special machines have therefore been developed for the biaxial testing of samples of material, welded seams and connection details (Figs. D 2.11 and D 2.12). Slitting the sample of material at the sides and clamping the resulting separate strips in the jaws of the testing machine guarantee the homogeneous introduction of the tensile force.
To ascertain the maximum state of stress under external loads, in which the stress in one direction of the fabric is often much greater than in the other direction, the tensile strengths in the warp and weft directions are tested separately in uniaxial testing machines. The strengths of seams are also tested uniaxially transverse to the seam (Fig. D 2.13).
Every batch of membrane material used in a project must be tested for an Individual Approval (ZiE). A testing institute approved by the DIBt determines the uniaxial tensile strengths in the warp and weft directions at room temperature (23 °C) and at a higher temperature (70 °C) according to DIN 53354 or EN ISO 1421 (Fig. D 2.15). Strips of material 50 mm wide are normally used for the tests; however, some samples 100 mm wide are tested in order to minimise the extent to which manufacturing tolerances and the number of fibres in the fabric could affect the results.
In addition to testing the material itself and connections such as stitched or welded seams, the tear propagation resistance is also tested in some instances by way of uniaxial and biaxial tests. However, this value is often simply specified by the manufacturer and testing within the scope of the approval is not compulsory.

Creep and relaxation behaviour

The creep and relaxation behaviour of textile membranes and foils can vary considerably depending on the backing material, the coating and the magnitude of the permanent loads (prestress). Important to mention are the high creep figures of PTFE coatings and PTFE threads. The exact creep and relaxation values are determined in uniaxially tensioned samples in fatigue strength tests.

Reaction to fire

The combustibility of textile membranes essentially depends on their coatings, and that of foils depends on the foil itself. Most membrane materials can achieve class B1 to DIN 4102 or DIN EN 13501. Each material is tested for its flammability, smoke development and formation of droplets.

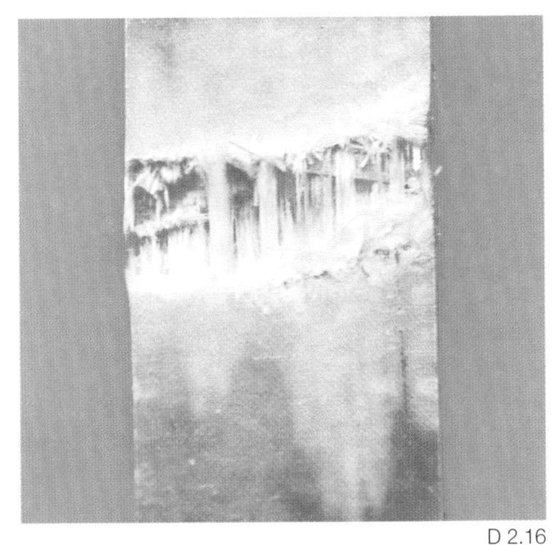

D 2.16

D 2.17

D 2.11 Biaxial tensile test on material
D 2.12 Biaxial tensile test on laced seam
D 2.13 Uniaxial tensile test on welded joint
D 2.14 Relevant testing standards for assessing polymers and fibre-reinforced polymers
D 2.15 Relevant testing standards for assessing foils and membranes
D 2.16 Tensile test on a manually laminated GFRP
D 2.17 Three-point bending test for determining the short-term strength of polymers of fibre-reinforced polymers

Polymers

Universally applicable standards for materials and quality directives, as are available for structural steelwork or concrete or masonry, for example, have not yet been published for polymers or fibre-reinforced polymers. The suitability of a material for a particular requirements profile, including its long-term behaviour, must be investigated in every individual case. Fig. D 2.14 (p. 155) shows an example of the series of tests recommended for investigating fibre-reinforced polymers.

Mechanical properties (short-term strength)

The basic variables required for structural calculations (tensile, compressive, shear and bending properties) are first tested at room temperature without the application of any external actions in short-term tests (Figs. D 2.16 and D 2.17, p. 155). Five small specimens (cut from the laminate) for each parameter are often adequate for machine-made components. But for manually laminated components, a wider scatter of the characteristic values can be expected, depending on the position in the laminate or the particular batch, and so in this case several series each consisting of five tests are recommended. It is important to test samples from different areas, e.g. at the overlaps between reinforcing mats or at small radii.

Durability with respect to environmental influences

Environmental conditions such as temperature or the weather have an effect not only on the mechanical properties of a polymer, but also on the quality of its surface. For architectural applications this is frequently just as important as guaranteeing the load-carrying capacity. As buildings and structures are used for a much longer length of time than other everyday artefacts or vehicles, the figures required are frequently unavailable and therefore have to be estimated through experiments.
Such tests often help in selecting the polymer or the surface coating best suited to a particular application.

Storage underwater

The specimens are stored underwater for several days. The surfaces of painted components should be scratched first in order to simulate potential damage. Following the period of immersion, the mechanical and visual or optical effects of the underwater storage are investigated. The specimens may lose some of their strength or their visual appearance or optical properties may be impaired by the formation of blisters or discolouration.

Freeze-thaw cycles and temperature loads

The performance of surface coatings, e.g. painting, can be investigated in a freeze-thaw cycle test, which involves immersing a sample alternately in icy water and hot water. The abrupt change in temperature can lead to cracking of the coating or to the coating becoming detached from the backing material.
In addition, the material should be subjected to high and low temperatures in order to determine whether and to what extent such cycles affect the strength and elastic modulus. This also enables the maximum service temperature to be ascertained.

Accelerated weathering

Accelerated weathering tests are employed to estimate how moisture, temperature and UV radiation affect a polymer. The specimens are tested in a climatic test chamber (Fig. D 2.20) in which three environmental conditions are varied over a cycle lasting, for instance, more than 1000 hours. Afterwards, the specimens are tested or examined to establish how such conditions have affected their mechanical, visual or optical properties.
It should be noted, however, that a direct correlation between accelerated and natural weathering is impossible. Instead, the tests can only provide estimations of tendencies and provide a means of selecting the product best suited to the respective location from a range of products. Spray tests are normally used for assessing the resistance to de-icing salts (see "Weathering resistance", p. 55).

Dynamic loads

Dynamic loads such as vibrations or impacts can lead to fatigue failures. Adequate fatigue strength must be guaranteed for structures or bridges susceptible to vibration. The fatigue strength is determined by way of dynamic testing. For painted components in particular, it is also important to investigate whether the coating can accommodate the strains that ensue or whether visible cracking occurs.

Fire tests

The combustibility of a polymer is frequently a critical factor for a building application. Fire class B to DIN EN 13501, which is frequently specified for buildings, can only be achieved with selected materials or components. The fire resistance requirements should therefore always be established right at the start of the planning phase. The tests for verifying class B are very wide in their scope: besides combustibility, the resulting energy, the development of smoke and fumes and the occurrence of (flaming) droplets must all be assessed. A fire class is seldom specified for a civil engineering structure.

Load-carrying capacities of connections

Three tests are generally sufficient but these must be carried out on full-size mock-ups of the actual connections. The load-carrying capacity of a connection depends not only on the mechanical properties of the bolts or the adhesive, but also on those of the laminate, plus the geometry and the combination of the applied loads.

Quality control and industrial safety

All the members of the design team should be conversant with the fundamental principles of quality control and industrial safety with respect to site supervision duties and the coordination of health and safety matters. A quality assurance plan must be drawn up for the individual project in consultation with the manufacturer.

Manufacturing quality and erection

Whereas membrane and foil materials comply with standards of quality that are very consistent, the fabrication, transport and erection operations can lead to considerable damage to materials. Folding for shipping can result in broken fibres in the material (especially in glass-fibre fabrics), which sometimes do not become obvious until after a long period of exposure to the weather.

D 2.18 Permanent damage to the glass fibres by folding a PTFE/glass membrane twice
D 2.19 Irregularities in a glass fibre-reinforced polymer caused during production; the textile inlay is not in its proper position, is wavy instead.
D 2.20 Climatic test chamber for accelerated weathering
D 2.21 The use of adhesive over a very large area with a template for controlling the thickness
D 2.22 Drilling through a glass fibre-reinforced polymer section

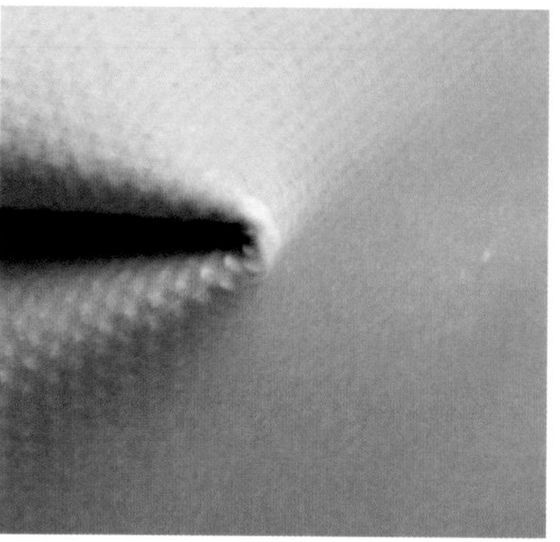

D 2.18

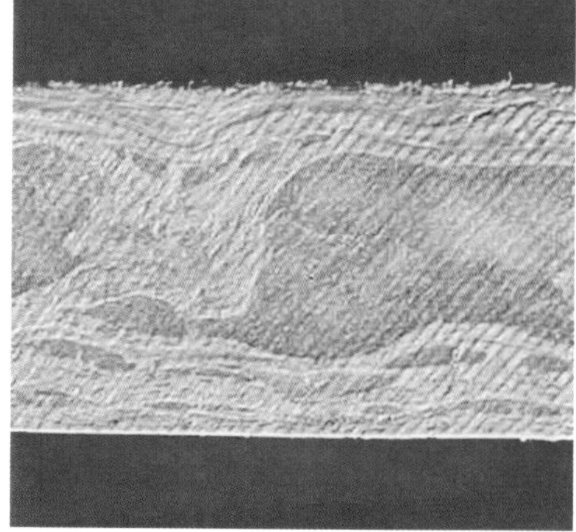

D 2.19

It is therefore very important to transport and erect membrane materials susceptible to flex cracking, e.g. PTFE/glass and ETFE foil, without folds or creases. Folding twice is especially problematic because it involves very tight radii (Fig. D 2.18).
During erection, members of the erection crew may only wear soft, clean footwear when walking on the membrane, and all workers must be secured by safety harnesses or other measures. Semi-finished thermoplastic products are manufactured in factories and are therefore subject to only minor quality fluctuations. In fibre composites, however, the properties can sometimes vary quite considerably. During their production it is important to carry out continuous monitoring with respect to the following criteria:
- Dimensional deviations
- Fibre reinforcement orientation, fibre content and saturation of the fibres by the matrix (polymer)
- The surface characteristics of the laminate

Industrial methods of manufacture such as pultrusion are always subjected to tighter production tolerances than manual methods such as hand lay-up. But even in industrial methods, irregularities in the orientation of the fibres can occur, e.g. areas with insufficient saturation of the fibres or foreign matter inclusions (Fig. D 2.19). Burning off the matrix in a furnace enables the fibre reinforcement to be revealed for examination.
Flaws such as air pockets in the matrix itself must be determined by non-destructive means, i.e. on the intact specimen, e.g. by way of ultrasonic testing or by measuring the thermal transmittance. This latter method involves heating the material on one side with a flash of light and determining the thermal transmittance by means of thermography in order to localise flaws or irregularities.
The surface characteristics are important for ensuring that the fibres have adequate protection against environmental influences. Severe shrinkage of the matrix can lead to the appearance of cracks in the surface during curing. A flawed or unsealed surface can eventually lead to the formation of blisters. In both cases the problem areas must either be replaced or repaired.

Maintenance and repairs

Loadbearing structures made from polymers should be maintained at regular intervals in order to detect the following changes in good time:
- Mechanical damage
- Visible cracks in the laminate
- Swelling and blisters
- Severe deformations and bulges

The recommendation is to replace areas of mechanical damage, or at least to repair them by providing a new, undamaged surface. Cracks are an indication of either errors during production (shrinkage cracks) or excessive loads. Areas that have absorbed a high amount of water must certainly be replaced. Exposed cut edges can absorb water and so all such edges must be sealed. This also applies to openings cut at a later date and to drilled holes.
Any flaws in the coating to a membrane must always be repaired.

Health and safety advice

Industrial safety during the fabrication of membrane materials is not normally a critical area. Only during the processing of PTFE-coated membranes is it important to ensure good ventilation at the place of work because poisonous fumes can be released during welding. For this reason, smoking must be prohibited in all areas where membrane materials containing fluoropolymers such as ETFE and PTFE are in use because otherwise the PTFE dust could be burned in a cigarette, leading to the inhalation of the ensuing toxic smoke.

Fibres with a length > 5 μm and a diameter < 3 μm can be inhaled and penetrate the tissue of the lungs. Carbon fibres are therefore produced as standard with a diameter > 7 μm; glass fibres have a much larger diameter anyway (Fig. B 2.10, p. 50). During cutting and machining operations, both types of fibre break transversely and therefore maintain their diameter and are not respirable. However, the polymer matrix can decompose into smaller particles while it is being worked and lead to itching and to irritation of mucus membranes. Dust from cutting and grinding operations should therefore always be suppressed with water or extracted immediately at source.
Various protective measures can be considered for working with polymers:
- Special clothing to protect skin and mucous membranes
- Dust extraction equipment
- Tools with water sprays to bind dust, or water jet cutting

Water that contains dust should be disposed of in airtight containers immediately after completing the work. Storing the dust in containers is not really advisable because the water evaporates and the remaining dust could then be inhaled again.

References:

[1] Bundesvereinigung der Prüfingenieure für Bautechnik e.V.: BÜV-Empfehlung, Tragende Kunststoffbauteile im Bauwesen (TKB). Berlin, 2010, p. 28 (www.bvpi.de/bvpi-content/ingenieur-box/richtlinien/richtlinien.htm; 26 Aug 2010)
[2] Oppe, Matthias: Zur Bemessung geschraubter Verbindungen von pultrudierten faserverstärkten Polymerprofilen. Dissertation. RWTH Aachen 2008. In: Schriftenreihe Stahlbau, No. 66, p. 77
[3] Vallée, Till: Adhesively bonded lap joints of pultruded GFRP shapes. Dissertation. Composite Construction Laboratory (CCLAB), EPFL Lausanne, 2003, p. 78

D 2.20

D 2.21

D 2.22

Part E Building with polymers and membranes

Fig. E Roof covering to a shopping centre in the form of air-filled ETFE cushions, Amadora (P), 2009, Promontorio Architects

Building with semi-finished polymer products

E 1.1

Building with semi-finished products made from polymers or fibre-reinforced polymers means, first and foremost, selecting suitable components and suitable connections between them. However, the use of prefabricated semi-finished products does limit the design freedoms. Prefabricated semi-finished products are normally less expensive than individual, tailor-made components and require little planning input. Such components are therefore preferred for economic reasons when building with polymers. In contrast to designs employing free-form elements (see "Building with free-form polymers", pp. 174–187), semi-finished products are simply added together in order to create buildings and structures. To do this, they are worked, e.g. cut to length, drilled, or in some cases even shaped, within the scope of their assembly or erection. So the choice of connections and the design of the connection details are critical aspects. It is not necessary to distinguish between polymers and fibre-reinforced polymers for the majority of basic details, and therefore the term "polymer" is used to cover both groups of materials on the following pages.

Design principles

Polymers can be cut, drilled and glued, welded, too, in some cases, with simple tools. However, cutting through fibre-reinforced polymers means interrupting the protective outer layers. The ensuing cut edges can absorb water and so must be sealed afterwards.
The detailing of joints and junctions can frequently be carried out directly on the building site. Some semi-finished products already include integral push-fit or clip-in connections that enable easy assembly without the need for further materials or components. Standardised means of connection such as screws, bolts, rivets or adhesives are often used. For fibre-reinforced polymers in particular, pin-type fasteners frequently lead to unsatisfactory results because, compared with other materials such as steel, only relatively low loads can be transferred across such joints. Glued joints generally result in connections with a high load-carrying capacity and should therefore always be preferred. However, they are not approved for all types of application.

Thermal expansion

The coefficients of thermal expansion of unreinforced polymers are much higher than those of glass and most metals. Expansion joints of adequate width must be provided where a construction has to be supported free from restraint. The coefficients of thermal expansion of fibre-reinforced polymers are lower, depending on the nature, orientation and proportion of fibres in the material. Polymers reinforced with carbon fibres can be adjusted during production so that they do not expand at all as the temperature rises.
The high thermal expansion does not necessarily lead to high restraint stresses because polymers are comparatively resilient. Therefore, in some circumstances zero-restraint supports are unnecessary. Comparing the mechanical parameters of various polymers (Fig. E 1.6), we see that polymers have relatively high tensile strengths but low elastic moduli. In bars or sheets restrained at both ends, restraint stresses occur in the material as a result of a change in temperature. These stresses depend on the elastic modulus of the material as well as its coefficient of thermal expansion. And the degree of utilisation can be calculated by comparing these stresses with the admissible stresses. The degree of utilisation in turn indicates the behaviour of the material if it is not able to expand, and, in theory, at a value of 100 % it breaks. For example, unreinforced polymers can be utilised to maximum of 17 % with a temperature difference of 50 K, glass fibre-reinforced polymers to a maximum of 21 %. Float glass, on the other hand, exhibits a stress utilisation of 70 % in this case, i.e. more than four times that of acrylic sheet.
However, this simplified derivation cannot be directly transferred to real structures; material safety factors and the effect of long-term loads must be considered as well. In addition, components can buckle or warp at even quite low loads, or the means of connection might fail. With a temperature of 20 °C at the time of installation, a temperature difference of 50 K corresponds to a maximum component temperature of 70 °C, but this value can also be exceeded under real boundary conditions.

Means of connection

The choice of a suitable means of connection represents a compromise between optimising the transfer of forces and the robustness and reliability of the design. Another aspect that must be considered for temporary structures in particular is the detachability of the connection. Essentially permanent connections such as gluing, grouting or welding often permit the design of high-strength, inconspicuous connections, which also provide a sealing function at the joint. However, they also call for greater accuracy during fabrication and in most cases are irreversible. It is for these reasons that pin-type connections still tend to dominate. Many polymers, and fibre-reinforced polymers in particular, are, however, less ductile than, for example, steel and so bolts, screws and rivets tend to be unsatisfactory. The development of methods of connection that do justice to the material is still ongoing, however, and many current connection details for semi-finished products have been borrowed from steel or timber engineering.

Pin-type fasteners

Connections employing bolts, screws or rivets are easily assembled, are easy to check, and are reliable. They can be readily used on the building site and even completed in inclement weather conditions. Apart from a few thermoplastics, most of the polymers used in architecture are brittle. Redistribution of the stress concentrations that occur around pin-type fasteners is therefore limited, and that is why a large number of fasteners is frequently required for one connection. Drilling holes severs the fibres of fibre-reinforced polymers and therefore, unlike with metals, an even transfer of the load around the hole is impossible. In addition, drilling weakens the protective surface layer, which makes the connection susceptible to moisture and requires the subsequent application of a sealing material. Suitably resistant fasteners, e.g. made from stainless steel, should be used in order to match the good weathering resistance of polymers.

Bolts

Bolted connections carry the loads via shear stresses and the diameter of the bolt tends to be related to the thickness of the components being joined. A simple lap joint results in an eccentric connection and hence an additional moment at the connection plus an obvious visual offset (Fig. E 1.9a). Bending one of the components at the connection at least overcomes the visual offset problem, but the local bending moment still remains (Fig. E 1.9b). It is better to use splice plates to create a symmetrical joint (Fig. E 1.9c). Bending the edges of the components through 90° or including a steel angle in the joint can make such a bolted connection less conspicuous (on one side anyway, see Figs. E 1.9d and e). However, the forces that can be transferred across such a connection are lower than those of an axial connection because the splicing components are subjected to bend-

1 Cap for screw
2 Capping piece
3 Special screw
4 Sealing washer
5 Corrugated sheet

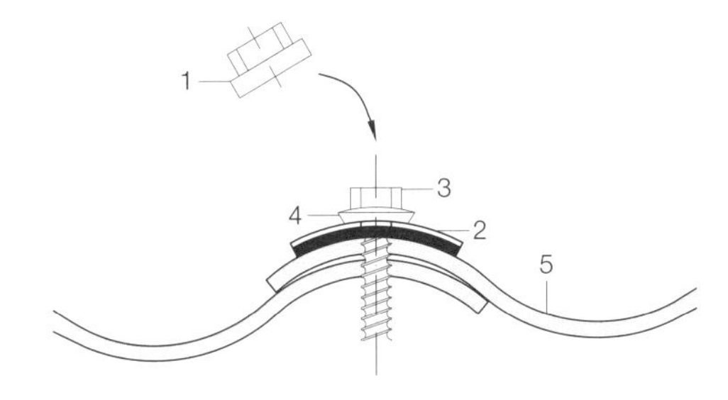

E 1.2

E 1.3

1 Polymer component
2 Shaft of solid rivet
3 Collar
4 Break point
5 Body of blind rivet
6 Mandrel head retained in rivet
7 Preformed head
8 Head formed in situ

a

b

c

E 1.4

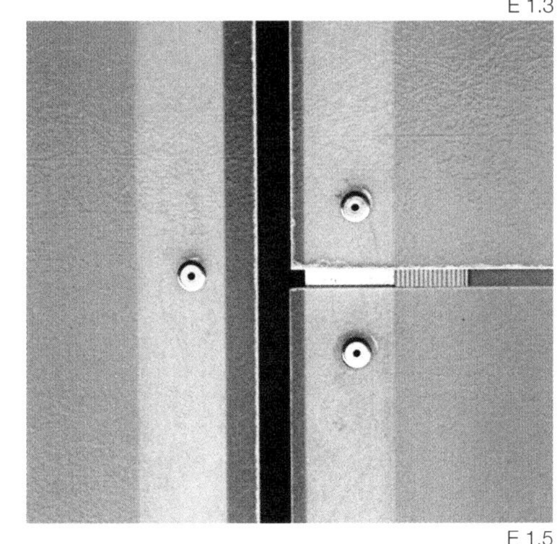

E 1.5

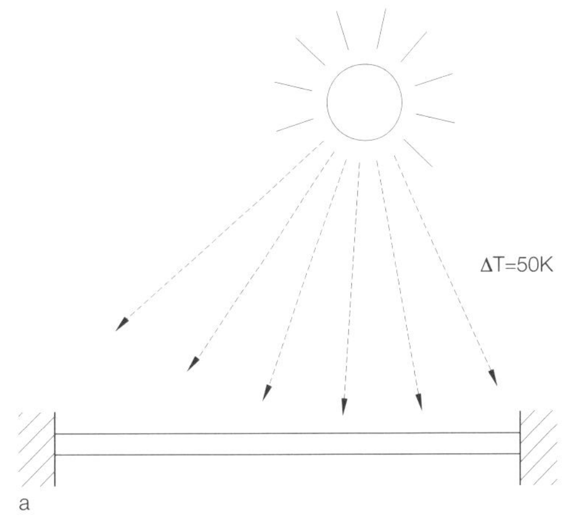

a

E 1.1 Polycarbonate facade to production building, Bobingen (D), 1999, Florian Nagler Architekten
E 1.2 Screw fixing for corrugated sheets
E 1.3 Polymer facade with screwed corrugated sheets
E 1.4 Various riveted connections
a Rivet nut
b Blind rivet
c Traditional countersunk solid rivet
E 1.5 Polymer facade with riveted sheets
E 1.6 Degree of utilisation η of various materials as a result of a temperature difference of 50 K with expansion in the longitudinal direction restricted
a Schematic diagram
b Guidance values for various materials for determining the risk of temperature-induced restraint stresses

Material		Tensile/yield strength (typical value) f_k [N/mm²]	Elastic modulus (typical value) E [N/mm²]	Coefficient of thermal expansion α_T [10^{-6}/K]	Degree of utilisation[1] η [%]
PMMA		63	2600	80	17
Polycarbonate		66	2250	65	11
GFRP, pultruded	longitudinal	240	23000	9	4
	transverse	50	7000	30	21
GFRP, manually laminated		80	7000	30	13
Steel		235	210000	12	54
Float glass		45	70000	9	70
Aluminium		140	70000	23	58

[1] Degree of utilisation $\eta = \frac{\alpha_T \cdot \Delta T \cdot E}{f_k}$ for ΔT = 50 K

b

E 1.6

1 GFRP section
2 Steel plate
3 Hexagon-head bolt

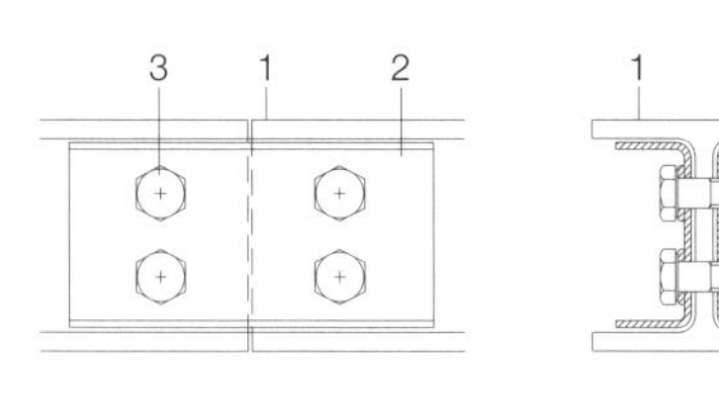

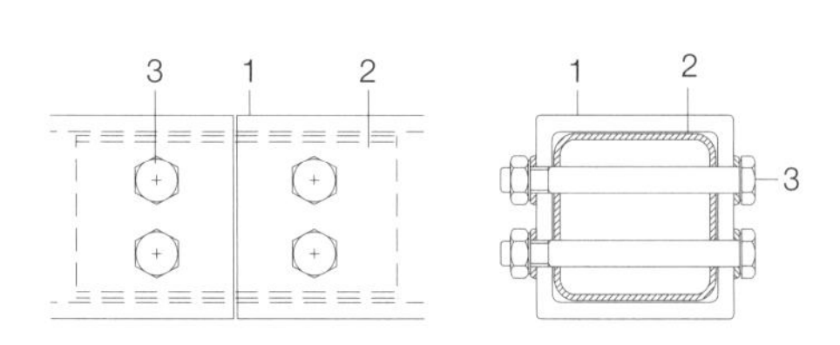

E 1.7

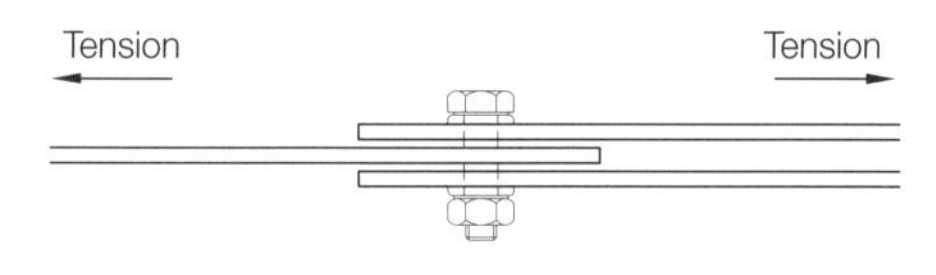

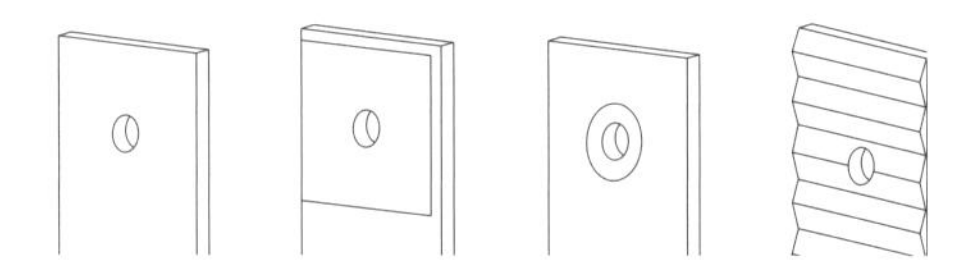

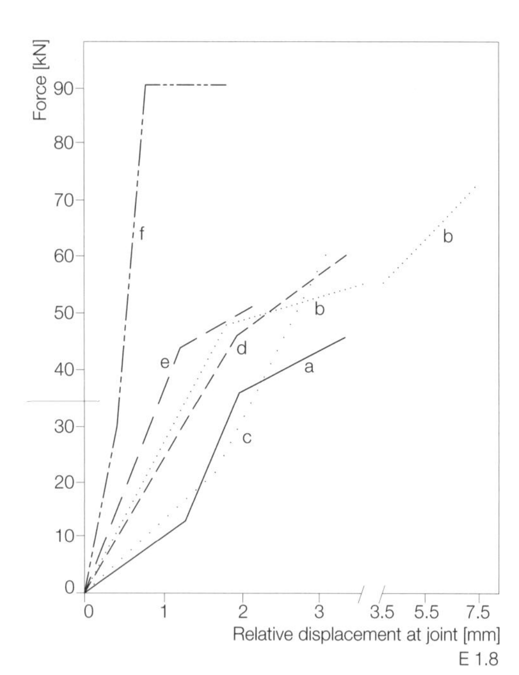

E 1.8

ing. Another variation is fasteners embedded in the components in combination with one splice plate (Fig. E 1.9f).

Rivets
The load-carrying capacities of rivets are basically comparable with those of bolts. The diameters of rivets are mostly smaller than those of bolts and therefore rivets are seldom used singly for connections, but rather in larger numbers. Stainless steel rivets with diameters between 2.4 and 6.4 mm are common. The traditional solid rivet consists of a shaft plus the set and snap heads. Whereas the former is preformed, the latter has to be formed out of the shaft once the rivet has been driven through the components to be joined (Fig. E 1.4c, p. 161). Blind rivets are used where only one side of the component is accessible. These rivets are inserted through a predrilled hole with the head on the other end being subsequently formed by withdrawing the mandrel (through the centre of the rivet) with a special tool. The sleeve, which forms the body of the rivet itself, thus deforms, pressing itself up against the component (Fig. E 1.4b, p. 161). The mandrel snaps off.
A rivet nut has a thread on the shaft and a collar that is screwed on after the rivet has been inserted (Fig. E 1.4a, p. 161). In contrast to bolts, rivets cannot usually be detached once they have been fitted.
The pressure exerted by a rivet on the components results in a further increase in the load-carrying capacity in fibre-reinforced polymers because the interlaminar shear strength is increased by the fact that the individual plies of the composite are pressed together. Rivets at close spacings can achieve a reasonably homogenous force transfer. But the small heads of rivets result in a low tear-through resistance, i.e. rivets are easily pulled out when subjected to tension. This is another reason why many rows of rivets have to be used at each connection.

Splice plates
Generously sized splice plates made from steel or stainless steel simplify the jointing of semi-finished products, especially sections. The parts to be connected can be butted together without the need for any kind of offset (Fig. E 1.7). Steel plates or angles can be used to join together several components at one point (Fig. E 1.18, p. 165). In contrast to the majority of polymers, steel plates can be bent or welded without any problems. As with the fasteners themselves, stainless steel is a good choice for the plates because it matches the good corrosion resistance of the polymers at the connections. The steel components can accommodate the stress concentrations from the bolts better than the polymer components and therefore relatively thin plates are usually adequate for such connection details. Nevertheless, relatively large numbers of fasteners are still necessary.

New types of bolted connection
The low bearing strength of a bolted connection usually leads to an unsatisfactory result. In many cases cross-sections have to be enlarged for this reason alone in order to accommodate the necessary number of fasteners, which has serious consequences for the details and the construction as a whole. But as the simple handling of bolted connections and the easy assembly and dismantling of the structure are very attractive benefits, adhesive joints are frequently not a viable alternative. There have therefore been numerous attempts to optimise the load-carrying capacity of bolted connections. By way of an example, Fig. E 1.8 shows the capacity of a bolted connection between pultruded GFRP flat bars measuring 5 x 1 cm employing various strengthening methods such as collars, glued splice plates or newly developed friction fittings. [1]

Reinforcing splice plates
Steel spice plates attached with adhesive can strengthen the drilled holes for bolts (Fig. E 1.12). These plates carry the concentrated stresses from the bolt and transfer them evenly via the adhesive to the other component. Significant increases in load can be achieved with this method. In addition, the splice plates protect the GFRP against mechanical damage during assembly and dismantling. This type of connection was developed for pultruded GFRP sections but can be used for other polymers as well. [2]

Friction fittings
In the newly developed friction connection, the load transfer takes place via the serrations, which are attached to the components to be joined beforehand (Fig. E 1.8f). The bolts merely hold the components in position, they could even be replaced by loops. This type of connection permits quick assembly and dismantling while ensuring an even transfer of the forces across the joint. Under load, the angled mating surfaces give rise to a compressive force perpendicular to the component. This is beneficial for fibre-reinforced polymers because it increases the bond strength between the individual plies of the laminate. Friction connections have a higher load-carrying capacity than adhesive joints. [3]

Adapting the fibre reinforcement
An optimum bolted connection between fibre-reinforced polymer components can be achieved by adjusting the fibre reinforcement itself. However, the prerequisite for this is that the exact position of the connection and the flow of forces must be defined prior to production of the semi-finished products (see "Adapting the fibre reinforcement", p. 181). Additional threaded sockets or force-transfer elements can help to distribute the stresses involved evenly to the fibres and hence increase the load-carrying capacity.

Glued joints

Loadbearing adhesive joints are still a rarity in the construction industry. Apart from a few exceptions such as structural sealant glazing, glued connections are employed only for fixing linings and cladding. The disadvantage that often prevents the use of adhesive is the fact that the quality of a glued joint cannot be checked afterwards. Damage or problems as a result of poor workmanship can occur long after the joint is finished. Failure is then usually abrupt and brittle. On the other hand, glued joints enable an even transfer of the forces involved and therefore usually exhibit a better load-carrying capacity than connections with pin-type fasteners. The high load-carrying capacity of adhesive joints is primarily due to the generous size of the mating surfaces. For example, although the silicone adhesives commonly used in the building industry (see “Silicone adhesives”, p. 57) have a low shear strength, such connections can still develop a high loadbearing capacity because of their large surface area.

Functions of glued joints

Glued joints can perform other functions in addition to transferring the forces. For example, a weather-resistant adhesive can also seal the joint between the components. In addition, with a sufficiently thick joint and a soft adhesive it is possible to compensate for thermal expansion and contraction, especially at joints between different materials. And indeed, a glued joint is also able to accommodate dimensional tolerances to a certain extent.

Design of glued joints

A glued joint should be aligned parallel with the direction of loading and the area of the mating faces should be as large as possible. This is achieved by allowing for a suitably large overlap between the parts to be joined (Fig. E 1.10a). It should be remembered, however, that the load-carrying capacity cannot be increased *ad infinitum* simply by enlarging the length of the overlap in the direction of loading because it is the peak stresses at the edges that govern the strength of the joint (see “Glued connections”, p. 153). A glued joint should always be loaded in shear and not tension if at all possible.
As with bolted connections, a symmetrical joint should be preferred, e.g. by way of glued splice plates (Fig. E 1.10b). Where it is only possible to attach a splice plate on one side, this should be thicker than the components being joined in order to accommodate the moment due to the eccentricity (Fig. E 1.10c).
A butt joint should be avoided because of the small contact surfaces available and, furthermore, the glued joint is loaded in tension. If such an end-to-end connection is unavoidable, it should at least be splayed (Fig. E 1.10d).
Gluing together edges that have been bent through 90° results in tensile stresses in the adhesive joint, which reduces the load-carrying capacity of the connection. Such connections can be strengthened with splice plates or channel sections (Fig. E 1.11).

1 Polymer component
2 Hexagon-head bolt
3 Polymer splice plate
4 Sheet steel angle
5 Steel splice plate
6 Built-in fastener

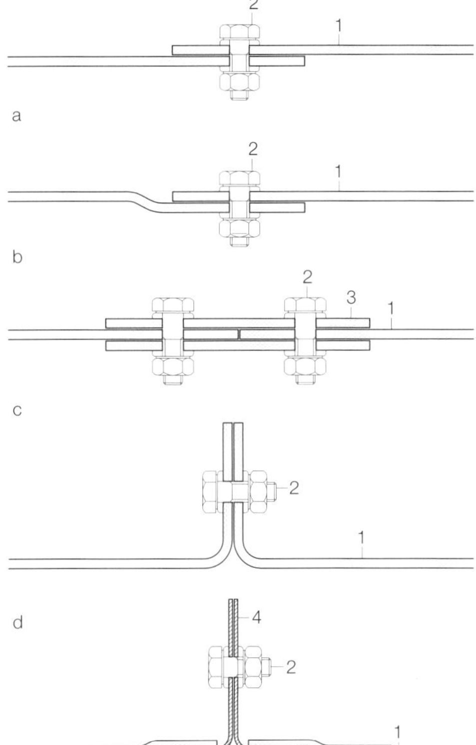

E 1.9

1 Polymer component
2 Adhesive
3 Splice plate both sides
4 Splice plate on one side
5 Channel section

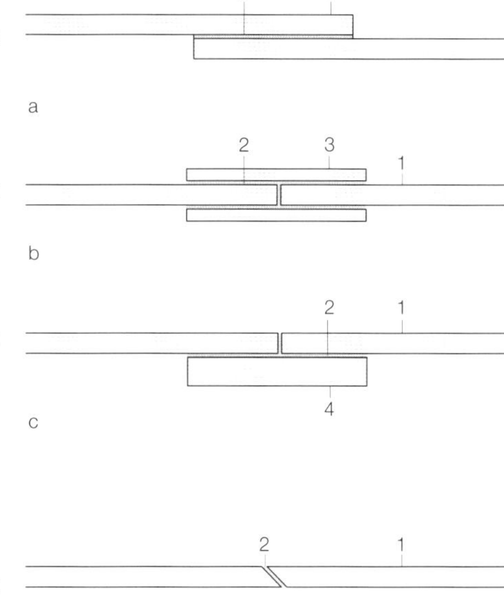

E 1.10

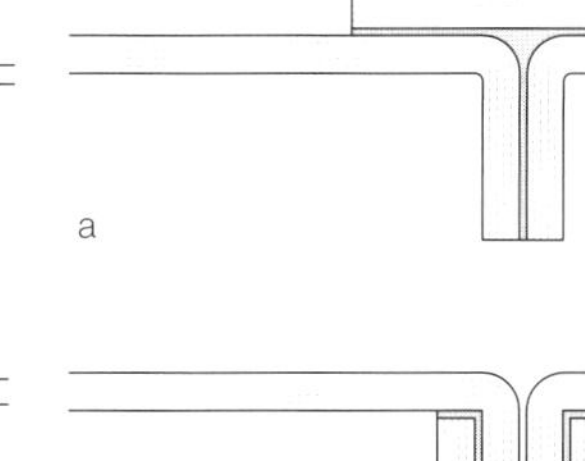

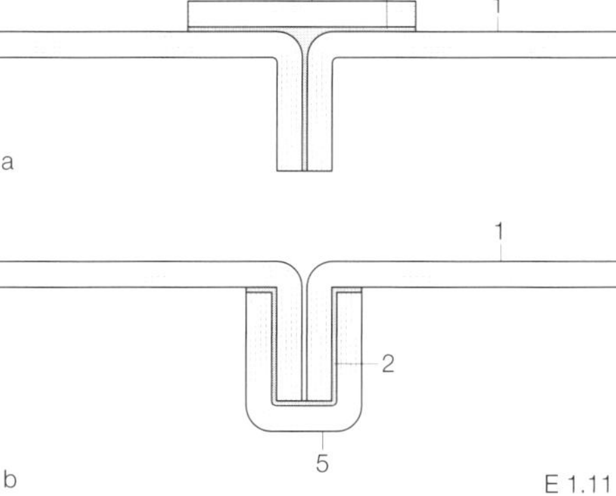

E 1.11

1 Polymer proponent
2 Hexagon-head bolt
3 Glued sheet steel

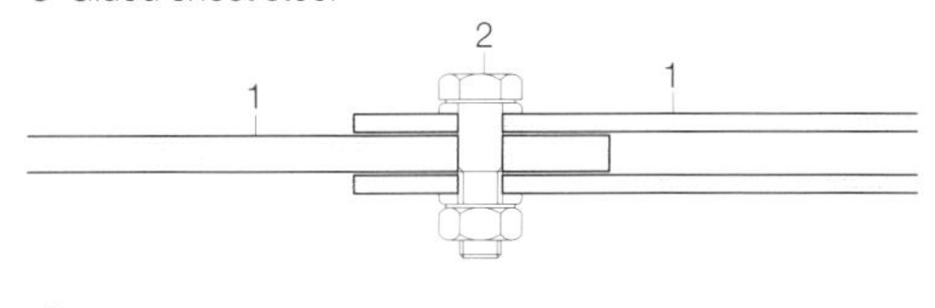

a

b

E 1.12

E 1.7 Use of spice plates for an axial joint
E 1.8 Loadbearing behaviour of various bolted connections
a Unreinforced
b Steel splice plate
c CFRP splice plate, longitudinal
d CFRP splice plate, transverse
e Steel collar
f Friction connection
E 1.9 Details of bolted connections
a Simple overlap, with offset
b Simple overlap, without offset
c with splice plates
d with edges bent through 90°
e with steel angles
f with built-in fasteners and splice plate
E 1.10 Various adhesive joints
a with overlap
b with splice plates on both sides, symmetrical butt joint
c with splice plate on one side only
d Splayed butt joint
E 1.11 Adhesive joints with component edges bent through 90°
a with splice plate
b with channel section
E 1.12 Reinforcing a bolted connection with steel splice plates

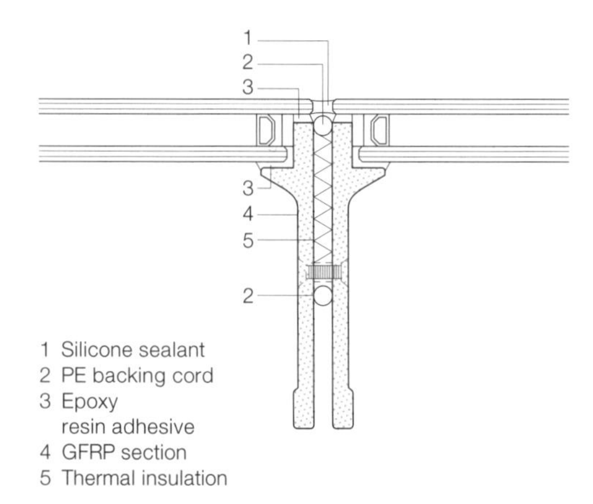

a

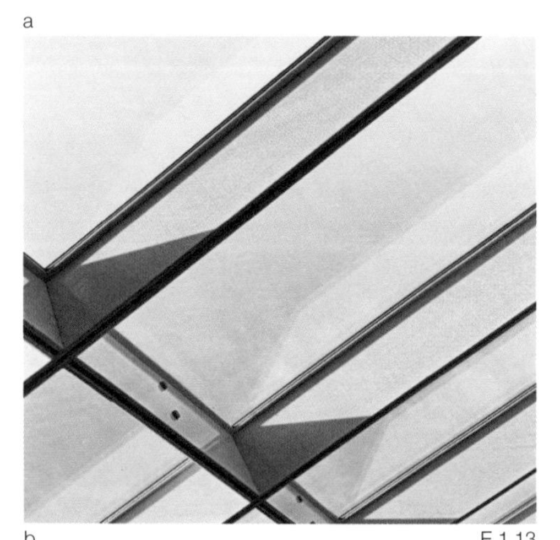

b E 1.13

a

b E 1.14

Assembling glued joints
The surfaces to which the adhesive is to be applied must be free from dust and grease. In addition, the relative humidity of the air should be < 80% and the ambient temperature > 10°C. Component surfaces that are to be ground (or least roughened with an abrasive material) prior to applying the adhesive must be degreased beforehand. Roughening the outer layer of wax or the gelcoat is advantageous for fibre-reinforced polymers. But grinding as far as the fibre reinforcement has proved to be a disadvantage because the adhesion between the glue and the fibres is poorer than the adhesion between the glue and the surrounding polymer matrix. Where a primer (bond enhancer) is being used, then its compatibility with the material must be checked beforehand because incorrect application or use with the wrong materials can substantially reduce the strength of the adhesive joint.

Combinations of materials
Polymers can be glued to materials such as steel, concrete, glass or timber. But the coefficients of thermal expansion and the elastic moduli of the materials to be joined should be compatible. A flexible adhesive (e.g. silicone) can be used to join materials with different thermal expansion behaviour; but the result is a shear-flexible connection with a low load-carrying capacity and larger deformations. Stiff adhesives (e.g. epoxy) can produce composite constructions with a higher load-carrying capacity; but only materials with similar thermal expansion behaviour can be joined because otherwise high restraint stresses can occur.

GFRP-glass composite
With a high glass fibre content, pultruded GFRP sections have – in the longitudinal direction – a similar coefficient of thermal expansion to that of glass. The two materials can therefore also be connected with a stiff adhesive applied in a relatively thin layer. Complex constructions employing GFRP and glass (Figs. E 1.13 and E 1.14) can make use of slim framing members because the inherent stiffness of glass within the plane of the pane can be fully activated. [4] In such constructions, the pane of glass carries the compressive stresses, the GFRP section the tensile stresses. A thermal break between framing and glazing is unnecessary because of the low thermal conductivity of the GFRP.

Further jointing techniques
In fibre-reinforced polymers it is primarily the fibres that are responsible for carrying the loads. And in order to guarantee an effective load-bearing system, the loads should be transferred directly to the fibres. A number of jointing techniques have therefore been developed specifically for fibre-reinforced polymers. In contrast to connections with pin-type fasteners or adhesive joints, the properties of the polymer matrix play only a subsidiary role in these connections. Friction is responsible for transferring the forces between components in a clamped or interference-fit connection. Additional compression perpendicular to the fibre-reinforced polymer enables the load-carrying capacity of the joint to be increased further.
Interlocking connections such as loops or grouting achieve even better results. The latter is similar to the anchorage head on a wire rope. The exposed fibres are embedded in compound formed into a conical shape which transfers the loads to the anchorage. All these types of connection must, however, be implemented during the fabrication of the semi-finished products and are therefore almost exclusively restricted to free-form components (see "Fibre-reinforced polymers", pp. 176–184).

Combining means of connection
As with other materials, combining different means of connection does not cause any special problems. The stiffer means of connection carries most of the load, whereas the less stiff components do not make a significant contribution to the load-carrying capacity of the joint. Joints where different means of connection are responsible for the loads in different directions represent an exception. For example, adding bolts to a glued joint is ineffective because the adhesive is stiffer and therefore the bolts do not carry any load. But where a combination of tension and shear loads has to be accommodated, the bolts can carry the tensile stresses and the adhesive the shear stresses. Combining different means of connection is an approach employed when a higher redundancy against failure is necessary. In Germany, for example, glued facade elements > 8 m above the ground must be additionally secured with mechanical fasteners.

Sections

In the building industry, pultruded GFRP is very important for designs employing polymer sections. Other linear-type semi-finished polymer products made from PMMA or carbon fibre-reinforced polymers (CFRP) either have a poor load-carrying capacity or represent uneconomical alternatives. Pultruded sections made from GFRP are mainly used for structures in industrial plants where excellent corrosion resistance must be combined with economy (Fig. E 1.15). Since the 1990s they have also been increasingly used in bridges, buildings and facades (Fig. E 1.16). The design options are limited to a few standard systems such as trusses, arches or compound sections, and the design language used so far tends to follow that of traditional steelwork, although the dimensions of GFRP sections are larger than those of equivalent steel sections because of the material's lower elastic modulus. Forms of construction and cross-section geometries more appropriate to this material are still in the early stages of development. The well-known jointing techniques of structural steelwork have only limited suitability for fibre-reinforced polymers; generally, more bolts are required to transfer the forces across connections (Fig. E 1.18).

Compound sections

The GFRP sections available as standard are frequently only available in sizes up to about 30 x 30 cm. And the spans possible when using such sections as beams (in bending) are really quite short. The load-carrying capacity can be increased, however, by forming compound sections, i.e. two or more standard sections fitted together (Fig. E 1.17). The individual sections or sheets are glued, occasionally riveted or bolted, together to form larger sections. This approach enables tension members, beams or symmetrical columns to be created. And if additional CFRP lamellae are attached to the outer faces of such compound sections, then a further improvement in the load-carrying capacity and reduced deformations are the result. However, the material consumption and work involved are both high with such compound sections, which frequently renders such forms of construction uneconomic.

E 1.15

E 1.16

1 GFRP section
2 Adhesive
3 CFRP lamella as reinforcement
4 GFRP twin-wall sheet

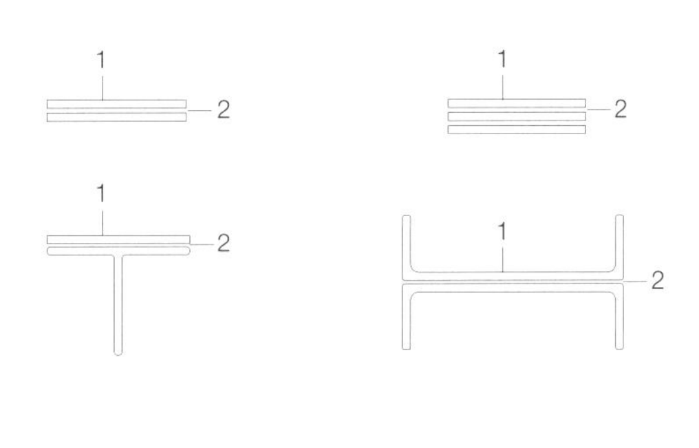
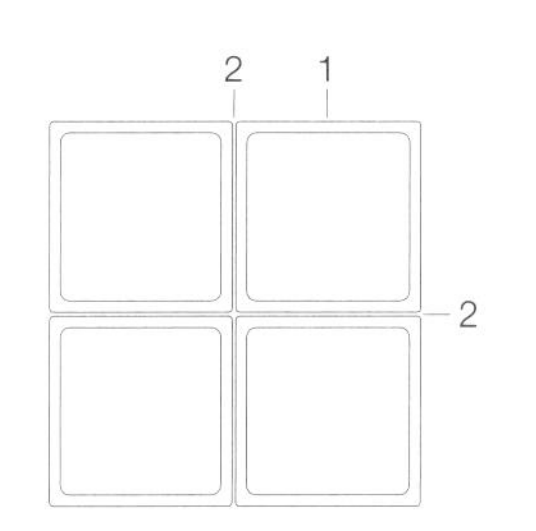
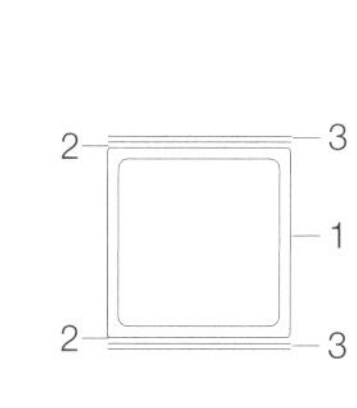
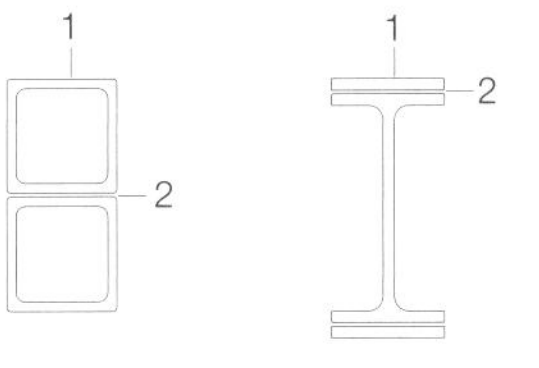
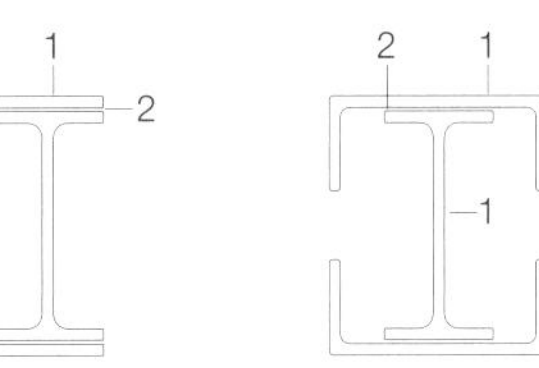
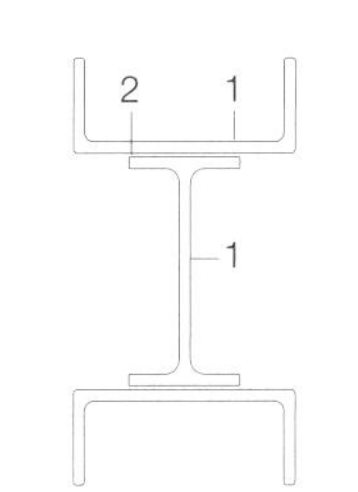
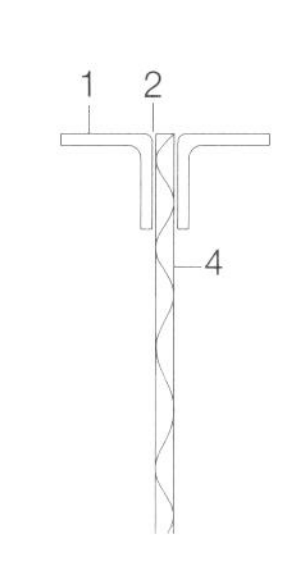

E 1.17

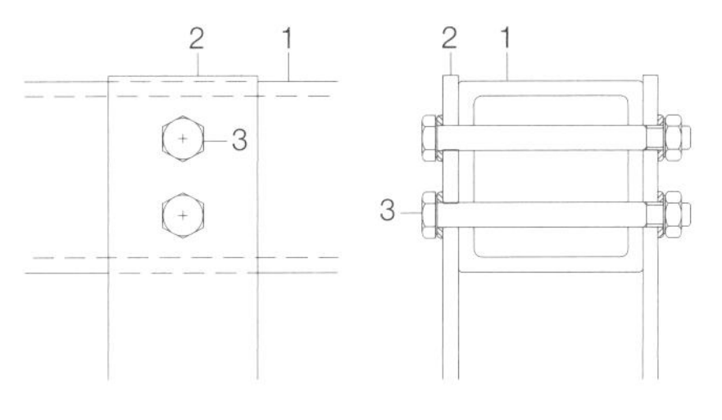
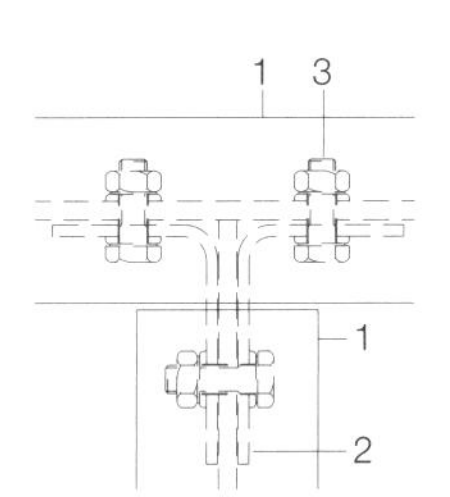
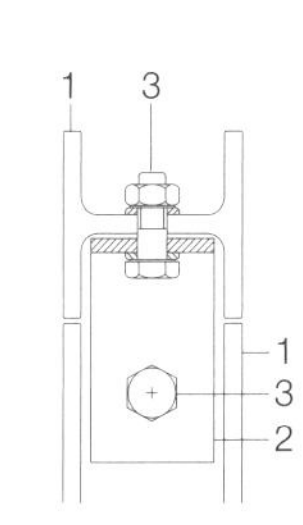

1 GFRP section
2 Steel plate/angle
3 Hexagon-head bolt

E 1.18

E 1.13 Insulating glass glued to GFRP frame sections, with screwed butt joint between adjacent frame sections
a Detail
b View of finished construction

E 1.14 Glass reinforced with glued GFRP sections, pavilion made from glass and GFRP
a Overall view
b Close-up view

E 1.15 Structure made from bolted GFRP sections for use in aggressive environments

E 1.16 Arch bridge made from bolted GFRP sections; Lleida (E), 2001, Pedelta Structural Engineers

E 1.17 Compound GFRP sections

E 1.18 Using splice plates to connect components at T-joints

a

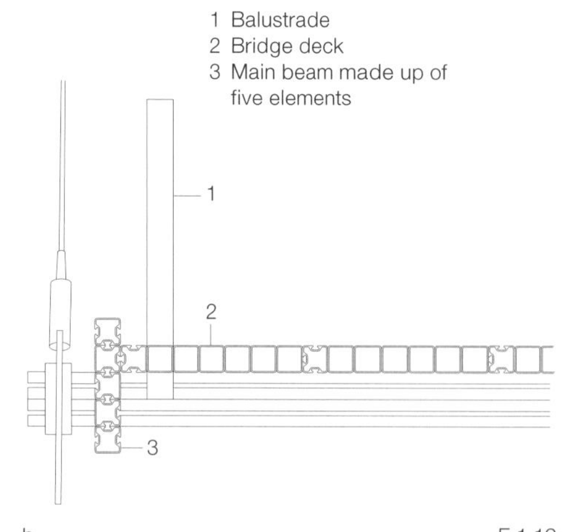

b

E 1.19

a

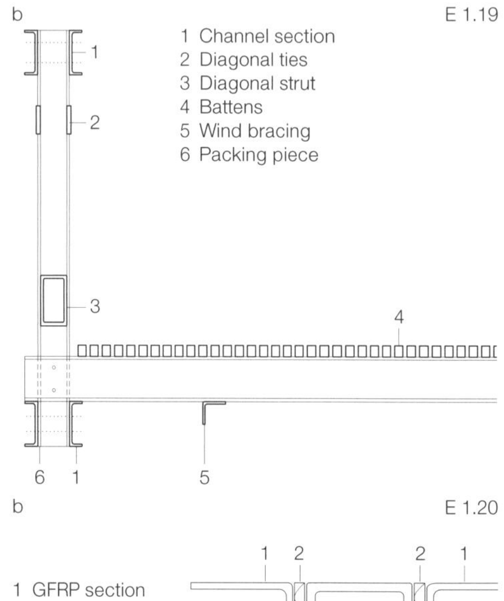

b

E 1.20

a

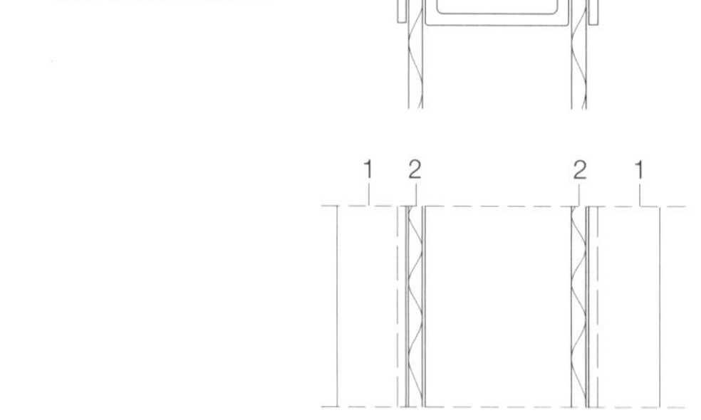

b

E 1.21

a

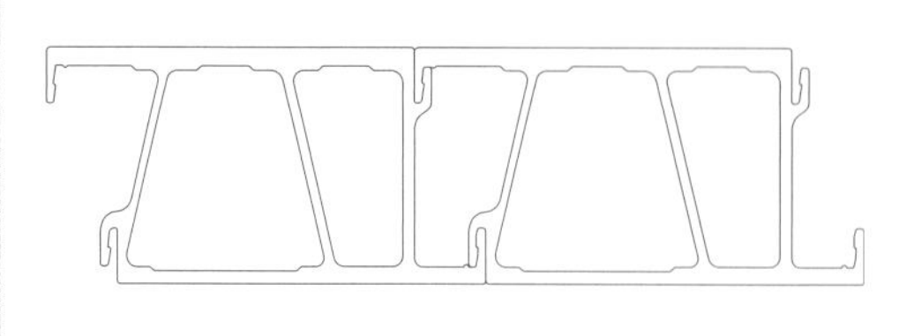

b

E 1.22

Deep beams

In beams it is primarily the outer zones of the cross-section that are effective in carrying the loads in bending, whereas the inner zones are loaded to a lesser extent. Therefore, when using compound sections it would seem sensible to use GFRP sections with a high fibre content for the flanges, and sheets with a lower fibre content, or indeed unreinforced polymers, for the web. The use of translucent or transparent sheets for the web improves the appearance by making the beam seem less "stocky". In the design of footbridges, such beams can also serve as balustrades and handrails in addition to performing a loadbearing function (Fig. E 1.21). Adhesive applied over a large area transfers the stresses. The combination of sections and twin- or multi-wall sheets has proved to be a viable solution, but the buckling stability of the sheets is not unproblematic, which is why additional stiffeners, i.e. ribs glued to the sheet to add stability, are sometimes necessary. [5]

Lattice beams

Lattice beams can be relatively easily assembled from GFRP sections (Fig. E 1.20). The holes required can be drilled during assembly. The members are all subjected to axial forces, which is ideal for pultruded sections with their longitudinal fibres. One problem, however, is that there is not usually enough material at the joints for the number of bolts or area of adhesive required. It is therefore often necessary to use very large sections simply to overcome this problem, which consequently results in a high consumption of material. Connections should be designed as symmetrical and steel plates can be helpful at complicated nodes (Fig. E 1.18, p. 165).
On trussed bridges the deck can be fabricated from GFRP planks or open-grid flooring panels, which distribute the loads between the beams.

Push-fit systems

Modular push-fit systems have integral joints with loose tongue and groove details. Such systems require fewer bolts or less adhesive. Several sections can be combined to form one beam. In the ideal case, repeated assembly and dismantling of a structure is possible. To do this, each of the hollow sections to be connected has a slot. A smaller bar with a dovetail-shaped cross-section is fitted into both slots to link the two hollow sections together. As a rule, such push-fit systems are used for cladding, linings and other components not forming part of the primary loadbearing system. The small dimensions of the connecting bars limit the forces that can be transferred across the joint. These systems have occasionally also been used for footbridges (Fig. E 1.19). In contrast to non-compound sections, it is fairly easy to construct bridge decks or balustrades with such push-fit systems. This form of construction is especially suitable for temporary and experimental forms of construction.

Clip-in connections
Integral clip-in connections represent another useful way of joining sections together. The means of connection is formed in the component during the automated production process. Such sections can be connected to form larger panels, e.g. for building bridge decks (Fig. E 1.22). In contrast to glued joints (see "Special semi-finished products for engineering applications", pp. 92–93), components with clip-in connections are quickly and easily assembled on site in any weather conditions. On the other hand, clip-in connections can carry only relatively low loads. And apart from that, brittle thermosets are generally used for fibre-reinforced polymers, which means that repeated assembly and dismantling is not normally possible because the clip-in parts tend to break off.

CFRP sections
Carbon fibre-reinforced polymers (CFRP) are used only occasionally in construction projects because of the high cost of these materials. However, if they are used, then their outstanding mechanical properties are fully exploited. Designing beams completely from CFRP would not make economic sense. In the meantime, the use of CFRP lamellae just a few millimetres thick for strengthening existing concrete components has become a standard method. This reinforcement, glued to the outside of the component, can replace corroded steel reinforcing bars or supplement them to increase the imposed load the structure can carry. Bars made from CFRP have also been used as prestressing tendons or suspension rods in some structures; such bars can accommodate much higher stresses than steel (see "Special semi-finished products for engineering applications", pp. 92–93).

CFRP-concrete composite
The combination of fibre-reinforced polymers and concrete enables the design of comparatively economic forms of loadbearing construction. There are various reasons for choosing this combination of materials. On the one hand, the more durable fibre-reinforced polymers can replace the steel reinforcement so vulnerable to corrosion. And in contrast to steel, the reinforcement does not have to be protected by the concrete, but instead can be fixed to the outside. On the other hand, an outer covering of a polymer material can serve as formwork for the concrete. In some cases the easy machinability of fibre-reinforced polymers, compared with steel, is an advantage when, for example, retaining walls have to be penetrated at a later date. CFRP has a higher elastic modulus than GFRP and so it is better suited to being combined with concrete. The high strains required to activate the tensile strength of GFRP frequently cannot be accommodated by the concrete.
Up until now, this combination of materials was principally used in the form of concrete-filled CFRP tubes. To achieve the composite action, the inside of the tube has to have an irregular surface to achieve an adequate bond, e.g. transverse ribs. The carbon fibres are initially braided to form a hose, shaped to suit the particular specification and subsequently impregnated with the polymer. The cured tubes have a low self-weight, which enables them to be installed on site without the need for heavy equipment prior to being filled with in situ concrete. The bridge system shown in Fig. E 1.23 is based on this form of construction. The CFRP-concrete arches in this example were subsequently backfilled with a loose material up to deck level. [6]
Further developments are focusing on the use of CFRP panels as permanent formwork. In a similar fashion to steel-concrete composite slabs, first of all thin sheets are laid which serve as formwork for the concrete. Serrations on the surface of the panels ensure the necessary bond. In the final condition, the CFRP functions as tension reinforcement on the underside of the slab.

E 1.19 Footbridge, Aberfeldy (UK), 1991, Dundee University
a View of node
b Section
E 1.20 Footbridge, Pontresina (CH), 1997, Swiss Federal Institute of Technology Zurich, Institute of Building Technology, Thomas Keller (design)
a View of balustrade
b Section
E 1.21 GFRP sandwich composite beam, 1997, EPFL Lausanne, CCLAB, Thomas Keller
a Production
b Section
E 1.22 GFRP section for use in bridge decks, Kookmin University (KR), Sung Woo Lee
a Production
b Section
E 1.23 Bridge system with CFRP-concrete composite tubes, 2009, University of Maine, Habib J. Dagher
a Axonometric view
b Erection

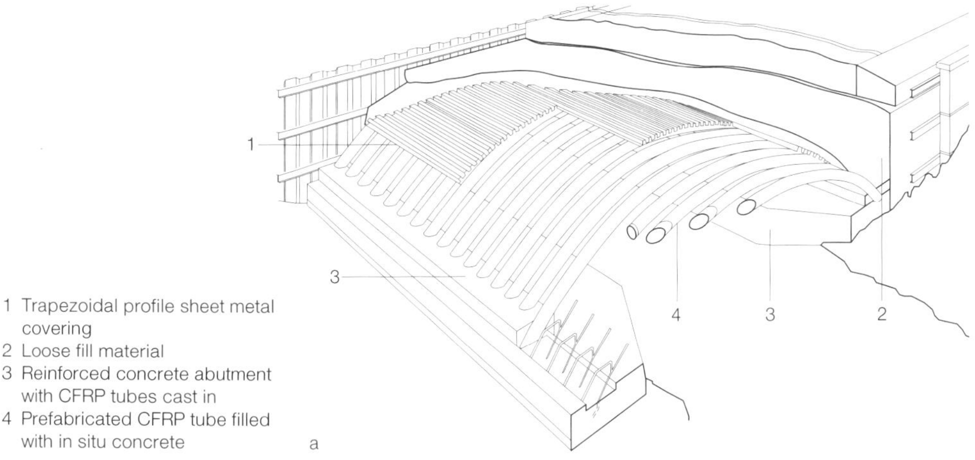

1 Trapezoidal profile sheet metal covering
2 Loose fill material
3 Reinforced concrete abutment with CFRP tubes cast in
4 Prefabricated CFRP tube filled with in situ concrete

a

b

E 1.23

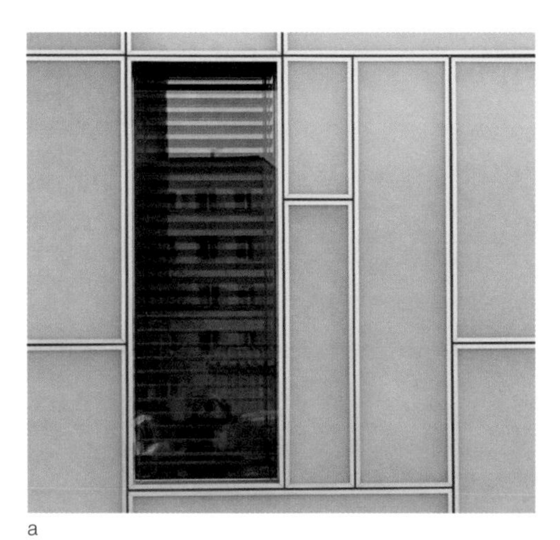
a

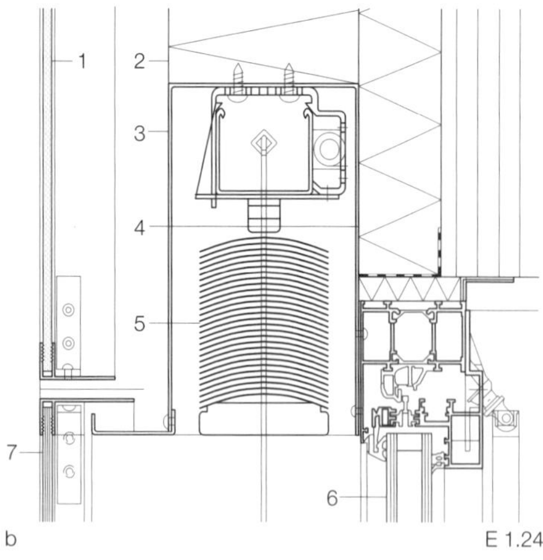

b E 1.24

1 GFRP sheet in aluminium frame
2 Mineral wool
3 Housing for louvre blind
4 Rigid insulation
5 Louvre blind
6 Low E glazing
7 Single glazing

Sheets

Facades and pitched roofs are the principal applications for transparent, translucent or opaque polymer sheets. They are also suitable as internal partitions, for shielding electrical equipment alongside railway facilities or for balustrade infill panels. The facade panels in everyday use can be made from brittle thermoplastics or fibre-reinforced polymers or other composites such as mineral boards. All these sheets are available in solid or hollow variations, which has an effect on the details. In principle, sheets can be used to build both watertight envelopes and also facing leaves with a ventilation cavity.
Forms of construction based on polymer sheets sometimes borrow details such as point fixings or elastomeric strips from glass construction because there is a lack of details designed specifically for polymers. But in contrast to brittle glass, such elaborate measures are actually unnecessary. Compared with glass, polymer sheets are relatively easy to drill and cut to size. Especially interesting here is the option of being able to incorporate the connection details into the sheets themselves during production. One essential difference when compared with glass or metal is that polymer sheets are not diffusion-resistant. The associated risk of condensation should be dealt with by construction measures such as a ventilation cavity.

Solid and corrugated sheets
Sheets made from solid or fibre-reinforced polymers are generally between 3 and 7 mm thick. They are usually produced in large formats and only cut to size in the course of the final erection on site. The cut edges of fibre-reinforced polymers should be sealed afterwards.

Fixing
Outer envelopes that serve merely as protection against the weather and for appearance purposes can be relatively straightforward forms of construction. The sheets can be bolted, screwed or riveted to the supporting framework (Figs. E 1.26 and E 1.27). Owing to the lower elastic modulus of the material, it is in many cases unnecessary to include expansion joints and elongated holes, especially with corrugated sheets, because the restraint stresses due to thermal movements are comparatively small (Fig. E 1.6, p. 161).
Joints between flat panels can often be simply overlapped and, like with panes of glass, the sheets laid on elastomeric strips (Fig. E 1.25), which achieves an even load transfer. Apart from that, the forms of construction can be built watertight. The supporting construction required is, however, more involved than with other methods of fixing.
Special fixing systems are worth considering for facades with a ventilation cavity; such systems are not visible from outside (Fig. E 1.31). Another alternative is to provide sheets with metal rails on all sides that are then fixed to the supporting structure (Fig. E 1.24). This solution protects the edges of the sheets against mechanical damage and in the case of fibre-reinforced polymers prevents the exposed edges from absorbing water.
Point fixings are very suitable in principle and their details are simpler than with glass because the holes are much easier to drill (Fig. E 1.28). It is also possible to embed threaded sockets in the sheets to ease the fixing to the supporting framework (Fig. E 1.29).

Waterproofing
Solid polymer sheets are generally not designed to be watertight, but instead make use of open (drained) joints. Sheets that must be supported without restraint require relatively wide joints in order to accommodate the large movements of the polymer as a result of temperature fluctuations. Silicone sealants are therefore mostly unsuitable for polymer sheets.
One simple option for a horizontal joint design is to overlap the sheets or to use preformed sealing strips (Figs. E 1.30a and b). Vertical joints can also be designed with preformed sealing or cover elements (Figs. E 1.30c and d). Screws and bolts with elastomeric sealing washers are required to achieve a watertight envelope.

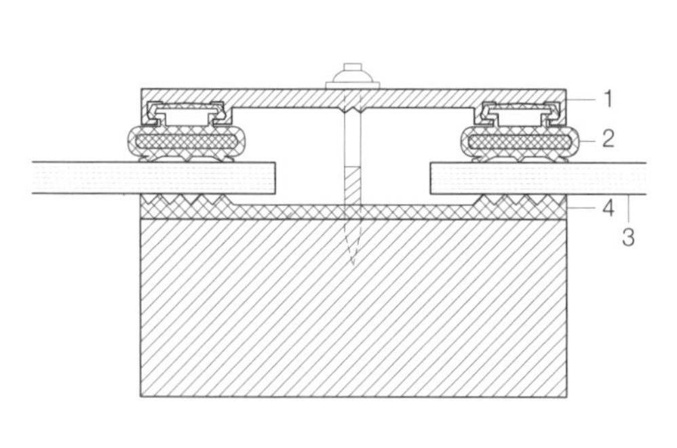

1 Aluminium clamping bar
2 Lipped sealing gasket
3 Polymer sheet
4 Lipped sealing strip

E 1.25

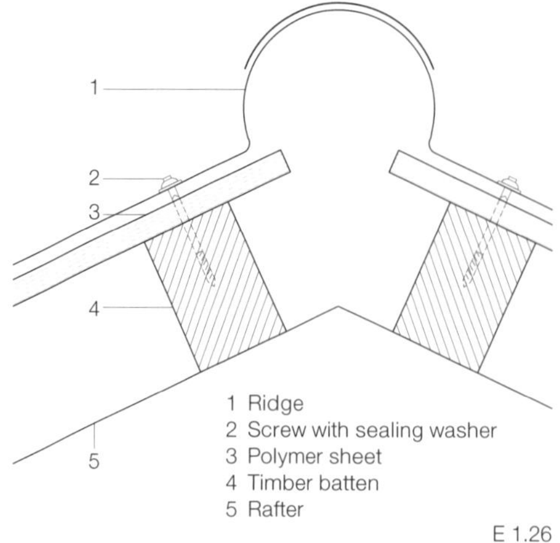

1 Ridge
2 Screw with sealing washer
3 Polymer sheet
4 Timber batten
5 Rafter

E 1.26

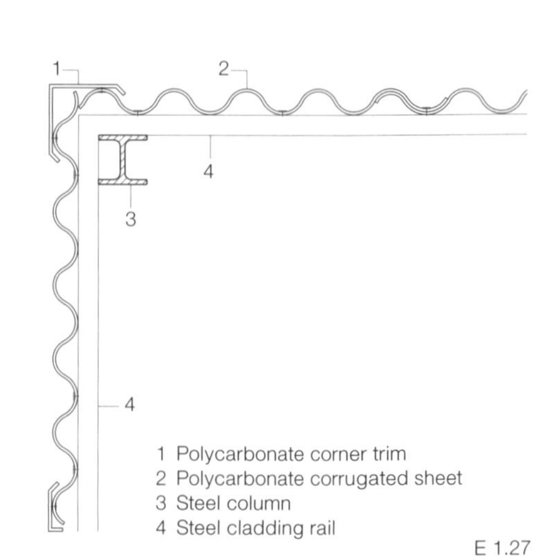

1 Polycarbonate corner trim
2 Polycarbonate corrugated sheet
3 Steel column
4 Steel cladding rail

E 1.27

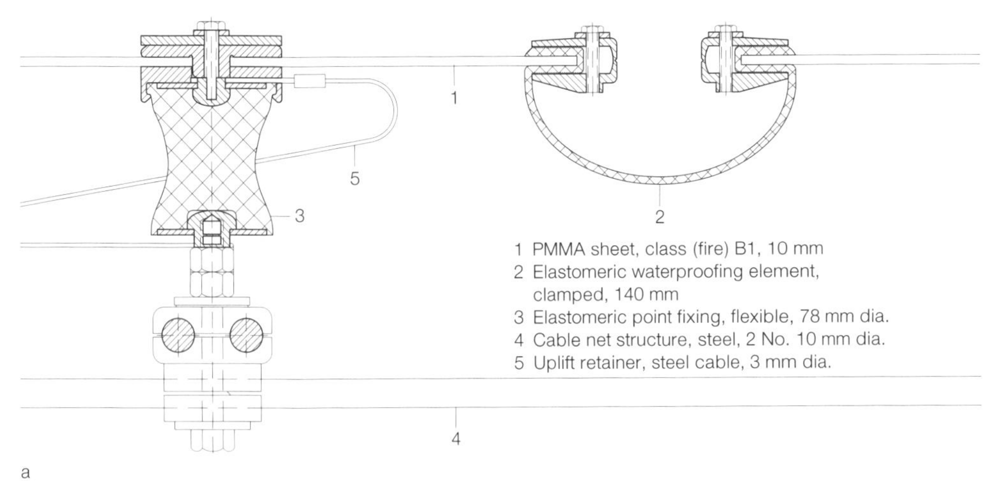

a

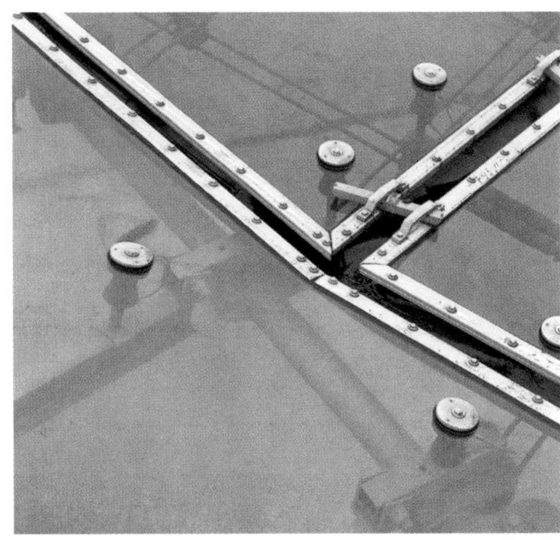

b E 1.28

Planks

Facade planks, in contrast to flat sheets, are prefabricated especially for uses in facade construction (see "Planks", p. 90). They are suspended from the supporting construction via their webs, the vertical joints are sealed by way of a built-in overlap.

Twin- and multi-wall sheets

The fixing and jointing methods for twin- and multi-wall sheets are more complicated than those for solid sheets because of the more complex geometries and the thin walls involved. This is especially true when the thermal insulation properties of the sheets must be retained by avoiding open joints or penetrations.
There are limits to the widths of twin- and multi-wall sheets that can be produced, but they can be produced in any length (subject only to transport restrictions). They are simply lined up side by side to form facades. Butt-jointed twin- and multi-wall sheets do not result in satisfactory results because either the thermal insulation effect is interrupted or it is impossible to create a watertight joint (Fig. E 1.39a, p. 171). Integral joints or special connecting sections have proved advantageous. Individual details have to be developed for corners as well as the top and bottom edges of sheets, although preformed corner and edge trims are available for certain products (Fig. E 1.36, p. 170).

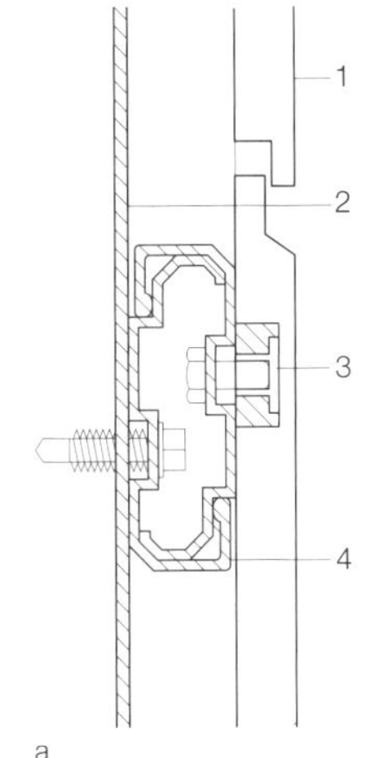

1 Mineral board
2 Supporting framework
3 Threaded socket, glued in place
4 Aluminium rail

a

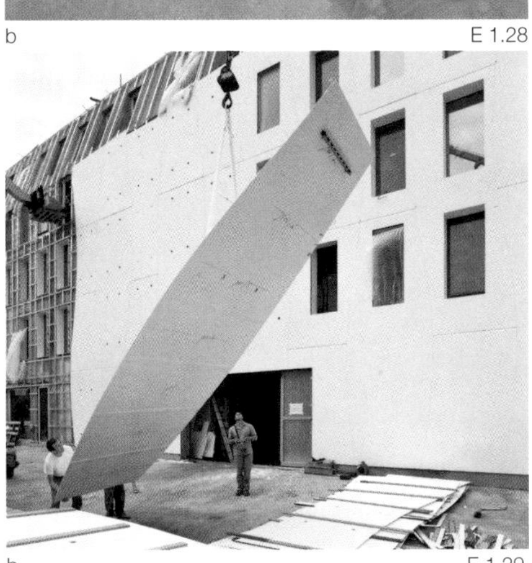

b E 1.29

E 1.24 Fraunhofer Institute, Ilmenau (D), 2008, Staab Architekten
a Facade of GFRP sheets in metal frames
b Section through window head
E 1.25 Clamp fixing for solid sheets
E 1.26 Screw fixing for solid sheets
E 1.27 Corner and edge details for corrugated sheets
E 1.28 Point fixing and waterproofing; roof to Olympic Stadium, Munich (D), 1972, Behnisch + Partner, Frei Otto et al.
a Detail
b View from outside

E 1.29 Facade panel made from mineral board; Seeko'o Hotel, Bordeaux (F), 2007, Atelier Architecture King Kong
a Vertical section
b Erecting a facade panel
E 1.30 Joint details for solid sheets
a Rebate, horizontal joint
b Sealing profile, horizontal joint
c Top-hat profile, vertical joint
d Groove and loose tongue, vertical joint
e Open (drained), vertical joint
E 1.31 Special fixing system for solid sheets

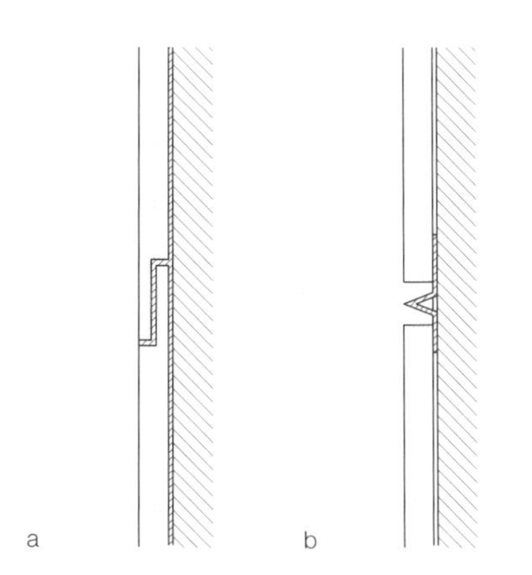

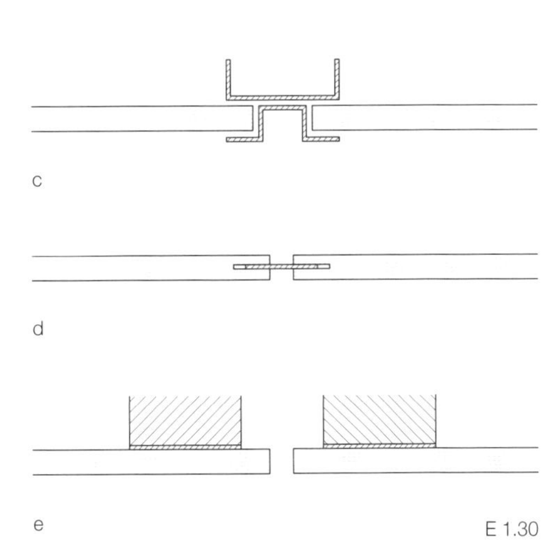

E 1.30

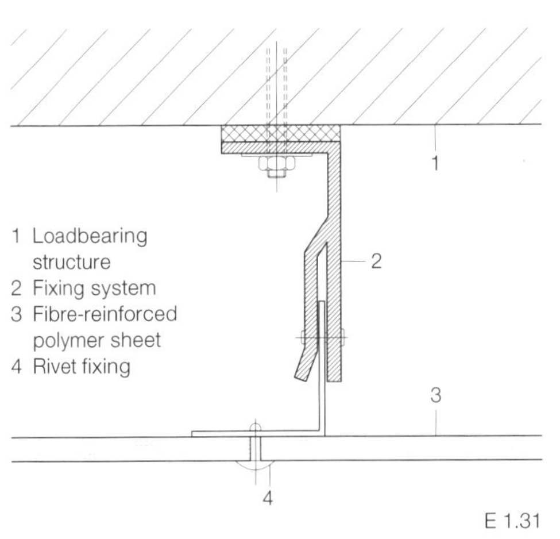

E 1.31

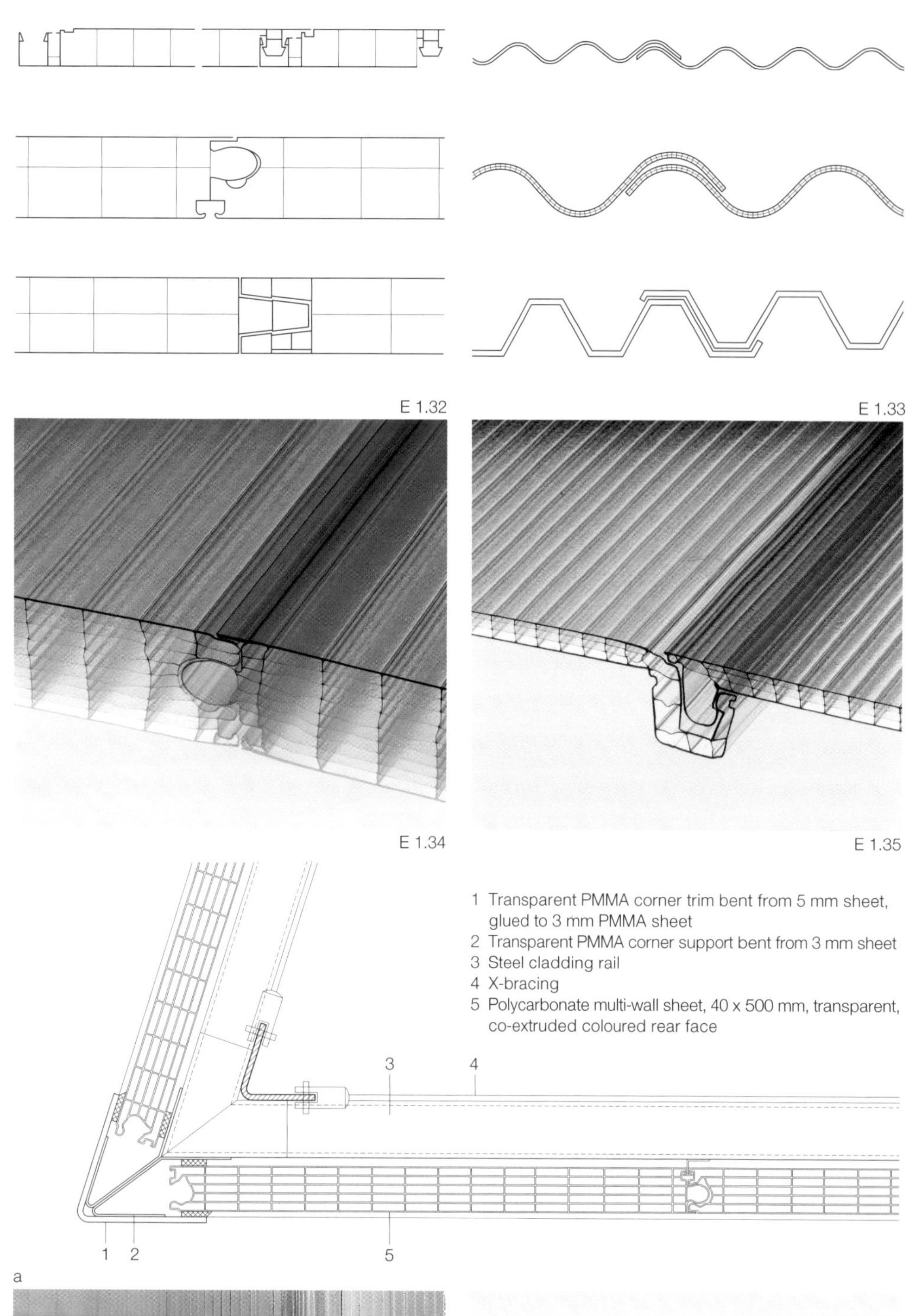

b

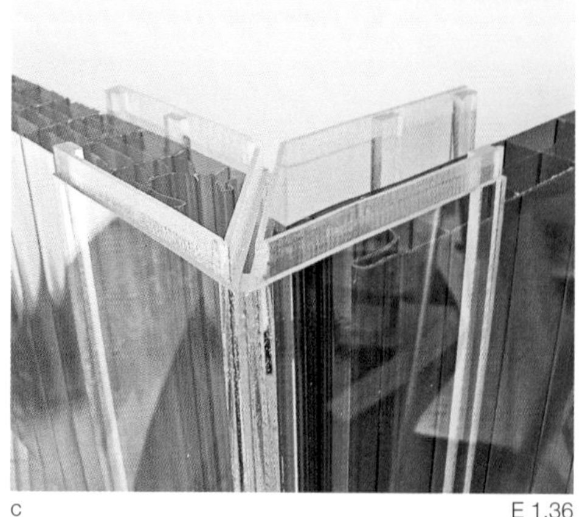
c

E 1.36

Fixing

Simple bolted connections are unsuitable for twin- and multi-wall sheets. The thin webs buckle when subjected to compression and the penetration leads to a thermal bridge. The sheets can be clamped along the edges, like panes of glass, but integral joints similar to tongue and groove joints are better (Figs. E 1.39c and e). It is also possible to use specially shaped aluminium or PVC sections in conjunction with twin- and multi-wall sheets (Fig. E 1.38). As the means of connection does not penetrate the sheet, thermal bridges are ruled out, the appearance from outside is more uniform and the facade is watertight.

Integral joints

Twin- and multi-wall sheets are generally several centimetres thick, which means that it is possible to integrate clip-in or clamp-type joints into the structure of the sheets (Fig. E 1.32). The ductility of the polycarbonate used for the majority of twin- and multi-wall sheets is sufficient to allow the sheets to be assembled and dismantled more than once. These integral joints considerably simplify erection and detailing because the individual sheets only need to be pushed together on site to form an interlocking joint. The thermal insulation and sealing characteristics of such a connection are better than those of a butt joint. Additional profiling at the joint improve the thermal insulation effect even further and in the form of ribs increase the bending stiffness of the elements. These ribs can be reinforced with PVC or aluminium sections (Fig. E 1.38). And when using such sheets for the roof covering, additional profiling helps to ensure a watertight envelope. Further measures such as silicone joints or other sealants are superfluous because the raised position rules out the risk of water collecting in the joint. However, the long, narrow form of these sheets with their clearly defined widths does restrict architectural design freedom. The vertical joints and the numerous webs within the sheets are clearly visible from the outside and they can also substantially reduce the quality of the view through the material. The prismatic cross-sections of these sheets mean that integral joints are possible in one direction only; special details are required for the ends of the panels, likewise

E 1.32 Various polycarbonate twin- and multi-wall sheets with clip-in joints
E 1.33 Various corrugated sheets for pitched roofs
E 1.34 Polycarbonate multi-wall sheet with clip-in joint
E 1.35 Polycarbonate multi-wall sheet with clip-in joint and preformed bent edge
E 1.36 Multi-wall sheet with integral joints; Laban Centre, London (UK), 2003, Herzog & de Meuron, Basel
a Section through corner
b View of facade
c View of corner detail
E 1.37 Twin- or multi-wall sheets butt-jointed over aluminium framing member, isometric views
a Aluminium bar
b Aluminium bar with polymer clamping cap

corners and vertical joints. The ensuing boundary conditions for erection should be considered during the planning phase. Twin- and multi-wall sheets are confined to rigid orthogonal patterns and therefore unsuitable for complex geometries or small-format facades or roofs.

Temporary structures
Twin- and multi-wall sheets with integral joints are ideal for non-permanent structures such as mobile pavilions or temporary accommodation. The fixings and joints are easily detached and sealing compounds or drilling are generally unnecessary. The integral clip-in connections can be put together and taken apart again and again without suffering any damage. Facades and roof constructions can be rebuilt in their entirety at other locations or certain parts of the designs can be reused in other structures, within certain limits.

Moulded items

Building with moulded parts can be compared with building with flat sheets. Three-dimensional trays or components in double curvature are usually made from a solid polymer material and therefore the fixings can be very simple: screws, bolts, rivets, adhesives or clamping elements. One special aspect of using thermoplastics is that moulded parts can be produced from standard flat sheets by a forming process, usually deep-drawing, during the final processing or even during erection.

Rooflights
Moulded polymer items are frequently used for forming rooflights, either individual units or continuous strips. Transparent or translucent thermoplastics such as acrylic sheet (PMMA), polycarbonate (PC) or glycol-modified polyethylene terephthalate (PET-G) are the most popular materials for such applications, but glass fibre-reinforced polymers are occasionally employed (Fig. E 1.42, p. 172). The desired geometry is generally achieved via a hot-forming process; a curving form is preferred so that rainwater and melting snow run off easily. The bottom edge of a rooflight must be positioned above the level

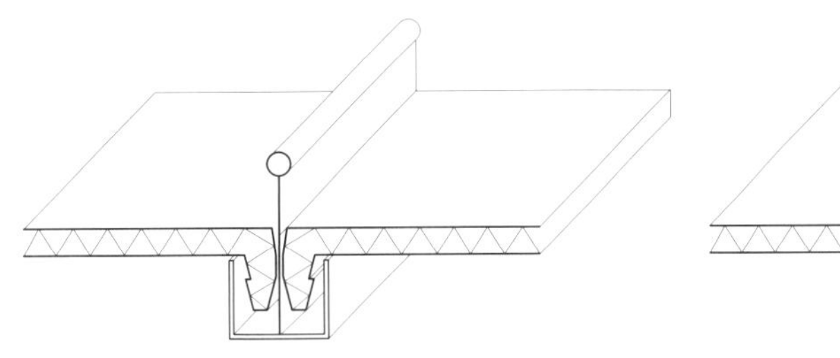

a

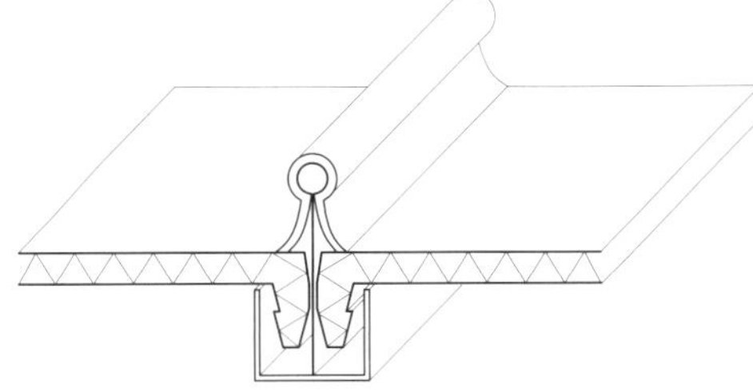

b

E 1.37

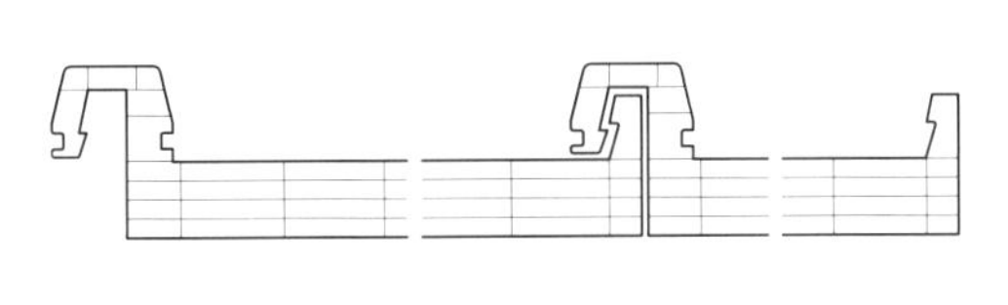

a

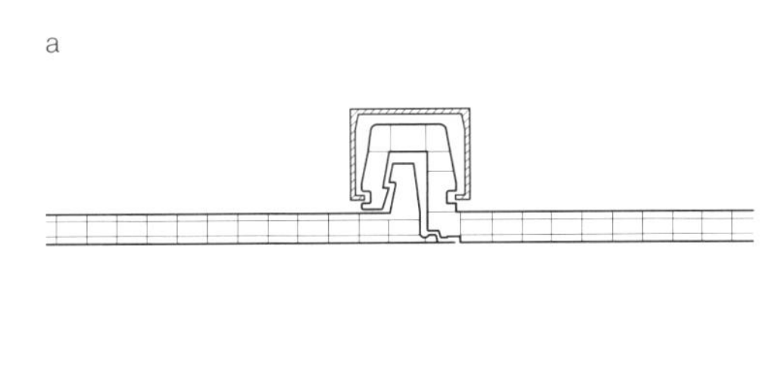

b

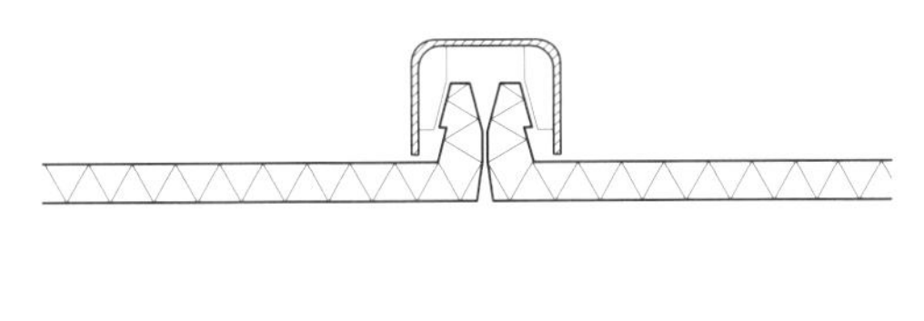

c

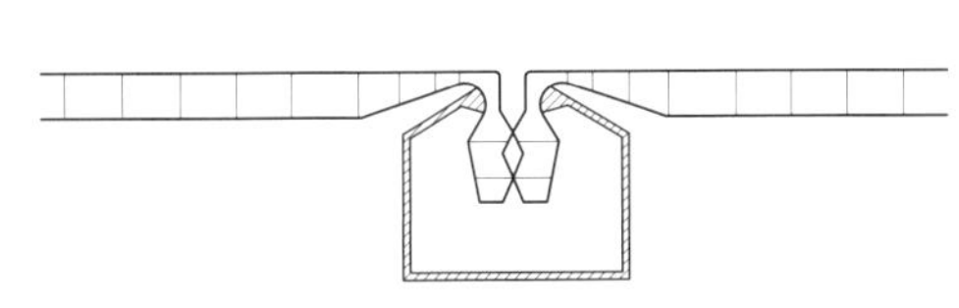

d

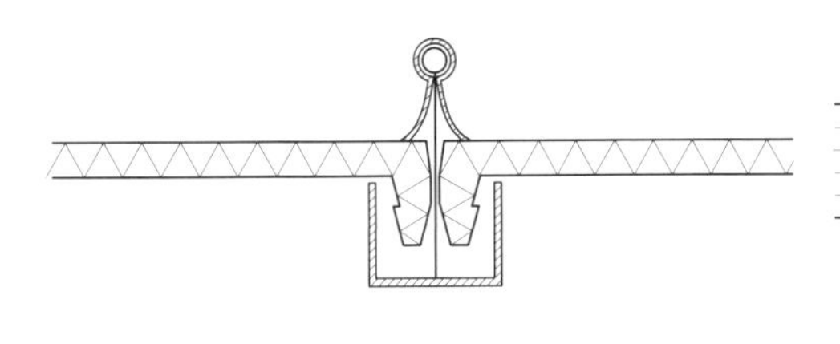

e

E 1.38

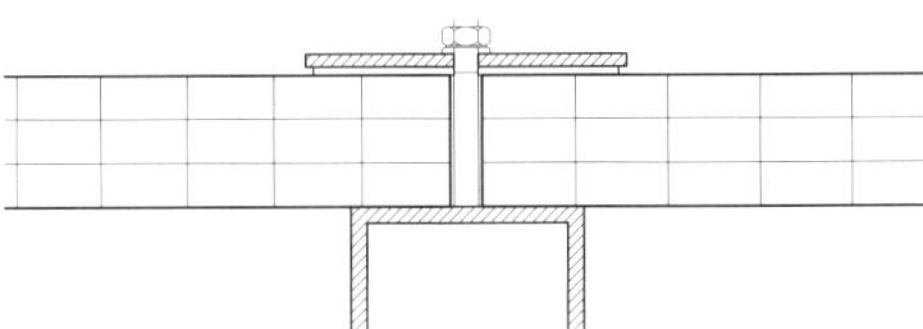

a

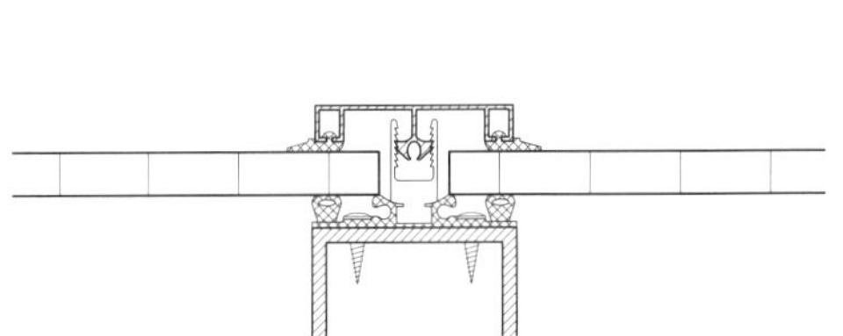

b

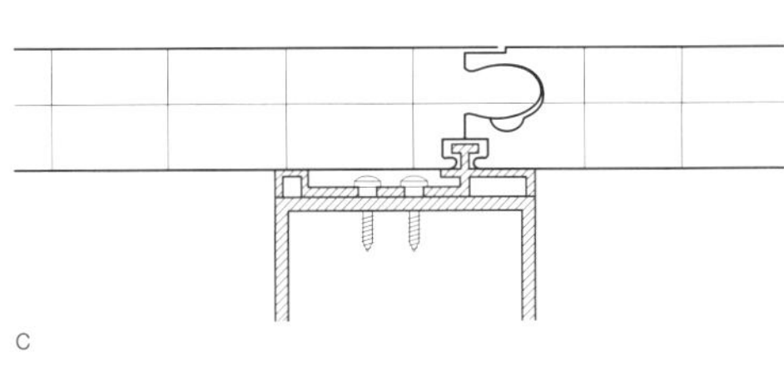

c

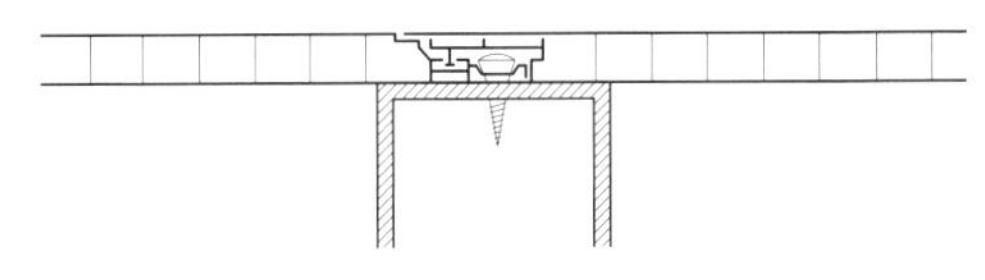

d

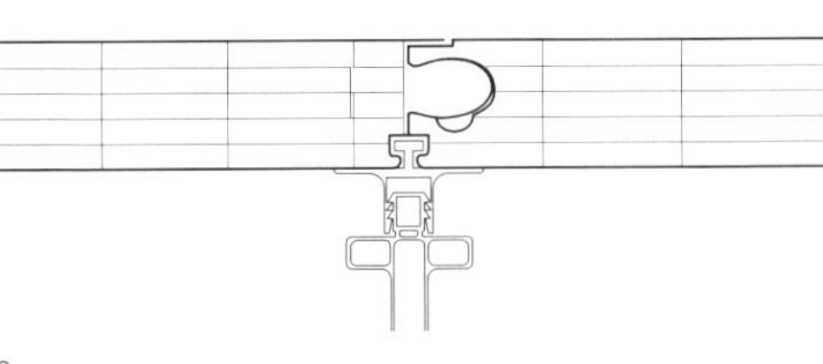

e

E 1.39

E 1.38 Butt joints between and strengthening of twin- and multi-wall sheets for pitched roofs, horizontal sections
a Interlocking butt joint
b Joint strengthened with external aluminium capping rail
c Joint strengthened with external polymer capping rail
d Joint strengthened with internal aluminium section
e Penetrating polymer strengthening section with clamping cap

E 1.39 Butt joints between and fixing of twin- and multi-wall sheets for facades, horizontal sections
a Butt joint with screwed aluminium clamping bar
b Butt joint with clip-in aluminium clamping bar
c Sheets interlocking with aluminium member
d Concealed screw fixing
e Sheets interlocking with PVC section

of the surrounding roof surface in order to prevent the infiltration of any water that might build up on the roof.
In principle, simple overlap and individual fixings are adequate at the junction between roof structure and rooflight. Rooflights consisting of up to four leaves, one over the other and connected via a special hermetic edges seal, are specified to comply with higher thermal performance specifications. Solid sheets are normally used for forming rooflights because they respond better to the hot-forming process. But twin- and multi-wall sheets can be used for continuous rooflights to improve the thermal insulation.

Side-by-side assembly and series production
Three-dimensional semi-finished products are in most cases modular items added together to form a larger entity, e.g. a facade. At the planning stage the total area is divided orthogonally into geometrically identical modules as far as possible. This enables series production of the elements, which in turn results in an economical design. Critical here is the number of moulds required. Fig. E 1.41 shows a prefabricated lining of PMMA trays. To reduce the cost of the moulds, only a few different modules were combined for this project. The trays are glued to flat PMMA bars that have first been screwed to the steel supporting construction. The joints are finished with transparent silicone gaskets so that the screws are not visible from the outside.

Forming
Only thermoplastic materials can be used for producing moulded elements in virtually any form from flat sheets. Twin- and multi-wall sheets are usually unsuitable because the thin webs are destroyed when subjected to large strains or the cross-section may be deformed. Hot-forming takes place at high temperatures but in the ideal case the process is free from stresses. The thermoplastics can even be forced into a new form at room temperature, a process that is also known as "cold-forming".

Hot-forming
Prior to forming, the thermoplastic material is first heated to a few degrees above the thermo-elastic temperature, i.e. the temperature at which the material becomes plastic. However, this temperature lies well below the melting point. The sheet, with a thickness of 0.3–10 mm, can subsequently be formed by hand or by machine, and after cooling it retains its new shape.
PET-G and PMMA are ideal for hot-forming – the forming temperatures of both these materials are comparatively low. A somewhat higher temperature is necessary for polycarbonate (PC). Other thermoplastics such as polystyrene (PS) and its copolymers (ASA, ABS) plus polyethylene (PE), polypropylene (PP) and polyvinyl chloride (PVC) can also be hot-formed.
One method frequently used is vacuum forming, a method also commonly used for building architectural models. First of all, a mould made from cardboard, wood, unsaturated polyester resin (UP) or aluminium is made, usually just a female tool without a matching male part. The polymer sheet is laid on the mould and heated from above by hot air. The air is then evacuated from the mould which causes the sheet to take up the shape of the mould. This method of production is primarily used for moulded parts with simple geometries and no ribs (Fig. E 1.40).
Although the cost of a vacuum-formed item is higher than an injection-moulded one, for instance, the high cost of the tools for injection moulding is saved.

"Cold-forming"
The low elastic modulus and the ductility of some thermoplastics means that, up to a point, it is possible to force flat sheets into three-dimensional shapes. This process can be carried out directly on the building site without the need to apply heat. The tendency of polymers to creep has the effect that the restraint stresses decrease over time (relaxation), and the component retains the shape that has been forced upon it.

Jointing
Three-dimensional moulded items do not generally include any integral joints, but rather, like panes of glass, have to be held in place by point fixings or clamping elements along the edges. The sheets used are mostly solid and

a

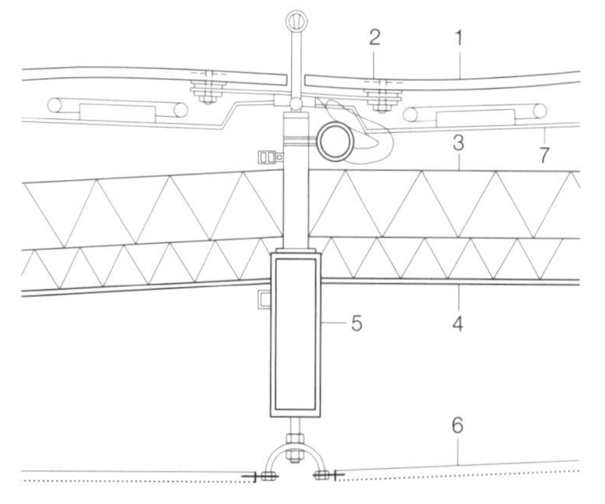

b
E 1.40

1 Hot-formed PMMA sheet
2 Point fixing
3 Foamed glass insulation, plastic sheet waterproofing
4 Sheet steel
5 Steel structure
6 Wire mesh tensioned between perimeter frame
7 Fixing for lighting unit
8 Steel rectangular hollow section
9 Steel flat
10 Steel channel
11 Lamp
12 Moulded PMMA panel, vacuum-formed
13 PMMA hanger, glued
14 Silicone gasket, transparent

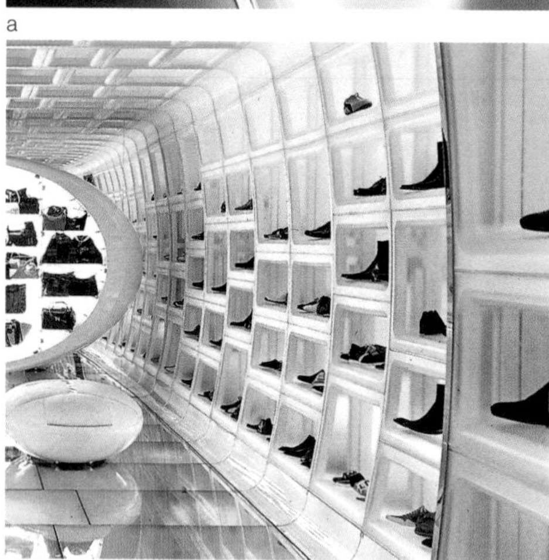
a

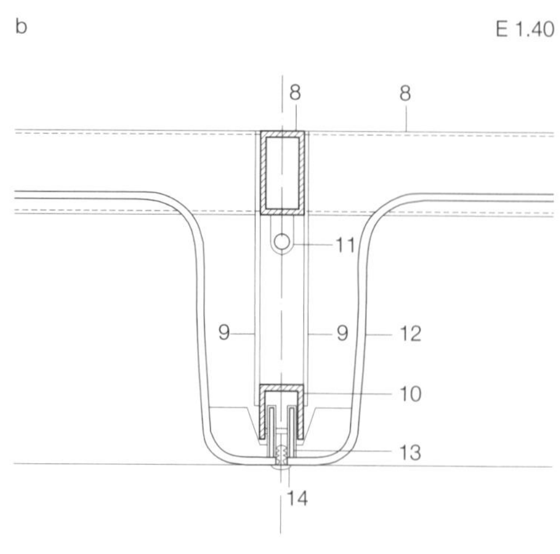

b
E 1.41

E 1.42

therefore do not provide enough depth to include clip-in connections. In addition, moulded parts are subjected to greater tolerances than flat sheets, which makes integral joints more difficult. Simple bolted or riveted connections are more common. It is hardly possible to make universal statements about building with moulded parts because very diverse solutions are used all the time.

Modular GFRP bridge

The modular footbridge shown in Fig. E 1.44a unites detachable and fixed connections for moulded parts. Each oval main beam section has end plates with multiple integral interlocking joints which are simply butted together and tightened against each other with integral steel cables (Fig. E 1.44b). The curved planks made from translucent GFRP, on the other hand, are attached to the vertical GFRP ribs with rivets. The ribs in turn lie in the plane of the joints between the main beam sections and are likewise connected via an interlocking joint only.

CFRP stairs

The example of a delicate staircase construction with treads of CFRP and stringers of glass illustrates the different jointing techniques of polymers and glass particularly clearly (Fig. E 1.43). Whereas the point fixing for the brittle glass requires a generously sized disc with appropriate bearing pads, simple screws are all that are required for the just 4 mm thick, more robust CFRP treads.

References:

[1] Park, Don-U., Knippers, Jan: Application of a new GFRP jointing method for an exhibition membrane spatial structure. 9th Asian Pacific Conference of Shell and Spatial Structures (APCS 2009), Nagoya, May 2009

[2] Oppe, Matthias: Zur Bemessung geschraubter Verbindungen von pultrudierten faserverstärkten Polymerprofilen. In: Stahlbau, No. 66/2008

[3] ibid. 1

[4] Peters, Stefan: Kleben von GFRP und Glas für baukonstruktive Anwendungen. Stuttgart, 2006, pp. 147ff.

[5] Keller, Thomas et al.: Adhesively Bonded and Translucent Glass Fiber Reinforced Polymer Sandwich Girders. In: Journal of Composites for Construction 5/2004, pp. 461ff.

[6] Dagher, Habib J.: Bridge in a Backpack. Project Presentation, Advanced Structures & Composite Center, University of Maine (USA), 19 Aug 2010

E 1.40 Curved PMMA sheets for a facade; art gallery, Graz (A), 2003, spacelab Peter Cook/Colin Fournier
a View from outside
b Schematic section, simplified

E 1.41 Shoebaloo, Amsterdam (NL), 2003, Meyer en Van Schooten
a Translucent PMMA trays mounted on steel framework
b Schematic section, simplified

E 1.42 Rooflights made from polymer sheet material

E 1.43 Staircase with CFRP treads, London (UK), Geoffrey Packer/EeStairs
a View of finished stair
b Fixing detail for CFRP treads
c Detail of stainless steel point fixing

E 1.44 Bridge system "Variocell 02"; "In the Clouds" footbridge, expo.02, Yverdon (CH), 2002
a View of finished bridge
b Isometric view of GFRP oval hollow section
c Section through bridge

a

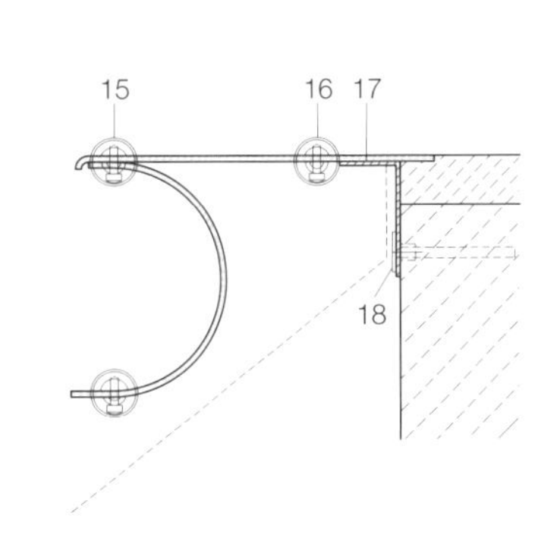

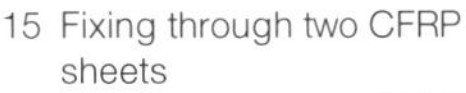

b

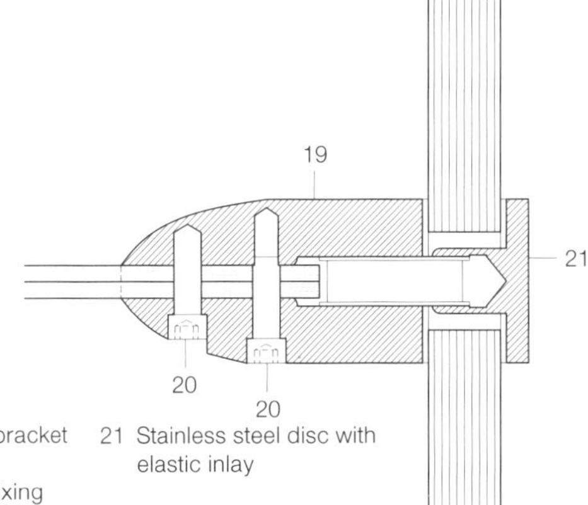

c

E 1.43

a

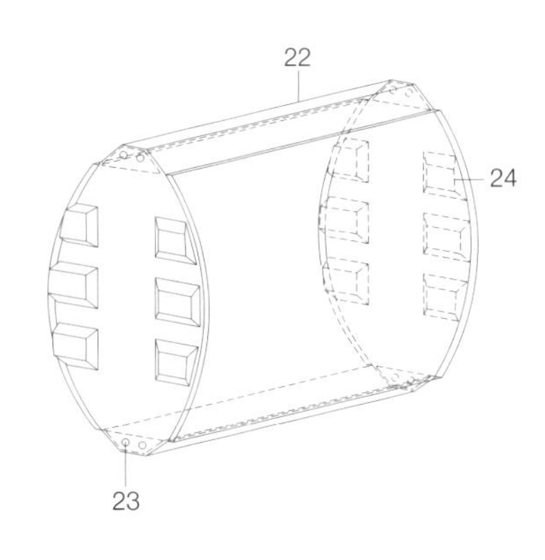

b

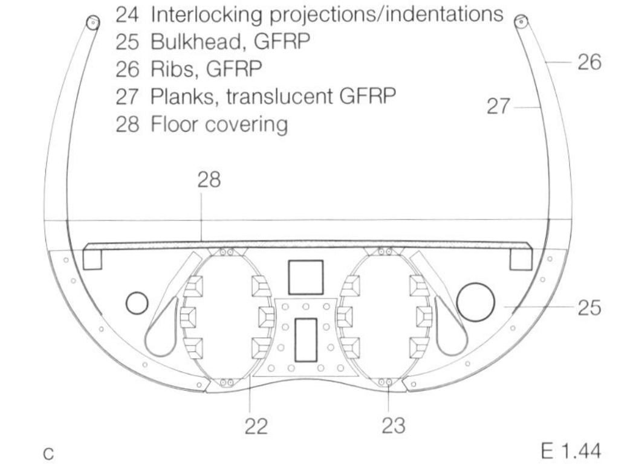

c

E 1.44

Building with free-form polymers

E 2.1

Polymer materials offer the planner design freedoms that are second to none: various colours, surface finishes, dimensions and mechanical properties can be specified. Furthermore, the free-form options enable several functions to be combined in one component and the geometry to be optimised to suit the requirements. Multi-functional polymer components are intrinsic to our everyday lives; even just a simple bottle closure performs several functions (Fig. E 2.1). Living hinge, clip-fit closure, thread and seal are formed in one operation in this typical, industrially fabricated product. It is an injection-moulded component that requires no additional work. The hinge in this case is not a traditional linkage consisting of several parts, but rather a thin polymer strip that is formed together with the parts it joins in one and the same moulding operation. Ductile thermoplastics are ideal for such a so-called living hinge. Comparable multi-function designs are impossible with conventional materials.

Compared with metals, polymers are lightweight building materials with high strengths and are therefore predestined for lightweight designs. However, the elastic moduli of these materials – apart from carbon fibre-reinforced polymers (CFRP) – are relatively low and so polymers require specific constructional measures to be taken to ensure that components attain the necessary stiffness. This is achieved, for example, by creating a sandwich structure, by forming ribs, or through choosing a design that is stiffened by way of its geometry. Most polymers can be formed into any random or irregular shape at temperatures far lower than those required for metals or glass, which means that forming and any subsequent work required can be carried out with relatively simple tools. Polymer processing operations can also be carried out in small plants.
The particular features arising from the nature of polymers themselves result in a series of aspects that must be considered if we are to achieve a design that does justice to the materials:

- Flowing and generously dimensioned structures instead of the isolated jointing of small-format elements
- Planar, thin-wall structures (exception: foams)
- Rounded forms, instead of arrises and corners, due to the method of production (Fig. E 2.2)
- Stiffening by way of webs, ribs or sandwich structures instead of massive, heavyweight components
- Flanged edges and load-transfer points instead of a thickening of the material
- Flexible, thin, living hinges instead of true hinges with high stress concentrations
- Alignment of the fibre reinforcement (in fibre-reinforced polymers) to match the flow of forces

When building with polymers, the method of production must be selected early on in the planning process and the geometries of the components adapted to suit if the designer does not wish to make use of prefabricated semi-finished products (see "Building with semi-finished polymer products", pp. 160–173). Moreover, the requirements of mouldmaking have an effect on the component geometry for the vacuum-forming of thermoplastics and also planar fibre-reinforced polymers. In a similar way to the production of formwork for reinforced concrete, mouldmaking can represent a decisive factor in the production process and hence the cost of building with polymers. For this reason, it is usually imperative to design components in such a way that a mould or mould segments can be used more than once. Modular building or series production is always an optimisation goal in building with polymers.

Unreinforced polymers

Choosing a suitable material is just as important as the geometry and the method of production when building with unreinforced polymers. All three factors are directly interrelated and influence each other. Acrylic sheet (PMMA), for example, requires thick walls, can be moulded or extruded, and is highly transparent. But it is comparatively brittle and therefore less suitable for resisting impact loads. Polypropylene (PP), on the other hand, can be designed with very thin walls. Injection-moulding is the main technique used for processing PP, which can be

E 2.1 Closure for a plastic bottle
E 2.2 Design principles for polymers: rounded corners and arrises and curved surfaces
E 2.3 Stiffening principles for polymer sheets
a Solid, flat sheet (severe deformations)
b Corrugated or trapezoidal profile sheet
c Twin-wall panel or sandwich element
d Curved surface with various support conditions
E 2.4 Weight reduction through component design
a Solid sheet
b Ribbed element

produced in milky to transparent variations. Its high ductility makes it perfect for absorbing shocks and impacts.

Stiffening surfaces

First of all, it is necessary to clarify how the comparatively flexible polymer design can be stiffened because flat polymer surfaces tend to buckle and warp. Solid, flat sheets are only advisable in exceptional circumstances (Fig. E 2.3a). In order to reduce deformations and use the load-carrying capacity to the full, polymer components should be designed as resolved structures. Thick walls can lead to air inclusions and hence poor mechanical properties. Restraint stresses can ensue at transitions between zones of different thickness because the polymer does not cool evenly after production (see "Sources of errors in injection-moulding", p. 92).

Profiling

Unreinforced polymers are frequently processed to form sheets with corrugated or trapezoidal profiles (Fig. E 2.3b). Their prismatic cross-sections make these sheets ideal for series production. The profiles can be sine-wave, triangular or trapezoidal, forms that are primarily suitable for components spanning in one direction. The weak axis remains flexible because of the lack of stiffening but this allows the sheets to be bent to a curved form around a supporting structure.

Sandwich and ribbed forms

In contrast to simple profiling, a sandwich form is strong in two directions (Fig. E 2.3c). Whereas in designs employing fibre-reinforced polymers the sandwich elements generally have a foam core, in designs based on unreinforced polymers it is more common to have sandwich elements with honeycomb cores, ribs or webs. In principle, transparent designs are also possible with this latter type of sandwich. In contrast to corrugated sheets, however, flat surfaces are also possible.
Ribbed designs result in a considerable reduction in weight compared with a solid sheet (Fig. E 2.4). It is worthwhile strengthening the construction with ribs in zones with a high degree of utilisation, e.g. edges, connections, frame corners (Fig. E 2.5, p. 176).

Curved surfaces

Curved surfaces can be achieved with relatively simple means (Fig. E 2.3d). With suitable supports, the geometry of the component is stabilised by the double curvature. Basically, the design principles for lightweight plate and shell structures apply (see "Curvature of the surface", p. 146).

Edge and corner details

Most polymer components have thin walls, which is why unsupported edges and penetrations need additional strengthening. Bending up the edge at 90° to the plane of the material is a relatively simple way of achieving the necessary stiffness. In the end, it is the resulting structural lever arm of the bent edge that governs the loadbearing effect (Fig. E 2.7, p. 176). A whole range of different cross-sections is possible, but the semicircular form is frequently the best. The production methods used for polymers mean that rounded arrises and corners are to be preferred because this enables the thickness of the material to be kept constant and guarantees easier demoulding. Other forms may prove more suitable depending on the other functions required, e.g. for joining the components. However, the requirements of mouldmaking make undercuts undesirable.

Connections

Subsequent bolted, screwed, riveted or glued joints can, in principle, be employed in a similar way to those for semi-finished products (see "Building with semi-finished polymer products", pp. 160–173). However, means of connection that are integrated during the production of the component are to be preferred. These not only reduce the amount of work required during erection, but generally also enable much higher forces to be transferred across the joints because any strengthening elements required are produced at the same time.

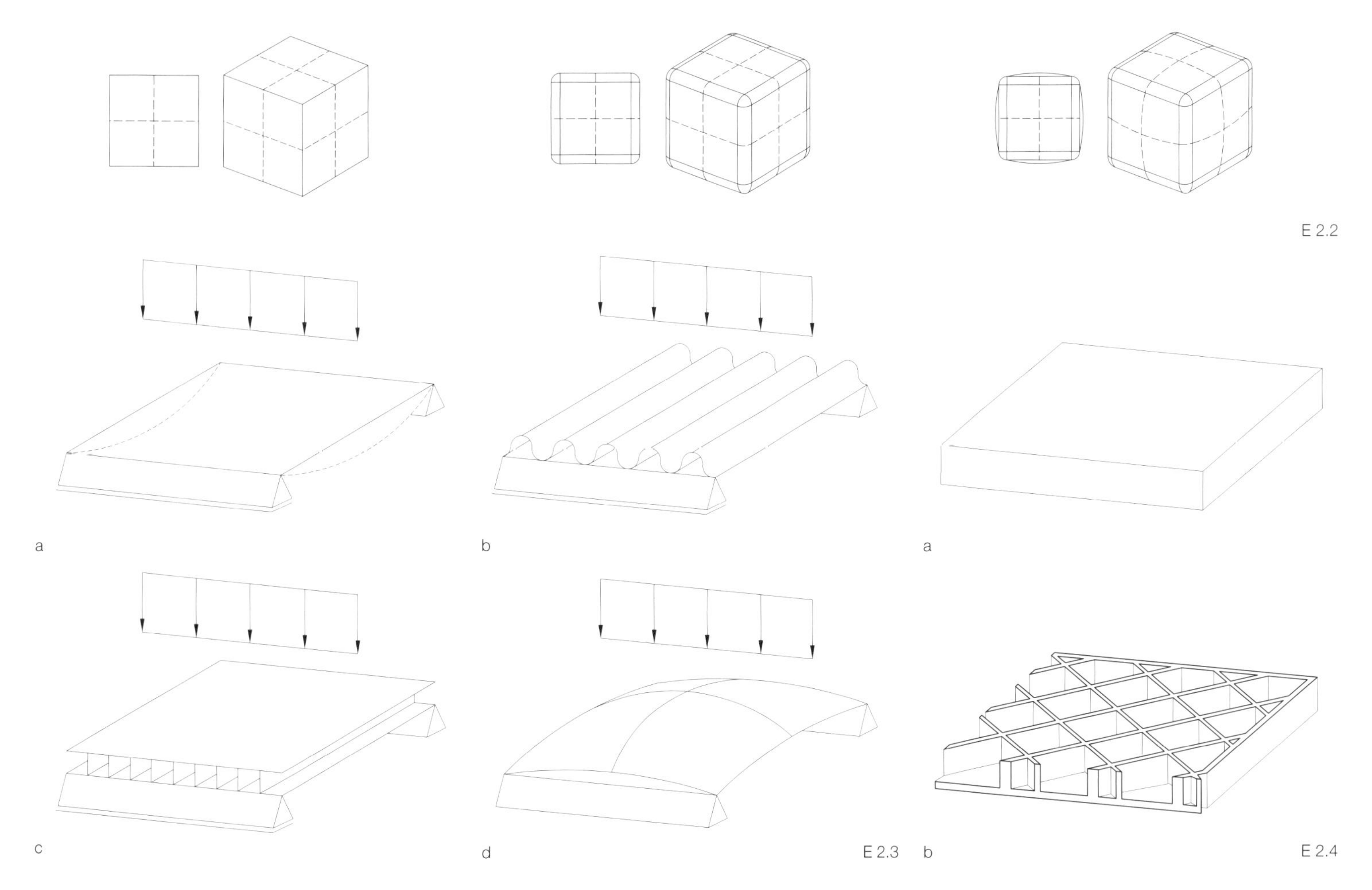

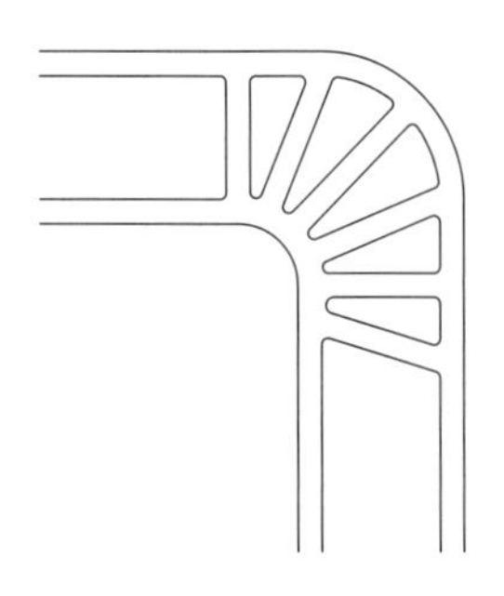

E 2.5

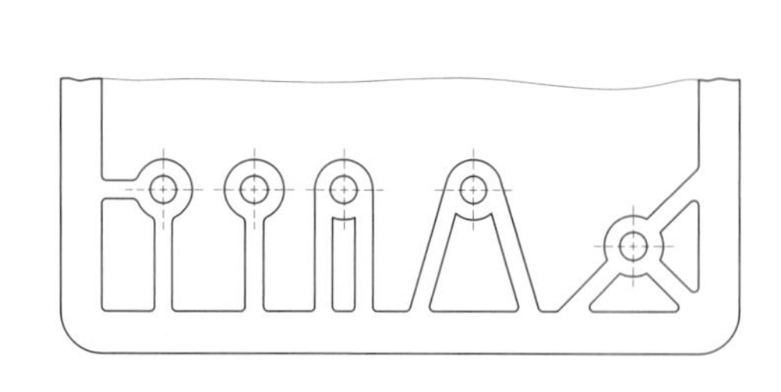

E 2.6

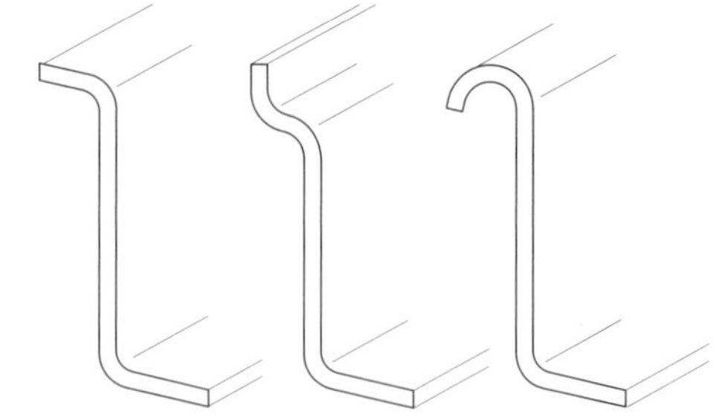

E 2.7

1 Spring
2 Barbed hook

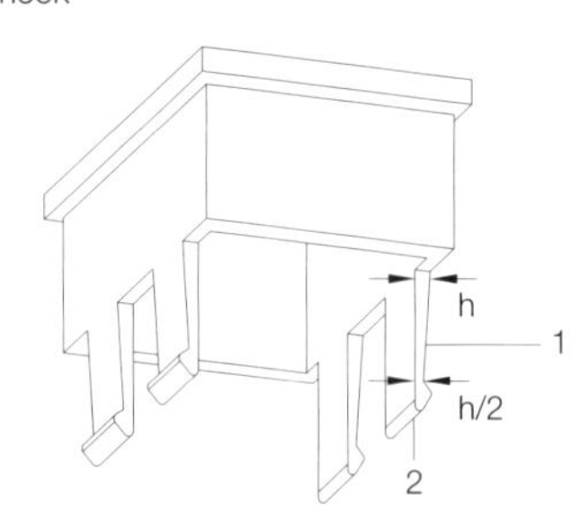

E 2.8

1 Plastic pipe
2 Radial spring
3 Axial barbed hook

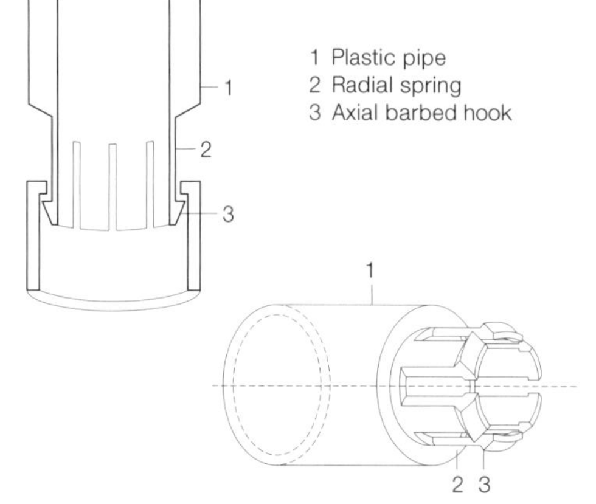

E 2.9

1 Living hinge
2 Smooth transition

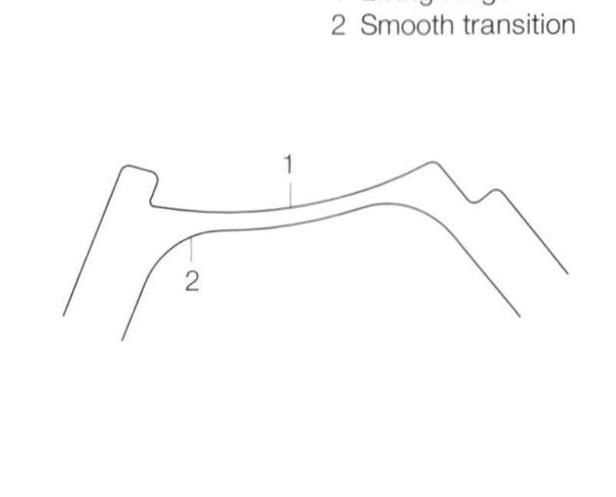

E 2.10

Clip-in connections
Clip-in or clip-fit connections are very important in building with polymers when trying to achieve a design that does justice to the material. The polycarbonate twin- and multi-wall sheets so popular in the building industry also make use of this type of connection (Fig. E 1.34, p. 170). Clip-in connections can be designed to be put together and taken apart many times. But non-detachable connections are suitable for permanent structures and such connections are frequently used when a component, for production reasons, must be assembled from two or more parts but in the final condition is regarded as one component.
A clip-in connection consists of a barbed hook and a corresponding female element. One of the two elements is linked to an elastic spring, usually formed from a thin strip of polymer material. The connection should be designed in such a way that both components only deform elastically, i.e. are not permanently deformed or damaged, when they are fitted together. A polymer with sufficient ductility, e.g. polypropylene (PP), should always be preferred where multiple assembling and dismantling operations are intended. In most instances the elastic spring is combined with the barbed hook (Fig. E 2.8). The spring works as a cantilever arm here, which must be sufficiently thin and long to enable the connection to be made without the elastic limit stress being exceeded. The rule of thumb is: the thickness of the spring at its point of fixity should taper to half this thickness at the barbed hook. Plastic pipes can be joined together via a concentric arrangement of clips (Fig. E 2.9).

Bolted connections
Appropriate strengthening should be designed into the component when intending to use bolts (or rivets) so that the concentrated load can be transferred evenly to the component. Integral collars or ribs can be formed at the position of the later joint (Fig. E 2.6). Thicker sections with great accumulations of mass should be avoided, however. Plastic threads do not usually exhibit sufficient strength for loadbearing connections, and the manufacturing tolerances are relatively generous as well. Metal threaded sockets, screwed, welded or glued into the polymer material, are the better choice and enable the use of metric threads with their superior durability. However, the socket itself should not be relied upon to strengthen the component; additional flanged edges or ribs are still required.

Living hinges
In metal structures, stiff members are joined together with discrete linkages or hinges where some movement is necessary. Such connection details are in most cases very massive because this is where all the forces are concentrated and the hinges themselves have to be connected to the members. But with polymers, it is possible to design elastic living or integral hinges. The hinge is integrated into the structure of the polymer component by varying the thickness at the position of the linkage, but the component and the hinge are made from exactly the same material. A smooth transition between the different thicknesses is crucial if local stress concentrations are to be avoided (Fig. E 2.10). Only sufficiently ductile polymers can be considered for living hinges, materials that do not suffer brittle failure as a result of repeated usage. But the thin walls of living hinges limit the forces that can be transferred across the articulated joint. Torsion is the most critical type of load, which can easily lead to failure of such a hinge.

Fibre-reinforced polymers

Fibre-reinforced polymers are used like unreinforced polymers, i.e. in planar form with relatively thin walls. To achieve a form of construction that does justice to the material, particular attention should be paid to the fibre reinforcement itself, which is in most cases in the form of several plies. A composite material made up of fibres and a polymer matrix is generally referred to as a laminate.
In practice, laminates consist almost exclusively of thermosets, also known as (synthetic) resins. Free-form fibre composites are produced using the hand lay-up technique plus methods based on this manual method, e.g. resin infusion (see "Resin infusion and vacuum methods", p. 79). With a few exceptions, the design guidelines

presented here can also be applied to automated methods of production. However, there are geometrical limitations to some of these methods.

Laminate lay-up
Fibre-reinforced polymers, like wood, cannot be considered to be homogeneous materials. The fibre plies are drawn as lines in the sectional drawings in this chapter. In a planar laminate one line corresponds to a layer of textile, in linear members with long fibres (rovings or continuous fibres) the lines symbolise the direction of the fibres within the component.
With more complex cross-sections, as in a sandwich panel (Fig. E 2.12), the orientation of the fibres must be "designed". For instance, the fibre plies in the vertical webs of such sandwich panels continue into the horizontal flanges. This results in a high load-carrying capacity at the web-flange junction. At the same time, it can be seen that webs are generally designed to be thinner than flanges because otherwise it is not possible to incorporate enough fibre plies at the junction. Nevertheless, the web-flange junction still represents a potential weak point in the structure because there is an accumulation of unreinforced resin in the centre of the junction.

Stiffening surfaces
As with unreinforced polymers, thin-wall laminates must always be stiffened because flat sheets are too flexible for longer spans. Stiffening can be achieved by profiling the cross-section, by including reinforcing ribs or by employing a sandwich form of construction (Fig. E 2.11). It is also possible, with appropriate support conditions, to stiffen the construction by way of its geometry, i.e. by forming a shell.

Sandwich elements
Structures employing fibre-reinforced polymers are frequently in the form of sandwich elements. The provision of a lightweight core increases the structural lever arm of the laminate, which in turn increases the load-carrying capacity and stiffness considerably for only a small increase in the weight per unit area (Fig. E 2.13). The central zone of a component carrying the loads in bending plays only a minor structural role anyway and so the core can be made from a material with a lower strength which is more flexible and usually less expensive than the fibre-reinforced polymer.

Manufacture of sandwich components
Various materials can be considered for the cores of sandwich elements (see "Core materials", pp. 72–75). Rigid foams (Fig. E 2.16d, p.178) enable the production of sandwich components with a high load-carrying capacity. The laminate is applied directly to the core material, the bond between the two being created by the resin itself. It is important to realise that some foams, e.g. polyurethane (PUR), absorb relatively large quantities of resin. Better results in

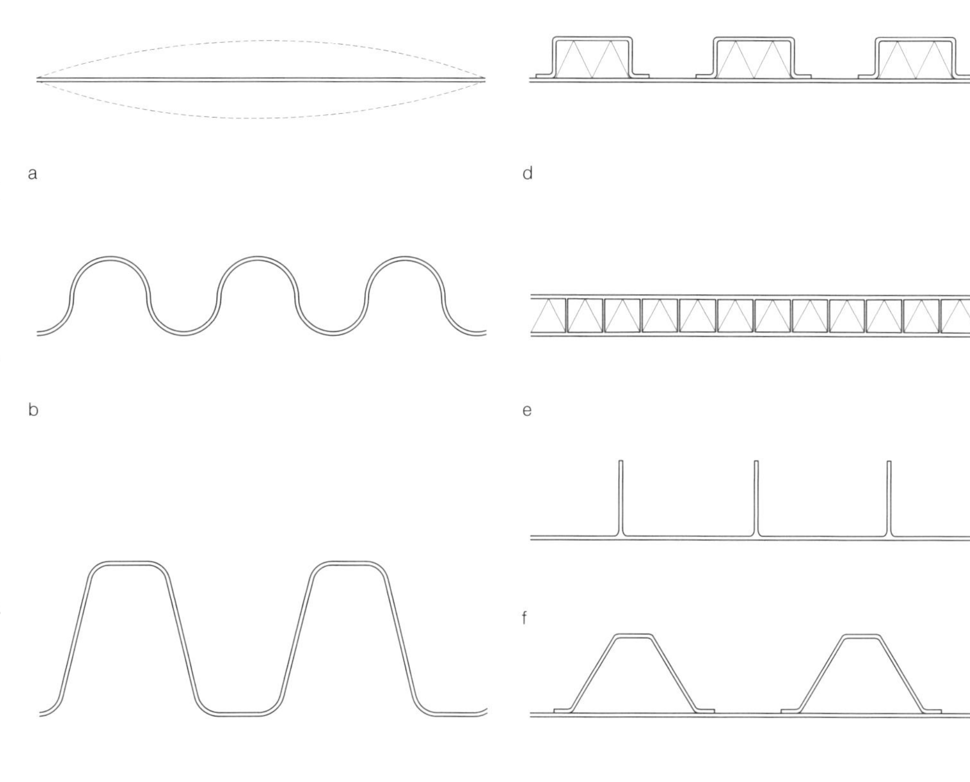

E 2.11

E 2.5 Ribs for strengthening a frame corner
E 2.6 Strengthening for connections
E 2.7 Unsupported edges strengthened by bending
E 2.8 Design of clip-in connections
E 2.9 Concentric clip-in connection
E 2.10 Living or integral hinge
E 2.11 Stiffening of planar, fibre-reinforced polymer components
a Flat solid sheet, vulnerable to deformation
b, c Profiled sheets
d Separate ribs
e Sandwich form
f Ribs laminated into sheet
g Trapezoidal ribs laminated into sheet
E 2.12 Alignment of the fibre reinforcement in a resolved cross-section with flanges and webs
E 2.13 Employing the sandwich principle to increase stiffness and load-carrying capacity, schematic diagrams

1 Fibre reinforcement in webs continues into flanges
2 Accumulation of resin
3 Rigid foam core

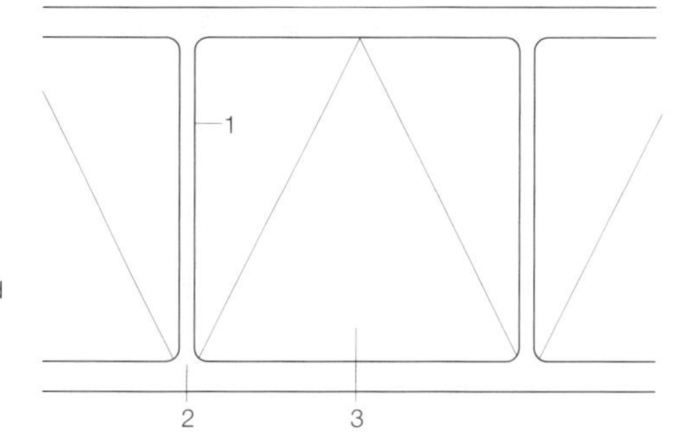

E 2.12

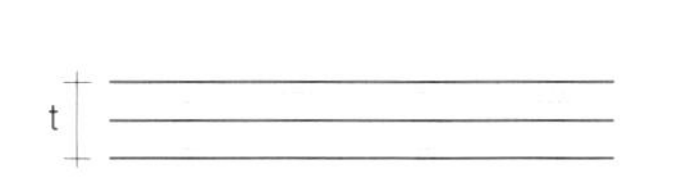

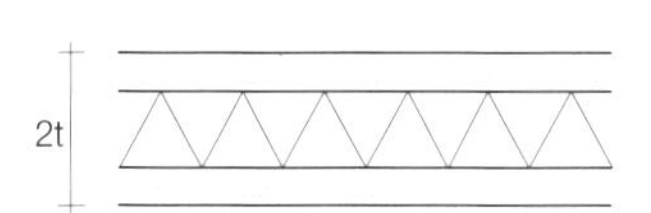

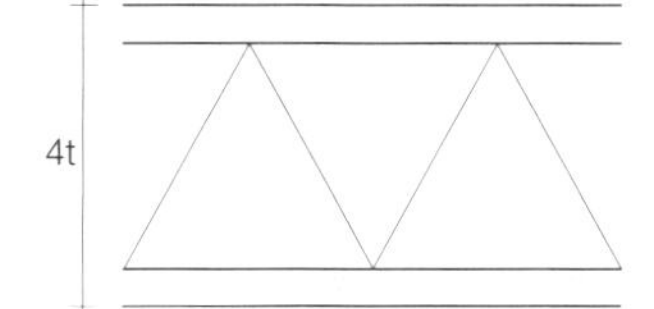

Depth of element	t	2 t	4 t
Stiffness [1]	1.0	7.0	37.0
Load-carrying capacity [1]	1.0	3.5	9.2
Weight	1.0	1.03	1.06

[1] in bending

E 2.13

a

b

E 2.14

1 Pipe made from fibre-reinforced polymer
2 Fibre-reinforced polymer, laminated in place
3 Foam core
4 Bulkhead glued in place

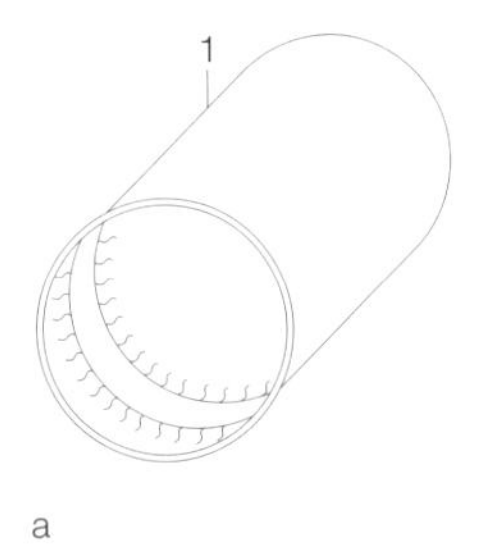

a

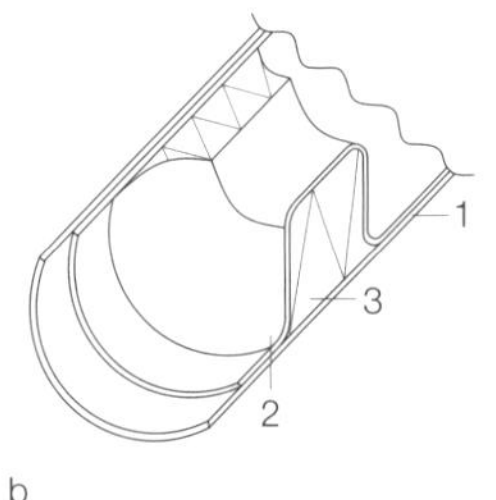

b

c

E 2.15

a

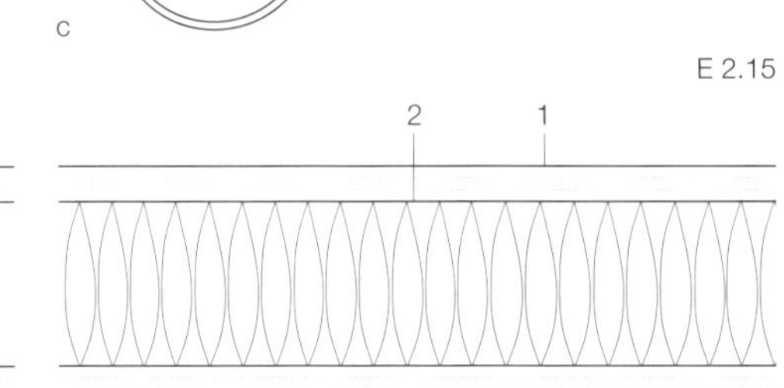

b

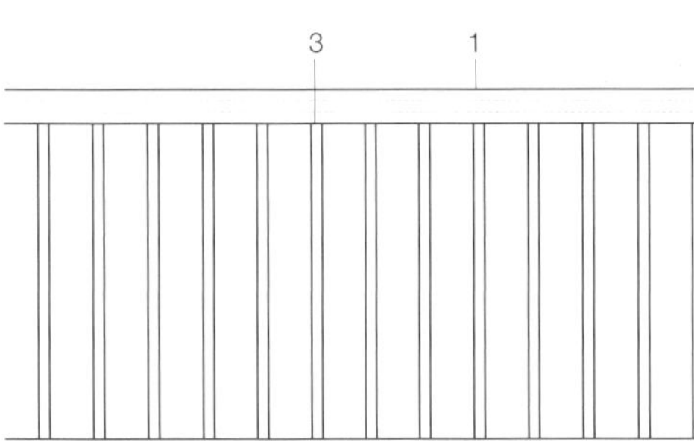

c

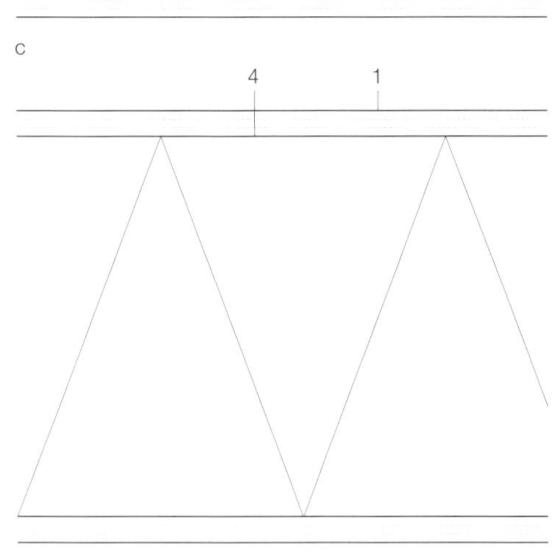

d

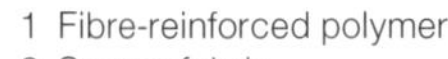

1 Fibre-reinforced polymer
2 Spacer fabric
3 Honeycomb core
4 Rigid foam core

E 2.16

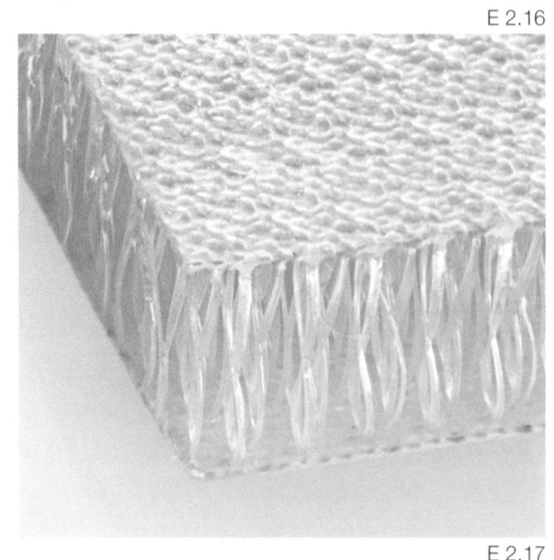

E 2.17

terms of processing and load-carrying capacity are achieved with PVC foam, which is, however, much more expensive. One advantage of rigid foams is that they can be fully automatically preformed with CNC milling machines prior to laminating. They therefore also function as the mould (indeed, permanent formwork) for the fibre-reinforced polymer component (see "Rigid foams", p. 185). Foams are relatively expensive materials and therefore voids with ribs or transverse bulkheads have proved to be more economic for components with larger dimensions (Fig. E 2.15).
Honeycomb structures, core fleeces and spacer fabrics can be used for thinner sandwich elements up to a thickness of a few centimetres (Figs. E 2.16b and c). In most cases the weight per unit area of the resulting sandwich is even less than when using rigid foam, and honeycomb cores are certainly the best choice for demanding lightweight construction specifications. As a rule, however, the thickness of the component must remain constant throughout. And tight bending radii or components in double curvature are difficult to achieve with such core materials.
Spacer fabrics (Fig. E 2.17) are initially compressed when applying the resin with a brush or roller, which ensures an even wetting of the material. Afterwards, the fabric regains its natural thickness automatically, thus creating the voids in the material. The facing plies and vertical threads impregnated with resin stabilise the structure. Further plies can then be laminated over the surfaces.

Profiling and ribs
Geometrical stiffening by way of profiling and ribs corresponds to the design principles for components made from unreinforced polymers. A direct connection between internal web, or bulkhead, and external surface should be preferred, i.e. continuing the fibre reinforcement through the junction, where the geometry permits this (Fig. E 2.18a). It is frequently the case, however, that – for production reasons – ribs are added to the finished laminate afterwards. To do this, a shaped core of rigid foam, metal or timber is glued to the component and then permanently integrated by laminating over this (Figs. E 2.18b–d). It is also possible to attach stiffening lamellae or sections with adhesive (Figs. e 2.18e–g) or to create a rib by profiling the cross-section itself locally (Fig. E 2.18h). When using metal, wood or a combination of different composites, restraint stresses can build up under certain circumstances as a result of the disparate thermal behaviour of the different materials.

Arrises

To take into account the change in direction of the reinforcing fibres and the requirements of mouldmaking, designers are advised to round off all arrises with a sufficient radius (Fig. E 2.20). This radius should be at least 5 mm and not less than the thickness of the laminate for pultruded sections. A radius of min. 20 mm is recommended for manually laminated components. Choosing a radius that is too tight can result in the textile reinforcement becoming folded or creased during production (Fig. E 2.19), which disrupts the loadbearing behaviour significantly. As with unsupported edges, additional strengthening of the planar laminate is often required along arrises. Thickening the material should be avoided, however, because continuous fibre reinforcement is then impossible. Instead, the thickness of the laminate should be kept constant and stiffening achieved by way of profiling.

Edge details

Unsupported edges are difficult from the constructional viewpoint because they are sensitive to deformations (Fig. E 2.21a, p. 180). Furthermore, the fibres are inevitably exposed along the edge and without extra protective measures are vulnerable to moisture. A flanged or reinforced edge is recommended for visual and mechanical reasons. But as with the rib stiffeners, simply doubling the thickness should be avoided. A flanged edge can be omitted in exceptional cases only, i.e. where the sheet is precisely manufactured, the edge is sealed and also rests on a continuous support. This is the case with cladding materials, for example.

Strengthening the edge

The simplest way of strengthening an edge is to form a 90° bend in the laminate (Fig. E 2.21b, p. 180). And a higher load-carrying capacity can be achieved by providing a core material that defines the shape of the edge. The core can be made from a hollow metal section, a foam or a balsa wood dowel (Figs. E 2.21c–e, p. 180). The laminate is wrapped around the core material during production; alternatively, the core can be added afterwards and additional plies of laminate added over this. Besides the stiffening function, the edge member can also be used to attach the component to the supporting construction, for instance.

E 2.14 Reinforcing rings in GFRP "stalks"; "Market Houses", Mainz (D), 2008, Massimiliano Fuksas
a Stalk prior to erection
b View of GFRP stalks in position

E 2.15 Methods for stiffening pipes and tubes
a Circumferential ring
b Reinforcing ring with sandwich core
c Reinforcing bulkheads

E 2.16 Sandwich elements made from fibre-reinforced polymers
a Fibre-reinforced polymer
b with spacer fabric
c with honeycomb core
d with rigid foam core

E 2.17 Elastic spacer fabric

E 2.18 Reinforcing ribs
a–h Various options
1 Fibre-reinforced polymer
2 Rib laminated to sheet
3 Wooden batten
4 Fibre-reinforced polymer laminated to sheet
5 Rigid foam core
6 Steel section
7 Adhesive
8 Flat plate made from fibre-reinforced polymer, e.g. CFRP
9 Hollow section formed from fibre-reinforced polymer

E 2.19 GFRP production error due to inadequate radius at an arris

E 2.20 Rounded corner principle for fibre-reinforced polymers

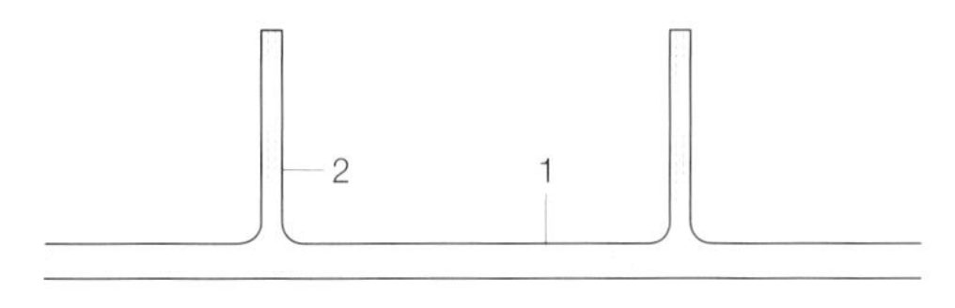

a

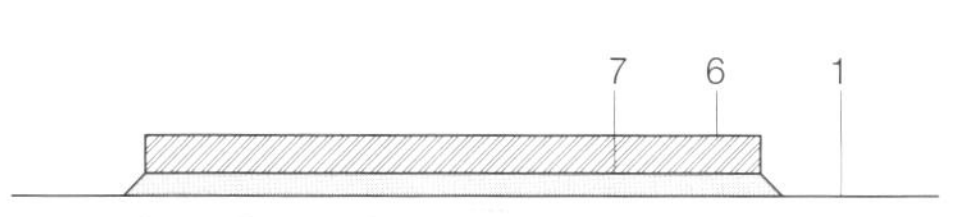

e

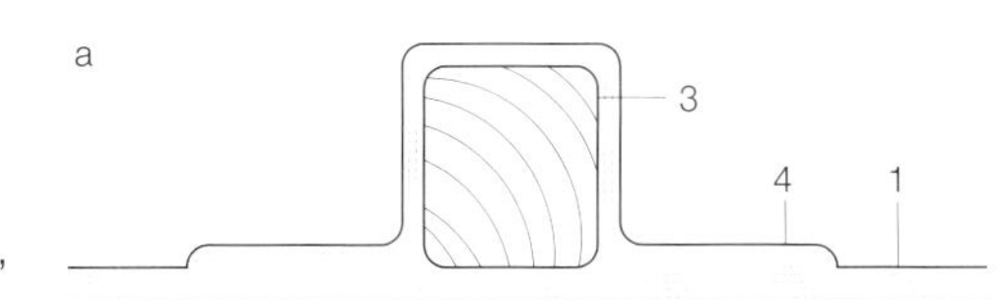

b

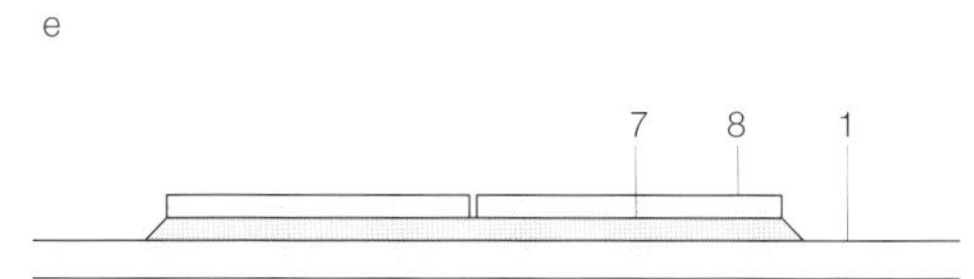

f

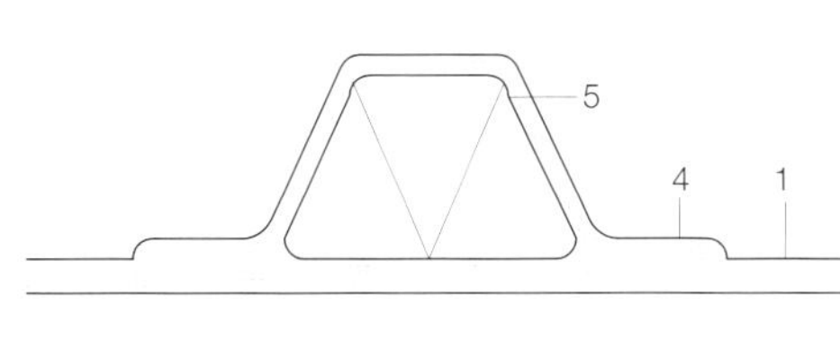

c

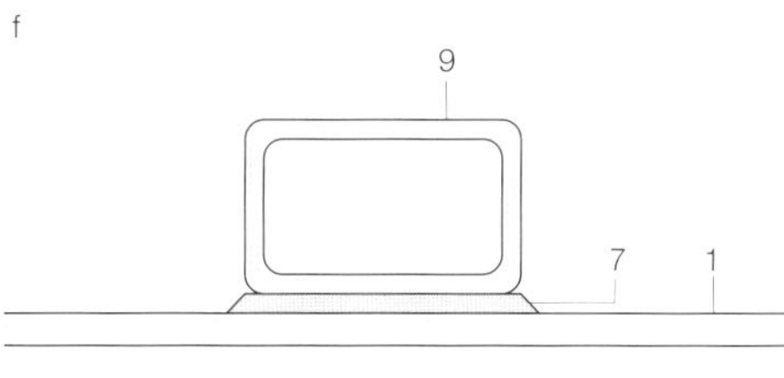

g

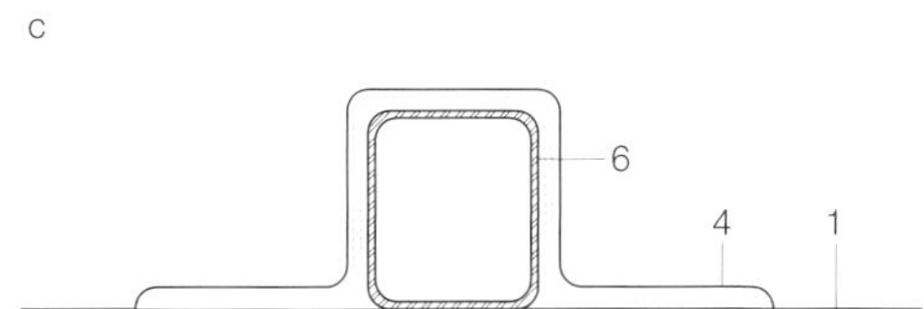

d

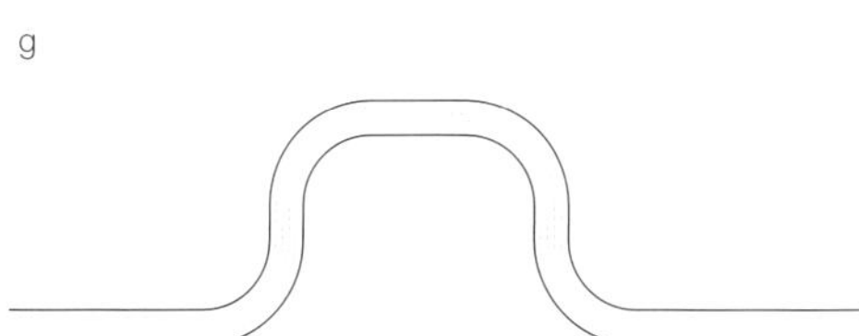
h

E 2.18

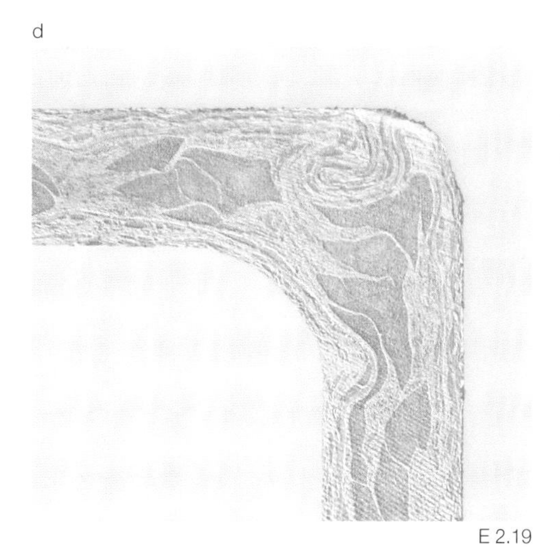
E 2.19

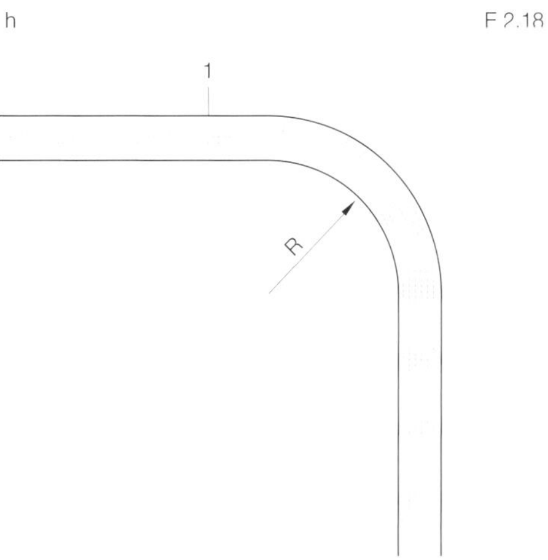

E 2.20

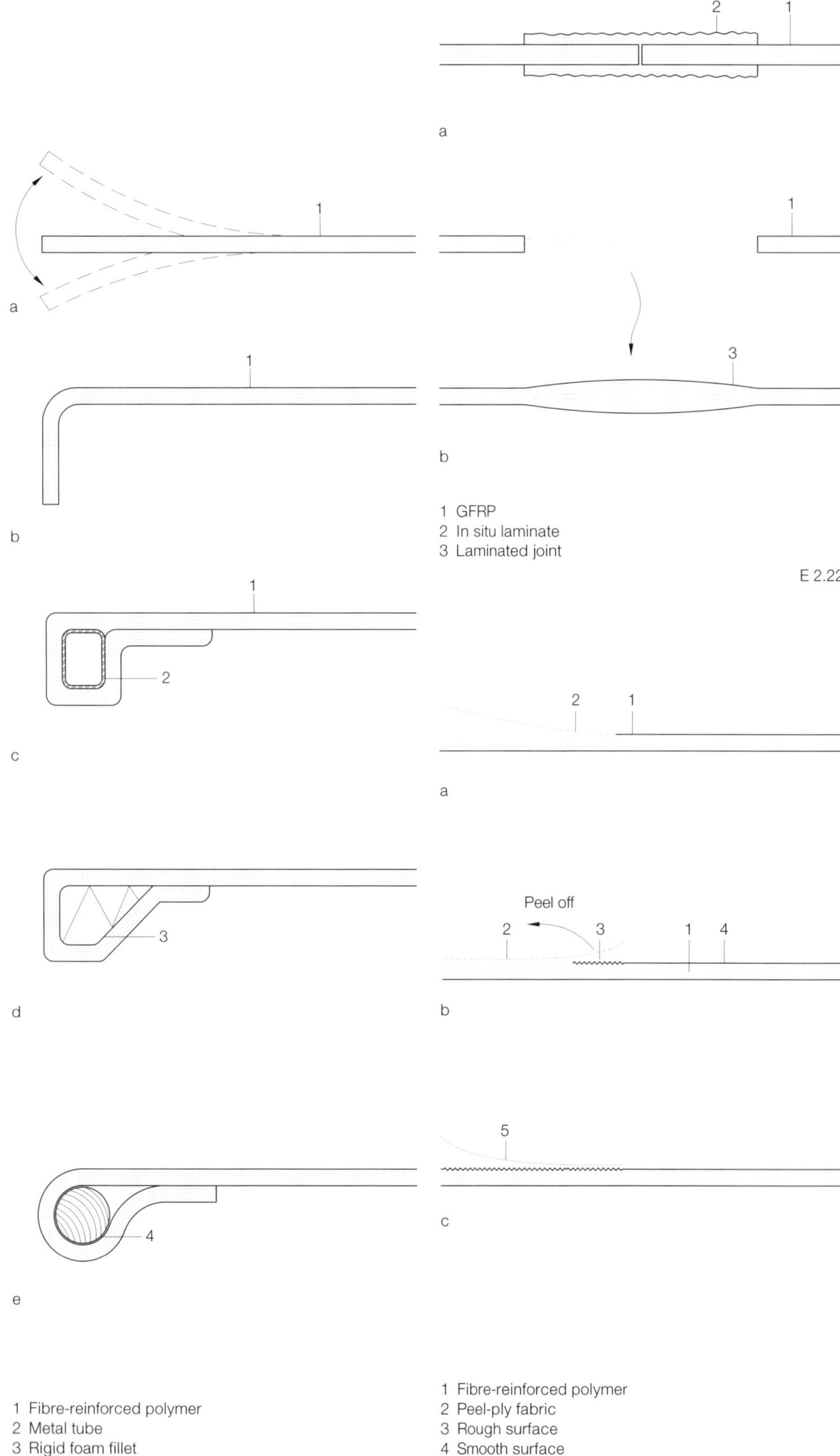

E 2.21 Reinforced edges for fibre-reinforced polymers
a Unsupported edge
b Edge bent through 90°
c Metal tube laminated to edge of sheet
d Rigid foam fillet laminated to edge of sheet
e Wooden dowel laminated to edge of sheet

E 2.22 Laminated joints
a Butt joint laminated both sides
b Laminated joint formed by leaving fibres projecting and subsequently overlapping them and impregnating with resin

E 2.23 Laminated joint with peel-ply fabric

Shadowline joints

Butt joints between large-format components made from fibre-reinforced polymers are difficult to achieve in practice because of the inevitable manufacturing tolerances. The advantage of designing shadowline joints is that the flanged edges of the components serve as strengthening ribs both during erection and in the final structure. At the same time, the means of connection can be concealed within the construction (Figs. E 2.25a and E 2.26).

This form of construction was common to the first buildings made from fibre-reinforced polymers in the 1960s, but is unsatisfactory from the building physics viewpoint because it creates an open joint and at the same time a thermal bridge. This problem is even more significant when joining together sandwich elements because the layer of thermal insulation is interrupted. A shadowline joint also eases the detailing when setting up a fibre composite component on the ground; installing an elastomeric strip in the joint helps to ensure an even load transfer (Fig. E 2.25b). If the means of connection at a joint between elements is to remain accessible from outside, then the shadowline joint should be designed as shown in Fig. E 2.25c.

Connections

Joints required for erection purposes can be closed off afterwards by laminating over them. Ideally, the joint will then have mechanical and building physics properties identical with those of the components on either side. However, individual components can also be connected by way of pin-type fasteners or adhesives (see "Means of connection", pp. 161–164). It is possible to integrate lugs, splice plates, fittings or sockets into the material during production, and also to adapt the orientation of the fibres to suit the means of connection. Such detailing improves the load-carrying capacity of the joint and in some cases the building physics properties as well.

Laminated joints

At a laminated joint, the components to be joined are initially butted together and then connected by laminating plies across the joint (Fig. E 2.22a). The additional layers of fibres

a Attaching the peel-ply fabric as the final layer
b Removing the peel-ply fabric before the resin has fully cured
c Laminating over the rough surface at a later date

E 2.24 Measures for increasing the bearing strength of bolted connections

E 2.25 Design of shadowline joints
a Vertical shadowline joint
b Shadowline joint on ground
c Recessed joint

E 2.26 "D-Tower", Doetinchem (NL), 2004, Lars Spuybroek/NOX

should be attached on both sides wherever possible in order to ensure an even load transfer. The surfaces of the components must be sufficiently rough to ensure good adhesion for the additional plies at the joint. A peel-ply fabric can be used to achieve this (see "Peel-ply fabrics", p. 71). The peel-ply fabric is first attached in the factory as the final layer but removed before the resin has fully cured. This creates a rough surface with small polymer serrations to which further plies can be attached during erection (Fig. E 2.23).
Alternatively, it is also possible to leave dry fibres protruding from the edges. During erection, these are overlapped alternately and impregnated with resin layer by layer (Fig. E 2.22b). Both methods result in a thickening of the laminate at the joint.

Adapting the fibre reinforcement
In contrast to building with semi-finished products, the use of free-form laminates enables the designer to adjust the construction to suit the anticipated loads. It is possible to improve the shear strength at a hole for a bolt or screw in order to increase the bearing strength of a bolted or screwed connection. Including textile fibre reinforcement at an angle of 45° to the axis of the component increases the bearing strength irrespective of the direction of the load and the exact position of the connection. Even more effective are prefabricated helical or star arrangements. However, the exact position of the connection must be known beforehand. Looping the fibres around the hole achieves the best results (Fig. E 2.24). Fitting a metal sleeve into the hole as well increases the load-carrying capacity even further. These measures rely on positioning the fibres so accurately that they are not severed when drilling the hole. The forces are transferred tangentially from the screw or bolt to the fibres and from there directly to the rest of the laminate. However, the geometry and direction of the force at the connection must be known in advance.

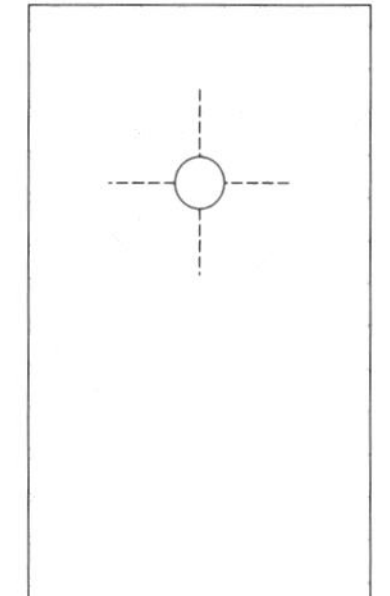
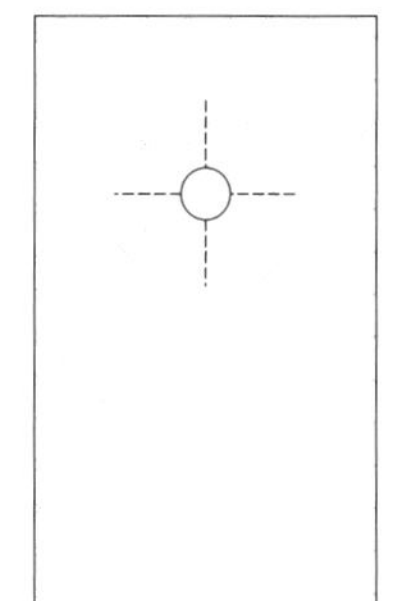

Helical

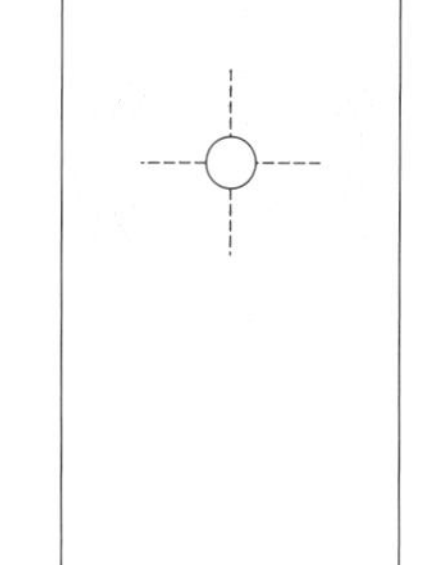

Star

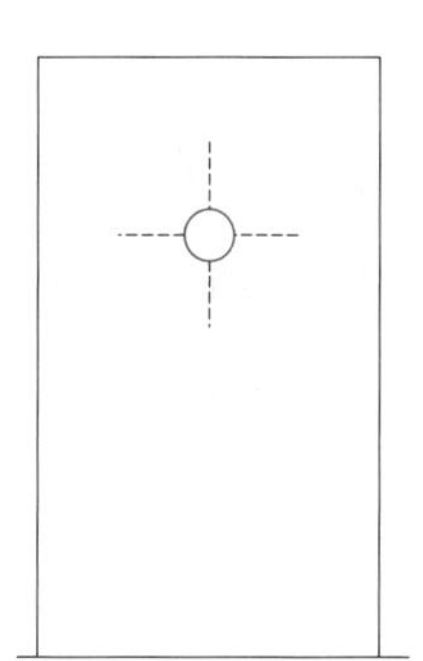

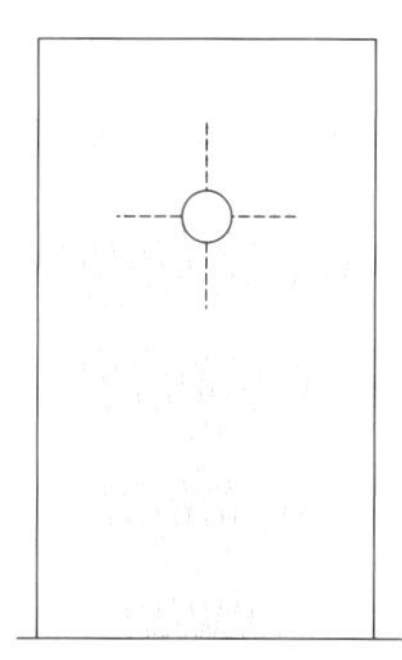

E 2.24

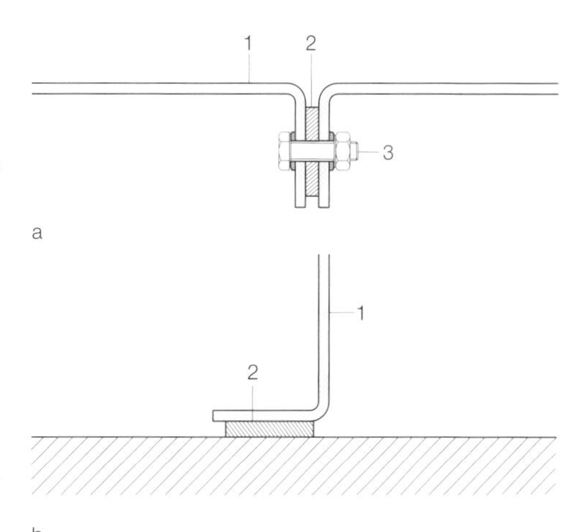

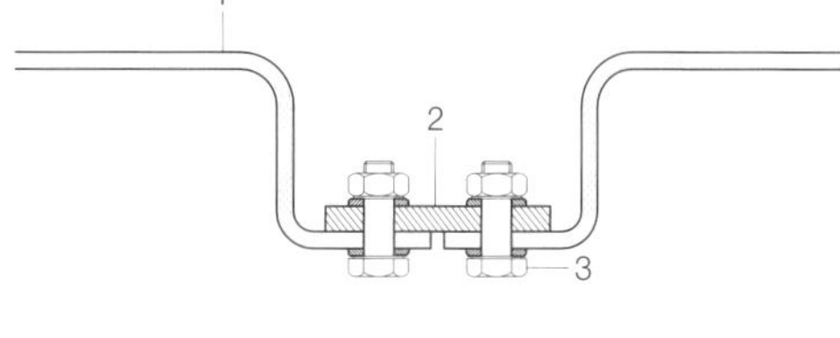
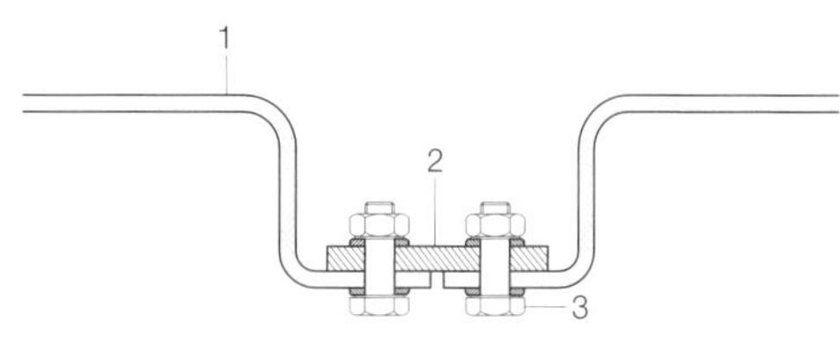

1 Fibre-reinforced polymer
2 Spacer made from elastomer, steel, etc.
3 Bolt or rivet

E 2.25

E 2.26

E 2.27 Metal connecting parts attached with adhesive
a Plate
b Angle
E 2.28 Building in plates or perforated sheet metal to optimise a connection, with rovings looped through perforations
a Axonometric view
b Section
E 2.29 Proprietary fittings for building into fibre-reinforced polymers
E 2.30 Threaded built-in part
E 2.31 "fg 2000", Altenstadt (D), 1968, Wolfgang Feierbach
a View of facade
b Corner detail
E 2.32 Stepped joint for sandwich elements
E 2.33 Laminated joint between sandwich elements
E 2.34 Hemispherical radomes (for housing antennas) made from GFRP sandwich elements
a Assembling the individual components
b Completed dome

1 Fibre-reinforced polymer
2 Steel plate or angle
3 Adhesive

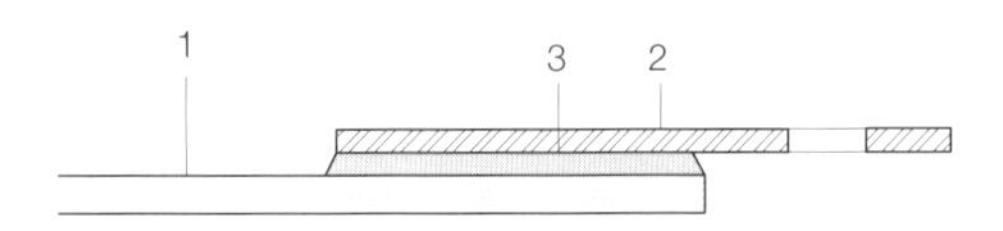

a

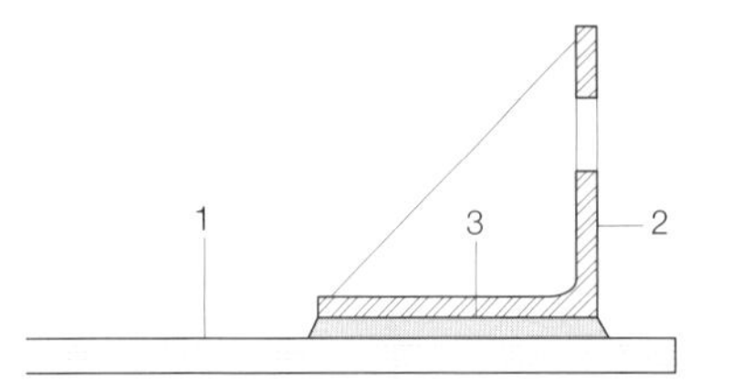

b

E 2.27

1 Fibre-reinforced polymer
2 Lug made from thin sheet steel
3 Long fibres (rovings), looped through perforations
4 Normal planar fibre reinforcement

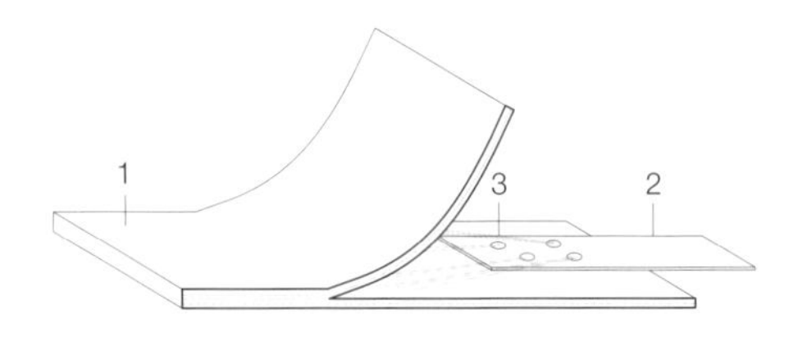

a

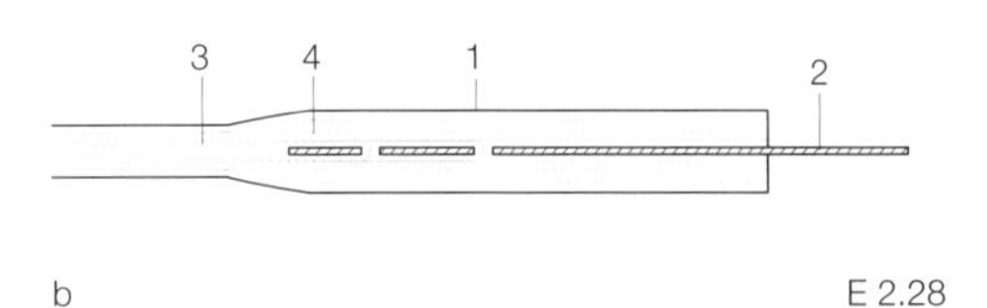

b

E 2.28

E 2.29

1 Fibre-reinforced polymer
2 Threaded built-in part with thin sheet steel disc

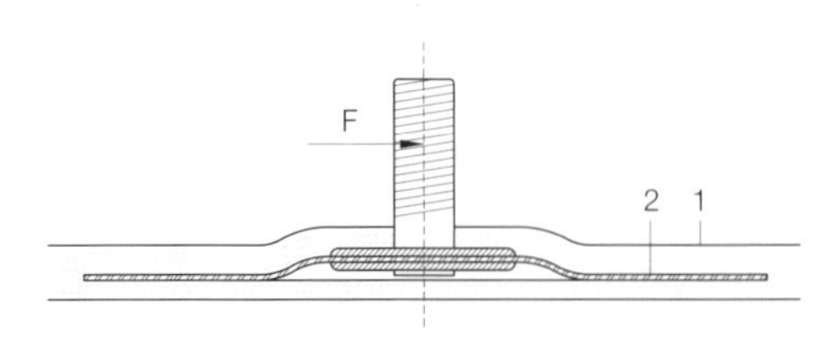

E 2.30

Built-in metal fittings
Built-in fittings made from steel, stainless steel or aluminium are useful for individual connections with a concentrated load transfer. The coefficients of thermal expansion of the laminate and the built-in part should be compatible with each other in order to minimise restraint stresses. The thermal expansion coefficients for fibre-reinforced polymers vary over a wide range depending on type of fibre and laminate lay-up, which is why it is not possible to make any global recommendations regarding materials. Aluminium tends to be the most suitable material for planar GFRP hybrid laminates, whereas steel or stainless steel are better for pultruded GFRP. The very low coefficient of thermal expansion of CFRP makes it less suitable for combining with metals.
Metal lugs and plates should be kept as thin as possible in order to minimise the disruption to the laminate lay-up (Fig. E 2.28). Perforated sheet metal enables a better penetration of the polymer during production and the long fibres (rovings) can also be looped through the perforations, which increases the load-carrying capacity yet further. Screws and threaded sleeves can be anchored in the laminate with prefabricated built-in components. As with lugs and plates, thin perforated sheet metal produces the best results (Figs. E 2.29 and E 2.30).
Large built-in fittings are also possible with sandwich elements. They are positioned within the core material.

Glued joints
Steel lugs and angles can also be attached with adhesive as an alternative to using built-in components (Fig. E 2.27). High forces can be transferred with a sufficiently large adhesive joint.

Details for sandwich elements
Sandwich elements are responsible for two main functions when building with fibre-reinforced polymers: increasing the load-carrying capacity beyond that of a thin laminate, and thermal insulation. A design without joints is therefore desirable in order to avoid degrading

a

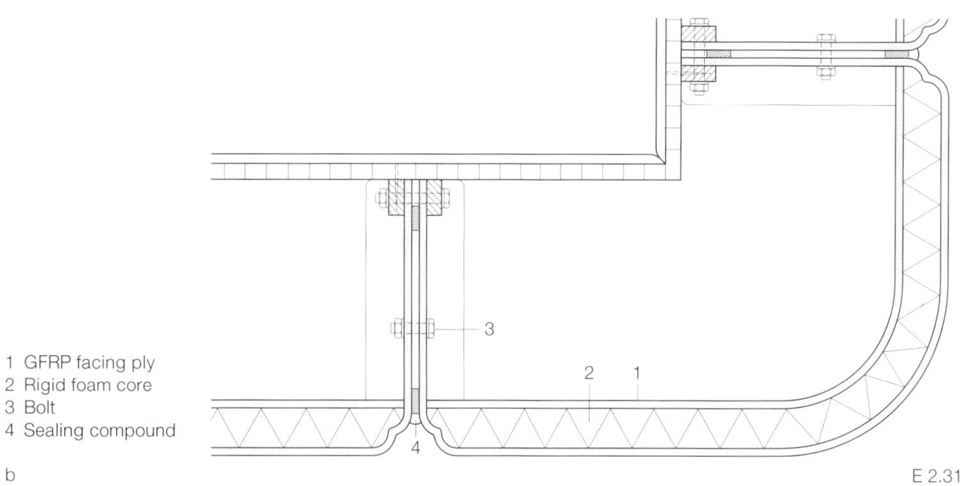

1 GFRP facing ply
2 Rigid foam core
3 Bolt
4 Sealing compound

b

E 2.31

the mechanical and building physics characteristics. One option here is to provide a loose tongue and groove joint for the core and subsequently laminate over the joints (Fig. E 2.33). During construction, the forces are transferred exclusively via the joint in the core material, which calls for the use of a material with a suitable loadbearing capacity, e.g. PVC or PUR. Once the joint has been finished, the facing plies of fibre-reinforced polymer are continuous and the joint is concealed, the sandwich element essentially continuous. It may be necessary, however, to add a final ply over the entire structure in order to achieve an adequate load-carrying capacity.

Bolted joints
Sandwich elements can also be connected via bolts or screws where economic criteria dictate or where the construction is not permanent. Local reinforcement is necessary to cope with the stress concentration at the joint, which usually results in a lower loadbearing capacity and a lower thermal insulation value, however. A stepped joint (Fig. E 2.32) can help to compensate for the building physics disadvantages to some extent, and such a joint can be regarded as a hinge. The bolted connection can be strengthened with an integral steel collar. Alternatively, an integral flange can be formed in the sandwich element (Fig. E 2.31), but although this creates a rigid connection, it results in a thermal bridge.

Large format built-in steel parts
Large-format built-in parts can replace the core material locally in a sandwich element, which achieves an increase in the load-carrying capacity but without this being visible from the outside. For example, the roof shell to the Itzhak Rabin Center is made from sandwich elements with integral steel trays for connecting to the columns (Fig. E 2.36a, p. 184). The first step in the production is to assemble all the fibre plies, the rigid foam core and the built-in parts. The entire cross-section is then impregnated with the polymer using the resin infusion method in a second step (Fig. E 2.36b). On site the finished

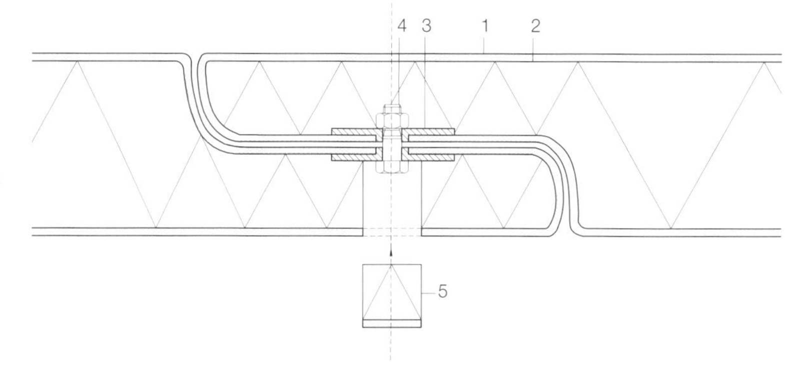

1 GFRP facing ply
2 Rigid foam core
3 Steel built-in part
4 Bolt
5 Plug of material to conceal connection

E 2.32

1 Facing ply made from fibre-reinforced polymer
2 Rigid foam core
3 Loose tongue made from rigid foam, glued in place
4 Facing ply laminated in situ after joining elements

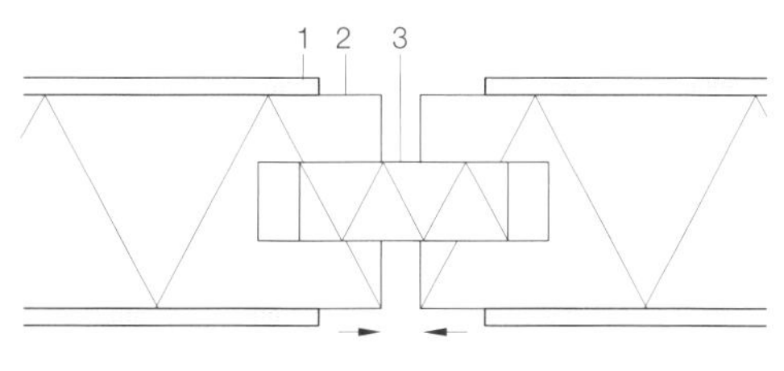

a

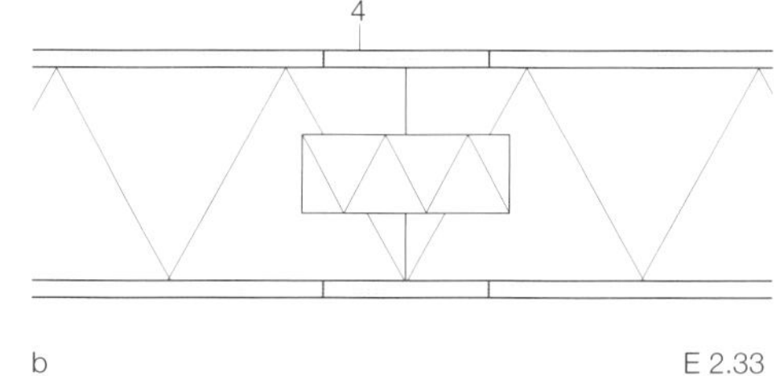

b

E 2.33

a

b

E 2.34

segments of the shell are simply lifted into position and attached to the structure (Fig. E 2.36c).

Integrating functions

Fibre-reinforced polymers are built up in layers and processed either cold or at comparatively low temperatures. Integrating further components and functions during the initial production process would seem to be an obvious move. Built-in light fittings, decorative features, thermal mass, sensors for measuring strains and temperatures plus a sunshade control system are just some examples of the possibilities (see "Potential, trends and challenges", pp. 24–27). And with sandwich elements it is also possible to incorporate electric cables or water pipes during production (Fig. E 2.35). For this purpose, service ducts can be formed in the sandwich element through which the pipes and cables are routed. Completely enclosed or accessible ducts are possible depending on the need to gain access to the services at a later date.

Mouldmaking

The polymer becomes viscous during the production of fibre composites components and so a sealed mould is essential. A one-part mould is sufficient for the hand lay-up of planar components, also for fibre spraying and the resin infusion and vacuum methods. On the other hand, the automated compression-moulding method requires a two-part mould. The surface of the laminate in contact with the mould is smooth, whereas the other surface usually has a rough or irregular finish. A foil can be laid over the surface not in contact with the mould when using the resin infusion and vacuum methods in order to achieve a smooth finish on this surface as well, but it is very important – and difficult – to lay the foil without folds or creases.

Mould design

The mould can be developed from the component geometry, although it may be necessary to divide up the mould or the component into several segments to suit production requirements. For example, at least two segments are required when laminating a circular cross-section (Fig. E 2.37). Considering the demoulding aspects for a component are vital when designing a mould, e.g. for undercut geometries. Instead of dividing the component into pieces, it is also possible to divide the mould into several sections. The individual parts are fixed firmly together during laminating. To do this, the edges of the mould segments are provided with flanges that are bolted together.

Moulding process

The moulding process normally takes place in three steps. Firstly, the original or master mould, i.e. the prototype, is produced. The original mould can be produced by additive or subtractive means, i.e. by respectively adding or removing material from the mould step by step. It is made from materials such as rigid foam, balsa wood, clay or gypsum, which although easy to work are unsuitable for multiple uses. A negative mould is produced from this original mould in the second step. To do this, the surface of the original mould is coated with a release agent such as silicone oil or wax and the negative mould laminated or cast on this. Various robust materials – fibre-reinforced polymers or metals – can be used for the negative mould depending on the size of the production run. The third step is the production of the actual component (with a surface geometry identical to that of the prototype) in the negative mould. Here again, a release agent is necessary in order to ensure easier demoulding (Fig. E 2.41, p. 186).

Instead of the three-stage moulding process, it is also possible to build the negative mould directly. Rigid foam shaped with a CNC milling machine can be used, for example, but negative moulds made from wooden boards are also worth considering for large-format laminates. One special type of mould is permanent formwork, which is coated with the plies of laminate material and remains as the core material in a sandwich element.

Materials

Moulds are expensive in terms of their materials and production, and can in some cases exceed the cost of the actual component quite consid-

1 Facing ply made from fibre-reinforced polymer
2 Rigid foam core
3 Access panel
4 Pipes or cables
5 Integral services duct made from fibre-reinforced polymer

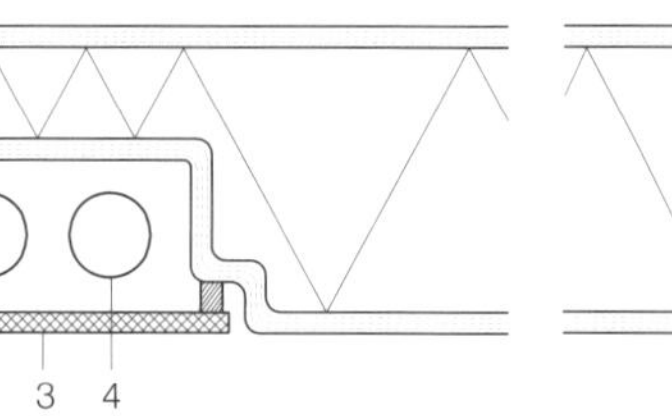

a

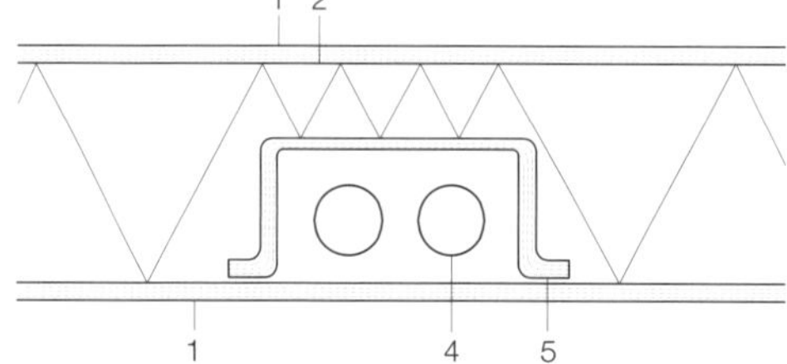

b

E 2.35

E 2.35 Integrating services into sandwich elements
a Accessible
b Concealed

E 2.36 Itzhak Rabin Center, Tel Aviv (IL), 2005, Moshe Safdie, Mick Eekhout
a Steel built-in component
b Production using the vacuum bag method
c Lifting a prefabricated segment into position on site

E 2.37 Dividing a component into more than one segment

E 2.38 Rounded corners in the mould enable better laminating

E 2.39 Avoiding high friction forces during demoulding: no surfaces parallel with demoulding direction

E 2.40 Multiple uses of an oversize form for components with the same cross-section but different lengths

a

b

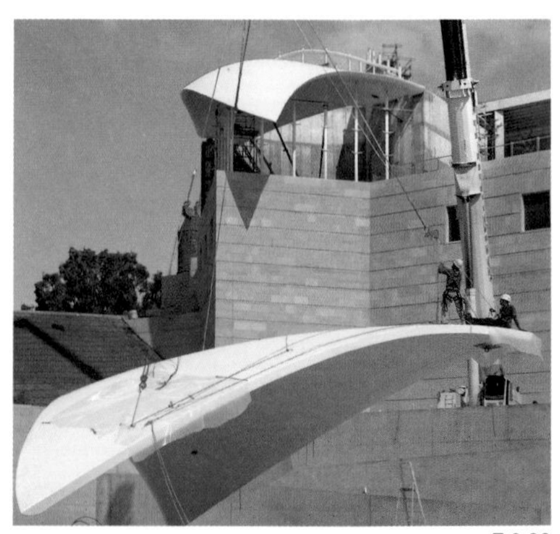

c

E 2.36

erably. The least expensive material is therefore chosen depending on the dimensions of the component, the desired surface quality and the number of reuses required. In addition, the cost of mouldmaking should be minimised by designing the component geometry accordingly, e.g. by using the same moulds for components with the same shape but different dimensions (Fig. E 2.40).

Gypsum and clay
Gypsum is an inexpensive material that is easily formed into the shape required. It is suitable for both original and negative moulds. But its low strength means it is only suitable for small components and a few reuses. Dry gypsum absorbs water and release agent, which makes demoulding difficult on many occasions. Gypsum moulds are fragile and are frequently damaged beyond repair during demoulding.
Clay is likewise an inexpensive, easily worked mould material. Under the right temperature and moisture conditions, it is easy to shape, and after drying, or rather cooling, it can be worked with simple tools.

Rigid foams
The advantage of fine-pore foams (PVC, PUR, XPS) is that these can be shaped with a computer-controlled CNC milling machine. The cost of the material is comparatively high and so the quantity of rigid foam required must be reduced to a minimum. The rigid foam is frequently left in the finished component as the core material. But where it is required for moulding only, then it must be sealed with a filling compound and wax. Moulds made from rigid foam are likewise only suitable for a few reuses. Although foams with larger pores (EPS, Styropor) are among the cheapest, they are difficult to work. EPS combined with gypsum or clay is suitable for simple moulds.

Fibre-reinforced polymers
Fibre-reinforced polymers, mainly GFRP materials, are suitable for making negative moulds. Different resin systems are used depending on the number of reuses required, i.e. the durability demands placed on the mould. GFRP has established itself as a material for negative moulds where 100+ reuses are required. One advantage of GFRP is that it is possible to integrate additional handles, flanges and fixings in the mould to simplify handling and assembly.

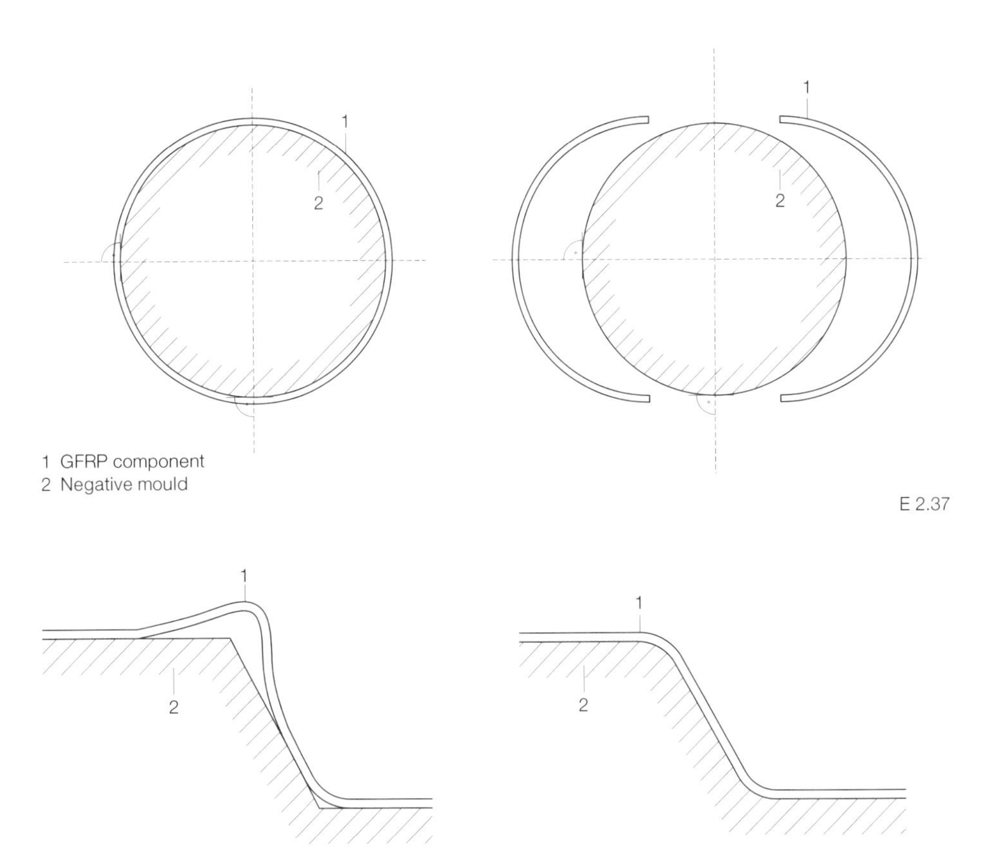

1 GFRP component
2 Negative mould

E 2.37

1 GFRP component
2 Negative mould

E 2.38

Difficult demoulding

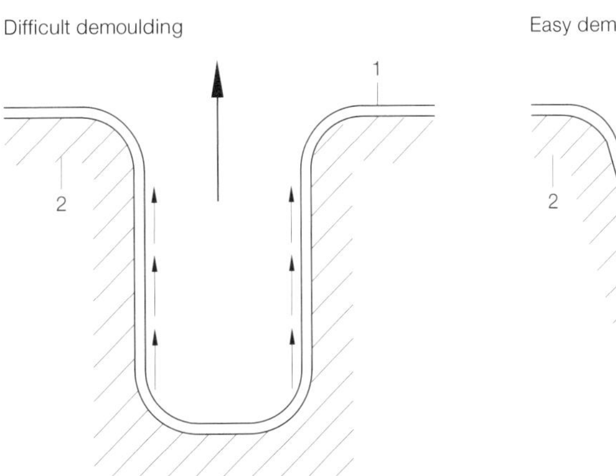

Easy demoulding

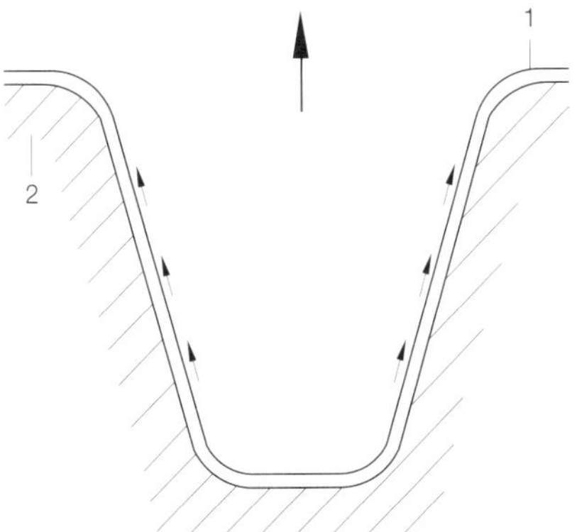

E 2.39

1 Negative mould made from GFRP
2a, b Components with different lengths but otherwise identical

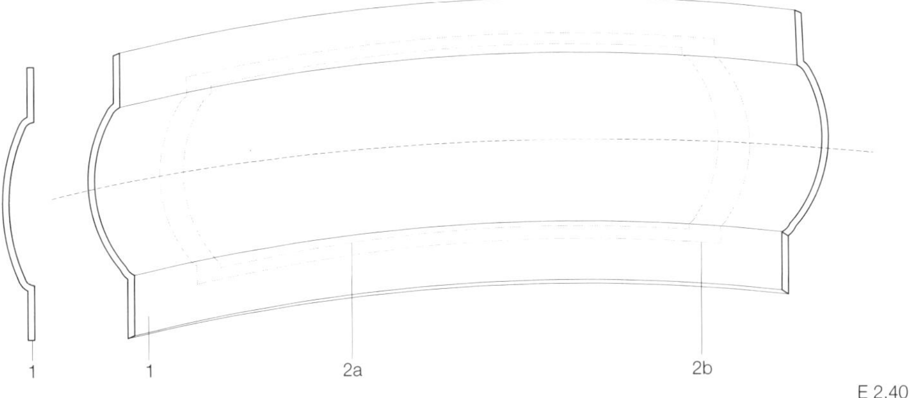

E 2.40

Metals
Moulds made from steel or aluminium are only relevant for very large production runs or demanding tolerance requirements. Such moulds are expensive to produce but are stable and durable.

Wood
Moulds made from timber represent a reasonable alternative for especially large components and where moulds do not have to satisfy requirements regarding dimensional accuracy. The actual face of the mould can be made from thin veneer plywood or planed boards fixed in position by an orthogonal arrangement of framing members. These can be manufactured exactly in a computer-controlled process.

Polymers
Polyurethane casting resin is used where high-precision moulds are needed. This material has an excellent surface finish and is relatively robust. However, the mould itself is on the whole comparatively heavy and expensive, and the resin cannot be re-formed afterwards.
Elastomers, e.g. silicone rubber, represent alternatives to casting resins for making moulds, but only for relatively small components. One advantage is that undercuts are possible with these extensible materials. In addition, no release agent is required when using silicone.

Design principles for moulded parts
The materials normally used for mouldmaking result in negative moulds and components that are comparatively stiff. The geometry should therefore be designed in such a way that there are no undercuts (Fig. E 2.37, p. 185). If necessary, several segments must be combined to form a mould that is separated again afterwards. Surfaces parallel with the demoulding direction must be avoided because they cause high friction forces when removing the component from the negative mould (Fig. E 2.39, p. 185). Small moulds up to 20 cm deep should be designed with an angle of min. 2° to the vertical, larger moulds > 1 m deep with an angle of min. 5°. Rounded arrises with adequate radii must be included so that laminating with a consistent thickness is possible (Fig. E 2.38, p. 185).

Hollow components
Intermediate steps are necessary when producing hollow components from fibre-reinforced polymers (Fig. E 2.45). First of all, two half-shells (female moulds) are laminated, with the lower segment being produced with the laminate projecting from the mould. Before the laminate cures, a prefabricated pressure bag (male mould) is laid in the lower mould and partially inflated. The projecting laminate is laid over the bag and the second (upper) half of the laminate component mounted on the lower mould. The two female moulds are connected and the pressure bag fully inflated. The two laminate halves therefore bond over the length of the overlap and the pressure bag compacts them and forces out any air bubbles. Components with high strengths and exact geometries can be produced using this method. The joint between the two is a wet lay-up connection and therefore exhibits a good load-carrying capacity. Fig. E 2.41 shows the various production steps using the example of concave GFRP lamellae. Prior to laminating, the original mould is first cut out of a block of rigid foam fully automatically with a CNC milling machine. Afterwards, the GFRP negative mould is produced from this mould. And in the third step the pressure bag method described above is applied. The negative mould can be used for components of different lengths.

Sandwich core as mould
Sandwich elements do not necessarily require a mould if the laminate material is applied directly to the core material. The core functions as mould, loadbearing component and thermal insulation. The use of CNC machining allows virtually any shape to be produced.
To do this, the block of rigid foam must be cut first, e.g. with a CNC milling machine (Fig. E 2.42). The fibre-reinforced polymer is laid directly on the rigid foam without the need for a release agent and the laminate bonded to the foam via the resin. The amount of liquid resin absorbed by the foam depends on its porosity; this fact must be allowed for in the production. Separate blocks of rigid foam can be glued together to produce large-format components.

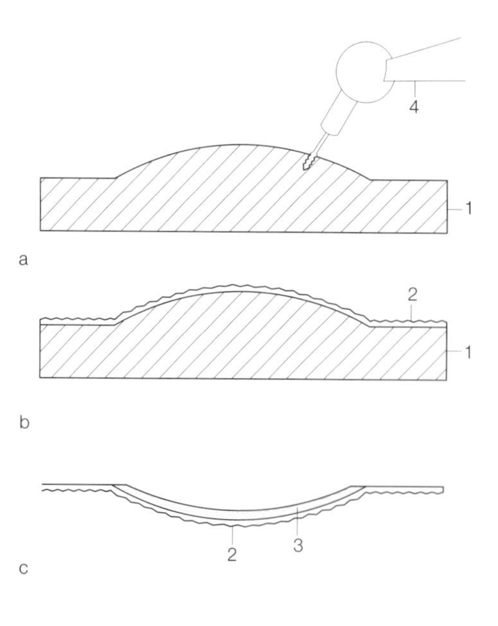

1 Original mould made from rigid foam
2 Negative mould made from GFRP
3 Component made from GFRP
4 CNC milling tool

E 2.41

E 2.42

a

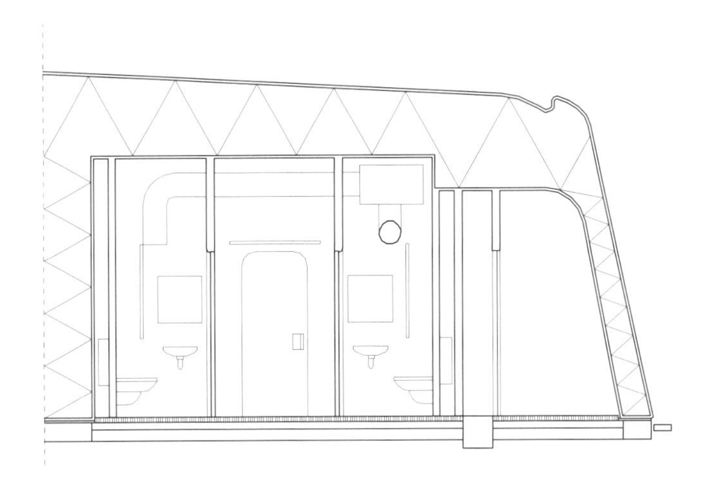
b

E 2.43

The high cost of such foam materials makes this form of construction relatively expensive. It therefore makes economic sense to integrate the mould into the component only in the case of irregular, one-off geometries. Another disadvantage is that the part is laminated on the outside, i.e. the comparatively rough and inaccurate final ply of the laminate forms the final surface. However, this disadvantage can be compensated for to some extent by using the resin infusion or vacuum methods (see "Resin infusion and vacuum methods", p. 79).

The bus terminal in Hoofddorp near Amsterdam was made from large foam blocks shaped with CNC milling machines (Fig. E 2.42). The blocks were glued together on site and the GFRP laminate added afterwards. The work was carried out inside a temporary tent that guaranteed dry working conditions. The finished surface is relatively rough and therefore vulnerable to soiling. The rest room for bus drivers incorporated into the structure was produced in one operation together with the entire structure (Fig. E 2.43).

E 2.41 Typical procedure for the series production of GFRP components
a Producing the original mould by means of CNC milling
b Casting the negative mould
c Casting the component in the negative mould
E 2.42 CNC machining of rigid foam
E 2.43 Large-format sandwich structure; bus terminal, Hoofddorp (NL) 2003, NIO Architects
a View of completed structure
b Section through integral room
E 2.44 Compressing the laminate with a pressure bag
E 2.45 Producing a hollow component from two half-shells
a Lower part of component produced with projecting laminate
b Simultaneous laminating of upper part of component
c Installing the pressure bag
d Joining the two parts prior to curing
e Inflated pressure bag

E 2.44

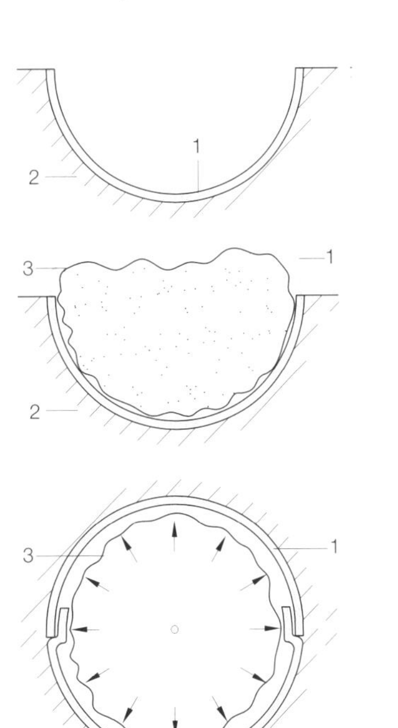

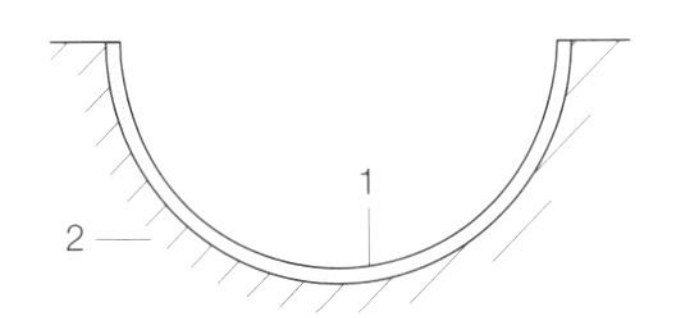

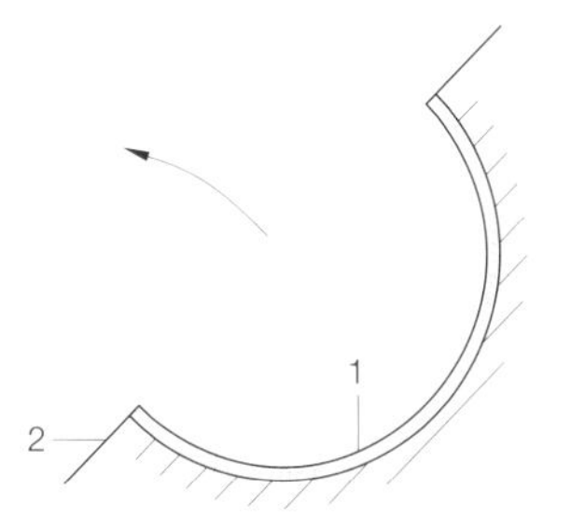

1 Component made from GFRP
2 Negative mould
3 Inflatable pressure bag

E 2.45

Building with foil

E 3.1

When they form part of the loadbearing structure, foil materials are mainly employed in the form of pneumatically prestressed cushions. The clamping details along the edges are therefore particularly important because they must satisfy not only structural requirements, but also comply with various constructional and building physics conditions. Other important facets of the design, apart from these edge details, are the technical components and various principles for the air supply to the cushions. These aspects apply to cushions made from textile membranes as well as hybrid designs made from fabric and foil. Designs using foil materials stabilised pneumatically with a pressure below atmospheric pressure are also conceivable in principle. However, this type of application must be considered very carefully when using foil because unfiltered air, and hence dust and dirt, too, could be sucked in, which would ruin the optical quality and the appearance. Owing to the low strength, high elongation and creep behaviour of foil materials, mechanically prestressed foil designs have been used on only a few occasions in the past. Ethylene tetrafluoroethylene (ETFE) is the material mainly used for foil designs, and therefore the following descriptions of the constructional details relate to this material in the main, although most of them could be used for other foil materials.

Cushion lay-up and form

For the typical wind and snow loads of Central Europe, the maximum span of pneumatically prestressed ETFE foil cushions, which currently can only be manufactured with an adequate optical quality in thicknesses up to 300 µm, is approx. 4.50 m. As air-filled cushions also remain stable when prestressed in one direction only, this recommended maximum span dictates the shorter span, i.e. elongated rectangular formats are also possible. For example, air-filled foil cushions measuring 4.50 × 46.00 m were used to roof over the inner courtyard of a bank in Bratislava and shelter it from rain and snow (see "Bank", pp. 253–255).
Various options can be considered when cushion designs with a larger format are desired (Fig. E 3.3):

- Increasing the rise of the cushion reduces the loads acting on the top and bottom layers somewhat. However, manufacturing and constructional conditions place limits on this increase because of the ensuing greater curvature.
- The span of the foil can be increased by providing additional cable nets. For example, in order to carry the snow loads acting on horizontal cushions it is possible to strengthen the lower layer, which is more heavily loaded, by spanning a cable net underneath (see "Pneumatically prestressed surfaces", p. 143). A further cable net can improve the load-carrying capacity of the top layer (Fig. E 3.20, p. 195).
- In some cases doubling the upper and/or lower layers is worth considering in order to improve the load-carrying capacity of the cushions. The very large cushions (approx. 10 × 10 m) over a shopping mall near Lisbon represent one example of this approach (see "Shopping centre", pp. 256–257).
- The foil of the upper and/or lower layers can be replaced by a material with a higher strength, e.g. a reinforced fabric such as polyester-PVC or PTFE/glass. The significantly higher strengths of woven fabrics enable much longer spans when using pneumatically prestressed designs. This means, however, that the cushions can no longer be transparent.

Combinations of these various measures are also conceivable. A cushion measuring 50 m in diameter (and almost 2000 m^2 in area) was produced for the roof over the "Vista Alegre" bullfighting arena in Madrid. In this design a top layer of polyester-PVC was combined with a lower layer of ETFE foil reinforced by a cable net.

Cushions are nearly always prefabricated in factories protected from the weather and then installed as complete units on the building site. It is the cutting pattern that defines the form (see "Cutting pattern", pp. 147–148) and when the layers are welded together the result is a three-dimensional assembly. Depending on the dimensions of the layers, there are limitations to how much this assembly can be folded for transport without causing wrinkles that would impair the optical quality of the cushion once installed. In particular, the folding of cushions

E 3.1 Erecting roof cushions; Allianz Arena, Munich (D), 2005, Herzog & de Meuron
E 3.2 Overview of foil details and technical elements
a Seam
b Clamp extrusion (cushion)
c Edge (prestressed situation)
d Cable net support
e Air supply (cushion)
E 3.3 Overview of cushion forms in various sizes and with different numbers of layers

made from welded layers of transparent ETFE foil could be a factor that limits the format, and this must be taken into account early on in the planning.

Multi-layer cushions

Multi-layer cushions offer a chance of improving the insulating effect because of the separate layers of air. The inner layers of foil can be much thinner than the outer ones because they are subjected to a lower prestress and make only a minimum contribution to carrying the loads. They are mostly fabricated with a cutting pattern that gives them the necessary form because otherwise installing them without any creases or wrinkles is extremely difficult. However, flat, prestressed central plies (no cutting pattern) are also possible depending on the appearance requirements.
Individual cushion layers made from the same material can be factory-welded along their edges to form a complete cushion following their fabrication (i.e. cutting according to the pattern and welding the individual segments together) and therefore do not have to be clamped separately. It is even possible to join more than two layers together. This type of production represents the least costly variation for ETFE foil because it substantially reduces the work required on the building site. In addition, the erection work is less dependent on the weather because the inside of the cushion is already sealed against the infiltration of moisture, dust and dirt, thus avoiding the need to carry out expensive and time-consuming cleaning.
The alternative – and unavoidable when using different materials for the various layers – is to clamp the individual layers separately. The advantages of this approach are that the layers can be replaced separately if necessary and, first and foremost, significant thermal bridges are avoided at the welded joints between the layers. It is also possible to combine the two variations in a multi-layer cushion design.

Movable central layer

Printing white or silver dots – the usual choice but, indeed, any other patterns or colours (see "Colouring, printing and coating", p. 97) are possible – on the foil can reduce the radiation transmittance through the cushion. With a multi-layer cushion design it is worth considering printing a pattern on the upper layer that is offset with respect to that on the central layer. Pressurising the lower chamber causes the central layer to rise to the underside of the upper ply so that the printed areas of each layer close off the gaps in the printing in the other layer (so-called intelligent printing). This can be achieved, for example, with an offset chessboard pattern, but other, even far more complex, patterns are possible (Fig. E 3.5, p. 190). This requires separate pressure controls for the two chambers of the cushion. We must distinguish between repositioning (Fig. E 3.4a, p. 190) and the elastic elongation (Fig. E 3.4b, p. 190) of the central layer as a result of the pressure increase in the lower chamber. The principle of the operation of the movable central layer is described in more detail in the chapter entitled "Foil cushions with integral sunshade" on p. 221.

Supporting structure

Foil cushions have a very low weight per unit area and – compared with mechanically prestressed membranes – transfer only very low prestressing forces to their supporting construction. As a result, loadbearing structures for foil cushions can be designed to be very delicate and lightweight. The cushions are generally attached to aluminium sections that are in turn mounted on a timber, steel or aluminium primary structure for generously dimensioned roof and facade surfaces. The clamping sections can themselves span certain distances (depending on the particular design), meaning that they only have to be fixed to the primary structure at discrete points, which achieves a certain visual separation between cushions and structure (e.g. cushions clamped to timber primary structure). Occasionally, the cushions are supported directly on a cable net structure (see "Bank", pp. 253–255).

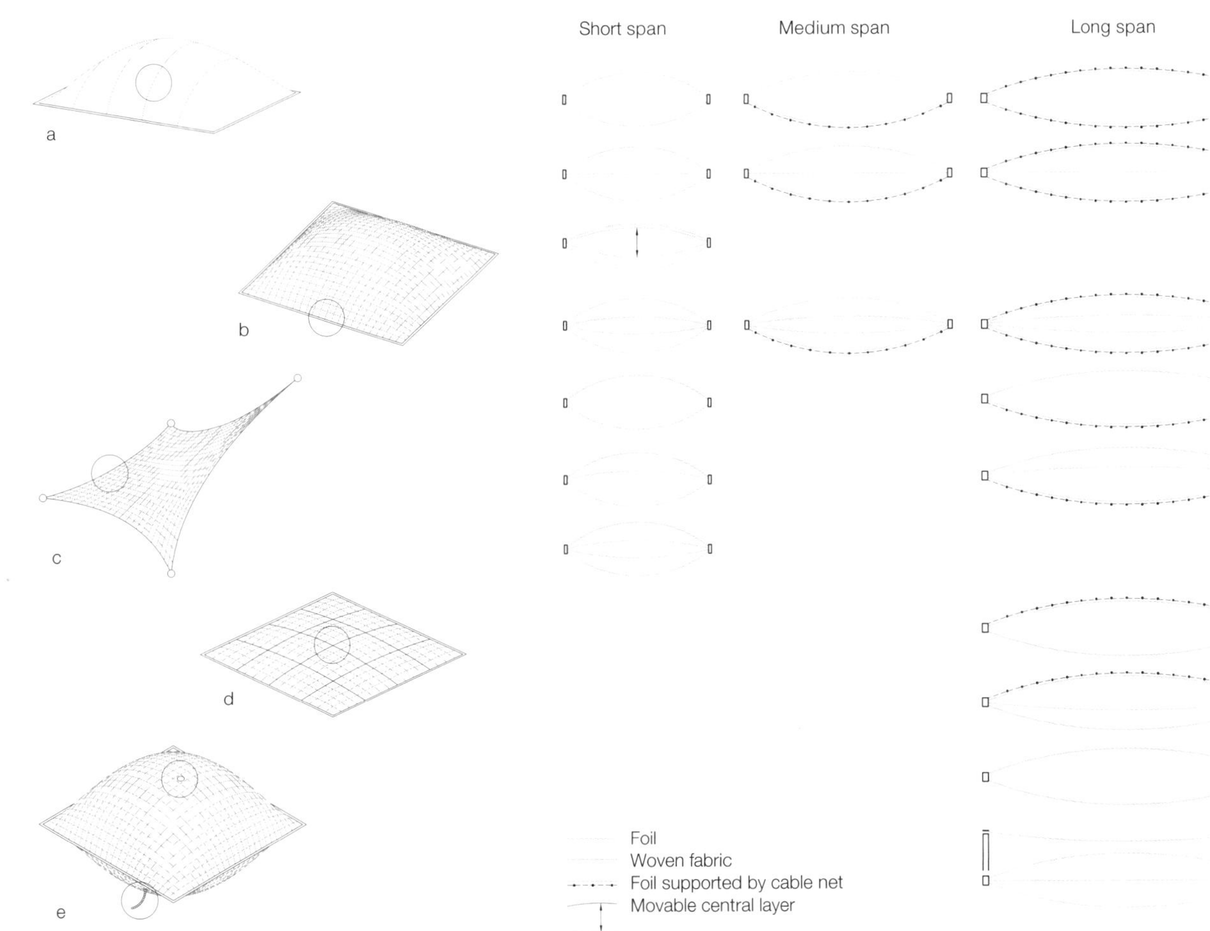

E 3.2

E 3.3

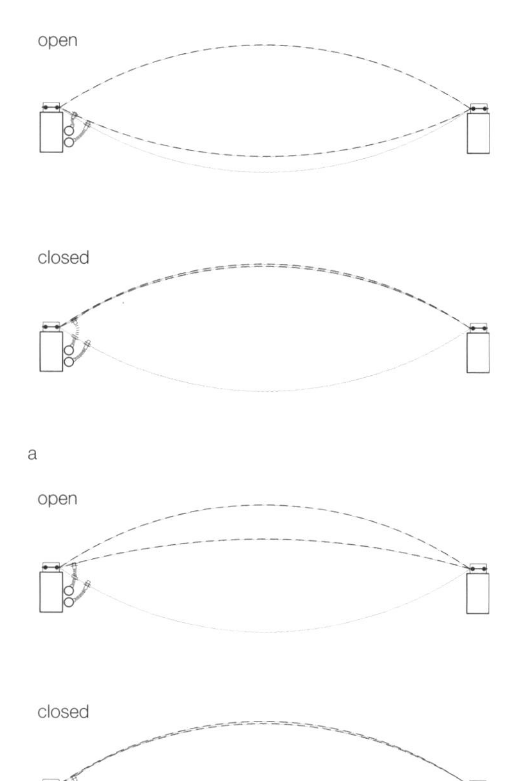

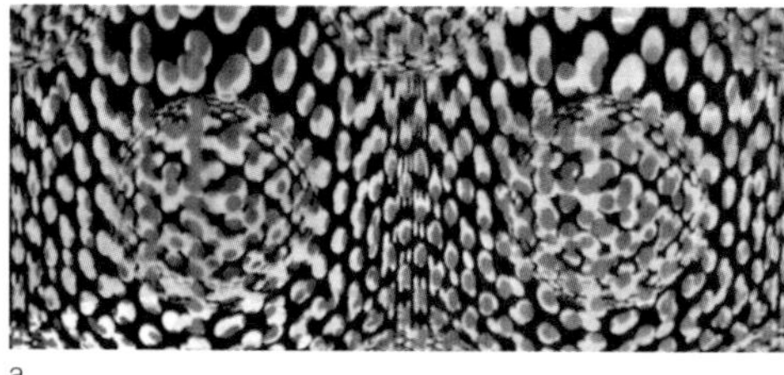
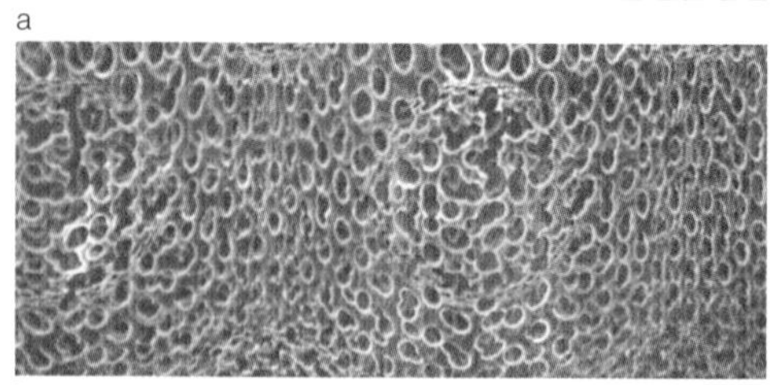

E 3.4 Movable central layer
a Moved by repositioning
b Moved by elastic elongation
E 3.5 Movable central layer with intelligent printing
a open
b closed
E 3.6 Simple edge clamp detail
a with flat bar
b with extruded aluminium section
c with extruded aluminium section above and below timber member for better thermal insulation along the edge
E 3.7 Welded seam and covered edge clamp detail
E 3.8 Edge clamp detail with condensation channel and factory-fitted polymer edge bead
E 3.9 a, b Edge clamp details with factory-fitted polymer edge bead and clamping bar as erection aid
E 3.10 Cushion corner detail with keder interrupted
E 3.11 Stainless steel wires above a clamped edge detail for protecting against birds

As the final shape of the cushion depends not only on its cutting pattern, but also on the elongation of the material itself, it is essential to make sure that there is sufficient clearance between the underside of each cushion and the primary loadbearing structure or other components. This is because the sag of the cushion can be expected to increase over time due to the creep of the material caused by constant, sometimes high, loading.

Details

This section deals mainly with the construction details for air-filled cushion assemblies. As the perimeter and corner details of mechanically prestressed foils are hardly any different to those of textile membranes, the reader should refer to the chapter entitled "Building with textile membranes" (pp. 196–211).

Seams

In contrast to coated woven fabrics, welding foil materials results in a homogeneous joint. The tensile strength and waterproofing quality at the seam could therefore be achieved, in theory, with a welded seam no wider than the thickness of the material. The prerequisite for this, however, is that the areas adjacent to the seam are perfectly formed. So, as the welded seam is absolutely crucial to the safety and reliability of the structure, welded seams 10–15 mm wide are the norm (see "Fabrication of ETFE foil", p. 98).

Edges

Foil materials are clamped along their edges or held in place by edge cables or webbing belts in pockets – all similar details to those of textile membranes. But as foil is employed mainly for pneumatic cushion designs, rigid edges with clamping sections represent the commonest solutions. These sections are generally extruded, anodised aluminium products. Sections with rough surface finishes or sharp edges or affected by galvanic corrosion must be avoided at all costs because such defects can cause mechanical damage to the foil and changes in its microstructure. The stiffness and load-carrying capacity of ETFE decrease significantly at high temperatures (see "Mechanical properties of ETFE foil", p. 97) and so heat losses via conduction at connections between foil and metal components represent a further risk. Clamping details can include strips made from elastomeric materials such as ethylene propylene diene monomer rubber (EPDM) laid between the foil and the metal clamping sections in order to protect the foil against all mechanical, chemical and thermal actions. Such elastomers can be integrated directly into clamping elements in the form of factory-fitted polymer edge beads (Fig. E 3.8).

The clamping along the edges of foil cushions can satisfy several constructional, technical and building physics requirements at the same time:

- Accommodating tensile stresses
- Transferring loads to the supporting structure
- Self-supporting requirements
- Clamping several separate layers, also when made from different materials
- Accommodating thermal expansion
- Providing thermal insulation/break along the edge
- Functioning as a gutter for rainwater
- Functioning as a gutter for condensation
- Fixing air supply components and lighting units
- Accessibility for maintenance work
- Bird control (Fig. E 3.11)
- Support during erection

Many different edge clamping sections are available for ETFE cushions, which undergo constant development by their manufacturers so that all the functions listed above can be properly covered and integrated.
We can distinguish between a number of different types of edge clamp. A keder welded into the edge of the foil (see "Keders", p. 99) is clamped either directly (Fig. E 3.6) or in an elastic edge bead (Figs. E 3.8 and E 3.9).
A thermal break is achieved by incorporating thermal insulation in the clamping section and/or by clamping the inner and outer foil layers separately on the top and bottom of a rectangular section (e.g. timber) (Fig. E 3.6c). When using a thermally insulated clamping section, it is important to remember that the insulating value of the cushion decreases severely towards its edges and more condensation will collect on the underside of the cushion here. Such edge details should therefore include a drainage channel below the clamping section (Fig. E 3.8). Condensation is less of a problem where the upper and lower layer are clamped separately.

Simple edge clamp details
In principle, we distinguish between clamping with simple flat bars (Fig. E 3.6a) and clamping with extruded aluminium sections (Figs. E 3.6b and c). With the former detail, the keder is fitted behind the bar itself and therefore the fixing screws or bolts have to pass through holes in the edge of the foil. With extruded aluminium sections, the keder can be held in place in front of the fasteners, which avoids having to penetrate the foil, and therefore damaging it. This latter type of detail is also used in conjunction with mechanically prestressed membranes (see "Clamped edge", p. 205).

Edge clamp detail with factory-fitted polymer edge bead
In this type of detail, the fabricated foil with its welded keder is already threaded into a polymer edge bead (usually made from EPDM) at the factory, and the polymer edge bead itself later clamped in a two-part aluminium section (Fig. E 3.8). This type of edge clamp detail has a number of advantages over the simple edge clamp described above:

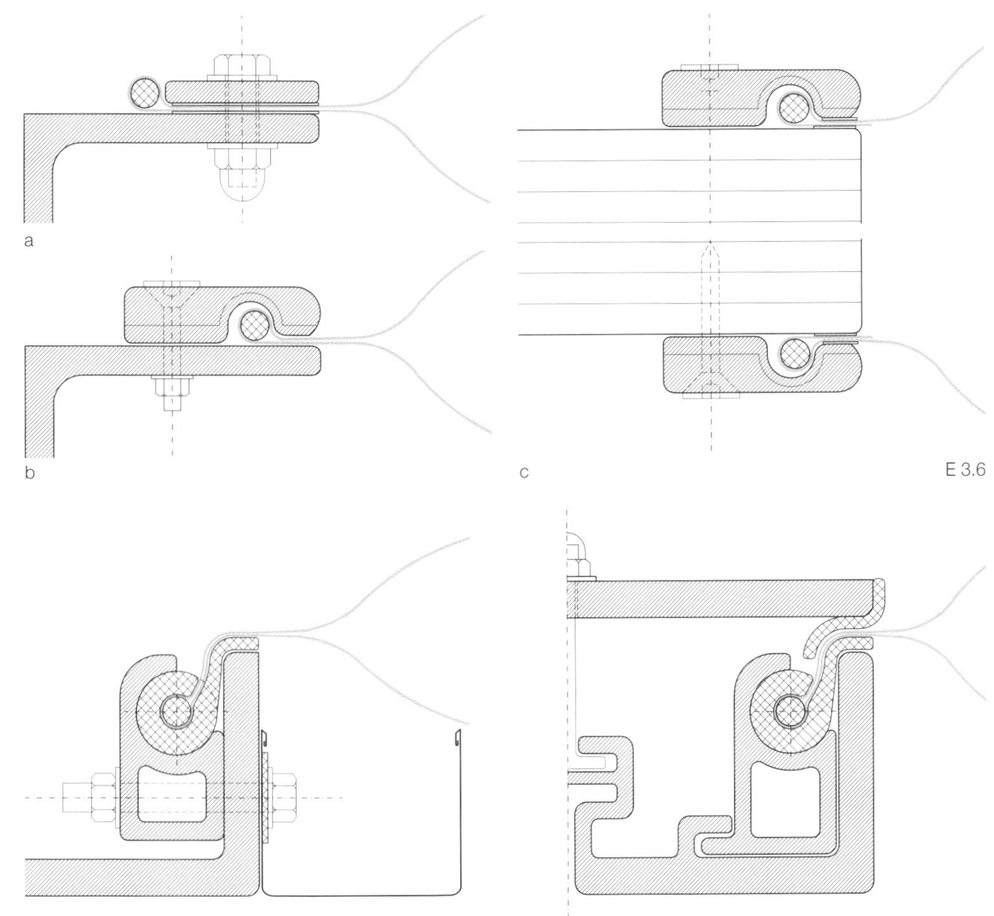

E 3.6

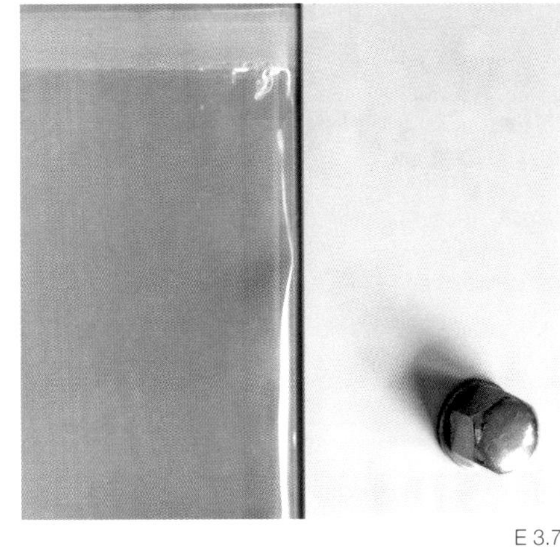
E 3.7

E 3.8

E 3.9

- Quicker erection
- Protection for the foil pocket at the clamp
- Lower stress peaks at the clamped edge
- The ability to accommodate thermal expansion because the EPDM edge bead is clamped in the two-part aluminium section.

Edge clamp detail with erection aid
Separate clamping bars can be integrated into the clamping section in order to simplify the installation of the cushions. These separate bars are clipped into the sections attached to the loadbearing structure without the need for any screws or bolts and are either fitted directly to the keder or clamped to a polymer edge bead (Fig. E 3.9a). Once all the sections on one side of a cushion and the neighbouring cushion are clipped in place, a capping strip is screwed or bolted to the section so that the cushions are properly fixed in place and waterproofed (Fig. E 3.9b and Fig. E 5.12, p. 217).

Corners
As the angle at the corner of a foil cushion becomes more acute, so it becomes more and more difficult to achieve a homogeneous transfer of the stresses in the surface to the corner and thus avoid wrinkles and creases. In the case of very acute angles, the keder in the edge should be turned around the corner with a polygonal or rounded form. Sharp corners are in practice sometimes pretensioned and heated with hot air to approx. 70–80 °C in order to minimise wrinkles. Heating causes plastic deformation of the foil, which results in a state of stress equilibrium.
At open corners the keder is stopped short of the corner; the welded seam continues, however, as far as the corner itself and therefore ensures that the foil remains watertight (Fig. E 3.10).

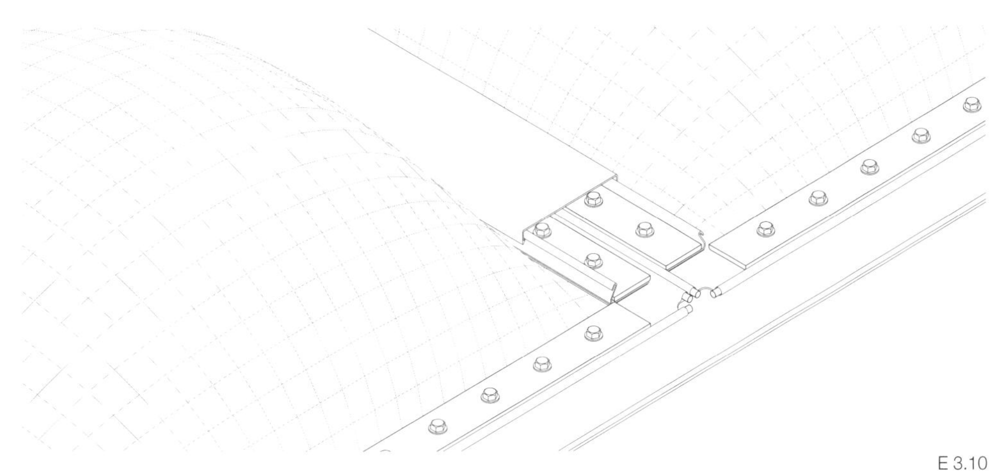
E 3.10

E 3.11

Bird control

Birds with their sharp beaks can indeed represent a risk for foil cushions. The surface of an ETFE cushion is generally too slippery for birds and so they always land on the clamping sections. Perched here, they could damage cushions, especially when they peck at insects that are actually on the other side of the foil. Keeping birds away from the roof surface is therefore normally achieved with thin stainless steel wires, which are attached directly to the clamping sections and are practically invisible beyond a certain distance (Fig. E 3.11, p. 191).

Air supplies for pneumatic structures

The principle of pneumatic forms of construction is based on creating a pressure difference between two areas. We divide such structures into two categories, which can also be combined:

- Air-supported structures, in which the entire usable interior space is at a pressure higher than that of the outside air
- Air-inflated structures, in which certain parts are stabilised by an overpressure (designs with air-filled cushions and tubes)

An air supply must be provided for both types of pneumatic structure so that they remain usable and stable (see "Pneumatically prestressed surfaces", p. 143). All the information and concepts given here apply equally to cushions made from polymer foils and woven fabrics.

Pressure level

The pressure in a pneumatic structure must be maintained at a constant level. However, pneumatic structures built from conventional foil and membrane materials can never be constructed completely airtight. Leaks are unavoidable in the following areas:

- via the material itself (low)
- via faults in the material
- via the joints in the material (welded or glued seams)
- via the air supply connections
- possibly via the clamping and edge details

In practical situations these leaks are considerably affected by the quality of fabrication and workmanship on site plus the geometry of the cushion itself, e.g. acute angles generally lead to high air losses at the corners. The internal pressure must be regulated continually to cope with the constant losses and the pressure fluctuations of the outside air.
Depending on the size of the structure, one inflation unit could be responsible for all the cushions, or several units may be required, each of which is connected to a particular group of cushions. The installation can be designed in such a way that it is able to increase its output considerably to cope with high snow loads by raising the internal pressure in all or certain cushions.

Air supplies for maintaining the pressure

The air inlet to each cushion is generally close to the edge clamp because this is where the supply hoses can be easily routed and fixed (Fig. E 3.12). The connection itself must be flexible in order to cope with the inflation procedure and the unavoidable movements of the cushions in use; ETFE hoses or other elastic polymer hoses are the best choice. Hoses made from a material that withstands ultraviolet radiation are certainly compulsory for ETFE cushions; a transparent PUR hose with steel convolutions is generally used in practice. The main lines and the secondary duct system are typically made from spiral-wound pipes. If these remain exposed and the aesthetics are important, pipes made from polymers or other materials (e.g. stainless steel) can be used. Very small hose diameters of 10–20 mm would be adequate for normal operations, for maintaining the air pressure at the necessary level. However, it is very difficult for systems with small hoses to cope with the drop in pressure if a cushion is damaged. Therefore, air hose diameters of 40 mm and more have become established in practice.

A pressure-controlled air supply, with compensation for losses, is usually necessary in order to reach the level of pressure required and maintain it at that level. Minor pressure fluctuations help to achieve a maximum service life for the cushion structure. Occasionally, additional outlet safety valves are fitted and normally equipped with silencers to suppress any disturbing whistling noises (Fig. E 3.12c). It may be necessary to fit such valves when a certain pressure level must be maintained very accurately or the inevitable leaks in the structure are not adequate for the necessary flushing of the cushion with the fresh air. Cushions consisting of two or more layers can be kept inflated by a common pressure level in the individual chambers (Fig. E 3.12b). Separate connections for the chambers enables the pressure levels to be graduated (Fig. E 3.12d). This latter solution is used when the central layer is to be moved by changing the pressure (see "Movable central layer", p. 189) or various materials are being used (e.g. woven fabric for outer layer, foil for inner layers) or where this approach has advantages for carrying the loads.

If several chambers are maintained at the same pressure level, then it is normal to provide holes, i.e. leakage air openings, in the intervening layers which for hydrodynamics reasons should not be positioned too near the air inlets. Including such openings ensures that the pressure in the cushion is distributed faster and more evenly, also in the event of a change in the external pressure (e.g. wind pressure and suction). The air inlet to each cushion should include a check valve to maintain the pressure for up to 8 hours even if the fans are not functioning.

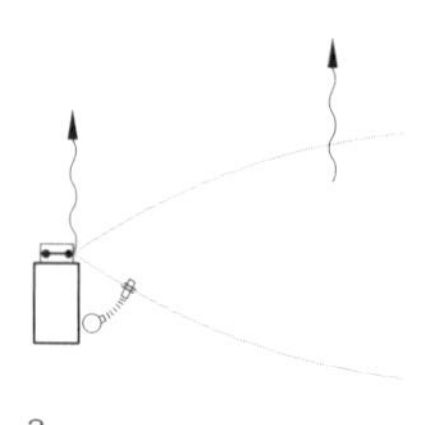

a

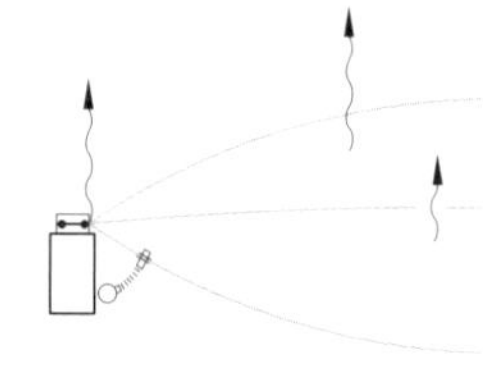

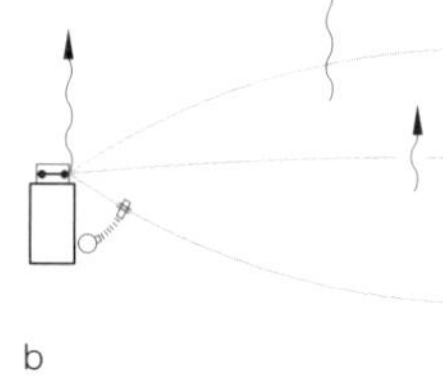

b

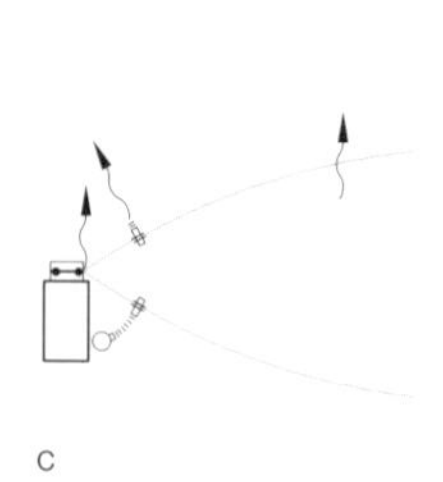

c

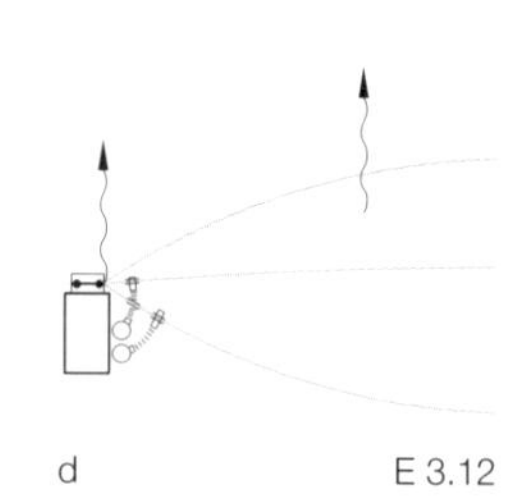

d

E 3.12

E 3.12 Options for connecting the air supply to cushions
a Single air inlet; air escapes via leaks in the surface and at edges
b Cushion with two chambers and single air inlet; leakage air opening in central layer
c Air supply with control valve; the air escapes via leaks in the surface and at edges and also via a silenced outlet valve (air pressure in cushion regulated)
d Cushion with two chambers each with its own air supply (various pressure levels possible)

E 3.13 Air supply systems with parallel (a), series (b), return air + parallel (c), return air + series (d) connections
1 Backup supply
2 Primary air supply
Filter
Inflation unit
Dehumidifier
3 Return air system with sensors
P = sensor for air pressure
F = sensor for humidity

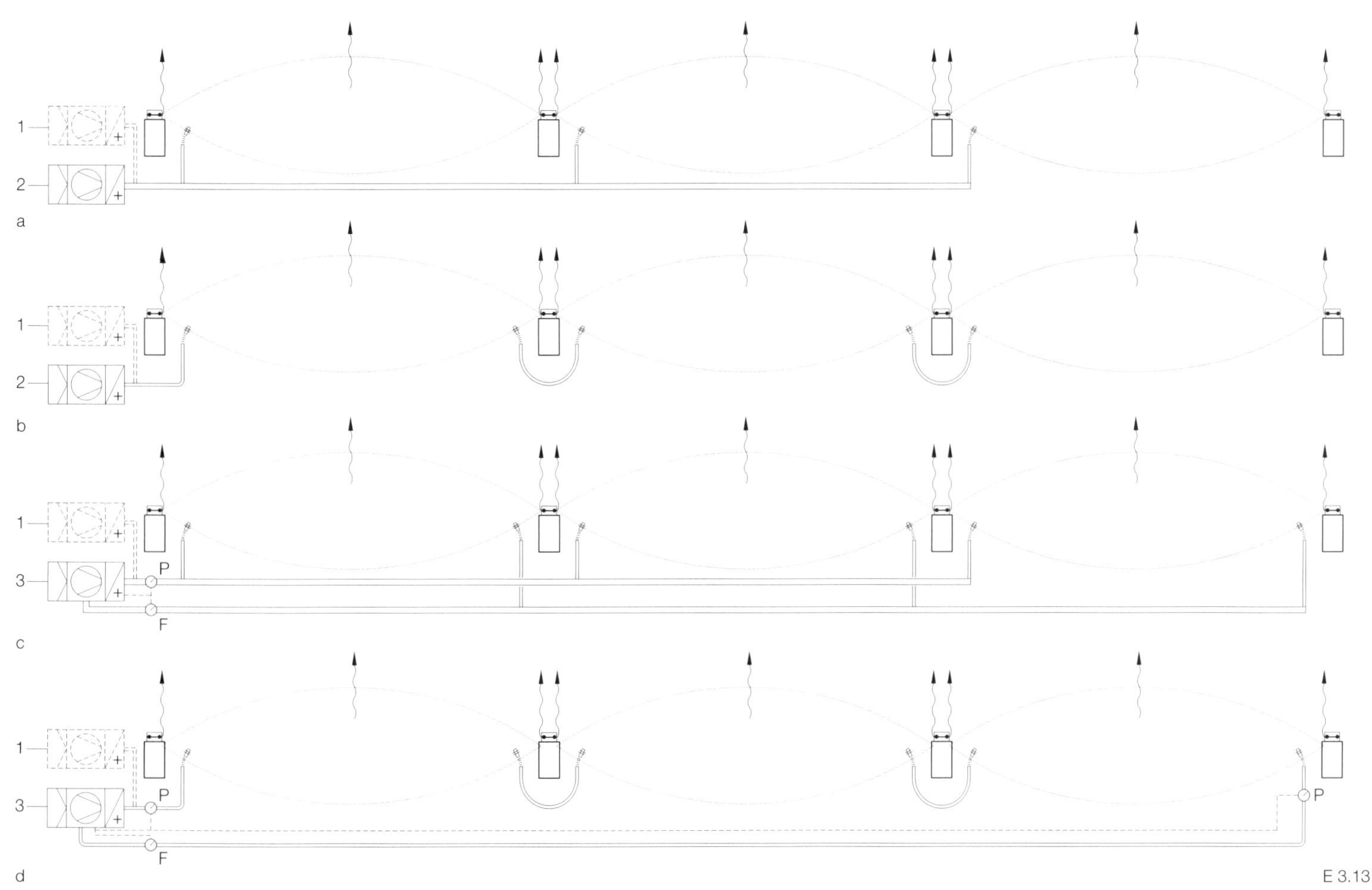

E 3.13

Air supply systems

The air supply is not provided purely for maintaining the pressure in the cushions, but also for ensuring that the air within the cushions is sufficiently dry. This prevents condensation and algae growth inside the cushions. Pneumatic structures should therefore be supplied with pretreated air and so the plant normally consists of filter, fan/compressor and a condenser drier or a dehumidification unit with a heating battery (absorption dehumidifier; Fig. E 3.15, p. 194). Dehumidifying the air accounts for a considerable proportion of the energy consumed by the air-supply system; there is room for developing alternative concepts here that require only a minimum amount of primary energy.

Filtering the air is important because otherwise dust and dirt could enter the cushions, from where it is impossible to remove. All the components of the plant should therefore be accessible for regular maintenance and repairs. The system should be flushed through with dry air to remove any dust, dirt, foreign matter or pollutants prior to connecting the hoses to the cushions for the first time. In air-supported structures the requirements for the quality of the air tend to be dictated by the comfort criteria for the occupants (primarily with respect to hygiene, humidity and temperature).

It is usual to connect several cushions together to form a group which is then supplied by common systems in a series or parallel arrangement. A parallel system (Fig. E 3.13a) achieves a very constant pressure level in the individual cushions with just one connection. Furthermore, individual cushions are easily replaced because they can be readily disconnected from the system without interrupting the supply to the other cushions. An additional common supply pipe is required, the size of which normally has a much greater diameter (approx. 100–150 mm) than the branches (approx. 40–50 mm).

In a series installation, all the cushions (apart from the last one in each series) requires two connections (Fig. E 3.13b). The pressure level generally drops gradually from the first to the last cushion. Both systems are regulated by the pressure, sometimes combined with humidity control, and both suffer from losses. This type of system generally includes absorption dehumidifier.

Quick detection of major breakdowns and leaks is achieved with a timer control, i.e. an unusually long operating time (e.g. > 1 min continuously) triggers an alarm. Such detection systems are becoming increasingly important for safety reasons.

For calculation purposes, a power supply between approx. 0.4 and 3 W/m^2 can be assumed for fan and dehumidifier, and the actual annual energy requirement should be taken as approx. 3–20 kWh/m^{2}a for rough calculations. The wide ranges of these figures are due to the fact that, on the one hand, various technical concepts are possible and, on the other, the low number of structures built so far means that only a few measurements regarding actual consumption are available.

Return air systems

Return air systems, the characteristic feature of which is the return flow line, are being used more and more in order to save energy in air supply installations (Figs. E 3.13c and d). Most of all, this reduces the energy required for dehumidifying the air because this unit only functions when activated by signals from sensors. Measuring the relative humidity in the cushion, which is usually carried out at the centre of the circuit, enables the system to respond to the changing weather conditions. Series (Fig. E 3.13c) and parallel (Fig. E 3.13d) systems are possible with return air installations as well, with the same advantages and disadvantages as for those systems with inherent losses. Two pressure sensors are generally recommended for a series installation, which measure the values at the start and end of the chain and, for example, calculate a mean value for the control.

Although return air systems are essentially designed for continuous operation in order to guarantee a constant pressure level, they often result in considerable energy-savings of up to 60 %, which justifies the higher initial cost of such systems.

a

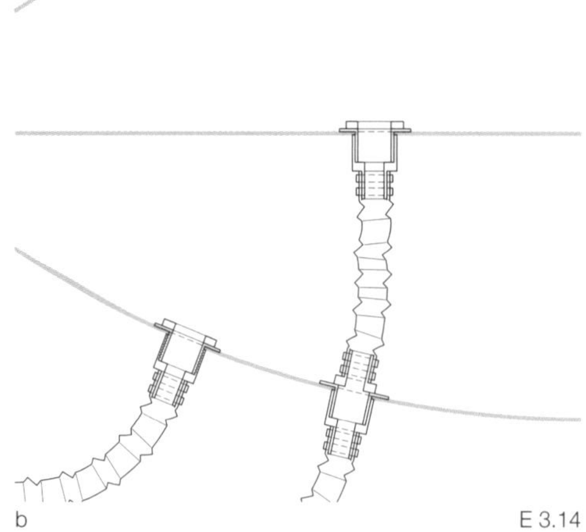
b E 3.14

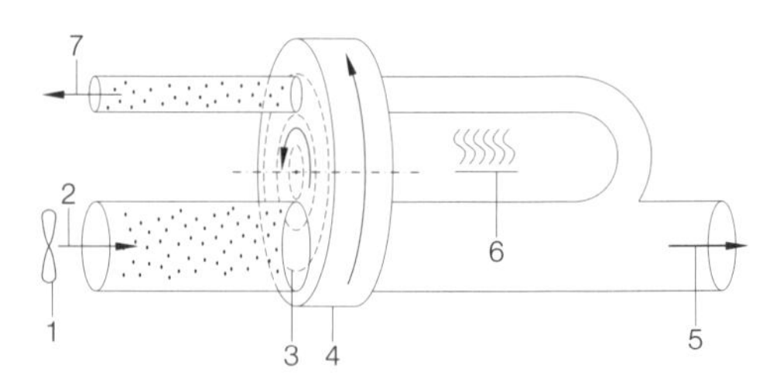

1 Fan
2 Moist supply air
3 Moisture absorption
4 Silica gel rotor
5 Dehumidified air
6 Heating battery
7 Moist exhaust air

E 3.15

E 3.14 a, b Connecting the air supply to a multi-layer cushion with a separate air supply to each chamber
E 3.15 Inflation unit with absorption dehumidifier
E 3.16 a, b Emergency overflow for a foil cushion
E 3.17 Cable clamps for cable nets
E 3.18 Close-up of a node in a prefabricated cable net
E 3.19 Tensairity beam, EMPA Materials-Testing & Research Institute, Zurich
E 3.20 Foil cushion supported by cable net; hydrogen filling station, Munich (D), 2007, frank & probst architekten
E 3.21 Funnel-type canopy with printed ETFE foil strengthened by cable net, Chamber of Trade & Industry, Würzburg (D), 2003, Franz Gröger/ Georg Redelbach
E 3.22 Retensioning system for the mechanically prestressed ETFE facade to the Gerontology Technology Centre, Bad Tölz (D), 2003, D. J. Siegert

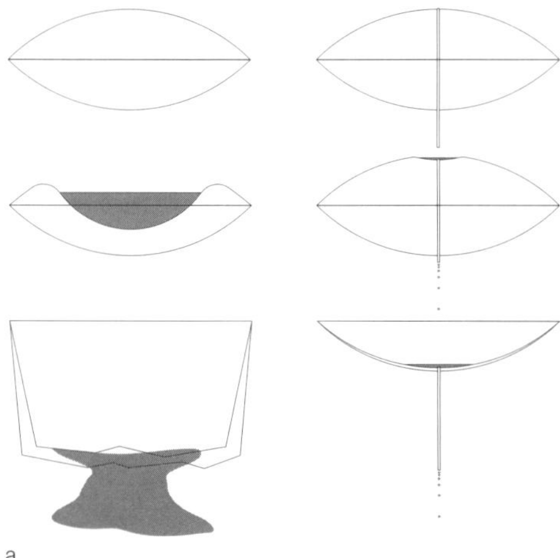
a

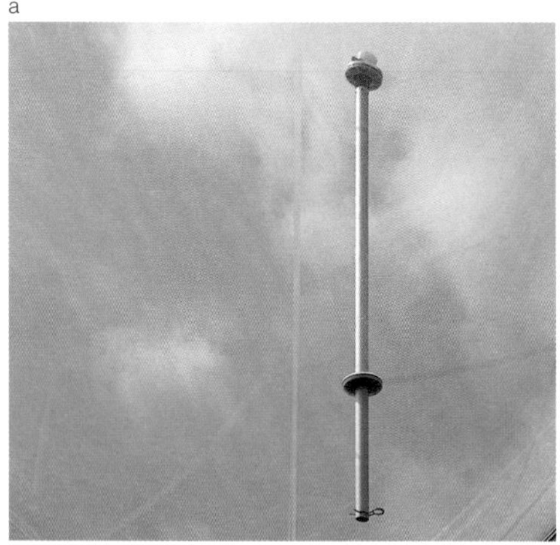
b E 3.16

Safety of cushion structures

Cushion structures are stabilised by internal overpressure. If this pressure cannot be maintained, the load-carrying capacity of the cushion can no longer be guaranteed. This can lead to the material fluttering and, in strong winds, to irreparable damage. With rain or snow at the same time this could lead to ponding or snowdrifts and possibly to the overloading of the material. The primary structure must be designed for this loading case so that failure is ruled out. Corresponding studies have shown that relatively large asymmetrical loads result in practice which in turn can govern the development of the structural concept.

Two scenarios are relevant in practice: failure of the air supply and local damage (holes) in the outer layer of a cushion. Neither leads to sudden failure of the construction. Instead, it tends to be the case that, even if the air supply has failed or the material has been damaged, an overpressure is maintained in the cushions for quite some time and they lose their prestress only slowly. Most systems include pressure sensors that detect such problems and output an alarm so that the necessary remedial measures can be taken. Cushion assemblies are also comparatively safe in the event of a major accident: even a badly damaged cushion overhead does not represent a serious danger because of its low self-weight. In a worst-case scenario, a cushion sagging under the weight of snow or water rips and empties its contents onto the floor below.
Air supply systems to cushion structures must be designed with inherent redundancy in order to be able to maintain the overpressure in event of a fan breakdown or the failure of an individual cushion. This means that every inflation unit must be fitted with two fans that guarantee constant operation, controlled by a timer switch that alternates the fans every few days (Fig. E 3.13, p. 193). In addition, the inflation units are often backed up by emergency generators so that full functionality is guaranteed even in the event of a power failure.
Regular inspections and maintenance of the foil and the bird control measures are necessary if mechanical damage is to be avoided or at least detected in good time. Holes can be repaired by welding on pieces of ETFE material locally, which are no more conspicuous than the other seams.
A multi-layer cushion design can increase the level of safety. If the outer layer is pierced, the next, inner layer is automatically forced upwards towards the underside of the damaged layer by the pressure and can therefore close off the opening temporarily.

Overflows

An overflow concept for extreme situations was included for the first time in the design for the Allianz Arena in Munich. This is designed for the unlikely situation that a large pool of water collects in an unpressurised cushion. Sudden failure of the foil could result in a large quantity of water being discharged onto persons below. But in Munich a pipe permanently welded to the top of the cushion enables the water to drain away continuously in such an emergency situation without causing any serious problems (Fig. E 3.16). The extra cost of a detail that penetrates the foil is only justified in those instances where a quick repair cannot be guaranteed and large quantities of water falling from great heights represent an obvious safety risk.

Mechanically prestressed foil

Up until now, ETFE foil has been used primarily for building envelopes with air-filled cushions. The material has a better elasticity than textile membranes, but a lower strength, and so mechanically prestressed foil is currently only feasible for short spans. But in some cases a clearly anisotropic prestress renders possible longer, strip-like foil membranes. Special attention must be given to the creep behaviour of the foil material. Whereas in cushion structures the internal pressure can compensate for any loss of prestress as a result of creep, a mechanically prestressed design must include retensioning elements such as threaded parts with adequate travel. At the Gerontology Technology Centre in Bad Tölz, for example, this is achieved with leaf springs and adjusting screws on the

E 3.17

E 3.18

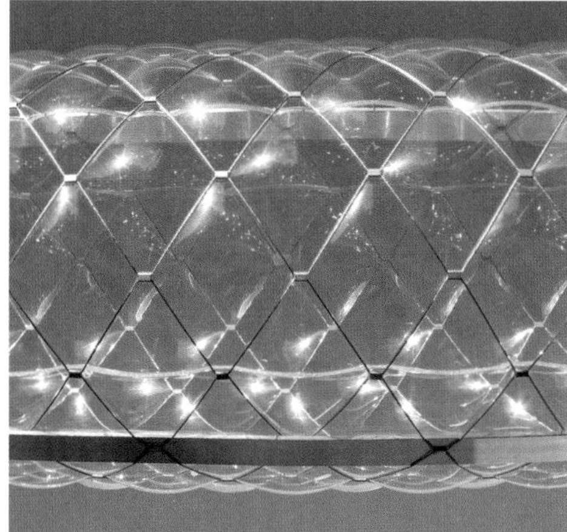

E 3.19

long edges of the mechanically prestressed strips of foil (Fig. E 3.22 and Fig. E 5.25, p. 222). One very promising new type of application for foil is as a stretch material over modular frames. Here, the foil is first fixed to a frame with mechanical fasteners and then, in a second operation, tensioned by inserting an arch (see, for example, "Training centre for mountain rescue service", pp. 260–261). Such framed membrane modules are also suitable for double-leaf facades, where they can be used in a similar way to a frame structure but have a considerable weight advantage over glass.
Other applications for mechanically prestressed foil are as ceilings and internal partitions, also for improving room acoustics (see "Room acoustics", p. 118). PVC foil is also possible in such instances because of the lower mechanical stresses and the low UV exposure (see "PVC foil", p. 99).

Cable net support systems

Cable nets can be used in conjunction with foil in order to achieve longer spans – for both mechanically and pneumatically prestressed designs. In the case of the latter, a cable net either above or below the foil enables the individual cushions to be designed with a shallower curvature, which, however, means a higher stress in the surface that cannot be accommodated solely by a foil (see "Pneumatically prestressed surfaces", p. 147).
The points of contact between the foil and the steel cables or cable net can – in a similar way to edge clamp details – lead to mechanical damage, galvanic corrosion, heat transfer and hindering the expansion of the material. Accordingly, it is advantageous to create a shear-resistant connection between the cable net and the foil, which, however, has proved to be difficult in practice. Cable nets with large apertures are therefore preferred because these allow the foil to curve outwards quite distinctly, which fixes it in position (Fig. E 3.20). Cable nets with small apertures (Figs. E 3.18 and E 3.19) are only suitable when the foil exhibits sufficient elasticity and can still bulge outwards between the more closely spaced cables. This has been achieved very successfully with the transparent Tensairity beams in the research project carried out at the EMPA Materials-Testing & Research Institute in Zurich (see "Tensairity", p. 144, and Fig. E 3.19). As a rule, however, specially fabricated large-aperture cable nets are used, with standardised cable clamps at the nodes (Fig. E 3.17).
The other difficulty with mechanically prestressed foil materials is that a cable net underneath provides support for one loading direction only. The net should therefore be laminated between two layers of foil in a mechanically prestressed design, or at least one group of parallel cables should be fitted into pockets attached to the foil. This latter solution was used for the foil stretched over the canopies at the Chamber of Trade & Industry in Würzburg. Here, the cable net makes use of meridian and circumferential cables in diameters of 8–10 mm (Fig. E 3.21). The meridian cables are fitted into pockets integrated into the seams, which couples together foil and cables to cope with uplift and compression loads.

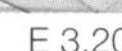

E 3.20

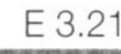

E 3.21

E 3.22

Building with textile membranes

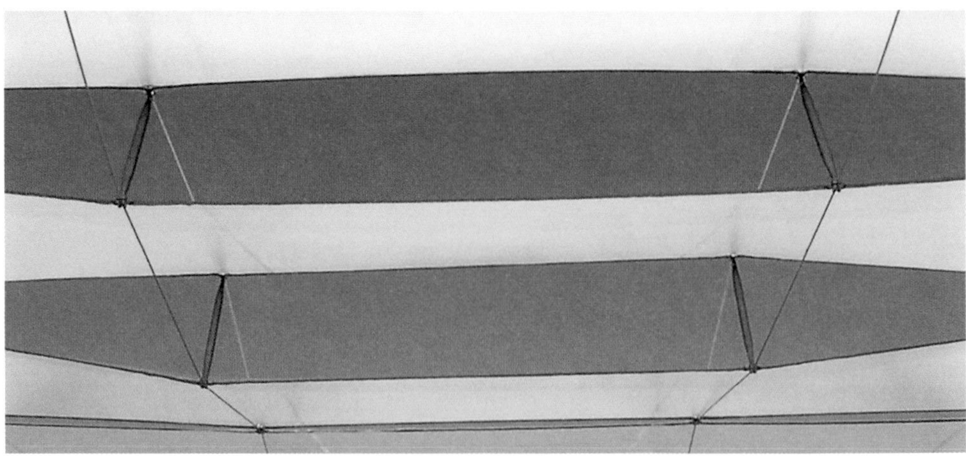

E 4.1

Membranes are prefabricated in large formats and folded or rolled for transport. This means that the number of joints, seams and connections is comparatively low when compared with other forms of construction. But this also means that the details are even more significant for the overall loadbearing structure because this is where high tensile forces must be transferred from membranes with complex geometrical forms, and just a few millimetres thick, to the rest of the structure.
The form of a mechanically prestressed membrane is essentially determined by the laws of physics once the boundary conditions have been defined (see "Form-finding", pp. 138–140). But the details worked out by the designer can influence the appearance of a membrane loadbearing structure significantly. Design offices and fabricators experienced in the design and construction of membrane structures often develop their own unmistakable styles for the details. The details described on the following pages show all the basic constructional features of building with membranes in relation to the materials used, although the details shown here are restricted to a number of standard situations and standard geometries. More complex details can be seen in the photographs and in the case studies presented in Part F (pp. 225–285). Special solutions for convertible structures are not dealt with in detail because such designs are always very specific to the particular project (see, for example, "Open-air Theatre, Josefsburg Arena", pp. 282–285, and "Convertible membrane structures", p. 149).

The forms of construction and features of membrane details depend on many factors, which the engineer and architect must fine-tune and agree upon in close collaboration in an iterative planning process:

- Geometry of planar structure
- External loads
- Membrane material
- Magnitudes and directions of forces
- Erection and maintenance concepts
- Form
- Costs

Fig. E 4.2 provides an overview of the typical details that need to be considered for mechanically prestressed membranes, and Fig. E 4.3 shows how the respective details depend on which membrane material is used. It is important to categorise the details according to whether the loads are transferred as linear loads or point loads. The former occur at edges, seams and linear supports, the latter at corners. The basic principles for anchoring the stresses in the plane of the membrane at these details are often similar and so the basic constructional elements such as wire ropes, webbing belts and clamping bars can therefore be employed in similar ways at the various details.

Generally speaking, the fundamental principle of membrane structures, i.e. using a minimum amount of material, should be reflected in the details as well: their geometry and positioning should match the flow of forces and render the structural system "legible". The consistency of the proportions between the individual components is very important here. For example, the dimensions of a corner plate should be defined by the components that meet at this point and also by the diameters of the cables connected to the plate.
Owing to the comparatively large deformations that membrane structures undergo upon the application of external loads (see "Mechanically prestressed surfaces", pp. 140–143), all details should allow for the necessary movement – also during erection. And allowance for movement at the details is of course especially important in convertible structures.

The prestressing of the membrane surface is generally introduced at the details, which should therefore also include appropriate fittings for connecting the temporary tensioning equipment required. It is often possible to attach portable winches or ratchet straps to eyes or edges that are available anyway. But where this is not possible, temporary or permanent (welded) attachment points must be provided. Furthermore, it is often necessary to allow for adjusting the prestressed or retensioning the incoming cables, which means cables must include turnbuckles or must be attached to threaded fittings.

E 4.1 Resolved traditional Spanish awning (*toldo*) with "flying masts"; Medina (KSA), 2003, Rasch + Bradatsch
E 4.2 Overview of typical details for mechanically prestressed membranes
E 4.3 Relationships between details and material

All edges and corners and arrises of metal parts used in conjunction with membranes must be rounded off. This applies not only to parts that are designed to be in contact with the membrane, but also to any metal parts that could come into contact with the membrane during erection.

Elements of the construction

Membrane structures inevitably make use of semi-finished metal products as well as textiles and semi-finished polymer products such as membrane materials, webbing belts (see "Webbing belts", p. 107) and keders (see "Keders", p. 99).

Cables and cable fittings

Edge cables are mostly in the form of steel or stainless steel wire ropes, only rarely ropes made from synthetic materials such as polyester or aramid. To protect against corrosion, every individual steel wire is hot-dip galvanised. Special aluminium-zinc coatings offer the best protection against corrosion.
Stranding is the process of forming a strand from several individual wires laid (wound) in a helical arrangement around an axis or another wire to produce a symmetrical section. When this strand is used directly as a wire rope, we speak of a spiral rope, but if several strands are laid around each other, this is known as a stranded rope.

Wire ropes (generally referred to as cables) for the edges of membranes should be as flexible as possible so that they can match the curve of the edge. Special round strand ropes and open spiral ropes made up of large numbers of thin wires are available for this. Where very high forces are expected in the cables, e.g. guy ropes, fully locked spiral ropes are used, which are characterised by their z-shaped wires on the outside (Fig. E 4.4, p. 198). These shaped wires interlock with each other and create a dense surface that protects the wires in the core of the rope and hence improves the corrosion protection. In addition, fully locked spiral ropes are given a filling of zinc dust paint. The wires of such ropes are packed more tightly together and so achieve a high load-carrying capacity for a relatively small diameter.

End terminations for cables take the form of spelter sockets or swaged fittings (Fig. E 4.5, p. 198). The latter are used for round strand ropes and open spiral ropes in diameters up to approx. 36 mm, whereas the former are required for anchoring larger rope diameters and fully locked ropes. Spelter sockets are shorter and bulkier than swaged fittings and are filled with a molten metal (e.g. usually a zinc alloy) or a synthetic material (epoxy or polyester resin). Spelter sockets and swaged fittings can be anchored in various ways; we distinguish between three types: open, closed and cylindrical.
An open fitting is attached to a corner plate with a bolt or pin, a closed fitting is anchored between two plates. Both may require turnbuckles at the end of the rope where adjustability is necessary. Cylindrical fittings or sockets are installed as clamps (no thread) and with internal or external threads.

Cylindrical swaged terminations with an external thread, the so-called threaded fitting adjusted directly via the screw thread, are typical for membrane details. These fittings are inserted through sleeves and secured with a nut on the other side. With a sufficiently large sleeve inside diameter and spherical washers between nut and end of sleeve, they can also accommodate rotation.

Clamping and keder details

Detachable linear details are generally in the form of clamping bars or keder rails. These are interlocking connections in which the keder, welded into the edge of the membrane, presses against the sides of the clamping bar or keder rail. Fig. E 4.6 (p. 198) shows the different edge detail arrangements and how the loads are carried; the red arrows represent the actions and reactions, the blue ones the clamping forces of the clamping element. The advantage of polymer keders, e.g. PVC, is that they exhibit similar elongation characteristics to those of the membrane and therefore do not lead to any stress- or temperature-related restraint stresses. A keder made from a steel rope should be encased in a

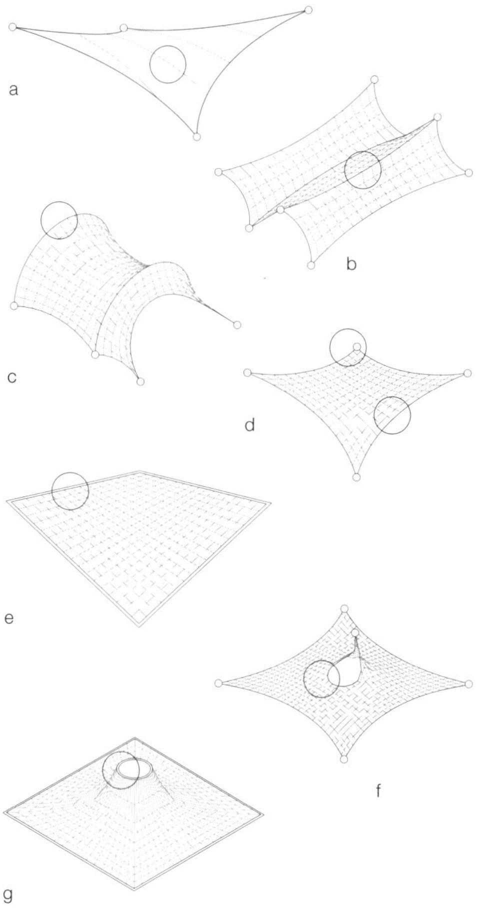

E 4.2

	Fig. E 4.2		Polyester-PVC	PTFE/glass	Glass-silicone	Coated PTFE	PTFE
Seam	permanent (a)	stitched	+	–	–	+	++
		welded	++	++	–	+	–
		glued	(+)	–	++	–	–
	detachable (a)	laced	+	(+)	(+)	+	+
		clamping bar	++	(+)	(+)	+	+
		keder rail	+	++	++	+	+
Linear support	flexible (b)	webbing belt	+	–	–	+	+
		wire rope	+	+	+	+	+
	rigid (c)		+	+	+	+	+
Edge	flexible (d)	webbing belt	+	–	–	+	++
		rope in pocket	++	(+)	+	+	+
		separate edge cable	+	++	+	+	(+)
	rigid (e)	laced	+	(+)	(+)	+	+
		clamping bar	++	+	+	+	+
		keder rail	+	++	++	+	+
Corner	open (d)		++	+	+	+	+
	closed (d)	ring/eye	+	–	–	+	++
		plate	+	++	+	+	+
High/low point	flexible (f)	cable loop	+	+	+	+	+
		scalloped	+	(+)	(+)	+	++
	rigid (g)	ring	++	++	+	+	+
		hump	+	+	+	+	+

++ typical + possible (+) rare – not possible

E 4.3

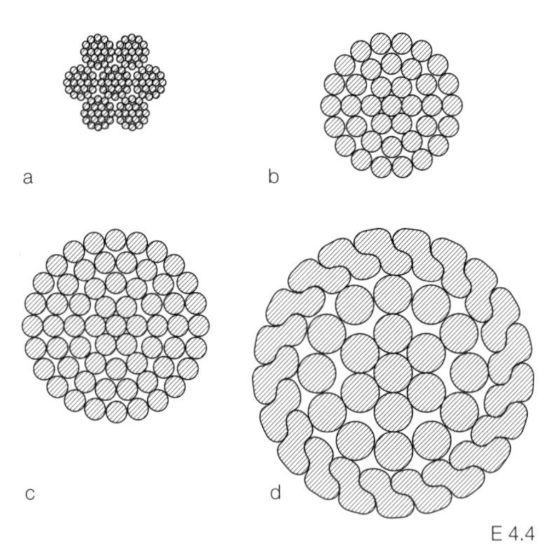

E 4.4

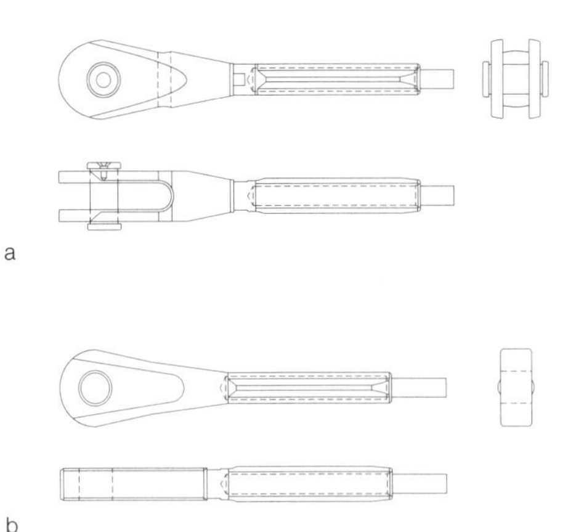

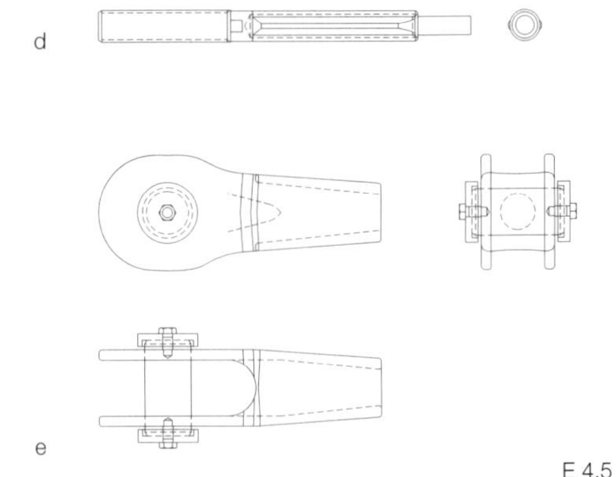

E 4.5

shrink-wrap plastic sleeve to prevent damage to the membrane.
Clamping bars are typically made from steel and are 30–40 mm wide and 5–8 mm thick (Fig. E 4.7a); their length depends on the degree of movement required at the connection.
Holes pre-punched in the membrane for the fasteners should be much larger than the diameter of the fastener in order to avoid fraying around the edges of the hole. Tightening the fastener and thus exerting a clamping force on the membrane results in a connection held together by a combination of the applied force and the interlocking form; the edge can therefore be pulled taut and clamped in position.

Keder rails and clamps are aluminium extrusions. Small notches are provided in these components as an aid for drilling the holes for the fasteners (Figs. E 4.7b–d). In contrast to a joint with clamping bars, the fasteners do not penetrate the membrane with this type of detail. The extrusion includes a recess into which the keder is threaded. The membrane is therefore held in place but at the same time can still expand in the direction of the joint, i.e. a longitudinally; this is purely an interlocking joint (Figs. E 4.7b–f). With a one-piece keder rail, the membrane with its welded keder is threaded in from the side; applying wax helps to overcome the frictional resistance. Two-piece keder clamps are fitted either side of the keder and then fixed to the rigid supporting structure.

We must distinguish between open and closed clamping details. In the former, a small gap remains between the fixed and detachable parts of the clamping detail, which allows the membrane to expand and contract (Figs. E 4.6b and E 4.7f); in the latter, there is no gap and the result is again a connection held together by a combination of the applied force and the interlocking form (Figs. E 4.6c and E 4.7g) which allows the edge of the membrane to be pulled taut. As the area in contact is much smaller than in the case of a clamping bar, thin strips of membrane or synthetic rubber are sometimes inserted to cushion the clamping action and therefore prevent damage to the fabric.

Seams

The various sections of membrane material are joined together via seams. A permanent seam is a factory-made junction between two pieces of material, designed to produce a coherent surface from the pieces of material cut according to the cutting pattern. A detachable seam is a connection that is made during erection so that the prefabricated sections of membrane material can be assembled on the building site.

Permanent seams
Large membrane surfaces are joined together in the factory from individual segments prepared according to the cutting pattern to form a curved membrane section (see "Cutting pattern", pp. 147–148). All seams must satisfy stringent demands because their mechanical and visual characteristics must be as close as possible to those of the membrane material itself. The main requirements are:

- High mechanical strength (similar to the membrane) when subjected to short- and long-term actions
- Similar elongation behaviour and flexibility as those of the membrane
- Watertightness, and also airtightness in the case of pneumatic structures
- As narrow as possible
- Consistent visual and mechanical qualities
- Economic fabrication

The techniques used for permanent seams are welding, stitching and, occasionally, gluing as well (see "Fabrication", pp. 106–107).

Welded seams
Welded seams are generally carried out in the factory using large welding plant that can produce high-quality seams very quickly (see "Welding", p. 106). When welding is carried out on site, it is only for attaching cover strips over detachable joints between membrane sections, or over rigid edges, corner details or other openings.

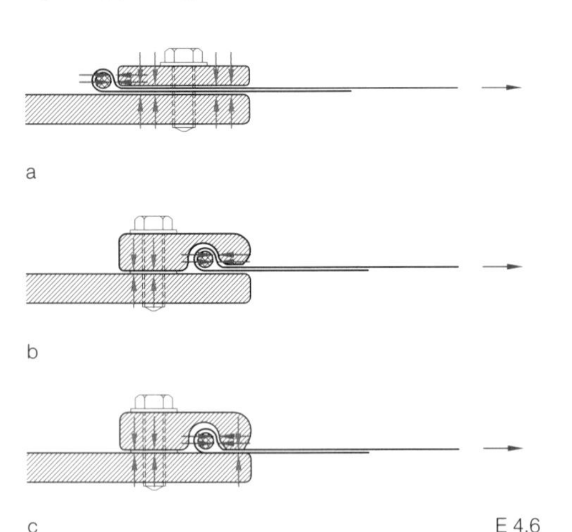

E 4.6

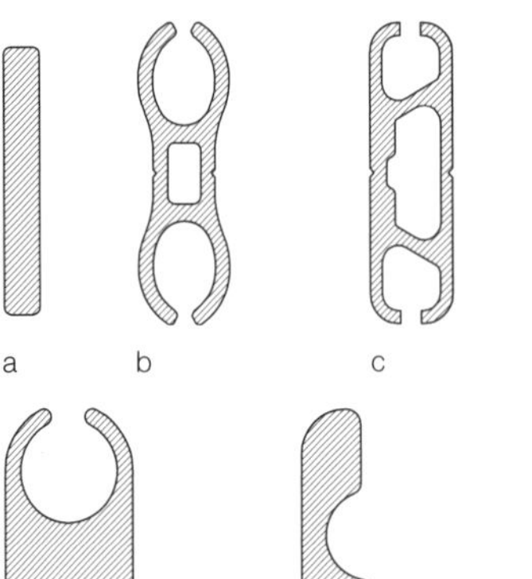
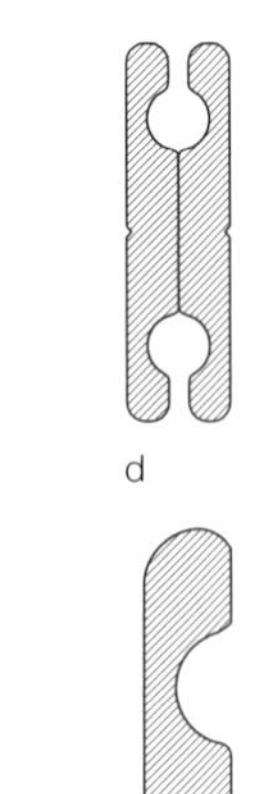
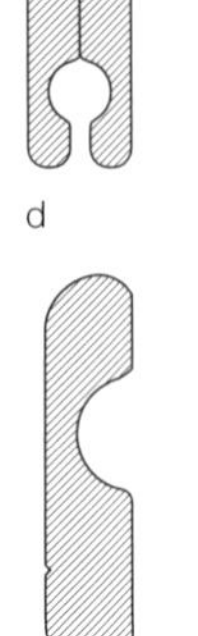

E 4.7

E 4.4 Wire rope cross-sections
a Round strand rope
b, c Open spiral rope
d Fully locked spiral rope
E 4.5 Wire rope fittings
a Open
b Closed
c Turnbuckle
d Threaded fitting
e Open Spelter socket
E 4.6 Load-carrying mechanisms
a Clamping bar
b Keder clamp with open gap
c Keder clamp with closed gap
E 4.7 Keder clamping options
a Clamping bar
b, c Double keder rails

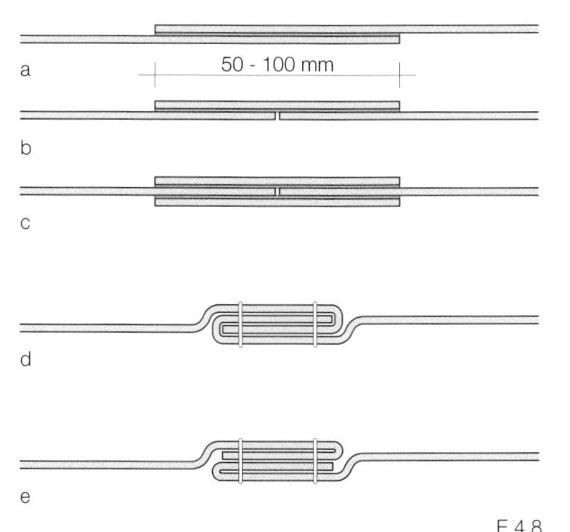

E 4.8

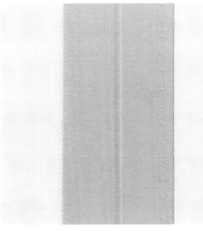

E 4.9

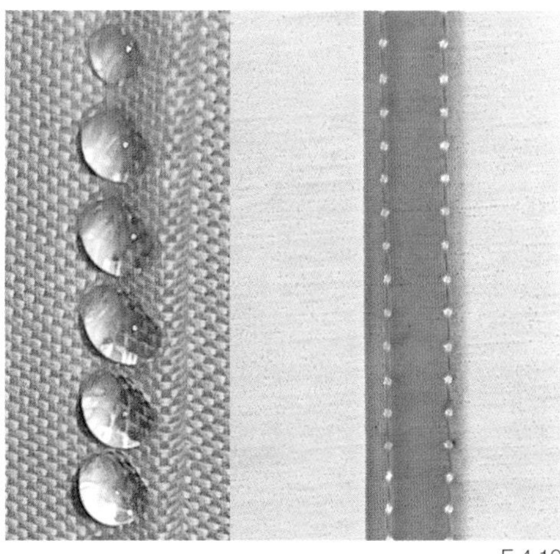

E 4.10

Welded seams are the most common type of seam in use because of their high quality and cost-effective production; these days, only materials unsuitable for welding are still stitched or glued. Welded seams can achieve a strength that is equal to about 90 % of that of the membrane itself. However, the prerequisite for this is loads in the plane of the membrane, i.e. the material is being used properly from the structural viewpoint. Shear forces due to local load concentrations and peeling forces perpendicular to the plane of the membrane lead to seams with much lower load-carrying capacities and should be avoided.
As a rule, a welded seam is produced simply by overlapping the pieces of material by 50–100 mm in order to avoid excessive differences in stiffness between the seam and the main area of the material (Figs. E 4.8a and E 4.9).

It is also possible to produce splices with one or two separate pieces of material covering a butt joint between the two pieces of membrane (Figs. E 4.8b and c). With such a splice joint, there is no need to take the seam into account in the cutting pattern, so the full width of the roll of material available can be used. Welded splices with separate pieces of material above and below the joint can in some cases achieve even higher strengths. The disadvantage, however, is their more time-consuming and costly fabrication.

Stitched seams
Stitched seams are primarily used for uncoated woven fabrics that cannot be welded. We distinguish between plain, flat-fell and double-stitched flat-fell seams. Only the latter of these three can achieve the strength and watertightness necessary for membrane structures (Figs. E 4.8d and e). Such a seam can be produced either with interlocking or overlapped hems. The width of the stitched seam is limited by a homogeneous utilisation of all adjacent seams. With too many rows of stitches, the inner rows are only loaded once the outer rows fail. Two, three or four rows of stitches is normal.
The holes for the stitches widen as the membrane is prestressed, which reduces the watertightness at these points considerably (Fig. E 4.10). Subsequently welding or gluing separate cover strips over stitched seams helps to improve their watertightness. Special adhesives are also available that are spread directly over the stitched seam to improve the watertightness.

Glued seams
Glued seams are only used when no other method is suitable. They are still used for glass-silicone membranes, either combined with stitching or in the form of special adhesive tape. The material is overlapped in a similar way to welded seams.

Intersections
Joining together the separate pieces of material to form a coherent membrane can lead to intersections between two or more welded seams (Fig. E 4.11). These nodes are thicker, which can lead to problems during fabrication and also with respect to transferring the forces at these points. On the other hand, it is often desirable, from the aesthetics viewpoint, that intersecting seams meet at one point in order to create a neater appearance. The solutions chosen to overcome such problems depend very much on the material. Whereas it is possible to overlay and join together even four, five or six layers of a lightweight material at one point, alternative solutions must be found for heavier materials. One option is to create a common seam where each intersecting seam is offset by the width of one seam.

Overlapping membrane sections
Overlaps at seams should always be arranged such that run-off water drains from the uppermost piece of material to the lower one in order to minimise the amount of water impinging on the actual joint between the layers and hence the risk of water infiltrating (Fig. E 4.12). The reverse arrangement also allows dust and dirt to collect at such points and in some circumstances even infiltrate the woven fabric at open edges.

d Two-part double keder clamp
e Special keder rail with slot for bolt head (see Fig. E 4.29f, p. 204)
f One-sided keder clamp with open gap
g One-sided keder clamp with closed gap

E 4.8 Various seam arrangements
a Simple overlap, welded
b One-sided splice, welded
c Double-sided splice, welded
d Double-stitched flat-fell seam, interlocked
e Double-stitched flat-fell seam, overlapped

E 4.9 Welded seam in a polyester-PVC membrane

E 4.10 Stitched seam in an open-weave PTFE fabric, with water seeping through the holes for the stitches

E 4.11 Intersections between welded seams,

E 4.12 Overlapping seams in the direction of water run-off

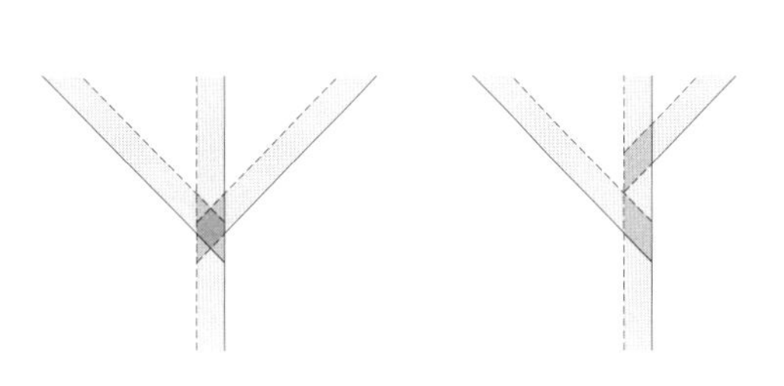

E 4.11

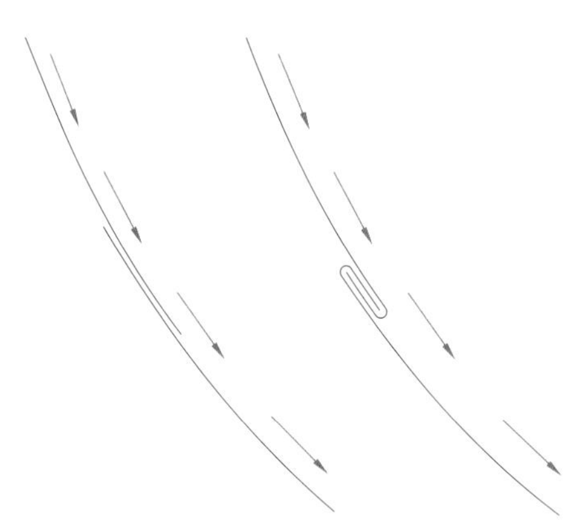

E 4.12

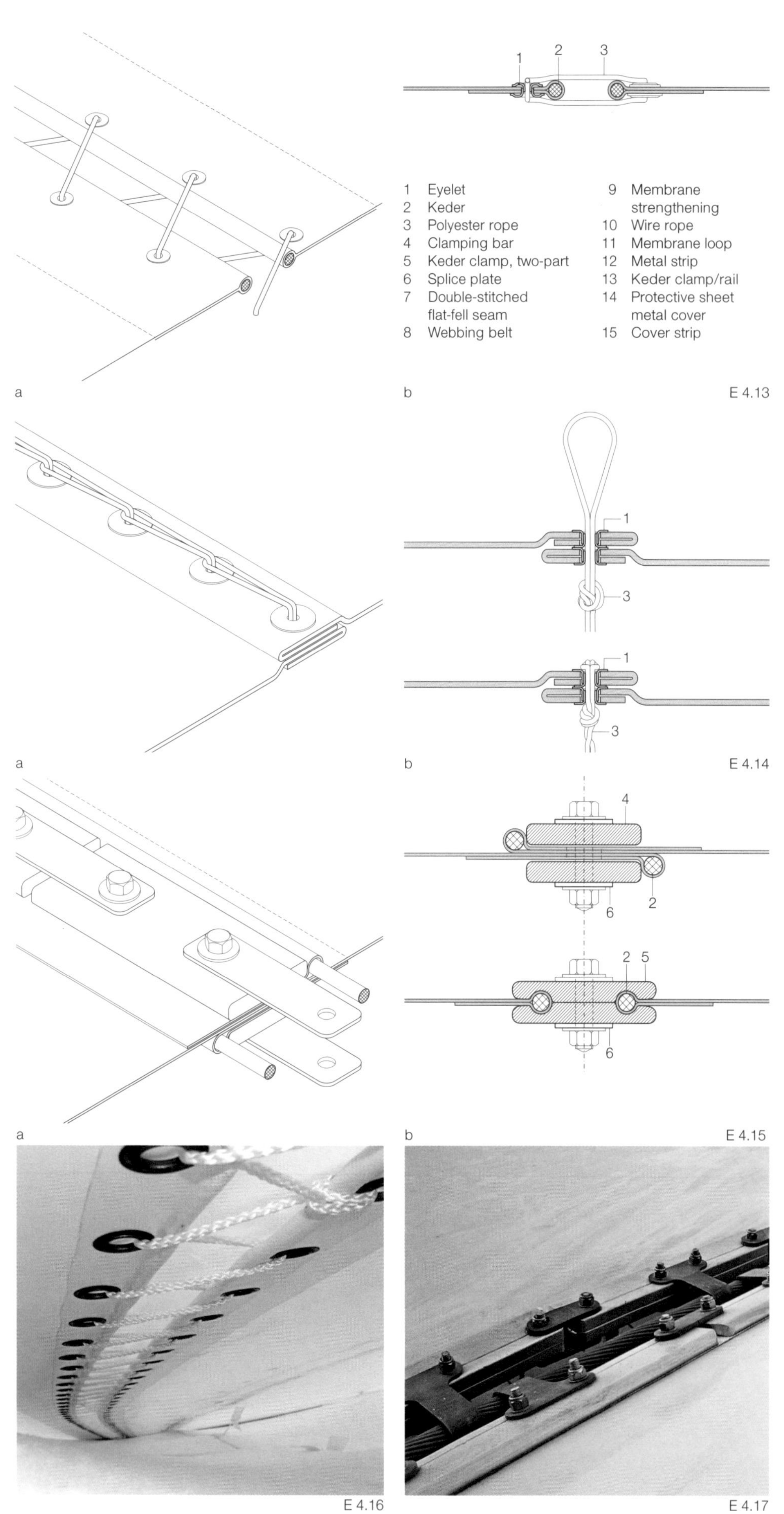

E 4.13

E 4.14

E 4.15

E 4.16

E 4.17

Detachable seams

Detachable seams are used where fabrication, transport or erection requirements dictate that a membrane surface must be subdivided; otherwise, detachable seams should be avoided. The maximum area of membrane therefore depends not only on the geometry of the structure and the erection sequence, but also on the weight and the rollability or foldability of the material being used. This can vary considerably and it is not possible to specify a maximum size that applies to all situations. However, coherent membrane surfaces measuring up to 1500 m² in area are certainly normal.

The detachable seam is initially prepared during fabrication and only completed on the building site. An additional strip of membrane over the seam is required in order to guarantee complete watertightness. This strip can be factory-welded to one side of the joint and site-welded to the other side after erection and after introducing the prestressed. In certain cases, e.g. temporary membrane structures or places difficult to reach, it is possible to fix the second side of the cover strip with an adhesive tape. The separate cover strip could be damaged by the fasteners underneath during erection or maintenance work, even by heavy snow loads, and so separate protection is required for these. Bent sheet metal, timber battens or foam represent viable solutions. Additional protection is unnecessary at laced seams or when using keder rails with countersunk-head screws.

Laced seams

One particularly simple and flexible form of detachable on-site connection is the laced seam, which is achieved by tying together parallel sections of membrane. Braided polyester ropes are typically used for tying together the two membrane surfaces, which are fed through eyelets. These offer the least frictional resistance during retensioning.

The low UV resistance of polyester means that such a seam is primarily suited to temporary structures. A strip of membrane material must be fixed across the joint in order to protect the rope against UV radiation and guarantee a watertight seam.

A laced seam is very easy to handle, requires hardly any additional material and can be both retensioned and adjusted. One disadvantage is the low redundancy of the seam, i.e. if the rope breaks at one point, the seam generally comes apart over its entire length.

A keder threaded fitted in a pocket in the edge of the membrane in this case serves to reinforce the edge and prevent the eyelets being torn out of the edge, which are fitted directly adjacent to the keder in the hem of the membrane (= double thickness).

There are various types of laced seam: like a shoelace, the rope can be either threaded backwards and forwards between the eyes in a zigzag manner or perpendicular to the edge of the membrane (Figs. E 4.13 and E 4.16).

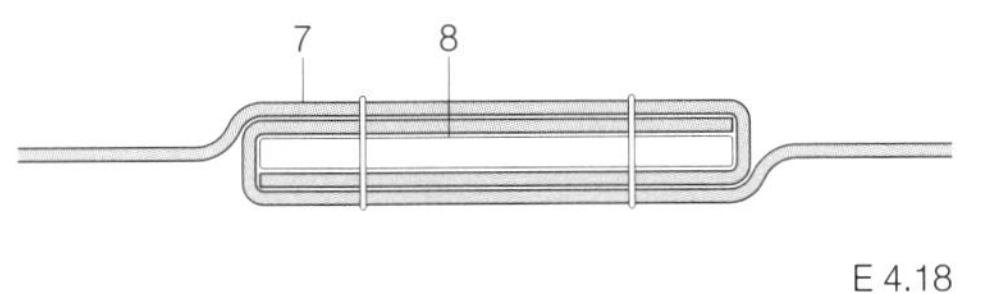

E 4.18

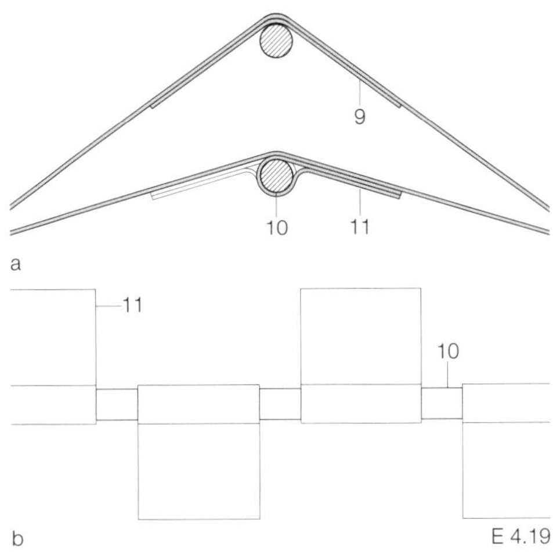

E 4.19

E 4.13 Standard laced seam
a Isometric view
b Section through seam
E 4.14 Laced seam with "crocheted" rope loops
a Isometric view
b Sections through seam
E 4.15 Clamped seam and seam with two-part keder clamp
a Isometric view of clamped seam
b Sections through seams
E 4.16 Standard laced seam with cover strip

E 4.17 Clamped details either side of valley rope
E 4.18 Webbing belt stitched into membrane to form ridge or valley
E 4.19 Ridge details (sections and plan)
a with membrane strengthening
b with membrane loops
E 4.20 Ridge detail with two-part keder clamps
a Isometric view
b Section
E 4.21 Arch detail with double keder rail

Another option is to tie the edges together with short, "crocheted" loops of rope that are fed through the eyelets (Fig. E 4.14). The advantage of this type of connection is that the membrane sections are overlapped like a clamped seam.

Clamped seams

A seam that requires a high load-carrying capacity but at the same time must still remain flexible can be clamped, i.e. the edges of the sections of membrane and clamped in place between metal bars, possibly with the membrane sections overlapping (Fig. E 4.15). At a seam within a membrane panel the clamping bars are kept relatively short in order to guarantee sufficient flexibility; 100–150 mm is a typical length. Leaving gaps of 5–10 mm between adjacent bars along the length of the joint ensures adequate flexibility.
Short clamping bars and large joints allow the membrane to expand along the joint. Normally, however, the clamping bars at seams and edges are attached in such a way that the edge of the membrane is stretched to the prestressing amount. The gaps between the clamping bars are then bridged over with pieces of sheet metal and thus kept constant. The advantage of this is that no higher stresses can occur between the bars and the lengths of the edges as built can be checked. Owing to the need to punch holes in the membrane, this type of detachable seam is mainly used for polyester-PVC membranes because of the low tear propagation resistance of PTFE/glass-membranes.

Seams with keder clamps

A seam with a keder clamp (Fig. E 4.15b, bottom) is somewhat stiffer than a seam with clamping bars because the elements are longer in this case. This type of seam is therefore often chosen for those places where the membrane has a linear support in the form of an arch or ridge or valley cable (Figs. E 4.17 and E 4.20). Where such a seam is not at a support, the clamping element should not exceed a length of approx. 200 mm if sufficient flexibility of a membrane is to be guaranteed and the element is not to be subjected to bending.
With two-part clamps and no gap it is possible to pull the membrane taut and clamp it directly, as with a clamped seam.
Where the seam is visible internally, it may be worthwhile fixing the keder clamping bars from below in order to minimise the visual intrusion.

Linear supports

Membrane surfaces are often supported by additional linear elements such as ridge or valley cables or arches (see "Surfaces with elements forming ridges and valleys", p. 142). A membrane connected directly to an arch or cable makes use of a detail that is essentially the same as the detail at an edge, but with a second, mirrored version of the detail as well (Figs. E 4.20 and E 4.21). If a webbing belt is being used, then this can be stitched directly to the membrane, fitted within the overlapping hems of the membrane sections according to the principle of the double-stitched flat-fell seam in order to protect it against UV radiation (Fig. E 4.18). Cables and arches can also be left exposed beneath the membrane, secured by lacing or welded loops or pockets in order to prevent movement of the membrane relative to the supporting element (Fig. E 4.19). However, the risk of such relative movement decreases as the curvature of the membrane increases. In such instances it may be adequate to reinforce the membrane locally with a second strip of material.

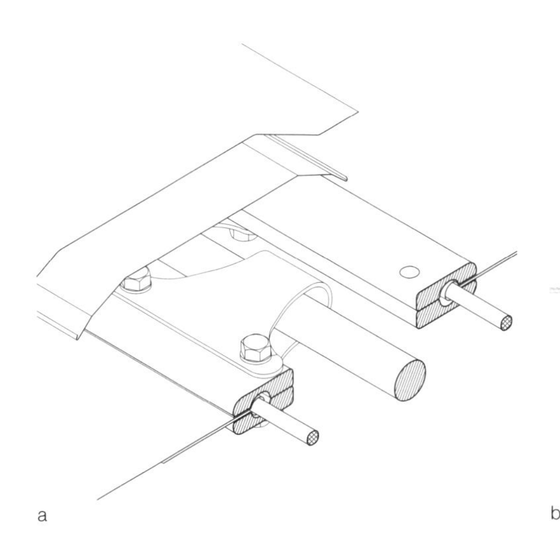

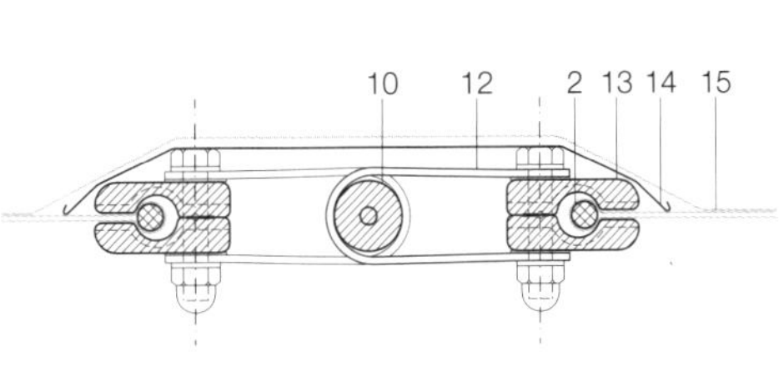

E 4.20

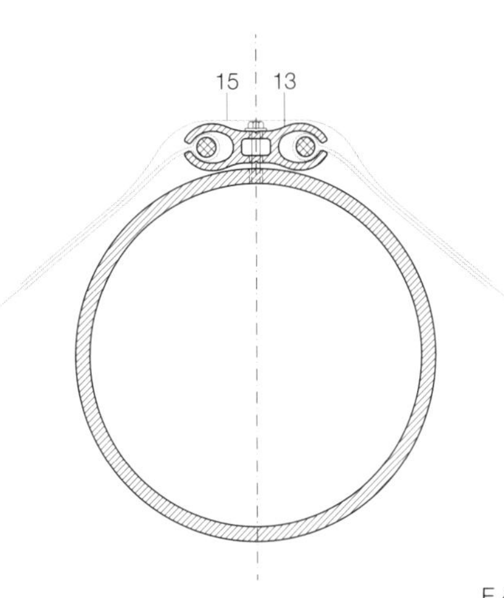

E 4.21

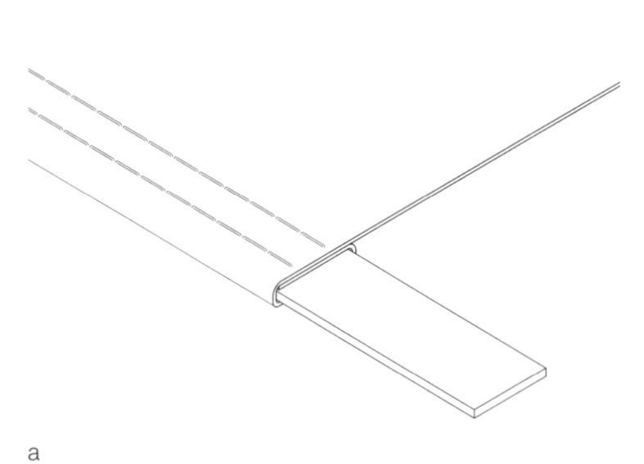
a

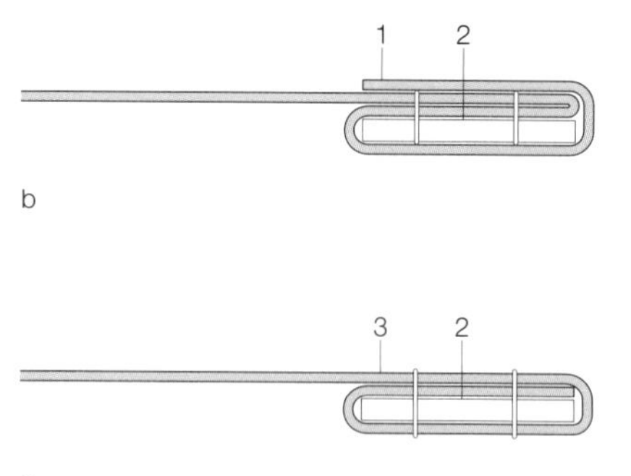

E 4.22

E 4.22 Webbing belt
a Isometric view
b, c Sections, scale 1:2
E 4.23 Edge cable in pocket large enough for open fitting
a with hemmed edge, isometric view
b with hemmed edge, section, scale 1:5
c with separate welded pocket and strengthening
E 4.24 Separate edge cable
a Isometric view
b Section through edge, scale 1:5
E 4.25 Section through rainwater gutter adjacent to separate edge cable, scale 1:5
E 4.26 Rainwater gutter
a with preformed foam cord
b with aluminium flat
E 4.27 Rainwater gutter alongside separate edge cable
E 4.28 Rainwater gutter with preformed foam cord

Edges

The task of a membrane edge, or rather its strengthening, is to accommodate the stresses from the surface of the membrane and transfer these to the corner details where they are then anchored.

Flexible edges

Flexible edges are those curved edges where cables or belts carry the membrane stresses perpendicular to the edge and transfer these to the corners as tensile forces. The relationship between prestress in membrane, force in rope and curvature of edge is explained in detail in the section entitled "Curvature of edge cables" (pp. 145–146).

Webbing belt

The edge detail with a webbing belt is an ideal solution for small and medium-sized membrane structures with flexible edges. This is a very flexible arrangement that accommodates the parallel tangential forces directly. In this exclusively textile solution, the webbing belt is stitched on to form a type of strengthened edge (Fig. E 4.22). The difference in stiffness between membrane and edge is relatively small. All convertible membrane roofs are fabricated with webbing edge belt because of the high flexibility demands. Webbing belts are generally woven from polyester or polyamide fibres (see "Webbing belts", p. 107). Neither of these materials is resistant to UV radiation and so the belts must be protected against direct exposure to sunlight and the weather. Belts should therefore always be wrapped completely in membrane material. Extra material must be allowed for at the edge of the membrane in order to be able to wrap this around the belt and weld it in place (Fig. E 4.22b). No further components are required provided the membrane itself and the stitching are made from weather-resistant PTFE – simply folding the material around the belt is adequate (Fig. E 4.22c). At the corners, a special membrane pocket must be fabricated for the loop of belt material. In addition, the different compensation values of belt and membrane must be taken into account when stitching on the belt (see "Compensation", p. 148).

Edge cable in pocket

With this type of edge detail, a cable is integrated into a pocket formed by folding over the edge of the material (Fig. E 4.23b) or forming a pocket with an extra strip of material (Fig. E 4.23c). This edge pocket transfers the membrane stresses perpendicular to the edge to the edge cable. During erection in particular, tangential forces that cannot be transferred via friction in the pocket must be anchored at the corners (see "Corner details", pp. 206–210). The membrane pocket must be large enough to allow the cable and its end fittings to be fed through without overstressing the material. The greater the width of the pocket, the shallower the angle between the upper and lower strips of membrane material and the lower the peeling forces acting on the weld fixing the pocket in place. The profiled surface of the cable presses severely into the membrane and as this can cause flex cracking of the membrane, the edge pocket detail is preferred for member materials that are less susceptible to flex cracking, e.g. polyester-PVC. Adding an additional strip of membrane material or a webbing belt in the edge pocket can help to protect the loadbearing membrane and also increase the radius of the material around the cable (Fig. E 4.23c). Strips of membrane or webbing belts should be welded or stitched in position at the ends of the pocket to prevent them slipping within the pocket. A separate edge cable is preferred where the loads are very high, e.g. with long-span edge cables and a PTFE/glass membrane.

Separate edge cable

The cable is placed beyond the edge of the membrane and connected at separate points when using PTFE/glass membranes – especially in the case of long spans (Figs. E 4.24, E 4.27 and E 4.28). The methods used to connect the membrane to the edge cable resemble those of seams between membrane sections. Here, too, clamping bars or keder rails are employed, attached to the cable with metal strips. The individual clamping bars or keder clamps are connected to each other either by sheet metal or appropriately shaped metal strips. As the

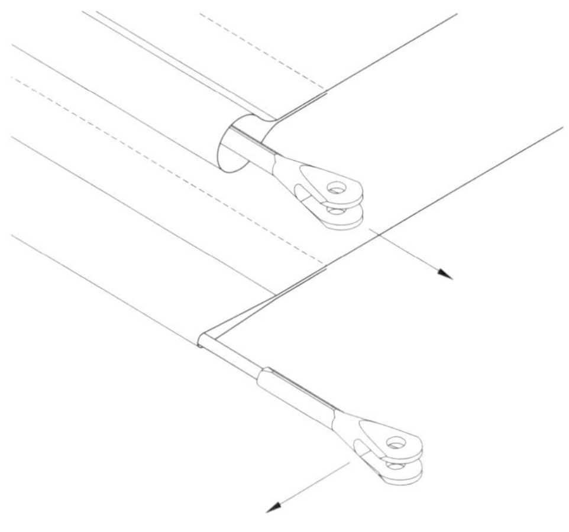
a

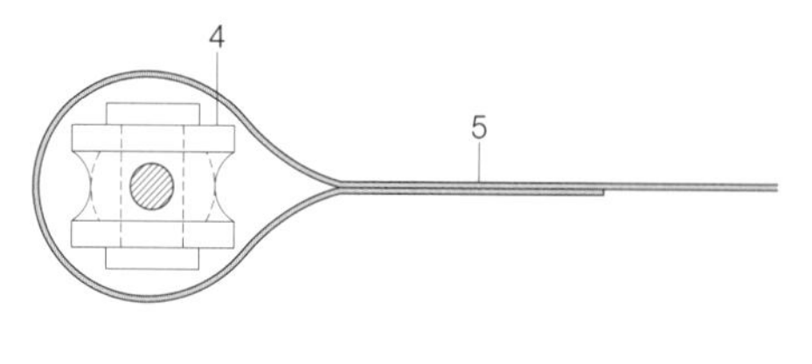

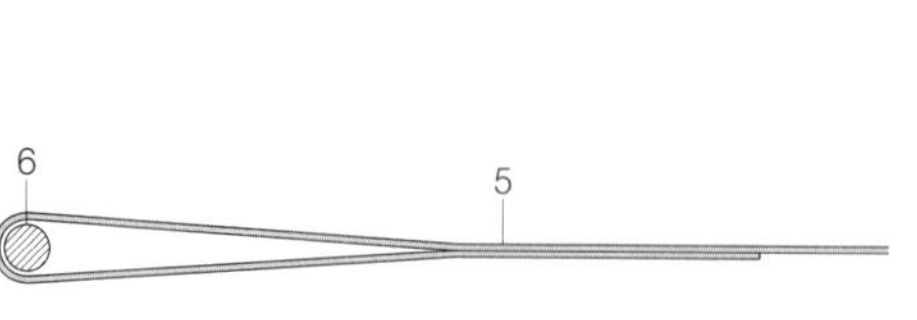

b

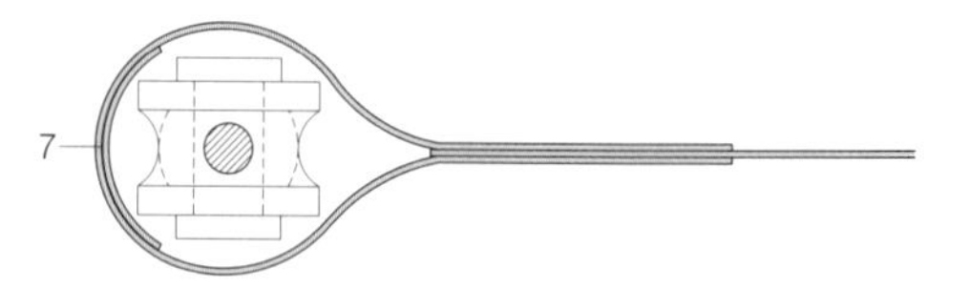

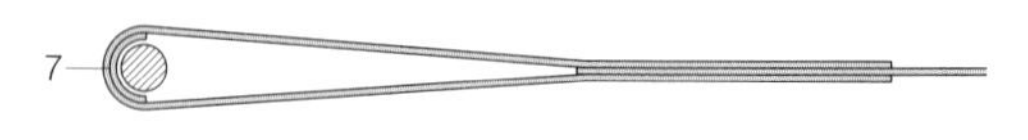

c

E 4.23

diameter of the edge cable does not always match the thickness of the clamped edge, any difference must be compensated for by inserting shims, for instance. If thin sheet metal strips are sufficiently long, then any difference can be compensated for by simply bending the sheet metal to suit.

Rainwater drainage at membrane edges
Various methods can be used to drain water from the edge of a membrane. The aim is to create some kind of upstand along the edge of the membrane so that run-off water is collected and channelled towards the corners. This upstand can be formed by a preformed foam cord (Figs. E 4.26a and E 4.28) or a flat aluminium bar, both enclosed in a separate strip of material (Fig. E 4.26b), with a flat bar remaining stable because of the curved line of the edge. The open edges of the strip of material should face outwards so that no water infiltrates the woven fabric, especially when using polyester-PVC membranes. Other options for draining rainwater are open membrane pockets or – with separate edge cables – strips of membrane material turned up and fixed taut to rigid aluminium angles (see Figs. E 4.25 and E 4.27, also "Roof over circulation zone at EXPO 2010", pp. 262–267, and "Open-air Theatre, Josefsburg Arena", pp. 282–285).

Rigid edges
A rigid edge is created when a membrane is connected to a rigid linear component, usually a steel section. Rigid edges make use of similar components to those of detachable seams. They should not be joined at acute angles because stress peaks and creases can then occur at these positions. The erection and prestressing of stiff membrane corners with acute angles has proved to be problematic as well because the geometry results in a clash between the means of tensioning which can then only be carried out from the opposite side. Circular and oval plan forms, or those with obtuse angles, represent the best solutions. If acute angles cannot be avoided, then a rounded segment can be cut out of the corner and closed off with a separate piece of material.
Watertightness at a rigid edge is often only achieved by welding on a separate piece of material, regardless of the particular type of rigid edge detail. This piece of material is connected directly to a gutter beyond the load-bearing detail (Fig. E 4.30, p. 205). However, this covering prevents access to the detail for maintenance. As an alternative, the membrane can also be fitted over a saddle and fixed directly to a rainwater gutter (see Fig. E 3.8, p. 191).

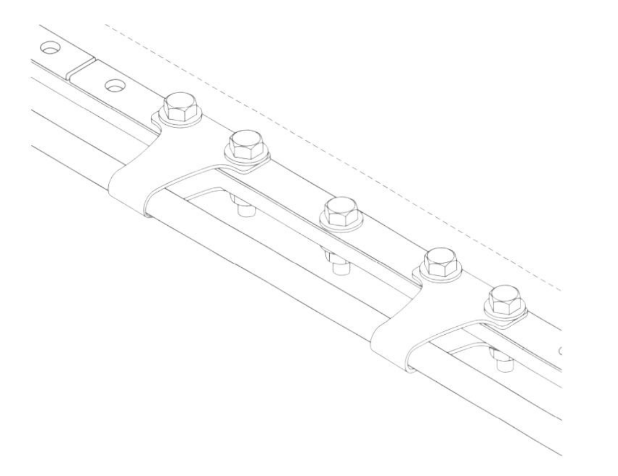

a

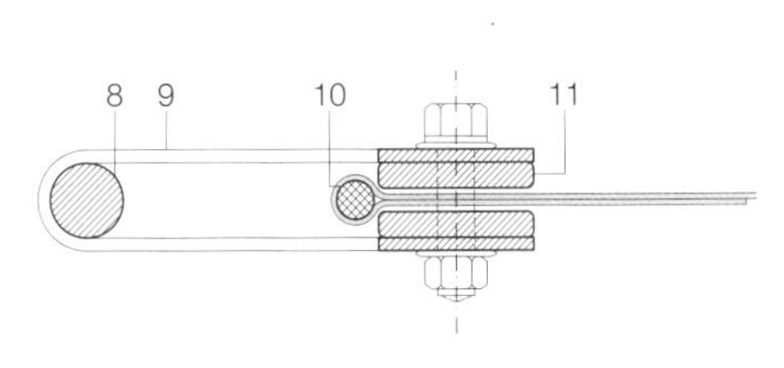

b

E 4.24

1 Double tuck with stitching protected
2 Webbing belt
3 Single tuck
4 Open fitting
5 Pocket for rope
6 Wire rope
7 Membrane strengthening
8 Edge cable
9 Metal strip
10 Keder
11 Clamping bar
12 Aluminium angle
13 Edge of membrane turned up
14 Preformed foam cord
15 Aluminium flat

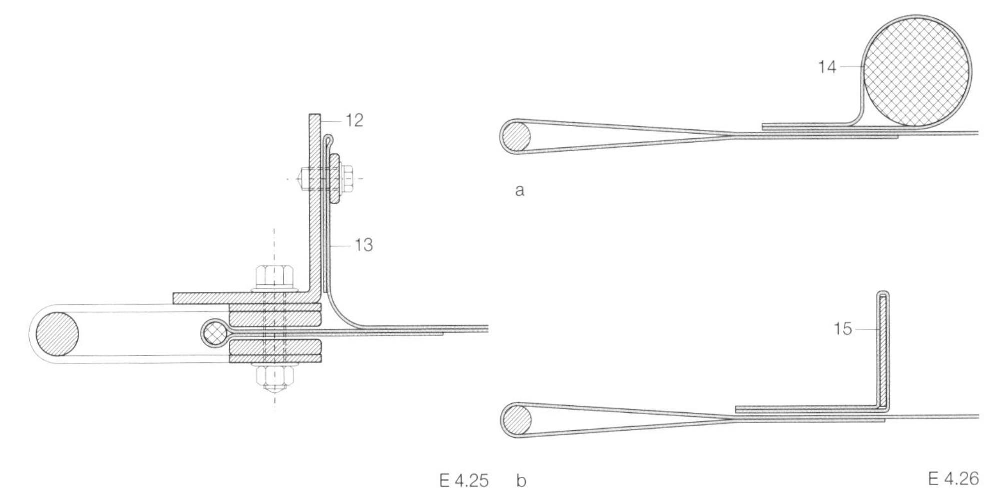

E 4.25

E 4.26

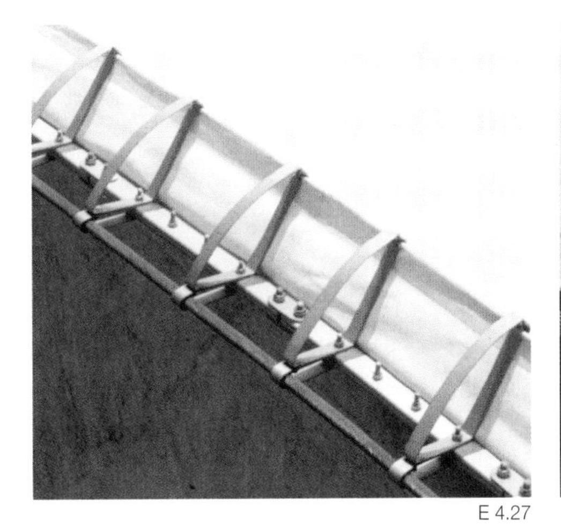

E 4.27

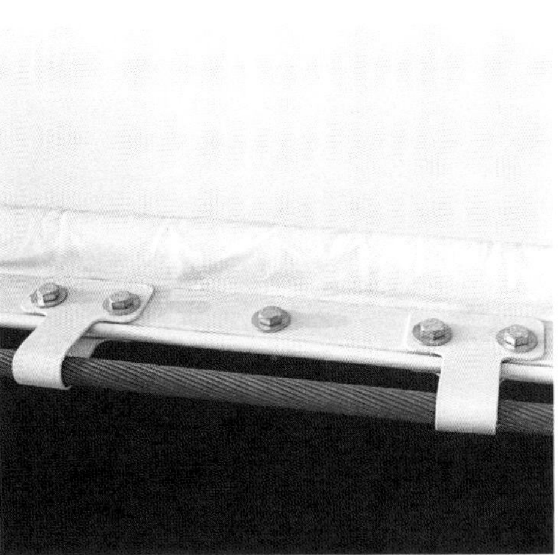

E 4.28

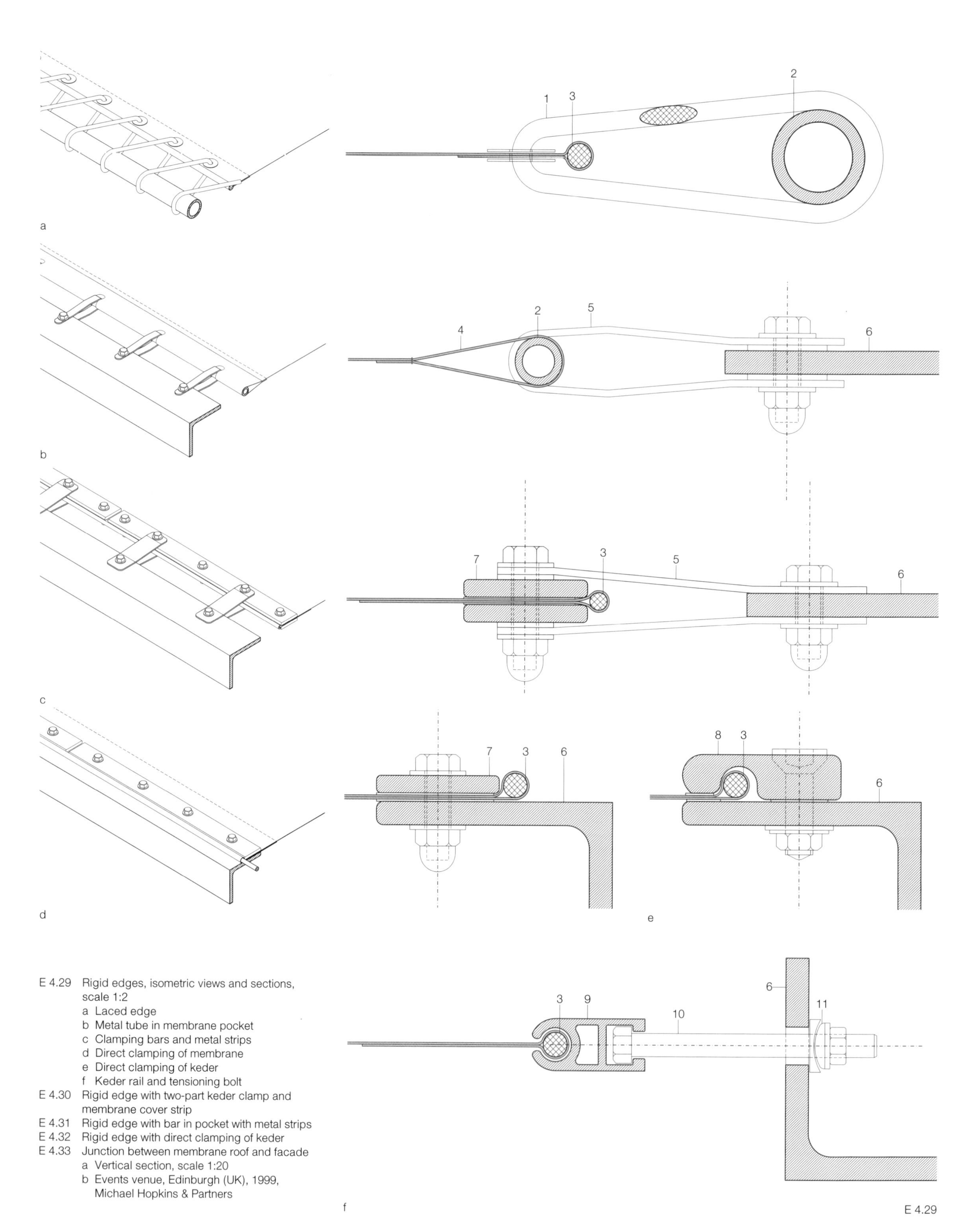

E 4.29 Rigid edges, isometric views and sections, scale 1:2
a Laced edge
b Metal tube in membrane pocket
c Clamping bars and metal strips
d Direct clamping of membrane
e Direct clamping of keder
f Keder rail and tensioning bolt

E 4.30 Rigid edge with two-part keder clamp and membrane cover strip

E 4.31 Rigid edge with bar in pocket with metal strips

E 4.32 Rigid edge with direct clamping of keder

E 4.33 Junction between membrane roof and facade
a Vertical section, scale 1:20
b Events venue, Edinburgh (UK), 1999, Michael Hopkins & Partners

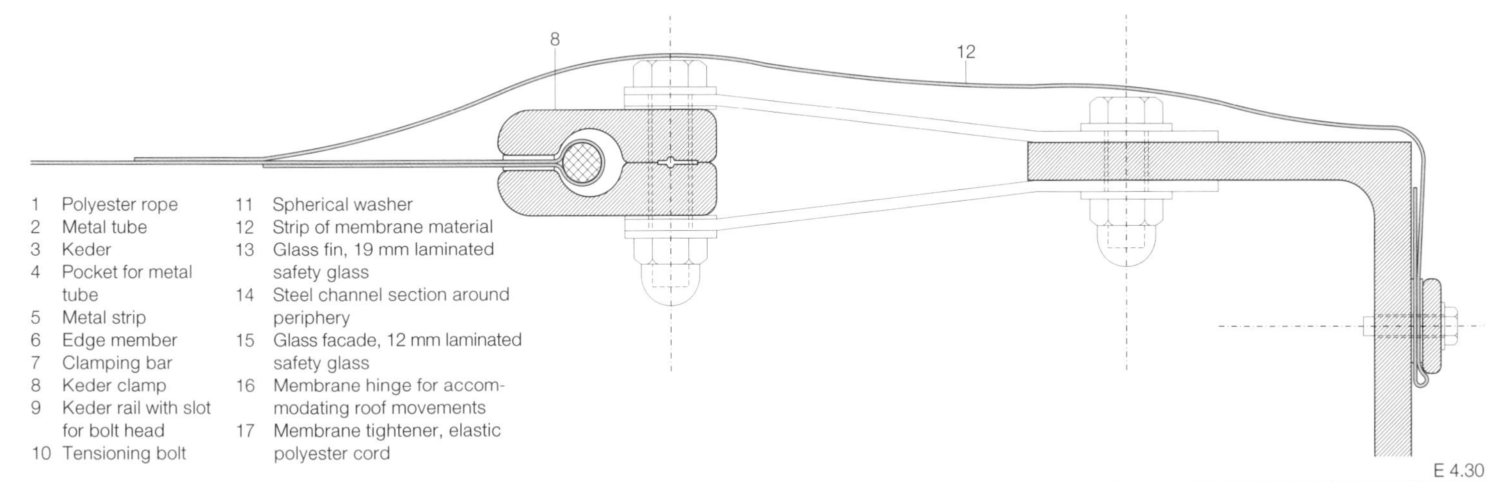

1 Polyester rope
2 Metal tube
3 Keder
4 Pocket for metal tube
5 Metal strip
6 Edge member
7 Clamping bar
8 Keder clamp
9 Keder rail with slot for bolt head
10 Tensioning bolt
11 Spherical washer
12 Strip of membrane material
13 Glass fin, 19 mm laminated safety glass
14 Steel channel section around periphery
15 Glass facade, 12 mm laminated safety glass
16 Membrane hinge for accommodating roof movements
17 Membrane tightener, elastic polyester cord

E 4.30

Laced edge
This represents a simple solution for temporary membrane structures: ropes joining a strengthened edge to a rigid solid round bar or circular hollow section, which is welded or bolted to the loadbearing structure via spacer components (Fig. E 4.29a). The lacing itself is similar to that of a detachable laced seam.

Tube in pocket
In this type of edge detail a rigid tube is fed through a pocket in the membrane. Small, regularly spaced openings in the pocket allow the tube to be connected to a rigid edge member via metal strips, belts or ropes (Figs. E 4.29b and E 4.31). Owing to the simple design and construction of this detail, but its low load-carrying capacity, this principle is very much favoured for air-supported structures. The opening between pocket and edge member is in this case closed off airtight with a strip of membrane material welded in place.

Clamped edge
Clamping bars and keder clamps can either be bolted directly to stiff edge beams of metal or timber (Figs. E 4.29d and E 4.32) or fixed clear of these by means of metal strips (Figs. E 4.29c and E 4.30). The metal strips can be used to pull the edge of the membrane taut and clamp it separately; tensioning and adjusting options are also easier with a separate clamped edge and metal strips. A very functional solution is possible with special keder rails, which include a slot for fitting a long bolt which can be used for tensioning (Fig. E 4.29f).

Roof–facade junction
Connecting a roof membrane to a stiff facade is a particularly challenging detail because the rigid facade structure may not hinder movement of the membrane bay. And vice versa: no loads should be transferred from the membrane to the facade. To do this, separate pieces of membrane material can be tensioned between the facade and the membrane, which are tensioned laterally with springs or elastic cords (Fig. E 4.33). Consequently, differences in height between the membrane bay and the edge of the facade can be compensated for.
A similar effect can be achieved, for example, with air-filled tubes or cushions positioned between facade and membrane (Fig. E 5.16, p. 218, No. 15). Creating a weak point in terms of the building physics is frequently unavoidable at the junction between a membrane and a facade.

E 4.31

E 4.32

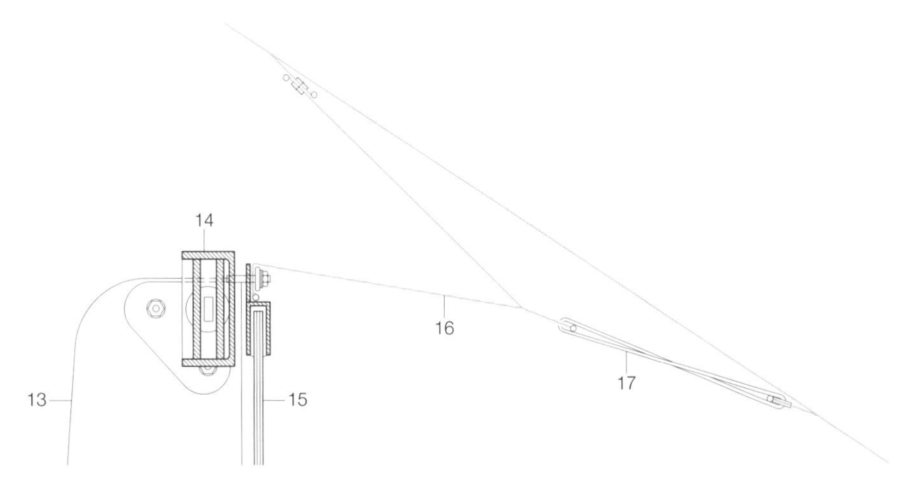

a

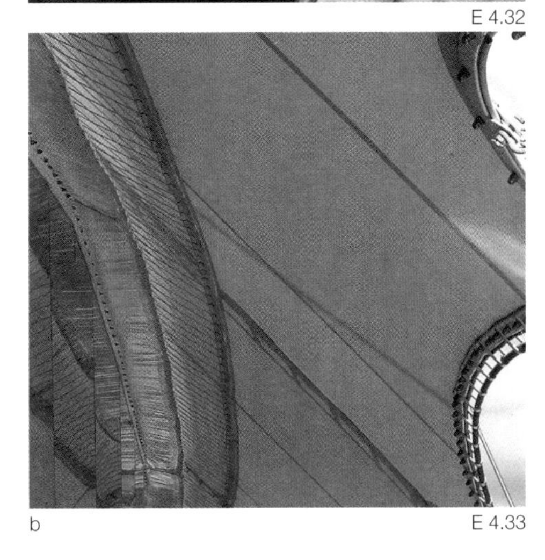

b

E 4.33

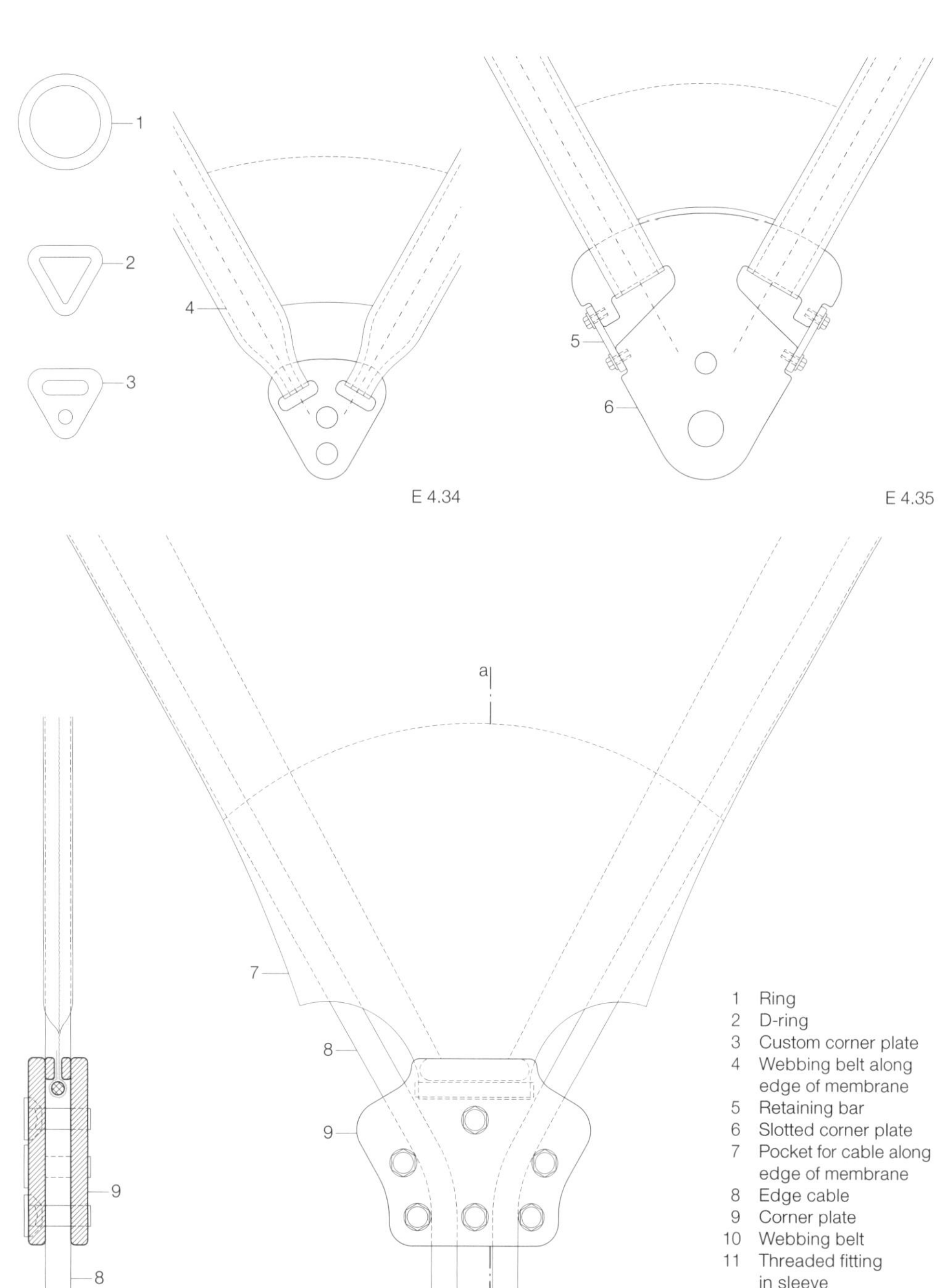

Corner details

Wherever two flexible membrane edges meet at a corner, the forces in the edge cables must be anchored and transferred to the loadbearing structure or foundations in the direction of the resultant reaction. The characteristics of corner details are therefore essentially determined by the design of the membrane edge. Corner details must satisfy the following demands:

- Flexibility of the connections about various rotational axes because large deformations can be expected during erection and usage
- Ability to accommodate edge cable forces plus the prestressing forces from the membrane
- Aligning the corner plates according to the angles of the forces in the cables
- Avoiding eccentricities (deviations from symmetry and the lines of the system)
- Adjustment options for the edge cables

All these requirements must be realised within a very confined space. For simplicity, the following descriptions are based on a typical corner detail with two edge cables in order to present the different forms of construction.
A membrane is always doubled at a corner in order to handle the unavoidable stress peaks, which can occur because the membrane cannot dissipate overstresses within the short span at the gusset, neither through elongation nor through racking of the weave of the fabric. The additional layer of membrane is permanently welded or stitched to the main membrane and fitted around the corner in an arc. Edge cable pockets should be widened at the corners so that they do not tear.
Corner plates are usually made from galvanised steel or stainless steel because anti-corrosion coatings on steel are inevitably damaged by tensioning equipment and movements of the cables.

Corner details for webbing belt edges

In contrast to steel cables, webbing belts are not sensitive to buckling and so can be fitted to corner details at very tight radii. This enables very compact details to be designed, with a steel ring or a custom corner plate with slits to be stitched into the corner during fabrication of

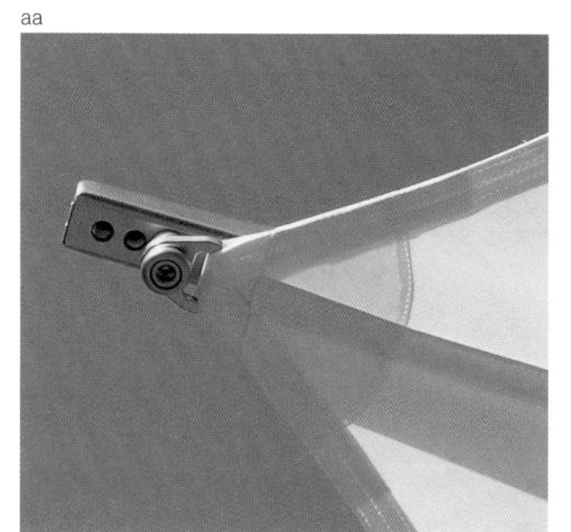
E 4.37

E 4.38

E 4.34 Webbing belt corner detail showing various corner plate options
E 4.35 Webbing belt corner detail with open slots in corner plate
E 4.36 Closed membrane corner with two continuous edge cables
E 4.37 Webbing belt corner detail with stitched-in plate; funnel-type canopy, Barbados, 2004, Rasch + Bradatsch
E 4.38 Open membrane corner, tent structure, Magdeburg (D), 1994, Rasch + Bradatsch
E 4.39 Open membrane corner with discontinuous edge cables
E 4.40 Closed corner detail with two ridge and two edge cables; membrane roof to hotel, Mecca (KSA), 2007, Rasch + Bradatsch
E 4.41 Open membrane corner with exposed ridge cable; Waldau tram stop, Stuttgart (D), 1997, Unold/Schlaich Bergermann & Partner

the membrane (Figs. E 4.34 and E 4.37). Open slits can also be provided where later replacement or later fitting of the corner plates is desirable (Fig. E 4.35); however, these should be closed off with a bolted plate to prevent the belt from slipping out and also to enable the forces to be transferred to the plate via an open slit. Rounding off all edges and corners of custom plates is vital. In some circumstances a second hole must be provided for the tensioning equipment in addition to the hole for the actual fixing so that erection and tensioning of the corner can be carried out.

Corner details with cable connections
Both the membrane and the edge cables must be connected to the corner plate in this type of corner detail.
The following options are available for connecting the membrane:
- Open membrane corner, i.e. no direct connection (Figs. E 4.38, E 4.39, E 4.41; E 4.43, p. 208, and E 4.48, p. 209)
- Closed membrane corner, i.e. with direct connection (Figs. E 4.40, E 4.42, E 4.45, p. 209; E 4.46 and E 4.49, p. 210)

Connecting the edge cables to the corner plate is achieved using the following details:
- Separate continuous edge cables (Figs. E 4.36 and E 4.38)
- Continuous edge cables (Fig. E 4.46, p. 209)
- Discontinuous edge cables (Figs. E 4.39–E 4.42; E 4.43, E 4.45, E 4.48 and E 4.49, p. 210)

Open membrane corners
At open membrane corners the membrane is not connected to the corner plate directly, but rather via the edge cables and, if necessary, ratchet straps. With this type of detail, the membrane is cut around the corner plate in an arc shape and reinforced by a second layer of material in this zone. The tangential forces parallel to the edge cable at an open membrane corner must be transferred separately to the corner plate in order to prevent slippage of the membrane at the corner, especially during erection. This is achieved in most cases by stitching webbing belts into the membrane pocket which are tensioned against the corner

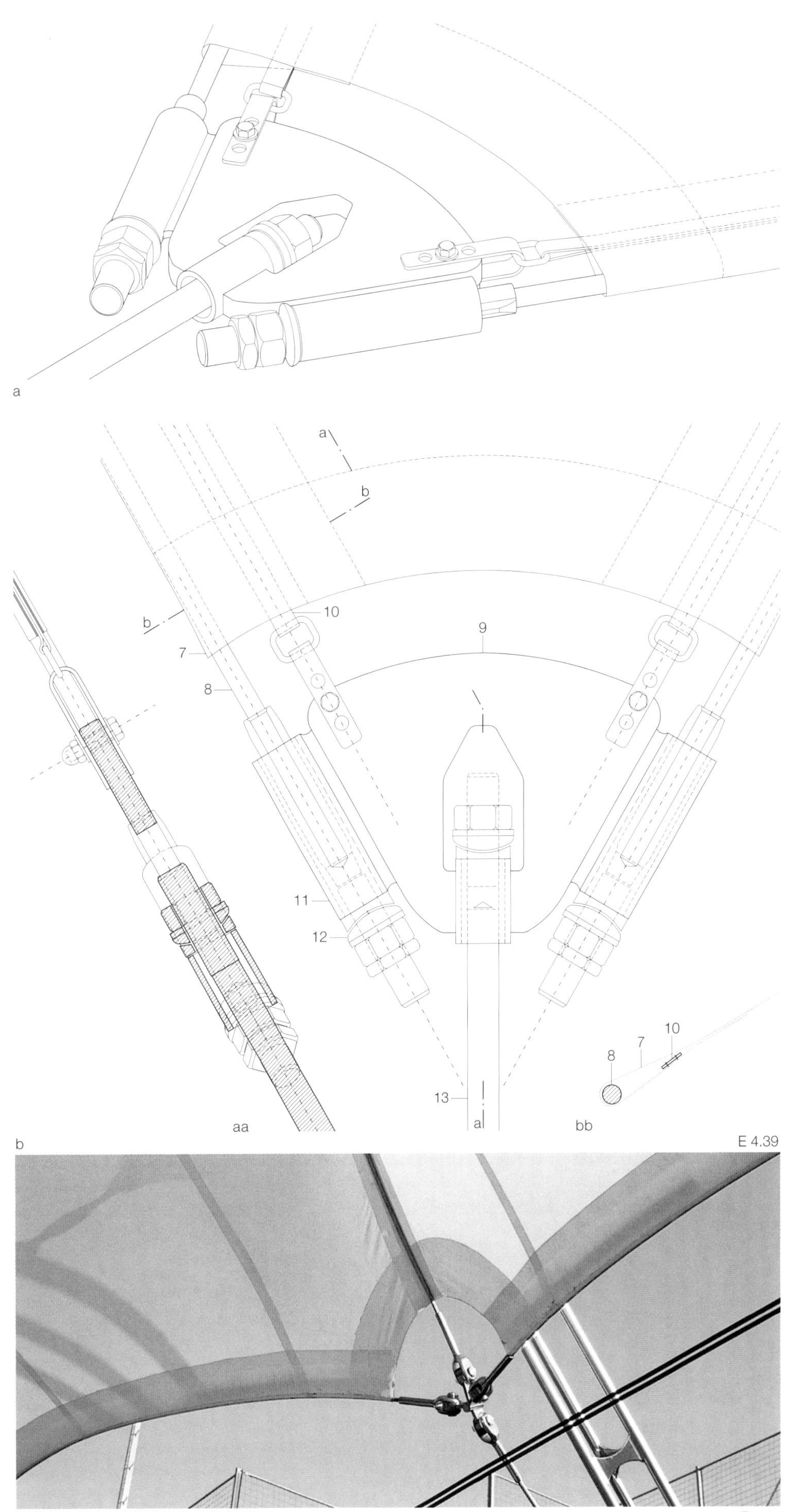

E 4.39

E 4.40

E 4.41

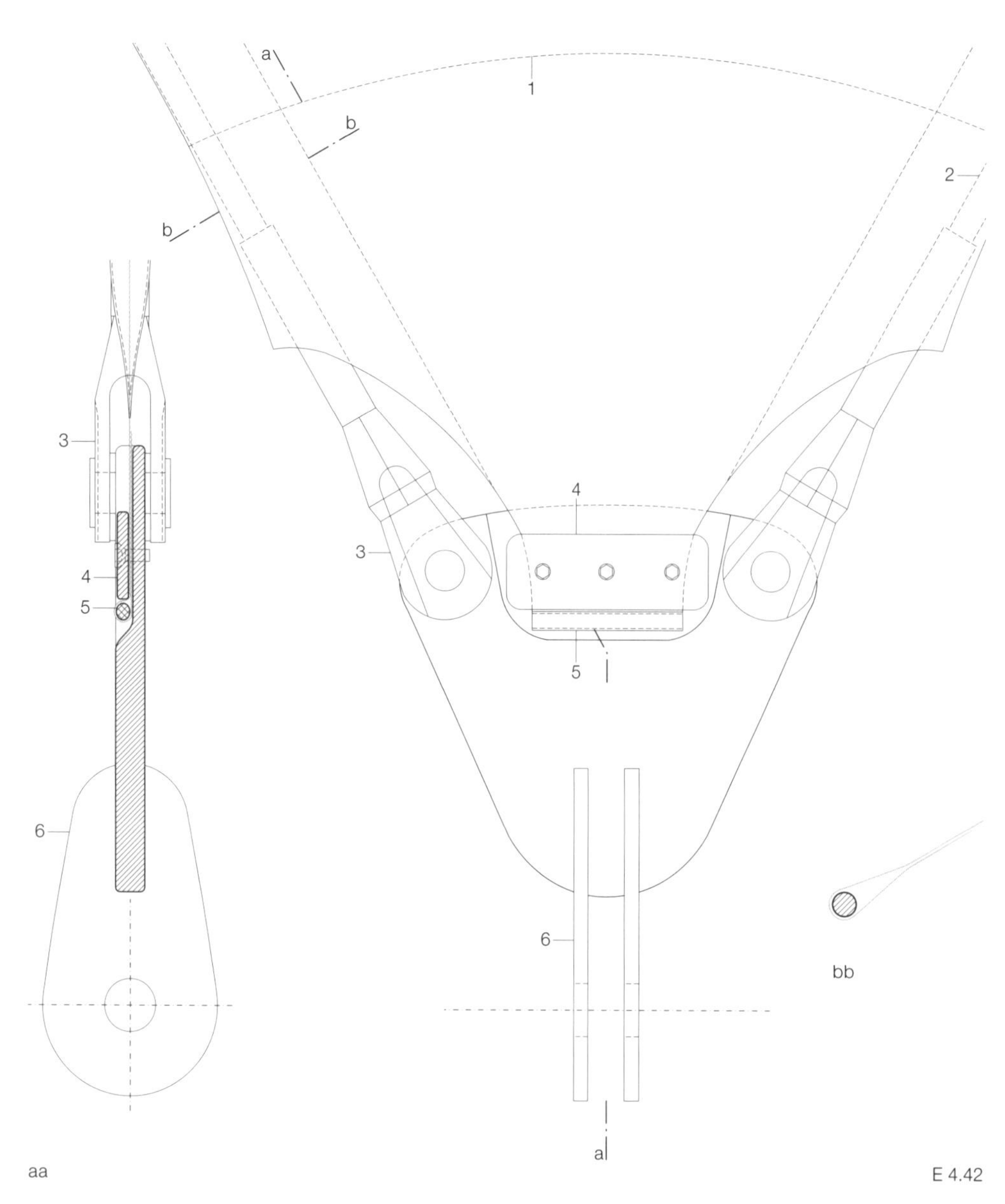

E 4.42

E 4.42 Closed membrane corner with discontinuous edge cables
E 4.43 Complex corner detail with double-layer membrane, exposed edge and valley cables; dockside shed, Brand (D), 2002, SIAT
E 4.44 Corner plate/guyed mast connection, scale 1:20
E 4.45 Closed membrane corner with exposed edge cable
E 4.46 Closed membrane corner with continuous edge cable
E 4.47 Corner plate/guyed mast connection, scale 1:20
E 4.48 Open membrane corner with guy rope, four-point sail, Rimsting (D), 2007, Jan Cremers/Klaus-Michael Koch/Hansjörg Zabel
E 4.49 Closed membrane corner with threaded fitting (adjustable); arts centre, Puchheim (D), 1999, Lanz Architekten

E 4.43

plate with turnbuckles or adjustable perforated plates. This method is used with polyester-PVC membranes, for example. As PTFE/glass membranes cannot be stitched, the tangential forces cannot be transferred through webbing belts, so in this case the membrane is either clamped with clamping bars similar to the edge details (in the case of larger corner cutouts), or clamped directly to the corner plate (smaller structures).

Closed membrane corners
A closed membrane corner is a corner detail where the membrane is fixed directly to the corner plate with the help of clamping bars or keder clamps over the longest possible length. It is not usually possible to retension the membrane at the corner with this approach, which tends to be preferred for smaller structures.
A membrane lying in the same plane as the top side of the corner plate creates a problem because the system line for the edge cable must be aligned with the top edge of the corner plate in order to avoid an asymmetric detail. Where the cable is aligned with the centre of the corner plate, then the plate can be milled down to half its thickness in the region of the membrane clamping detail, for instance (Figs. E 4.42 and E 4.49), or designed in two halves so that the membrane is aligned with the system line of the cable (Fig. E 4.46). When using discontinuous edge cables and threaded fittings, the outer sleeves can also be welded eccentrically to the corner plate.

Separate continuous edge cables
In this type of corner detail the edge cables are redirected to form the guy ropes (Figs. E 4.36 and E 4.38, p. 206). The redirection is achieved either via a cable fitting or through a suitable mast head detail. As the cables continue past the corner plate and therefore no cable fittings are necessary here, this edge detail is minimal, but not adjustable.

Continuous edge cable
Obtuse corner angles (> 90°) or low forces in the cables enable the edge cable to be routed around a rounded corner plate so that it can continue beyond the corner (Fig. E 4.46). This saves cable fittings and therefore results in more

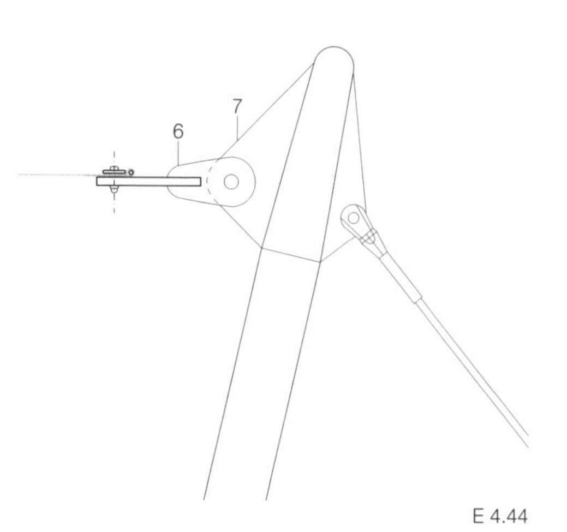

E 4.44

compact corner details. The disadvantage is that there are no separate retensioning options for the edges to the left and right of the detail. Bolted metal plates secure the cable in position. The corner detail with continuous cable is often designed with a corner plate made from two halves that clamp the membrane directly between them. To do this, as with clamped seams, holes must be punched in the membrane beforehand so that the two halves of the corner plate can be bolted together.

Discontinuous edge cable
An edge cable that is not continuous around the corner must be attached to the corner plate with cable fittings (Fig. E 4.5, p. 198). When connected via an open fitting, each fitting is attached directly to the corner plate with a bolt or pin (Fig. E 4.42). Steel shims should be welded to the plate if it is thinner than the opening in the fork fitting in order to close the gap (Figs. E 4.42 and E 4.43). Threaded fittings are fixed to the corner plate via sleeves welded to the sides (Figs. E 4.45 and E 4.49). The screw thread enables the cable length to be adjusted easily and directly at the corner plate. And attaching the cables at the side in this way means that the plate can be narrower than with an open fitting. Some details make use of corner plates made from two halves, with the edge cables fitted between these using closed fittings.

Connecting the corner plate to the loadbearing structure
Corner plates are connected to the foundations either directly via a guy rope or indirectly via a guyed mast.
A tie bar, fitted with a screw thread for adjustment, is generally used when connecting the corner plate to a rigid structure such as a wall or beam (Fig. E 4.39, p. 207). Steel cables, i.e. guy ropes, are the usual choice for long distances between corner plate and anchorage (Fig. E 4.36, p. 206, and E 4.45, p. 209).
Corner details are frequently lifted higher by a guyed mast. In this situation the corner plate is attached directly to the mast and adjusted by changing the angle of the mast by means of the guy ropes on the other side. The connection must be pinned to allow the necessary rotation

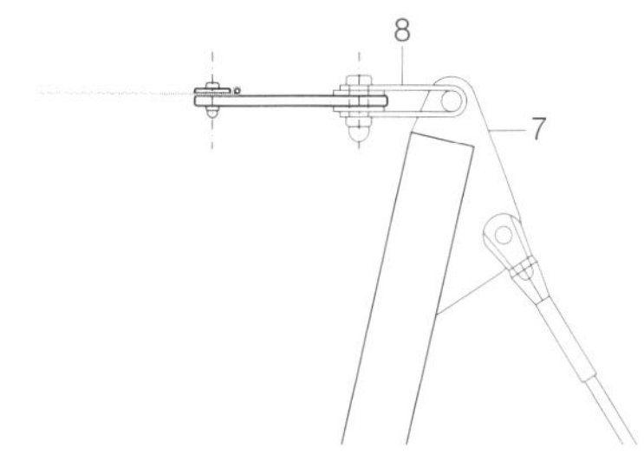

1 Membrane strengthening
2 Edge cable
3 Open fitting
4 Clamping plate
5 Keder
6 Closed fitting
7 Head of mast with connecting plate
8 Metal strip
9 Keder clamp, two-part
10 Threaded fitting in sleeve
11 Spherical washer

E 4.47

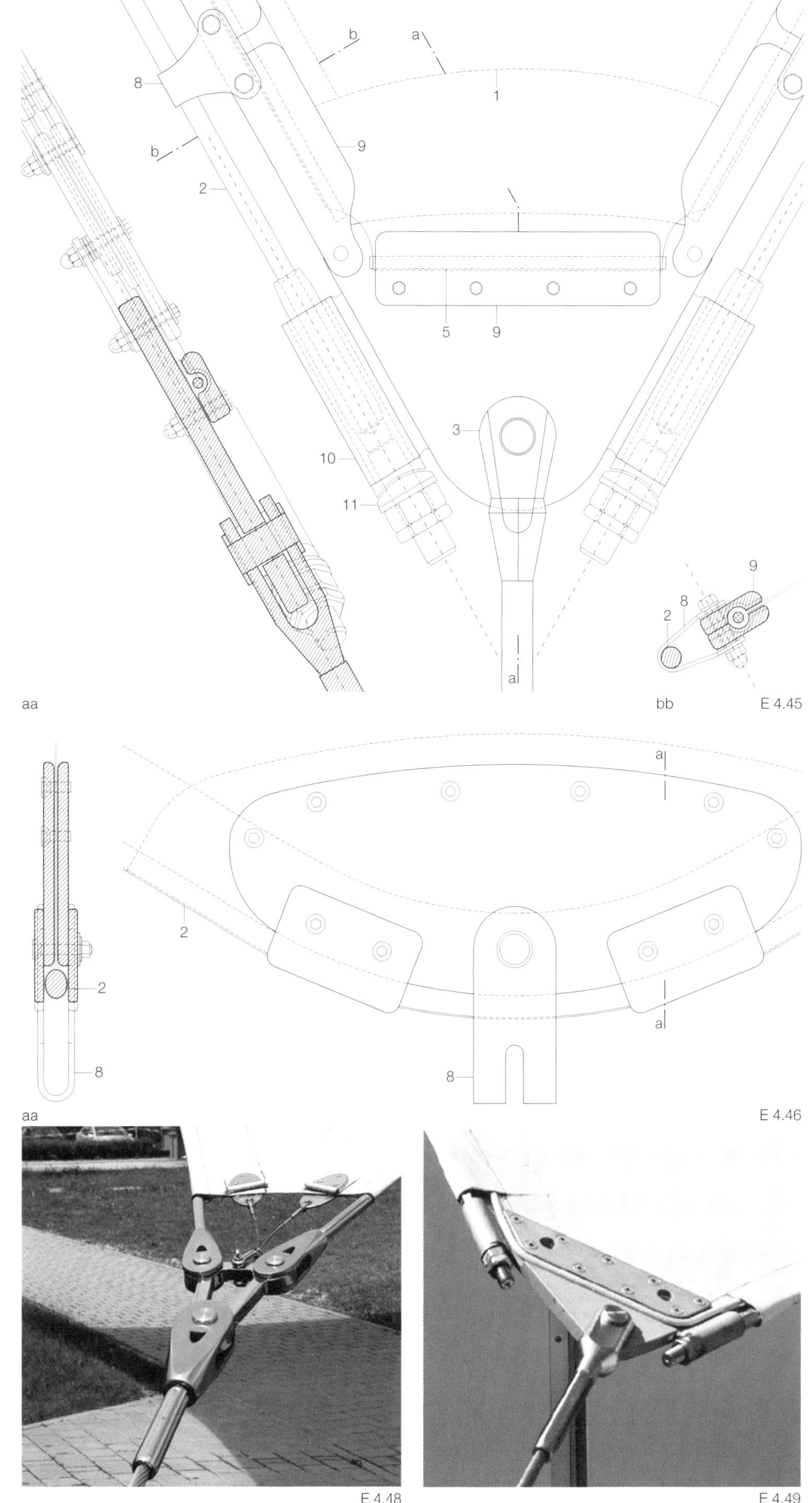

E 4.45

E 4.46

E 4.48

E 4.49

a

b E 4.50

E 4.51

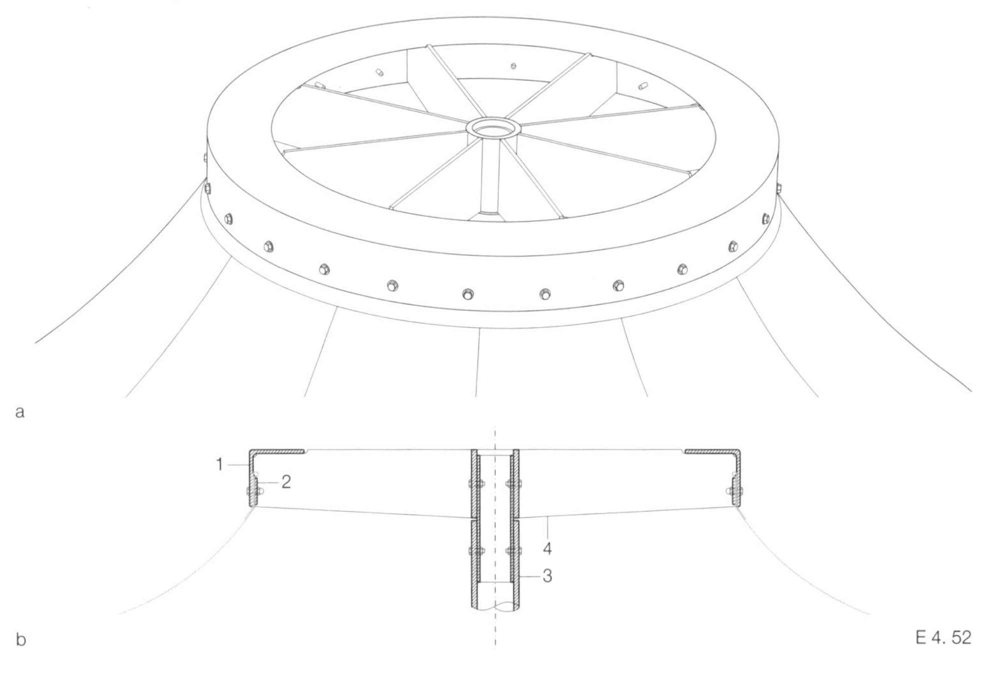

a
b
E 4. 52

1 Rigid ring
2 Clamping bar
3 Column
4 Spoke
5 Webbing belt
6 Steel cable
7 Steel flat ring
8 Clamping ring
9 Head of column
10 Electric cable for heating
11 Rainwater downpipe, lagged to prevent condensation
12 Pinned-end column
13 Ridge cable
14 Bent bar along inner edge of membrane
15 Cable clamp
16 Saddle with cable clamps

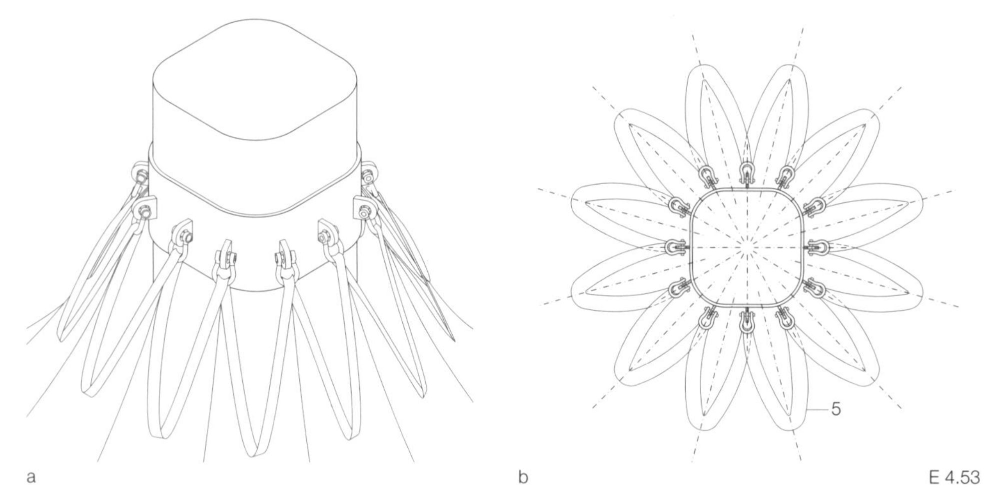

a b E 4.53

(Figs. E 4.44, p. 208, and E 4.47, p. 209).
The optimum position of a guyed mast is on the bisector of the angle between the edge ropes and the guy ropes and/or in line with the resultant of the forces at this node.
The base of the mast should always be designed as a pinned connection in order to compensate for deformations during prestressing and as a result of external loads (see "Erection", p. 148).

High and low points

The membrane surface is raised or lowered locally at high or low points respectively. This is generally achieved by connecting the membrane to either a mast or ropes.
When considered in the sense of the construction details, these points can also be defined as internal edges. High and low points can be in the form of circular rings or looped or scalloped cables. The design principles for rigid edges apply to rings (Figs. E 4.52 and E 4.54), whereas looped or scalloped arrangements can be classed as flexible edges (Figs. E 4.50, E 4.51, E 4.53, E 4.56 and E 4.59).

Decompensation of the membrane is necessary at the clamping detail when using a stiff ring (see "Compensation", p. 148) and prestressing the membrane from outside via the ring (Fig. E 4.54). Alternatively, it can be prestressed from inside, via the ring itself (Fig. E 4.52). In doing so, the ring can either be suspended from the structure or fixed rigidly to a mast.

One special form of the high point is the "hump" (Fig. E 4.55). With this form, the membrane is pushed upwards or pulled downwards over a large area by means of discs or leaf springs. The high point does not need any special cutting pattern when the curvature of the membrane surface is only minimal. This type of local displacement is frequently used for membranes that, for example, form a suspended ceiling supported at many individual points below a rigid roof construction (Fig. E 5.16, p. 219). Very high, heavily loaded high-point masts can be resolved into lattice masts (Figs. E 4.56 and E 4.58), which consist of three or more

E 4.54

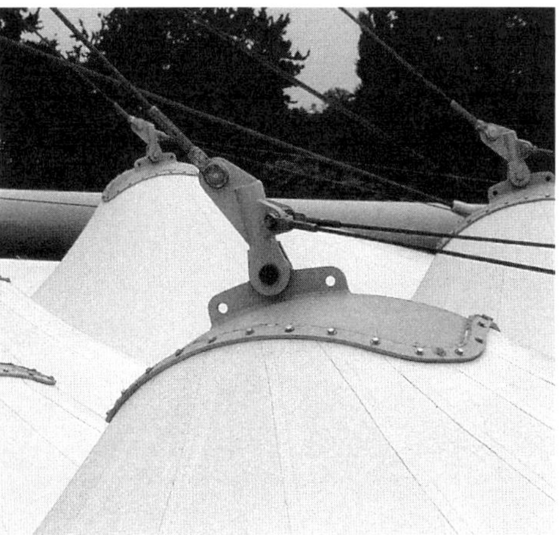

E 4.55

E 4.56

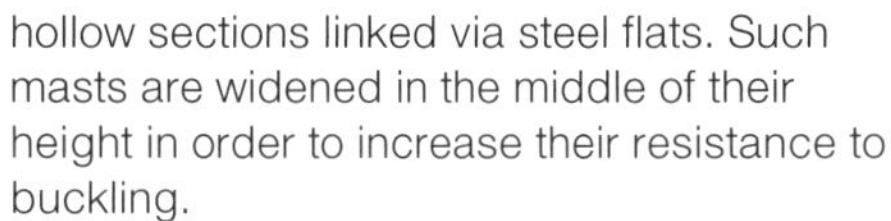

hollow sections linked via steel flats. Such masts are widened in the middle of their height in order to increase their resistance to buckling.

Covering to high points

An opening remains in the membrane at all high points (apart from a hump) and this must be closed off if a rainproof structure is required. The covering to the opening can be in the form of a separate section of membrane material with a low prestress which is then connected directly to the main membrane (Fig. E 4.50).

Stiff canopy or roof structures made from glass or metal represent alternative options.

Drainage at low points

Rainwater collects at low points and so some form of drainage must always be incorporated here. Irrespective of the way in which the forces are transferred at the detail (e.g. clamping the membrane at a rigid edge or a scalloped edge), a funnel with a low prestress for collecting the rainwater will have to be separately clamped (Fig. E 4.51). Rainwater downpipes at low points are often integrated into columns (Fig. E 4.57).

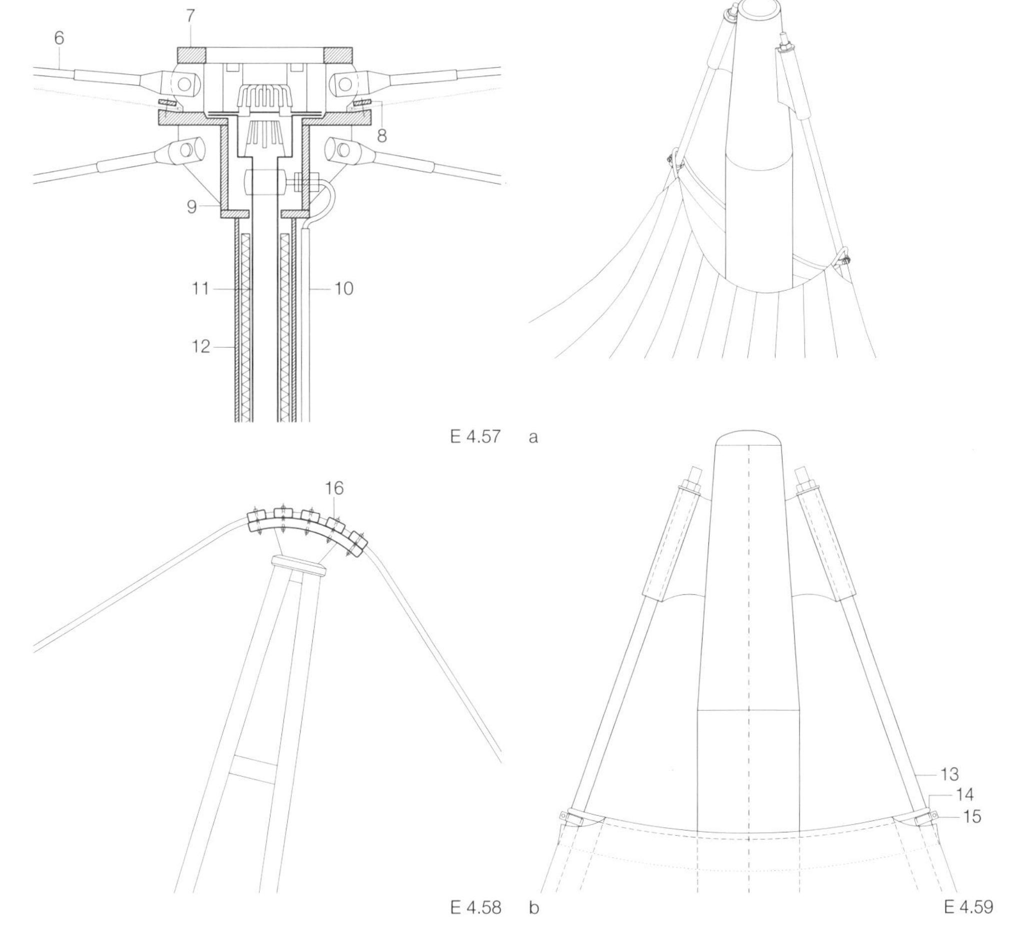

E 4.57 E 4.58 E 4.59

E 4.50 High point, exhibition pavilion, Leonberg (D), 2000, Rasch + Bradatsch
a Double-layer membrane cap to cover opening at high point
b Scalloped internal edge to multi-layer high point
E 4.51 Low point with scalloped edge; funnel-type canopy, Barbados 2004, Rasch + Bradatsch
E 4.52 High point with rigid ring
a Isometric view
b Vertical section, scale 1:20
E 4.53 High point with scalloped webbing belt
a Isometric view
b Plan, scale 1:20
E 4.54 High point with rigid ring; luxury accommodation at Ayers Rock (AUS), 2004, Cox Richardson
E 4.55 High points as "humps"; tennis stadium, Hamburg-Rothenbaum (D), 1997, Schweger + Partner
E 4.56 High point with cable loop and ridge cable continuous over saddle: tent in garden of Ministry for Urban & Rural Development, Riyadh (KSA), 2001, Rasch + Bradatsch
E 4.57 Low point drainage, rainwater downpipe in column
E 4.58 Cable saddle on lattice mast
E 4.59 High point with cable loop

Complex building envelopes

E 5.1

The building envelope is often likened to a "third skin", after our actual skin and our clothing. This comparison of course refers to the protective, regulatory and controlling functions of the individual "skins" and at the same time implies a hierarchy and a differentiated allocation of tasks resulting solely from the different distances from the building's occupants. Precise knowledge of the characteristics and mechanisms of the human skin and its individual layers has for some years been a key requirement for the development of functional clothing in particular and an essential ingredient in its design. However, this knowledge has not really found its way into the design of building envelopes.

The envelope design brief

Exhaustive studies into the subject of comfort in building interiors were carried out as long ago as the 1960s and 1970s. However, these investigations, so vital to an integrative understanding of the requirements placed on the building envelope, concentrated mainly on symptoms and were intended to assist in the design of air-conditioning systems. And the notion of a standardised "perfect" environment for the human organism, be it of a static or dynamic nature, has been dealt with by science fiction on many occasions. For the individual demands placed on all three levels of investigation – skin, clothing and building envelope – are affected by dynamic processes from both sides, i.e. are never static processes. Normally, both the conditions in the human body and also those of the exterior climate are subjected to constant fluctuations. This chapter will not attempt to carry out a study of the complex demands placed on building envelopes and arrive at a conclusion; readers interested in such investigations are referred to the appropriate section of the bibliography (p. 289). It will instead deal with particular issues and potential solutions relevant to the use of polymers and membranes, which will be illustrated here by way of examples. Some of the solutions have already been employed and are supplemented here by vital fundamental information. Polymer materials are used in the building envelope in the form of semi-finished products (e.g. sheets and panels) and also as foils and membranes. However, thermal insulation made from synthetic materials is also very important, and so the first part of this chapter is devoted to the subject of thermal performance.

Thermal performance for buildings

The information given in the chapter entitled "Building physics and energy aspects" (pp. 108–123) in the first place relates to homogeneous material structures and thermal processes. But when considering these aspects in relation to an actual construction, it is multi-layer, multi-leaf constructions, combinations and penetrations, which are intrinsic to virtually every building or structure, plus their interactions with other building subsystems (e.g. building services or loadbearing structure) that should be our focus of attention. Furthermore, in terms of building physics, the distribution of water vapour partial pressures and saturation vapour pressures must also be investigated, for example, because such considerations must always be based on the actual humidity of the air.
Thermal conductivity, thermal transmittance and thermal resistance have already been referred to elsewhere in this book. Further principles and terminology must now be briefly explained in order to understand the study of the practical, constructional level.

Surface resistance and heat transfer coefficient
The heat transfer coefficient per unit area α [W/m²K] specifies the amount of heat energy that flows to the adjacent layer of air or next layer of material through 1 m² of a material structure in 1 h for a temperature gradient of 1 K. We distinguish here between α_a (external) and α_i (internal). The surface resistance per unit area (R_a or R_i) specifies the extent to which the surface of the respective material structure resists the heat transfer. Although this effect occurs at all boundary layers, in practice it is primarily the transitions between interior air and first layer and between last layer and external air that are important. The following applies:

$$R_i = 1/\alpha_i \text{ and } R_a = 1/\alpha_a \text{ [m}^2\text{K/W]}$$

E 5.1 ETFE cushions measuring 10 × 10 m, shopping centre roof, Amadora (P), 2009, Promontorio Architects
E 5.2 The relationship between thickness of layer of insulation and U-value (Europe, left) or R-value (North America, right) for insulating materials with different thermal conductivities (simplified: no covering layers, no edge effects, no surface resistances)
E 5.3 Thermal bridge principles
a Geometrical thermal bridge (2D)
b Geometrical thermal bridge (3D)
c Linear-type thermal bridge
d Point-type thermal bridge

The values to be used are given in DIN 4108-2, section 6.2, and in DIN 4108-3, Annex A, section A.2.3.

Total thermal resistance and thermal transmittance
The total thermal resistance per unit area R is calculated from the thermal resistance of the material structure and the surface resistances of its two sides R_i and R_a. When considering a multi-layer construction, the corresponding layer-related thermal resistances (e.g. s_1 to s_3) should be added together in the ratio of their individual layer thicknesses:

$$R = \frac{1}{\alpha_a} + \frac{s_1}{\lambda_1} + \frac{s_2}{\lambda_2} + \frac{s_3}{\lambda_3} + \frac{1}{\alpha_i}$$

This standard procedure is simplified because we assume that the thermal resistances of individual layers are constant and homogeneous, and that the surface resistances between the individual layers can be ignored.
The inverse of the thermal resistance is the thermal transmittance U, normally simply referred to as the U-value (previously known as k-value in Germany):

$U = 1/R$ [W/m²K]

It is important to realise that this value is related to a surface area only and any loss effects, for example, can only be taken into account by way of global or proportional surcharges or detailed individual calculations. The relationship between the thicknesses of layers of insulation and the U-values that can be achieved is not linear because of the inverse relationship $U = 1/R$. This fact is not wholly irrelevant for architectural design freedoms when considering the energy efficiency aspects, as is illustrated graphically for various insulating materials in Fig. E 5.2 (U-value on left-hand y-axis).
Designers in North America use the total thermal resistance (R) instead of the European U-value. The North American R-value therefore increases with the quality of the thermal insulation, exhibits an approximately linear relationship with the thickness of the thermal insulation and, moreover, is specified in US customary units [F · ft² · h/Btu]. The relationship is clearly illustrated in Fig. E 5.2: the R-values for the relationship between thermal conductivity and thickness of insulation are on the right-hand y-axis.

Temperature and partial vapour pressure gradients
The water vapour partial pressure p is the product of the temperature-related saturation vapour pressure p_s and the relative humidity of the air ϕ.

$p = p_s \cdot \phi$ [Pa]

Air can continue to absorb water vapour until the saturation vapour pressure is reached. However, the saturation vapour pressure also depends on the temperature (relative humidity). Once the saturation pressure is exceeded, the water vapour condenses out (condensation). Knowledge of the temperature and partial vapour pressure gradients across a multi-layer construction is primarily important for estimating the potential occurrence of condensation (especially *where* it might occur). This can be determined relatively easily for a purely two-dimensional structure by using the Glaser method (see DIN 4108-3). But in the case of linear and, first and foremost, complex three-dimensional geometries, and also when very accurate results are needed, computer-assisted hygrothermic calculations based on finite element models (FEM) will be necessary.

Thermal bridges
A thermal bridge is a local position at which – viewed on a relative scale – the heat flow is significantly higher than that of the construction considered as a whole. Consequently, a homogeneous two-dimensional structure cannot have any thermal bridges, even if the thermal conductivity is very high in absolute terms. "Geometric thermal bridges" can ensue in three-dimensional, non-planar structures (Figs. E 5.3a and b). The higher heat flow at such positions is due entirely to the ratio of the internal surface area to the larger external surface area. On a molecular level (see "Conduction", p. 108) we could say, for example, that each web in the microstructure of an insulating material is a thermal bridge. Generally, however, the term is used only in constructional relationships, i.e. in the combination and jointing of various materials. We therefore also refer to structural or constructional thermal bridges, which are either linear-type (Fig. E 5.3c), point-type (Fig. E 5.3d) or a combination of these.

Calculation of thermal bridges, U-value
Under certain circumstances, thermal bridges are the result of the geometry of insulating elements, the edges of which, by way of their very nature, exhibit a higher thermal conductivity than that of the (undisturbed) middle of the system. The effect depends on the exact configuration of the edge of the system, the geometry and the dimensions, plus the respective installation situation as well.
The heat flow via such "non-standard places" is either estimated using a simplified method or calculated accurately by means of FEM, and then included in the overall design by way of linear (length-related) U-values or an effective (modified) thermal conductivity (λ_{eff}). The result is an effective (modified) U-value which depends on the parameters length of periphery, surface area and thickness, and consequently is different for every system; the effective thermal conductivity (λ_{eff}) is a mean value valid for one particular system only.
According to the current state of the art, it is therefore advisable to specify U-values for standard cross-sections and to calculate the length-related linear U-value Ψ_K for the respective installation situation, i.e. the specific thermal bridge configuration, separately (e.g. also with the help of FEM), and to take these into account within the scope of the total energy balance according to DIN EN 832.
Considering the area-based thermal conductivity and the linear thermal bridge effect separately means that the area-related proportions can be compared with other insulating materials. The thermal bridge problem is aggravated when using high-performance thermal insulation, e.g. vacuum insulation systems. Such systems are much thinner and minimise the conduction through the surface area, which results in every thermal bridge becoming more significant – in relative terms – than is the case with conventional insulating materials.

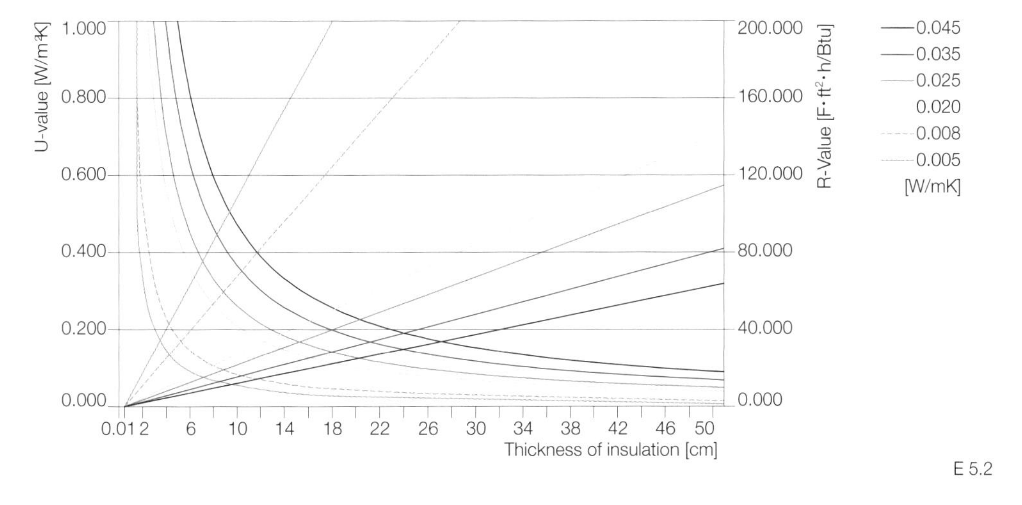

E 5.2

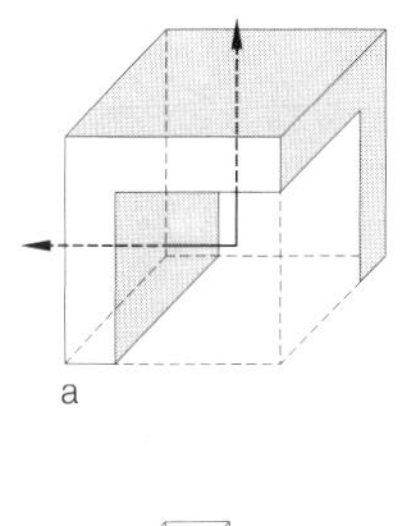

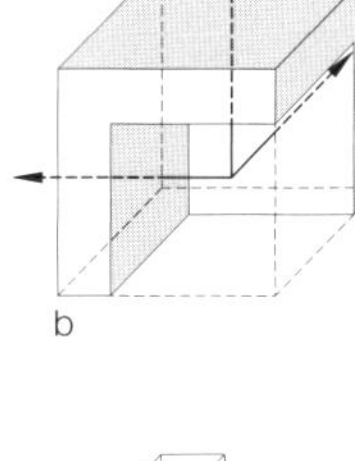

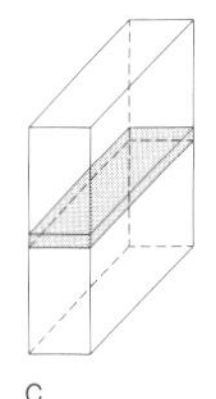

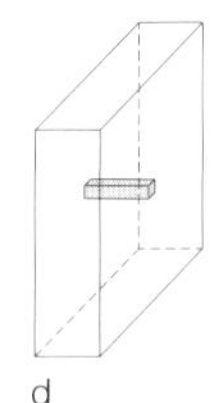

E 5.3

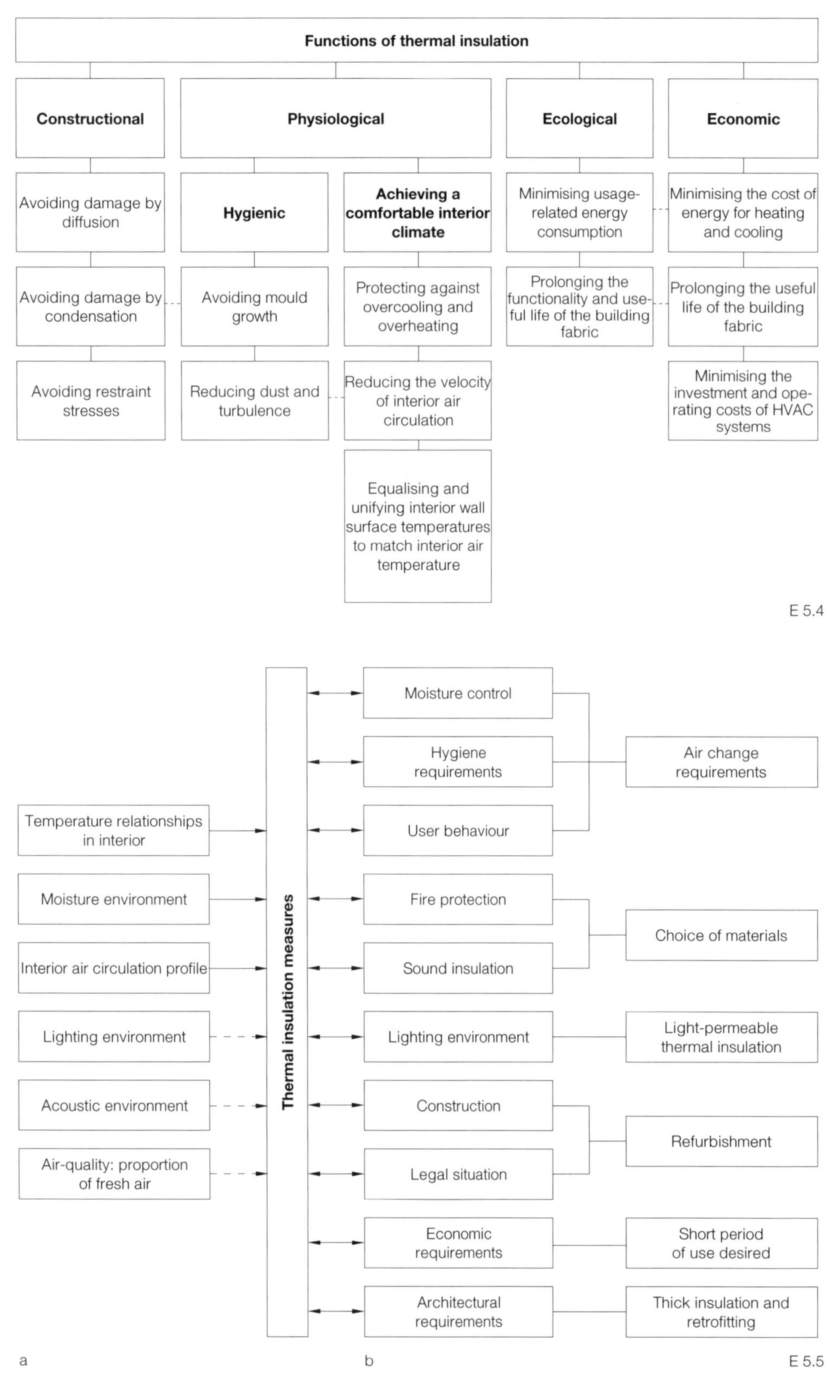

E 5.4 The functions of thermal insulation
E 5.5 a, b Areas that can have interactions with thermal insulation measures and could present potential conflicts within the scope of thermal insulation measures
E 5.6 How radiation-permeable designs are dependent on the weather
a Typical opaque design with mass or thermal insulation
b Radiation-permeable design with separate layers and low mass
E 5.7 Building physics aspects of cushions made from polymer foil

Objective and effect of thermal insulation measures
Why do we actually try to reduce the heat transfer through the building envelope? The reasons are varied and go well beyond the alleged primary inducement of saving energy, and many are related to each other (Fig. E 5.4). The physiological functions of the human body serve as the starting point for creating a sufficiently hygienic and comfortable interior climate. Various areas are touched on and influenced within the scope of any thermal insulation measure (Fig. E 5.5a). These effects must be addressed and checked. At the same time, there are many potential conflicts to be overcome (Fig. E 5.5b).

As the governing external conditions acting on a building are of a dynamic nature, a purely static approach to thermal insulation measures is inappropriate, even though this type of approach has been used hitherto in all the relevant standards and regulations. Dynamic interactions between exterior, building envelope and interior – and hence consequences for the heat flow – result from, in particular, solar energy gains via translucent and transparent areas of the building envelope and the heat storage properties of building components (thermal mass). Thermal insulation measures make a valuable contribution to evening out day/night fluctuations in the interior temperature – especially in the presence of little thermal mass.

Special aspects of foil and membrane designs

The development of efficient building envelopes using foil and membrane materials to provide protection from the climate requires the consideration of diverse aspects that are perhaps unnecessary when working with conventional building materials and forms of construction. In conjunction with the further specific characteristics of these extremely thin and flexible materials, these special aspects in turn result in unique solutions to many issues, only some of which are presented here, with no claim to be exhaustive.
Thermal performance is an important aspect for a building envelope and, as foil and membrane materials for reasons of their minimal thickness alone (0.1–2 mm) cannot themselves offer adequate thermal resistance, one obvious solution is to employ a multi-layer design. This is the case with air-filled (pneumatic) membrane cushion structures in particular, but with tensile surface structures the normal answer is to provide additional thermal insulation.

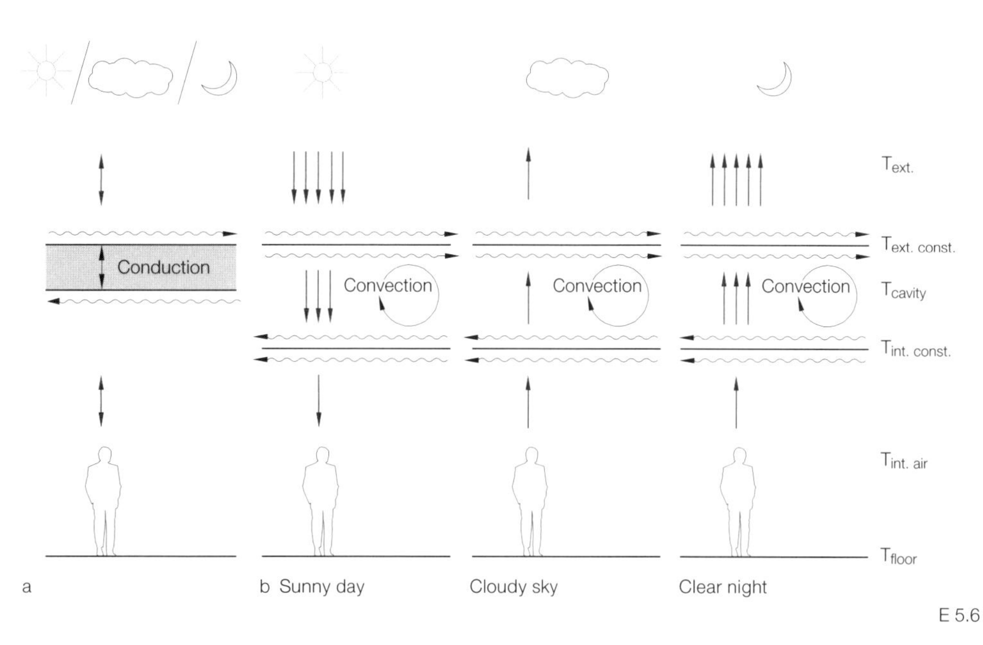

E 5.6

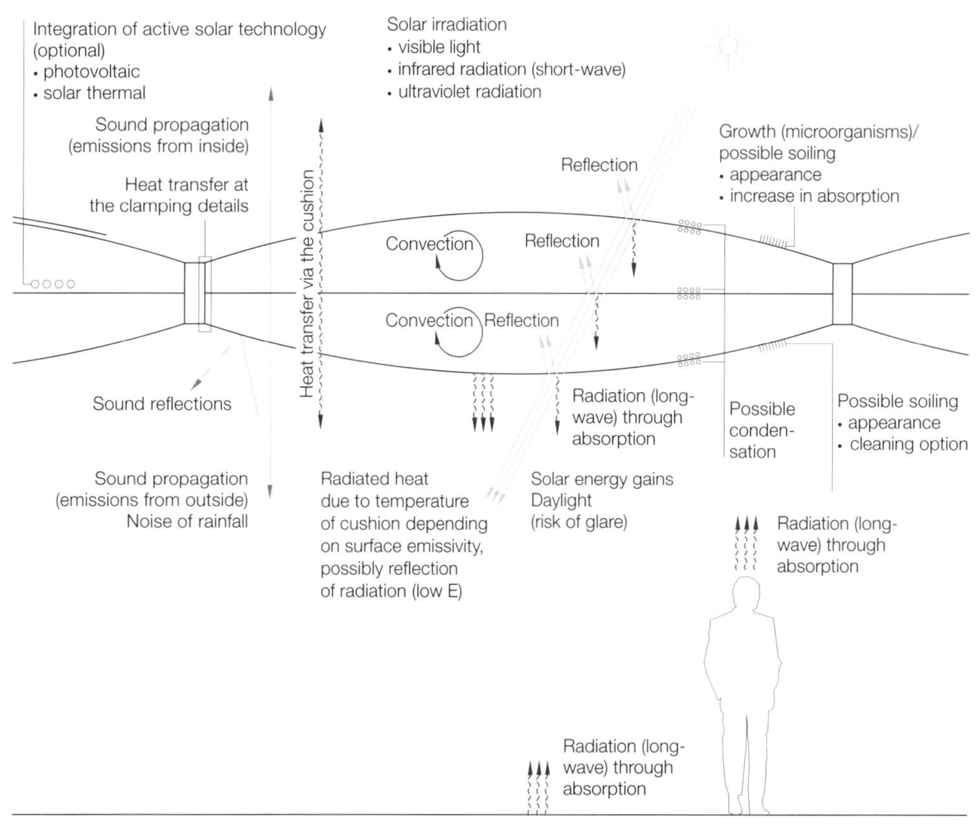

E 5.7

Heat transfer in designs with several layers and very low mass

In an opaque envelope construction with comparatively heavyweight building materials and, possibly, thermal insulation as well, it is conduction that is the dominant component in the total heat transfer. By comparison, in permeable, lightweight, multi-layer designs, i.e. primarily single- and multi-leaf membrane building envelopes, it is the convection and radiation components that are critical (Fig. E 5.6). The thermal conductivities of the materials used, as with all thin, planar polymer materials, are practically irrelevant because of the minimal thickness of each material and its position perpendicular to the heat flow.
The large proportion of heat transfer by way of radiation leads to a differentiated behaviour of the envelope in relation to the radiation environment. It is this behaviour that must be considered when optimising the energy efficiency of the design (Fig. E 5.6).
A considerable energy transfer via radiation can be expected in the absence of clouds to attenuate the radiation effect, i.e. on a sunny day or during a clear night. As a result, the temperature of certain exposed surfaces, for example, can drop well below that of the surroundings. The condensation that may occur must be taken into account when designing the envelope.

Heat transfer in membrane cushions

Air-filled cushion designs are frequently chosen not for their structural and constructional benefits, but rather because their intrinsic multi-layer construction leads to a vast improvement in the thermal insulation properties. When transparency, i.e. an unobstructed view through the material, and not just translucency, i.e. diffuse light permeability only, is desired, then membrane cushions and the glass-ETFE foil designs described on p. 223 are the only options for achieving comparatively low U-values. Important here are the surface resistances at the air/material interfaces and, first and foremost, the convection within the cushion, which is inevitable at certain temperature differences because of the large volume of air between the layers of material.
As Fig. E 5.8a (p. 216) shows, the convection effects caused by the rising warmer air differ depending on the orientation of the cushion and the direction of the heat flow (horizontal or vertical). Every additional layer of material, and hence every additional air chamber, in the cushion reduces the volume and introduces two further surface resistances (air/membrane/air). Consequently, this represents an improvement (Fig. E 5.8b, p. 216).
Nonetheless, the cushion edge details are still important for the heat transfer through a building envelope composed of membrane cushions. Besides the thermal insulation quality of the (clamping) frame detail (e.g. achieved with a thermal break), it is also important to consider the proportion that the framing represents in terms of the total surface area – just like any other thermal bridge calculation and similar to the pane/frame situation at a window – in order to arrive at a total U-value. Critical here is the U_f-value, i.e. the U-value of the frame construction, or rather the length-related thermal transmittance Ψ [W/mK].
One fundamental frame optimisation option that can be used for membrane cushions is to separate the individual layers and clamp them separately (Fig. E 5.8d, p. 216). The potential improvement in the U_f-value depends on the distance between the layers and the intervening materials (usually the loadbearing structure). However, this solution involves considerably more design and construction input (two clamping elements, airtightness, protection from weather during erection), which inevitably results in higher costs. The standard variation of a factory-welded cushion with a common clamping arrangement, fixed directly to the

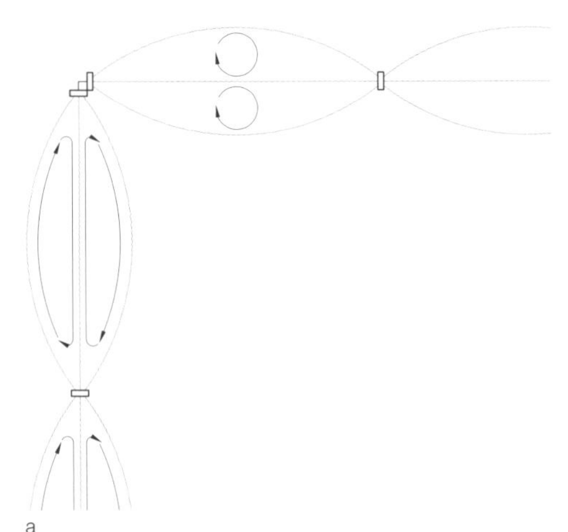
a

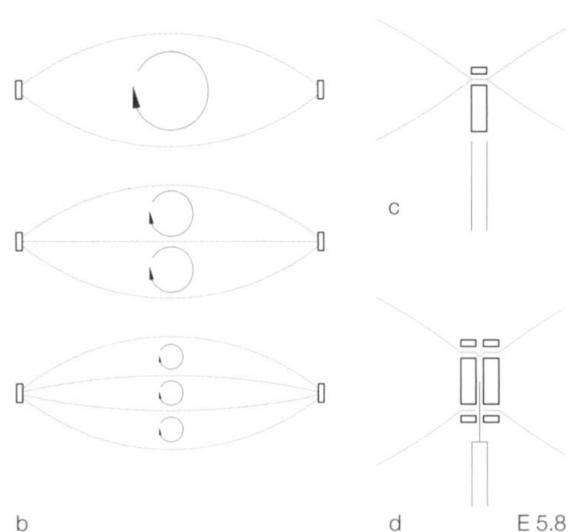

b d E 5.8

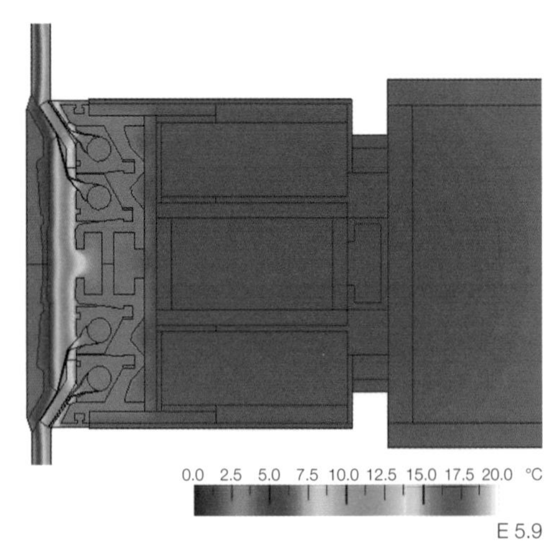

E 5.9

framing, always results in a considerable thermal weak spot; a high local U-value can be expected here (U_f-values in some instances > 4 W/m²K). A gutter beneath the clamping detail will normally be necessary in order to deal with the unavoidable condensation (Fig. E 3.8, p. 191). The supposed disadvantage must, however, be looked at in the following context. Firstly, the cushion clamping detail usually accounts for a very small proportion of the total surface area when compared with the alternatives, e.g. glass; the framing may well be < 2% of the area when using cushions with a favourable geometry (Fig. E 5.14). Secondly, this type of design guarantees that the thermal weakness is certainly along the edges, at the clamping details, and not within the surface of the cushion. Inconspicuous condensation gutters beneath the clamping details may well represent a cost-effective answer to coping with any moisture in these areas; the condensation can generally evaporate and does not need any elaborate drainage measures.

Calculating U-values

Up until now, most research projects concerning membrane cushions concentrated on their wintertime thermal performance. The studies have established that both the standards applicable to heavyweight wall constructions (DIN EN ISO 6946) and windows (DIN EN 673) contain conditions that restrict their applicability to membrane cushion designs. Work carried out by the Fraunhofer Institute for Building Physics (IBP) has revealed a distinctly non-steady-state heat transfer mechanism. The reasons for this are the very low mass and the large volume of air between the membrane layers (much greater than that of multi-pane glazing), with the ensuing convection. This means that the U-value in the centre of the cushion is independent of the thickness of the layer of air and therefore the absolute size of the cushion, at least for customary cushion dimensions.
Comparing the two standards mentioned above and measured U-values leads us to suspect, however, that both standards could be used in a roughly similar way in order to estimate a mean U-value. This does not allow the range of variation in the non-steady-state U-value to be considered, however. A better alternative for calculating the thermal transmittance has not been available so far.
Fig. E 5.10 therefore illustrates the results of calculations for various heat transfer directions (horizontal, upwards and downwards) based on DIN EN ISO 6946 and DIN EN 673. The results differ only marginally within each direction. However, the differences between the various directions are much more obvious. We can therefore conclude that it is not so much the method used that is critical for accessing the U-value of a membrane cushion, but rather the installation situation. If our calculations exclude the heat flow from outside to inside, which only applies in hot regions or in summer, and consider the Central European wintertime case, we only need to distinguish between horizontal and upward heat flows.
Membrane cushions can be constructed from polymer foil, woven fabrics or combinations of these materials. Fig. E 5.13 contains comparative optical values for such combinations.
Where cushions use both foil and woven fabric, then these materials must be clamped separately because they cannot be welded together. Besides the possibility of designing separate clamping details (Fig. E 5.8d), it is also possible to use special double keder rails, like those of the visitor pavilion at Alnwick Garden in southern England (Fig. E 5.11).
The envelope of this building had to comply with various specifications regarding the light transmittance and thermal insulation for different internal zones. The cushion design in some areas therefore consists of a combination of transparent ETFE foil and a glass/PTFE fabric, with additional thermal insulation applied to this latter material on the outside of the cushion. A newly devised double keder rail, which can span

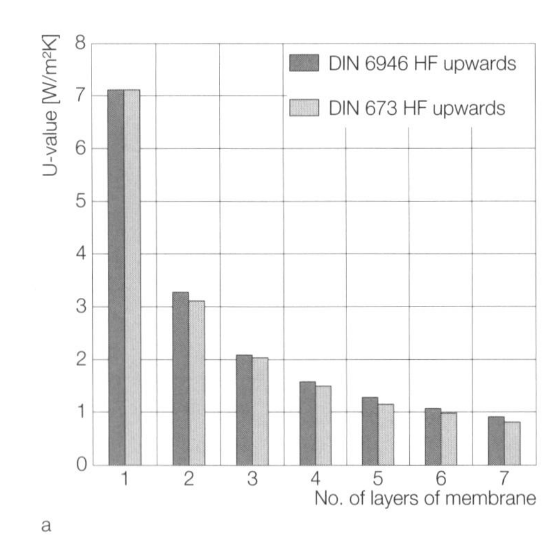

a

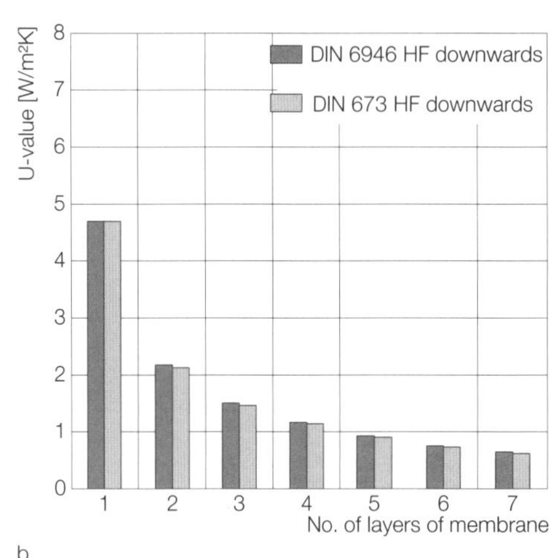

b

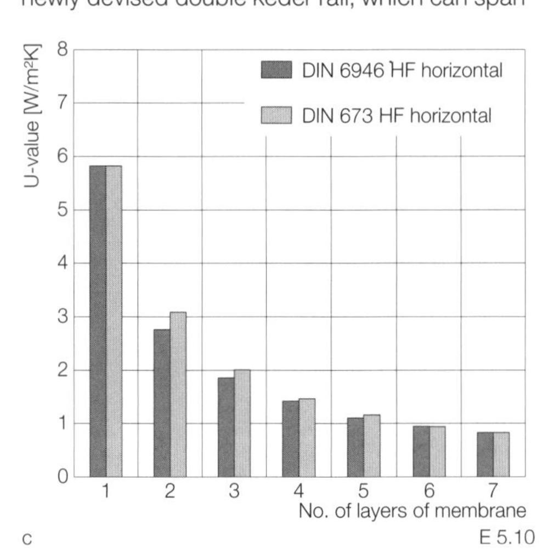

c
E 5.10

E 5.11

E 5.12

more than 4 m without support, fixes both materials in a common and hence much slimmer section (Fig. E 5.12).

Use of additional thermal insulation materials in foil and membrane designs

One of the chief advantages of textile materials is the ability to combine particular construction options (e.g. long spans and unusual forms) and at the same time achieve a high light transmittance. Designers often strive to maintain this latter characteristic even if additional thermal performance requirements must be satisfied. This in turn leads to attention being given to translucent, i.e. light-permeable, insulating materials. There is a fundamental relationship between U-value and potential light transmittance: increasing the thickness of the insulation decreases the light transmittance achievable with this form of construction.

On the other hand, there are also examples that use conventional, opaque insulating materials because light transmittance is not always desirable; venues and places of assembly often require an opaque enclosure. For example, the two-ply PVC membrane roof to the health spa clinic in Masserberg in central Germany, completed in 1994, uses two layers of 8 cm thick mineral wool with offset joints and a covering of PE foil. Individual unplasticised PVC mountings fix the insulation at least 50 cm clear of the upper ply of PVC in order to create a ventilation cavity. A very similar design was used for the roof to the Musical Dome in Cologne (1996). Here, 16 cm of mineral wool enables the roof to achieve a U-value of approx. 0.23 W/m²K and a mean sound reduction index of 45 dB. The arts centre in the Munich suburb of Puchheim (1999) has a complex roof construction with two layers of sand-filled spacer fabric each 20 mm thick and two layers of mineral fibre insulation (8 + 10 cm). This results in a U-value of approx. 0.2 W/m²K and a sound reduction index of approx. 51 dB. All three roofs are completely opaque.

As with all insulation measures, the building physics aspects must be considered in membrane designs as well, particularly the possibility of condensation and especially at thermal bridges, e.g. at fixings, penetrations and junctions with other components. The actual light transmittance of membrane structures with translucent insulation is frequently very low (e.g. around 1 %), especially in older examples. However, this can have an advantage in terms of the lower heat gains.

One example of such a structure is the Olympic swimming pool in Munich dating from 1972, which forms one of the enclosed spaces beneath the famous Olympic roof. The insulated "suspended ceiling" (approx. 8250 m²) over the swimming pool was renewed between 2003 and 2006 (Fig. E 5.17a, p. 219). Fig. E 5.16 (p. 218) shows sections through the insulated membrane construction following the refurbish-

Material/Combination of materials	Transmisson solar T_{sol} (direct)	Reflection solar R_{sol} (direct)	Transmission visual T_{vis} (direct)	g-value	U-value
1 EFTE foil, 200 µm, clear	92 %	4 %			
2 EFTE foil, 150 µm, printed with 5 mm dots	60 %	25 %			
3 PTFE/glass, 0.5 mm	16 %	77 %			
1 + 1	84 %		81 %	85 %	3 W/m²K
1 + 1 + 1	77 %		73 %	80 %	2 W/m²K
3 + 1 + 2			12 %	14 %	2 W/m²K
3 + 1 + 1 + 1			14 %	15 %	1.5 W/m²K

E 5.13

E 5.8 Different manifestations of convection
a Horizontal and vertical cushions
b Cushions with two and more layers
c Cushions with welded layers
d Cushions with separate layers

E 5.9 Clamping section, U_f-value 4.26 W/m²K / Ψ-value 0.06 W/mK, "La Miroiterie", Lausanne (CH), 2007, Brauen + Wälchli

E 5.10 U-values for foil structures with different numbers of layers, orientations and...
a heat flow (HF) upwards
b heat flow downwards
c heat flow horizontal

E 5.11 Garden pavilion, Alnwick (UK), 2006, Hopkins Architects

E 5.12 Garden pavilion, clamping rail

E 5.13 U-values for the wintertime case

E 5.14 Example of how the clamping detail at the edge influences the total U-value of a foil cushion:
$U_{mid\text{-}cushion}$ = 2 W/m²K
(e.g. ETFE foil cushion, 3-layer)
U_{clamp} = 5 W/m²K
clamp width: 4 cm
cushion area: 5 × 30 m = 150 m²
clamp length: 70 m
clamp area: 2.80 m²
clamp area proportion: 1.86 %
U_{tot} = (98.14 % × 2) + (1.86 % × 5) = 2.06 W/m²K
relative change = approx. +3 %

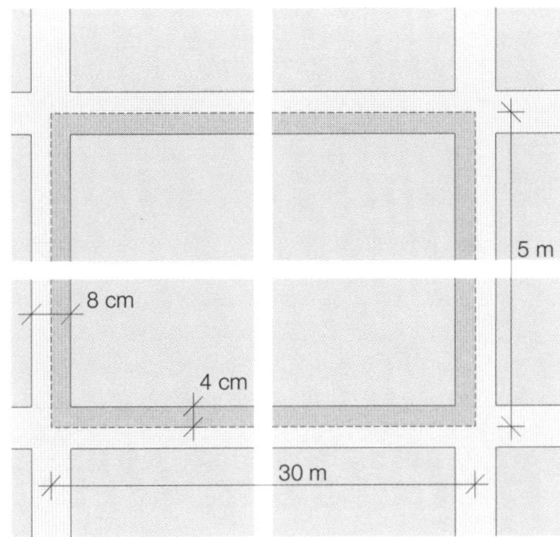

E 5.14

ment measures. Below the cable net roof with its covering of PMMA panels there is now a new suspended ceiling with the following make-up (from inside to outside): a polyester/PVC membrane as the inner leaf, insulation in the form of two layers of 35 mm thick impregnated polyester fleece with offset joints and an active ventilation system for controlled ventilation of the insulation, and an ETFE foil as waterproofing beneath the PMMA-covered cable net. The total light transmittance of this roof construction is approx. 1.5 %. An indoor swimming pool is always subjected to large temperature differences between inside and outside, and the high interior humidity and corrosive atmosphere place considerable demands on the structure. The mechanical ventilation system, which prevents the construction becoming saturated, increases convection and hence lowers the surface resistances, which in turn causes a worsening of the U-value from 0.42 to approx. 0.47 W/m²K during wintertime conditions (outside -5 °C, inside +30 °C).
The refurbishment work also included replacing the original approx. 400 m long PMMA fascia panel at the junction between membrane roof and post-and-rail facade. Movements of up to 1.5 m occur at this point and these are now accommodated by an air-filled, flexible ETFE tube, which forms both an impervious and insulated transition between the fixed glazing of the facade and the membrane roof which is constantly in motion (Fig. E 5.17b).

The main aspects and advice with respect to insulated membrane designs can therefore be summarised as follows:

- Translucent thermal insulation results in a certain light transmittance through the total construction. The light inside is normally diffuse and therefore glare effects must be investigated.
- Insulation should be laid in two layers if possible, with offset joints. This approach helps to reduce thermal bridges caused by gaps and inaccurate installation.
- Insulation may well have to satisfy various requirements depending on the particular application: flexibility, heat and moisture resistance, translucency, suitability for foot traffic (erection, maintenance), UV resistance, low water absorption.
- Membrane and foil materials are not vapour-tight. The topic of condensation and potential saturation of the insulation must therefore be looked at very carefully. Besides using the principle of increasing the vapour-permeability of the layers from inside to outside, it is also possible to provide a large cavity (> 50 cm) for intensive ventilation.
- Fire protection, sound insulation and room acoustics aspects must be considered.
- Connecting the insulation to the membrane must be achieved with minimal thermal bridges. This is best achieved via a mechanical detail, e.g. with special anchors. Large bonded joints, e.g. adhesives, have not been tried so far.
- Flexible connections around the edges are indispensable. Membrane structures can in some cases exhibit considerable movements along the edges, too (wind pressure and thermal expansion), which must be accommodated by the details at junctions, e.g. with rigid facades. As explained in conjunction with the example of the Olympic swimming pool in Munich, this can be solved with a cushion-like junction, which can absorb a considerable amount of movement and at the same time provide a certain degree of thermal insulation.

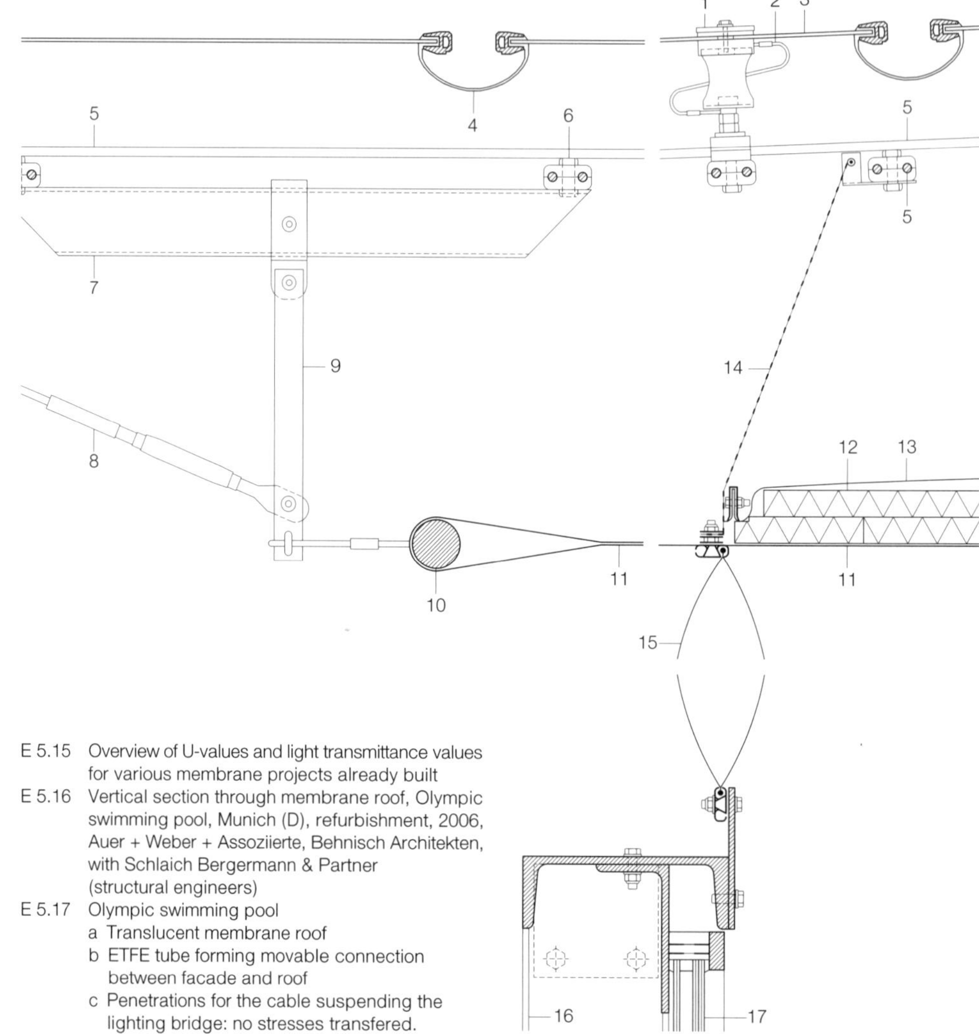

E 5.15 Overview of U-values and light transmittance values for various membrane projects already built
E 5.16 Vertical section through membrane roof, Olympic swimming pool, Munich (D), refurbishment, 2006, Auer + Weber + Assoziierte, Behnisch Architekten, with Schlaich Bergermann & Partner (structural engineers)
E 5.17 Olympic swimming pool
a Translucent membrane roof
b ETFE tube forming movable connection between facade and roof
c Penetrations for the cable suspending the lighting bridge: no stresses transfered.

Project	Thermal insulation	U-value [W/m²K][1]	Light transmittance
Health spa clinic, Masserberg	8 + 8 cm mineral wool	0.23 W/m²K	0 %
Arts centre, Puchheim	8 + 10 cm mineral wool	0.2 W/m²K	0 %
Refurbishment of Olympic swimming pool, Munich	3.5 + 3.5 cm polyester fleece	0.42 W/m²K	1.5 %
Dedmon Athletic Center, Radford	Aerogel fleece between PTFE/glass, 5 cm	0.47 W/m²K	3.5 %
Pavilion, Solar Decathlon 2007, Atlanta	Aerogel granulate between ETFE foil, approx. 8 cm	0.25 W/m²K	15 %

[1] U-values do not take into account the thermal bridge defects and mechanical ventilation (if applicable)

E 5.15

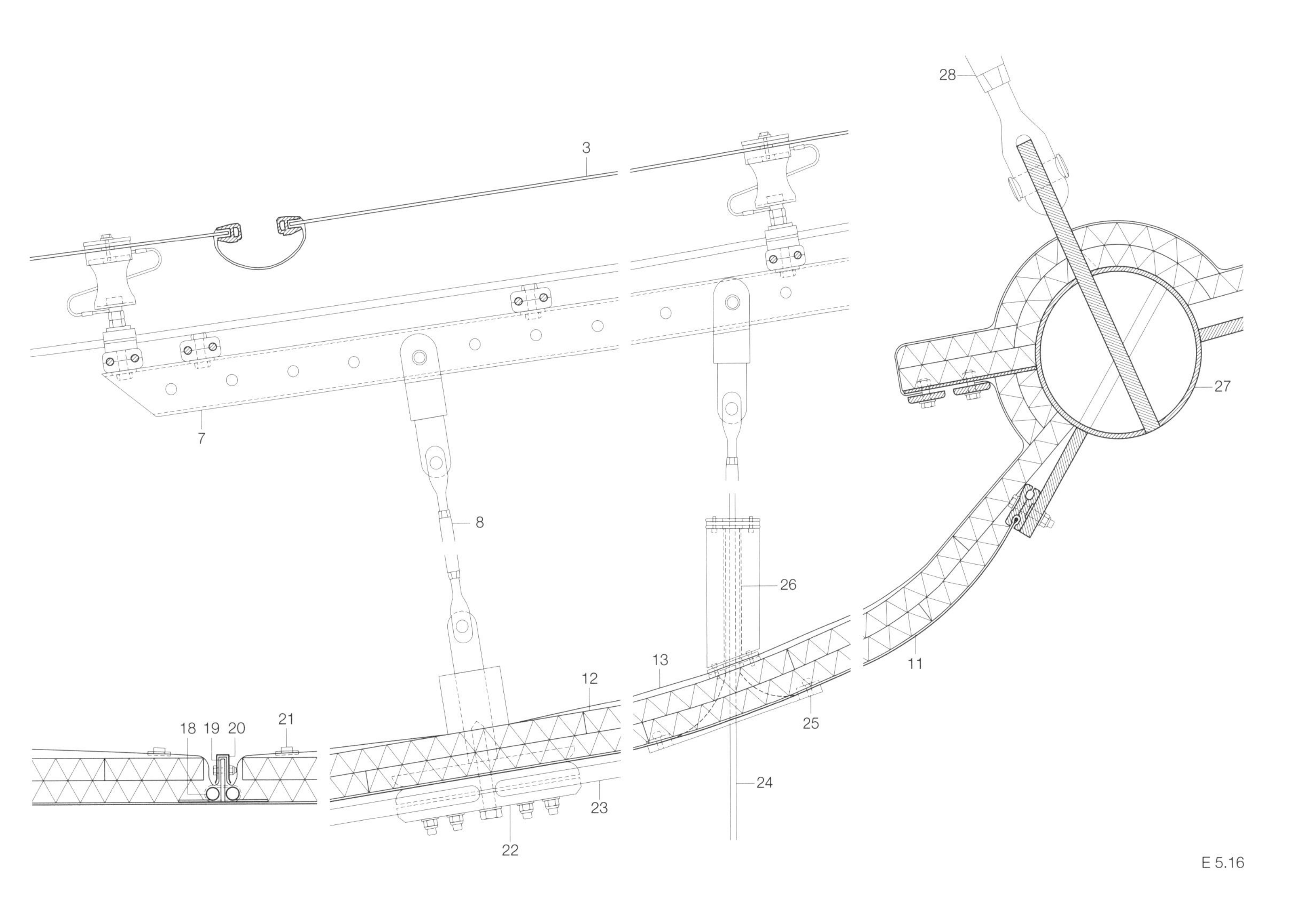

E 5.16

Section – Scale 1:10

1 Point fixing for PMMA sheet, Ø 78 mm
2 Uplift retainer, point fixing, Ø 3 mm steel cable
3 PMMA sheet, class (fire) B1, transparent, 10 mm
4 Waterproofing element, chloroprene rubber, 140 mm wide
5 Cable net structure, 2 No. Ø 10 mm steel cables
6 Cable clamp on cross-beam, movable
7 Cross-beam, steel rectangular hollow section, 100 × 50 × 6.3 mm
8 Turnbuckle, 10 mm
9 Prop, circular hollow section, Ø 40 mm
10 Round steel bar, Ø 65 mm, 1500 mm long
11 Internal suspended membrane roof: PVC-coated polyester cloth, translucent, as loadbearing layer
12 Polyester insulating fleece, translucent, 2 No. 35 mm with offset joints, ventilated
13 Waterproofing, ETFE foil, transparent
14 Bird screen, polyamide, 30 × 30 mm mesh
15 ETFE air-filled cushion, 2-layer, variable height
16 Steel facade, IPE 200
17 Insulating glass, 45 mm
18 Ventilation instead of vapour barrier: Ø 20 mm branch pipes along webs Ø 1 mm hole drilled every 2000 mm warm, pretreated air, approx. 2–3 bar
19 PVC web at each seam
20 Clip-on bar for securing ETFE foil against uplift
21 Ventilation outlet, polypropylene, Ø 12 mm
22 Cloverleaf clamping element, 300 mm
23 Cloverleaf hanger, spring steel, Ø 25 mm
24 Hanger for lighting walkway, Ø 10 mm steel cable
25 Clamping ring, 8 mm aluminium, Ø 220 mm
26 Collar, PVC, welded to loadbearing membrane
27 Supporting ring at high point, Ø 4000 mm, Ø 273 × 8 mm steel circular hollow section
28 Hanger from cable structure, Ø 22 mm steel cable

a

b

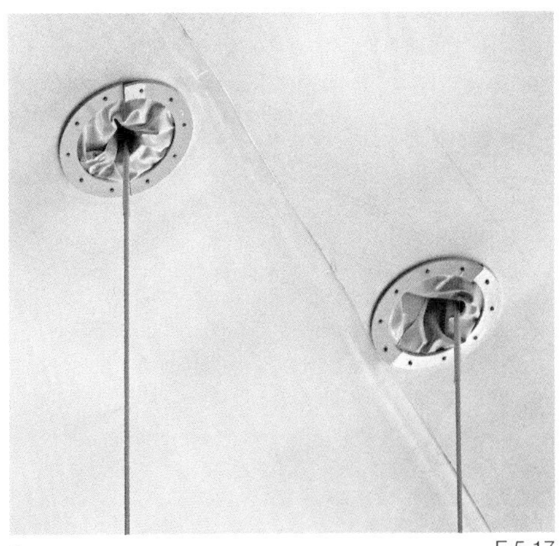
c

E 5.17

Material thickness aerogel granulate [cm]	Properties Light transmittance	g-value	U-value [W/m²K]
1.3 cm	73%	0.73	1.4
2.5 cm	53%	0.52	0.7
3.1 cm	45%	0.43	0.57
3.8 cm	39%	0.39	0.47
5.0 cm	28%	0.26	0.35
5.4 cm	21%	0.21	0.28

E 5.18

Properties of aerogel fleece in uncompressed state

Thickness	3.5 mm and 8 mm
Width of roll	56 cm
Length of roll	up to 100 m
Thermal conductivity	0.021 W/mK for an average temperature of 12.5 °C
	0.0235 W/mK for an average temperature of 37.5 °C
	0.025 mW/mK for an average temperature of 62.5 °C
Density	approx. 75 kg/m³

E 5.19

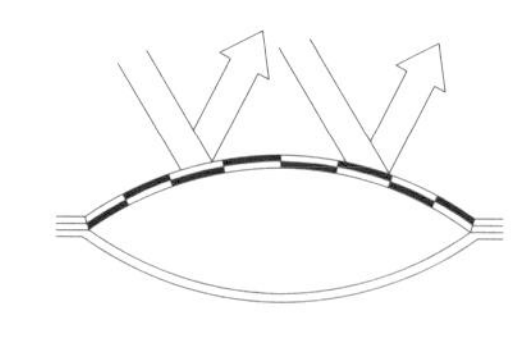

a

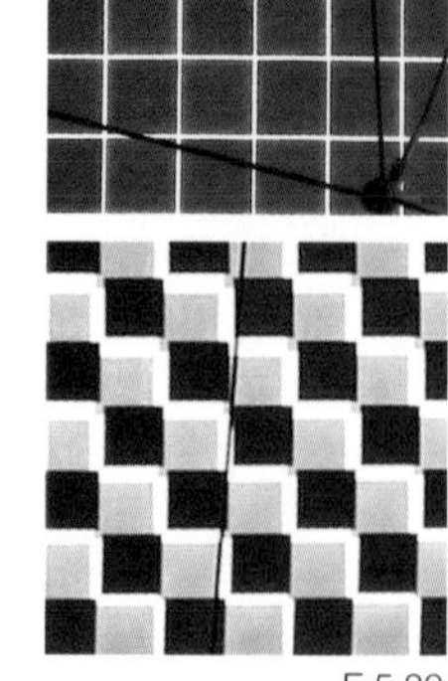

b

E 5.20

Aerogels in tensile structures

The use of highly translucent aerogel granulate in membrane structures is a relatively new topic (Fig. C 6.17, p. 112). This high-performance material exhibits not only excellent thermal insulation properties, but, in contrast to most conventional insulating materials, is also translucent (see "Transparent thermal insulation", pp. 112–113).

Opaque insulating materials are usually undesirable in structures employing foil or textile materials. The light transmittance of an aerogel layer is approx. 80 % per centimetre material thickness; the insulating properties in relation to the thickness of the layer are about twice as good as those of polystyrene foam with a similar thickness. A layer just 3 cm thick achieves a U-value of 0.57 W/m²K and at the same time a light transmittance of 45 % (Fig. E 5.18).

Silica aerogels are available in powder, granulate and solid block forms; powder is generally only suitable for opaque applications, but granulate can also be used for transparent thermal insulation in conjunction with membranes. The architectural design qualities are just as interesting as the energy aspects. The light-scattering properties of aerogel ensure not only a homogeneous inner surface, but also pleasant, non-glare lighting conditions in the interior. Translucent aerogel granulate is therefore high on the list of potential solutions for an air-filled ETFE cushion design where daylighting needs to be exploited.

The ETFE foil and its perimeter fixing details are not vapour-tight, and therefore small amounts of water vapour can infiltrate into the insulation. But thanks to its hydrophobic properties, the aerogel granulate does not bind the water, which can therefore escape from the insulation again through diffusion. However, the good insulating properties of aerogel mean that the inner face of the structure is generally not cold enough for condensation to collect.

The specially developed roof to the Georgia Institute of Technology for the Solar Decathlon 2007 made use of aerogel in conjunction with an ETFE cushion structure and at the time was a worldwide first. The outstanding energy efficiency and aesthetic characteristics of aerogel were exploited in an exemplary fashion in this highly insulated, semi-transparent roof design (Fig. E 5.21).

In order to keep the constructional elements of the roof as simple as possible, the designers divided the construction into two functional levels. The lower level, which is the ceiling, consists of nine highly insulated panels each measuring 4.00 × 1.50 m. Aerogel-filled ETFE foil spans between the timber frames to these panels, which have an optimised cross-section plus thermal break. This results in a luminous ceiling with a homogeneous appearance over the entire area of each panel, achieving a light transmittance of approx. 15 % and a U-value < 0.3 W/m²K. The upper level, merely providing protection against the weather, is an ETFE-covered arch arrangement. This layer is independent of the insulating layer and spans only a short distance (1.50 m), which means it could be kept correspondingly simple (no cutting pattern necessary) and built with a minimal cross-section – major advantages for transport to the building site and handling during erection. The result is a comparatively lightweight and highly insulated roof construction which owing to its translucency exploits daylight to the full. As the aerogel is installed in a horizontal element, and is even under a very light pressure due to it being enclosed in ETFE foil, it remains firmly in place. Unattractive sagging of the aerogel filling over time, an effect that can occur in sloping insulating glass units due to the constant movement of the panes as the atmospheric pressure fluctuates, is therefore ruled out.

It should be added at this point that the photovoltaic modules mounted above the roof to this pavilion at the Georgia Institute of Technology act as sunshades and cut out most of the solar radiation (Fig. E 5.21b).

a

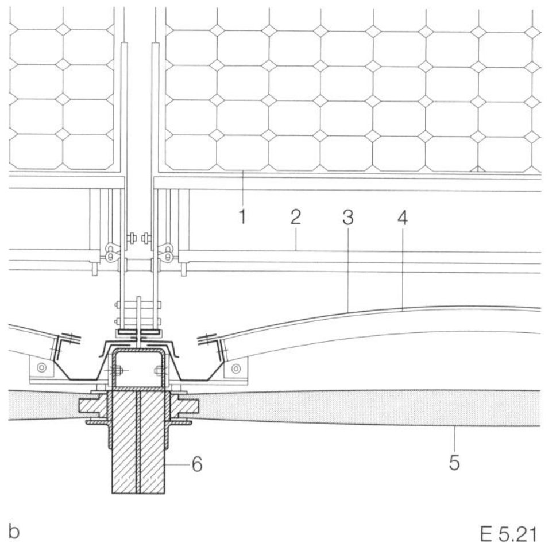

b

E 5.21

1 Photovoltaic module
2 Supporting framework for photovoltaic module
3 Weather protection
ETFE foil, 250 µm
4 Galvanised steel square hollow section, 50 × 50 mm
5 Aerogel panel, 4.00 × 1.50 m
250 µm ETFE foil
70 mm silica aerogel
250 µm ETFE foil
timber frame, 60 × 60 mm spruce
6 Loadbearing structure
60 × 240 mm timber joist

Aerogel fleece as further option
A further variation on aerogel insulation is employed with mechanically prestressed designs because of the lack of the stabilising overpressure. This type of aerogel is in the form of a fleece consisting of two types of fibre mixed with aerogel particles. The result is a flexible but non-compressible mat with excellent insulating properties (Fig. E 5.19). This fleece can be used in conjunction with transparent ETFE foil and also translucent membrane materials such as PTFE-coated glass-fibre fabric (Fig. E 5.22). The layer of translucent insulation is preferably laid directly on the lower membrane and reduces the light transmittance only marginally. There is no need to ensure an even distribution, as is the case with a granular material. In contrast to the very homogeneous appearance possible with granulate, the seams between the individual rolls of material can spoil the overall look. This effect may indeed be undesirable in structures made from transparent ETFE foil. The remedy here is to install two or more layers of the fleece and offset the joints. This is also recommended for avoiding the weakening of the layer of insulation at the butt joints (linear thermal bridges).
These fleeces are available in different thicknesses in order to achieve the U-value required; using two or more layers allows further variation. The first project to make use of this aerogel fleece in combination with PTFE/glass in a building envelope was the thermally insulated membrane roof (4800 m^2) over the Dedmon Athletic Center of the University in Radford, USA (Fig. E 5.23). Less than 50 mm thick, it replaced the single-skin roof built in 1981 and achieves a U-value of 0.47 W/m^{2}K with a light transmittance of 3.5 %.

Foil cushions with integral sunshade
Foil cushions with at least three plies can be designed so that a central layer can be moved to achieve a sunshading effect. The upper and central layers in this case are printed (e.g. a chessboard pattern) in such a way that when the two layers are brought together, the patterns supplement each other and thus reduce the amount of incoming solar radiation (Fig. E 5.20). This requires separate pressure controls for the two chambers in the cushion. The central layer is either repositioned, i.e. it is raised from a position below the geometrical centre-line of the cushion via a non-tensioned intermediate phase and pressed against the underside of the upper layer, or the central ply can be raised from a position not far below the upper layer and pressed against the underside of the upper layer by increasing the pressure in the lower chamber. Both these processes are of course reversible. However, it is extremely complicated to fabricate (cutting pattern and jointing) the two layers of foil for either of these two solutions so that the patterns match up exactly as intended in the as-built condition. But only then is it possible to achieve g-values with a significant difference and hence the desired "switchable" shading effect. Furthermore, it should be realised that the effect also depends on the reflective qualities of the printing used and that the moving central layer may well lead to different U-values for the open/closed conditions.

Example of a facade design with good thermal insulation and high light transmittance
The "La Miroiterie" building in Lausanne, which was built to accommodate high-quality retail outlets, has a facade of four-layer translucent cushions made up of a PTFE/glass cloth on the outside and three layers of ETFE foil behind (Fig. E 5.24, p. 222). The facade measures 900 m^2 in area and is attached to a steel loadbearing structure. Some of the triangular panels between the diagonal bracing members of the facade have a glass infill. The infill material for the other panels is a membrane material with a U-value of 1.3 W/m^{2}K and a light transmittance of approx. 15 %. The membrane material is fixed on the outside and lends the building a "textile" appearance. The high light transmittance enables the interior to be provided with a good level of daylight during the day, and at night the membrane scatters the light from the interior lights to create a very uniform and bright level of lighting. One remarkable feature of this project is the air supply to the cushions, which is based on a return air system (Fig. E 5.24b, p. 222, and E 3.13, p. 193; see also "Air supplies for pneumatic structures", pp. 192–193).

Membranes as materials for double-leaf facades
So far, membrane materials have been used only very occasionally for the outer leaf of double-leaf facades. This topic introduces diverse new options, the full potential of which has not yet been fully explored; it is currently the object of a number of research projects. It is not so much acoustic improvements that are of prime importance here, for which membranes are less suitable, but rather the energy- and usage-related aspects, e.g. safeguarding the function of an external sunshade even during strong winds at the Unilever building in Hamburg (Fig. C 6.1, p. 108). The extremely low self-weight of membranes is one of the key focal points in the theme of upgrading existing buildings.

One of the first projects in which ETFE foil was used for such an application was the Centre for Gerontology in Bad Tölz in southern Germany (Fig. E 5.25). The offices are located on the upper floors above the retail zone. One particular feature is the broad vertical circulation zone on the outside of the thermally insulated walls. This area, which provides access to the offices and shops, is protected from the weather by a second leaf with a movable sunshading system. Designed as a highly transparent membrane facade with a minimal loadbearing framework, the visual relationship between inside and outside is hardly obstructed. In addition, this "climate-control envelope" creates a frost-free and energy-saving buffer zone with an intermediate temperature, which can be ventilated naturally via the

a

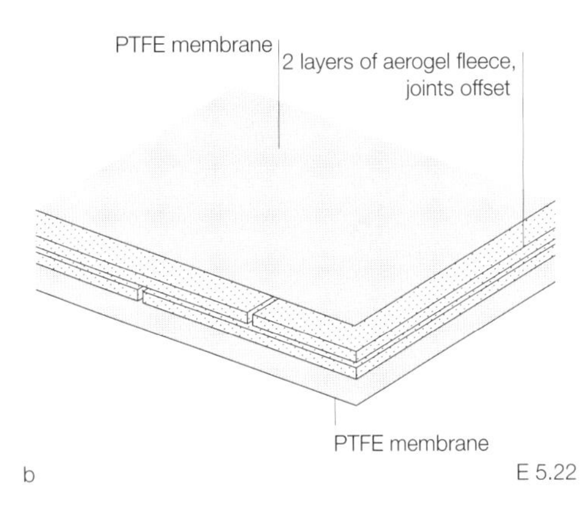

b
E 5.22

E 5.18 Properties of translucent aerogel granulate
E 5.19 Properties of aerogel fleece
E 5.20 The principle of a movable ("switchable") central layer in a foil cushion
a closed
b open
E 5.21 Solar Decathlon Pavilion of the Georgia Institute of Technology, Atlanta (USA), 2007
a View of aerogel panels after installation, with covering layer of ETFE foil
b Section through roof construction, scale 1:20
E 5.22 Using aerogel fleece as an insulating layer between two membrane layers
a Materials
b Principle
E 5.23 Thermally insulated membrane roof, Dedmon Athletic Center, University, Radford (USA), 2009

E 5.23

a

b

c E 5.24

controllable, glazed flaps at the top and bottom of the facade.
The second leaf measures approx. 1550 m² in area and is made from prestressed ETFE foil with a fixing and retensioning system, using minimised clamping bars, that was specially developed for this application. A pattern of silver dots printed on the transparent foil provides protection from the sun and also scatters and reflects the incoming light. It is only through the artificial lighting at night that the printing on this immaterial facade is really perceived by the observer.

Combinations of polymer and glass

Single leaves of glazing made from rolled or float glass are in most cases inadequate for modern building envelopes. It is nearly always a synthetic material that is used to improve the efficiency of glazing, e.g. in the region of the hermetic edge seal around insulating glass units. If the edge of the glass is to be optimised with respect to the linear thermal conductivity (a so-called warm edge solution), then the proportion of synthetic material is increased yet further, e.g. by using a TPS (Thermo Plastic Spacer) or silicone foams.
As with other glass applications, the use of synthetic materials increases the efficiency. Retrofitted foils, for example, can improve the properties of glazing in existing buildings (Fig. E 5.26a, 1, 2). A taut, selective low E-coated foil in the cavity produces an insulating glass with an efficiency that corresponds to that of all-glass products but is lighter and slimmer (Fig. E 5.26b, 3, 4).
Winding mechanisms incorporated in the cavity convert such foils into adjustable sunshades (Fig. E 5.26b, 5). Owing to the extremely low thermal mass of these very thin foils, the secondary heat transfer by way of radiation is extremely low. The geometries of optimized, and therefore complex, light-redirecting elements fitted in the cavity are only economic when produced from synthetic materials as extruded (Fig. E 5.26c, 6, 7) or injection-moulded (Fig. E 5.26c, 8) items.
The surfaces of these products are then treated in a second operation, e.g. vacuum metallisation (aluminium), to create a highly reflective finish. These properties are maintained for a very long time because the elements are installed in the cavity, in a protective atmosphere of dry air, possibly even a noble gas (Figs. C 6.34 and C 6.35, p. 117).
Foils play a decisive role in the production of laminated safety glass, which is made from panes of float glass, toughened safety glass or heat-strengthened glass that are joined together with a special adhesive foil, mostly 0.38 mm thick polyvinyl butyral (PVB), in an autoclave under the action of heat and pressure (> 100 °C, > 10 bar) to form a composite material. The adhesive foil, which is available in different designs (transparent, translucent, opaque, coloured, patterned, etc.), melts. A further material can be laminated into this adhesive joint, e.g. low E-coated PET foil, as is common in the production of windscreens for vehicles, in order to achieve a significant reduction in the solar heat gains. Other polymers can be used as the adhesive interlayer instead of PVB; some of these have much higher initial stiffnesses and strengths. Insulating glass made from laminated safety glass is suitable for overhead glazing that must comply with special safety requirements (Fig. E 5.26d, 10).
All other types of laminated glass make use of other materials for the interlayer, e.g. reactive resins for acoustic glazing, gels for fire-resistant

E 5.25

E 5.24 "La Miroiterie" building, Lausanne (CH), 2007, Brauen + Wälchli
- a Translucent facade at night
- b View of facade from inside
- c Air supply system to cushions

E 5.25 Centre for Gerontology, Bad Tölz (D), 2003, D. J. Siegert

E 5.26 Examples of possible combinations of synthetic materials and glass for building glazing applications
- a Adhesive foils for insulating glass
  - 1 Applied to inside, e.g. for reducing the view through or for reflecting heat radiation
  - 2 Applied to outside, e.g. for reducing solar gains
- b Coated foil in cavity
  - 3 For improving the thermal insulation
  - 4 As for 3, but with two foils
  - 5 Movable, e.g. in the form of an integral roller blind
- c Light-redirecting systems in the cavity
  - 6 Prismatic sheet
  - 7 Redirecting louvres
  - 8 3D grid
- d Adhesive foil between two panes of glass
  - 9 Laminated safety glass
  - 10 Insulating glass unit with one pane made from laminated safety glass
- e Laminated glass made from glass panes and PMMA sheets
- f Transparent polymer sheet (e.g. PMMA) with thin pane of glass applied to outside

E 5.27 "FoilGlass" concept
- a "FoilGlass" section made from polymer material for connecting ETFE foil and glass
- b Clamping detail for "FoilGlass" elements
- c Roof to a glasshouse

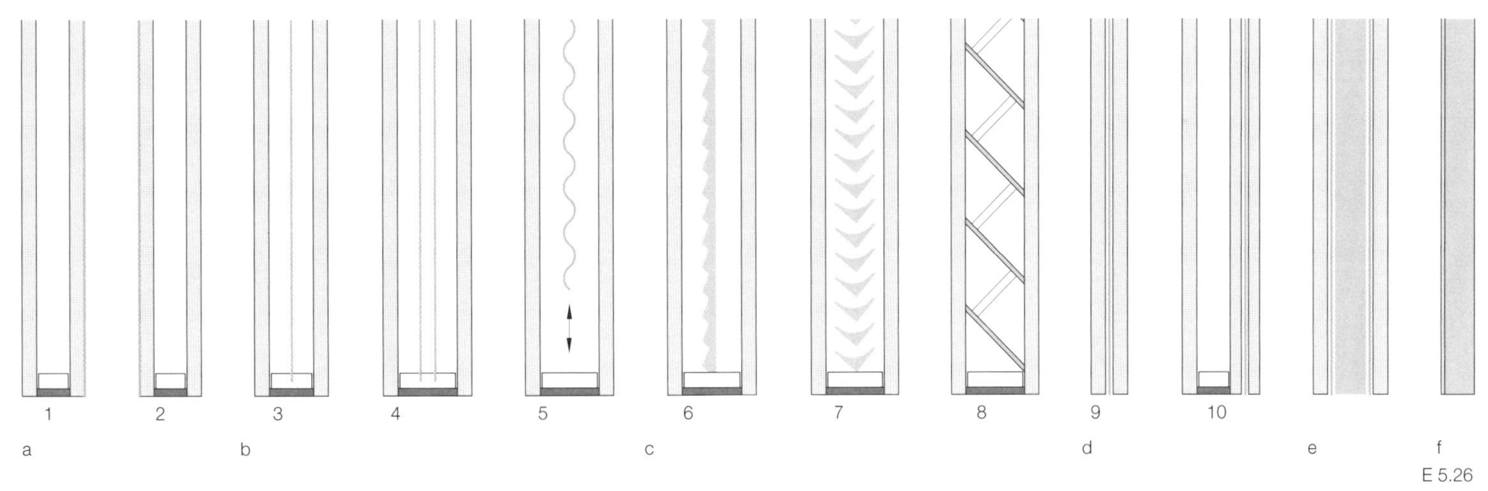

E 5.26

glasses, or fabric inlays between PVB foils. Other adhesives, mostly ethylene vinyl acetate (EVA), can be used to embed thicker elements such as photovoltaic modules.
Applications for such types of laminated glass include diverse security glazing products (e.g. anti-bandit or bullet-resistant glass). Replacing one or more of the panes of glass with transparent PMMA sheets (Fig. E 5.26e) can bring about a saving in weight of up to 50%.
For some applications it is the lower chemical resistance and, first and foremost, the lower surface hardness of polymers that represent disadvantages for their long-term usage. This can lead to scratches causing optical impairments, for example. Very thin panes of glass laminated onto the polymer can help to improve the surface characteristics of sheets of polymer material in such cases (Fig. E 5.26f).

Combinations of glass and ETFE foil

Marketed under the name of "FoilGlass", one current development is the use of glass (always toughened safety glass) as a loadbearing element in conjunction with one or two plies of ETFE foil. The object of this is to improve the insulating properties (through the multi-layer effect), although the foil can also provide a safety function for overhead applications. In addition, the system is switchable, i.e. the thermal insulation effect can be minimised by extracting the air from the cavity between glass and foil and therefore forcing the foil against the glass (Fig. E 5.27). The prime objective of this development, which has had a limited number of applications so far, is glasshouses (Fig. E 5.27c), where the main benefit is the favourable soiling behaviour of the ETFE foil on the outside but also the good, permanent condensation behaviour of the glass on the inside.
However, this product also opens up new options for architecture in general, mainly in the field of overhead glazing, for which ETFE foil is attached to both sides of the glazing. A special polymer frame section has been developed for this combination of glass and foil (Figs. E 5.27a and b). As the strength of toughened safety glass is several times that of float glass or laminated safety glass and its permissible deflection is also much higher, panes of glass with larger dimensions but lower weight can be installed than is the case when using conventional overhead glazing. And in the event of breakage, the ETFE foil guarantees the necessary residual loadbearing capacity. With respect to the potential thermal insulation effect, glazing designed according to the "FoilGlass" principle can be produced with a very high UV-B permeability (see "Greenhouse effect", pp. 114–115), which can be advantageous for areas of planting or leisure facilities.
At the Cramer facility, for example, the thermal insulation can be switched on or off within a period of about 15 minutes (Fig. E 5.27c). The foil remains stable in the wind in both positions: it is either stabilised by the overpressure in the system or the vacuum causes it to attach itself to the pane of glass, which prevents it from fluttering.

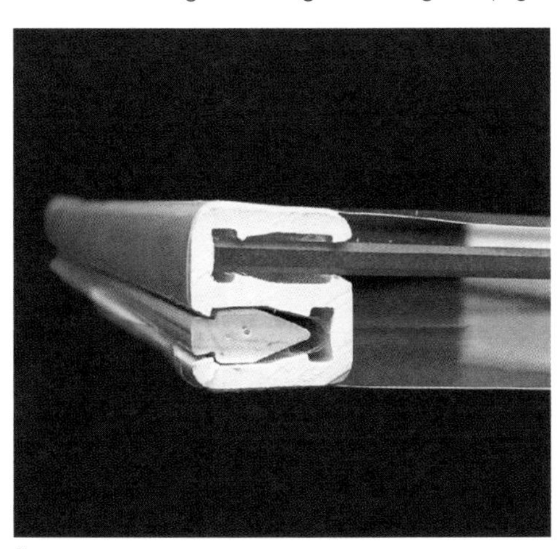
a

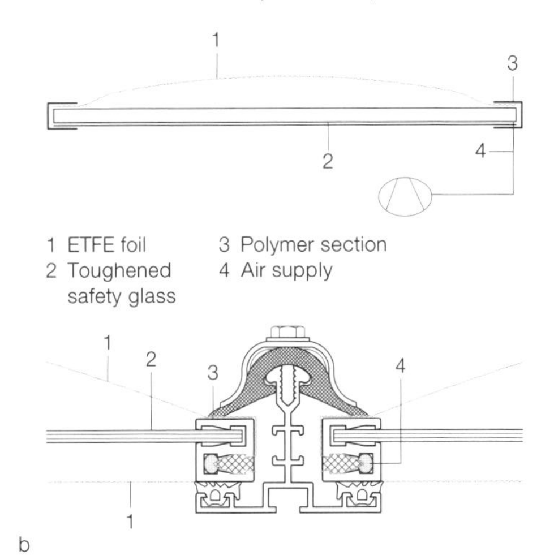

b

c

E 5.27

Part F Case studies

Fig. F Manually laminated GFRP panels, Mobile Art – Chanel Contemporary Art Container, Zaha Hadid Architects

Facade design and interior fitting-out, "Sportalm" fashion boutique

Vienna, Austria, 2009

Architects:
Baar-Baarenfels, Vienna
Project team:
Petr Vokal, Martin Reis, Bernhard Trummer, Utku Mutlu
Structural engineers:
Werkraum Wien

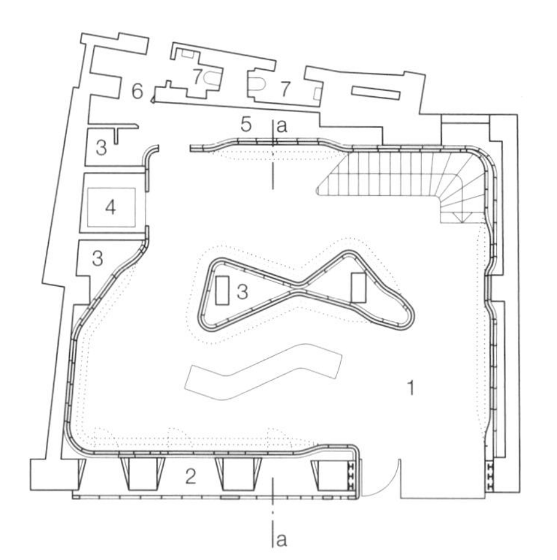

1 Sales area
2 Display window
3 Plant
4 Lift
5 Store
6 Corridor
7 WC

Plan
Scale 1:250

Horizontal section
Scale 1:20

The honeycomb-like facade forming the front of this retail outlet is certainly an eye-catcher in the inner-city streetscape. The dynamic form of the diamond-shaped perforations makes the facade seem to curve towards the glazed entrance – the only part of the facade where passers-by gain an unobstructed view of the interior. Both the exterior cladding and the interior lining are made completely from white acrylic-bonded mineral boards. The display window is a loadbearing plane frame consisting of a diamond-shaped stainless steel lattice stiffened by enclosed hollow elements. These are positioned at random and appear as plain panels in the facade, contrasting with the other panels, which are glazed. Four laminated layers of mineral boarding are used on the facade in order to achieve the necessary depth with webs and rounded transitions. Following CNC milling to produce the necessary profiling to the facade, the boards were glued to the loadbearing lattice. The rebates at the joints increase the contact area and halve the depth of the penetration at each joint. The dimensions and weights of the facade elements were chosen so that the entire facade could be prefabricated prior to delivery to the building site.
The exterior seems to flow through to the interior without a break. In keeping with the corporate philosophy of this chain, the sales area is an abstract, sculpted winter landscape. The white lining to the walls consists of fully bonded mineral boards. Certain boards are apparently "twisted" out from the vertical wall to form horizontal shelving with concealed hanging rails and LED lighting underneath. A steel frame guarantees the necessary stability. At the end of each shelf, this dynamic transition is achieved with a moulded hollow segment formed in a CNC-milled negative mould. The only coloured accent in the interior is provided by Macassar ebony wood behind and below the shelving. The non-insulated display window serves as a climate buffer and is provided with mechanical ventilation.

- Facade of acrylic-bonded mineral boards
- Mineral boards for interior lining

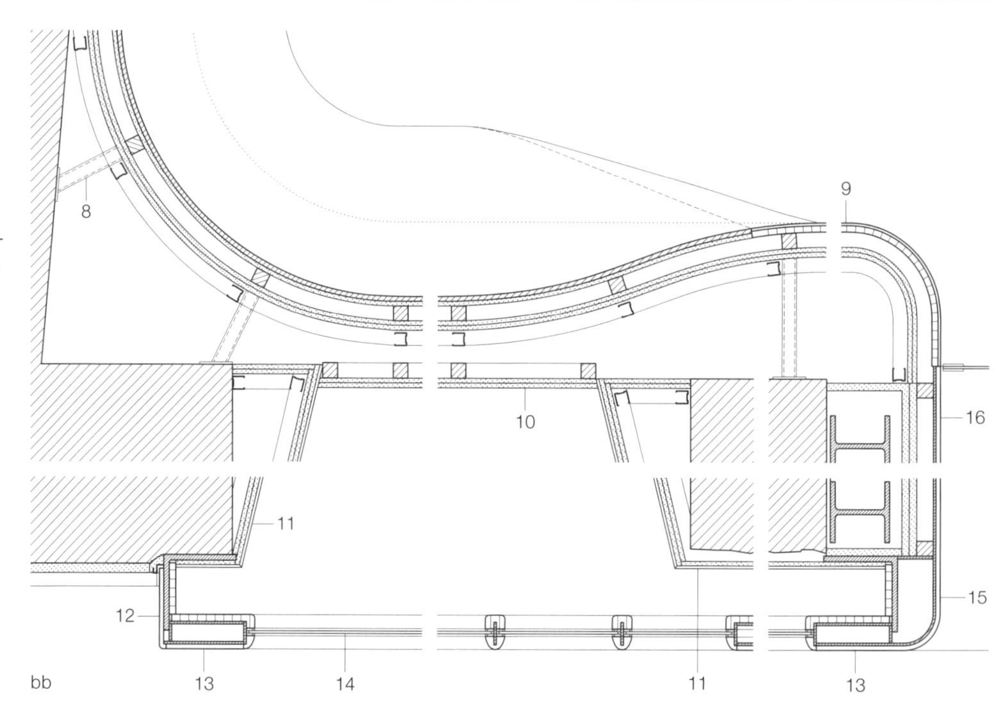

bb

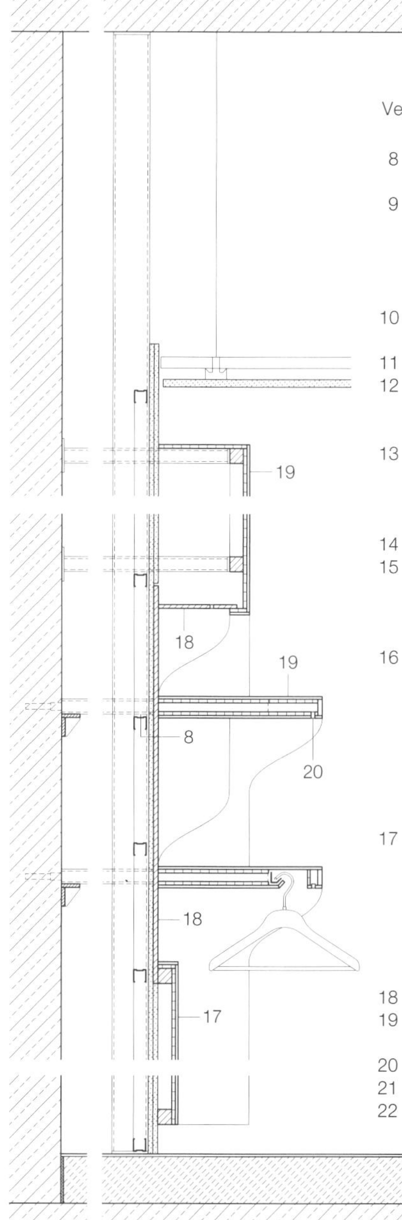

Vertical section Scale 1:20

8 Steel square hollow section, 40 × 40 × 3 mm
9 Mineral board, glued, 6 mm
18 mm MDF board
40 × 40 mm timber frame
2 No. 12.5 mm plasterboard
50 mm metal studs and rails
10 Plasterboard, 2 No. 12.5 mm, with 1000 × 1000 mm access opening
11 Mirror, glued
12 Mineral board, glued, 12 mm
230 × 200 × 12 mm steel angle
18 mm MDF board
13 Mineral board, glued, 12 mm
6 mm stainless steel, 48 mm cavity
6 mm stainless steel, 18 mm MDF board
14 Toughened safety glass, 6 mm
15 Mineral board, glued, 12 mm
6 mm stainless steel, 100 mm cavity
230 × 200 × 12 mm steel angle
18 mm MDF board
16 Mineral board, glued, 12 mm
6 mm stainless steel
40 × 40 mm timber frame
2 layers of 20 mm rock wool
20 mm F 90 fire-resistant casing
HEB 160 steel column welded to 200 × 800 × 3 mm base plate
existing masonry
17 Mineral board, glued, 6 mm
10 mm particleboard
40 × 40 mm timber battens
2 No. 12.5 mm plasterboard
50 mm metal studs and rails
100 × 100 × 15 mm steel square hollow section
18 Macassar ebony wood lining
19 Mineral board, glued, 6 mm
10 mm particleboard
20 LED lighting
21 Hanging rail, 3 mm, bent sheet steel
22 PUR coating, 5 mm, painted
existing screed

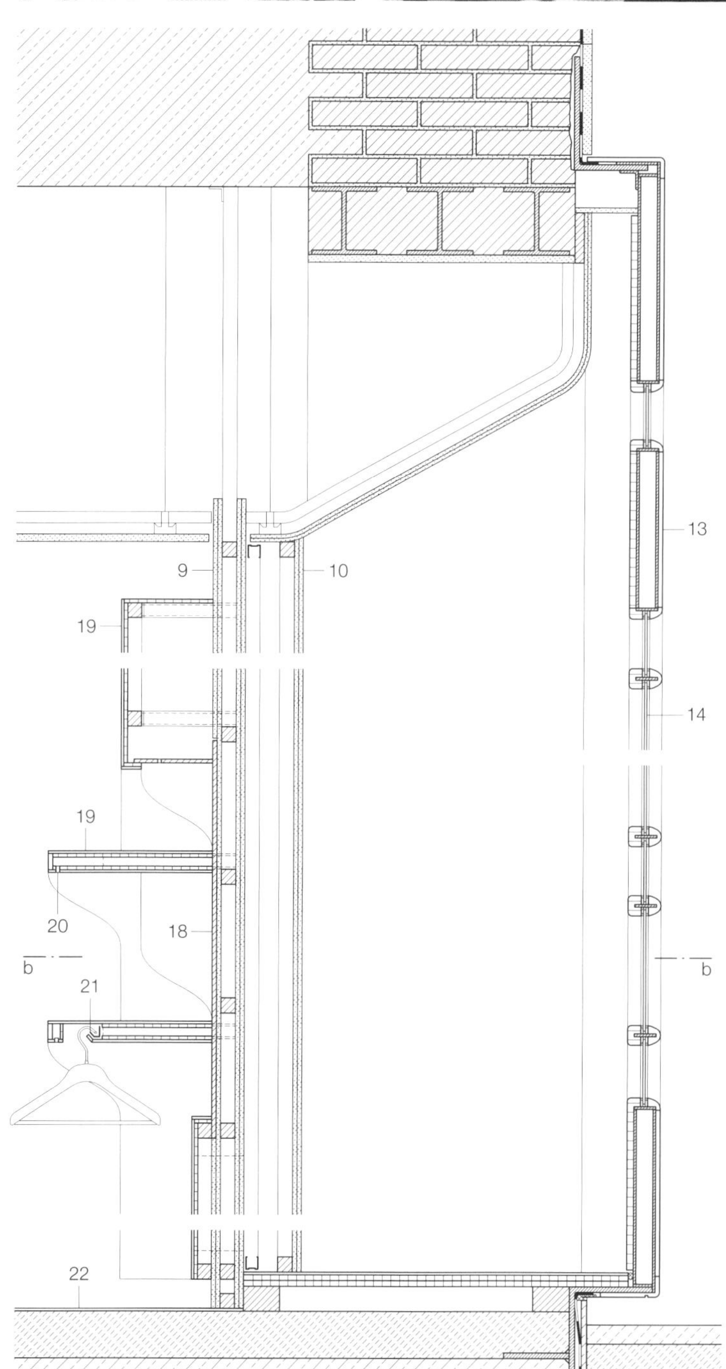

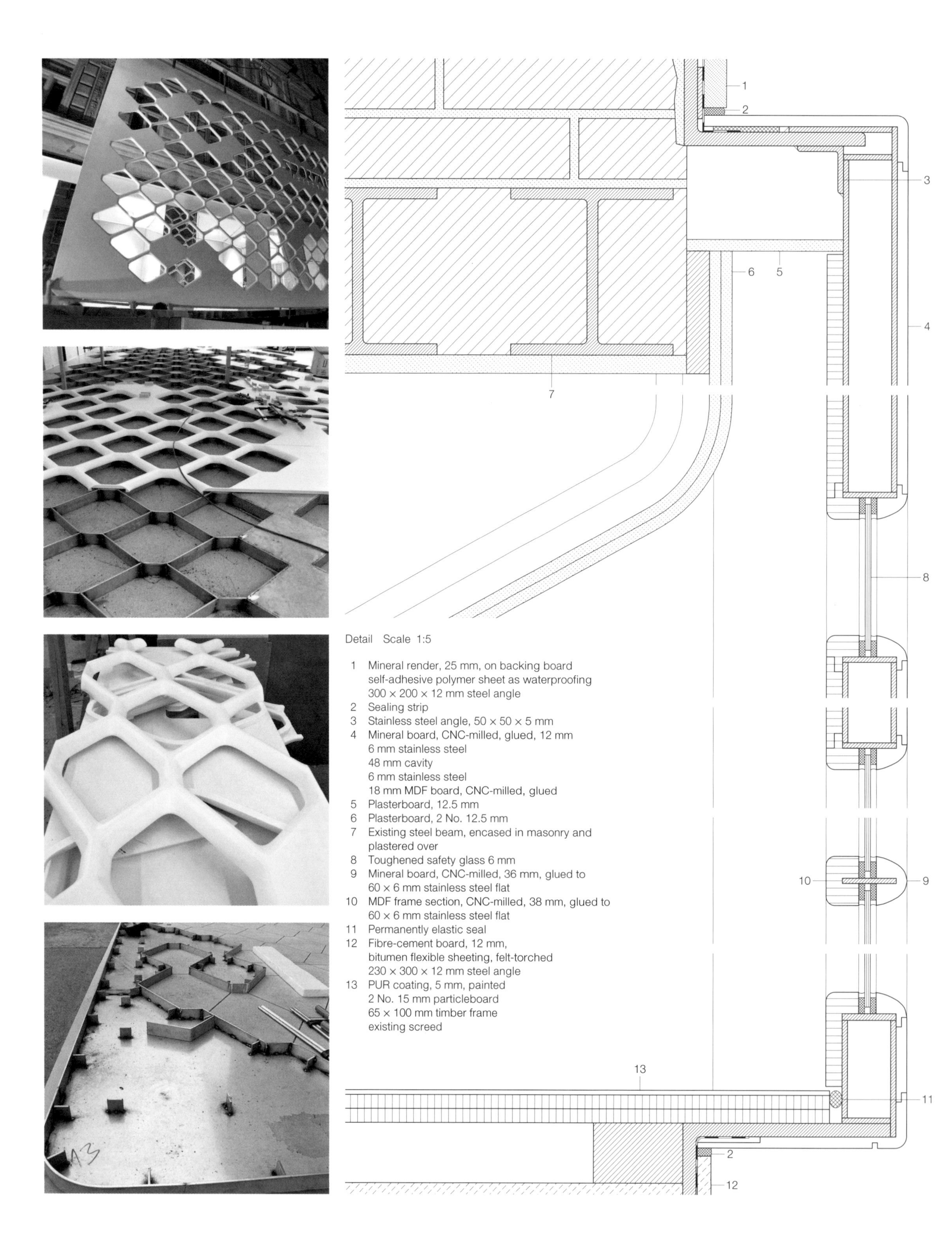

Detail Scale 1:5

1 Mineral render, 25 mm, on backing board
self-adhesive polymer sheet as waterproofing
300 × 200 × 12 mm steel angle
2 Sealing strip
3 Stainless steel angle, 50 × 50 × 5 mm
4 Mineral board, CNC-milled, glued, 12 mm
6 mm stainless steel
48 mm cavity
6 mm stainless steel
18 mm MDF board, CNC-milled, glued
5 Plasterboard, 12.5 mm
6 Plasterboard, 2 No. 12.5 mm
7 Existing steel beam, encased in masonry and plastered over
8 Toughened safety glass 6 mm
9 Mineral board, CNC-milled, 36 mm, glued to
60 × 6 mm stainless steel flat
10 MDF frame section, CNC-milled, 38 mm, glued to
60 × 6 mm stainless steel flat
11 Permanently elastic seal
12 Fibre-cement board, 12 mm,
bitumen flexible sheeting, felt-torched
230 × 300 × 12 mm steel angle
13 PUR coating, 5 mm, painted
2 No. 15 mm particleboard
65 × 100 mm timber frame
existing screed

Reception pavilion

Basel, Switzerland, 2007

Architect:
Marco Serra, Basel
Assistant:
Stephan Schoeller
Structural engineers:
Ernst Basler & Partner AG, Zurich
Ecole Polytechnique Fédérale de Lausanne, Prof. Thomas Keller

The reception pavilion on the site of the Novartis company has a very simple overall form, but it is the choice of materials and construction that give this building its distinctive character. The monolithic roof made from a glass fibre-reinforced polymer and polyurethane foam is supported directly on the loadbearing glass facade without the need for any further beams or columns. It is loadbearing structure, waterproofing and thermal envelope in one, and it is the wing-like outline that lends this structure the lightness desired by the architect. The roof surface consists of 460 CNC-milled PUR foam blocks, each one with a unique shape. In accordance with the structural requirements, the PUR foam modules, measuring 90 × 90 cm, have different densities. The modules were wrapped in up to 12 layers of glass-fibre cloth in a hand lay-up process. This created webs at the joints between the individual blocks which together with the plies on the top and bottom faces form the loadbearing structure. The blocks were glued together and covered with a further layer of glass fibre in the factory to form prefabricated roof elements 18.50 m long which were then joined together in the same way on the building site to form one continuous component. The roof is 400 m² in area and weighs 28 t. It transfers the vertical loads to the facade via the integral double-thickness webs. Sliding bearings and steel strips compensate for the different thermal behaviour of glass and GFRP. Each steel strip is fixed rigidly to the roof in the middle of each side in order to transfer the wind loads to the facade. The facade consists of insulating glass units stiffened by vertical glass fins attached with silicone sealant forming a structural joint between the two. The laminated safety glass panes were factory-glued to stainless steel frames that are concealed in slots in the roof and the ground to transfer the forces. Vertical tie bars between the glass fins prevent deformation of the roof and secure it against wind uplift. At the top they are bolted to a steel plate laminated into the roof, at the bottom a stainless steel spring compensates for temperature-induced changes in length.

- GFRP as loadbearing structure and waterproofing
- Thermal envelope with manually laminated PUR foam blocks

Section • Plan
Scale 1:200

1 Main entrance
2 Reception
3 Staff entrance
4 Access to underground parking
5 Access to company site

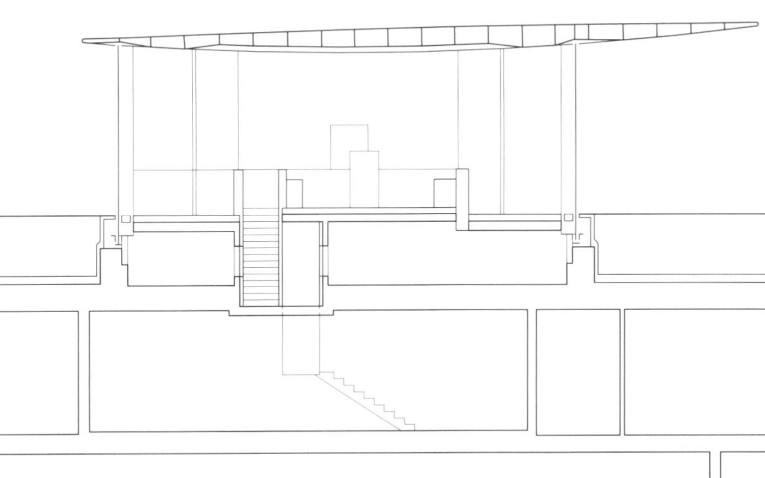

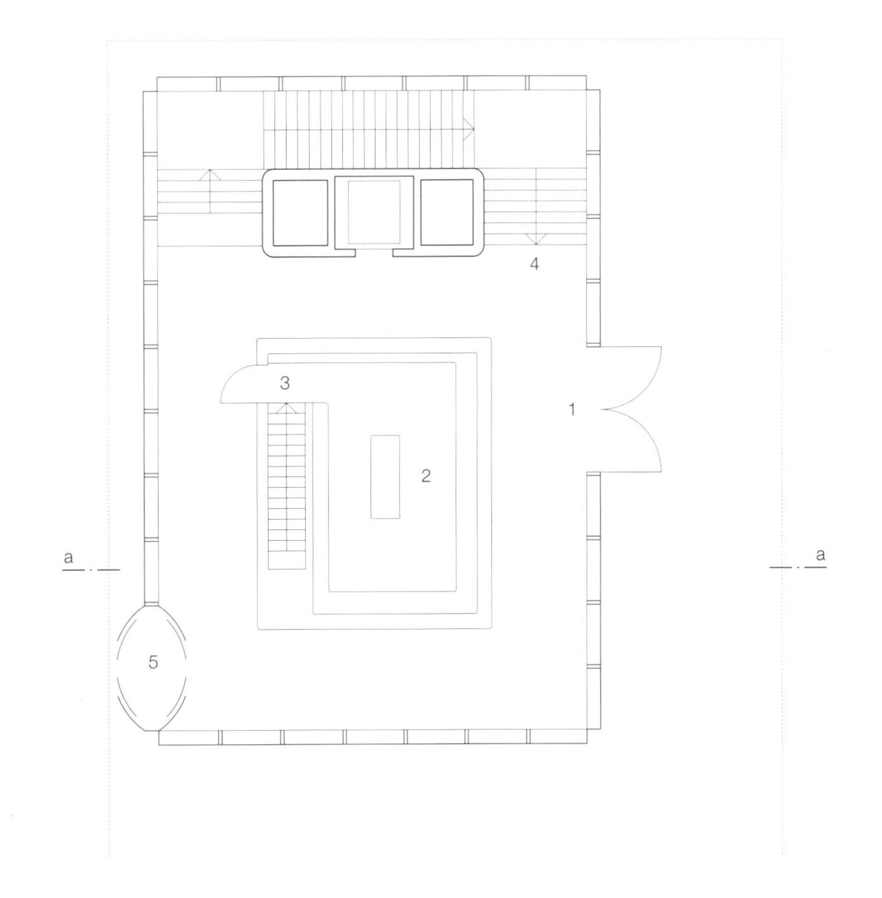

Vertical section
Scale 1:20

Details
Scale 1:5

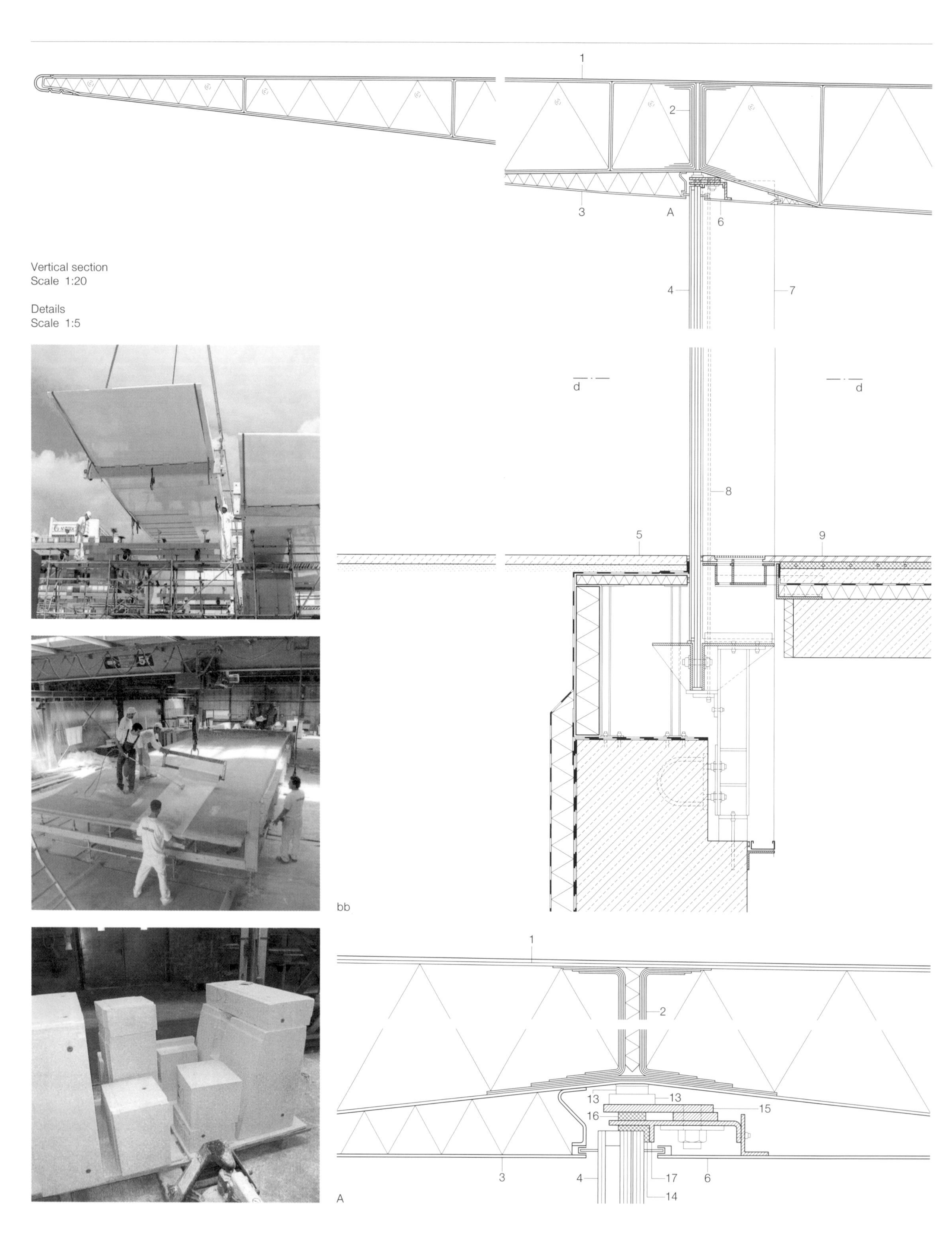

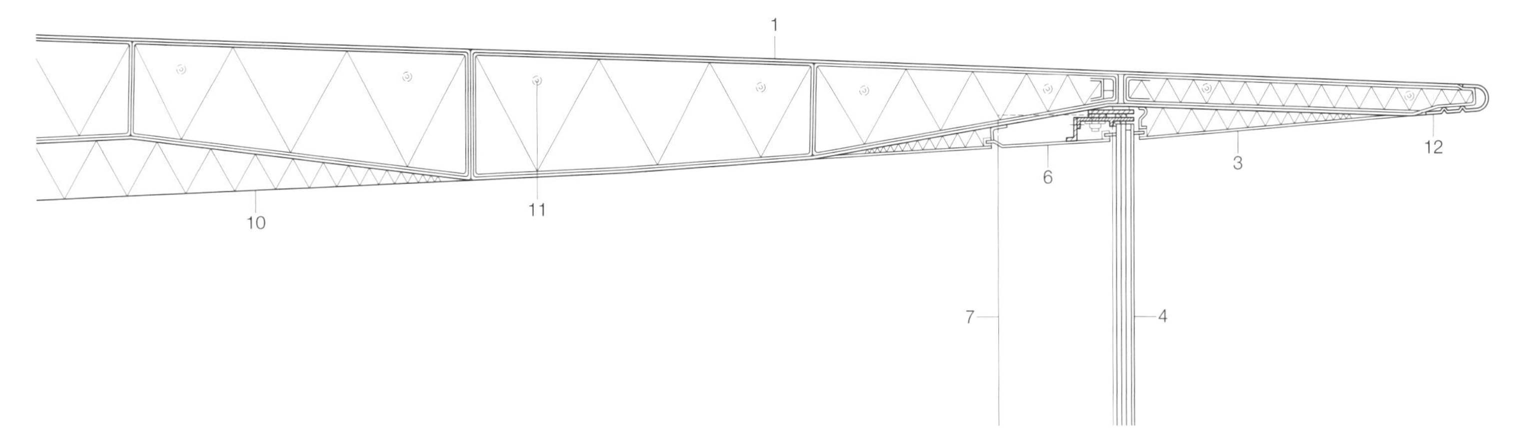

1 PUR block, 70–600 mm, facing laminate of GFRP, 6–10 mm, loadbearing, coated finish, UV-resistant polyester top coat, self-extinguishing
2 Double-thickness web, GFRP, 2 No. 6 mm to 2 No. 9 mm, with 15 mm rigid foam in between
3 GFRP, non-loadbearing
4 Loadbearing insulating glass facade:
8 mm tough. safety glass + 16 mm cavity +
lam. safety glass, (2 No. 12 mm heat-strength. glass w. 1.52 mm PVB interlayer)
5 Asphalt, 65 mm
6 Removable cover, non-loadbearing GFRP
7 Glass fin, lam. safety glass: 3 No. 8 mm heat-strength. glass w. 2 No. 1.52 mm PVB interlayers; 60 mm stainless steel channel frame at base
8 Steel tie bar, ∅ 12 mm, in PMMA sleeve, bolted to steel element in roof, flexible fixing at base
9 Giallo Siena stone, 25 mm,
underfloor heating, 7 + 18 mm
70 mm concrete subfloor, 0.2 mm PE sheeting
60 mm thermal insulation, 250 mm RC slab
10 Acoustic ceiling: 3 mm fabric + mineral wool acoustic mat
11 Close-tolerance bolts, for CNC-controlled fabrication
12 Rainwater drip, moulded GFRP
13 Separate sliding bearings, sheet steel, adjustable longitudinal position
14 Silicone sealant, loadbearing
15 Steel flat, 120 × 8 mm
16 Synthetic resin injected to compensate for tolerances
17 Stainless steel section, 5 mm
18 GFRP, 6 mm
19 Separate steel inlays, 186 × 50 × 40 mm
20 Stainless steel channel, 50 × 35 mm, glued to lam. safety glass
21 Compressive strip
22 Stainless steel flat glued to laminated safety glass
23 Edge trim, grey, enamelled
24 Corner column, insulating glass: 6 mm tough. safety glass + 12 mm cavity + lam. safety glass (12 + 15 + 12 mm heat-strength. glass)

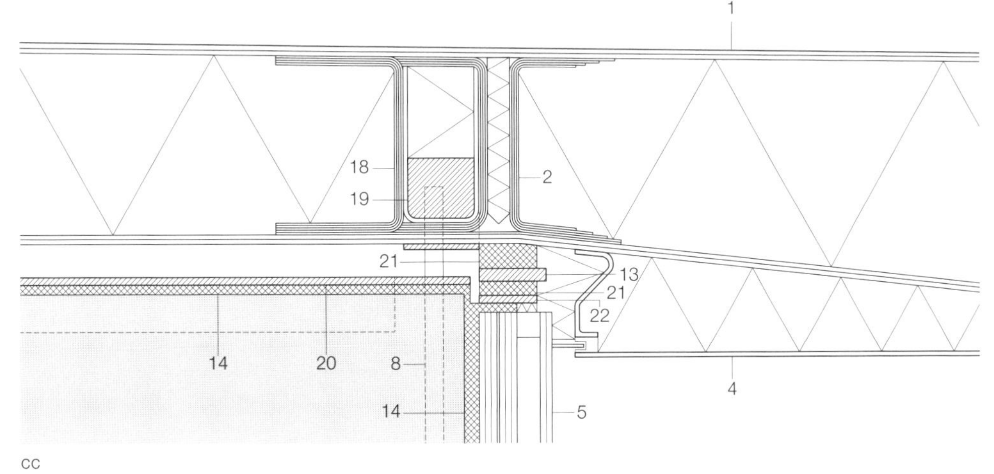

cc

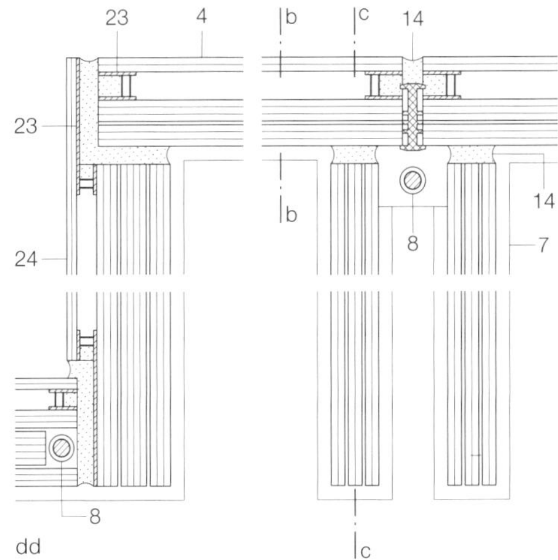

dd

"The Walbrook" office and retail development

London, UK, 2009

Architects:
Foster + Partners, London
Structural engineers:
Arup, London

This office and retail development, with a total of 42 000 m² of lettable floor space distributed over 10 storeys, is located on an important site in the City of London. Two atria ensure ample daylight within the building. The "organic" curving outer form with its silver cladding to the facade suggests that metal has been used here. However, the 14 000 m² of facade is composed entirely of glass fibre-reinforced polymer (GFRP) louvres. "The Walbrook" is therefore the first structure in which this material has been used on this scale.
GFRP can be moulded into any shape, can be used as a loadbearing material and can also be employed in the form of delicate elements with a low self-weight and high weathering resistance. The vertical strips break up the facade and support the horizontal sunshading louvres positioned every 1 m up the side of the building. Direct sunlight is screened off depending on the time of year and time of day, but the metallic paint finish on the surface reflects scattered light into the interior.The louvres are elliptical in section and measure 50.0 × 12.5 cm on the side facing the sun, 20.0 × 6.2 cm on the north side.
The geometry of the building envelope was developed in a digital, parameterised 3D model. This was the only way of handling the large number of different moulded parts and obtaining the data required for the fabrication plant. The facade elements were manufactured in three steps: the production of original moulds in CNC-milled rigid PUR foam, from which the GFRP negative moulds for the louvres could be formed, into which the textile fibre reinforcement was laid and impregnated with polyester resin in a manual process. Each hollow louvre is made up of two half-shells. A pressure bag was used to give the GFRP its final form while still wet. The tolerances due to the hand lay-up work were compensated for by the CNC-milling. Some 4000 louvres and about 750 lesene elements were produced in this way. These were attached to aluminium facade elements in the factory to create fully prefabricated subassemblies.

- Building envelope of GFRP louvres
- From digital, parameterised 3D model to manually laminated facade elements

Section
Scale 1:800
Details
Scale 1:20

A Parameterised model
B Impregnating the fibre reinforcement with the polyester resin
C Inflating the pressure bag to compress the wet GFRP
D Prefabricated facade element after painting

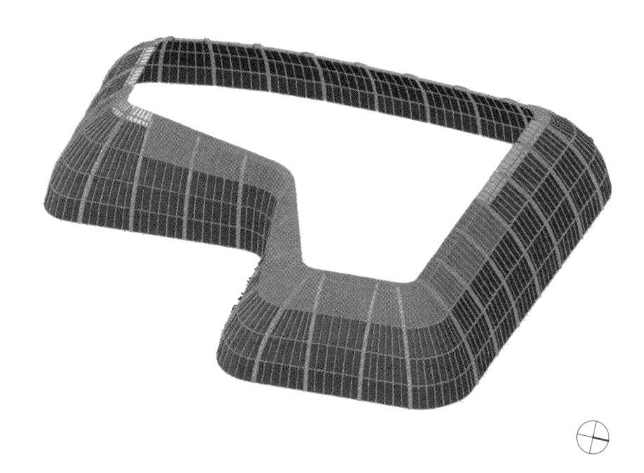

A

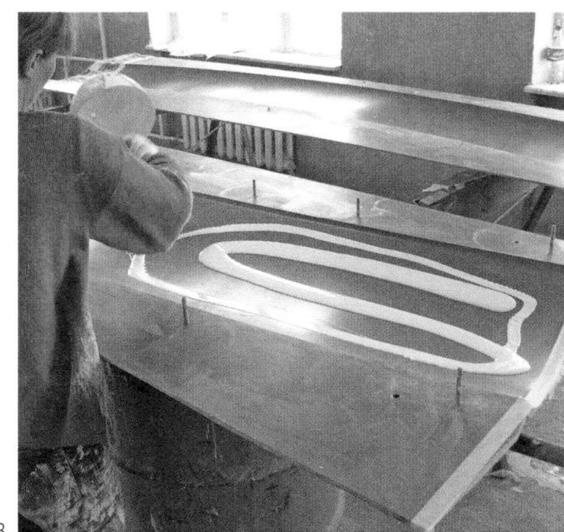

B

1 Aluminium post-and-rail framework
2 Hollow floor, 150 mm, reinforced concrete slab, 130 mm, suspended ceiling
3 Facade mounting
4 Sheet steel, 2 mm, bent to suit, with permanently elastic joint for sound insulation
5 Sheet steel, 2 mm, powder-coated, for bracing the facade and for the subsequent sunshade
6 Facade bracing, 50 × 50 × 4 mm steel SHS
7 Sunshading louvre, GFRP
8 Insulating glass: 8 mm heat-strength. glass + 14 mm cavity + 12 mm lam. safety glass w. solar-control coating
9 Louvre mounting, 10 mm aluminium, powder-coated, bolted to end of louvre
10 Lesene, GFRP, 3.50 m long
11 Aluminium frame: 1 support & 1 wind anchor per lesene
12 Sheet aluminium, 2 mm, bent to suit
13 Mineral wool thermal insulation, 120 mm
350 × 250 × 10 mm galvanised steel sheet

aa

C

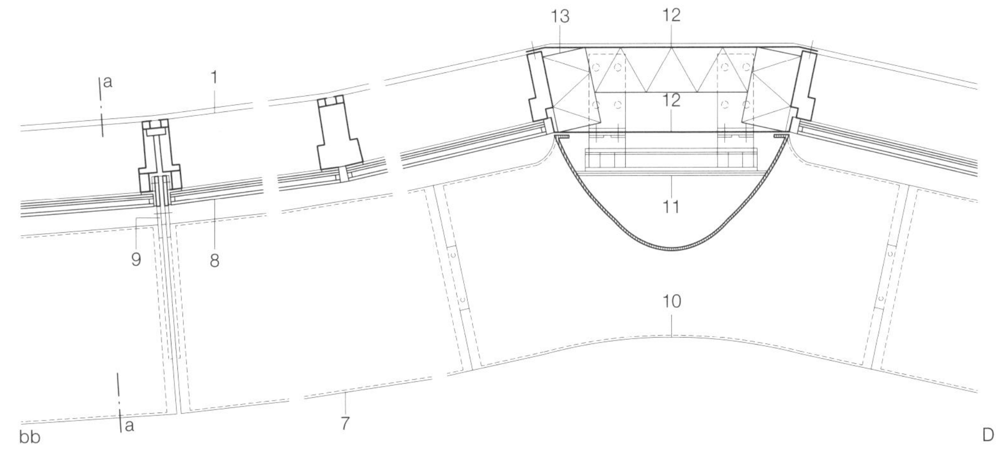

bb

D

Private house

Minamituru-gunn, Japan, 2006

Architect:
Takeshi Hosaka, Yokohama
Assistant:
Megumi Hosaka
Structural engineer:
Hirofumi Ohno, Tokyo

This house with its abstract form of white blocks apparently floating in the air represents a powerful contrast to the rural surroundings. From this location, near Mount Fuji and an attractive lakes landscape, the client can enjoy delightful views of the mountains but also ensure that the young family is not too close to the nearby scenic route for tourists and the other houses scattered around the neighbourhood. What appears to be the ground floor at first sight actually turns out to be nothing more than a solid fair-face concrete wall surrounding the garden to ensure the necessary privacy. On the upper floor, another solid wall around the terrace again provides a private enclosure for the family.
Whereas the plot is fully screened off from the outside world, the building itself seems to merge with the garden. A vital element in the architect's concept was to design the boundary between interior and exterior to be as transparent and invisible as possible. This impression is achieved with the help of two continuous transparent facade sections made from 20 mm thick PMMA, which form a lightweight envelope adequate for the Japanese climate. This material reflects hardly any light and so the view of the outside world from inside, or vice versa, is hardly disrupted. Disturbing vertical posts were also unnecessary, and so the boundary between interior and exterior vanishes almost entirely. The living quarters are grouped around a central core; each area has a glazed sliding door providing access to the outside. Only the bedrooms have internal, white sliding doors so that they can be closed off from the other areas. The apparently solid areas of the facade conceal a steel framework clad in plywood coated with a glass fibre-reinforced polymer.

- PMMA continuous facade sections
- Coating of glass fibre-reinforced polymer

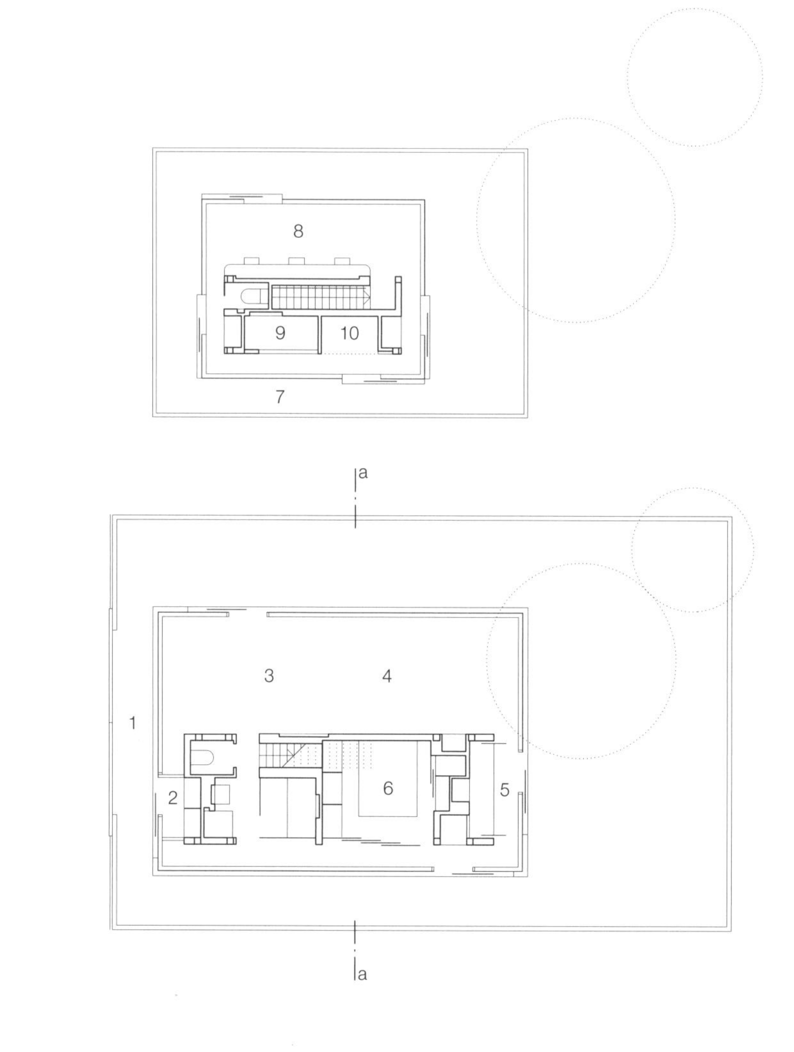

Section • Plans
Scale 1:200

1 Garden
2 Entrance
3 Living room
4 Dining area
5 Kitchen
6 Bedroom
7 Terrace
8 Children's room
9 Bunk bed
10 Storage

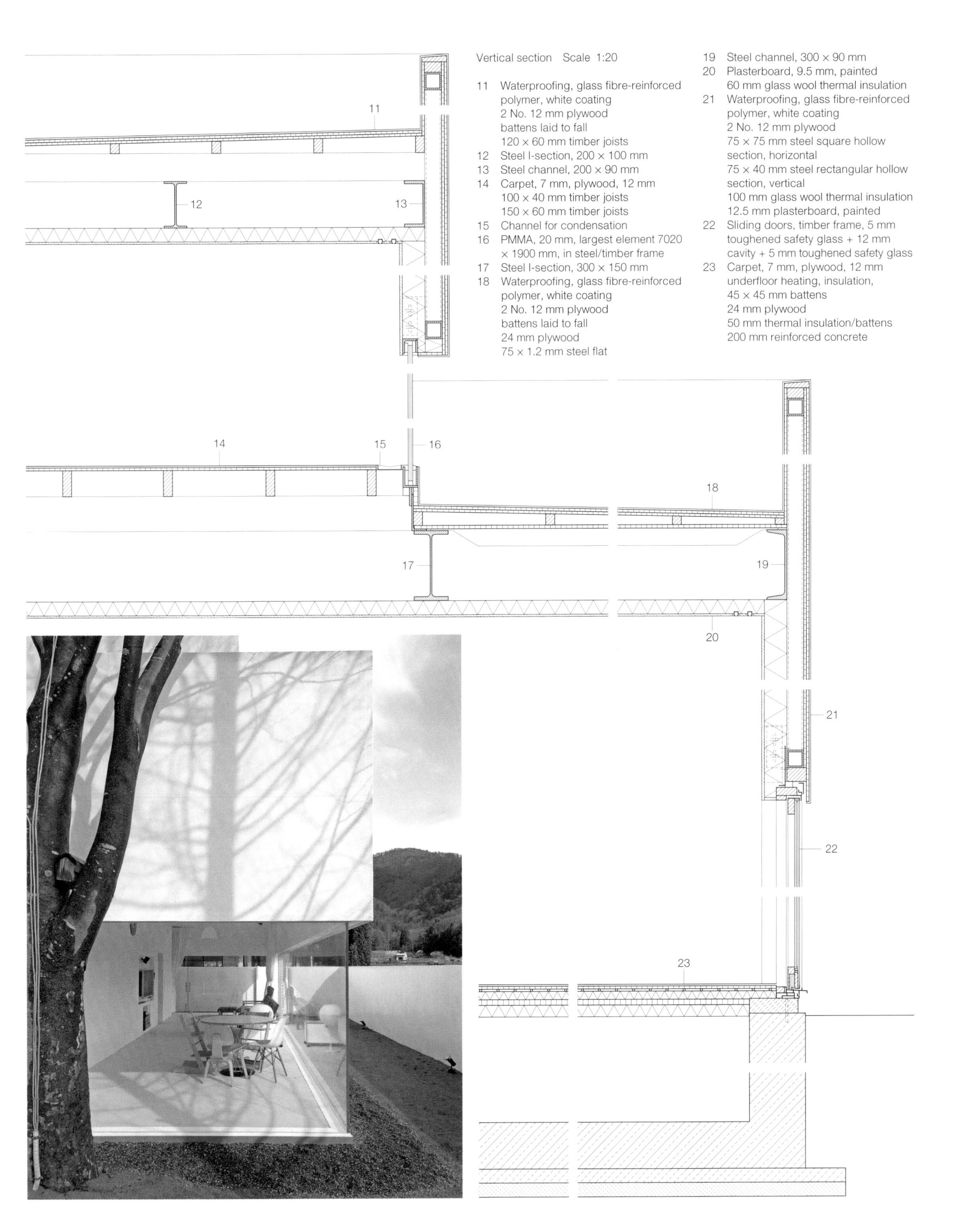

Vertical section Scale 1:20

11 Waterproofing, glass fibre-reinforced polymer, white coating
2 No. 12 mm plywood
battens laid to fall
120 × 60 mm timber joists
12 Steel I-section, 200 × 100 mm
13 Steel channel, 200 × 90 mm
14 Carpet, 7 mm, plywood, 12 mm
100 × 40 mm timber joists
150 × 60 mm timber joists
15 Channel for condensation
16 PMMA, 20 mm, largest element 7020 × 1900 mm, in steel/timber frame
17 Steel I-section, 300 × 150 mm
18 Waterproofing, glass fibre-reinforced polymer, white coating
2 No. 12 mm plywood
battens laid to fall
24 mm plywood
75 × 1.2 mm steel flat
19 Steel channel, 300 × 90 mm
20 Plasterboard, 9.5 mm, painted
60 mm glass wool thermal insulation
21 Waterproofing, glass fibre-reinforced polymer, white coating
2 No. 12 mm plywood
75 × 75 mm steel square hollow section, horizontal
75 × 40 mm steel rectangular hollow section, vertical
100 mm glass wool thermal insulation
12.5 mm plasterboard, painted
22 Sliding doors, timber frame, 5 mm toughened safety glass + 12 mm cavity + 5 mm toughened safety glass
23 Carpet, 7 mm, plywood, 12 mm
underfloor heating, insulation,
45 × 45 mm battens
24 mm plywood
50 mm thermal insulation/battens
200 mm reinforced concrete

Seeko'o Hotel

Bordeaux, France, 2007

Architects:
Atelier Architecture King Kong, Bordeaux
Paul Marion, Jean-Christophe Masnada,
Frederic Neau, Laurent Portejoie
Project team:
Olivier Oslislo, Fontaneda Calzada David,
Max Hildebrant
Structural engineers:
ETBA, Bordeaux

The dockyards on the banks of the River Garonne in Bordeaux are one of the city's landmarks. The decision to erect a "designer" hotel on this historical site initiated a heated debate. The result is a building that fits in well with its urban environment even though its form and exterior is a deliberate contrast to the sandstone facades of the nearby buildings. The smooth, white surface of the hotel's facade is an interpretation of its name: "Seeko'o" is the Inuit word for iceberg and glacier. The kinks in the facade line up with the eaves of the adjacent buildings and run straight across the facade regardless of any openings. The window formats of the historic surroundings have been incorporated in principle, but given a new interpretation by either setting back the panes of glass or fitting them flush with the facade surface.
This was the first time that pigmented, acrylic-bonded mineral boards were used for external cladding on a large scale. The vertical board formats are fitted together at the sides by means of an alternating convex/concave detail. They were assembled from standard boards and cut to a maximum panel size of 2.2 × 5.5 m as specified by the architects; the edges are rebated. The chamfered arrises on all sides are designed as movement joints and compensate for temperature-induced changes in length of approx. 3 mm per metre. The joints are reinforced at the back with 6 mm thick × 50 mm wide strips, which accommodate the movements and transfer the loads to the loadbearing aluminium framework. Concealed Squirrel® fixings are used for attaching the synthetic panels. Squirrel® fixings are round plugs made from a mineral material which are glued into the back of each panel, accurately fitted into milled cut-outs. C-form aluminium sections are screwed into the central metal insert and then clipped to the supporting framework for the facade every 45 cm. Consequently, only the fine structure of the curving panel formats is visible from the outside.

- Facade panels made from mineral board
- Concealed fixings made from a mineral material

Vertical sections
Scale 1:20

1 Facade panel, mineral board, UV-resistant, 12.3 mm, with aluminium fixing rail on back aluminium supporting frame (vertical and horizontal rails) 250 mm reinforced concrete external wall 100 mm mineral wool internal insulation 13 mm plasterboard
2 Window frame, aluminium
3 Opening light, aluminium frame with insulating glass
4 Window sill, aluminium, 3 mm, painted
5 Lining to window reveal 12.3 mm mineral board aluminium supporting frame screwed to reinforced concrete
6 Fixing bracket, aluminium
7 Point fixing, aluminium
8 Toughened safety glass with silk-screen printing
9 Plasterboard, 13 mm 50 mm mineral wool internal insulation
10 Aluminium angle, 120 × 70 × 5 mm
11 Insulating glass: 8 mm laminated safety glass + 12 mm cavity + 8 mm float glass glued to aluminium window frame

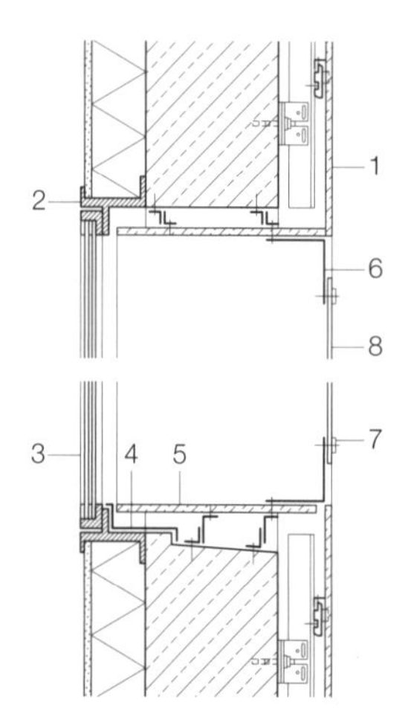

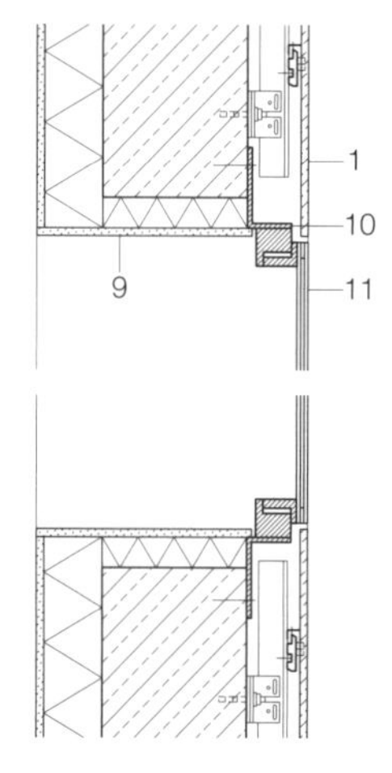

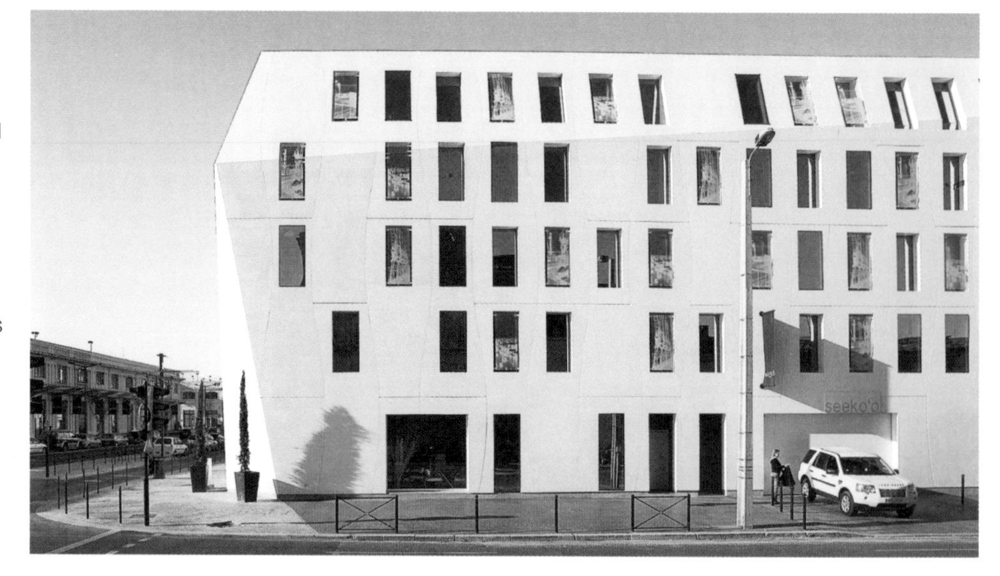

Private house

Müllheim, Germany, 2005

Architects:
Pfeifer Roser Kuhn, Freiburg
Project team:
Thomas Gillich (project manager),
Nils Schinker, Simone Wechsler
Structural engineers:
Greschik + Falk + Partner, Berlin
Energy concept:
Delzer Kybernetik, Lörrach
Building services:
Balck + Partner, Heidelberg

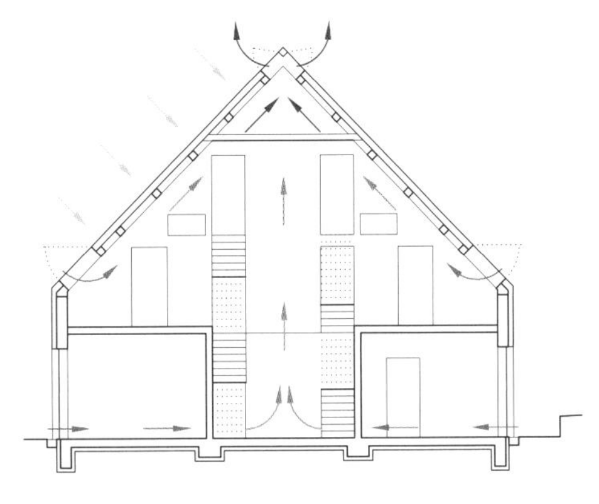

aa Air flows in summer

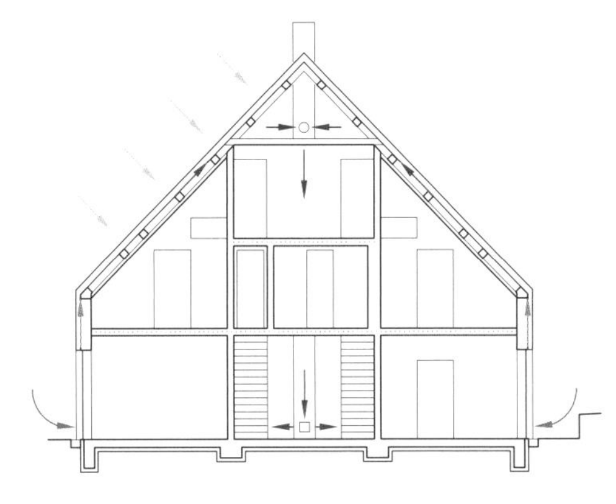

bb Air flows in winter

Behind its shimmering bluish exterior, this house with its traditonal form measuring 12 × 12 m on plan offers ample space for two families. Two sets of stairs, facing in opposite directions, in the central, common hallway provide access to the separate living quarters. The plan layouts are turned through 90° on each floor so that both families benefit from the sun's light and warmth to the same extent.
Whereas the gable walls consist of rendered aerated concrete blocks, and therefore ensure a good level of thermal mass and good insulation, the walls below the eaves and the roof surfaces form the heart of the building's passive solar energy system. The walls are made up of an inner leaf of edge-fixed solid timber elements and an outer leaf of large-format, translucent multi-wall polycarbonate sheets, which continue across the entire roof to form a uniform envelope. The 8 cm wide cavity functions as an air collector: solar irradiation heats up the air very quickly, which then rises. The ensuing suction opens the simple check flaps at the base of the cavity, which draws in fresh air. In the roof space, the heated air is directed into the rooms below with the help of a fan and a flue. Six manually controlled roof windows either side of the ridge permit further simple temperature control; any hot air not required can simply escape by opening these windows. The high U-value of the polycarbonate sheets (1.15 W/m²K) makes further insulation in the facade unnecessary. The low self-weight and high hail impact resistance of the material are further benefits. In addition, the material's translucency is important for the roof; it allows sunlight to enter the central hallway, which keeps the house warm throughout the year. Thermoactive concrete floor slabs also contribute to heating the rooms.

- Building envelope made from multi-wall polycarbonate sheets
- Thermal insulating effect

Sections
Plan of ground floor
Scale 1:250
1 Hall
2 Kitchen
3 Living room
4 Bedroom
5 Storage

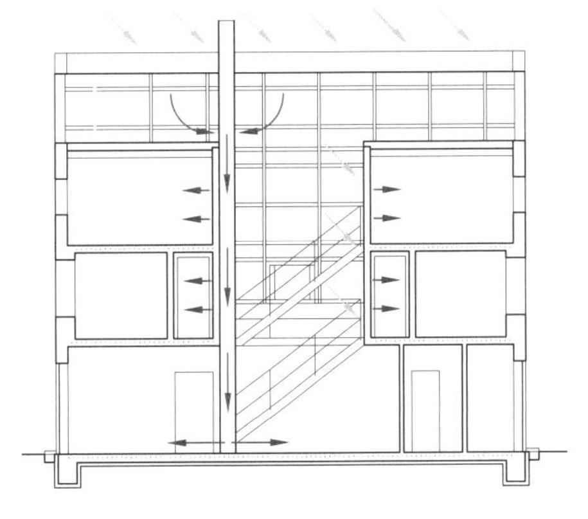

cc Heat distribution in winter

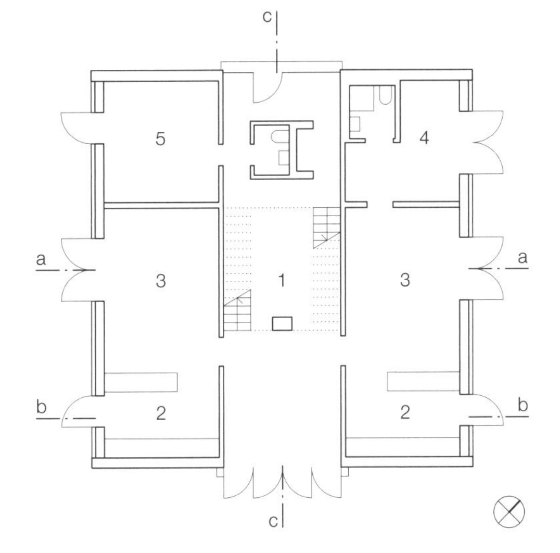

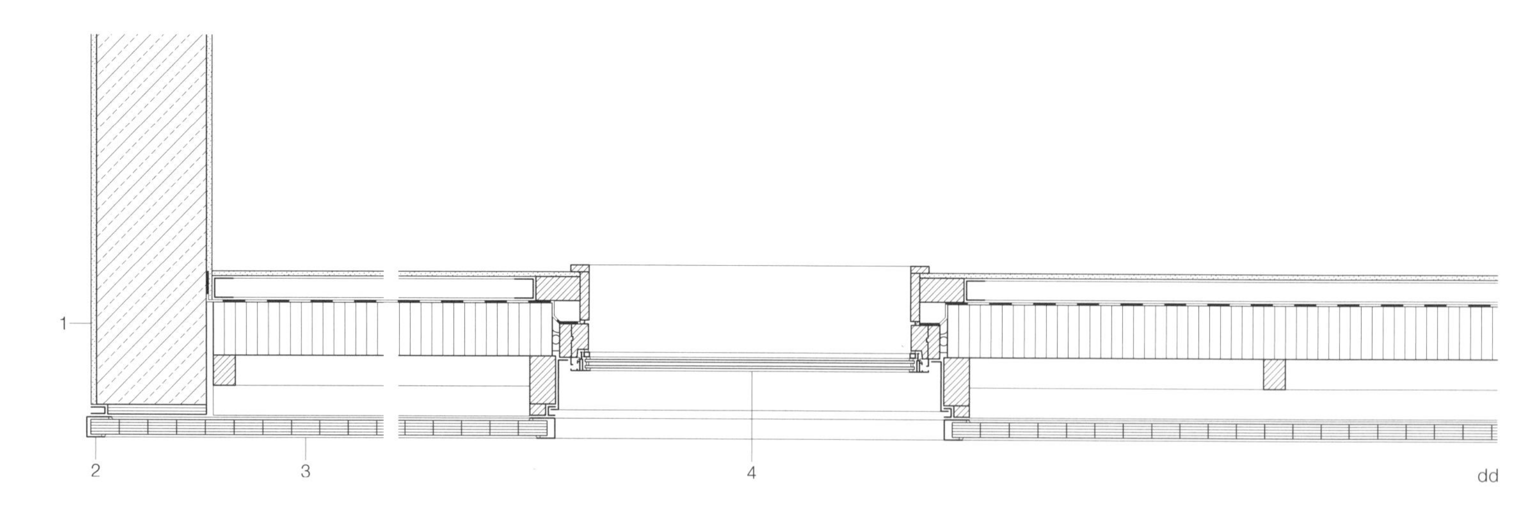

Horizontal section • Vertical section Scale 1:20

1 Gable wall: 15 mm render
300 mm aerated concrete plaster
2 Aluminium trim, 50 × 50 mm channel
3 Wall construction:
40 mm polycarbonate multi-wall sheets
flat suction anchor
60 × 80 mm battens
60 × 80 mm counter battens
140 mm edge-fixed solid timber elements
vapour barrier
50 mm steel channel framing
12.5 mm plasterboard
4 Insulating glass:
4 mm + 16 mm cavity + 4 mm
5 Roof construction:
40 mm polycarbonate multi-wall sheets
60 × 80 mm battens
60 × 80 mm counter battens
6 Sheet metal flashing
7 Floor construction, terrace:
50 mm concrete flags
150 mm granite ballast
8 Thermoactive reinforced concrete suspended floor slab, 190 mm
9 Check flap: PTFE-membrane, stainless steel insect screen
10 Floor construction, ground floor:
220 mm thermoactive reinforced concrete ground slab
100 mm thermal insulation
50 mm blinding
11 Sheet metal ridge capping
12 Top-hung roof windows
13 Purlin, 140 × 140 mm

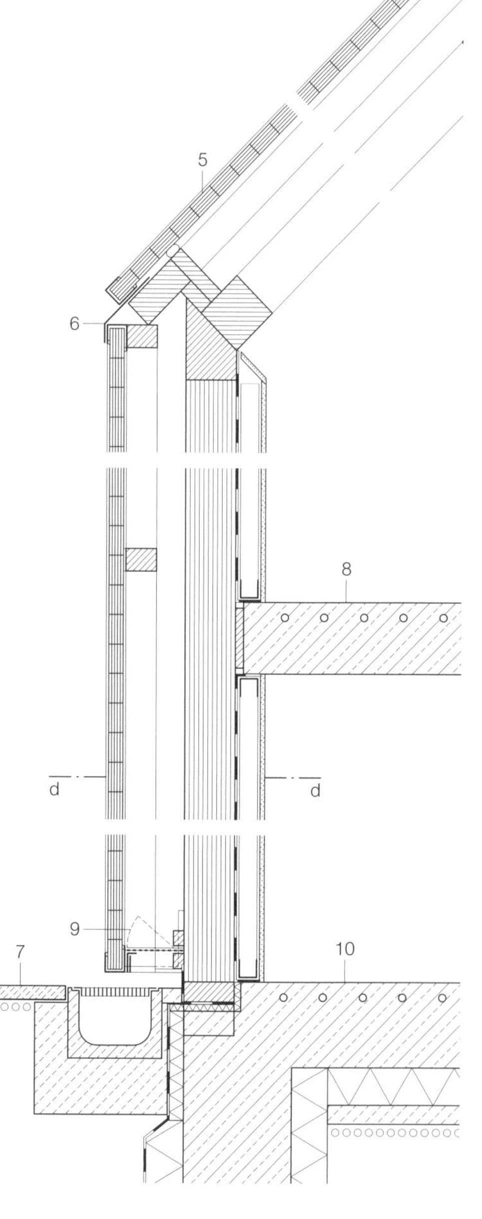

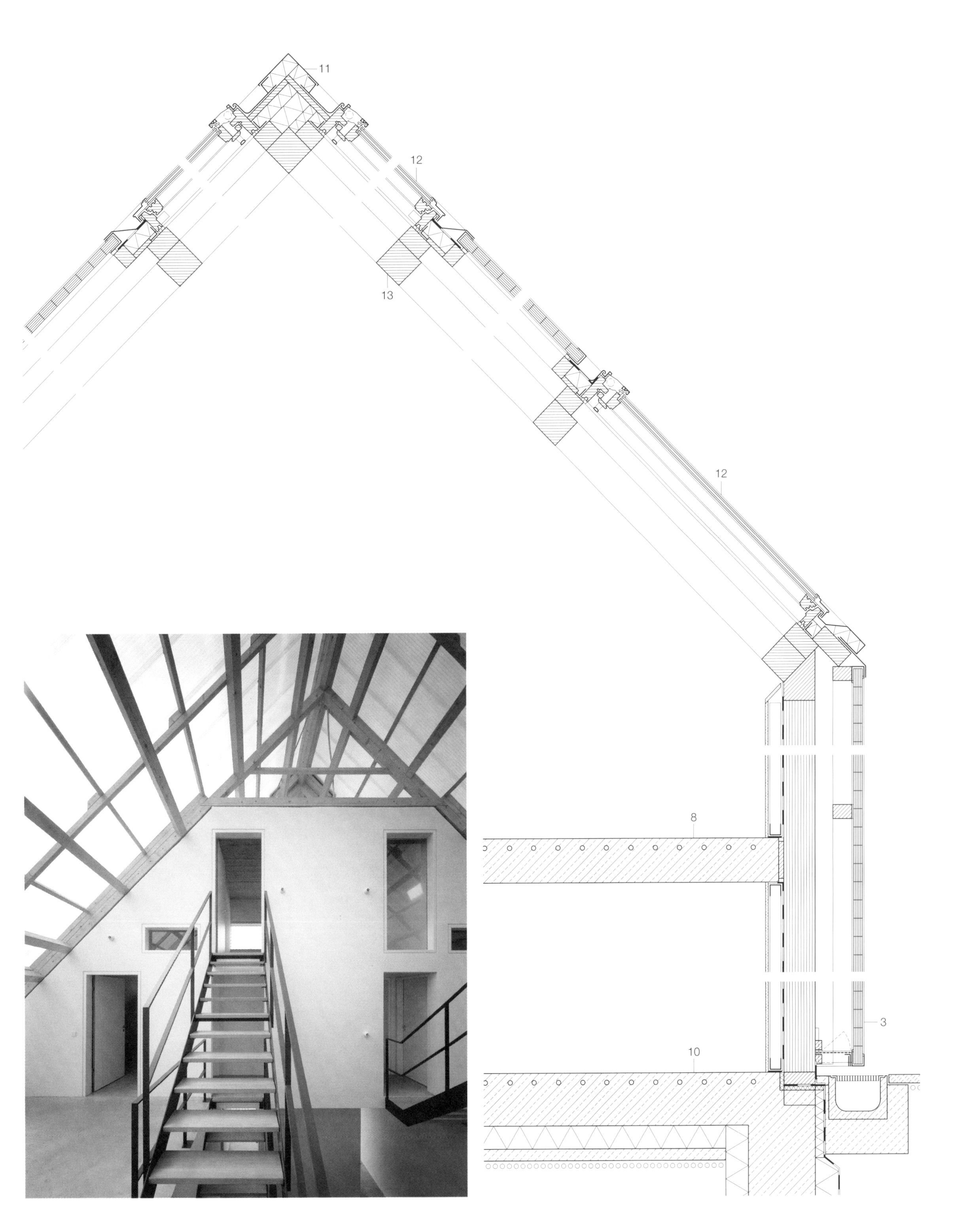
11
12
13
12
8
3
10

Flagship store and company headquarters

London, UK, 2008

Architects:
Squire & Partners, London
Project team:
A. Mangiavacchi (project manager),
Y. Chan, T. Gledstone, M. Larizadeh,
M. Levinson, A. Medland, F. Renton,
T. Sheridan, M. Squire, S. Steed
Structural engineers:
Fluid Structures, London

The new London headquarters of the fashion label Reiss combines various functions under one roof: the flagship store extending over three storeys, above that design studios, tailoring and dressmaking facilities, offices and a penthouse. Four British architectural practices were invited to take part in a competition to design an unmistakable exterior for the building, situated very close to Oxford Street, to ensure that the brand's image would be visible to the public. Squire & Partners, a London-based practice, succeeded with its concept for enclosing the various uses within an opaque veil of vertical PMMA sheets. The use of PMMA sheets 50 mm thick enabled vertical cut-outs of different widths and depths to be milled in the material to create a three-dimensional effect, enhanced by the alternating polished and matt surface finishes. Depending on the viewing angle and the lighting, the cladding either takes on a technical character, resembling a barcode, or the silky sheen of a folded material extending the full height of the building. During the day, the PMMA cladding ensures pleasant, non-glare illumination in the interior. But the facade at night offers the most impressive effect: individually controlled LED lighting strips behind each panel transform the facade into a semi-transparent curtain of light, helped by the high light-channelling effect of the material.
Every single panel is supported on two T-shaped brackets and also held at the sides by stainless steel bars fitted into milled slots, which are connected to the facade structure at three points. This sliding connection transfers the wind loads without causing any restraint stresses due to temperature-induced changes in length. The almost invisible fixing details for the elements emphasize the "floating" effect of this facade.

- PMMA sheets with individual profiling
- Different material thicknesses and surface finishes to create a three-dimensional effect

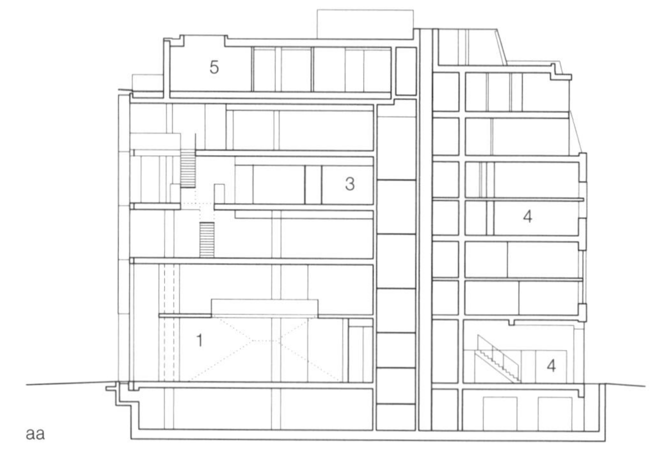

Section
Plans
Scale 1:500

1 Sales
2 Reception/office
3 Office/design studio
4 Apartment
5 Penthouse

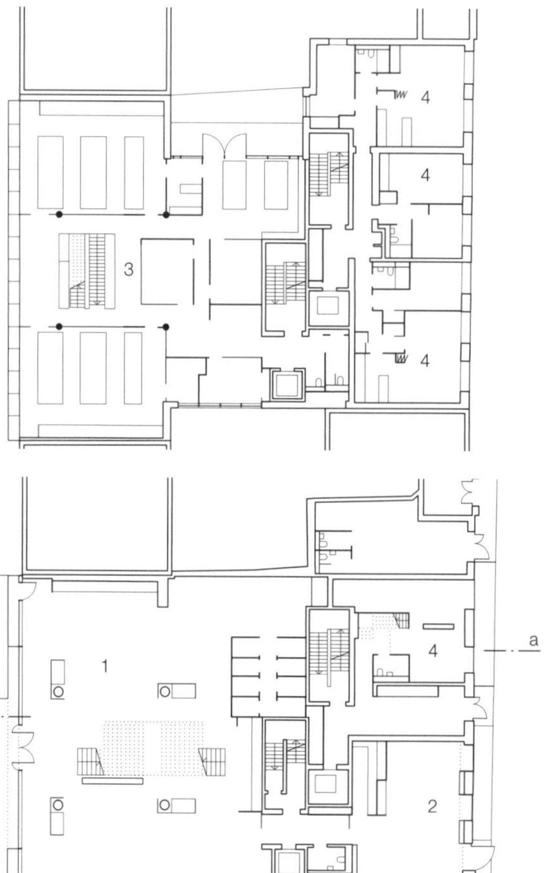

3rd floor

Ground floor

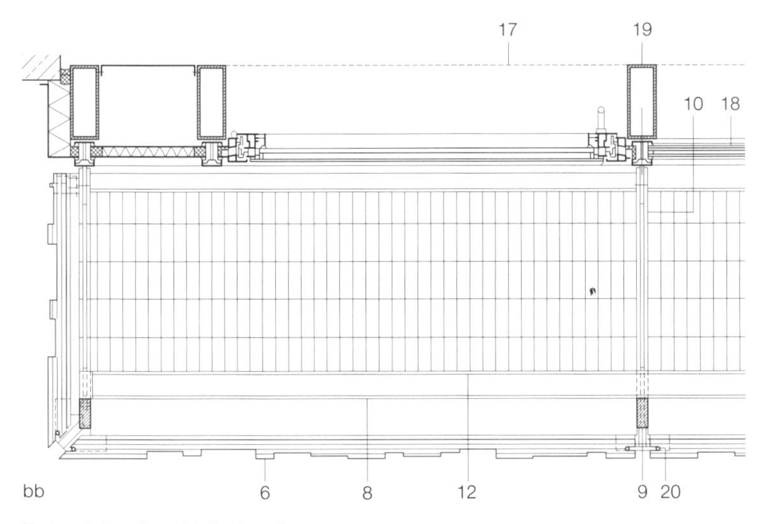

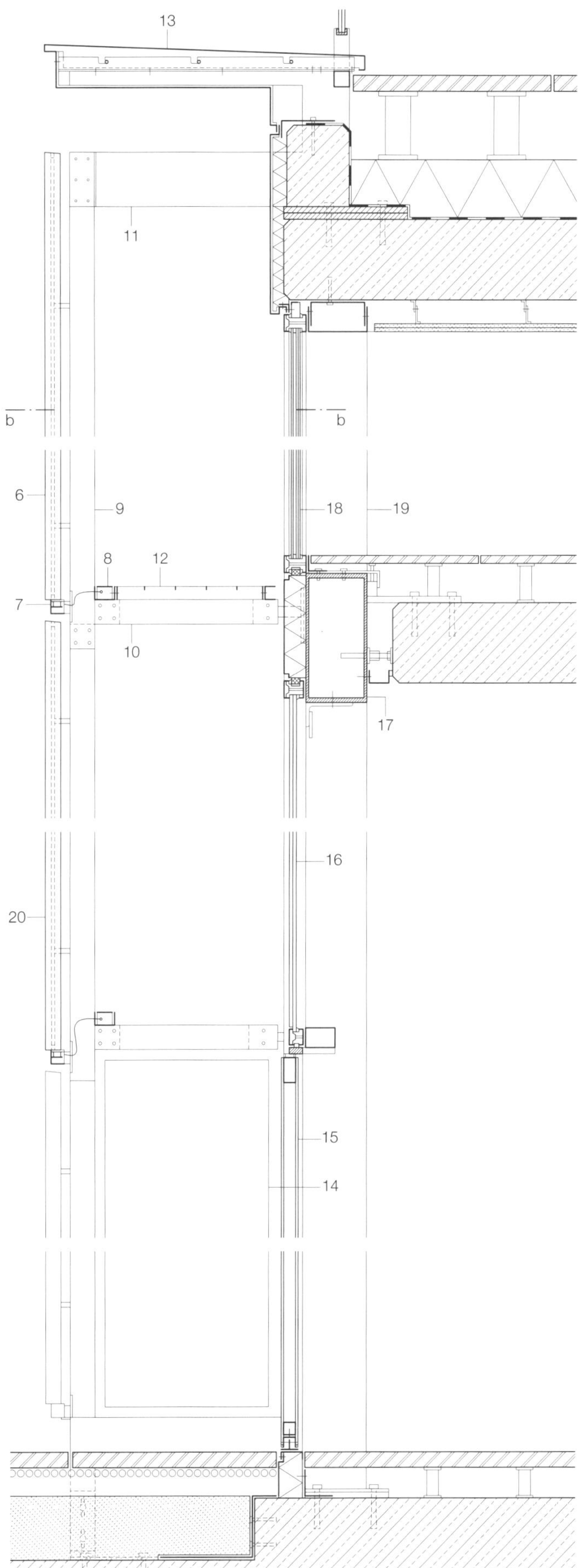

Horizontal section • Vertical section
Scale 1:20

6 PMMA sheet, 30–50 mm, milled, polished and matt finishes
7 Cover to LED mounting, 42 × 42 mm aluminium angle, brushed
8 Cable conduit, 40 × 70 mm steel channel, with cover
9 Facade post, 30 × 80 mm steel flat, powder-coated
10 Facade stay, 30 × 80 mm steel flat, powder-coated
11 Cantilevering support, 30 × 170 mm steel flat
12 Maintenance walkway, 40 × 10 mm open-grid flooring, powder-coated
13 Capping, sheet aluminium
14 Side panel in cavity, toughened glass
15 Entrance door, 2 No. 8 mm toughened safety glass, glued to steel frame both sides
16 Shop facade, single glazing, 2 No. 11 mm laminated safety glass
17 Perimeter floor beam, 200 × 400 × 5 mm steel rectangular hollow section
18 Office facade, insulating glass: 2 No. 6 mm laminated safety glass + 16 mm cavity + 6 mm toughened safety glass
19 Facade column, 200 × 80 mm steel rectangular hollow section (adjacent door only)
20 Retainer, stainless steel bar, ∅ 7 mm, fixed to facade posts

Manufacture and profiling of PMMA sheets by means of CNC milling

Vertical section • Horizontal section Scale 1:5

1 PMMA sheet, 30–50 mm, milled, polished and matt finishes
2 Retainer, stainless steel bar, Ø 7 mm, fixed to facade posts, 4 No. per storey
3 Steel fixing for retainer bar
4 Cover to LED mounting, 42 × 42 mm aluminium angle, brushed
5 LED lighting strip, individually controllable and programmable
6 LED cover, glass strip
7 Steel bracket for carrying the load of the PMMA sheets
8 Fixing screw, stainless steel, countersunk
9 Facade post, 30 × 80 mm steel flat, powder-coated
10 Facade stay, 30 × 80 mm steel flat, powder-coated
11 Cable conduit, 40 × 70 mm steel channel
12 Cover to cable conduit, 60 × 5 mm steel flat
13 Maintenance walkway, 40 × 10 mm open-grid flooring, powder-coated

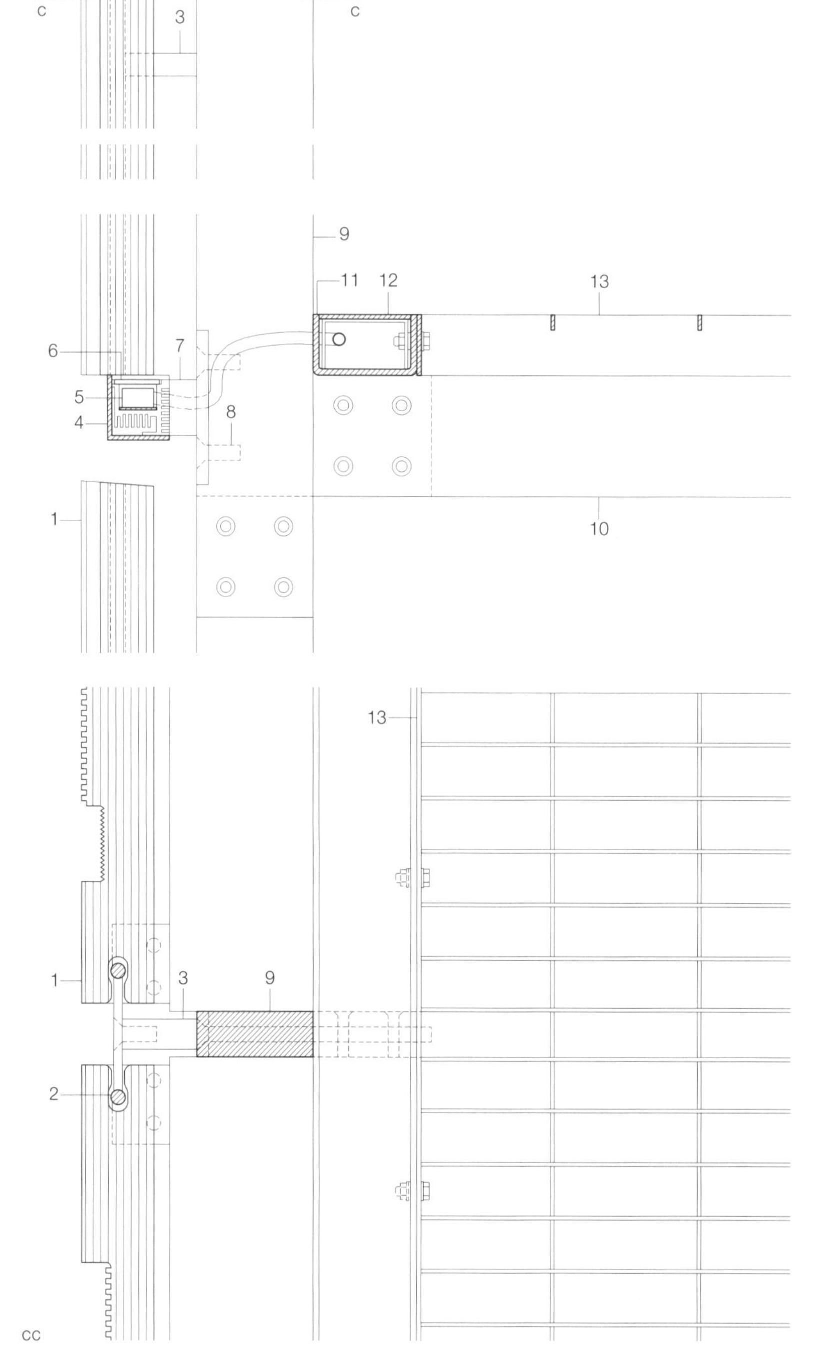

Office pavilion

Madrid, Spain, 2009

Architects:
Selgas Cano, Madrid
Jose Selgas Rubio, Lucia Cano Pintos
Assistant:
Jose de Villar

This unconventional office "tube", partly sunk below ground level, is in the immediate vicinity of the architects' home and guarantees an unobstructed view of the trees on this plot of land. The tube consists of two parts: on the north side curving 20 mm thick PMMA over the corridor zone, and on the south side a sandwich of polyester sheets with translucent polyethylene insulation to prevent glare in the working area. Such polyester sheets are used in some rolling stock running on German railways, but are not available in small quantities. The architects therefore had to wait for the Deutsche Bahn to order some of this material in order to obtain a section 12 m long! The work on site also proved to be much more difficult than had been originally envisaged; many different tasks had to be coordinated: one company was responsible for bending the sheets, another for installing them, and yet another for the gable ends. The latter are made from PMMA with a matt finish and can be opened for cross-ventilation with the help of pulleys and counterweights. The northern half of the tube, in transparent PMMA, is made from 10 standardised parts with slots in the edges only for inserting a loose tongue sealed with silicone. The view out is therefore unobstructed – only the rain leaves marks and is noisy overhead.

- Shaped PMMA
- Translucent polyethylene insulation

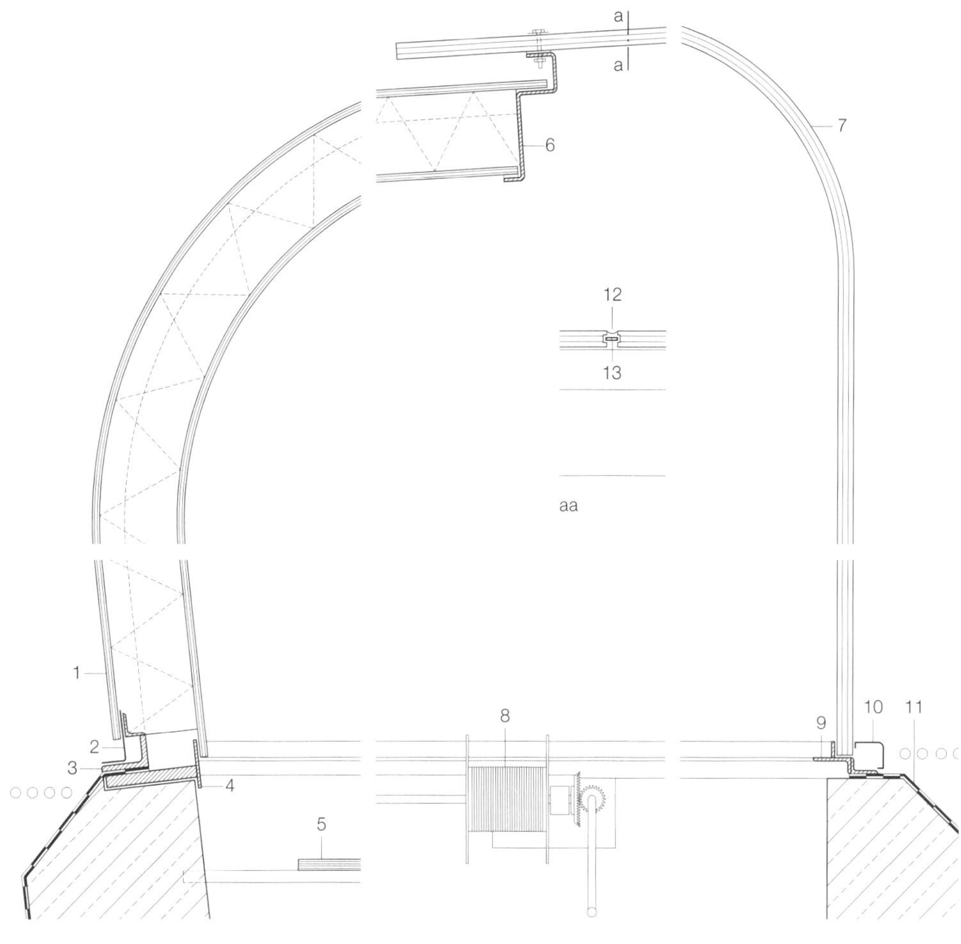

Vertical section
Scale 1:10

1 Glass fibre-reinforced polyester, 2 No. 10 mm, with translucent polyethylene thermal insulation in between, 100 mm
2 Flashing, bent galvanised steel sheet, 2 mm
3 Galvanised steel angle, 60 × 40 × 7 mm, welded to galvanised steel angle, 30 × 30 × 2.5 mm
4 Galvanised steel sheet, 4 mm, welded to galvanised steel plate, 15 mm
5 Shelf, 15 mm PMMA, on ∅ 16 mm round steel brackets
6 Galvanised steel sheet, 3 mm, painted white
7 PMMA sheet, 20 mm, transparent PVC support, transparent
8 Winch for polyamide rope: 2 No. ∅ 160 mm stainless steel discs with ∅ 80 mm drum in between and crank handle
9 Steel angles, 2 No. 40 × 20 × 3 mm, welded to 2 mm steel flat
10 Cover, bent galvanised steel sheet, 2 mm
11 Geotextile, 2 mm
2 mm waterproofing
250 mm fair-face concrete
(formwork: 70 mm rough tongue-and-groove boards)
12 Silicone seal
13 Loose tongue, 16 × 2 mm stainless steel

Company headquarters

Middelfart, Denmark, 2006

Architects:
KHR arkitekter, Copenhagen
Jan Søndergaard
Project team:
Henrik Danielsen, Emi Hatakana, Ole Jensen,
Claus Bang Lauridsen, Morten Vedelsbøl

The headquarters of this Danish manufacturer of glass fibre-reinforced polymers (GFRP) seems to form a gentle hill in the flat landscape. Development, production and offices are combined here under one roof, with an integral high-bay racking warehouse defining the maximum height of the building. All the functional areas of the production are grouped around this central element. Offices, development and marketing are housed in the three storeys on the east side of the building, separated from the production bay by glazing, which permits a visual link between the two areas.
Three large transparent "incisions" break up this elongated structure, lend it a certain dynamic. At the same time these atria ensure that plenty of daylight is distributed throughout the interior. The company's own products, some of them developed specifically for this project, were used for the building envelope. The outer leaf consists of vapour-tight sandwich panels clad with GFRP planks. Overlapping joints ensure that this outer leaf, in front of a ventilation cavity, remains rainproof. Specially formed GFRP sections were used for the window sills and window frames as well. The latter are very narrow on elevation yet still achieve a good insulation value. Both the pultruded sections and the facade panels are produced with a transparent resin so that the internal fibre reinforcement remains visible and lends the components a certain depth. The all-glass facades to the three atria also make use of GFRP sections, which are glued directly to the panes of glass. The prefabricated elements are merely bolted together and to the supporting structure underneath. The rigid adhesive joints enable the glass to be used for carrying the loads, which means that the frame dimensions could be much smaller than those of an aluminium facade.

- Facade planks made from glass fibre-reinforced polymer
- Very narrow window frames made from glass fibre-reinforced polymer

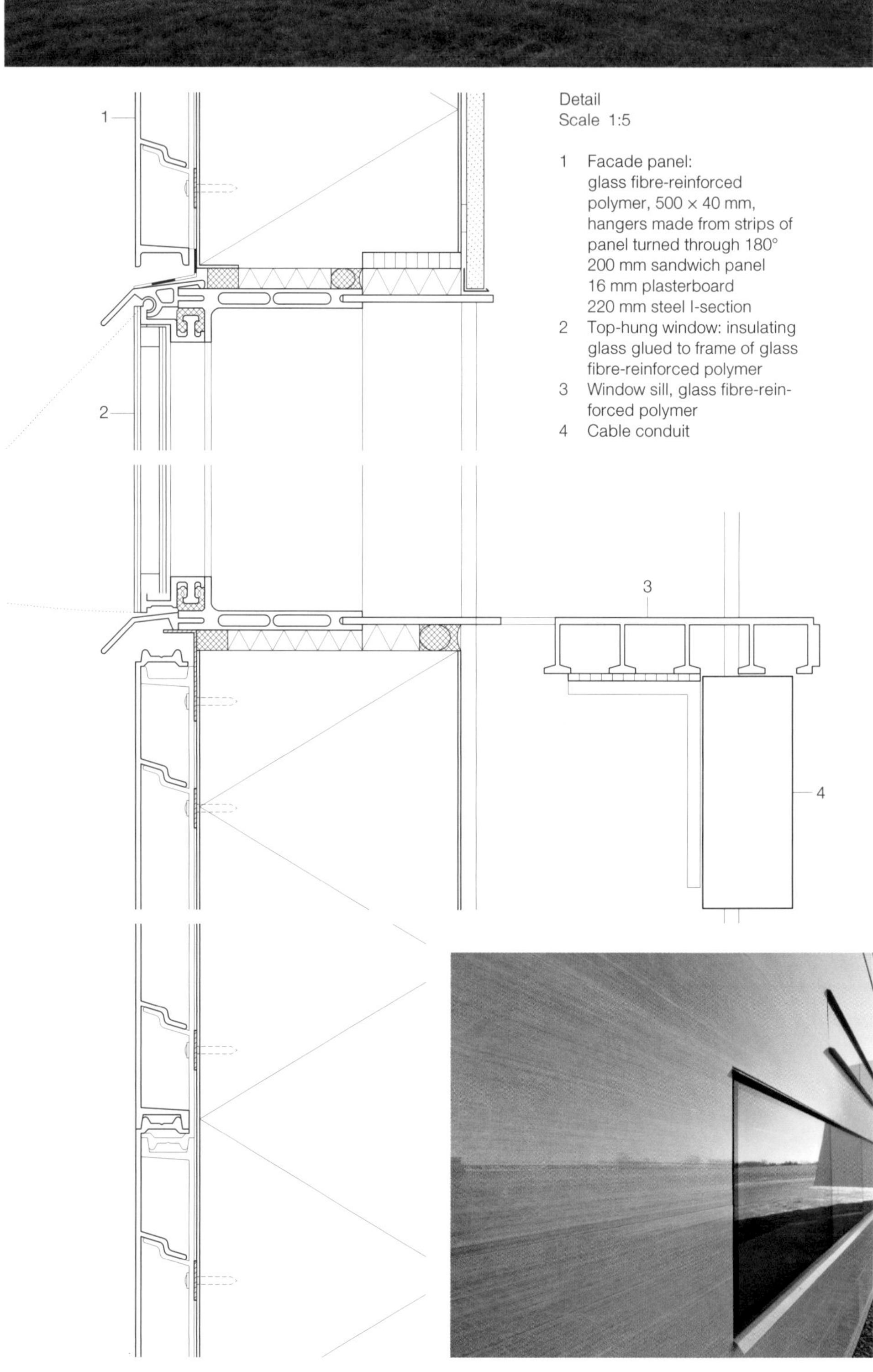

Detail
Scale 1:5

1 Facade panel:
glass fibre-reinforced polymer, 500 × 40 mm, hangers made from strips of panel turned through 180°
200 mm sandwich panel
16 mm plasterboard
220 mm steel I-section
2 Top-hung window: insulating glass glued to frame of glass fibre-reinforced polymer
3 Window sill, glass fibre-reinforced polymer
4 Cable conduit

House and office

Dachau, Germany, 2005

Architects:
Deffner Voitländer, Dachau
Project team:
Stefan Bohnengel, Julia Hertel, Kersten Waltz, Florian Zeitzler
Structural engineers:
Tischner & Pache, Dachau

This house and office belonging to the architects is located in the old quarter of Dachau. Almost half of the spacious open area on the eastern side of a building is sheltered beneath the long branches of a 100-year-old lime tree. This natural monument forms the focal point of this inner-city square and makes this site unique. All the habitable rooms of the building therefore face east. The view of the tree is the chief theme and the facade, too, reflects this. Photographs of the tree were projected onto the external leaf and so the contours of the tree seem to embrace the entire building.
The translucent envelope made from glass fibre-reinforced polymer makes this possible. The tree motif plotted on special paper is laminated into the manually laminated panels. The impregnation with synthetic resin means that the motif remains visible even though it is coated with the final layer of GFRP. Certain lighting conditions reveal the supporting framework behind, too. The multi-layer construction of the facade becomes visible, thus achieving a spatial effect and the lightness desired by the architects. The colour and form of the set-back top storey represent a stark contrast to the rest of the building even though the same materials have been used. Paint with a high pigment content was mixed into the synthetic resin to achieve the muted aubergine colouring. The individual panels have rounded arrises and corners, and include flanges that are overlapped and bolted together at the joints. The ensuing pattern of the joints lends the facade a certain structure. The negative moulds required for the individual GFRP elements were produced from polystyrene and polyurethane foam in unpretentious manual work with a file!
The building stands as a clear contrast to its surroundings without dominating them, and allows the old tree to take the limelight in this urban setting.

- Glass fibre-reinforced polymer
- Translucent building envelope with tree motif laminated into material
- Facade structure with rounded panels

Plans
Scale 1:250

1 Dustbins
2 Stairs
3 Office
4 Plotter room
5 Kitchen
6 Void
7 Meeting room
8 Bathroom
9 Room
10 Open-plan living/dining/kitchen
11 Pantry
12 Storage
13 Dressing room
14 Bedroom
15 Gallery
16 Rooftop terrace

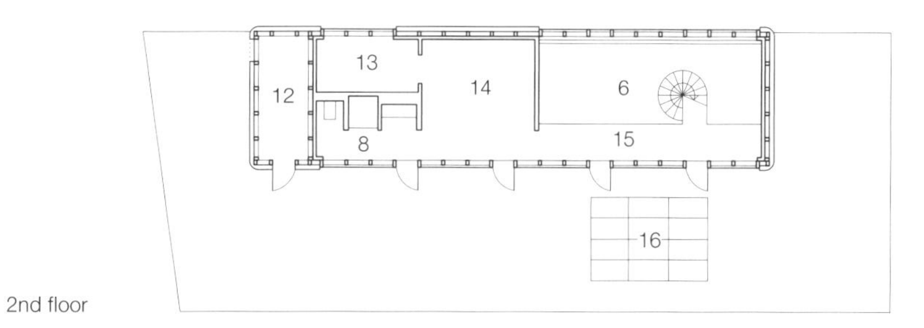

2nd floor

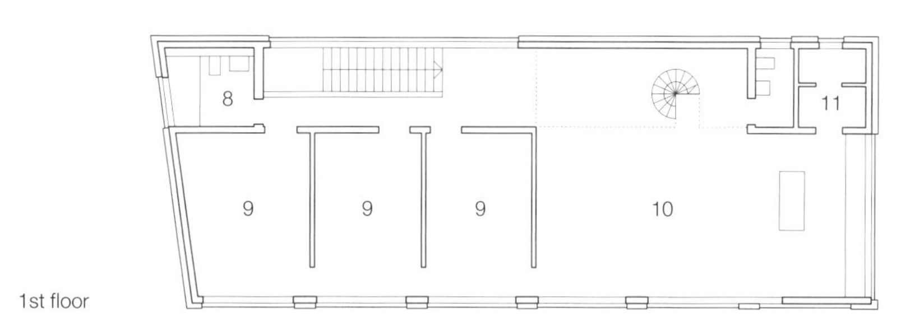

1st floor

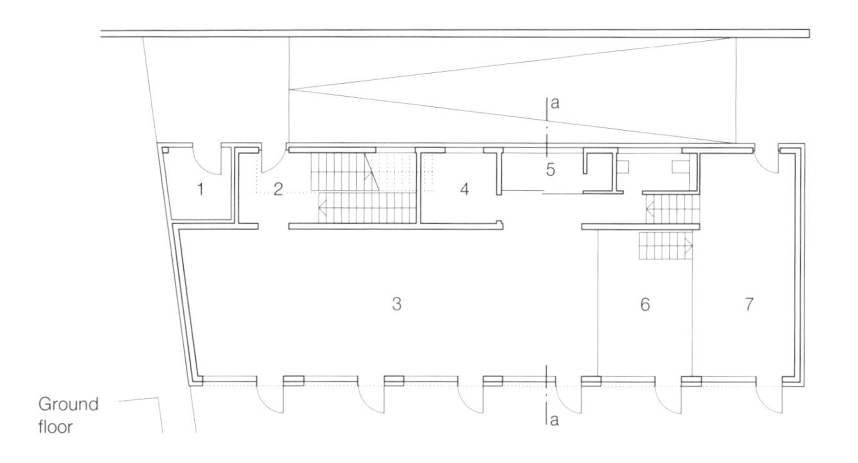

Ground floor

Vertical section
Scale 1:20
Horizontal sections
Scale 1:5

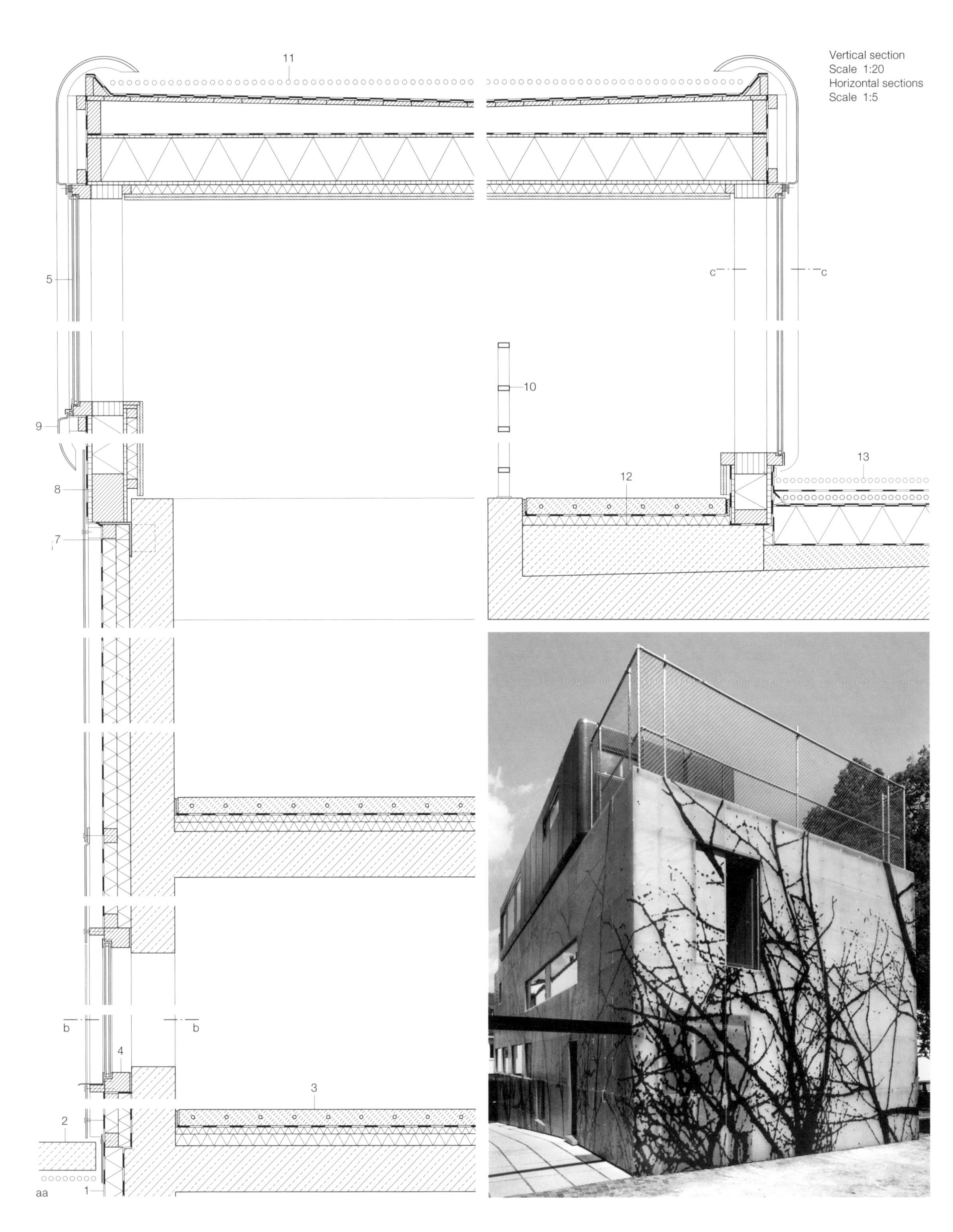

1 Thermal insulation, XPS, 80 mm
2 Paving flags, 120 mm, laid to falls
3 Cement screed, 80 mm, with underfloor heating
PE separating membrane, 30 mm impact sound insulation
50 mm thermal insulation, 200 mm RC
4 Wooden window frame, hemlock, 70 × 110 mm
5 Insulating glass: 4 mm tough. safety glass + 16 mm cavity + 4 mm tough. safety glass
6 GFRP panel, 4 mm, with spacers
40 × 60 mm battens, painted white
airtight membrane, diffusion-permeable
2 No. 60 mm mineral wool thermal insulation
200 mm reinforced concrete
7 Galvanised steel angle, 140 × 140 × 10 mm
8 Solid timber, 120 × 180 mm
9 airtight membrane, diffusion-permeable,
20 mm insulating board
140 mm cellulose thermal insulation
19 mm OSB, 40 mm MW thermal insulation
2 No. 12.5 mm plasterboard
10 Steel sections, 20 × 50 mm, coated
11 Gravel, 50 mm, 2 layers of bitumen waterproofing
20 mm timber sheathing
40–140 mm joists laid to falls
airtight membrane (building paper), 20 mm plywood
60 × 180 mm joists with 180 mm cellulose thermal insulation in between
20 mm OSB, 40 mm MW thermal insulation
2 No. 12.5 mm plasterboard
12 Lightweight concrete, 200–230 mm
13 Chippings, 50 mm, filter fleece, 50 mm gravel
2 layers of bitumen waterproofing, 180 mm thermal insulation, vapour barrier, screed laid to fall
180–300 mm reinforced concrete laid to fall
14 Steel plate, 10 mm, bedded on mortar
15 Galvanised steel circular hollow section, ∅ 48.3 mm
16 Plywood, 24 mm
17 Galvanised steel angle, 250 × 250 × 16 mm
18 Glazing bead, aluminium, 60 × 60 × 5 mm

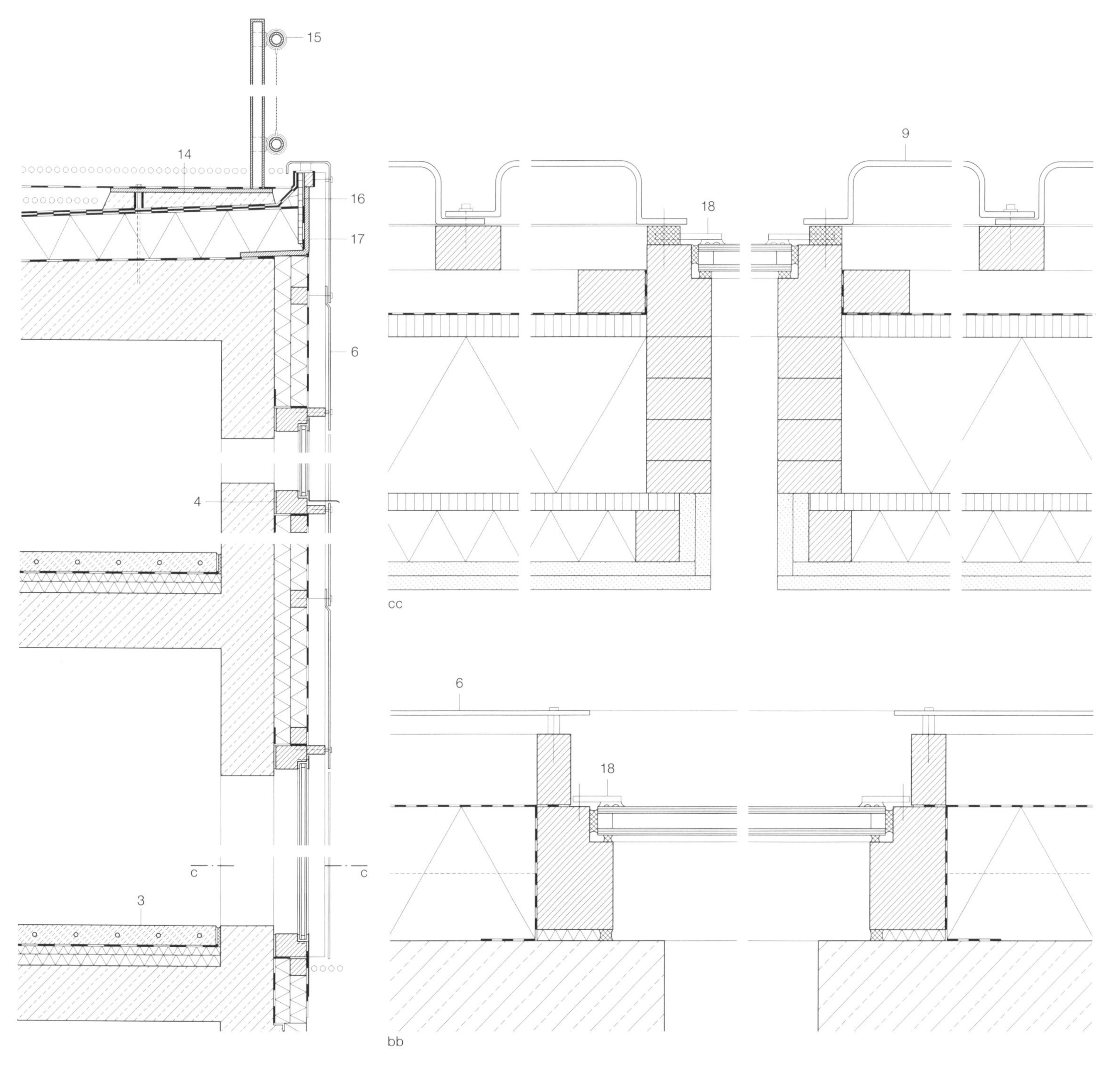

Mobile Art – Chanel Contemporary Art Container

Hong Kong, Tokyo, New York, 2008
and other locations worldwide

Zaha Hadid Architects, London
Zaha Hadid, Patrik Schumacher
Assistants:
Thomas Vietzke, Jens Borstelmann
Structural engineers:
Arup, London

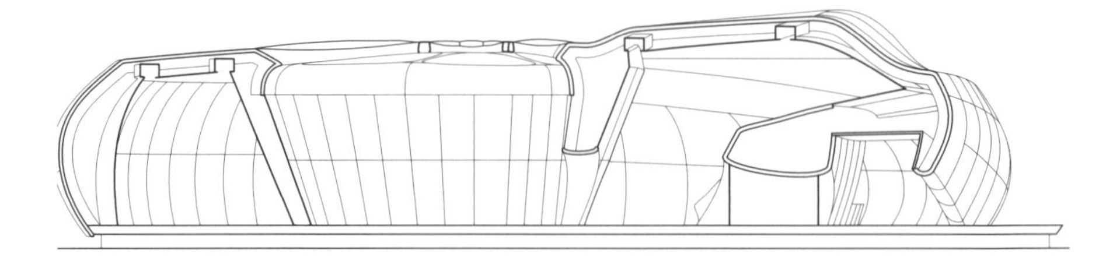

aa

Chanel's celebration of one of its cult objects, the "2.55" handbag, designed in February 1955, was reason enough for Karl Lagerfeld to invite artists to pay tribute to the company's founder and to create an exceptional ambience for the occasion. This took the form of a mobile pavilion which toured the world to underscore the cultural significance of Coco Chanel. The temporary building is no less a work of art than the exhibits it houses. The organic forms and homogeneous surfaces embody the transformability and elegance of Chanel. The arch-shaped facade elements are also tangible within the interior. They guide the visitor through the exhibition laid out around a central courtyard, which with its translucent roof is the perfect place to linger. A direct link between this and the glazed exit creates an association with the outside world. The transition is dynamic, flowing.
Designed in the computer as a 3D model, the building consists of approx. 7000 individual parts – a steel frame enclosed in an envelope of three different synthetic materials: translucent ETFE cushions to admit daylight into the interior, PVC-coated polyester fabric to cover the roof, and 400 manually laminated GFRP panels, each with a unique form, to clad the external walls. The latter were made possible with CNC-milled negative moulds. However, the greatest challenge was optimising the pavilion for transport and assembly. It had to travel around the world and so had to be reduced to compact segments that would fit into standard containers. Facade panels beyond a certain size are therefore split into three parts horizontally. It takes two weeks to erect the pavilion each time, 10 days to dismantle it. Ideas for saving time therefore had an influence on the form of construction and choice of materials. Mechanical ventilation plant installed beneath the platform ensures pleasant interior temperatures that responds to the particular climatic conditions of the pavilion's location.

- 3-ply ETFE cushions
- PVC-coated polyester fabric
- Manually laminated, painted GFRP panels

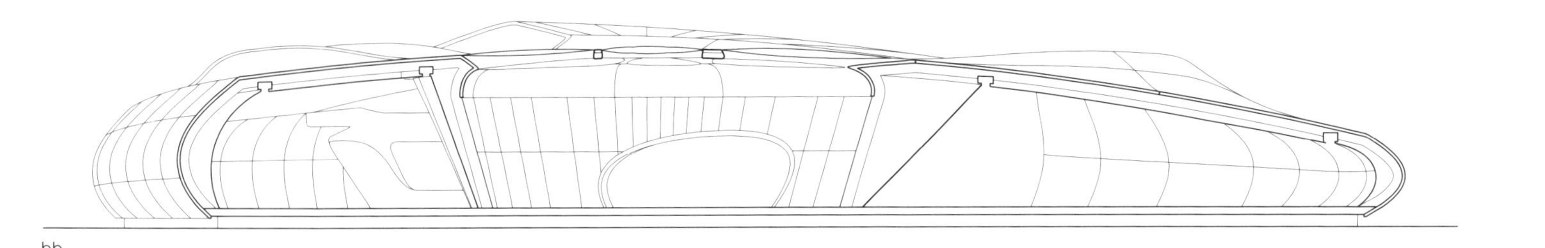

bb

Sections
Scale 1:250

Isometric view of roof
Plan
Scale 1:500

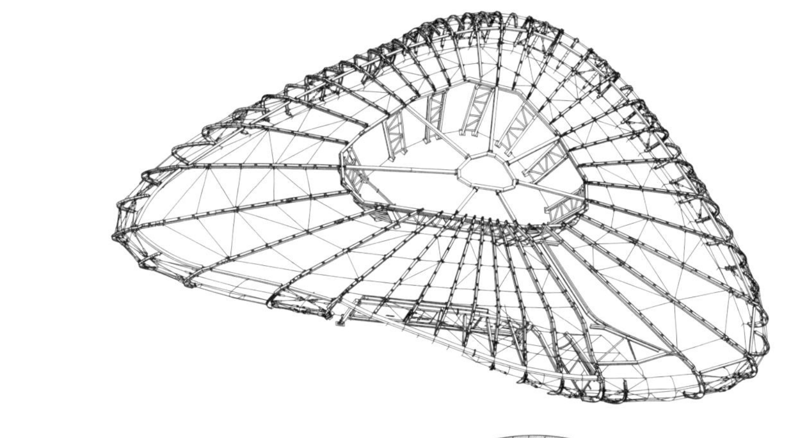

Fibre-reinforced polymer
Membrane made from PVC-coated polyester fabric
ETFE cushion

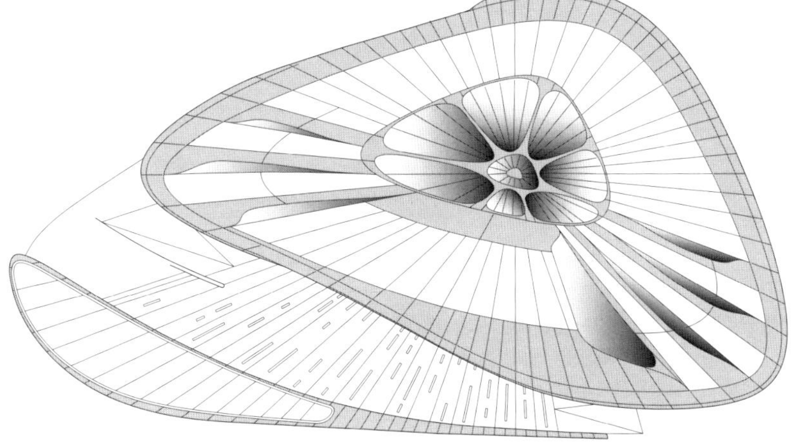

1 Ticket sales
2 Raised terrace
3 Entrance
4 Cloakroom
5 Exhibition
6 Central courtyard
7 Exit

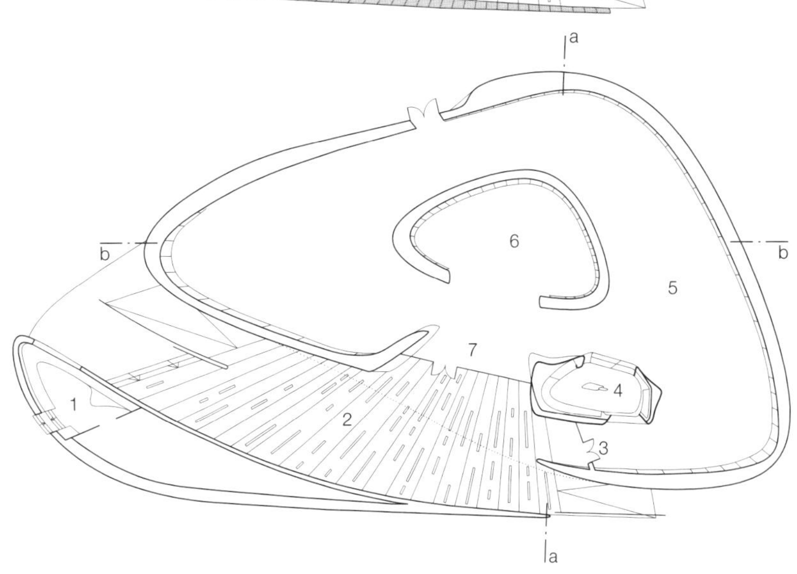

Vertical section
Scale 1:20

Details
Scale 1:5

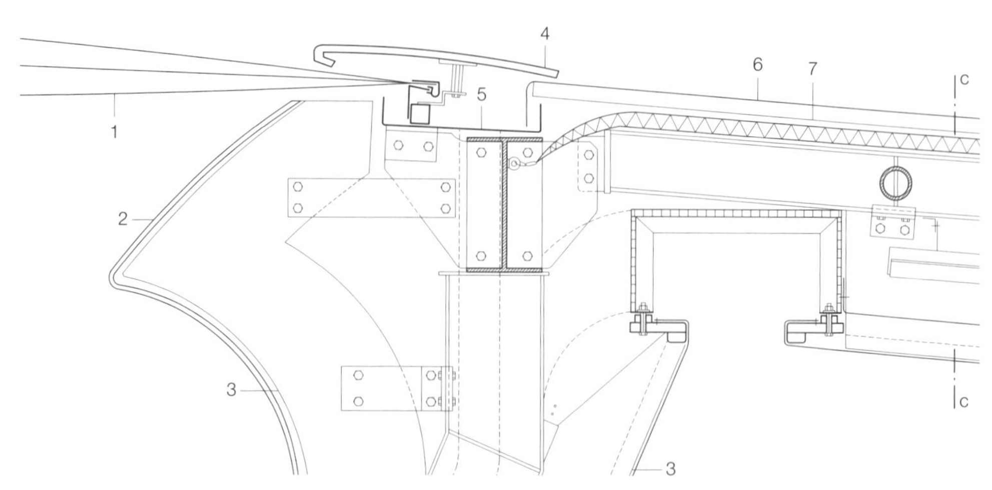

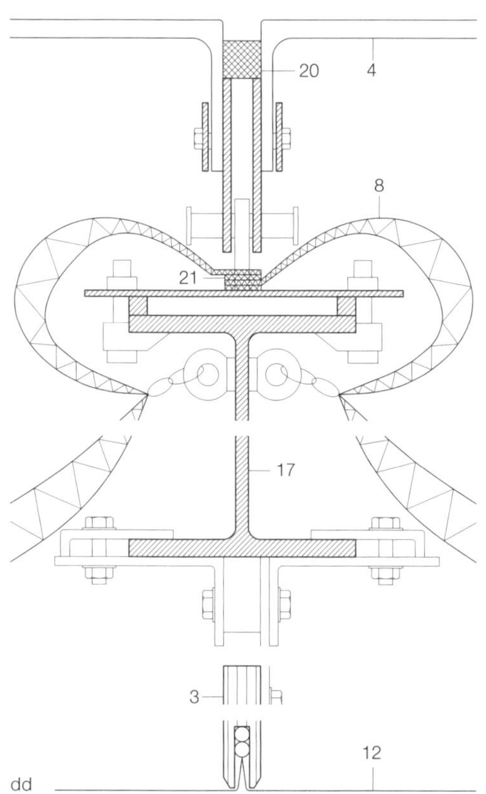

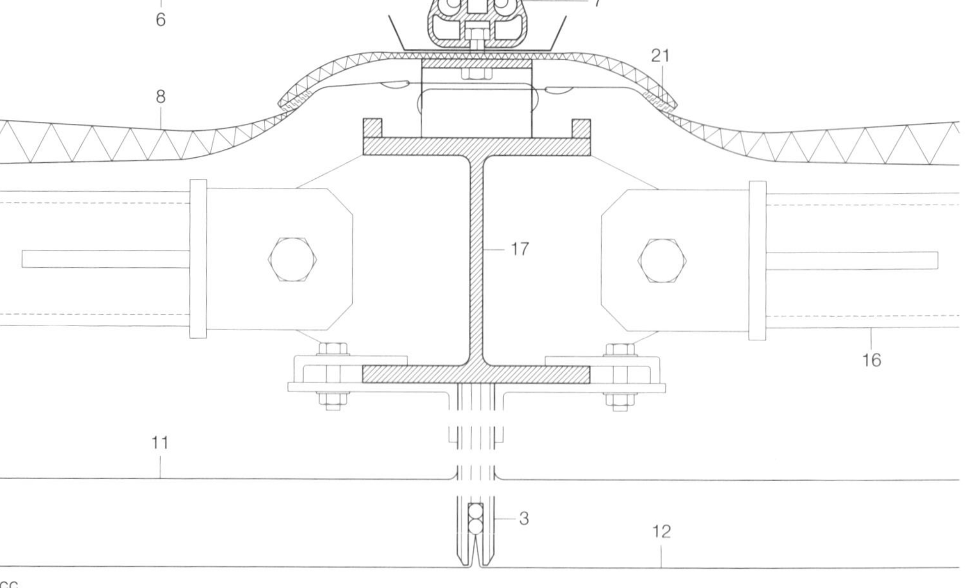

1 Air-filled cushion, 3-ply ETFE foil, outer ply 0.25 mm, rigid central ply 0.1 mm, inner ply 0.2 mm, tear strength: 5200 kg/m
2 GFRP panel, 12 mm
3 MDF, 22 mm
4 GFRP panel, 14 mm
5 Rainwater gutter, galvanised steel sheet, 2.5 mm
6 PVC-coated polyester fabric, 0.5 mm, tear strength: 6000 kg/m
7 Keder rail, aluminium
8 Flexible thermal insulation, 10–50 mm, multi-ply mat made from aluminium foil and foam
9 Steel I-section, 152 × 152 × 37 mm
10 Fluorescent lamp
11 Fabric, white, translucent
12 Fabric, white, stretchable, with pocket for keder
13 Services duct (exhaust air/lighting), painted plywood
14 Tensioning mechanism for membranes
15 Steel square hollow section, 150 × 150 mm
16 Steel circular hollow section, Ø 114.3 mm
17 Steel I-section, 150 × 200 × 10 mm
18 LED lighting
19 Linoleum floor covering, 4 mm, 21 mm plywood, 22 mm timber stage, 60 × 120 mm steel section
20 Silicone seal
21 Touch-and-close fastener

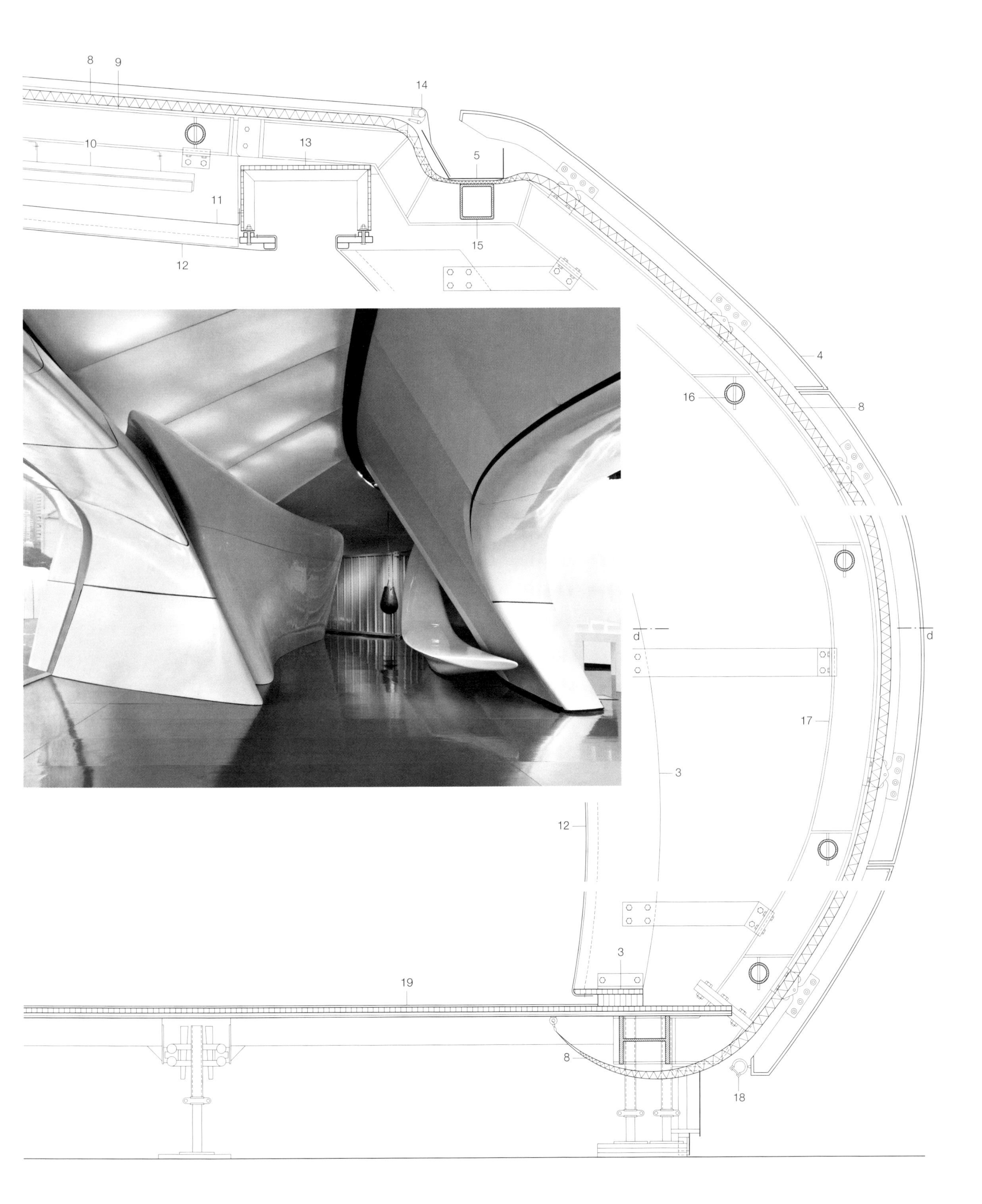
8
9
14
10
13
5
11
15
12
4
16
8
d
d
17
3
12
3
19
8
18

"Mobile Action Space"

2006

Architects:
raumlaborberlin, Berlin
Matthias Rick, Jan Liesegang with
plastique fantastique
Marco Canevacci

Examining how featureless and unattractive urban spaces can be upgraded with art is the mission of the campaigners from raumlaborberlin. Instead of conventional "monuments", which often go unnoticed, they rely on spectacular, temporary installations that require active involvement. The search for affordable shelter from the weather that is easy to set up and take down and is also transportable finally led to a pneumatic structure that since its inception has captured everyone's imagination. Erection and dismantling are part of the staging of this artistic artefact, which has room for up to 120 people. For the first "act" in this production, a converted wheeled building site cabin is left standing for a week in the urban scene – a mysterious, window-less sculpture made from sheet zinc. Passers-by hear the noise of a great banquet coming from inside, ask themselves how so many people can fit inside such a small cabin. Only after the doors open is the secret revealed: loudspeakers and the cabin's function as a storage container for the PE foil of the pneumatic structure. Once the material has been unrolled and inflated, the translucent tube becomes a housing for tables and chairs. Depending on the location, the inflated tube is either in the open air or squeezed under a bridge or pressed up against trees and buildings. The cabin, lined with grey felt, now becomes the entrance, an airlock complete with cloakroom, lighting and counter. A fan below the open-grid entrance ramp ensures that the 18 m long × 6.50 m high polymer tube remains inflated.

- Translucent, fibre-reinforced PE foil
- Fan for filling foil tube with air

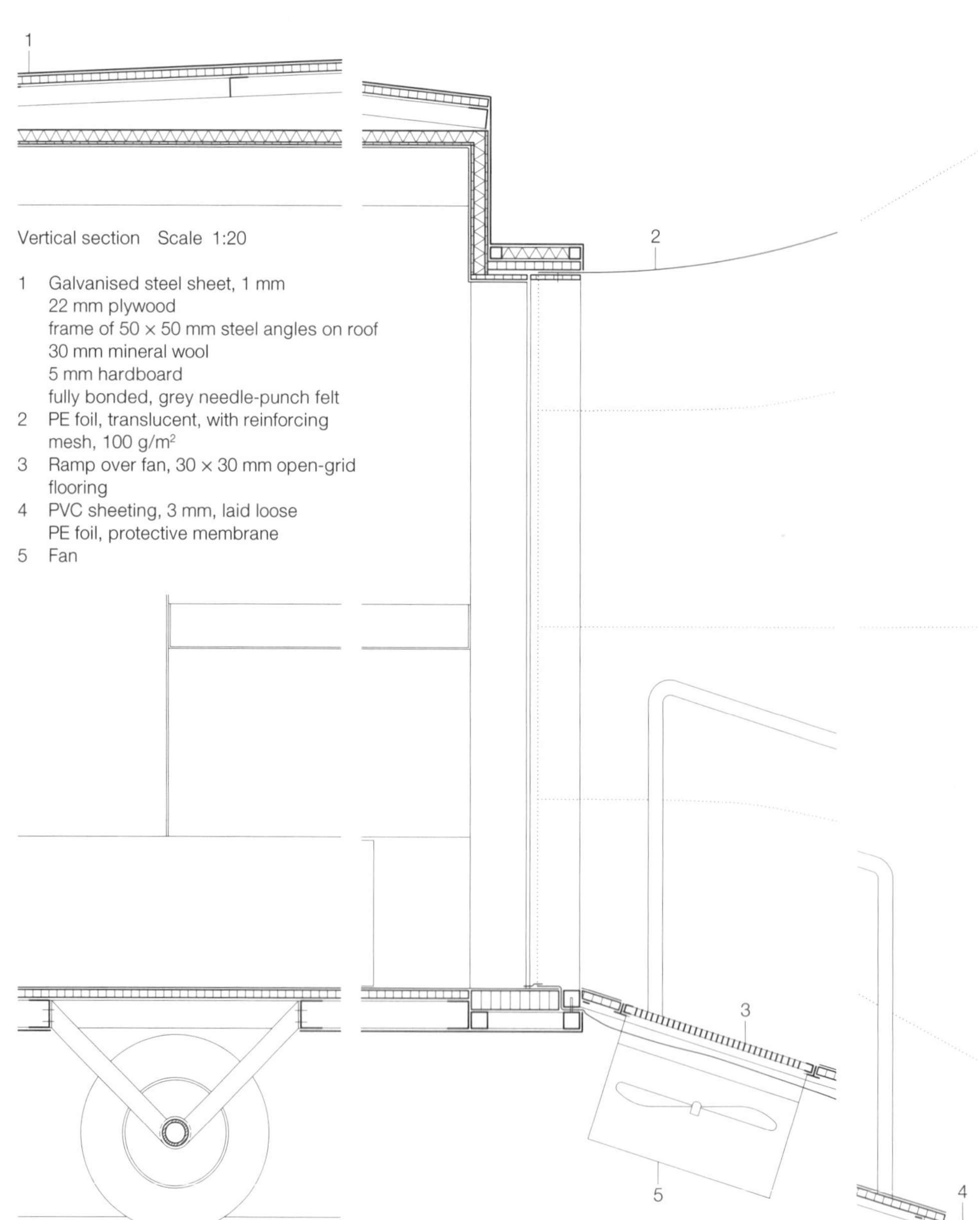

Vertical section Scale 1:20

1 Galvanised steel sheet, 1 mm
22 mm plywood
frame of 50 × 50 mm steel angles on roof
30 mm mineral wool
5 mm hardboard
fully bonded, grey needle-punch felt
2 PE foil, translucent, with reinforcing mesh, 100 g/m²
3 Ramp over fan, 30 × 30 mm open-grid flooring
4 PVC sheeting, 3 mm, laid loose
PE foil, protective membrane
5 Fan

Bank

Bratislava, Slovakia, 2008

Architects:
Jabornegg & Pálffy, Vienna
Christian Jabornegg, András Pálffy
Project team:
Željko Ivoševic, Ana Martin del Hierro, Julian Kerschbaumer, Juraj Mikulaj, Frank Müller, Florian Pfeifer, Gerhard Pfeiler, Felix Thörner

Traditionally, buildings for banks tend to be introvert constructions closed to the outside world. However, this new building in Bratislava housing a branch of the largest bank in Slovakia is the exact opposite. Transparency is the primary design feature of this nine-storey structure in the form of a square perimeter block around a covered courtyard. For many years, the administrative and business functions of this bank were distributed over a total of 12 buildings in the centre of the city. But now everything is under one roof.
The ground floor, semi-public, taller than the other storeys and set back within the building, contains the actual banking hall but also a lounge, a conference room and training and seminar facilities. Four main service cores extending the full height of the building constitute the only solid components in the structural framework. The eight fully glazed upper floors with their double-leaf facades are reserved exclusively for offices and meeting rooms.
Above the topmost floor, air-filled cushions made from transparent ETFE foil span across the open inner courtyard to shelter it from rain and snow. The courtyard becomes an atrium, the roof of which is in the form of pneumatic tubes measuring approx. 4.50 × 46.00 m. Each long side of each tube is fixed to a pair of parallel steel cables. These are supported by further steel cables (70 mm dia.) at 90° to these in a trussing arrangement with diagonal struts (76 mm dia.). The east and west ends of the roof structure have been left open to ensure natural ventilation via the roof. The air pressure in the ETFE foil tubes is kept constant at either 500 or 700 Pa. When lit by daylight from above, the cushions of the roof seem almost to disappear, as though the courtyard were open to the sky.

- Air-filled ETFE tubes forming roof over courtyard
- Delicate steel cable structure

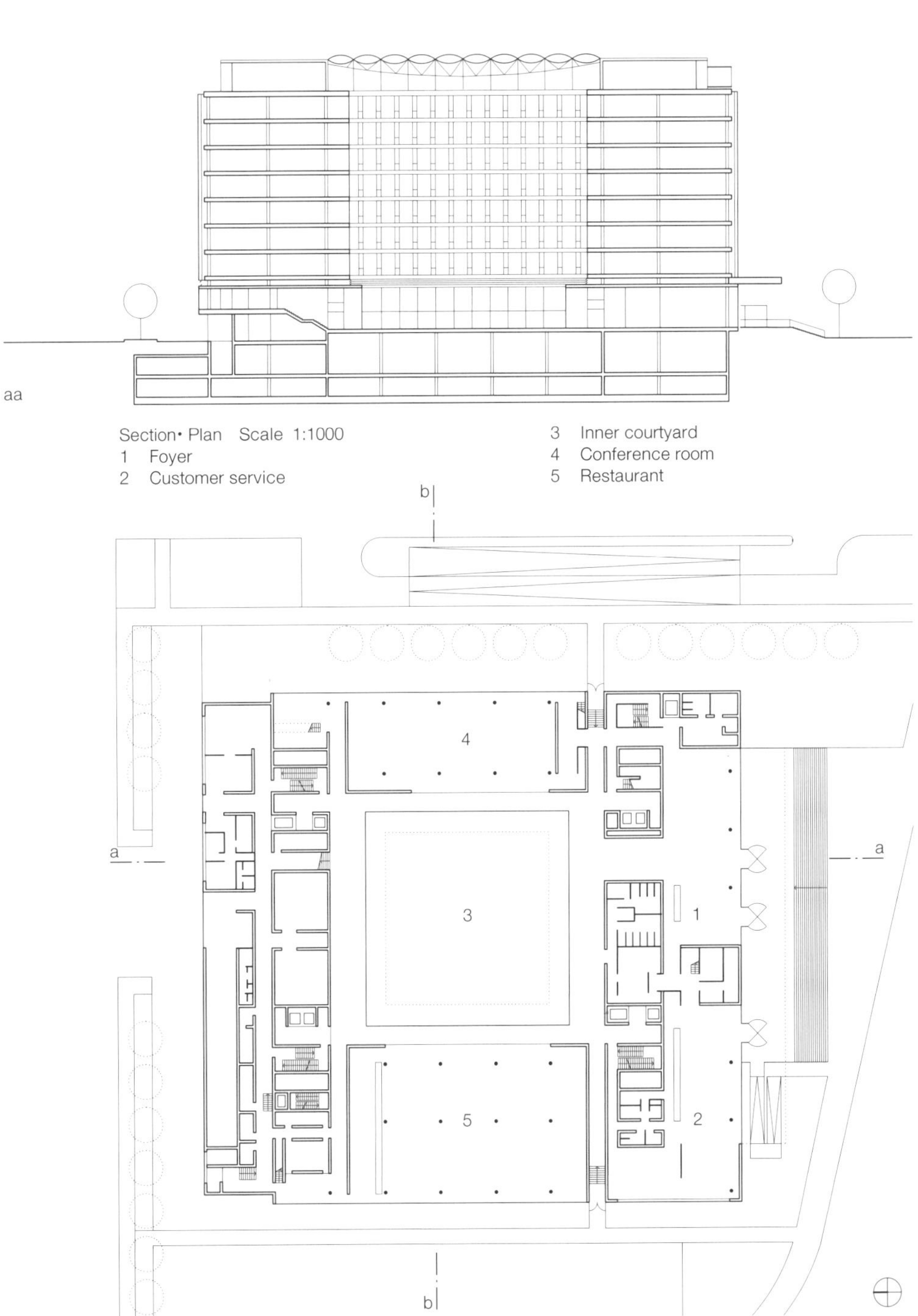

Section• Plan Scale 1:1000
1 Foyer
2 Customer service
3 Inner courtyard
4 Conference room
5 Restaurant

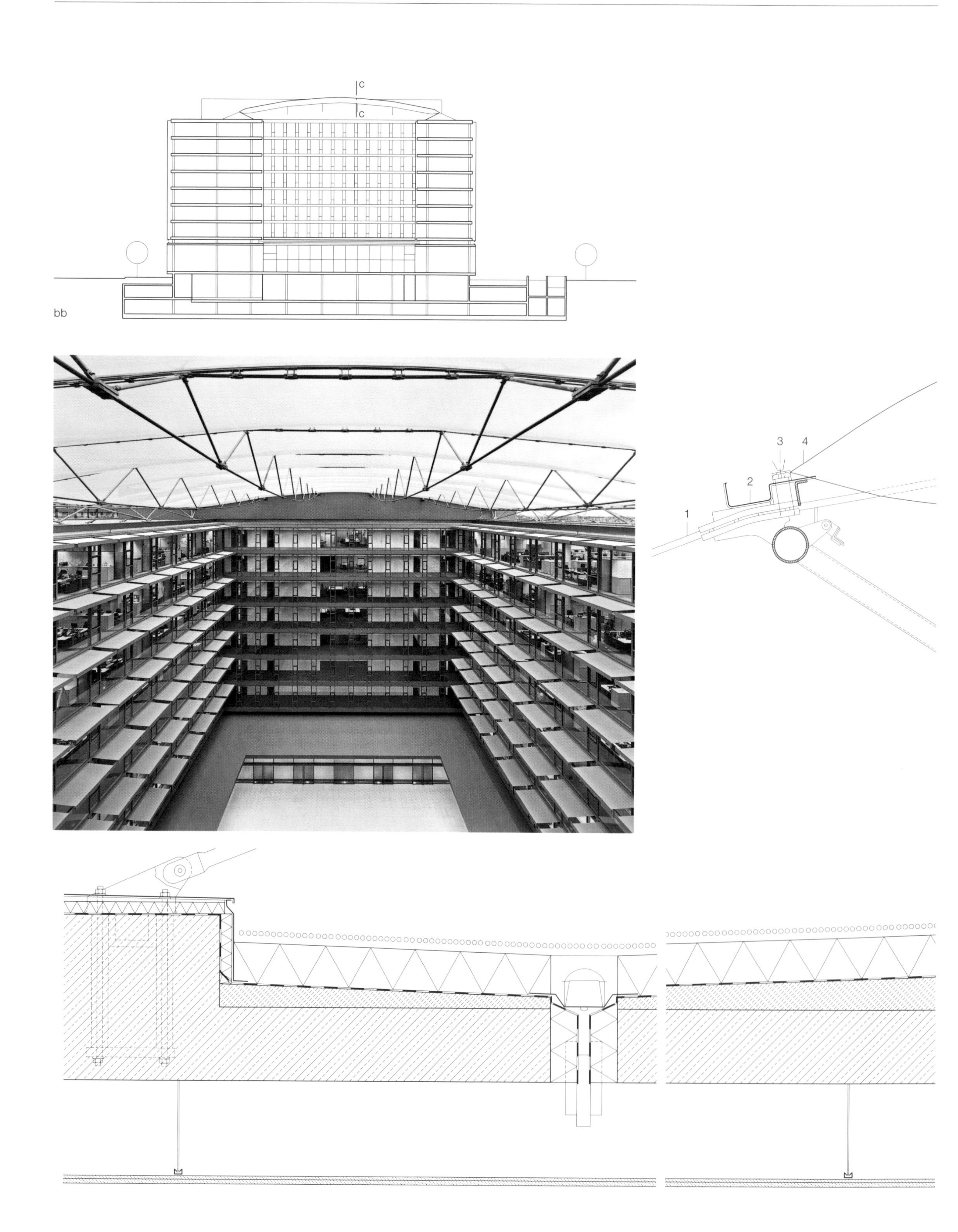
c
c
bb
3
4
2
1

Section
Scale 1:1000
Vertical section
Scale 1:20
Detail
Scale 1:5

1 Steel cable, galvanised, Ø 30 mm
2 Rainwater gutter
3 Keder rail, aluminium, with factory-fitted polymer edge bead
4 ETFE foil, 0.2 mm, U-value min. 0.2 W/m²K
5 Two-part clamping bar, aluminium, 260 × 170 × 26 mm
6 Air supply to cushion, transparent plastic pipe, Ø 50 mm
7 Air supply, main pipe, steel, Ø 150 mm

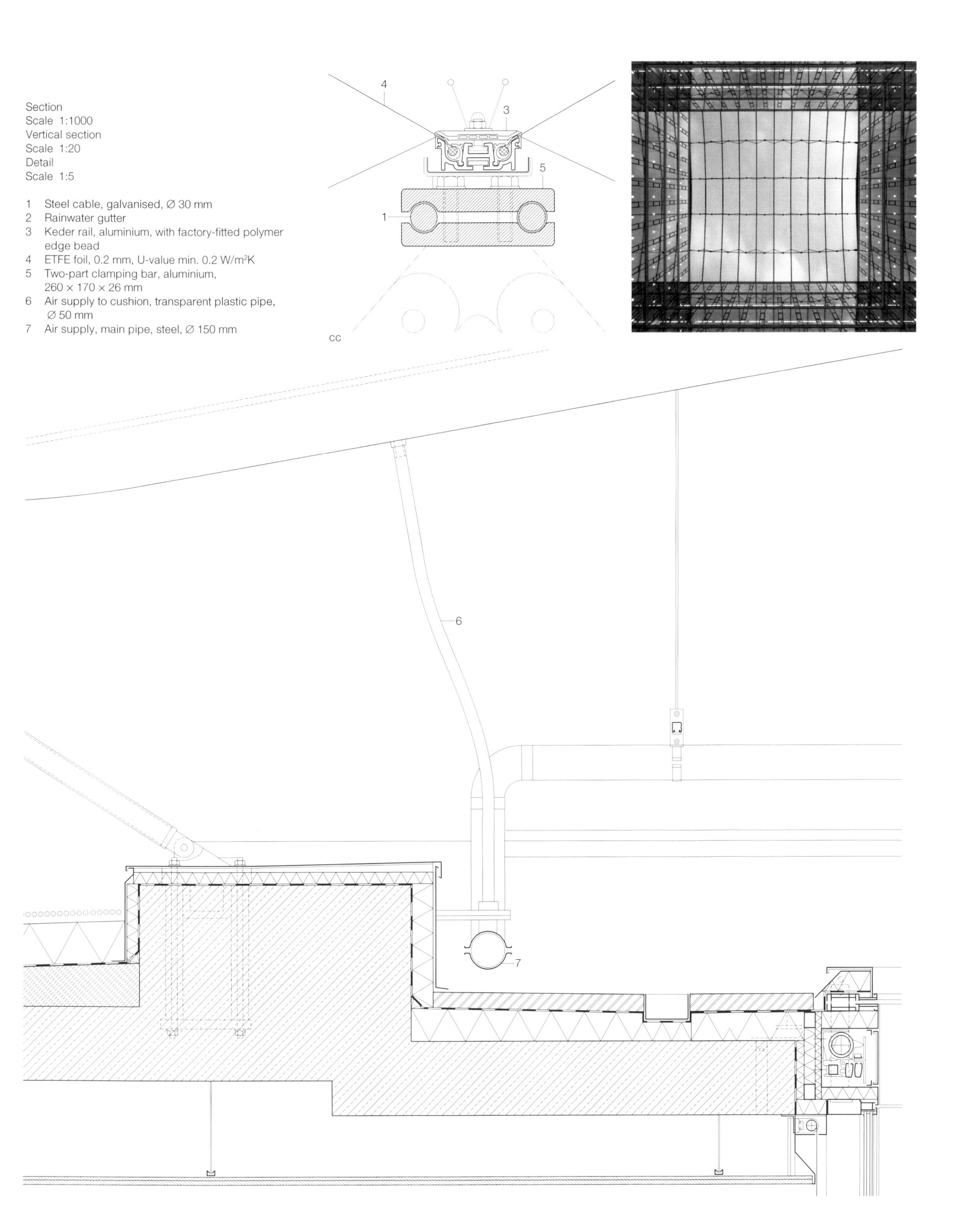

Shopping centre

Amadora, Portugal, 2009

Architects:
Promontorio Architects, Lisbon
Project team:
Nelson Paciencia, Sofia Araújo, Tiago Ferreira, Sónia Costa
Structural engineers:
Atelier One, London

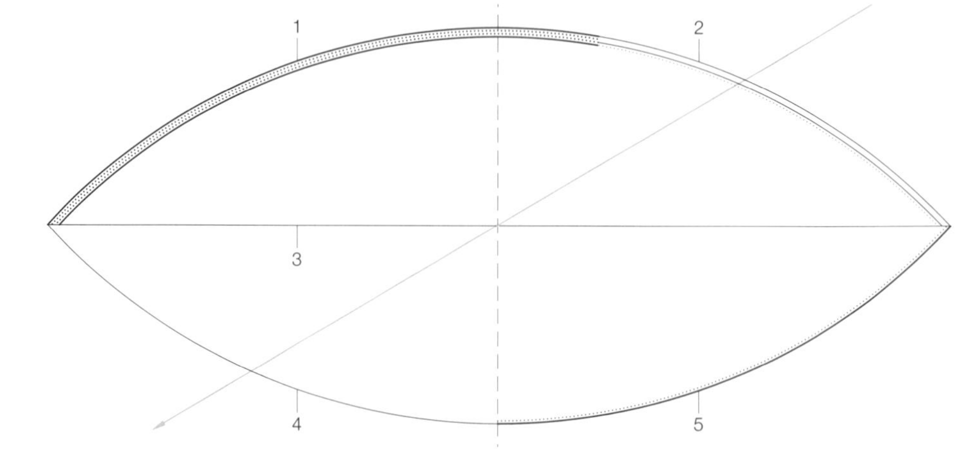

Daylight is extremely important for creating pleasant, comfortable conditions in a covered shopping centre. For the roof to this shopping centre near Lisbon, ETFE cushions proved to be a lighter and more cost-effective choice than conventional overhead glazing. Through an innovative combination and arrangement of up to five different foil variations in one single cushion, it was possible to combine good use of daylight with good thermal comfort. The different printing on the layers of foil represent an interpretation of the familiar sawtooth roof solution with exclusive use of daylight from the north side, achieved in this case via the diagonals in the geometry of the air-filled cushions.
With square cushions measuring approx. 10 × 10 m, very high stresses in the material are inevitable. The depth of each cushion was therefore restricted to 4 m in order to limit these stresses. Despite the long span, the double-skin top ply rendered additional support in the form of a cable net unnecessary.
The various foil plies of each cushion are printed depending on their orientation with respect to the sun. The central ply is transparent (3). That half of each cushion that faces south is fabricated from white ETFE foil. The double-skin upper ply is printed on the south side (1) as follows: 2 × 100 % silver on the underside of the upper foil, a 65 % hexagonal silver pattern plus subsequent 100 % silver on the top side of the lower foil. This latter printing is also used on the lower ply diagonally opposite (5). The cushion surfaces that face north are made from transparent ETFE foil so that daylight can enter the interior. In order to restrict the solar heat gains, however, there is a low E coating on the lower ply of the double-skin upper membrane (2).
Completely transparent cushions without any coating are used as a roof over an external area that can be ventilated naturally and therefore does not have to comply with any particular lighting and thermal insulation requirements.

- ETFE foil cushions measuring approx. 10 × 10 m
- Various finishes to ETFE foil

Schematic section through cushion
— transparent
— opaque
····· coated
Sections
Scale 1:4000
Vertical section
Scale 1:20

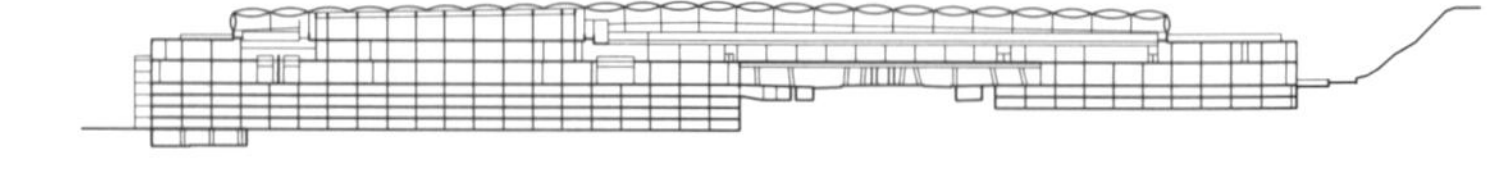

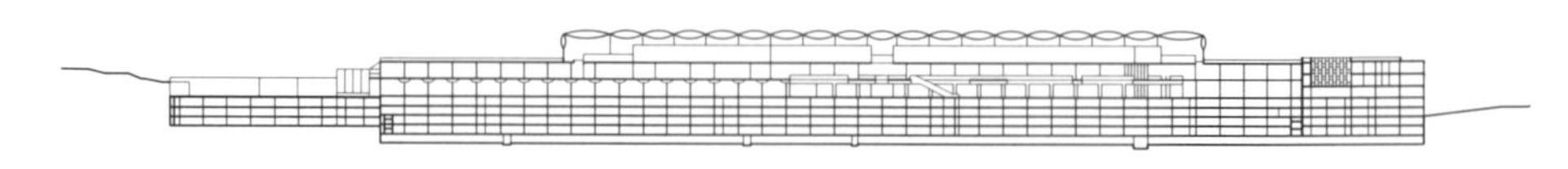

1. ETFE foil, white, 250 µm, underside printed with 2 × 100 % silver
   ETFE foil, white, 250 µm, top side printed with 1 × 65 % hexagonal silver pattern and 1 × 100 % silver
2. ETFE foil, transparent, 250 µm
   ETFE foil, transparent, 250 µm, low E coating to underside
3. ETFE foil, transparent, 150 µm
4. ETFE foil, transparent, 250 µm
5. ETFE foil, white, 250 µm, top side printed with 1 × 65 % hexagonal silver pattern and 1 × 100 % silver
6. Steel cable, ∅ 36 mm
7. ETFE cushion, 150–250 µm
8. Air supply to cushion, plastic hose, ∅ 50 mm
9. Steel pipe, ∅ 100 mm
10. Steel rectangular hollow section, 400 × 200 × 8 mm

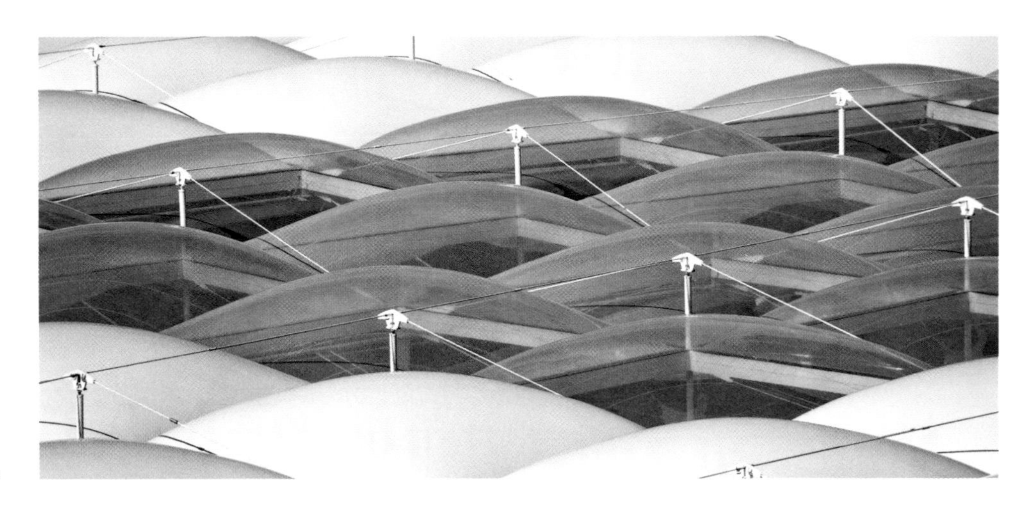

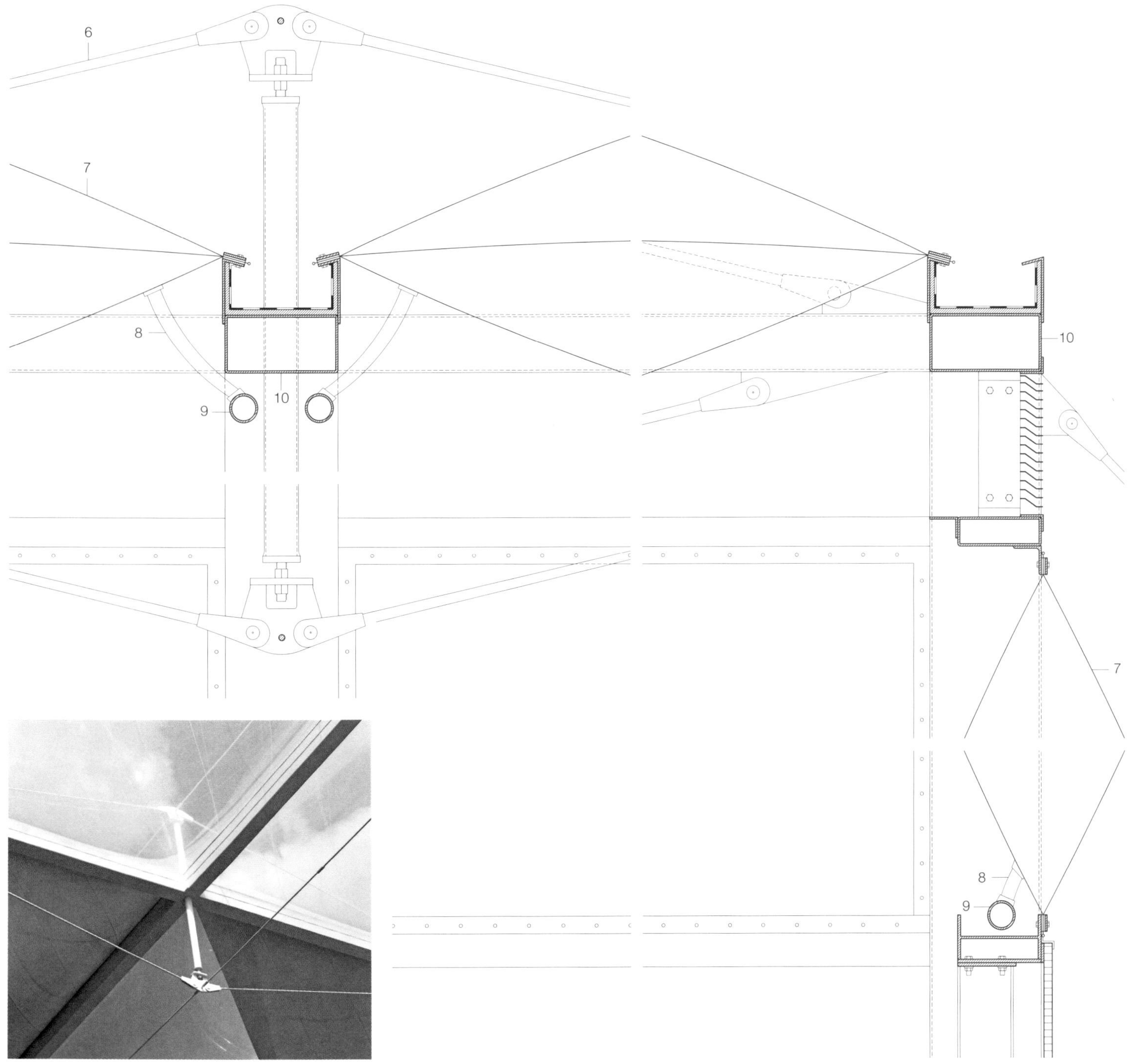

Leisure centre

Neydens, France, 2009

Architects:
L35, Barcelona/Paris
Ganz & Muller Architectes Associés, Geneva
GM2A Architectes, Paris
Structural engineers:
Charpente Concept, Geneva

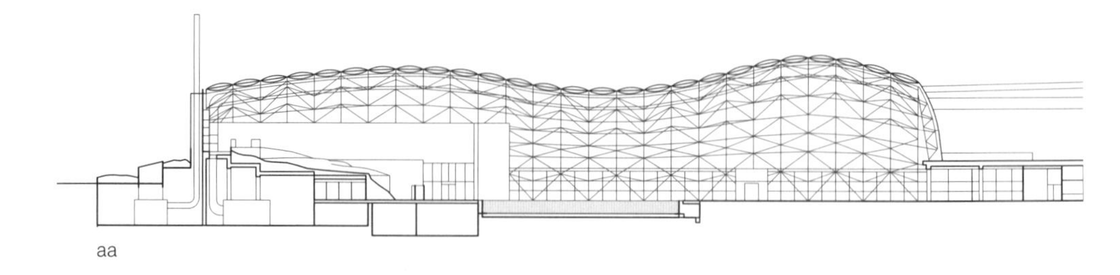

Section • Plan
Scale 1:500

Neydens is only a village on the French border with Switzerland, about 10 km south of Geneva. Nevertheless, it is the location of a major new leisure centre with swimming pools, outdoor areas, wellness facilities with sauna and Turkish bath, a fitness centre with climbing wall, plus shopping mall, hotel, restaurants and bars – a total area of approx. 35 000 m². The architects restricted the volume of the complex and added green roofs so that the leisure centre would not dominate the charming landscape of this area. The enclosure for the water park with its several pools is particularly worthy of note. With its unusual undulating form, the 120 m long × 65 m wide building reflects the topography of the surrounding landscape. The structure consists of 14 custom two-pin trussed arches made from curved, circular glued laminated timber sections. Between these there are 13 intermediate arches supported off the bottom chords of the main arches. The spacing between the lattice arches is 3.50 m and the rise of the arches varies between 14.50 and 18.00 m to produce the undulating effect of the roof. Three-ply ETFE foil cushions span between the arches. The 63 cushions are 3.50 m wide and up to 52 m long. They must accommodate not only the curvature of the arches, but also the twist due to the different radii of each pair of adjacent arches. This means that the geometry of every cushion is unique, which required a much greater design input. Despite the complexity of the building's form, the wavy alignment of eaves and crown enabled all clamping sections meeting at any one node to be connected without the need to offset incoming members. The cushions are fitted into aluminium keder rails supported on steel mountings fixed to the timber loadbearing structure. The air supply connection to each cushion is almost invisible. Two inflation plants, each with two fan units, keep the pressure in the cushions constant at approx. 300 Pa, and can increase it to max. 800 Pa to cope with wind and snow loads. If one plant fails, the other can supply the entire envelope with sufficient air.

- ETFE foil
- Wavy alignment of eaves and crown

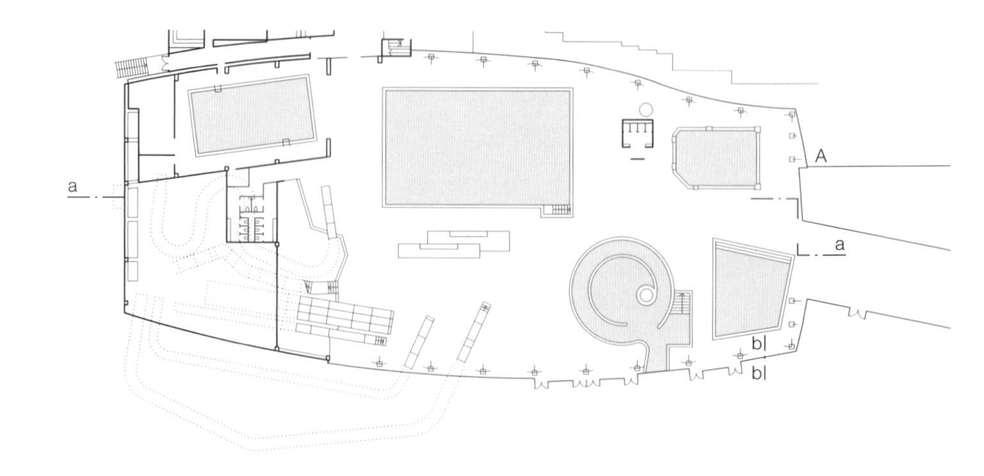

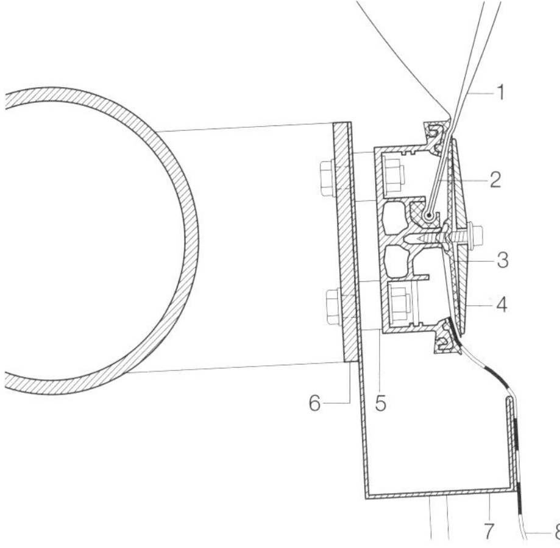

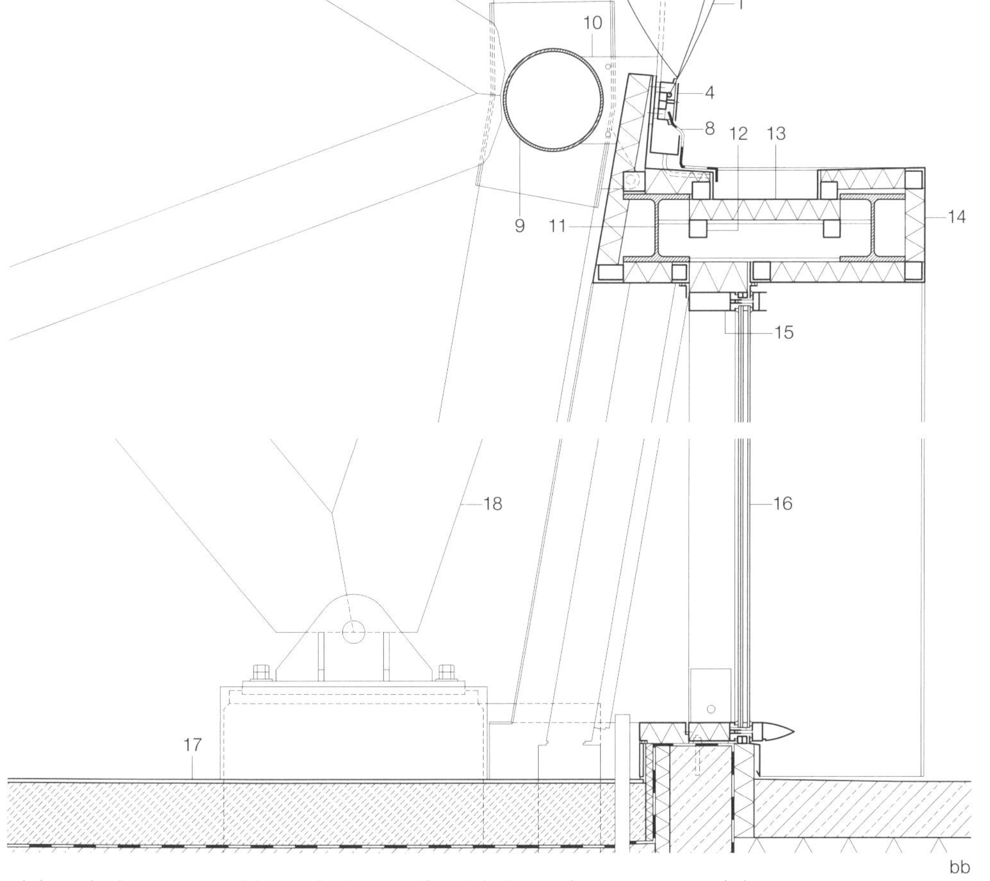

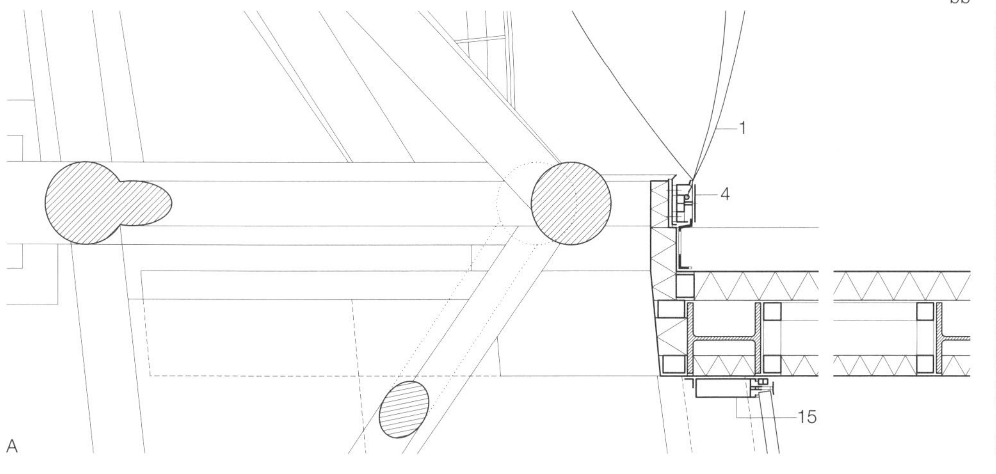

Vertical section • Horizontal section
Scale 1:20
Detail
Scale 1:5

1 Air-filled ETFE cushion
inner ply 0.25 mm
central ply 0.10 mm
outer ply 0.25 mm
2 EPDM keder, Ø 6 mm
3 First sealing layer: EPDM capping
4 Clamping element, aluminium, consisting of channel, cover and keder rail
5 Spacer block, EPDM
6 Steel flat, 130 × 5 mm
7 Second sealing layer: gutter of PVC-coated sheet steel, welded, 2 mm
8 Seal, textile-reinforced PVC membrane, 1.4 mm, connected to facade
9 Steel circular hollow section, Ø 273 × 6.3 mm
10 Steel flat, 230 × 10 mm, for fixing clamping element
11 Steel I-section, 180 mm
12 Steel square hollow section, 50 × 50 × 1.5 mm
13 Rainwater gutter, sheet aluminium, 3 mm
14 Sheet aluminium, 0.5 mm
50 mm insulation
15 Post-and-rail facade, extruded aluminium sections, 125 × 50 × 2 mm
16 Insulating glass: 6 mm toughened safety glass + 16 mm cavity + laminated safety glass (2 No. 6 mm)
17 Floor covering: 10 mm ceramic tiles
50 mm screed
waterproofing, 30–160 mm reinforced concrete
18 Primary loadbearing structure, glued laminated timber, curved, Ø 320 mm

Training centre for mountain rescue service

Gaißach, Germany, 2008

Architects:
Herzog + Partner, Munich
Thomas Herzog, Hanns Jörg Schrade
Assistant:
Xaver Wankerl
Structural engineers:
Sailer Stepan Partner
Beratende Ingenieure für Bauwesen GmbH, Munich

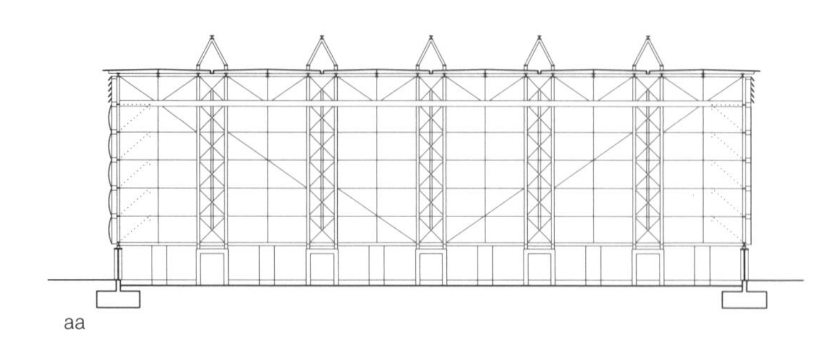

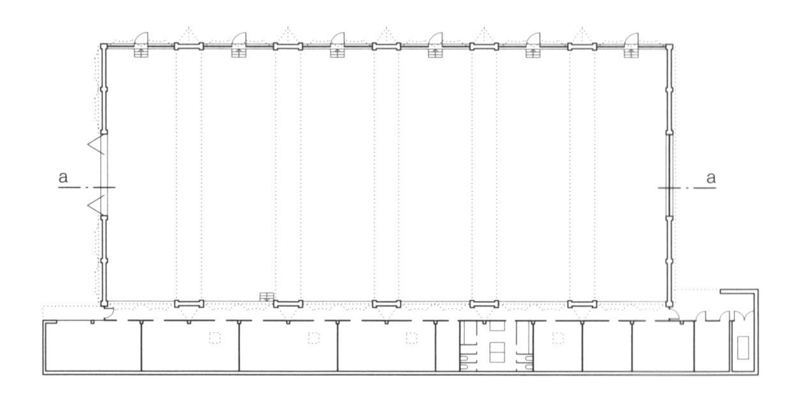

Section • Plan
Scale 1:750

The heart of this centre for the safety and training courses of the Bavarian mountain rescue service in Gaißach to the south of Munich is the simulation installation for helicopter rescue missions. This new building means that the costly outdoor training exercises with a real helicopter, which are so dependent on the weather, too, are no longer necessary. Furthermore, the 350 l of kerosene consumed during every hour of training can now be saved. Inside the building, two helicopter mock-ups enable rescue assignments to be practised: on the stationary simulator, which is mounted on a steel scaffold in one corner and is used for simpler training exercises, and, on the flight simulator, which is suspended from a crane and can be moved around the building as required. Training in conditions as realistic as possible is crucial, and so the facade is not insulated – it consists merely of transparent ETFE foil. The effects of the weather can therefore be felt inside the building. There are also further "special effects": the noise of the helicopter relayed via loudspeakers, fans to simulate the draught of the rotor blades, and flashing lights to imitate the flickering light from the sun – all intended to give trainees the feeling of a real rescue mission. At 20 m high, this block is exposed to considerable wind forces. Five three-chord steel portal frames, together with the gantry crane supporting the helicopter, form the primary loadbearing structure. Positioned between these are secondary beams that support the membrane facade. Modular frame elements specially developed for this project are covered with 0.3 mm thick, UV-resistant, self-cleaning ETFE foil. This material was wrapped around a Z-section and fixed with clamping bars. In a second operation, vertical arches were installed to stretch the foil outwards and tension it. The tie bar below each arch holds the frame exactly in position.
Sturdy concrete panels around the base of the building between the folding doors keep the membrane out of the reach of vandals. Besides the roof and the topmost bay of one gable end, the whole of the north side is clad in timber in order to support a climbing wall on the inside.

- ETFE foil, mechanically prestressed
- Modular frame of Z-sections and prestressing arches

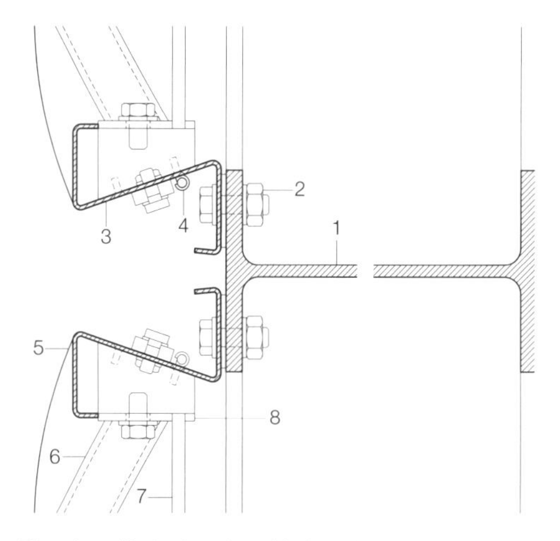

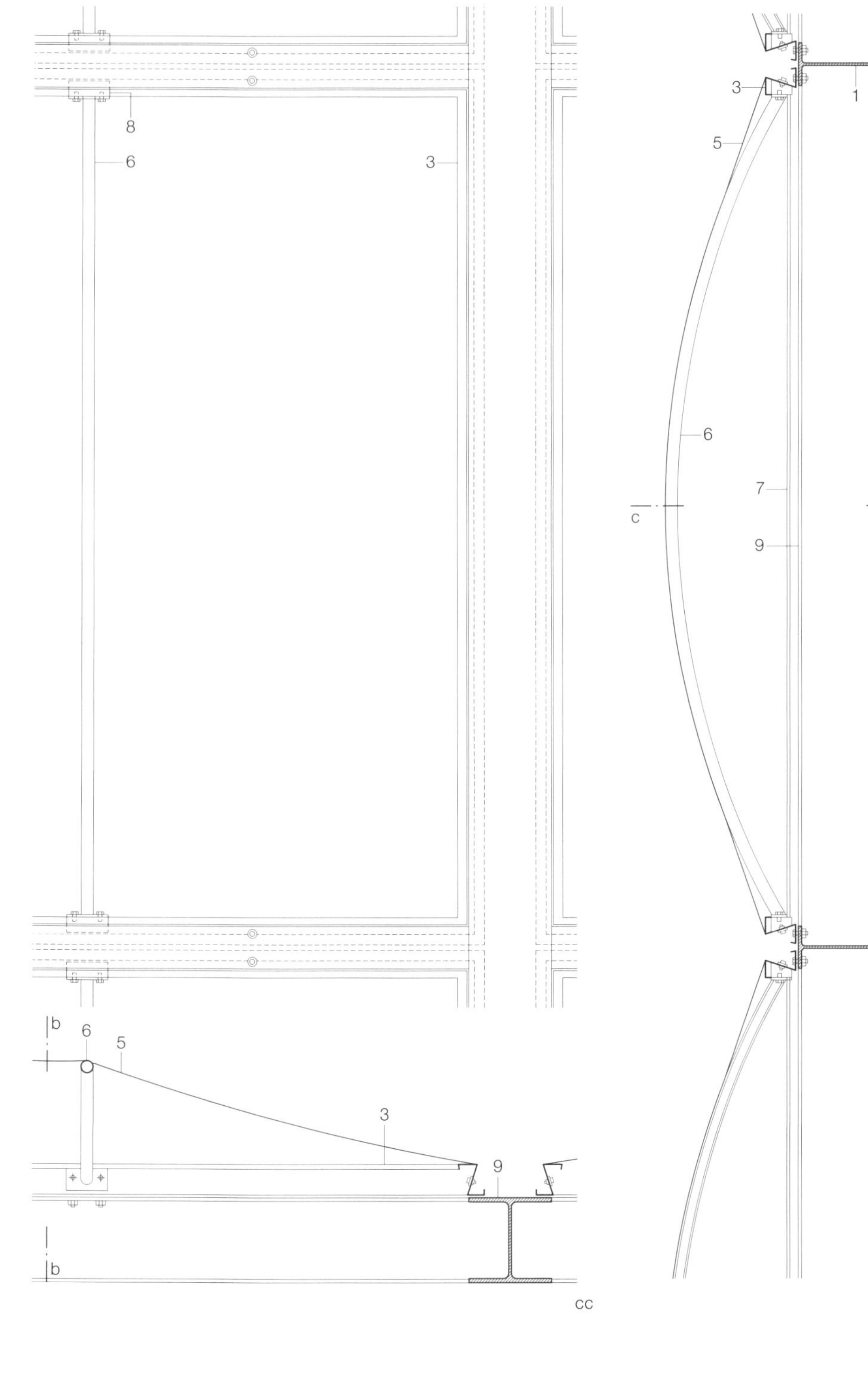

Elevation • Vertical section • Horizontal section
Modular frame element
Scale 1:20
Detail
Scale 1:2

1 Steel I-section, 240 mm
2 Bolt, M12
3 Bolted Z-section frame, steel, 3 mm
4 Keder, EPDM, ∅ 8 mm
5 ETFE foil, 0.20 mm, 0.25 mm or 0.30 mm thick depending on structural requirements
6 Prestressing arch, steel circular hollow section, ∅ 35 × 8 mm
7 Tie bar, steel, ∅ 8 mm
8 Steel flat, 60 × 120 × 5 mm
9 Steel section, HEB 240 mm

Roof over circulation zone at EXPO 2010

Shanghai, China, 2010

Architects:
SBA Architekten, Stuttgart
Hong Li, Bianca Nitsch
Project team: Cathrin Fischer, Reinhard Braun, Benedikt Köster, Lei Zhang, Yijun Qi
Structural engineers:
Knippers Helbig Advanced Engineering, Stuttgart/New York
Project team: Florian Scheible, Florian Kamp, Dirk Richter, Roman Schieber

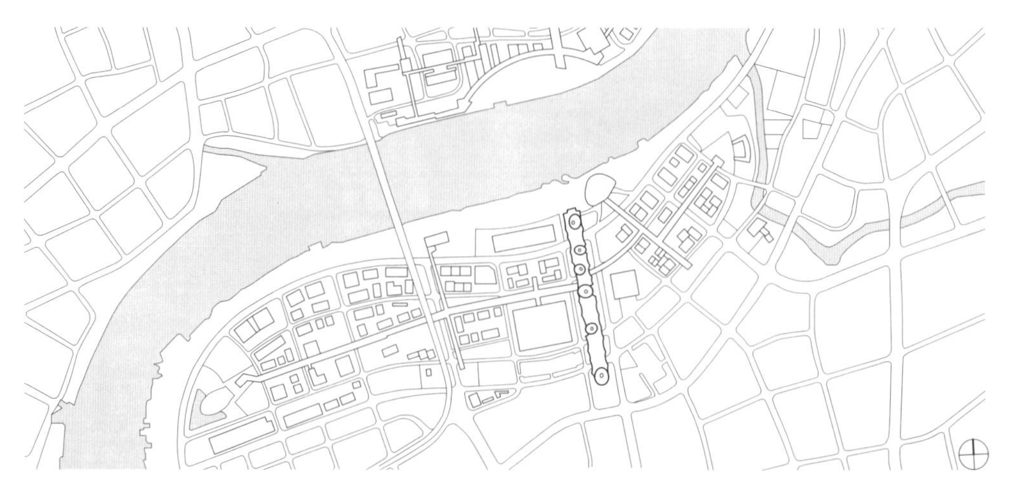

The central circulation zone at EXPO 2010 formed the route taken by all visitors as they arrived, guiding them towards the exhibition pavilions of the individual countries. Although EXPO 2010 is now over, this roof is one of the five structures that have been retained to become a focal point in a new district of Shanghai. A pedestrian precinct on four levels, this 1 km long, 100 m wide boulevard is covered by a membrane roof with a total area of 65 000 m². The roof is supported by 19 internal columns, 31 perimeter masts and six funnels of steel and glass with a free-form lattice structure in double curvature. Called "Sun Valleys", the funnels channel daylight into the subterranean levels and create a link between interior and exterior. They served as important points of reference on the huge EXPO site. The concept of a built landscape with flowing transitions between inside and outside called for a roof construction opening up to its surroundings. This could only be realised with a membrane of PTFE-coated glass-fibre cloth, which enables clear spans of almost 100 m – on the limits of technical feasibility. Structural aspects dominated the concluding form-finding process for the roof. The membrane essentially spans between the high points marked by the perimeter masts and the low points at the internal columns, where the main membrane is attached to a compression ring. There are also cables here to prevent uplift. This is where the largest vertical loads occur, and so two layers of membrane are provided here, the second in scalloped form. Three, sometimes four, retaining cables, which prevent the membrane punching downwards, meet at the top of each column, and three cables to the perimeter masts. The masts carry the main load of the membrane and each is tied back to a foundation via two guy ropes. The 2 × 2 m base plates could be readjusted over several months and the final adjustment of the foundations took place just before the EXPO was opened.

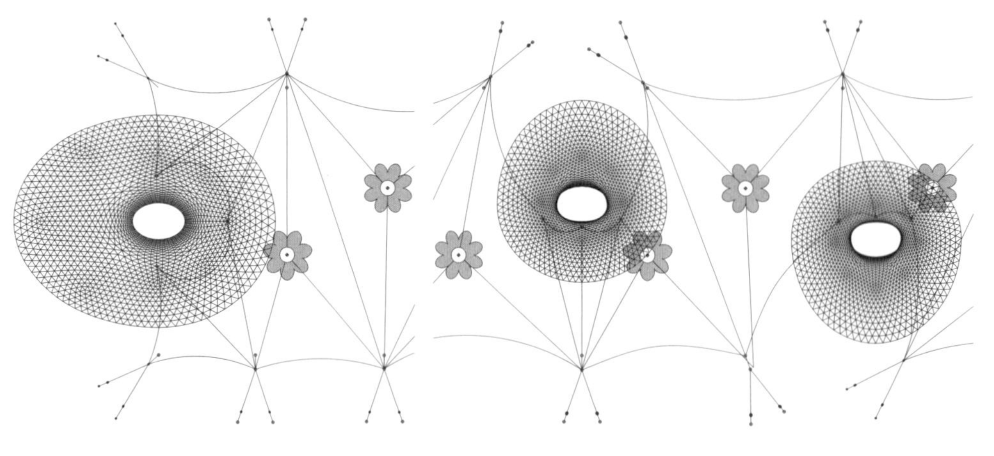

- PTFE-coated glass-fibre cloth
- Membrane roof with an area of 65 000 m² and clear spans of up to 100 m

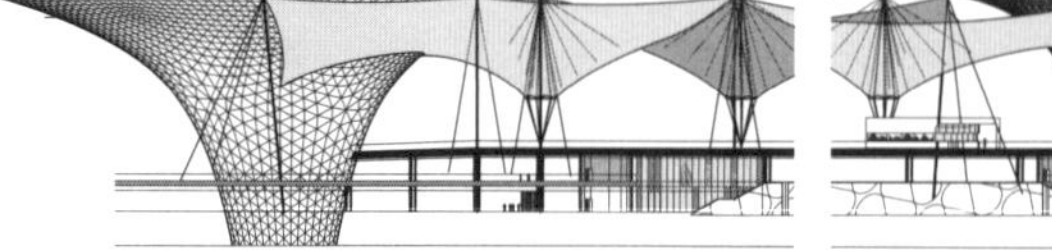

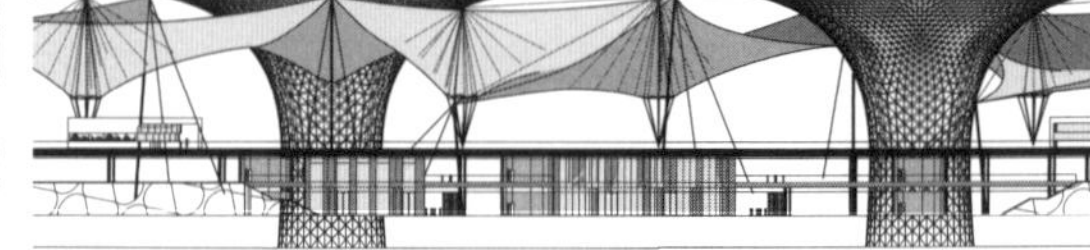

Site plan
Scale 1:40000
Plan • Elevation
Scale 1:2500
Section
Scale 1:1000

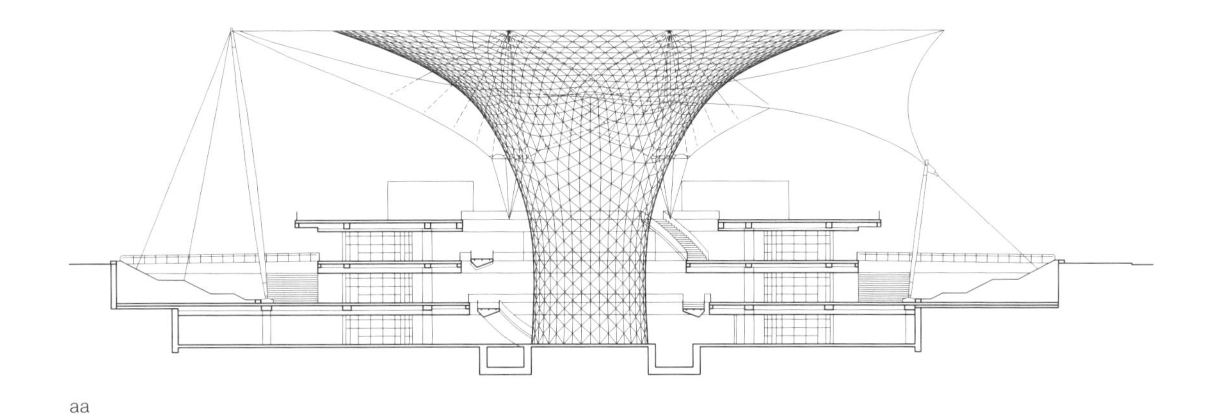

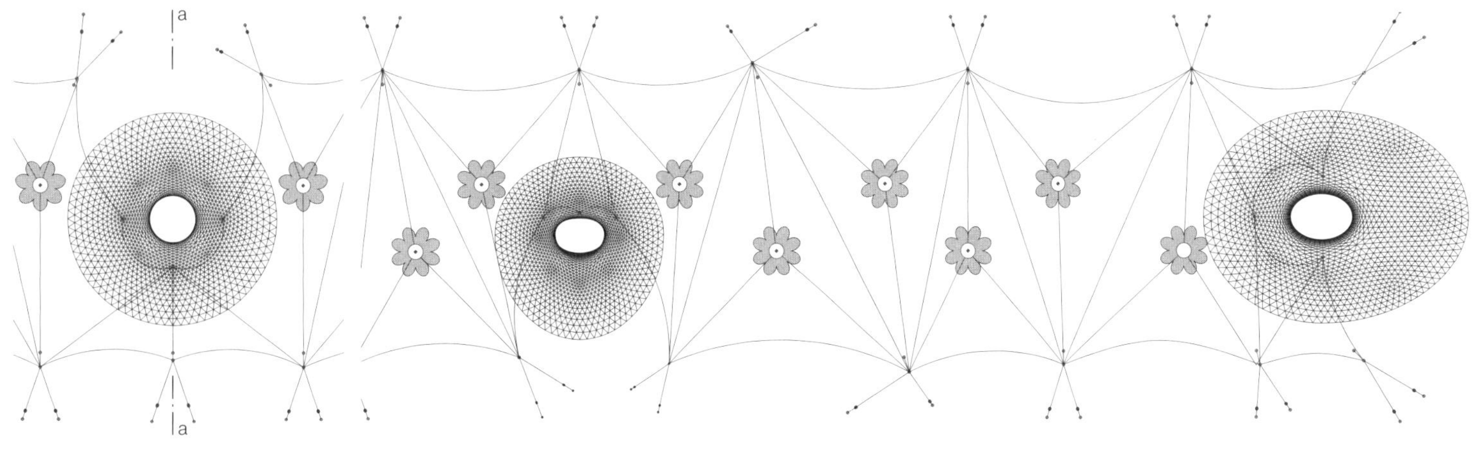

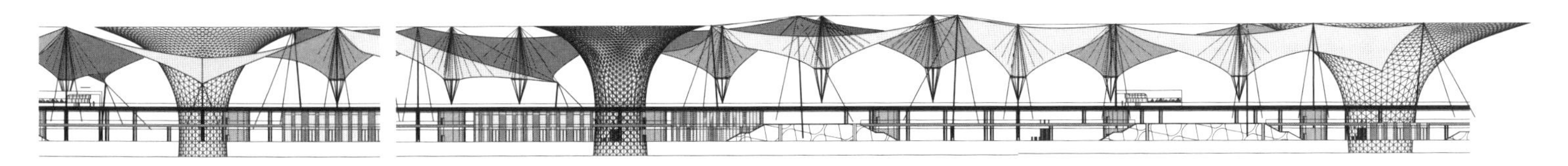

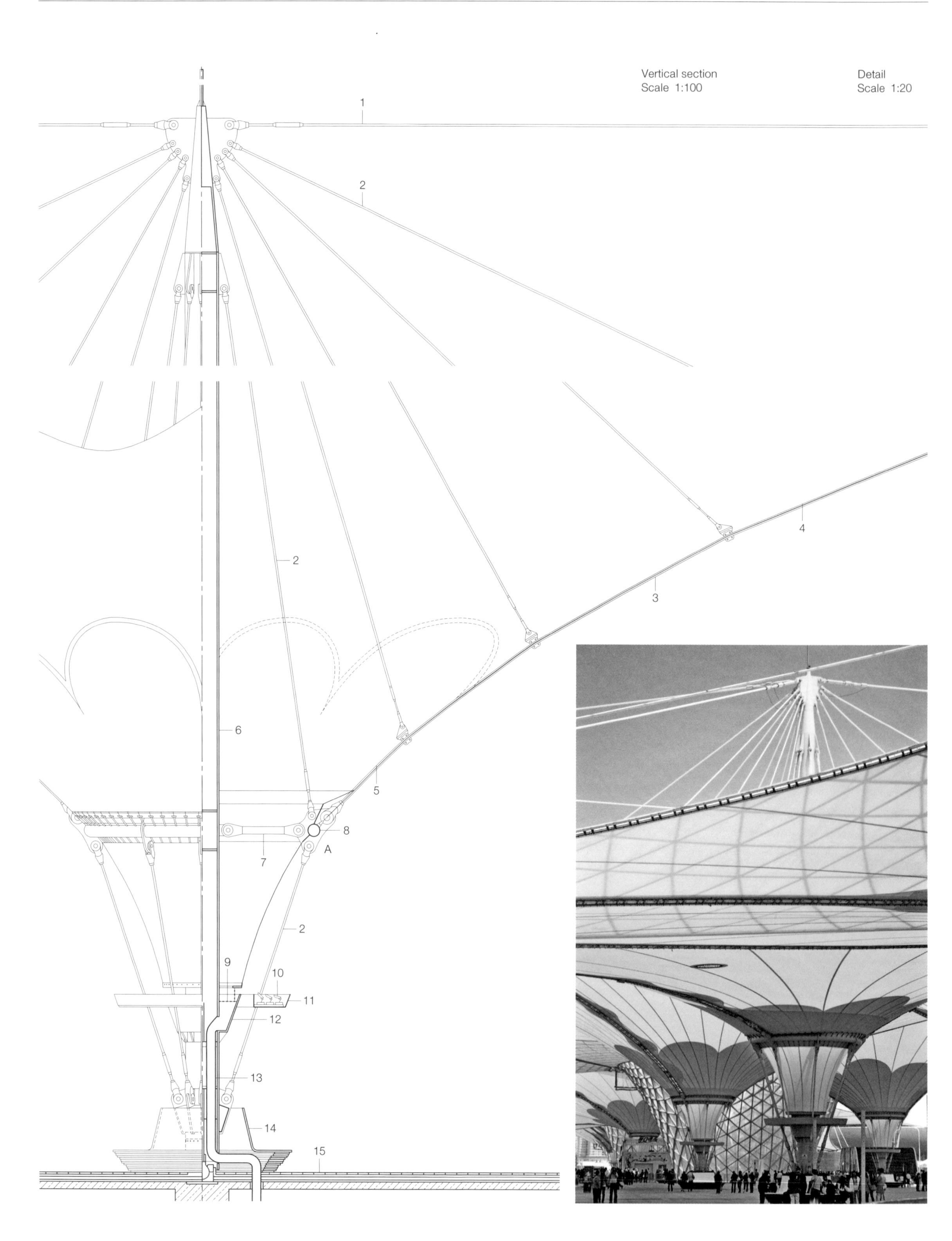
Vertical section
Scale 1:100
Detail
Scale 1:20
1
2
3
4
5
6
7
8
A
9
10
11
12
13
14
15

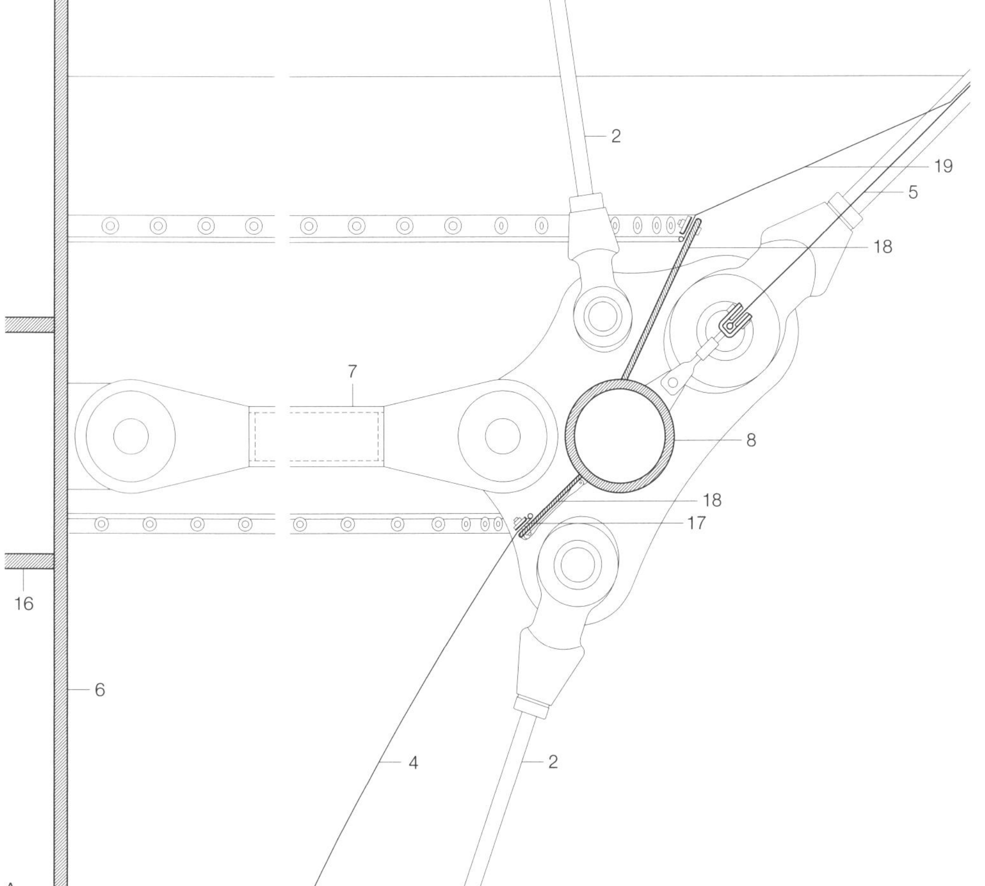

1 Cable between internal column and perimeter mast, steel in PVC sleeve, Ø 50 mm
2 Retaining cable, steel in PVC sleeve, Ø 41 mm
3 Wind uplift cable, steel in PVC sleeve, Ø 80 mm
4 Membrane: PTFE-coated glass-fibre cloth, 1.1 mm, natural white, tensile strength, warp/weft: 160/160 kN/m, light transmittance: 17.5 %
5 Membrane: PTFE-coated glass-fibre cloth, 2-ply (1.1 + 0.7 mm), natural white, welded
6 Galvanised steel circular hollow section, Ø 750 × 35 mm, coated
7 Strut, galvanised steel circular hollow section, Ø 159 × 16 mm, coated
8 Compression ring, galvanised steel circular hollow section, Ø 299 × 25 mm, coated
9 Galvanised steel grating, 10 mm
10 LED lamp, 45 W
11 Galvanised steel sheet, 8 mm, coated
12 Rainwater hopper, galvanised steel, 30 mm, coated
13 Rainwater downpipe, galvanised steel, Ø 200 mm, 4 No. per column
14 Bench
15 Suspended floor construction
30–50 mm granite flags
40 mm cement screed
PE sheeting, 20–66.5 mm rigid foam boards
20 mm cement mortar levelling bed
2 layers of bitumen flexible sheeting
20 mm cement mortar levelling bed
160 mm reinforced concrete slab
16 Stiffener, galvanised steel, 10 mm
17 Membrane clamping element, aluminium, 50 × 12 mm, bolted
18 Galvanised steel sheet, coated
19 Strip of membrane material welded to main membrane

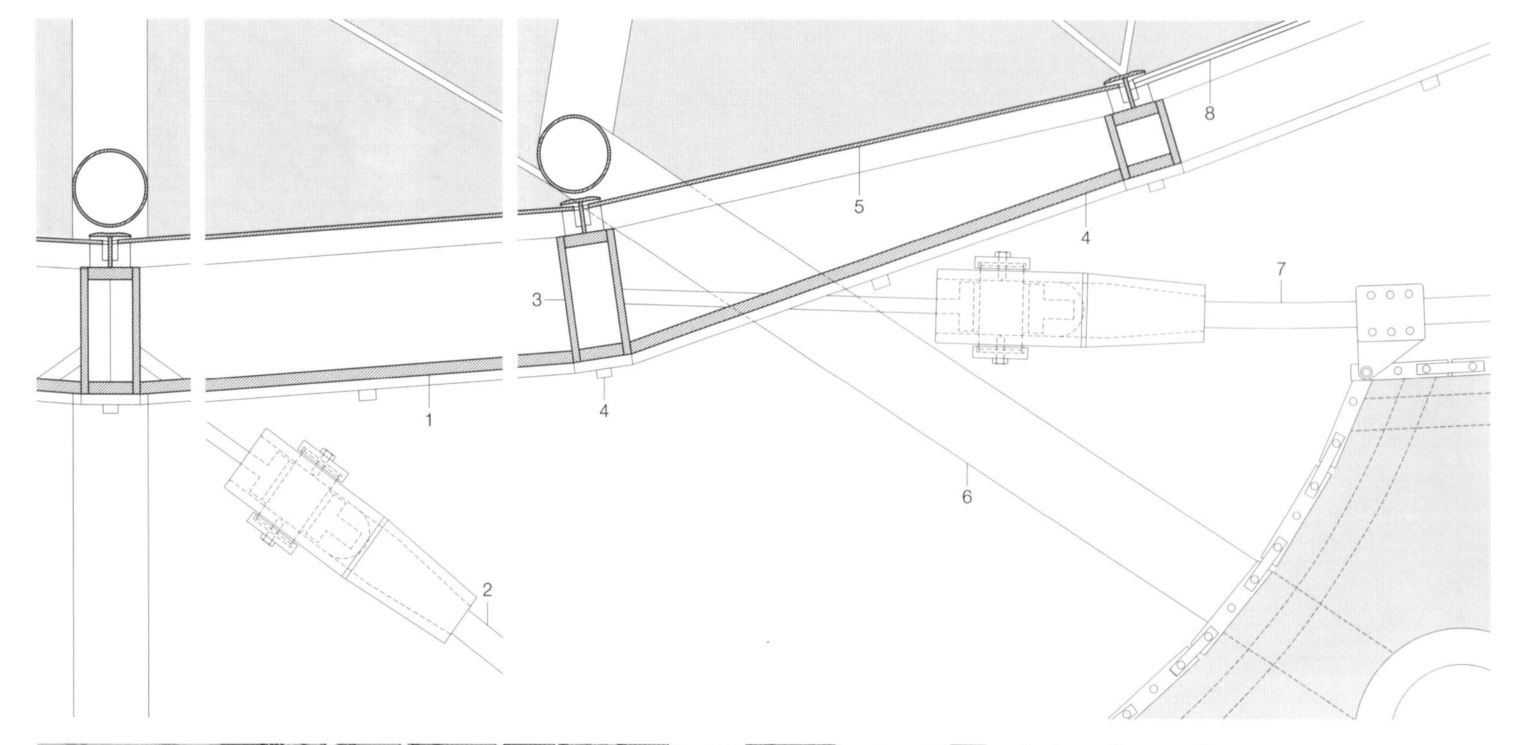

Sections • Plan on roof
Scale 1:20

1 Stiffener, galvanised steel plate, 32 mm
2 Ridge cable, steel in PVC sleeve, Ø 117 mm
3 Facade section, hollow steel box welded from steel flats, galvanised, coated, haunched, 360 × 130 × 20–32 mm to 180 × 65 × 5–10 mm
4 LED lamp
5 Galvanised steel plate, 10 mm
6 Rainwater drain, PE, Ø 200 mm
7 Perimeter cable, steel in PVC sleeve, Ø 90 mm
8 Glazing: laminated safety glass (2 No. 4 mm panes/1 mm PVB interlayer)
9 Guy rope, steel in PVC sleeve, Ø 155 mm
10 Cable socket with open fitting, galvanised steel
11 Perimeter mast, galvanised steel circular hollow section, 3 No. Ø 219.6 × 50 mm, coated, profiled steel stiffeners, 50 mm, galvanised/coated
12 Strip of membrane material, welded to main membrane
13 Ridge cable, steel in PVC sleeve, Ø 130 mm
14 Cable socket with open fitting, 1350 × 403 × 600 mm, galvanised steel
15 Membrane: PTFE-coated glass-fibre cloth, 1.1 mm, natural white, tensile strength, warp/weft: 160/160 kN/m, light transmittance: 17.5 %
16 Wind uplift cable, steel in PVC sleeve, Ø 80 mm
17 Steel square hollow section, 50 × 50 × 2.5 mm, galvanised
18 Keder rail, aluminium, 87 × 45 mm
19 Membrane fixing strip, 6 mm, galvanised steel
20 Rainwater gutter, aluminium, 6 mm

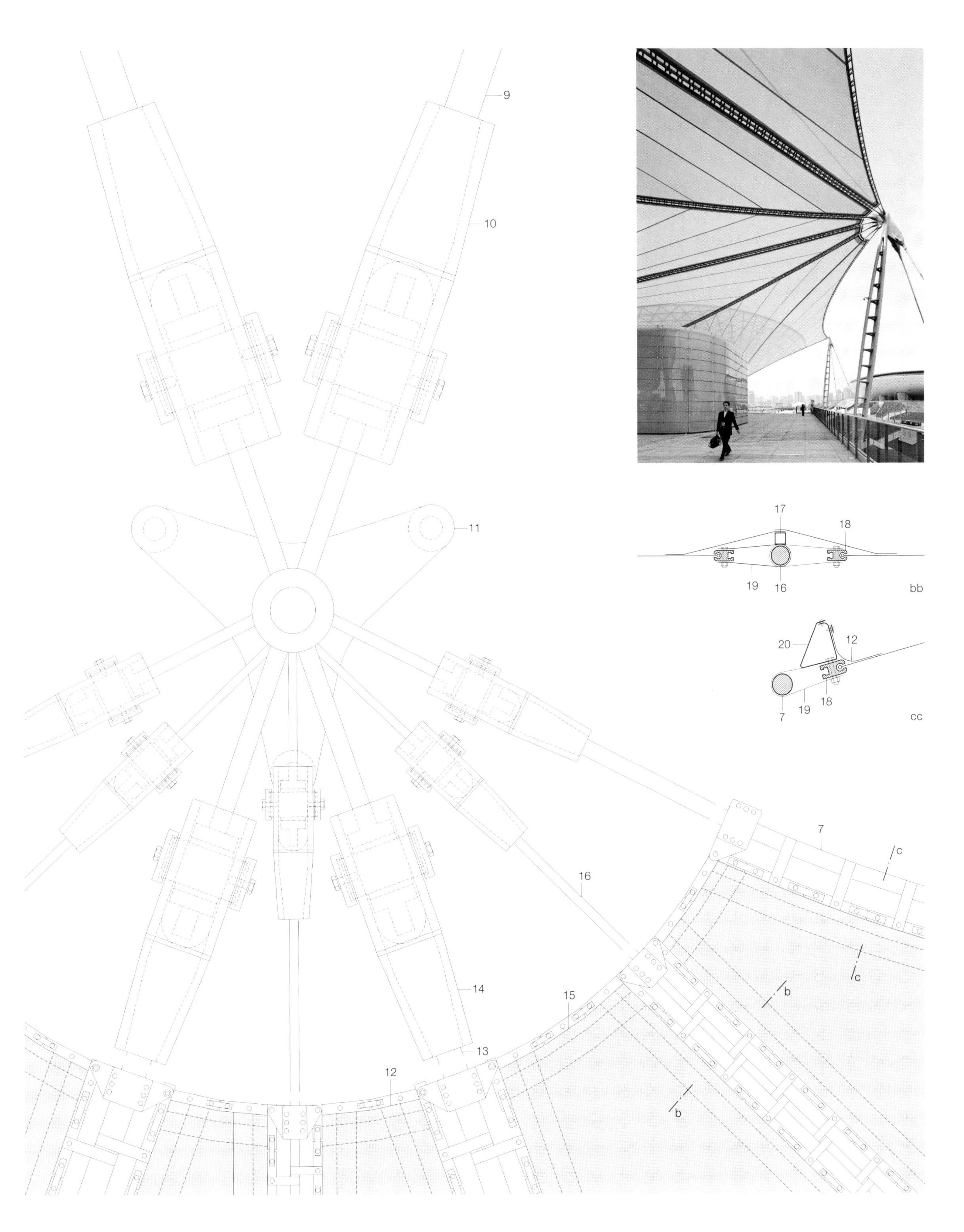
9
10
11
17
18
19
16
bb
20
12
7
19
18
cc
7
c
c
b
b
16
14
15
13
12

Memorial

Sachsenhausen, Germany, 2005

Architects:
hg merz architekten museumsgestalter, Stuttgart/Berlin
Project team:
Dietmar Bauer, Ulrich Lechtleitner, Mara Lübbert, Johannes Schrey, Michel Weber
Structural engineers:
Ingenieurgruppe Bauen, Berlin
Facade engineering:
Werner Sobek Ingenieure GmbH, Stuttgart

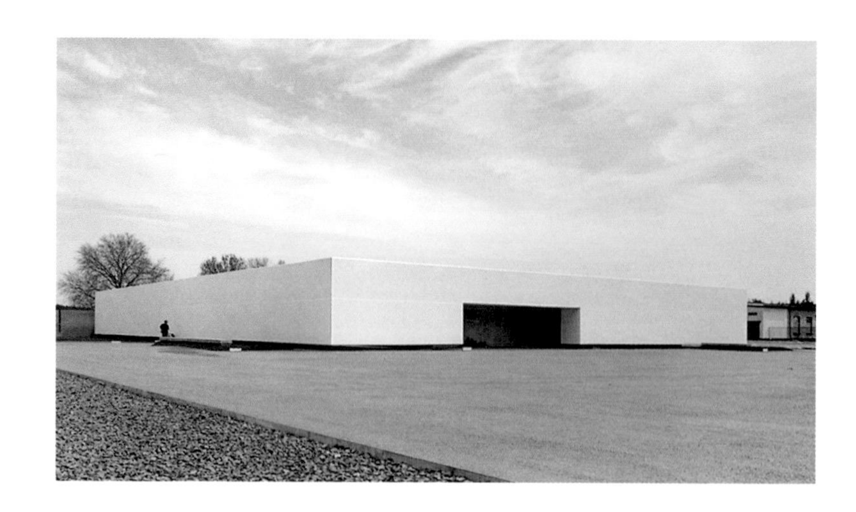

A flat, unassuming white block with just one entrance has been built to house the few original items left over from the former concentration camp in Sachsenhausen near Berlin – the so-called Station Z, the codename given to this extermination camp by Himmler's SS organisation. The architects of the memorial on the spacious site have tried to create a place of contemplation, a place of remembrance adjacent to the more traditional monument erected in 1961.
Although the layout of this clean-cut enclosure makes a reference to the existing topography, it does not attempt to reconstruct the original structure at this location. A clear ceiling height of just 2.60 m creates a compactness in the interior. Supported on just eight pad foundations, the walls stop 60 cm short of the ground and so the structure seems to float. The primary loadbearing structure, a steel space frame with welded joints, spans over an area measuring about 37 × 39 m, without any intervening columns. There is only one feature in the roof – a 22 × 10 m opening directly above the actual place of remembrance, which allows daylight into the interior.
The entire volume is enclosed in a translucent PTFE-coated glass-fibre membrane inside and outside; artificial lighting is therefore unnecessary. The steel structure can be discerned behind the seamless envelope, but plays only a secondary role visually. A special feature of this membrane design is the completely flat realisation without any visible details. A partial vacuum is maintained between the leaves of the envelope to ensure a continuous, smooth surface. The prestressing required is not maintained by the membrane in the usual way, i.e. by way of surfaces in double curvature, but rather by this partial vacuum and the concealed tensioning mechanisms at the corners. A grating between the primary loadbearing structure and the membrane serves as a backing for the membrane material.

- PTFE-coated glass-fibre cloth
- Stabilised by low pressure without curvature

Section • Plan
Scale 1:400

1 Entrance
2 Place of remembrance
3 Exhibition
4 Relics

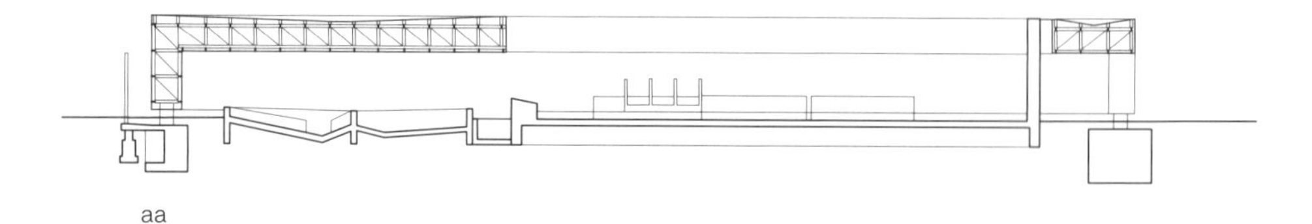

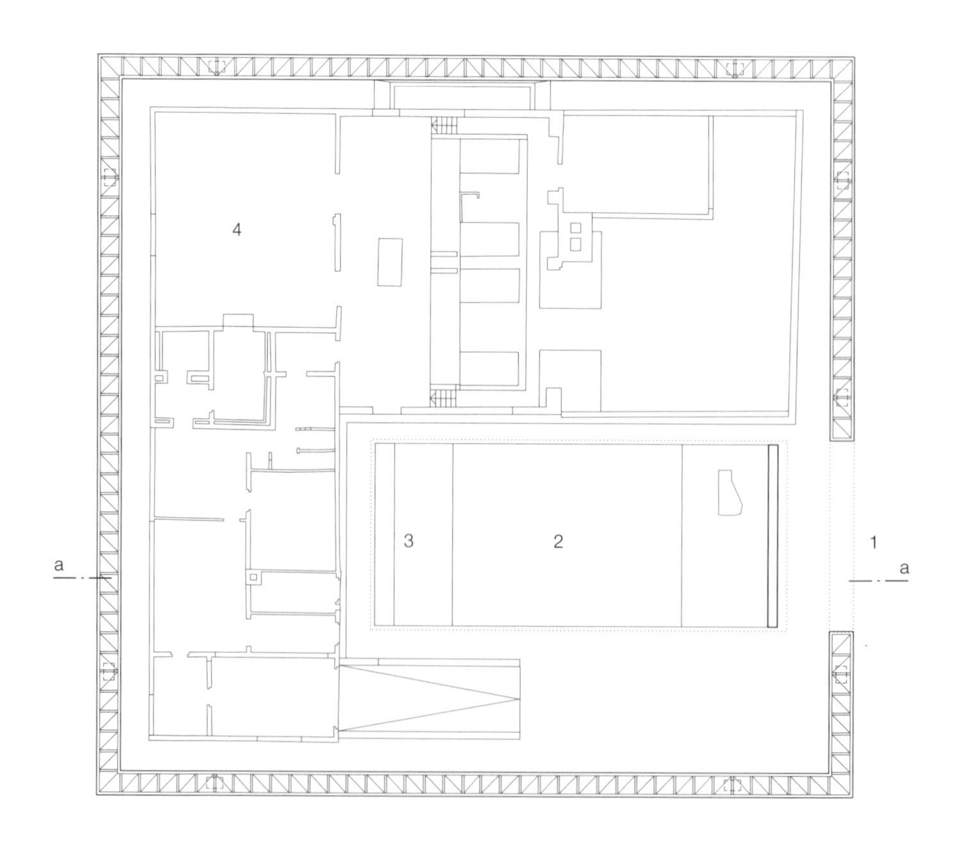

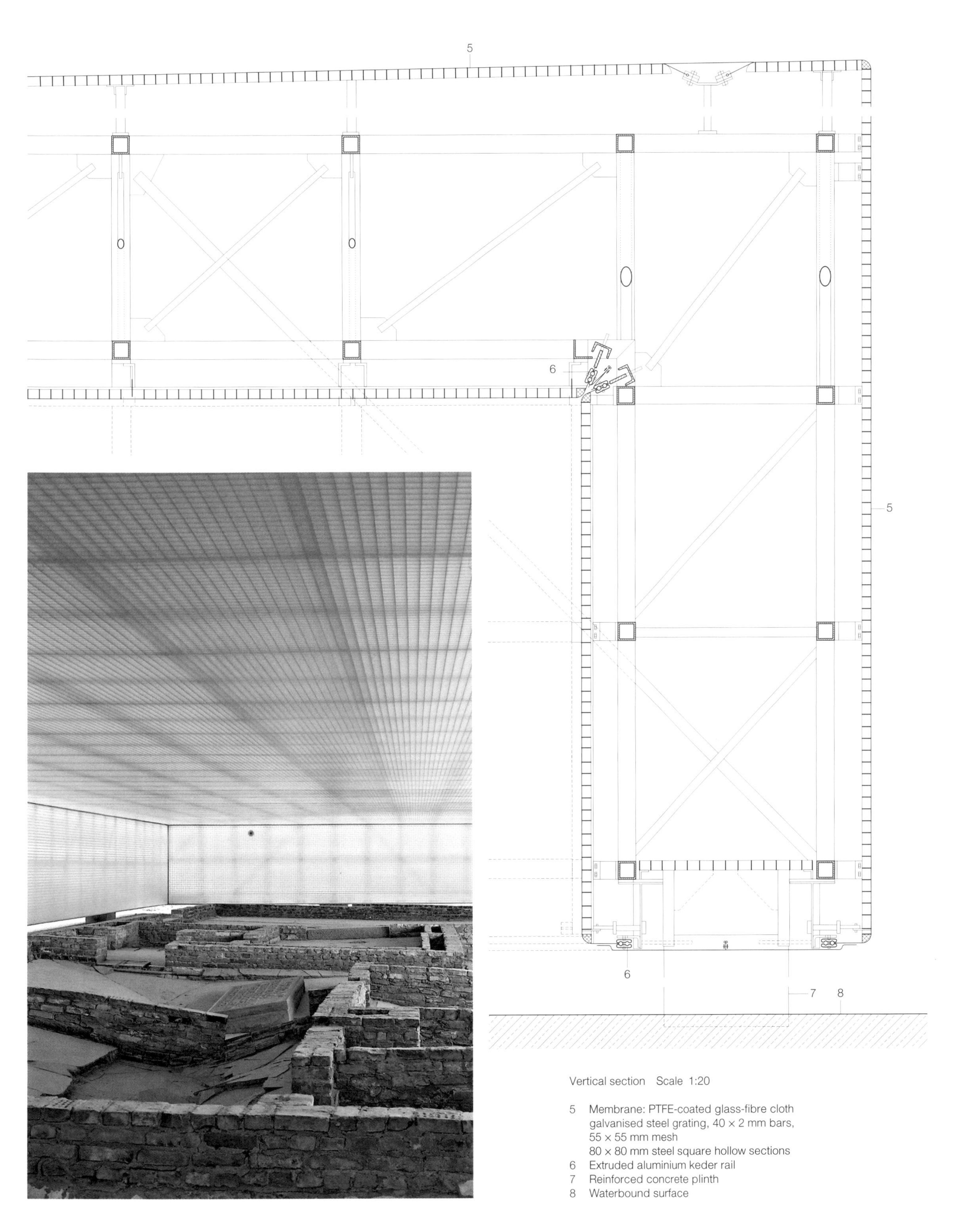

Vertical section Scale 1:20

5 Membrane: PTFE-coated glass-fibre cloth
galvanised steel grating, 40 × 2 mm bars, 55 × 55 mm mesh
80 × 80 mm steel square hollow sections
6 Extruded aluminium keder rail
7 Reinforced concrete plinth
8 Waterbound surface

Olympic stadium

Berlin, Germany, 2004

Architects:
von Gerkan, Marg & Partner, Berlin
Project team:
Jochen Köhn, Martin Glass, Ivanka Perkovic, Katja Bernert, Dagmar Weber, Ralf Sieber
Structural engineers:
Krebs & Kiefer, Darmstadt/Berlin
Schlaich Bergermann & Partner, Stuttgart

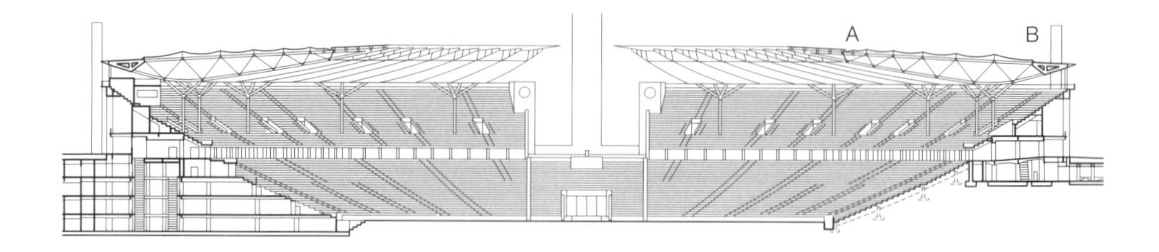

Originally built for the Olympic Games in 1936, this sports stadium in Berlin has remained a venue for major events and football matches to this day. A key element in the refurbishment project stretching over several years was the new membrane roof. It deliberately isolates itself from the heavyweight appearance of the existing structure but does pay homage to the historic axis of the whole complex by leaving an opening opposite the Bell Tower, above the Marathon Arch. This interruption to the roof ruled out the use of a circumferential ring, and so a lightweight cantilevering structure, with 76 radial trusses, was chosen. This roof structure is supported on 20 extremely slender steel columns in order to minimise the resulting obstruction to the view of the spectators. The roof trusses consist of a straight top chord and a curved bottom chord that reaches its maximum depth at the columns with their branching arms. Apart from the inner and outer edges of the roof, the entire area is covered by a double layer of membrane, one above, one below the roof structure. The upper membrane panels are fitted between the top chords of the radial trusses and are supported by tangential arches with a rise of 60–200 cm made from steel circular hollow sections. The membrane is tensioned over these arches and between the top chords of the radial trusses in such a way that the curved saddle surfaces necessary for membrane action ensue in the intervening areas. The lower membrane is tensioned between the lower chords to form a termination to the construction on the inside. Both membrane levels are characterised by high light transmittance and adequate strength, which is especially important for the lower membrane which must be able to accommodate maintenance foot traffic. Sound transmittance through the membrane also had to be guaranteed because the PA system is installed in the space between the membranes. The material that satisfies all these requirements is a PTFE-coated glass-fibre cloth, which is also favoured for its good self-cleaning behaviour.

- PTFE-coated glass-fibre cloth
- High light transmittance

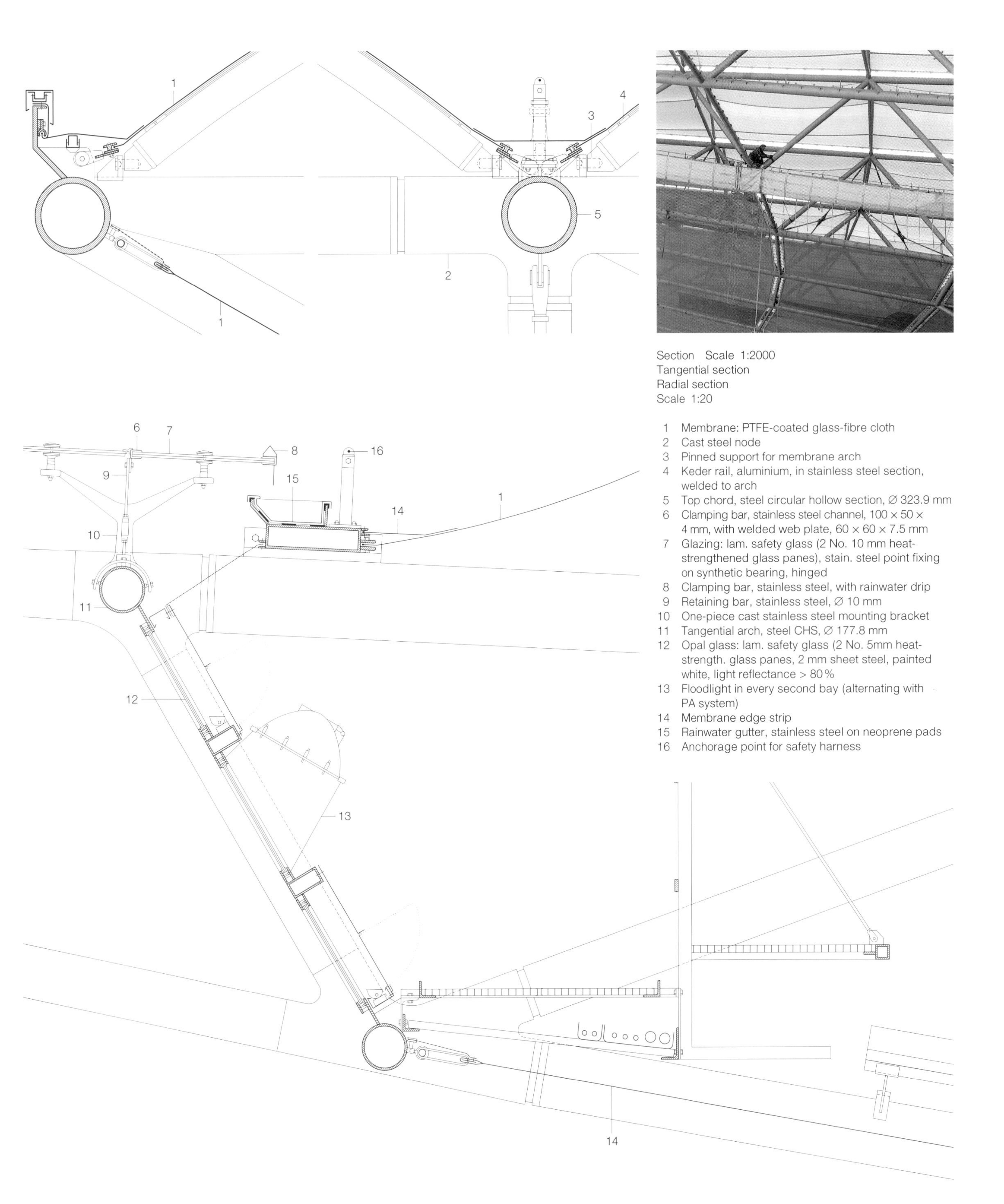

Section Scale 1:2000
Tangential section
Radial section
Scale 1:20

1. Membrane: PTFE-coated glass-fibre cloth
2. Cast steel node
3. Pinned support for membrane arch
4. Keder rail, aluminium, in stainless steel section, welded to arch
5. Top chord, steel circular hollow section, ∅ 323.9 mm
6. Clamping bar, stainless steel channel, 100 × 50 × 4 mm, with welded web plate, 60 × 60 × 7.5 mm
7. Glazing: lam. safety glass (2 No. 10 mm heat-strengthened glass panes), stain. steel point fixing on synthetic bearing, hinged
8. Clamping bar, stainless steel, with rainwater drip
9. Retaining bar, stainless steel, ∅ 10 mm
10. One-piece cast stainless steel mounting bracket
11. Tangential arch, steel CHS, ∅ 177.8 mm
12. Opal glass: lam. safety glass (2 No. 5mm heat-strength. glass panes, 2 mm sheet steel, painted white, light reflectance > 80 %
13. Floodlight in every second bay (alternating with PA system)
14. Membrane edge strip
15. Rainwater gutter, stainless steel on neoprene pads
16. Anchorage point for safety harness

A

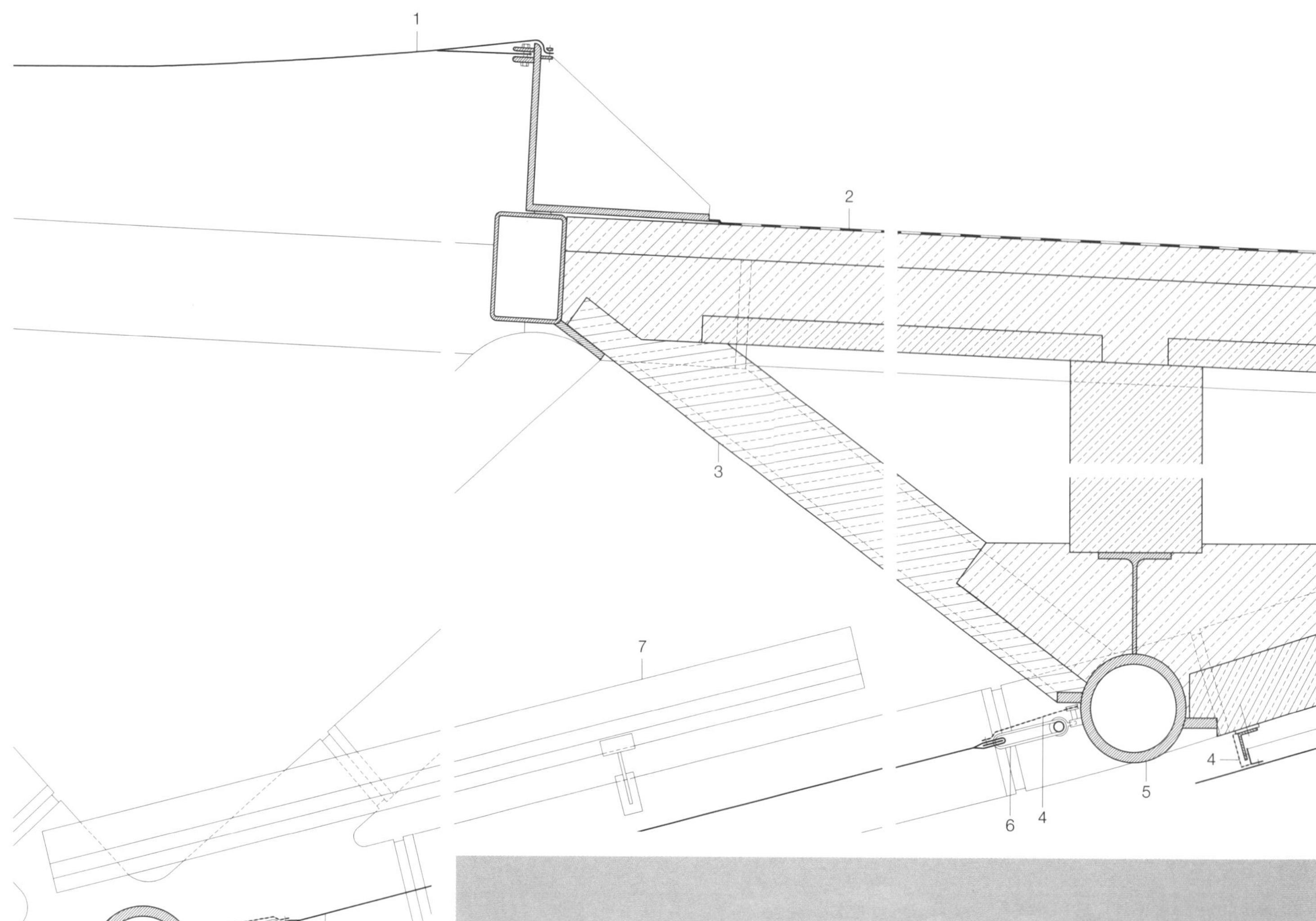

B

Radial section
Scale 1:20

1 Membrane: PTFE-coated glass-fibre cloth, 0.7 mm (1200 g/m²)
2 Waterproofing: synthetic coating, permanently elastic, UV-resistant
100 mm concrete topping
3 Edge bracing/counterweight, reinforced concrete
4 Insect screen
5 Tangential arch, steel circular hollow section, ⌀ 323.9 mm
6 Laced edge to membrane fitted around steel circular hollow section, ⌀ 38 mm
7 Fluorescent lamp on steel section, 40 × 100 mm
8 Membrane suitable for maintenance foot traffic: PTFE-coated open-weave glass-fibre cloth, 0.7 mm (1150 g/m²)
9 Cast steel node

Refurbishment and conversion of main railway station

Dresden, Germany, 2006

Architects:
Foster + Partners, London
Structural engineers:
Schmitt Stumpf Frühauf & Partner, Munich
Buro Happold, London

The overall concept for the refurbishment and conversion of the main railway station in Dresden calls for the preservation of the historic building fabric, but at the same time the enhancement of its effect and the introduction of innovative elements. All the additions and changes that had taken place over the years were therefore removed. What remained was the original iron structure and a few fragments from the 19th century. The new translucent roof, a total area of 30000 m², consists of PTFE-coated glass-fibre cloth. It was installed while trains continued to run underneath – the only time this has been done for a membrane of this size. But the greatest challenge was transferring the horizontal forces to the linear arch structure originally designed for vertical loads. The answer was to provide a new supporting structure for the membrane, which acts as an "adapter" to compensate for the three-dimensional prestressing forces, especially in the case of asymmetrical loads.
The existing loadbearing structure was divided into bays, each with two arches linked via horizontal bracing. The 10 m wide membrane panels are connected to the new pairs of steel circular hollow sections that transfer the forces via the space frame to the top chords of the existing trusses. Above the crown of each arch, the distance between the steel sections gradually widens to form a lens-shaped glazed rooflight. At every second arch between the central and side bays the roof covering is pulled down to form a conical low point. This enables drainage openings to be included and also results in a structurally favourable curvature in the longitudinal direction. At the other arches, the membrane is supported on steel cables hanging loosely between the rooflights and the side bays. If one membrane panel fails, extra cables at the top chords of the existing structure prevent excessive stresses. Following detailed tests, a PTFE-coated glass-fibre cloth was chosen for the roof covering. It satisfies the demands regarding fire protection, resistance to chemicals and fumes, plus self-cleaning and durability. The daylight filtering through the roof covering and the low sound reflectance create a pleasant atmosphere within the station.

- PTFE-coated glass-fibre cloth
- Erected without interrupting railway operations

Section
Scale 1:1000
Longitudinal section
Plan
Scale 1:2000

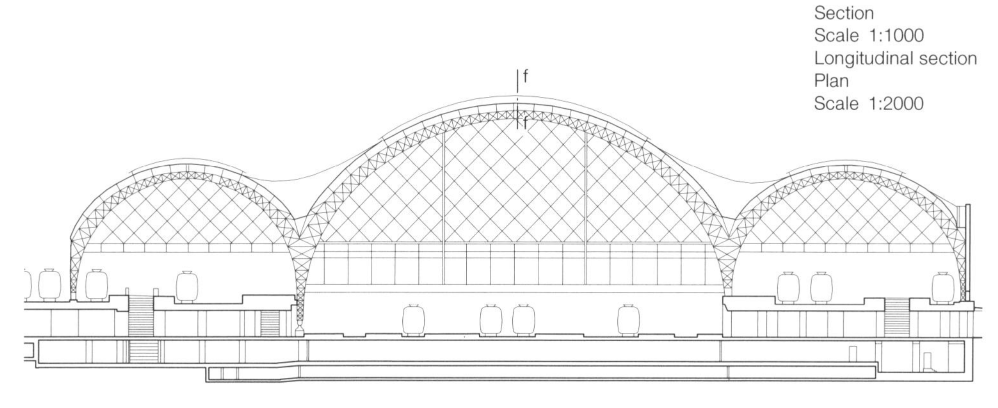

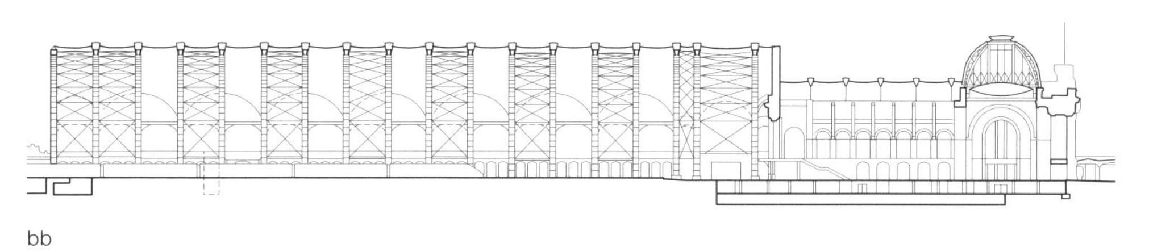

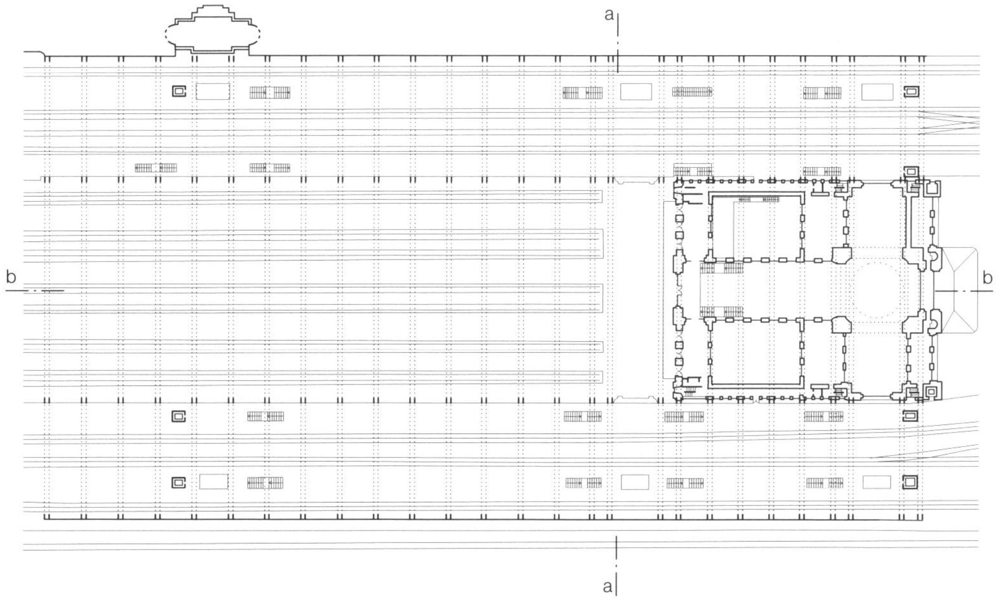

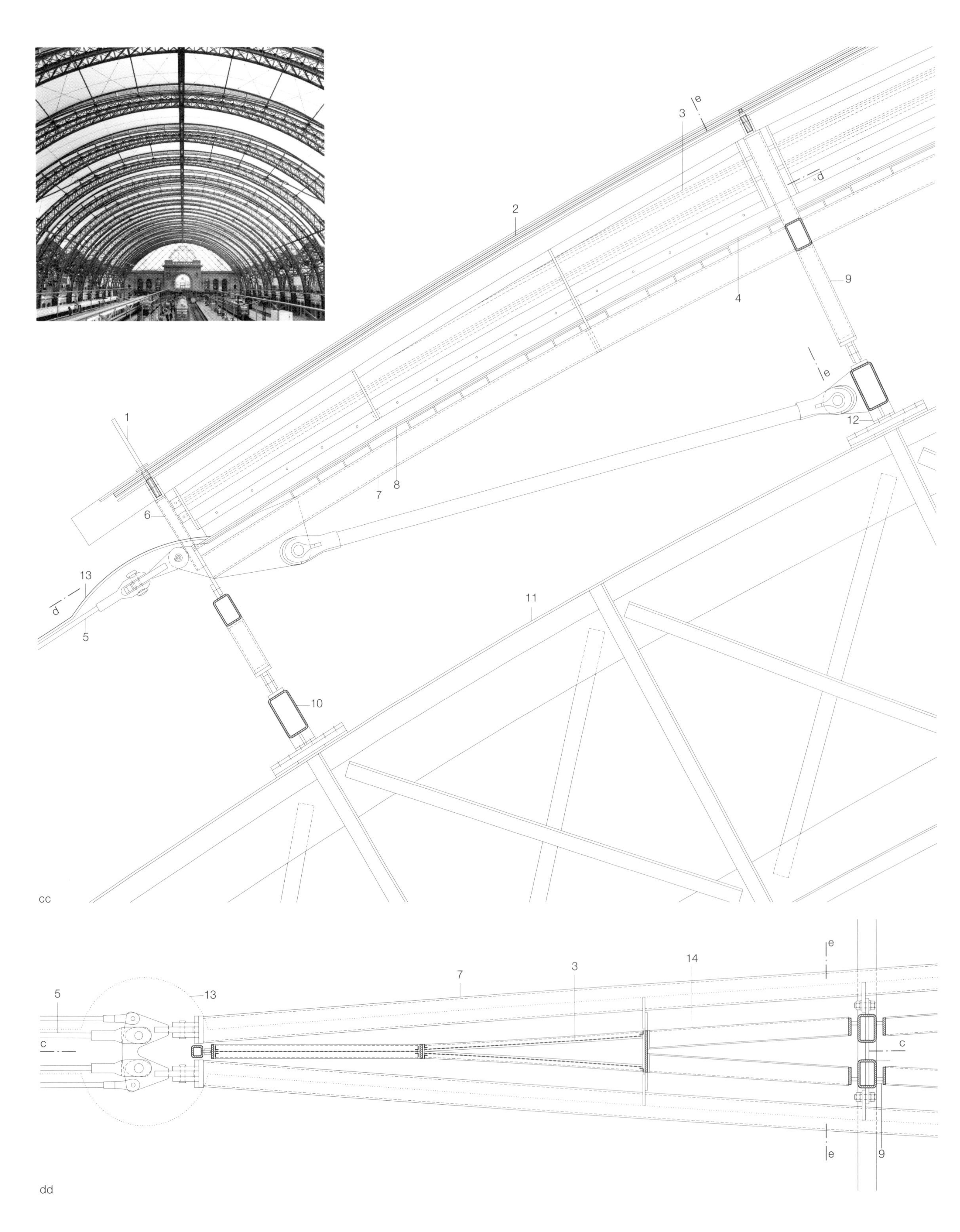
1
2
3
4
5
6
7
8
9
10
11
12
13
d
e
cc
5
13
7
3
14
c
e
9
dd

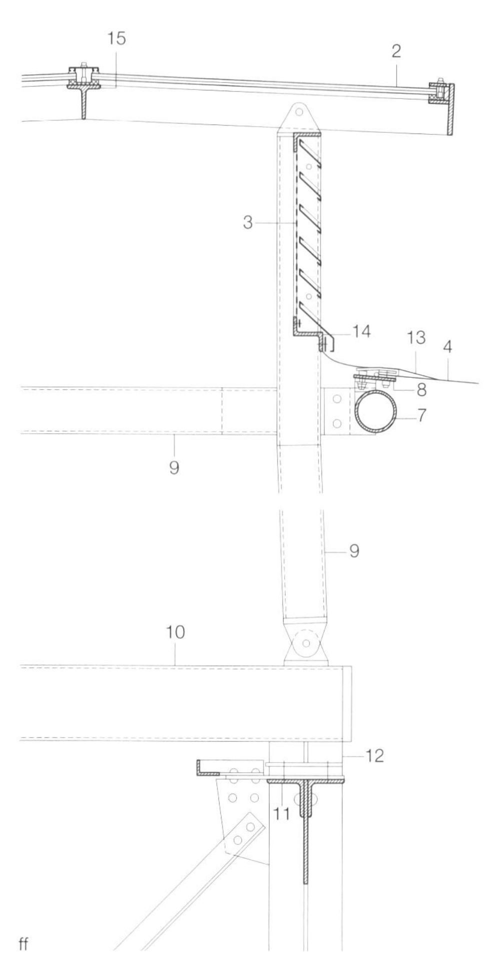

Vertical sections • Horizontal section (membrane omitted)
Scale 1:20

1 Lightning conductor, steel rod, ∅ 10 mm
2 Rooflight glazing: 16 mm laminated safety glass
3 Perforated sheet aluminium with riveted lamellae
4 Membrane: PTFE-coated glass-fibre cloth, 0.8 mm, white
weight: 1.2 kg/m²
tensile strength, warp/weft: 140/100 kN/m
light transmittance: 12.5 %
light reflectance: 73 %
5 Steel cable, electrogalvanised, ∅ 22 mm
6 Steel square hollow section, 50 × 50 × 4 mm
7 Steel circular hollow section, ∅ 114.3 × 12.5 mm
8 Clamping bar for fixing membrane, aluminium alloy, 115 × 10 mm
9 Steel rectangular hollow section, 120 × 80 × 12.5 mm
10 Purlin, steel rectangular hollow section, 200 × 100 mm
11 Top chord of existing arch: 2 No. 100 × 12 mm iron angles + 12 mm iron plate
12 Purlin adapter to compensate for tolerances, 10 mm steel plate, welded
13 Steel Z-section, 80 mm
14 Steel Z-section, 80 mm
15 Steel T-section, 90 mm

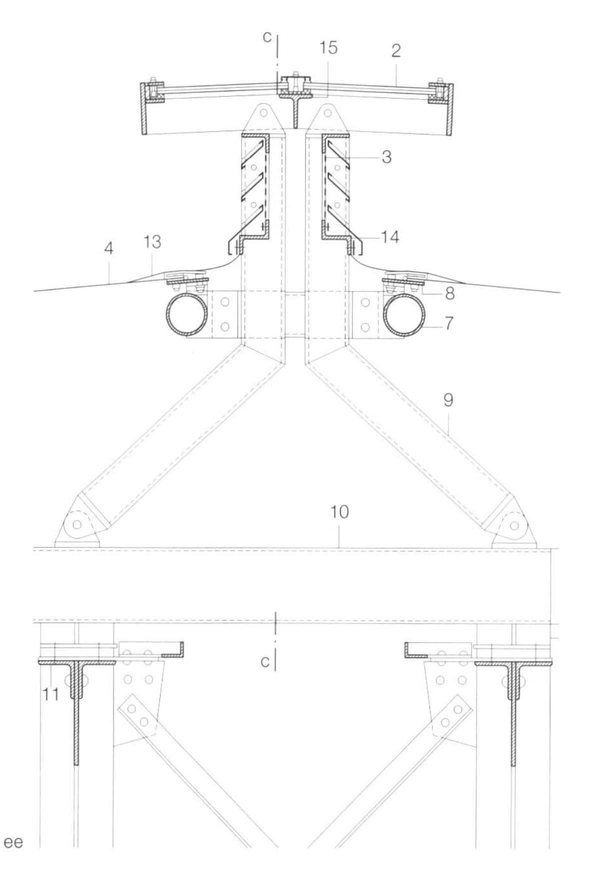

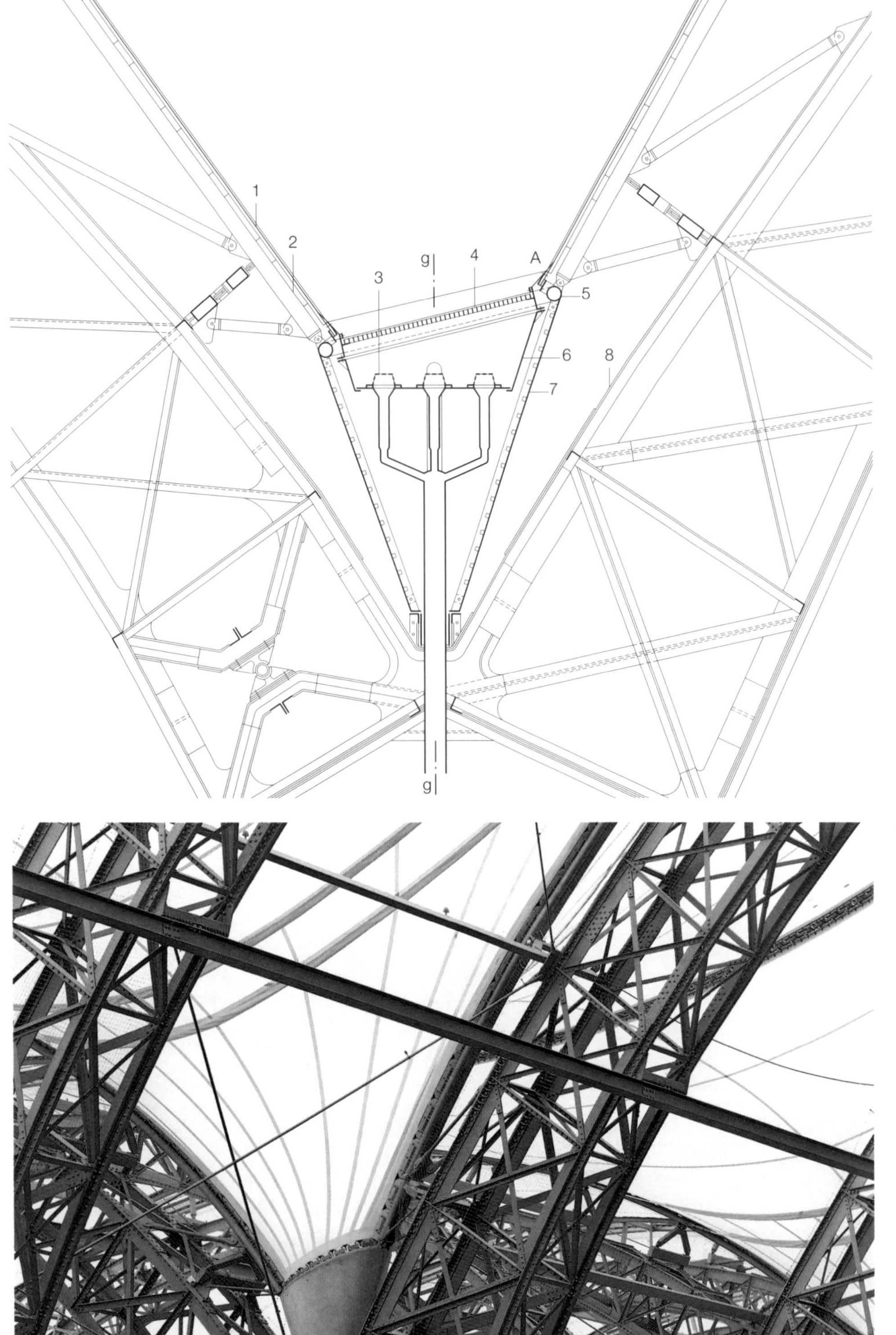

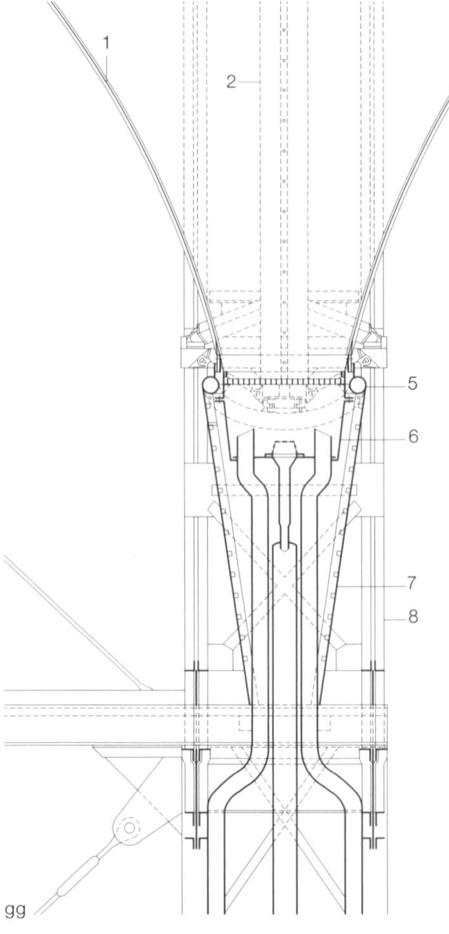

Vertical sections through low point Scale 1:50
Detail Scale 1:10

1 Membrane: PTFE-coated glass-fibre cloth, 0.8 mm, white
2 Steel circular hollow section, Ø 114.3 × 12.5 mm
3 Rainwater outlet
4 Grating, 30 × 30 × 3 mm
5 Oval ring, steel circular hollow section Ø 114.3 × 8 mm
6 Rainwater hopper, 6 mm sheet stainless steel
7 Funnel, 3 mm sheet steel
8 Top chord of existing arch
9 Seal, EPDM, 150 × 3 mm, for protecting membrane
10 Keder, EPDM, Ø 12 mm
11 Upper clamping bar, aluminium, 50 × 10 mm
12 Lower clamping bar, aluminium, 115 × 10 mm
13 Clamping bar, aluminium, 40 × 4 mm
14 Prefabricated membrane strip, welded to main membrane

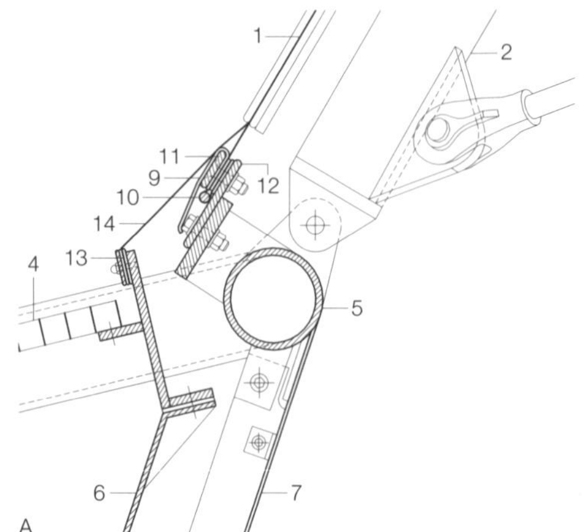

Passenger terminal complex, Suvarnabhumi International Airport

Bangkok, Thailand, 2005

Architects:
Murphy/Jahn, Chicago
ACT Consultants, Bangkok
TAMS Consultants / Earth Tech, New York
Structural engineers:
Werner Sobek Ingenieure, Stuttgart
Klimatechnik:
Transsolar, Stuttgart/Munich

The greatest challenge for the new Suvarnabhumi International Airport was to create a new gateway for Thailand that would be suited to the country's tropical climate. Temperatures between 25 and 35 °C prevail here over the whole year, accompanied by very high humidity and a sun that is always very high in the sky. The appearance of the airport is dominated by the central terminal building and the tube-like arms to the gates – the concourses. These essentially consist of a total of 104 identical three-chord trusses with a total length of approx. 3 km. Membranes span between these trusses in each case, an area of approx. 1000 m² spanning 27 m. Between the membranes there are areas of glazing. The membrane surfaces have to satisfy a demanding specification: on the one hand, the material must allow 1–2 % of the sunlight to pass through in the form of diffuse light so that there is an adequate level of background lighting in the interior during the day, on the other hand, however, it must limit the solar energy gains in the interior. The architects therefore developed a membrane envelope consisting of three layers.
On the outside, a hardwearing PTFE-coated glass-fibre cloth provides protection from the weather. This is characterised by its high reflectance, extremely high tear strength, dirt-repellent surface and excellent durability. Below this there is a grid of 1 × 1 m transparent polycarbonate panels, 6 mm thick, supported on a cable net. The joints between the panels are sealed for sound insulation. However, most functions are fulfilled by the inner membrane, which also relies on a glass-fibre backing material. Thanks to the perforations in this material, it is permeable to light and also acts as a sound attenuator. A silver low E coating on the inside reduces the radiation exchange between the outer membrane and components in the interior. In addition, the shimmering metallic surface reflects the pleasant cooling energy radiated from the thermoactive floor.

- 3-ply membrane envelope
- PTFE-coated glass-fibre cloth, polycarbonate panels, glass-fibre cloth with low E coating

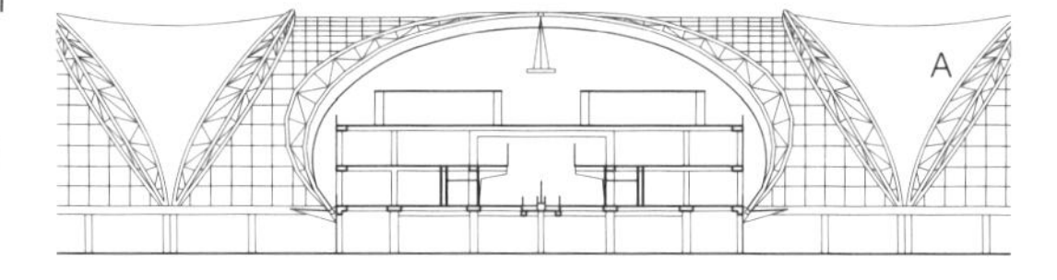

aa

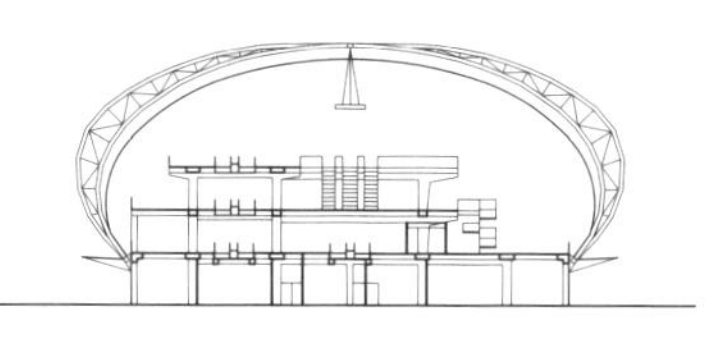
bb

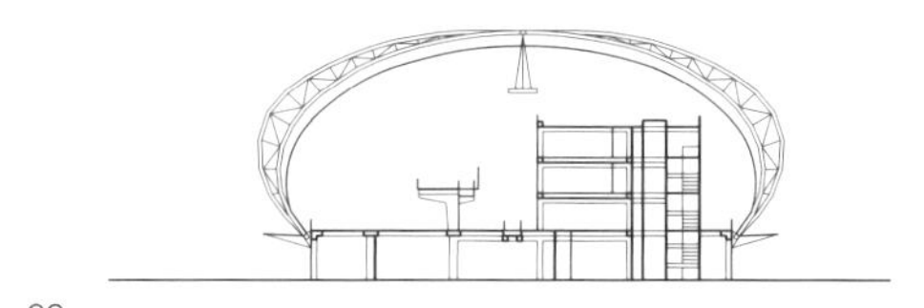
cc

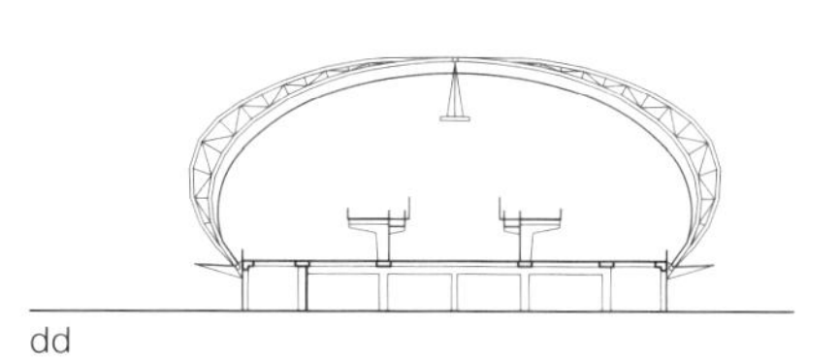
dd

Sections Scale 1:1500
Plan Scale 1:15 000

1 Three-level terminal approach structure
2 Multi-storey car park
3 Control tower
4 Palm garden
5 Low control tower
6 Terminal
7 Concourse

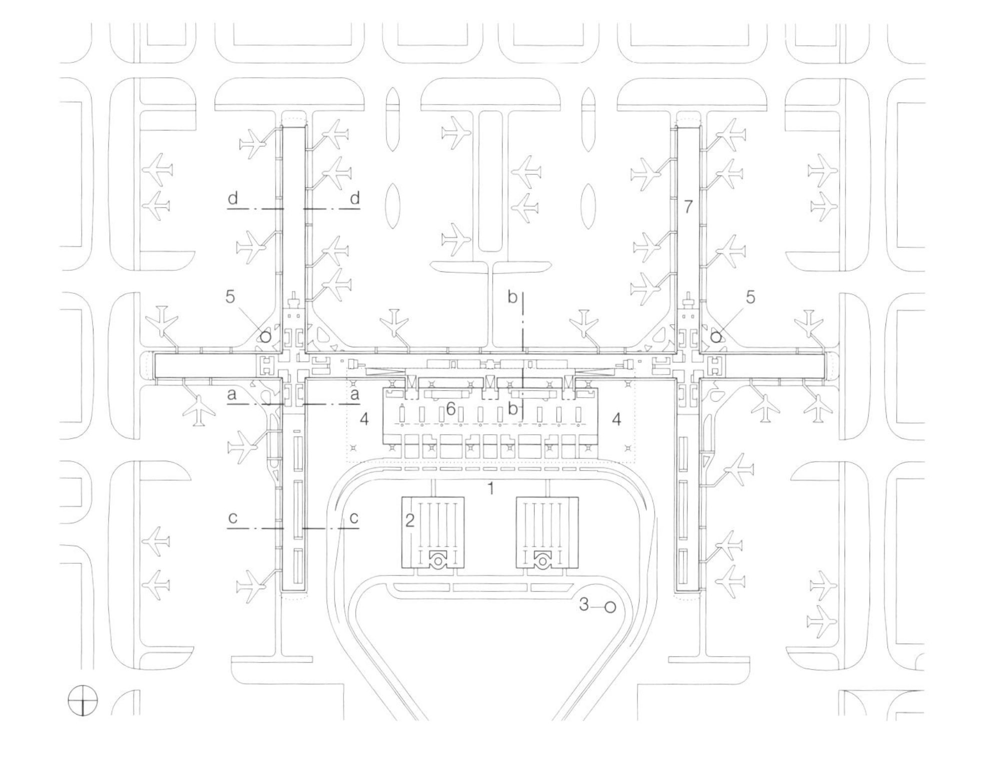

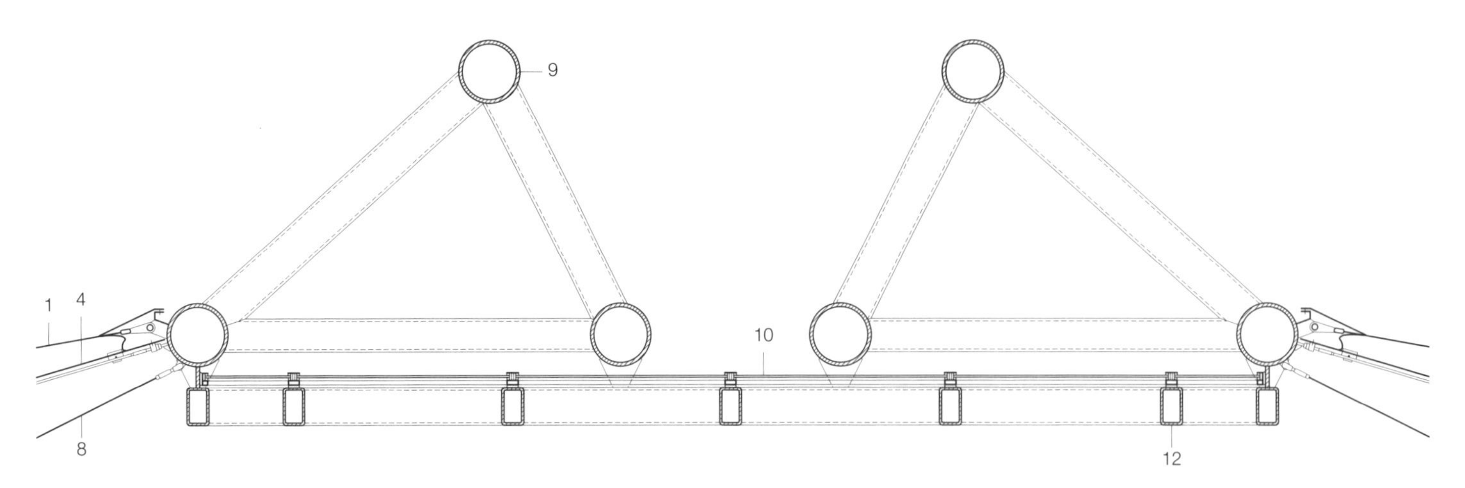

Section through membrane roof
Scale 1:50
Detail
Scale 1:10

1 Outer ply for weather protection: PTFE-coated glass-fibre cloth, 1.200 kg/m²
2 Tensioning mechanism attached to aluminium tube, Ø 40 mm
3 Edge strip: PTFE-coated glass-fibre cloth, attached after tensioning membrane
4 Central ply for insulating against aircraft noise: polycarbonate panels, 1000 × 1000 × 6 mm, transparent, 7.2 kg/m², R'_w = 35 dB, supported on cable net, class (fire) B1
5 Acoustic gasket, EPDM
6 Supporting cable net, steel, Ø 12 mm
7 Cable clamp, stainless steel
8 Inner ply as acoustic membrane: glass-fibre cloth with low E coating, open-pore aluminium, 0.320 kg/m², class (fire) A2
9 Three-chord truss, steel circular hollow sections, Ø 419 × 36 mm
10 Glazing: 15.5 mm laminated safety glass with low E coating, graduated printing as sunshade, from 20 % at eaves to 80 % at ridge
aluminium cover strips over vertical joints
silicone sealant in horizontal joints
11 Glazing bar, aluminium, 60 × 80 mm
12 Lattice structure, steel rectangular hollow sections, 150 × 250 × 16 mm

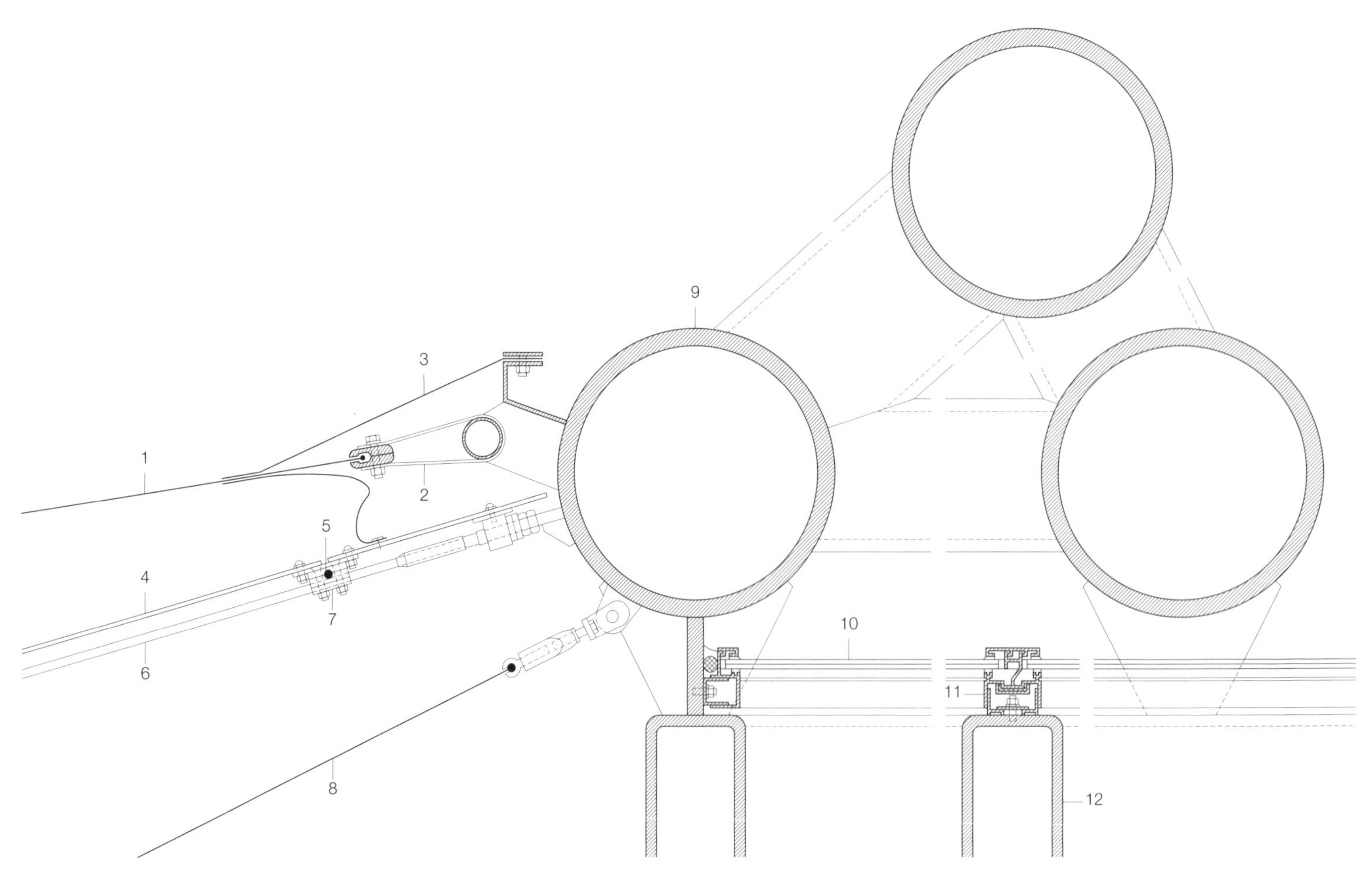

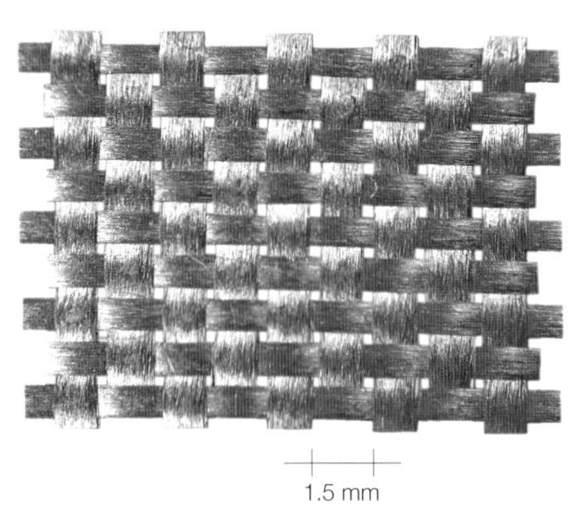

A

A Inner ply with low E coating
B 3-ply membrane envelope, acoustic principle
C Stepwise reduction in daylight permeability through 3-ply membrane envelope
D Relationship between building envelope, underfloor cooling and displacement ventilation
E Membrane lifted into position
F Membrane laid on central ply ready for spreading out
G Tensioned, temporary sliding membrane (PVC-coated polyester) with outer ply prior to laying
H Attaching the polycarbonate panels

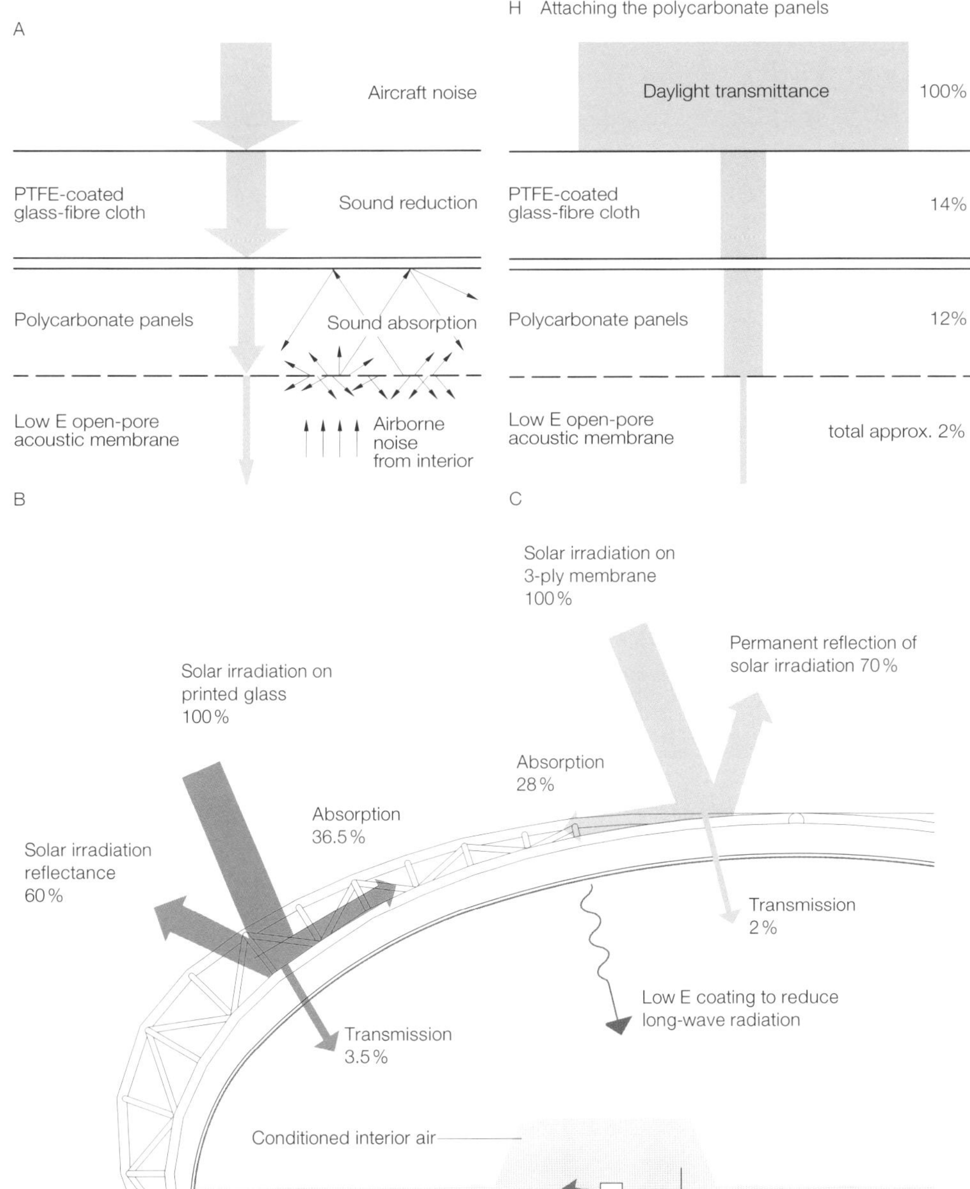

D

E

F

G

H

Canopy over Forum, "Old Spinning Mill"

Kolbermoor, Germany, 2010

Architects:
Behnisch Architekten, Munich
Stefan Behnisch, David Cook, Martin Haas, Robert Hösle
Assistants: Christian Glander, Wyly Brown
Site supervision:
Quest Architekten, Thomas Gerhager
Structural engineers:
Knippers Helbig Advanced Engineering, Stuttgart/New York
Project team:
Boris Peter, Klaus Pfaff, Ivan Tontchev

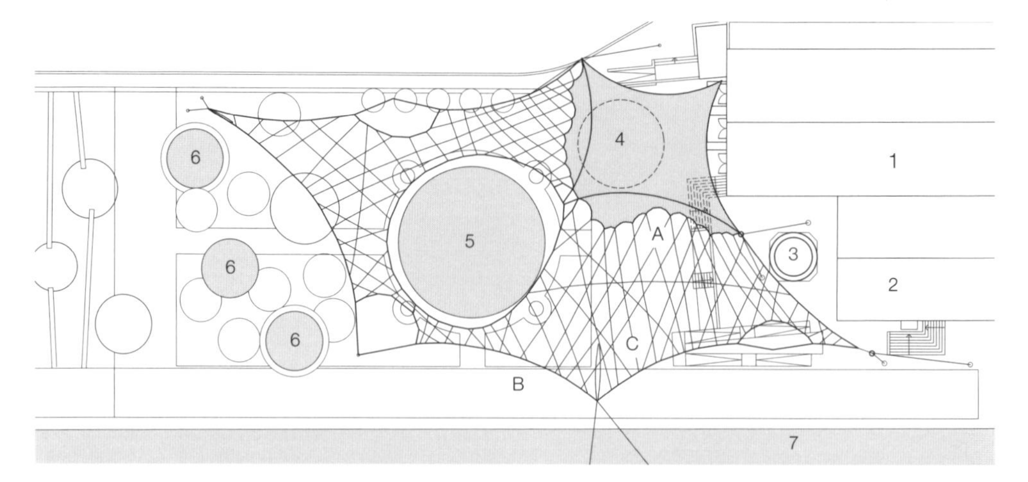

The town of Kolbermoor near Rosenheim owes its existence to the founding of the cotton-spinning mill here in the second half of the 19th century. The proximity of the railway line and the availability of water power were the deciding factors for choosing this location. A section of the River Mangfall was straightened over a length of nearly 3 km and a works canal of similar length was built. Following a chequered history, the company finally closed down in the 1990s. Many years of neglect followed before refurbishment, conversion and new building work started on this site, with the aim of creating a new urban district characterised by the remains of the area's industrial past.
The open space in the centre of this site, the new Forum, is intended as a venue for exhibitions and concerts, and to function as the vibrant hub of the "Old Spinning Mill". A PTFE-coated glass-fibre cloth provides a roof over part of this area. Around its perimeter, this membrane changes to a random, criss-crossing net of 10 cm wide membrane belts up to 40 m long – an interpretation of the "weaving" history of this location. This is not so much a roof, as more of a delicate sculpture linking the group of buildings, protected by conservation orders, on both sides of the canal. The net consists of fully bonded two-ply membrane belts held in place by stainless steel clamps specially designed for this project. At the intersections, the clamps are placed on top of each other and connected by a central bolt in order to carry the forces from different directions. Each pylon, made from glued laminated larch wood, has a ball-and-socket joint at the base which transfers the loads to the subsoil via a reinforced concrete pilecap and micropiles. Built-up welded membrane edges channel the rainwater to the two low points. At one of these points the water discharges freely into the garden, at the other there is a membrane pocket that transfers the water to the downpipe on the adjacent building.

- Canopy of PTFE-coated glass-fibre cloth
- Net structure of 2-ply, fully bonded membrane belts

Plan
Scale 1:750

Isometric views
Details
Scale 1:5

1 Boiler house
2 Café
3 Chimney
4 Area for events
5 Pagoda
6 Temporary pagoda
7 Works canal

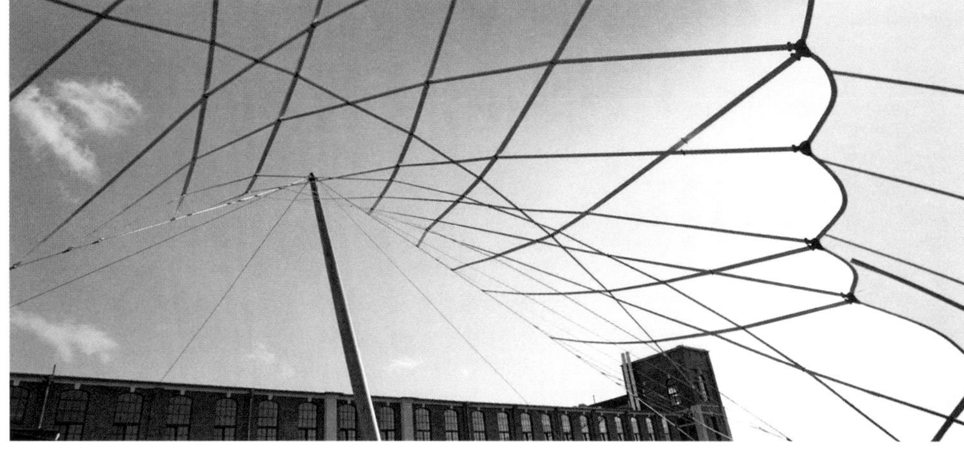

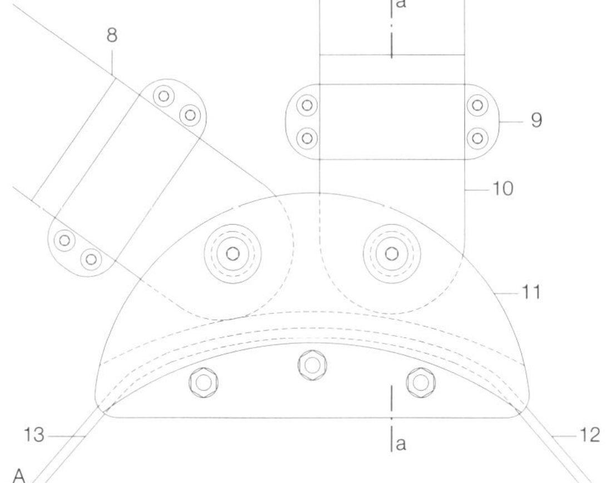

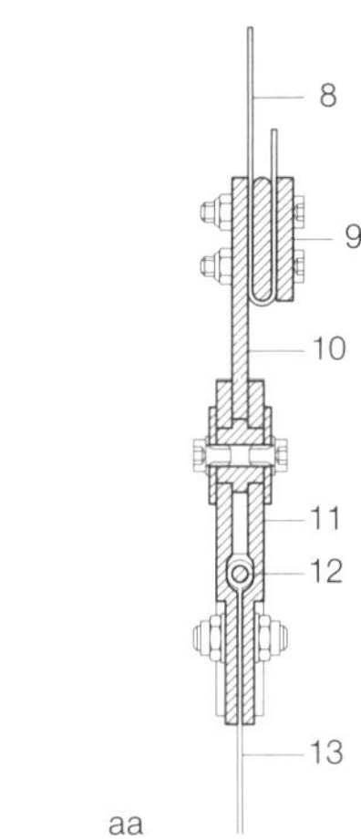

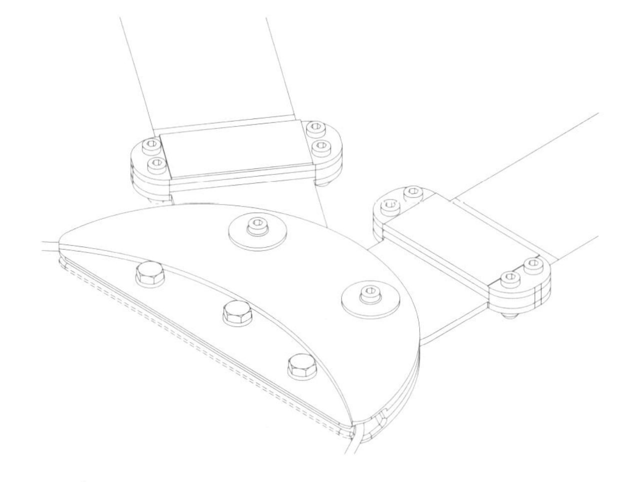

8 Membrane strap, 2-ply, PTFE-coated glass-fibre cloth, 2 No. 0.7 mm, fully bonded together by welding, tear strength of strap: 18.2 kN
9 Membrane clamp made from 2 profiled stainless steel plates: 140 × 50 × 6 mm and 140 × 50 × 8 mm, bolted together
10 Stainless steel plate, profiled, 135 × 140 × 3 mm
11 Stainless steel plate, profiled, 300 × 150 × 7 mm
12 Stainless steel cable, Ø 8 mm
13 Membrane, PTFE-coated glass-fibre cloth, 0.7 mm, tear strength, warp/weft: 140/120 kN/m
14 Membrane clamp made from 2 profiled stainless steel plates: 140 × 30 × 4 mm and 140 × 30 x 6 mm, bolted together
15 Countersunk-head bolt, M8, with hexagon socket
16 Stainless steel plate, profiled, 140 × 147 × 3 mm
17 Cable clamp made from 2 profiled stainless steel plates: 150 × 141 × 5 mm, bolted together
18 Edge cable, Ø 24 mm

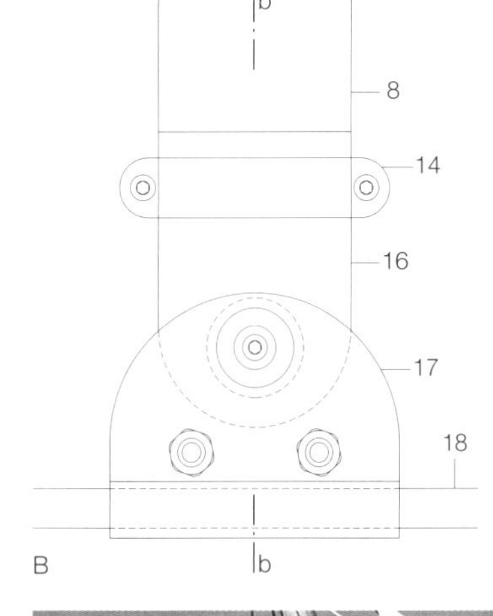

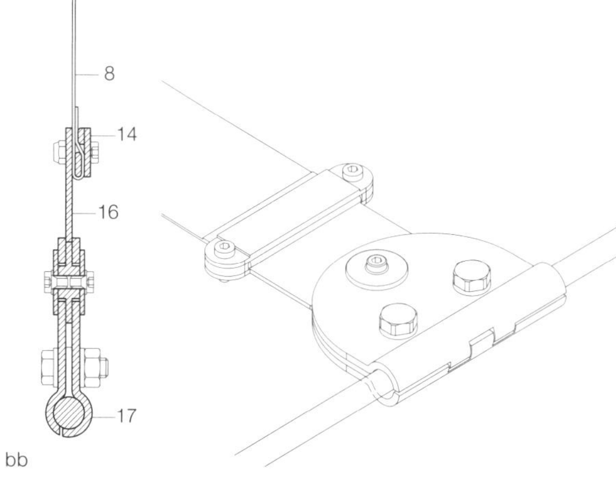

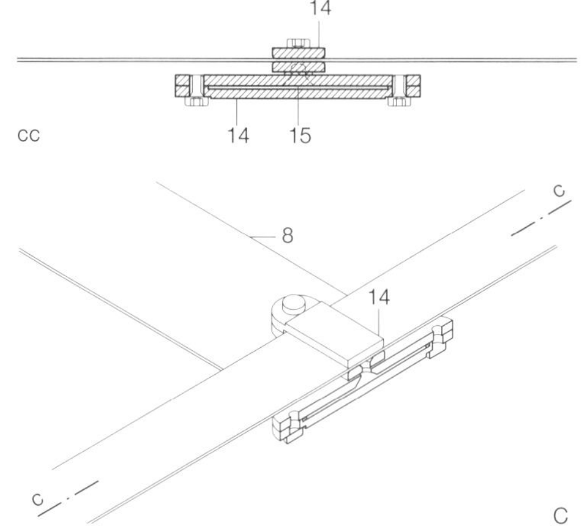

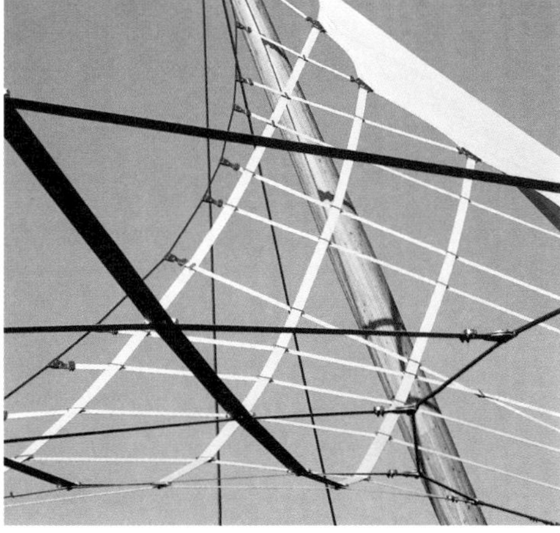

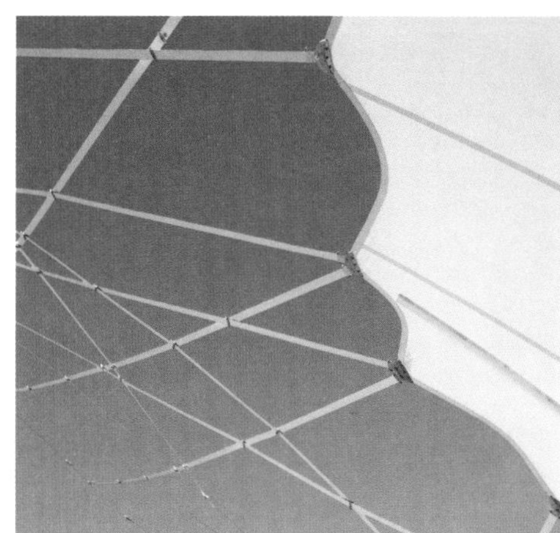

Open-air theatre, Josefsburg Arena

Kufstein, Austria, 2006

Architects:
Nikolai Kugel Architekten, Stuttgart
Structural engineers:
Alfred Rein Ingenieure, Stuttgart

Kufstein Fortress, originally built to serve as a means of defence, is today a popular tourist attraction. During the summer, open-air activities take place in the southern courtyard. A retractable canopy was planned so that events would not have to be cancelled due to inclement weather. However, it was important to ensure that the appearance of the complex as a whole was not spoiled. And the authority responsible for this heritage asset would also not agree to any anchorages in the historic walls. The answer was to design a delicate radial cable structure with the membrane stored in the centre when not in use. Activated by the touch of a button, it can be extended within four minutes.
The structure consists of 15 identical segments and is not unlike a spoked wheel lying on its side. Around the circumference, at a height of 10 m, is the "rim" – a polygonal compression ring supported on columns, five of which are "flying masts". The upper and lower radial cable "spokes" are fixed to a ring in the centre. Each membrane segment is suspended from 16 trolleys, eight on each lower radial cable. The first trolley in each group is fixed to the endless operating cable, which passes over pulleys parallel with the structural cables. Drive units controlled from a central point retract or extend the membrane as required via 15 separately controlled winches. Tensioning mechanisms stabilise the roof and ensure that it reaches the desired final position.
The movable membrane is made from a PTFE-coated fabric characterised by its good flexibility, flex cracking resistance and durability. The high light permeability and good soiling behaviour ensure a good appearance. In the extended position, a PTFE gutter welded along the edge collects the rainwater, which is then discharged via hoppers and downpipes at the columns. Two further aspects have become apparent since the roof was erected: in the extended position it improves the acoustics and with its atmospheric lighting installations it also underscores the uniqueness of this location.

- PTFE-coated fabric
- Convertible roof

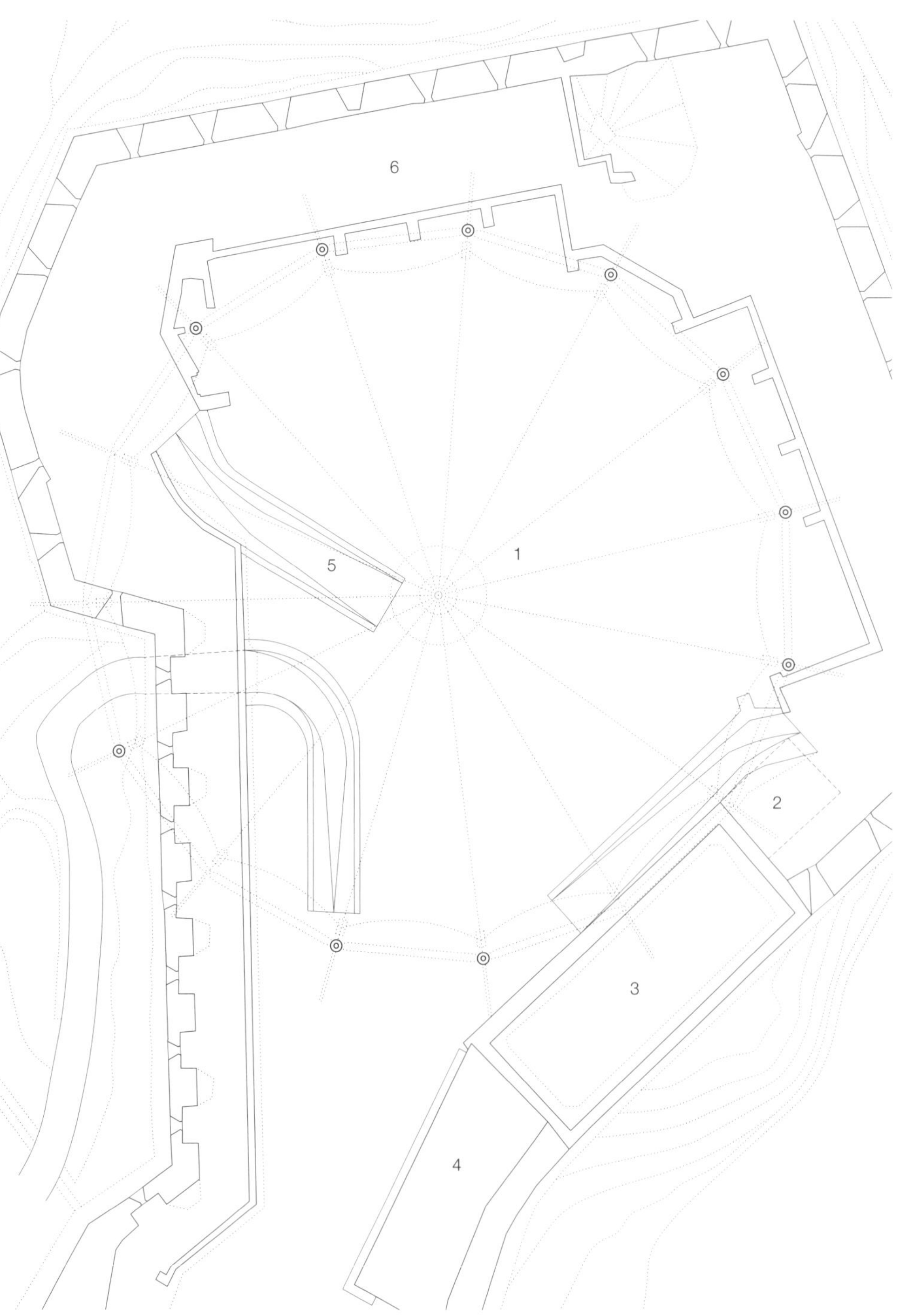

Site plan
Scale 1:2500
Plan • Section through roof system
Scale 1:500

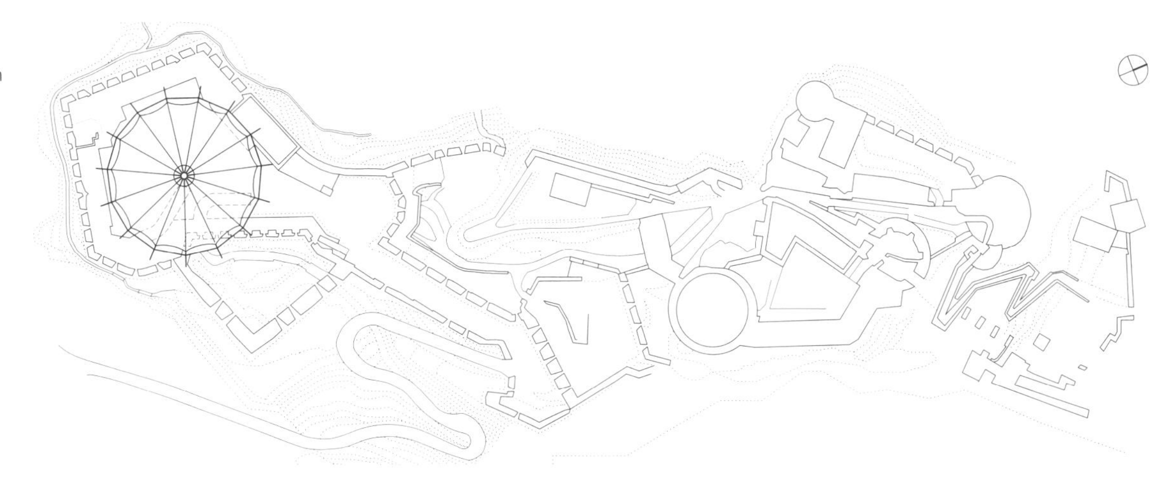

1 Courtyard
2 Director's box
3 Bar
4 WCs
5 Ramp
6 Casemate

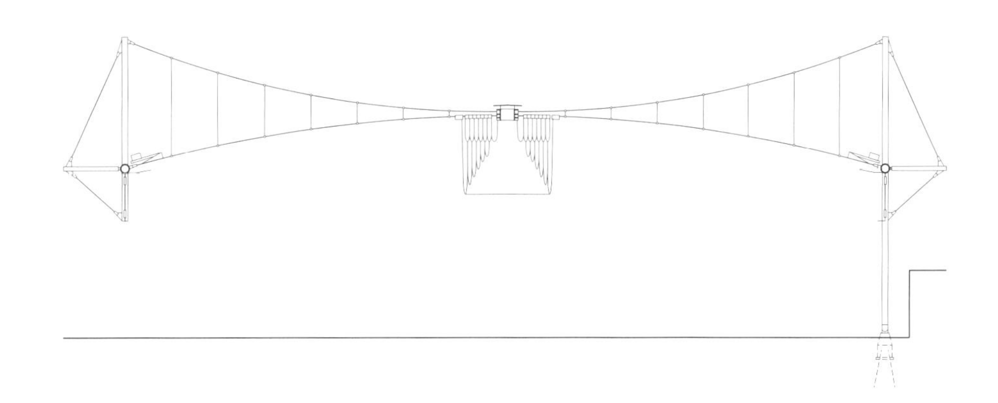

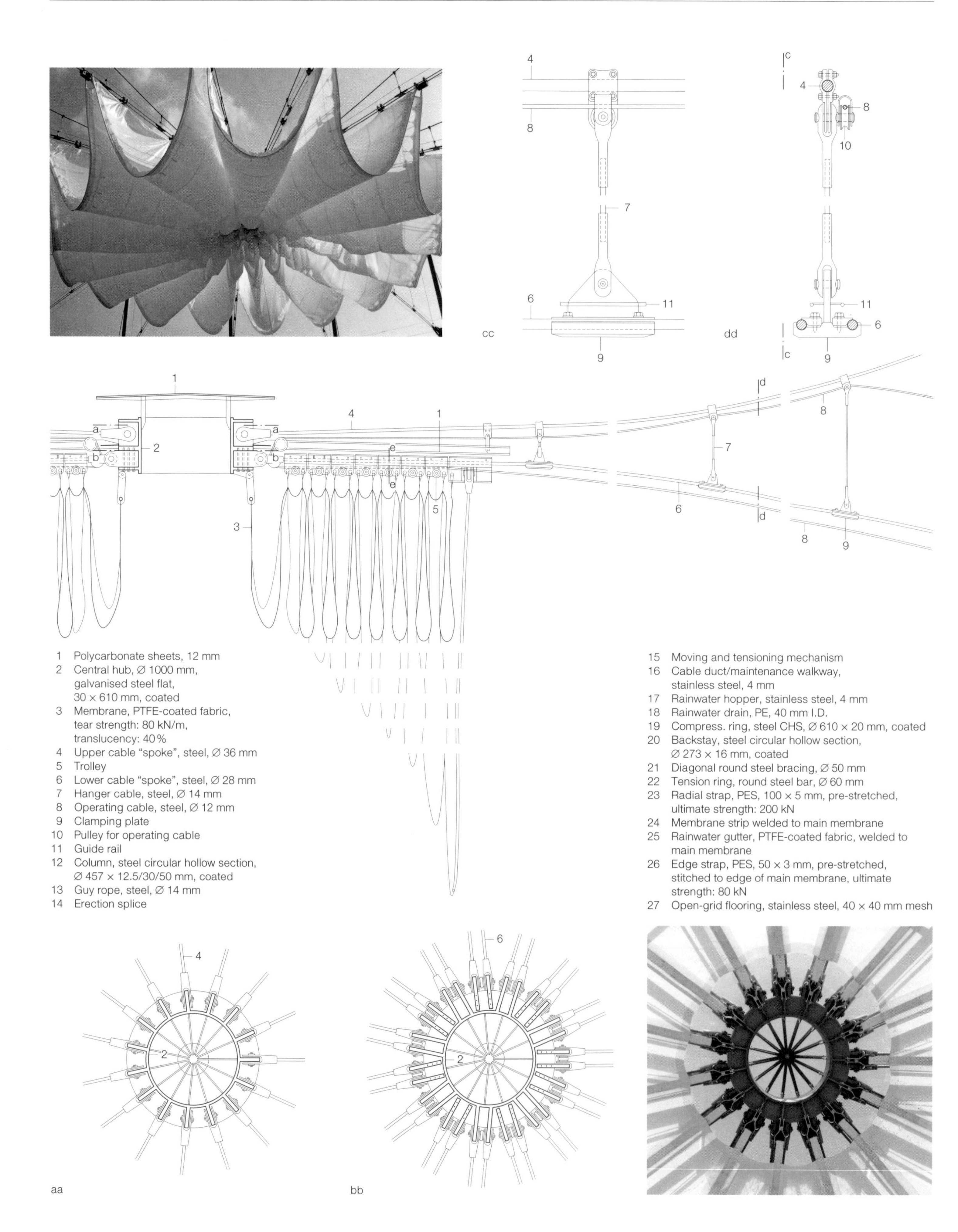

1 Polycarbonate sheets, 12 mm
2 Central hub, Ø 1000 mm, galvanised steel flat, 30 × 610 mm, coated
3 Membrane, PTFE-coated fabric, tear strength: 80 kN/m, translucency: 40 %
4 Upper cable "spoke", steel, Ø 36 mm
5 Trolley
6 Lower cable "spoke", steel, Ø 28 mm
7 Hanger cable, steel, Ø 14 mm
8 Operating cable, steel, Ø 12 mm
9 Clamping plate
10 Pulley for operating cable
11 Guide rail
12 Column, steel circular hollow section, Ø 457 × 12.5/30/50 mm, coated
13 Guy rope, steel, Ø 14 mm
14 Erection splice
15 Moving and tensioning mechanism
16 Cable duct/maintenance walkway, stainless steel, 4 mm
17 Rainwater hopper, stainless steel, 4 mm
18 Rainwater drain, PE, 40 mm I.D.
19 Compress. ring, steel CHS, Ø 610 × 20 mm, coated
20 Backstay, steel circular hollow section, Ø 273 × 16 mm, coated
21 Diagonal round steel bracing, Ø 50 mm
22 Tension ring, round steel bar, Ø 60 mm
23 Radial strap, PES, 100 × 5 mm, pre-stretched, ultimate strength: 200 kN
24 Membrane strip welded to main membrane
25 Rainwater gutter, PTFE-coated fabric, welded to main membrane
26 Edge strap, PES, 50 × 3 mm, pre-stretched, stitched to edge of main membrane, ultimate strength: 80 kN
27 Open-grid flooring, stainless steel, 40 × 40 mm mesh

Vertical section
Horizontal section
Scale 1:50
Details
Scale 1:10

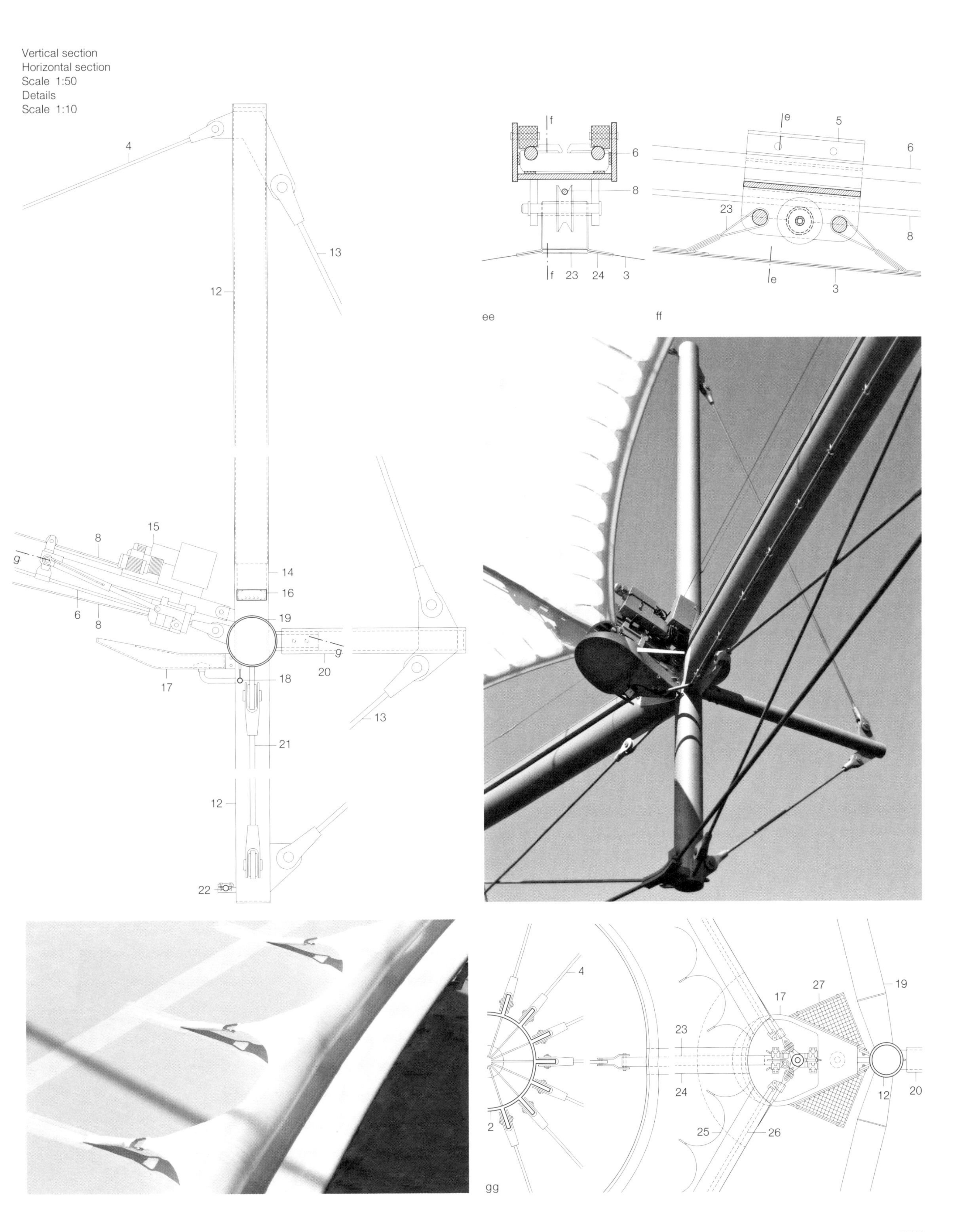

Statutory instruments, directives, standards

The EU has issued directives for a number of products, the particular aim of which is to ensure the safety and health of users. These directives must be implemented in the EU member states in the form of compulsory legislation and regulations.
The directives themselves do not contain any technical details, but instead only lay down the mandatory underlying requirements. The corresponding technical values are specified in associated sets of technical rules (e.g. codes of practice) and in the form of EN standards harmonised throughout Europe.
Generally, the technical rules provide advice and information for everyday activities. They are not statutory instruments, but rather give users decision-making aids, guidelines for implementing technical procedures correctly and/or practical information for turning legislation into practice. The use of the technical rules is not compulsory; only when they have been included in government legislation or other statutory instruments do they become mandatory, or when the parties to a contract include them in their conditions.
In Germany the technical rules include DIN standards, VDI directives and other publications such as the Technical Rules for Hazardous Substances.
The standards are divided into product, application and testing standards. They often relate to just one specific group of materials or products and are based on the corresponding testing and calculation methods for the respective materials and components. The latest edition of a standard – which should correspond with the state of the art – always applies. A new or revised standard is first published as a draft for public discussion before (probably with revisions) it is finally adopted as a valid standard.
The origin and area of influence of a standard can be gleaned from its designation:

- DIN plus number (e.g. DIN 4108) is essentially a national document (drafts are designated with "E" and preliminary standards with "V").
- DIN EN plus number (e.g. DIN EN 335) is a German edition of a European standard – drawn up by the European Standardisation Organisation CEN – that has been adopted without amendments.
- DIN EN ISO (e.g. DIN EN ISO 13786) is a standard with national, European and worldwide influence. Based on a standard from the International Standardisation Organisation ISO, a European standard was drawn up, which was then adopted as a DIN standard.
- DIN ISO (e.g. DIN ISO 2424) is a German edition of an ISO standard that has been adopted without amendments.

The following compilation represents a selection of statutory instruments, directives and standards that reflects the state of the art regarding building materials and building material applications as of March 2011.

Materials and semi-finished products

DIN EN ISO 1163-1 Plastics – Unplasticised polyvinyl chloride (PVC-U) moulding and extrusion materials – Part 1: Designation system and basis for specifications. Oct 1999
DIN EN ISO 1163-2 Plastics – Unplasticised polyvinyl chloride (PVC-U) moulding and extrusion materials – Part 2: Preparation of test specimens and determination of properties. Oct 1999
DIN EN 1778 Characteristic values for welded thermoplastic constructions – Determination of allowable stresses and moduli for design of thermoplastic equipment. Dec 1999
DIN EN ISO 1872-1 Plastics – Polyethylene (PE) moulding and extrusion materials – Part 1: Designation system and basis for specifications. Oct 1999
DIN EN ISO 1872-2 Plastics – Polyethylene (PE) moulding and extrusion materials – Part 2: Preparation of test specimens and determination of properties. May 2007
DIN EN ISO 1873-1 Plastics – Polypropylene (PP) moulding and extrusion materials – Part 1: Designation system and basis for specifications. Dec 1995
DIN EN ISO 1873-2 Plastics – Polypropylene (PP) moulding and extrusion materials – Part 2: Preparation of test specimens and determination of properties. Nov 2007
DIN ISO 2076 Textiles – Man-made fibres – Generic names. May 2001
DIN 7724 Polymeric materials; grouping of polymeric materials based on their mechanical behaviour. Apr 1993
DIN EN ISO 8257-1 Plastics – Polymethylmethacrylate (PMMA) moulding and extrusion materials – Part 1: Designation system and basis for specifications. Sept 2006
DIN EN ISO 8257-2 Plastics – Poly(methyl methacrylate) (PMMA) moulding and extrusion materials – Part 1: Designation system and basis for specifications. Jun 2006
DIN EN 13706-1 Reinforced plastic composites – Specification for pultruded profiles – Part 1: Designation. Feb 2003
DIN EN 13706-2 Reinforced plastic composites – Specifications for pultruded profiles – Part 2: Methods of test and general requirements. Feb 2003
DIN EN 13706-3 Reinforced plastic composites – Specifications for pultruded profiles – Part 3: Specific requirements. Feb 2003
DIN EN 14020 Reinforcements – Specification for textile glass rovings. Mar 2003
DIN 16944 Glass fibre reinforced reaction resin moulding materials; test methods. Jul 1988
DIN 16945 Testing of resins, hardeners and accelerators, and catalyzed resins. Mar 1989
DIN 16946 Cured casting resins. Mar 1989
DIN 18820-1 Laminates of textile glass-reinforced unsaturated polyester and phenacrylic resins for loadbearing structural members (GF-UP, GF-PHA); structure, manufacture and characteristics. Mar 1991
DIN 18820-2 Laminates of textile glass-reinforced unsaturated polyester and phenolic resins for loadbearing structural members (GF-UP, GF-PHA); physical parameters for standard laminates. Mar 1991
DIN 18820-3 Laminates of textile glass-reinforced unsaturated polyester and phenacrylic resins for loadbearing structural members (GF-UP, GF-PHA); protective measures for loadbearing laminates. Mar 1991
DIN 18820-4 Laminates of textile glass-reinforced unsaturated polyester and phenacrylic resins for loadbearing structural members (GF-UP, GF-PHA); tests and quality control. Mar 1991
DIN 61853-1 Textile glass; textile glass mats for plastics reinforcement; technical delivery conditions. Apr 1987
DIN 61853-2 Textile glass; textile glass mats for plastics reinforcement; classification and application. Apr 1987
DIN 61854-1 Textile glass; woven glass fabrics for plastics reinforcement; woven glass filament fabric and woven roving; technical delivery conditions. Apr 1987
DIN 61854-2 Textile glass; woven glass fabrics for plastics reinforcement; woven glass filament fabric and woven roving; types. Apr 1987

Analysis

DIN 4134 Air-supported structures; structural design, construction and operation. Feb 1983
DIN EN 13782 Temporary structures – Tents – Safety. May 2006
VDI 2014 Blatt 1 Design and construction of FRP components (fibre-reinforced plastics); basics. Jul 1989
VDI 2014 Blatt 2 Development of FRP components (fibre-reinforced plastics); concept and design. Sept 1993
VDI 2014 Blatt 3 Development of fibre-reinforced plastic components – Analysis. Sept 2006
Bau-Uberwachungsvereins e.V. (BUV): Tragende Kunststoffbauteile im Bauwesen – Empfehlung. Aug 2010 Download: www.bvpi.de/shared/pdf-dokumente/Kunststoff_Empf.pdf. 20 Aug 2010
Clarke, John L.: Structural Design of Polymer Composites – EUROCOMP Design Code and Handbook. London, 1996

Building physics

DIN EN 832 Thermal performance of buildings. Jun 2003
DIN 4102 Fire behaviour of building materials and building components. Nov 2004 to Mar 2011
DIN 4108-2 Thermal protection and energy economy in buildings – Part 2: Minimum requirements to thermal insulation. Jul 2003
DIN 4108-3 Thermal protection and energy economy in buildings – Part 3: Protection against moisture subject to climate conditions; Requirements and directions for design and construction. Jul 2001
DIN 4109 Sound insulation in buildings. May 2010 to Mar 2011
DIN 5034 Daylight in interiors. Sept 2010 to Mar 2011
DIN EN ISO 6946 Building components and building elements – Thermal resistance and thermal transmittance – Calculation method. Apr 2008
DIN EN ISO 7345 Thermal insulation – Physical quantities and definitions. Jan 1996
ISO 8302 Thermal insulation; determination of steady-state thermal resistance and related properties; guarded hot plate apparatus. Aug 1991
DIN EN ISO 10211 Thermal bridges in building construction – Heat flows and surface temperatures – Detailed calculations. Apr 2008
DIN EN 12898 Glass in building – Determination of the emissivity. Apr 2001
DIN EN 13125 Shutters and blinds – Additional thermal resistance – Allocation of a class of air permeability to a product. Oct 2001
DIN EN 13363-1 Solar protection devices combined with glazing – Calculation of solar and light transmittance – Part 1: Simplified method. Sept 2007
DIN EN 13363-2 Solar protection devices combined with glazing – Calculation of total solar energy transmittance and light transmittance – Part 2: Detailed calculation method. Jun 2005
DIN EN 13501-1 Fire classification of construction products and building elements – Part 1: Classification using data from reaction to fire tests. Jan 2010
DIN EN 13501-2 Fire classification of construction products and building elements – Part 2: Classification using data from fire resistance tests, excluding ventilation services. Feb 2010
DIN EN 13501-5 Fire classification of construction products and building elements – Part 5: Classification using data from external fire exposure to roofs tests. Feb 2010
DIN EN 14501 Blinds and shutters – Thermal and visual comfort – Performance characteristics and classification. Feb 2006
DIN V 18599 (preliminary standard) Energy efficiency of buildings – Calculation of the net, final and primary energy demand for heating, cooling, ventilation, domestic hot water and lighting. Feb 2007
VDI 2719 Sound isolation of windows and their auxiliary equipment. Aug 1987
Energieeinsparverordnung (EnEV) Verordnung uber energieeinsparenden Warmeschutz und energieeinsparende Anlagentechnik bei Gebauden. Mar 2009
International Glazing Database IGDB Version 17.1. Download: http://windows.lbl.gov/materials/igdb/. 20 Aug 2010

Testing standards: mechanical properties

DIN ISO 34-1 Rubber, vulcanised or thermoplastic – Determination of tear strength – Part 1: Trouser, angle and crescent test pieces. Jul 2004
DIN EN ISO 178 Plastics – Determination of flexural properties. Apr 2011
DIN EN ISO 291 Plastics – Standard atmospheres for conditioning and testing. Aug 2008
DIN EN ISO 527-1 (draft standard) Plastics – Determination of tensile properties – Part 1: General principles. May 2010
DIN EN ISO 527-2 (draft standard) Plastics – Determination of tensile properties – Part 2: Test conditions for moulding and extrusion plastics. May 2010
DIN EN ISO 527-3 Plastics – Determination of tensile properties – Part 3: Test conditions for films and sheets. Jul 2003
DIN EN ISO 527-4 Plastics – Determination of tensile properties – Part 4: Test conditions for isotropic and anisotropic fibre-reinforced plastic composites. Jul 1997
DIN EN ISO 527-5 Plastics – Determination of tensile properties – Part 5: Test conditions for unidirectional fibre-reinforced plastic composites. Jan 2010
DIN EN ISO 604 Plastics – Determination of compressive properties. Dec 2003
DIN EN ISO 899-1 Plastics – Determination of creep behaviour – Part 1: Tensile creep. Oct 2003

DIN EN ISO 899-2 Plastics – Determination of creep behaviour – Part 2: Flexural creep by three-point loading. Oct 2003
DIN EN ISO 1421 Rubber- or plastic-coated fabrics – Determination of tensile strength and elongation at break. Aug 1998
DIN EN 1875-3 Rubber- or plastic-coated fabrics – Determination of tear strength – Part 3: Trapezoidal method. Feb 1998
DIN EN ISO 2578 Plastics – Determination of time-temperature limits after prolonged exposure to heat. Oct 1998
DIN EN ISO 10350-1 Plastics – Acquisition and presentation of comparable single-point data – Part 1: Moulding materials. Jan 2010
DIN EN ISO 11403-2 Plastics – Acquisition and presentation of comparable multi-point data – Part 2: Thermal and processing properties. Jul 2004
DIN EN ISO 14125 Fibre-reinforced plastic composites – Determination of flexural properties. Jun 2003
DIN EN ISO 14126 Fibre-reinforced plastic composites – Determination of compressive properties in the in-plane direction. Jun 2003
DIN EN ISO 14129 Fibre-reinforced plastic composites – Determination of the in-plane shear stress/shear strain response, including the in-plane shear modulus and strength, by ±45° tension test method. Feb 1998
DIN EN ISO 14130 Fibre-reinforced plastic composites – Determination of apparent interlaminar shear strength by short beam method. Feb 1998
DIN EN ISO 22088 Plastics – Determination of resistance to environmental stress cracking (ESC). Oct 2009 to Mar 2011
DIN 53350 Testing of plastic films and coated textile fabrics, manufactured using plastics; determination of stiffness in bending, method according to Ohlsen. Jan 1980
DIN 53359 Testing of artificial leather and similar sheet materials – Flex cracking test. Nov 2006
DIN 53362 Testing of plastic films and textile fabrics (excluding non-wovens), coated or non-coated fabrics – Determination of stiffness in bending – Method according to Cantilever. Oct 2003
DIN 53363 Testing of plastic films – Tear test using trapezoidal test specimen with incision. Oct 2003
DIN 53442 Flexural fatigue testing of plastics using flat specimens. Sept 1990
DIN 53598-1 Statistical evaluation at off-hand samples with examples from testing of rubbers and plastics. Jul 1983
ASTM D 4851 Standard test methods for coated and laminated fabrics for architectural use. 2007

Testing standards: building physics
DIN EN 410 Glass in building – Determination of luminous and solar characteristics of glazing. Apr 2011
DIN EN 673 Glass in building – Determination of thermal transmittance (U-value) – Calculation method. Apr 2011
EN ISO 1182 Fire technical testing of building products, non-combustibility. Jan 2009
DIN EN 1634-1 Fire resistance and smoke control tests for door, shutter and openable window assemblies and elements of building hardware – Part 1: Fire resistance tests for doors, shutters and openable windows. Jan 2009
EN ISO 1716 Reaction to fire tests for building Products – Determination of the heat of combustion. Jan 2009
DIN EN ISO 11925-2 Reaction to fire tests – Ignitability of products subjected to direct impingement of flame – Part 2: Single-flame source test. Feb 2011
DIN EN 12865 Hygrothermal performance of building components and building elements – Determination of the resistance of external wall systems to driving rain under pulsating air pressure. Jul 2001
DIN EN 13501 Fire classification of construction products and building elements. Feb 2010 to Mar 2011
DIN EN 13823 Reaction to fire tests for building products – Building products excluding floorings exposed to the thermal attack by a single burning item. Dec 2010
DIN 53765 Testing of plastics and elastomers; thermal analysis; DSC method. Mar 1994
ASTM E 424 Standard test methods for solar energy transmittance and reflectance (terrestrial) of sheet materials. 1971

Testing standards: durability
DIN EN ISO 105 Textiles – Tests for colour fastness. Aug 2010 to Mar 2011
DIN EN ISO 305 Plastics – Determination of thermal stability of poly(vinyl chloride), related chlorine-containing homopolymers and copolymers and their compounds – Discoloration method. Oct 1999
DIN EN 673 Glass in building – Determination of thermal transmittance (U-value) – Calculation method. Apr 2011
DIN EN 1367 Tests for thermal and weathering properties of aggregates. Jun 2010 to Mar 2011
DIN EN ISO 4892-1 Plastics – Methods of exposure to laboratory light sources – Part 1: General guidance. Sept 2001
DIN EN ISO 4892-2 Plastics – Methods of exposure to laboratory light sources – Part 2: Xenon-arc lamps. Jan 2011
DIN EN ISO 4892-3 Plastics – Methods of exposure to laboratory light sources – Part 3: Fluorescent UV lamps. May 2006
DIN EN 13583 Flexible sheets for waterproofing – Bitumen, plastic and rubber sheets for roof waterproofing – Determination of hail resistance. Nov 2001
ASTM E 424 Standard Test Methods for Solar Energy Transmittance and Reflectance (Terrestrial) of Sheet Materials. 1971

Other testing standards
DIN 53370 Testing of plastics films – Determination of the thickness by mechanical scanning. Jun 2006

Environmental impact of polymers
DIN EN ISO 11469 Plastics – Generic identification and marking of plastics products. Oct 2000
DIN EN ISO 14021/A1 Environmental labels and declarations – Self-declared environmental claims (Type II environmental labelling) . Jan 2010
DIN EN ISO 14040 Environmental management – Life cycle assessment – Principles and framework. Nov 2009

Bibliography

Part A Polymers and membranes in architecture

Albus, Volker (ed.): Icons of Design: The 20th Century. Munich/London/New York, 2004
Blundell-Jones, Peter; Hübner, Peter: Peter Hübner – Building as a Social Process. Stuttgart, 2007
Burgard, Roland (ed.): Kunststoffe und freie Formen – ein Werkbuch. Vienna, 2004
Campos, Cristian: Plastic design. Cologne, 2007
Genzel, Elke; Voigt, Pamela: Kunststoffbauten: Teil 1: Die Pioniere. Weimar, 2005
Graefe, Rainer: Vela Erunt – die Zeltdächer der römischen Theater und ähnlicher Anlagen. Mainz, 1979
Herzog, Thomas: Pneumatic Structures: A Handbook of Inflatable Architecture. Stuttgart, 1976
Jeska, Simone: Transparent Plastics – Design and Technology. Basel/Boston/Berlin, 2008
Kaltenbach, Frank (ed.): Translucent Materials – Glass, Plastic, Metals. Munich, 2004
Koch, Klaus-Michael (ed.): Bauen mit Membranen – der innovative Werkstoff in der Architektur. Munich, 2004
Krausse, Joachim; Lichtenstein, Claude: Your Private Sky: R. Buckminster Fuller – Design als Kunst einer Wissenschaft. Baden, 1999
Lefteri, Chris: Kunststoff II. Material – Herstellung – Produkte. Ludwigsburg, 2006
Ludwig, Matthias: Mobile Architektur – Geschichte und Entwicklung transportabler und modularer Bauten. Stuttgart, 1998
Nerdinger, Winfried (ed.): Frei Otto: das Gesamtwerk – leicht bauen – natürlich gestalten. Basel, 2005
Roland, Conrad; Otto, Frei: Frei Otto – Spannweiten. Ideen und Versuche zum Leichtbau. Berlin, 1965
Schlaich, Jörg; Bergermann, Rudolf: Leicht weit – Light Structures. Munich, 2003
Tschimmel, Udo: Die Zehntausend-Dollar-Idee. Kunststoff-Geschichte vom Celluloid zum Superchip. Düsseldorf, 1991
Uffelen, Chris van; Steybe, Sophie: Pure Plastic – new materials for today's architecture. Berlin, 2008

Part B Materials

Polymers

Baur, Erwin et al.: Saechtling Kunststoff Taschenbuch. Munich, 2007
Bonnet, Martin: Kunststoffe in der Ingenieuranwendung: verstehen und zuverlässig auswählen. Wiesbaden, 2009
Bonten, Christian: Kunststofftechnik für Designer. Munich, 2003
Braun, Dietrich: Erkennen von Kunststoffen: qualitative Kunststoffanalyse mit einfachen Mitteln. Munich, 1998
Braun, Dietrich: Kunststofftechnik für Einsteiger. Munich, 2003
Braun, Dietrich et al.: Polymer synthesis: theory and practice: fundamentals, methods, experiments. Berlin/Heidelberg, 2005
Domininghaus, Hans: Die Kunststoffe und ihre Eigenschaften.
Berlin/Heidelberg, 2005
Domininghaus, Hans et al.: Kunststoffe. Eigenschaften und Anwendungen. Berlin, 2008
Ehrenstein, Gottfried W.: Mit Kunststoffen konstruieren. Munich/Vienna, 2007
Ehrenstein, Gottfried W.; Pongratz, Sonja: Beständigkeit von Kunststoffen. Munich, 2007
Elias, Hans-Georg: An introduction to plastics. Weinheim, 2003
Etzrodt, Günter: Die Farbenwelt der Kunststoffe: Farbmittel und Präparationen: Eigenschaften, Verarbeitung, Qualitätssicherung. Landsberg am Lech, 2003
Franck, Adolf: Kunststoff-Kompendium: Herstellung, Aufbau, Verarbeitung, Anwendung, Umweltverhalten und Eigenschaften der Thermoplaste, Polymerlegierungen, Elastomere und Duroplaste. Würzburg, 2006
Glenz, Wolfgang: Polystyrol-Hartschaumstoff (EPS, XPS).

In: Kunststoffe – Werkstoffe, Verarbeitung, Anwendung 10/2008, pp. 130ff.
Harper, Charles A.: Handbook of plastics, elastomers and composites. New York, 2002
Hellerich, Walter et al.: Werkstoff-Führer Kunststoffe – Eigenschaften, Prüfungen, Kennwerte. Munich, 2001
Kalweit, Andreas: Handbuch für technisches Produktdesign – Material und Fertigung. Berlin/Heidelberg, 2006
Köster, Lothar et al.: Praxis der Kautschukextrusion. Munich, 2007
Lindner, Christoph: Produktion, Verarbeitung und Verwertung von Kunststoffen in Deutschland (study). Alzenau, 2007; http://www.plasticseurope.de/document/produktion-verarbeitung-und-verwertung-von-kunststoffen-indeutschland-2007---kurzfassung--.aspx?Page=DOCUMENT&FolID=2; 26 Aug 2010
Ludwig, Carsten: Glasfaserverstärkte Kunststoffe unter hoher thermischer und mechanischer Belastung. Dissertation. Stuttgart, 2009
Moser, Kurt: Faser-Kunststoff-Verbund – Entwurfs- und Berechnungsgrundlagen. Düsseldorf, 1992
Müller, Albrecht: Coloring of plastics – fundamentals, colorants, preparations. Munich, 2003
Nanetti, Paolo: Lack für Einsteiger. Hannover, 2009
Pfaff, Gerhard: Spezielle Effektpigmente – Grundlagen und Anwendungen. Hannover, 2007
Schürmann, Helmut: Konstruieren mit Faser-Kunststoff-Verbunden. Berlin/Heidelberg, 2007
Schwarz, Otto; Ebeling, Friedrich Wolfhard; Furth, Brigitte: Kunststoffverarbeitung. Würzburg, 2002
Schwarz, Otto; Ebeling, Friedrich-Wolfhard (ed.): Kunststoffkunde – Aufbau, Eigenschaften, Verarbeitung, Anwendungen der Thermoplaste, Duroplaste und Elastomere. Würzburg, 2005

Fibres
Beckmann, Andreas; Kleinholz, Rudolf: Anforderungen an Naturfasern aus der Sicht eines Kfz-Zulieferers für Innenraumteile. Veranstaltung aus der Reihe "2nd International Wood & Natural Fibre Composites Symposium". Kassel, 1999
Bonnet, Martin: Kunststoffe in der Ingenieuranwendung: verstehen und zuverlässig auswählen. Wiesbaden, 2009
Bonten, Christian: Kunststofftechnik für Designer. Munich, 2003
Carus, Michael et al.: Einsatz von Naturfasern in Verbundwerkstoffen für die Automobilproduktion in Deutschland von 1999 bis 2005. pub. by Nova Institute, Hürth, 2006
Carus, Michael et al.: Naturfaserverstärkte Kunststoffe – Pflanzen, Rohstoffe, Produkte. Pub. by Fachagentur Nachwachsende Rohstoffe e.V. (FNR, Agency for Renewable Resources), Gülzow, 2008
Ehrenstein, Gottfried W.: Faserverbund-Kunststoffe: Werkstoffe, Verarbeitung, Eigenschaften. Munich, 2006
Flemming, Manfred et al.: Faserverbundbauweisen. Berlin, 1995
Fourné, Franz: Synthetische Fasern – Herstellung, Maschinen und Apparate, Eigenschaften. Munich, 1995
Hanselka, Holger; Hermann, Axel Siegfried: Technischer Leitfaden zur Anwendung von ökologisch vorteilhaften Faserverbundwerkstoffen aus nachwachsenden Rohstoffen am Beispiel eines Kastenträgers als Prototyp für hochbelastbare Baugruppen. Aachen, 1999
Michaeli, Walter; Begemann, Michael: Einführung in die Technologie der Faserverbundwerkstoffe. Munich,1990
Moser, Kurt: Faser-Kunststoff-Verbund: Entwurfs- und Berechnungsgrundlagen. Düsseldorf ,1992
Schurmann, Helmut: Konstruieren mit Faser-Kunststoff-Verbunden. Berlin/Heidelberg, 2007
Sperber, Volker E.: Trends für Naturfaser-Verbundwerkstoffe. In: Technische Textilien 2/2006, pp. 70ff.

Adhesives and coatings
Habenicht, Gerd: Kleben: Grundlagen, Technologien, Anwendungen. Berlin, 2009
Nanetti, Paolo: Lack für Einsteiger. Hannover, 2009
Pfaff, Gerhard: Spezielle Effektpigmente – Grundlagen und Anwendungen. Hannover, 2007
Peters, Stefan: Kleben von GFK und Glas für baukonstruktive Anwendungen. Stuttgart, 2006
Reichel, Alexander et al.: Putze, Farben, Beschichtungen. Munich, 2004
Rusam, Horst: Anstriche und Beschichtungen im Bauwesen – Eigenschaften, Untergrunde, Anwendung. Stuttgart, 2004

Natural fibre-reinforced polymer and biopolymers
Carus, Michael et al.: Naturfaserverstärkte Kunststoffe – Pflanzen, Rohstoffe, Produkte. Pub. by Fachagentur Nachwachsende Rohstoffe e.V. (FNR, Agency for Renewable Resources), Gülzow, 2008
Carus, Michael et al.: Studie zur Markt- und Konkurrenzsituation bei Naturfasern und Naturfaser-Werlstoffen (Deutschland und EU). Gülzower Fachgespräche, vol. 26. Pub. by Fachagentur Nachwachsende Rohstoffe e.V. (FNR, Agency for Renewable Resources), Gülzow, 2008
Domininghaus, Hans et al.: Kunststoffe. Eigenschaften und Anwendungen. Berlin, 2008
Endres, Hans-Josef; Siebert-Raths, Andrea: Technische Biopolymere: Rahmenbedingungen, Marktsituation, Herstellung, Aufbau und Eigenschaften. Munich, 2009
Riedel, Ulrich: Industrielle Fertigungsstrategien am Beispiel von automobilen Anwendungen. Pub. by Center of Excellence Composite Structures/Adaptronics, German Aerospace Center. Braunschweig, 2005
Shen, Li et al.: Product overview and market projection of emerging bio-based plastics. Study pub. by European Polysaccharide Network of Excellence & European Bioplastics. Utrecht, 2009
Wimmer, Robert et al.: Grundlagenforschung für die Entwicklung von Produktprototypen aus Naturstoffgebundenen Vliesen. Pub. by Austrian Ministry for Transport, Innovation & Technology. Vienna, 2007

Part C Semi-finished products

Primary products
Baur, Erwin et al.: Saechtling Kunststoff Taschenbuch. Munich, 2007
Braun, Dietrich: Kunststofftechnik für Einsteiger. Munich, 2003
Schwarz, Otto; Ebeling, Friedrich Wolfhard; Furth, Brigitte: Kunststoffverarbeitung. Würzburg, 2009

Fibre-reinforced polymers
Moser, Kurt: Faser-Kunststoff-Verbund – Entwurfs- und Berechnungsgrundlagen. Düsseldorf, 1992
Schurmann, Helmut: Konstruieren mit Faser-Kunststoff-Verbunden. Berlin/Heidelberg, 2007
Ehrenstein, Gottfried W.: Faserverbund-Kunststoffe: Werkstoffe, Verarbeitung, Eigenschaften. Munich, 2006
Flemming, Manfred; Roth, Siegfried: Faserverbundbauweisen. Eigenschaften. Berlin/Heidelberg, 2003
Flemming, Manfred et al.: Faserverbundbauweisen. Berlin/Heidelberg, 1995

Semi-finished polymer products
Domininghaus, Hans et al.: Kunststoffe. Eigenschaften und Anwendungen. Berlin, 2008
Flemming, Manfred et al.: Faserverbundbauweisen. Berlin/Heidelberg, 1995
Kaltenbach, Frank (ed.): Translucent Materials – Glass, Plastic, Metals. Munich, 2004
Knippers, Jan et al.: Brücken mit Fahrbahnen aus glasfaserverstärktem Kunststoff (GFK) – Neue Straßenbrücke in Friedberg (Hessen). In: Stahlbau 7/2009, pp. 462–470
Knippers, Jan; Hwash, Mohamed: Umgelenkte Lamellen aus kohlefaserverstärktem Kunststoff für freistehende Spannglieder im Konstruktiven Ingenieurbau. In: Beton- und Stahlbetonbau 10/2008, pp. 682–688
Lee, Sung Woo; Kee-Jeung, Hong: Experiencing More Composite-Deck Bridges and Developing Innovative Profile of Snap-Fit Connection. In: COBRAE Conference – Benefits of Composites in Civil Engineering. Stuttgart, 2007
Remmele, Mathias: Aus einem Guss: Die Entwicklung des Panton-Stuhls. In: deutsche bauzeitung 4/2006, pp. 27–32
Schwarz, Otto et al.: Kunststoffverarbeitung. Würzburg, 2009

Foil
LeCuyer, Anette: ETFE – Technology and Design. Basel/Boston/Berlin, 2008
Moritz, Karsten: ETFE-Folie als Tragelement. Dissertation. Munich, 2007
Nentwig, Joachim: Kunststoff-Folien: Herstellung – Eigenschaften – Anwendung. Munich/Vienna, 2006
Saxe, Klaus; Homm, Thomas: Mechanische Eigenschaften von ETFE-Folien für vorgespannte Strukturen, Proceedings, Techtextil Symposium. Frankfurt, 2007
Pearman, Hugh et al.: The Architecture of Eden. London, 2003

Textile membranes
Blum, Rainer et al.: Material Properties and Testing. In: Forster, Brian; Mollaert, Marijke:
European Design Guide for Tensile Surface Structures. Brussels, 2004
Seidel, Michael: Tensile Surface Structures – A Practical Guide to Cable and Membrane Construction. Berlin, 2009

Building physics and energy aspects
Cremers, Jan: Einsatzmöglichkeiten von Vakuum-Dämmsystemen im Bereich der Gebäudehülle – Technologische, bauphysikalische und architektonische Aspekte. Munich/New York, 2007
Cremers, Jan: Integration von Photovoltaik in Membrankonstruktionen. In: Detail Green 01/2009, pp. 61–63
Hegger, Manfred et al.: Construction Materials Manual. Munich/Basel, 2006
Hegger, Manfred et al.: Energy Manual – Sustainable Architecture. Munich/Basel, 2008
Jeska, Simone: Transparent Plastics – Design and Technology. Basel/Boston/Berlin, 2008
Kaltenbach, Frank (ed.): Translucent Materials – Glass, Plastic, Metals. Munich, 2004
Richter, Ekkehard; Fischer, Heinz M.: Lehrbuch der Bauphysik. Schall – Wärme – Feuchte – Licht – Brand – Klima. Wiesbaden, 2008
Schild, Kai; Weyers, Michael: Handbuch Fassadendämmsysteme – Grundlagen, Produkte, Details. Stuttgart, 2003
Troitzsch, Jürgen (ed.): Plastics flammability handbook: Principles, regulations, testing, and approval. Munich, 2004
Willems, Wolfgang M. et al.: Vieweg Handbuch Bauphysik. Wiesbaden, 2006
Zürcher, Christoph; Frank, Thomas: Bauphysik – Leitfäden für Planung und Praxis. Stuttgart, 2004

Environmental impact of polymers
Hegger, Manfred et al.: Construction Materials Manual. Munich/Basel, 2006
Hellerich, Walter et al.: Werkstoff-Führer Kunststoffe: Eigenschaften, Prüfungen, Kennwerte. Munich, 2004
Bauen und Umwelt e.V. (pub.): Leitfaden für die Formulierung der Anforderungen an die Produktkategorien der Umweltdeklarationen (Typ III) für Bauprodukte. Königswinter, 2006
Köpfler, Walter; Grahl, Birgit: Ökobilanzierung. Ein Leitfaden für Ausbildung und Beruf. Weinheim, 2009
LeCuyer, Anette: ETFE – Technology and Design. Basel/Boston/Berlin, 2008
Müller, Michael et al.: Ökologische/Ökonomische Bewertung zweier Fassadenkonzepte – Glasfassade versus Kunststofffassade. Research report. Remscheid, 2007
Preisig, Hansruedi: Massiv- oder Leichtbauweise? In: tec 21 42/2002, pp. 15ff.
Schittich, Christian et al.: Glass Construction Manual, 2nd ed. Munich, 2007
Sigg, Rene et al.: LUKRETIA – Lebenszyklus – Ressourcen – Technisierung. Zurich, 2006

Part D Planning and form-finding

Loadbearing structure and form
Barnes, Michael R.: Form-finding and analysis of tension structures by dynamic relaxation. In: International Journal of Space Structures, vol. 14 No. 2/1999, pp.89–104

Bradatsch, Jürgen et al.: Form. In: Forster, Brian; Mollaert, Marijke: European Design Guide for Tensile Surface Structures. Brussels, 2004
Brinkmann, Günther: Leicht und Weit – zur Konstruktion weitgespannter Flächentragwerke. Results from research area 64 "Weitgespannte Flächentragwerke", University of Stuttgart. Weinheim, 1990
Engel, Heino: Tragsysteme – Structure Systems. Ostfildern, 1999
Herzog, Thomas: Pneumatic Structures: A Handbook of Inflatable Architecture. Stuttgart, 1976
Höller, Ralf: FormFindung – architektonische Grundlagen für den Entwurf von mechanisch vorgespannten Membranen und Seilnetzen. Mähringen, 1999
Hughes, Thomas J.: The finite element method – linear static and dynamic finite element analysis. Mineola, 2000
Institute for Lightweight Structures & Conceptual Design (ILEK), University of Stuttgart (pub.): Mitteilungen: Wandelbare Dächer (IL5). Stuttgart, 1972
Institute for Lightweight Structures & Conceptual Design (ILEK), University of Stuttgart (pub.): Mitteilungen: Vela Toldos Sonnenzelte (IL30). Stuttgart, 1984
Joedicke, Jürgen et al.: Schalenbau – Konstruktion und Gestaltung. Stuttgart, 1962
Lewis, Wanda J.: Tension structures – form and behaviour. London, 2003
Luchsinger, Rolf H.; Crettol, René: Experimental and Numerical Study of Spindle Shaped Tensairity® Girders. In: International Journal of Space Structures, vol. 21, No. 3, 2006
Otto, Frei; Rasch, Bodo: finding form – towards an architecture of the minimal. Stuttgart, 1995
Scheck, H.-J.: The force density method for form-finding and computation of general networks. In: Computer Methods in Applied Mechanics and Engineering 3/1974, pp. 115–134
Seidel, Michael: Tensile Surface Structures – A Practical Guide to Cable and Membrane Construction. Berlin, 2009
Wakefield, David: Grundlagen und Berechnung von Membrankonstruktionen. In: Koch, Klaus-Michael (ed.): Bauen mit Membranen – der innovative Werkstoff in der Architektur. Munich, 2004

Detailed design aspects
Barnes, Michael R. et al.: Structural design basis and safety criteria. In: Forster, Brian; Mollaert, Marijke: European Design Guide for Tensile Surface Structures. Brussels, 2004
Blum, Rainer; Bögner, Heidrun: Testing methods and standards. In: Forster, Brian; Mollaert, Marijke: European Design Guide for Tensile Surface Structures. Brussels, 2004
Bau-Überwachungsverein e.V. (BÜV): Tragende Kunststoffbauteile im Bauwesen – Empfehlung. Aug 2010. Download: www.bvpi.de/shared/pdf-dokumente/Kunststoff_Empf.pdf, 20 Aug 2010
Clarke, John L.: Structural Design of Polymer Composites – EUROCOMP Design Code and Handbook. London, 1996
Ehrenstein, Gottfried W.: Faserverbund-Kunststoffe: Werkstoffe, Verarbeitung, Eigenschaften. Munich, 2006
Forster, Brian; Mollaert, Marijke: European Design Guide for Tensile Surface Structures. Brussels, 2004
Knippers, Jan; Gabler, Markus: Faserverbundwerkstoffe im Bauwesen. In: Stahlbau-Kalender 2007, pp. 456–498
Minte, Jörg: Das mechanische Verhalten von Verbindungen beschichteter Chemiefasergewebe. Dissertation. Aachen, 1981
Sobek, Werner; Speth, Martin: Textile Werkstoffe. In: Bauingenieur 70/1995, pp. 243–250

Part E Building with polymers and membranes

Building with semi-finished polymer products
Ehrenstein, Gottfried W. (ed.): Handbuch Kunststoff-Verbindungstechnik. Munich/Vienna, 2004
Ehrenstein, Gottfried W.: Mit Kunststoffen konstruieren. Munich/Vienna, 2007
Jeska, Simone: Transparent Plastics – Design and Technology. Basel/Boston/Berlin, 2008
Keller, Thomas et al.: Adhesively Bonded and Translucent Glass Fiber Reinforced Polymer Sandwich Girders. In: Journal of Composites for Construction 5/2004, pp. 461ff.
Toni, Michela: FRP architecture: Building by fiber-reinforced plastics. Florence, 2007

Building with free-form polymers
Ehrenstein, Gottfried W.: Mit Kunststoffen konstruieren. Munich/Vienna, 2007
Jeska, Simone: Transparent Plastics – Design and Technology. Basel/Boston/Berlin, 2008
Kalweit, Andreas: Handbuch für technisches Produktdesign – Material und Fertigung. Berlin/Heidelberg, 2006
Schurmann, Helmut: Konstruieren mit Faser-Kunststoff-Verbunden. Berlin/Heidelberg, 2007
VDI Wissensforum (pub.): Konstruieren mit Kunststoffen. Düsseldorf, 2006

Building with foil
Bubner, Ewald: Membrankonstruktionen – Verbindungstechniken. Essen, 2005
Lehnert, S.; Schween, T.: Bauen mit Folienkissen. In: Bauingenieur 6/2006, pp. 285–288
Moritz, Karsten: ETFE-Folie als Tragelement. Dissertation. Munich, 2007
Moritz, Karsten: Die Stadionhülle der Allianz Arena – Bauweise der ETFE-Folienpneus. In: Detail – Zeitschrift für Architektur + Konzept 9/2005, pp. 976–980
Moritz, Karsten: Bauweisen der ETFE-Foliensysteme. In: Stahlbau 5/2007, pp. 336–342

Building with textile membranes
Bubner, Ewald: Membrankonstruktionen – Verbindungstechniken. Essen, 2005
Drew, Philip: New Tent Architecture. New York, 2008
Forster, Brian; Mollaert, Marijke: European Design Guide for Tensile Surface Structures. Brussels, 2004
Forster, Brian: Planung und Entwicklung von Details. In: Koch, Klaus-Michael (ed.): Bauen mit Membranen – Der innovative Werkstoff in der Architektur. Munich, 2004
Göppert, Knut: Membrankonstruktionen – Form und Detail. In: Stahlbau 12/2004, pp. 990–1000
Ishii, Kazuo: Membrane Structures in Japan. Tokyo, 1995
Ishii, Kazuo: Membrane Designs and Structures in the World, Tokyo, 1999
Koch, Klaus-Michael (ed.): Bauen mit Membranen – Der innovative Werkstoff in der Architektur. Munich, 2004
Krüger, Sylvie: Textile Architecture – Textile Architektur. Berlin, 2009
Otto, Frei; Rasch, Bodo: Gestalt finden – auf dem Weg zu einer Baukunst des Minimalen. Stuttgart, 1995
Seidel, Michael: Tensile Surface Structures – A Practical Guide to Cable and Membrane Construction. Berlin, 2009

Complex building envelopes
Behling, Sophia et al.: Sol Power – the evolution of solar architecture. Munich/New York, 1996
Cremers, Jan; Lausch, Felix: Transluzente Hochleistungsdämmung aus sli-Aerogelen für Membranen. In: Detail – Zeitschrift für Architektur + Baudetail 5/2008, pp. 524ff.
Göppert, Knut; Linden, Sebastian: Erneuerung der abgehängten Decke in der Olympiaschwimmhalle in München. In: Detail – Zeitschrift für Architektur + Baudetail 5/2008, pp. 508ff.
Herzog, Thomas et al.: Facade Construction Manual. Munich/Basel, 2004
Herzog, Thomas: Transluzente Bauteile – Anmerkungen zu ihrer Wirkung. In: Almanach 90/92, Faculty of Architecture, TU Darmstadt. Darmstadt, 1992
Jahn, Helmut et al.: Suvarnabhumi Airport, Bangkok, Thailand. Ludwigsburg, 2007
Schittich, Christian et al.: Glass Construction Manual, 2nd ed. Munich, 2007

Authors

Jan Knippers
Born 1962
Studied structural engineering at the Technische Universität Berlin
1992 Completion of doctorate at the Technische Universität Berlin
1993–2000 Engineer, Schlaich Bergermann & Partner, Stuttgart
2000 to date Professor for structural engineering and structural design, University of Stuttgart
2001 to date Engineer, Knippers Helbig Advanced Engineering, Stuttgart/New York
Member of national and international committees and bodies

Jan Cremers
Born 1971
Studied architecture at the University of Karlsruhe and Westminster University, London
1999–2002 Architect, Koch+Partner, Munich, and other architectural practices
2002–2006 Scientific assistant, Chair of Building Technology, Prof. Thomas Herzog, Technische Universität Munich
2006 Completion of doctorate at the Technische Universität Munich
2006–2008 SolarNext AG, Rimsting, periodically as Chief Executive Officer
2008 to date Director of Technology, Hightex GmbH, Rimsting
2008 to date Professor for building technology and integrated architecture, Hochschule für Technik Stuttgart

Markus Gabler
Born 1977
Studied structural engineering at the University of Stuttgart
2000–2002 Institute for Lightweight Structures (ILEK), University of Stuttgart, also Novák consulting engineers, Sindelfingen
2003–2007 Project manager, Knippers Helbig Advanced Engineering, Stuttgart/New York
2007 to date Assistant and doctoral candidate at the Institute of Building Structures & Structural Design (ITKE), University of Stuttgart
Member of the working group of the DIN standard committee for fibre-reinforced polymers in building.

Julian Lienhard
Born 1980
Studied structural engineering at the University of Stuttgart
2004–2008 Engineer, Rasch + Bradatsch architectural practice, Leinfelden-Echterdingen
2007 to date Assistant and doctoral candidate at the Institute of Building Structures & Structural Design (ITKE), University of Stuttgart
2008 Founding of studioLD, Stuttgart

Picture credits

The authors and publishers would like to express their sincere gratitude to all those who have assisted in the production of this book, be it through providing photos or artwork or granting permission to reproduce their documents or providing other information.
The drawings in parts A to E that are not listed here were produced by the authors.
Photographs not specifically credited were taken by the architects or are works photographs or were supplied from the archives of the magazine DETAIL. Despite intensive endeavours we were unable to establish copyright ownership in just a few cases; however, copyright is assured. Please notify us accordingly in such instances. The numbers refer to the figures.

The photographs of the various materials in this Construction Manual are the result of a cooperation between the authors and the photographers of the University of Stuttgart.

Hans-Joachim Heyer + Boris Miklautsch/Werkstatt für Photographie/University of Stuttgart:

B B 1.1 B 1.8 B 1.13 B 1.23–25 B 1.27–33
B 1.36 B 1.39–40 B 1.42–44 B 2.1 B 2.11–13
B 2.16–21 B 2.1 B 2.11–13 B 2.16–21 B 3.7–9

C 1.1 C 1.4a–c C 1.6–11 C 1.17–21 C 2.4a–d
C 3.1 C 3.3–5 C 3.9–10 C 3.21–23 C 3.25–26
C 4.1 C 4.7–8 C 4.16 C 5.1 C 5.7–11

D 1.3 D 1.7–8 D 2.8

E 1.34–35 E 3.17–18

Part A Polymers and membranes in architecture

A Julian Lienhard, Stuttgart
A 1 Deutsches Museum archives, Munich
A 2 Kunststoffe, Carl Hanser Verlag, Munich
A 3 Tschimmel, Udo: Die Zehntausend-Dollar-Idee. Berlin, 1991, p. 69
A 4 http://www.liveauctioneers.com/item/5987732
A 5 Vitra, Birsfelden/Weil am Rhein
A 6 Hansen, Hans/Vitra, Hamburg
A 7–8 The Estate of R. Buckminster Fuller, Santa Barbara
A 9 The MIT Museum. In: Hess, Alan: Googie. fifties coffee shop architecture. San Francisco, 1986, p. 50
A 10 Wolfgang Feierbach, Altenstadt
A 11 Jean-Pierre Dalbéra, Paris
A 12a–b Paul Kramer, Berlin
A 13 Blundell-Jones, Peter; Hübner, Peter: Peter Hübner – Building as a Social Process. Stuttgart, 2007, p. 107
A 15a–b Institute for Lightweight Structures & Conceptual Design, Stuttgart
A 17a–c see A 15
A 18 Birdair Inc., New York
A 19 Walter Bird, University Archives, State University of New York at Buffalo
A 20 Koch, Klaus-Michael: Bauen mit Membranen. Munich, 2004, p. 44, Fig. 68
A 21a Horst Berger, New York
A 21b Taiyo Kogyo Co. Ltd., Tokyo
A 22a Yukio Futagawa, Tokyo
A 22b Verena Herzog-Loibl, Munich
A 23 Manfred Storck, Stuttgart
A 24b see A 15
A 25 see A 7
A 26 Winfried Nerdinger (ed.), Konstruktion und Raum in der Architektur des 20. Jahrhunderts. Munich, 2002, p. 76, Fig. 1
A 27a Herzog, Thomas: Pneumatic Structures: A Handbook of Inflatable Architecture. Stuttgart, 1976, p. 45, Fig. 33
A 27b George Cserna
A 28 Hightex GmbH, Rimsting
A 29 Tohru Waki/Shokokusha, Tokyo
A 32 Jan Cremers, Munich
A 33a–b see A 7
A 34a–b Renzo Piano Building Workshop, Genoa
A 34c Dini, Massimo: Renzo Piano. Progetti e architetture. 1964–1983. Milan, 1983, p. 15, Fig. 5
A 35a–b Gianni Berengo Gardin, Milan
A 36a–b Udd, Eric; Winz, Mike; Kreger, Stephen; Heider, Dirk: Failure Mechanisms of Fiber Optic Sensors Placed in Composite Materials. SPIE vol. 5758, 2005
A 37 according to Grohmann, Boris A.; Wallmersperger, Thomas; Kröplin, Bernd-Helmut: Lecture, adaptive structures. Institute for Statics & Dynamics (ISD), University of Stuttgart
A 38 Grohmann, Boris A.; Wallmersperger, Thomas; Kröplin, Bernd-Helmut: Adaptive Strukturen und gekoppelte Mehrfeldprobleme. In: Stahlbau, vol. 69, No. 6, p. 448, Fig. 6
A 39 Cremers, Jan: Performance-Steigerungen von Bestandsgebäuden durch innovative Membrankonstruktionen, Neumarkt i.d. Oberpfalz, 2010, p. 3
A 40 Werkstatt für Photographie, Faculty of Architecture & Urban Planning, University of Stuttgart
A 41 Uwe Walter/Courtesy EIGEN+ART Gallery, Leipzig/Berlin, and The Pace Gallery

Part B Materials

Polymers

B 1.2 Lindner, Christoph: Produktion, Verarbeitung und Verwertung von Kunststoffen in Deutschland. Alzenau, 2007, p. 6
B 1.6 Etzrodt, Günter: Die Farbenwelt der Kunststoffe: Farbmittel und Präparationen: Eigenschaften, Verarbeitung, Qualitätssicherung. Landsberg am Lech, 2003, p. 18, Fig. 11
B 1.7 Baur, Erwin et al.: Saechtling Kunststoff Taschenbuch. Munich, 2007, p. 695, Fig. 7.13
B 1.10 Pfaff, Gerhard: Spezielle Effektpigmente-Grundlagen und Anwendungen, Hannover, 2007, p. 141
B 1.11 http://www.ipt.arc.nasa.gov/finnfigures.html
B 1.16 Ludwig, Carsten: Glasfaserverstärkte Kunststoffe unter hoher thermischer und mechanischer Belastung. Dissertation. Stuttgart, 2009, p. 157
B 1.17 see B 1.16, p. 156
B 1.18 see B 1.7, pp. 235ff.
B 1.19 Braun, Dietrich: Erkennen von Kunststoffen: qualitative Kunststoffanalyse mit einfachen Mitteln. Munich, 1998, p. 42f.
B 1.21a–b see B 1.19, p. 35, Fig.3
B 1.22 Kalweit, Andreas et al.: Handbuch für technisches Produktdesign: Material und Fertigung, Entscheidungsgrundlagen für Designer und Ingenieure. Berlin/Heidelberg, 2006, p. 92
B 1.37 see B 1.19, p. 36, Fig. 4 B
B 1.38 see B 1.18, p. 654, Fig. 6.68
B 1.41 see B 1.19, p. 36, Fig. 4 A

Fibres

B 2.2 Schürmann, Helmut: Konstruieren mit Faser-Kunststoff-Verbunden. Berlin/Heidelberg 2007, p. 22
B 2.3 Moser, Kurt: Faser-Kunststoff-Verbund. Entwurfs- und Berechnungsgrundlagen. Düsseldorf, 1992
B 2.7 Ehrenstein, Gottfried W.: Faserverbund-Kunststoffe: Werkstoffe, Verarbeitung, Eigenschaften. Munich, 2006, pp. 19, 31, 39
B 2.8 Flemming, Manfred et al.: Faserverbundbauweisen. Berlin, 1995, p. 10, Fig. 2.1.5
B 2.10 see B 2.3
B 2.14 Faserinstitut Bremen
B 2.15 see B 2.7, p. 32

Adhesives and coatings

B 3.1 Jan Bitter Fotografie, Berlin
B 3.3 see B 1.22, p. 484, Fig. 31
B 3.4 Peters, Stefan: Kleben von GFK und Glas für baukonstruktive Anwendungen. Dissertation. Stuttgart, 2006, p. 123
B 3.5 see B 3.4, p. 87
B 3.10 Ludwig, Carsten: Glasfaserverstärkte Kunststoffe unter hoher thermischer und mechanischer Belastung. Dissertation. Stuttgart, 2009, p. 193
B 3.12 Rusam, Horst: Anstriche und Beschichtungen im Bauwesen – Eigenschaften, Untergrunde, Anwendung. Stuttgart, 2004, p. 111
B 3.14c BMW AG, Munich

Natural fibre-reinforced polymers and biopolymers

B 4.1 Swiss Cell/THE WALL AG, Ratingen
B 4.2 according to http://www.uni-kassel.de/fb15/ifw/wpc/zu_downloaden/Tagung_1999_PDF/30%20Beckmann.pdf
B 4.3 fabpics/Fernando Alda
B 4.4 Lucas Schifres/Finpro ry
B 4.5 Daimler Benz AG, Stuttgart
B 4.7 Mazda Motor Corporation, Teijin
B 4.8 Fachagentur Nachwachsende Rohstoffe e. V., Gülzow
B 4.10 Sergio Rossi, Milan
B 4.11 according to Endres, Hans-Josef; Siebert-Raths, Andrea: Technische Biopolymere. Rahmenbedingungen, Marktsituation, Herstellung, Aufbau und Eigenschaften. Munich, 2009, p. 206, Fig. 5.33
B 4.12 see B 4.11, p. 215, Fig. 5.46
B 4.13 NEC Deutschland GmbH, Düsseldorf
B 4.14 mehrwerk designlabor/Enrico Wilde, Halle (Saale)
B 4.15 Honda Deutschland GmbH, Offenbach

Part C Semi-finished products

Primary products

C Christian Schittich, Munich
C 1.2 Schwarz, Otto; Ebeling, Friedrich Wolfhard; Furth, Brigitte: Kunststoffverarbeitung. Würzburg, 2002, p. 19
C 1.14a–b BASF SE, Ludwigshafen
C 1.15 see B 1.17, p. 753, plate 8.19

Fibre-reinforced polymers

C 2.1 Fiberline Composites AS, Middelfart
C 2.2a Svenja Beye, RWTH Aachen University
C 2.3 according to DIN EN 13706, DIN 18820 and Sika Deutschland GmbH
C 2.6 see B 2.7, p. 164
C 2.9 see B 2.7, p. 176
C 2.10 see B 2.7, p. 177
C 2.12 BWH-Bücker Kunststoffe GmbH & Co., Emsdetten

Semi-finished polymer products

C 3.2 see C 1.2, p. 41
C 3.16 clear-PEP UV PC, Design Composite GmbH, Mittersill
C 3.27 see C 3.2, p. 81
C 3.29 SIEGERBAU, Vetschau
C 3.30a–b see C 2.1

Foil

C 4.2 Nowofol Kunststoffprodukte GmbH & Co. KG, Siegsdorf; Vector Foiltec GmbH, Bremen; Baur, Erwin, et al.: Saechtling Kunststoff Taschenbuch. Munich, 2007
C 4.3a according to Bongaerts, H. In: Handbuch der Kunststoff-Extrusionstechnik. vol. 2: Extrusionsanlagen. Munich, 1986
C 4.3b according to Nentwig, Joachim: Kunststoff-Folien: Herstellung, Eigenschaften, Anwendung. 3rd ed., Munich, 2006
C 4.4–5 Brückner Maschinenbau GmbH & Co. KG, Siegsdorf
C 4.9 Hodann, Robert: Fluorpolymer-Folien für Architekturkonstruktionen, Nowofol: presentation, DAGA 2007, Stuttgart.
C 4.10–12 Saxe, Klaus; Homm, Thomas (University of Duisburg/Essen): Mechanische Eigenschaften von ETFE-Folien für vorgespannte Strukturen. Presentation, Techtextil Symposium, 12 Jun 2007.

C 4.13–14 Novum Membranes GmbH, Edersleben
C 4.15 Karsten Moritz, Obing

Textile membranes
C 5.5a according to Seidel, Michael: Tensile Surface Structures. Berlin, 2009, p. 39
C 5.5b according to Forster, Brian; Mollaert, Marijke: European Design Guide for Tensile Surface Structures, Brussels, 2004, p. 227
C 5.12 Test results, ITKE, University of Stuttgart
C 5.13a–b according to test results of Bauer Membranbau, for Rasch + Bradatsch, Freising
C 5.14 Hareikon UG, Bellenberg
C 5.15 Koch Membranen GmbH, Rimsting

Building physics and energy aspects
C 6.2–3 Cremers, Jan.: Einsatzmöglichkeiten von Vakuum-Dammsystemen, Munich/New York, 2007, p. 16
C 6.7 Neopor BASF SE, Ludwigshafen
C 6.8 Cammerer, Walter: Wärme- und Kälteschutz im Bauwesen und in der Industrie. Berlin, 1995, pp. 415f., and Pupp, Wolfgang; Hartmann, Heinz: Vakuumtechnik. Leipzig, 1991
C 6.9 Porextherm Dämmstoffe GmbH, Kempten
C 6.11 see C 6.2, p. 20
C 6.12 see C 6.2, p. 45
C 6.13 according to Porextherm GmbH, Kempten
C 6.14 http://www.empa-ren.ch/ren/Projekte_Gebaeudehuelle/Pdf%20Gebaeudehuelle/sb%20hlwd.pdf; 30 Aug 2010, p. 11
C 6.15 ThyssenKrupp Steel Europe, Duisburg
C 6.17 Cabot Corporation, Boston
C 6.18 Wacotech GmbH & Co.KG, Bielefeld
C 6.20 Isoflex, Gustafs
C 6.21 OKALUX GmbH, Marktheidenfeld
C 6.22 Wacotech GmbH & Co.KG, Bielefeld
C 6.23 Manufacturer's information via Fachverband Transparente Wärmedämmung e.V.
C 6.27 Jan Cremers; according to data from ZAE-Bayern e.V.
C 6.30 Evonik Röhm GmbH, Essen
C 6.31 according to measurements from ZAE-Bayern e. V.
C 6.32 Jan Cremers; according to measurements from ZAE-Bayern e.V.
C 6.33 Labor Blum, Stuttgart
C 6.34 Peter Bartenbach, Munich
C 6.35 Peter Bonfig, Munich
C 6.36 Nigel Young, London
C 6.37 TEXAA raum AKUSTIKS Gbr., Eglsbach
C 6.38a Nimbus-Group/Andreas Körner, Stuttgart
C 6.38b–c according to KAEFER Isoliertechnik GmbH & Co. KG, Bremen
C 6.40 according to DIN EN 13501-1, Jun 2002
C 6.41 see C 6.33
C 6.44 Roth Werke GmbH, Dautphetal-Buchenau
C 6.45 Fraunhofer ISE, Freiburg
C 6.46 Kopf Solarschiff GmbH, Sulz-Kastell
C 6.47–48 see A 32
C 6.49 Samuel Cabot Cochran, Pratt Institute
C 6.50 see A 32
C 6.51 Kennedy & Violich Arch, Boston

Environmental impact of polymers
C 7.1 Rainer Schlautmann, Oberhausen
C 7.2 according to DIN EN ISO 14040
C 7.3 according to Institut für Bauen und Umwelt, Königswinter
C 7.5–7 according to Okobau.dat, http://www.nachhaltigesbauen.de/baustoff-und-gebaeudedaten/oekobaudat.html
C 7.8 Preisig, Hansruedi: Massiv- oder Leichtbauweise? Zurich, 2002, In: TEC21, No. 42/2002, p. 17
C 7.9 Andreas Braun/Vector Foiltec GmbH, Bremen
C 7.10 Adam Mørk, Copenhagen
C 7.11a Müller, Michael; et al.: Ökologische/Ökonomische Bewertung zweier Fassadenkonzepte – Glasfassade versus Kunststofffassade. Remscheid, 2007, p. 84
C 7.11b artur/Tomas Riehle
C 7.13 dRMM Architects & Designers, London

Part D Planning and form-finding

Loadbearing structure and form
D Mike Stoy, Bothell
D 1.2 École des Ponts ParisTech
D 1.15 see A 20, p. 89
D 1.17 Samuel Fournier, Lavaux
D 1.18 Hubertus Hamm, Munich
D 1.20 Fritz Busam, Berlin
D 1.21 Gerhard Hagen, Bamberg
D 1.32–33 Helen & Hard, Stavanger
D 1.36 according to Otto, Frei: IL 5, Wandelbare Dächer. Publications of the Institute for Lightweight Structures & Conceptual Design. Stuttgart, 1972, p. 45

Detailed design aspects
D 2.2 according to VDI 1989 (2006): Richtlinie 2014: Entwicklung von Bauteilen aus Faser-Kunststoff-Verbund
D 2.3 according to Blum, Rainer: Zeltbaumaterialien. In: Günter Brinkmann: Leicht und Weit. Weinheim, 1990, p. 204
D 2.11–13 see C 6.33
D 2.22 Pedelta, consulting engineers, Barcelona

Part E Building with polymers and membranes

Building with polymers and membranes
E Fernando Guerra /FG+SG, Lisbon
E 1.1 Stefan Müller-Naumann, Munich
E 1.3 Swissfiber AG, Zurich
E 1.4 Schürmann, Helmut: Konstruieren mit Faser-Kunststoff-Verbunden. Berlin/Heidelberg, 2007, p. 538
E 1.5 Beat Widmer, Swissfiber AG, Zurich
E 1.8 Park, Don-U., Knippers, Jan: Application of a new GFRP jointing method for an exhibition membrane spatial structure. 9th Asian Pacific Conference of Shell and Spatial Structures (APCS 2009), Nagoya, May 2009
E 1.13b see C 2.1
E 1.15–16 see E 1.13b
E 1.19a Toni, Michela: FRP architecture: Building by fiber-reinforced plastics. Florence, 2007, p. 82
E 1.20a Foto Flury, Pontresina
E 1.21a Keller, Thomas et al.: Adhesively Bonded and Translucent Glass Fiber Reinforced Polymer Sandwich Girders. In: Journal of Composites for Construction 5/2004, pp. 461ff.
E 1.22a Sung Woo Lee, Kookmin University, Seoul
E 1.23b Habib J. Dagher, University of Maine
E 1.24a Julia Liese, Munich
E 1.29b Arthur Péquin, Bordeaux
E 1.31 Wagner System, Safnern
E 1.36b Christian Schittich, Munich
E 1.36c Rodeca GmbH, Mülheim a.d. Ruhr
E 1.41a Jeroen Musch, Amsterdam
E 1.42 LAMILUX Heinrich Strunz GmbH, Rehau
E 1.43a–b Ee Stairs Nederland bv, Barnfeld
E 1.44a see E 1.5
E 1.44c Swissfiber AG, Zurich

Building with free-form polymers
E 2.14a–b Krake Technology Group, Dessau
E 2.17 Lange+Ritter GmbH, Gerlingen
E 2.26 Paul Pattijn, Doetinchem
E 2.29 Lange+Ritter GmbH, Gerlingen
E 2.31a Wiebke Elzel, Academy of Visual Arts, Leipzig
E 2.31b Genzel, Elke; Voigt, Pamela: Kunststoffbauten: Teil 1: Die Pioniere. Weimar, 2005, p. 203
E 2.32 see E 2.31b, p. 177
E 2.34a–b Hahlbrock GmbH, Wunstorf
E 2.36a–c Octatube International, Delft
E 2.42, 2.43a Maurice Nio, Rotterdam

Building with foil
E 3.1 Max Prugger, Munich
E 3.3 Cremers, Jan: interim research report: Membrane für die Energetische Sanierung von Gebäuden (MESG), Rimsting, 2009 (unpublished)
E 3.5a–b LeCuyer, Anette: ETFE – Technology and Design. Basel/Boston/Berlin, 2008, p. 108
E 3.12–13 see E 3.3
E 3.15 according to Baier, Bernd; Koenen, Reinhold; Müller, Joachim (ed.): Grenzbereiche: leichte Konstruktionen – Symposium interdisziplinar. University of Duisburg-Essen, 2005
E 3.16 b Marcus Bredt, Berlin
E 3.19 Rolf Luchsinger, Dübendorf
E 3.20 Florian Holzherr, Munich
E 3.21 seele holding GmbH & Co. KG, Gersthofen

Building with textile membranes
E 4.4–5 http://www.pfeifer.de/seilbau/download/
E 4.16–17, E 4.28 Rasch + Bradatsch, Leinfelden-Echterdingen
E 4.27 see A 20, p. 133
E 4.32, 4.41 Alexander Michalski, Stuttgart
E 4.43 see A 20, p. 200
E 4.51 Jakob Frick, Stuttgart
E 4.54 Patrick Bingham-Hall, Balmain

Complex building envelopes
E 5.1 see E
E 5.6 see E 3.3
E 5.7 see A 39, p. 2
E 5.9 MFPA Leipzig GmbH, Leipzig
E 5.10a Fraunhofer-Institut für Bauphysik, Holzkirchen
E 5.11 see A 28
E 5.13 see 6.31
E 5.18–19 Cabot Corporation, Boston
E 5.20 Vector Foiltec GmbH, Bremen
E 5.21a see A 28
E 5.23 Birdair, Inc. A Taiyo Kogyo Company, Williamsville
E 5.24a–b Thomas Jantscher, Colombier
E 5.24c see A
E 5.25 see A 32
E 5.27a–c Thomas Hofmann, Fürth/Gerhard Reisinger, Jülich

Part F Case studies

F Virgile Simon Bertrand, Hong Kong
pp. 226–228 Michael Alschner, Vienna
pp. 229, 231 Lukas Roth, Cologne
pp. 232, 233 top left Timothy Soar, Norfolk
p. 233 btm. left Josef Gartner GmbH, Gundelfingen
pp. 234–235 Sergio Pirrone, Tokyo
p. 236 Arthur Péquin, Bordeaux
pp. 237–239 Ruedi Walti, Basel
pp. 240–241 Will Pryce, London
p. 242 centre Markus Gabler, Stuttgart
p. 243 artur/Roland Halbe, Stuttgart
p. 244 top Torben Eskerod, Copenhagen
p. 244 btm. see C 2.1
p. 245 Deffner Voigtländer, Dachau
pp. 246–247 Dieter Leistner, Würzburg
pp. 248, 250 John Linden, Woodland Hills
p. 251 Marc Gerritsen, Taipei
pp. 256, 257 top see E
p. 257 btm. Eva Schönbrunner, Munich
pp. 258, 259 top Nicolas Pinzon
p. 259 btm. seele holding GmbH & Co KG, Gersthofen
p. 260 Verena Herzog-Loibl, Munich
p. 261 btm. see A 32
p. 262 Thomas Ott, Mühltal
p. 263 Christian Schittich, Munich
p. 264 Frank Kaltenbach, Munich
pp. 265–267 see p. 262
p. 268 Udo Meinel, Berlin
p. 269 Zooey Braun, Stuttgart
p. 270 Heiner Leiska, Hamburg
p. 272 Friedrich Busam, Berlin
pp. 273–276 Nigel Young, London
pp. 277–278 Rainer Viertlböck, Gauting
pp. 280–281 top & btm. left see p. 264
pp. 282–283, 285 btm. pro.media/smart design

Abbreviations for polymers

Abbrev.	Name	Page
ABS	acrylonitrile-butadiene-styrene	42
AFK	aramid fibre-reinforced polymer	76
ASA	acrylate-styrene-acrylonitrile	42
AU	polyester-urethane rubber	45
BR	butadiene rubber	45
CA	cellulose (tri)acetate	43
CAB	cellulose acetate-butyrate	38
CFK	carbon fibre-reinforced polymer	76
CN	cellulose nitrate	38
CP	cellulose propionate	38
CR	chloroprene rubber	45
EAM	ethylene-vinyl acetate rubber	45
EC	ethyl cellulose	38
EP	epoxy resin	47
EPDM	ethylene-propylene-diene monomer	45
EPS	expanded polystyrene	74
ETFE	ethylene tetrafluoroethylene	44
EU	polyether-urethane rubber	45
EVA	ethylene vinyl acetate	41
EVAC	ethylene vinyl acetate	41
FKM	fluorocarbon rubber	45
FVMQ	fluorosilicone rubber	45
GFK	glass fibre-reinforced polymer	76
IIR	butyl rubber	45
MF	melamine formaldehyde resin	46
MVQ	methyl vinyl silicone rubber	45
NFK	natural fibre-reinforced polymer	60
NR	natural rubber	45
PA	polyamide	43
PAN	polyacrylonitrile	51
PC	polycarbonate	42
PCTFE	polychlorotrifluoroethylene	122
PCL	polycaprolactone	61
PE	polyethylene	41
PE-HD	polyethylene, high density (HDPE)	41
PE-LD	polyethylene, low density (LDPE)	41
PES	polyether sulphone	74
PET	polyethylene terephthalate	42
PET-G	glycol-modified polyethylene terephthalate	43
PF	phenol formaldehyde resin	46
PHB	polyhydroxybutyrate	64
PLA	polylactic acid	63
PMI	polymethacrylimide	73
PMMA	polymethyl methacrylate	42
PP	polypropylene	41
PPE+PS	polyphenylene ether, modified	43
PS	polystyrene	42
PTFE	polytetrafluoroethylene	44
PUR	polyurethane	47
PVB	polyvinyl butyral	41
PVC	polyvinyl chloride	40
PVC-P	polyvinyl chloride, plasticised	40
PVC-U	polyvinyl chloride, unplasticised	40
Q	silicone rubber	45
SAN	styrene acrylonitrile	42
SB	styrene butadiene	42
SBR	styrene butadiene rubber	45
TFB	tetrafluoroethylene-hexafluoropropylene-vinylidenefluoride-fluoroterpolymer (THV®)	44
TM	polysulphide rubber	45
TPS	thermoplastic starch	63
UF	urea formaldehyde resin	46
UP	unsaturated polyester resin	46
VE	vinyl ester resin	47
WPC	wood plastic composite	61
XPS	extruded polystyrene	74
GF	suffix for glass-fibre reinforcement	
X	suffix for cross-linked thermoplastic	

Colour coding (parts C, D and E)

■ Fibres ■ Foil ■ Textile membrane

Index

Index of names

The authors and publishers would like to thank the following sponsors for their assistance with this publication:

Hightex GmbH
83253 Rimsting (D)
www.hightexworld.com

SAINT-GOBAIN
Compagnie de Saint-Gobain
La défense Cedex (F)
www.sheerfill.com
www.norton-films.com

SGL Technologies GmbH
86405 Meitingen (D)
www.sglgroup.com